WEST'S
PARALEGAL
TODAY

THE LEGAL TEAM AT WORK

THE ESSENTIALS

Second Edition

The West Legal Studies Series

Your options keep growing with West Legal Studies

Each year our list continues to offer you more options for every area of the law to meet your course or on-the-job reference requirements. We now have over 140 titles from which to choose in the following areas:

Administrative Law
Alternative Dispute Resolution
Bankruptcy
Business Organizations/Corporations
Civil Litigation and Procedure
CLA Exam Preparation
Client Accounting
Computers in the Law Office
Constitutional Law
Contract Law
Criminal Law and Procedure
Document Preparation
Environmental Law
Ethics

Family Law
Federal Taxation
Intellectual Property
Introduction to Law
Introduction to Paralegalism
Law-Office Management
Law-Office Procedures
Legal Research, Writing, and Analysis
Legal Terminology
Paralegal Employment
Real-Estate Law
Reference Materials
Torts and Personal-Injury Law
Will, Trusts, and Estate Administration

You will find unparalleled, practical support

Each book is augmented by instructor and student supplements to ensure the best learning experience possible. We also offer custom publishing and other benefits such as West's Student Achievement Award. In addition, our sales representatives are ready to provide you with dependable service.

We want to hear from you

Our best contributions for improving the quality of our books and instructional materials is feedback from the people who use them. If you have a question, concern, or observation about any of our materials, or you have a product proposal or manuscript, we want to hear from you. Please contact your local representative or write us at the following address:

West Legal Studies, 3 Columbia Circle, P.O. Box 15015, Albany, NY 12212-5015

For additional information point your browser at
www.westlegalstudies.com

WEST LEGAL STUDIES
Thomson Learning™

WEST

TM

THOMSON LEARNING

Africa • Australia • Canada • Denmark • Japan • Mexico • New Zealand • Philippines
Puerto Rico • Singapore • Spain • United Kingdom • United States

West Legal Studies Staff:

Business Unit Director: Susan Simpfenderfer
Executive Editor: Marlene McHugh Pratt
Acquisitions Editor: Joan Gill
Developmental Editor: Rhonda Dearborn
Editorial Assistant: Lisa Flatley
Executive Marketing Manager: Donna Lewis
Executive Production Manager: Wendy Troeger

Production Editor: Laurie A. Boyce
Production Service and Design: Ann Borman
Composition: Parkwood Composition Services, Inc.
Copyediting: Suzie Franklin DeFazio and Lavina Miller
Index: Bob Marsh
Cover Images:

Library of Congress Cataloging-in-Publication Data
Miller, Roger LeRoy
    West's paralegal today : the essentials: the legal team at work / Roger LeRoy Miller &
Mary Meinzinger Urisko.—2nd ed.
      p. cm.
    Includes bibliographical references and index
    ISBN 0-7668-1016-x
    1. Legal assistants—United States. I. Urisko, Mary S. II. Title.
KF320.L4M55   1999
340'.023'73—dc21   99-051373

DEDICATION

To my wife, Francette, who has
made textbook writing worthwhile.
Thanks for changing my life.
R.L.M.

To Jennifer W. Coté,

Kathy Needham,

Rick Dimanin, Amy Wolff,

and Anne Fassler—Thanks

for your friendship.

M.M.U.

Contents in Brief

Contents

PREFACE

One of the fastest-growing occupations in America today is that of the paralegal, or legal assistant. It seems fitting, then, that you and your students should have a new textbook that reflects the excitement surrounding paralegal studies today. *West's Paralegal Today: The Essentials*, Second Edition, we believe, imparts this excitement to your students. They will find paralegal studies accessible and interesting. This book is modern, colorful, and visually attractive, which encourages learning. We are certain that you and your students will find this text extremely effective.

West's Paralegal Today, Second Edition, makes the paralegal field come alive for the student. We use real-world examples, present numerous boxed-in features, and support the text with the most extensive supplements package ever offered for an introductory paralegal textbook.

Thomson Learning and West Group have been providing authoritative materials to the entire legal field for over 120 years. *West's Paralegal Today*, Second Edition, draws on the expertise of publishers that have had a long history of encouraging excellence in legal education.

All of the basic areas of paralegal studies are covered in *West's Paralegal Today: The Essentials*, Second Edition. These include careers, ethics and professional responsibility, pretrial preparation, trial procedures, criminal law, legal interviewing and investigation, legal research, computer-assisted legal research, and legal analysis and writing. In addition, there are a number of key features, which we describe in this preface.

A PRACTICAL, REALISTIC APPROACH

There sometimes exists an enormous gulf between classroom learning and on-the-job realities. We have tried to bridge this gulf in *West's Paralegal Today*, Second Edition, by offering a text full of practical advice and "hands-on" activities. Exercises at the end of each chapter provide opportunities for your students to apply the concepts and skills discussed in the chapter. Many of the book's other key features, which you will read about shortly, were designed specifically to give your students a glimpse of the types of situations and demands that they may encounter on the job as professional paralegals. A special introduction to the student, which appears just before Chapter 1, contains practical advice and tips on how to master the legal concepts and procedures presented in this text—advice and tips that your students can also apply later, on the job.

West's Paralegal Today, Second Edition, also realistically portrays paralegal working environments and on-the-job challenges. Ethical dimensions of the practice of law frame paralegals' work experiences to a significant extent. Because of this, we have made a special effort to show how seemingly abstract ethical rules affect the day-to-day tasks performed by attorneys and paralegals in the legal workplace.

TECHNOLOGY

We have attempted to make sure that *West's Paralegal Today*, Second Edition, is the most modern and up-to-date text available in today's marketplace. To that end, we have included in the Second Edition a number of new features and materials indicating how the latest developments in technology are affecting the law, the legal workplace, and paralegal tasks. Among other things, these features and materials will help your students learn how to take advantage of technology, including the Internet, to enhance their efficiency and productivity as paralegals.

A New Chapter on CALR

An entirely new chapter on computer-assisted legal research (Chapter 9) shows students how they can do legal research and investigation using CD-ROMs, the legal databases provided by Westlaw® and Lexis®, and online information available at various Web sites.

A New Feature Focusing on Technology

A new feature, titled *Technology and Today's Paralegal*, has been added for the Second Edition. Each of these boxed-in features, which appear throughout the text, focuses on how technology is affecting a specific aspect of paralegal work or on how paralegals can use technology to their benefit. For example, in Chapter 2 (Careers in the Legal Community) we have included a feature discussing "Online Job Searching." The feature offers guidelines to students on how they can find employment opportunities using the Internet. Titles of other features include the following:

- Is E-Mail "Confidential"? (Chapter 3).
- Filing Court Documents Electronically (Chapter 5).

From Chapter 1 . . .

TECHNOLOGY AND TODAY'S PARALEGAL
The Changing Paralegal Workplace

In many ways, technology has simplified the work of legal assistants. Documents can be easily drafted and revised on the computer. Mistakes can be eliminated with the stroke of a key, and changes can be made in a matter of just seconds. Computerized forms make generating the paperwork for routine legal transactions, such as bankruptcy filings or divorce petitions, a relatively simple matter. Database management systems allow paralegals to track or analyze hundreds—if not thousands—of documents without having to search through boxes filled with documents. E-mail messages can be created and sent in a fraction of the time it takes to create, reproduce, and distribute hard-copy memos or letters. Online databases have made it possible to conduct legal research and find information relevant to a legal investigation without leaving the office.

Indeed, it would seem that technology, by making legal work faster and easier to accomplish, might reduce the need for paralegals. That, however, is not true. Indeed, the opposite is occurring—technology is opening the door to new positions for paralegals. For example, some of today's paralegals are carving out a niche for themselves as Internet specialists. A paralegal who can conduct research efficiently, using online resources, is a valuable asset to any firm or agency. In a law office, efficient research saves time and money—for the firm and clients alike. Other paralegals are becoming experts in electronic evidence—encoding documents relating to a particular legal matter so that those documents can easily be retrieved in the event of a lawsuit.

Another emerging field in which paralegals may play a significant role has to do with the types of documents that should be entered into, or retained on, electronic systems. Even documents that have been previously deleted from a hard drive may be retrieved and used as evidence in a lawsuit, and companies that want to prevent future problems with electronic evidence increasingly are turning to their lawyers for advice on this issue. A paralegal knowledgeable in this area is a valuable member of the legal team in such situations.

Finally, technology has made it possible for some paralegals to perform at least some of their work at home. The virtual workplace, made feasible by telephones, faxes, and modems, is now becoming a reality.

We cannot predict what the future may hold, but one thing seems certain: as technology advances, there will be an increasing need for creative adaptations of technology to the field of legal work. High-tech paralegals who can fill this need will very likely be the highest-paid—and the most valued—legal assistants in the future.

- Indexing the Deposition Transcript (Chapter 6).
- Online "Plain English" Guidelines (Chapter 8).

Margin Web Sites

In every chapter, we have added several features titled *On the Web* in the margins. These features offer Web sites that students can access for further information on the topic being discussed in the text.

From Chapter 1 . . .

On the Web
NALA is implementing an online campus for continuing legal education (CLE) at **www.nalacampus.com.** For information on NFPA's online CLE offerings, go to **www.paralegals.org/ CLE/home.html.**

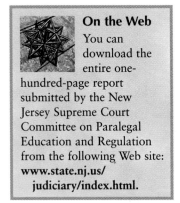

On the Web
You can download the entire one-hundred-page report submitted by the New Jersey Supreme Court Committee on Paralegal Education and Regulation from the following Web site: **www.state.nj.us/ judiciary/index.html.**

Chapter-Ending Internet Exercises

To help your students learn how to navigate the Web and find various types of information online, we have included at the end of each chapter one or more Internet exercises in a section titled *Using Internet Resources*. Each exercise directs the student to a specific Web site and asks a series of questions about the materials available at that site.

From Chapter 1 . . .

▧ USING INTERNET RESOURCES

Browse through the materials on the Web sites of the National Association of Legal Assistants, or NALA (at **www.nala.org**), and the National Federation of Paralegal Associations, or NFPA (at **www.paralegals.org**). Then do the following:

1. Look closely at the benefits of membership listed by each of these organizations. How do they compare? Are there any significant differences?

2. Examine the information that is included on each site about the organization's certification program. For each program, summarize the requirements that a paralegal must meet to become certified.

3. Select an article about a current development or issue in the paralegal profession from either NALA's "News &

Updates" or NFPA's "What's New?" pages. Write a one-paragraph summary of the article, indicating what the article is about and why the topic treated is significant.

4. Go to "What is a paralegal/legal assistant?" at the NALA Web site (at **www.nala.org**). Which of the following tasks might legal assistants perform, according to the information provided there?
   a. Draft legal documents.
   b. Try cases in court.
   c. Locate witnesses.
   d. Give legal advice.
   e. Set legal fees.
   f. Interview clients.
   g. Perform legal investigations.

WEST'S PARALEGAL ONLINE RESOURCE CENTER

The West Legal Studies Web site, at **www.westlegalstudies.com,** continues to offer numerous resources for paralegal professionals, instructors, and students. At this site, you and your students will find over 220 links to legal and paralegal information sites. This site also hosts a page dedicated to *West's Paralegal Today*, Second Edition, where you and your students can find text updates, hot links, and other resources.

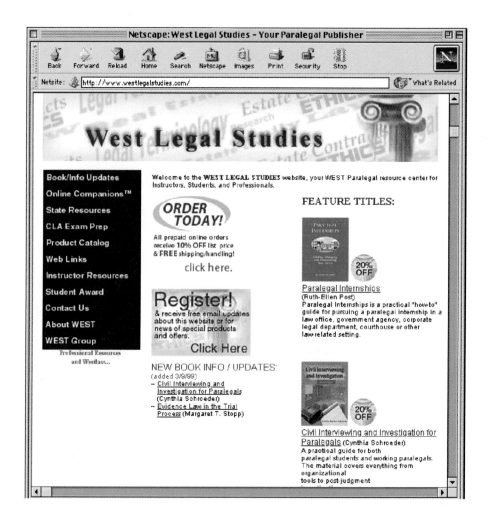

THE ORGANIZATION OF THIS TEXTBOOK

As every paralegal instructor knows, ideally materials should be presented in such a way that students can build their skills and knowledge bases block by block. This is difficult because, no matter where you begin, you will need to refer to some information that has not yet been presented to the student. For example, if you try to explain what paralegals do on the first or second day of class, you will necessarily have to mention terms that may be unfamiliar to the students, such as *litigation* or *substantive law* or *procedural law*. In writing this text, the authors have attempted, whenever possible, to organize the topics covered in such a way that the student is never mystified by terms and concepts not yet discussed.

We realize that no one way of organizing the coverage of topics in a paralegal text will be suitable for all instructors. It is our hope, however, that our organization of the materials will allow the greatest flexibility for instructors. Although to a certain extent each chapter in this text "builds" on information contained in previous chapters, the chapters can also be used independently. In other words, those instructors who wish to alter the presentation of topics to fit their course outlines, or who wish to use selected chapters only, will find it relatively easy to do so.

KEY FEATURES

In addition to the new *Technology and Today's Paralegal* features, which we have already discussed, every chapter in this text has the following features. Each feature is set apart and used both to instruct and to pique the interest of your paralegal students.

Developing Paralegal Skills

These boxed-in features present hypothetical examples of paralegals at work to help your students develop crucial paralegal skills. For the Second Edition, these features have been revised to include checklists and practical tips. Some examples are the following:

- Building an Ethical Wall (Chapter 3).
- Federal Court Rules—Creating a Complaint Checklist (Chapter 6).
- Keeping an Evidence Log (Chapter 7).
- Medical Research on the Internet (Chapter 9).

From Chapter 3 . . .

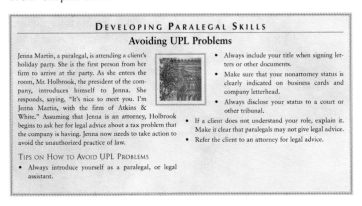

DEVELOPING PARALEGAL SKILLS
Avoiding UPL Problems

Jenna Martin, a paralegal, is attending a client's holiday party. She is the first person from her firm to arrive at the party. As she enters the room, Mr. Holbrook, the president of the company, introduces himself to Jenna. She responds, saying, "It's nice to meet you. I'm Jenna Martin, with the firm of Atkins & White." Assuming that Jenna is an attorney, Holbrook begins to ask her for legal advice about a tax problem that the company is having. Jenna now needs to take action to avoid the unauthorized practice of law.

TIPS ON HOW TO AVOID UPL PROBLEMS
- Always introduce yourself as a paralegal, or legal assistant.

- Always include your title when signing letters or other documents.
- Make sure that your nonattorney status is clearly indicated on business cards and company letterhead.
- Always disclose your status to a court or other tribunal.
- If a client does not understand your role, explain it. Make it clear that paralegals may not give legal advice.
- Refer the client to an attorney for legal advice.

Ethical Concerns

Every chapter presents three or more *Ethical Concerns*. These features typically take a student into a hypothetical situation that clearly presents an ethical problem. When possible, students are told what they should and should not do in particular situations being discussed. Some examples are the following:

- Saying "If I were you . . . " and the UPL (Chapter 3).
- Potential Arbitration Problems (Chapter 5).
- Communicating with Jurors (Chapter 6).
- The Importance of Finding Current Law (Chapter 8).

From Chapter 1 . . .

ETHICAL CONCERN
Paralegal Expertise and Legal Advice

Paralegals often become very knowledgeable in a specific area of the law. If you specialize in environmental law, for example, you will become very knowledgeable about environmental claims. In working with a client on a matter involving an environmental agency, you might therefore be tempted to advise the client on which type of action would be most favorable to him or her. Never do so. As will be discussed in detail in Chapter 3, only attorneys may give legal advice, and paralegals who give legal advice risk penalties for the unauthorized practice of law. Whatever legal advice is given to the client must come either directly from the attorney or, if from you, must reflect exactly (or nearly exactly) what the attorney said with no embellishment on your part. After consulting with your supervising attorney, for example, you can say to the client that Mr. X (the attorney) "advises that you do all that you can to settle the claim as soon as possible."

From Chapter 2 . . .

PARALEGAL PROFILE
Real-Estate Paralegal

DORA DYE has been a real estate/corporate paralegal since 1986. She has worked at several major San Francisco law firms and has transferred her skills to the corporate environment. She is currently the Dispositions Closing Coordinator at the RREEF Funds.

Dye was the president of the San Francisco Paralegal Association (SFPA) in 1993 and 1994 and currently serves on the Education Committee of both SFPA and the National Federation of Paralegal Associations, Inc. (NFPA). She is an active member of the NFPA's PACE Development Committee and co-authored the chapter, "Factual and Legal Research" in the Paralegal Advanced Competency Exam Study Manual with her husband, David Dye.

Dye also teaches legal writing, legal-assisting work experience, and commercial law via distance learning at City College of San Francisco's Paralegal/Legal Studies Program and is an associate professor of the paralegal program at California State University, Hayward.

Dye earned a bachelor of arts degree in Spanish, with distinction in general scholarship, and a master of arts degree in Spanish from the University of California, Berkeley. In addition, Dye received a master of business administration degree in International Business, with distinction, from Armstrong University.

What do you like best about your work?
"I enjoy the field of real estate, because I am able to bring in all of my experiences from the past to my current position. While working at various law firms, I became a senior paralegal specializing in multimillion-dollar real estate closings. That experience has allowed me to transfer my knowledge and skills in real estate, business, and the law to a corporate environment and to work more effectively with internal and external legal counsel. Becoming a part-time paralegal instructor has enabled me to share my knowledge and skills with future paralegals. I have even used my Spanish skills when doing pro bono work."

What is the greatest challenge that you face in your area of work?
"Satisfying the twin goals of cost efficiency and the generation of a superior work product represents the greatest challenge. To meet these goals, it is important to 'get it right' the first time. Today, paralegals have a more personal relationship with clients. Clients call paralegals directly to handle issues that require the attorney's attention, thus improving the quality of legal services being delivered and keeping costs down."

What advice do you have for would-be paralegals in your area of work?
"Be as detail oriented as possible, and be the best that you can be in all things that you do. Bringing to your position all experiences that you have had will add to your value as a paralegal.

Paralegal students should get work experience. Without work experience, students do not have an idea of office culture and environment, which are important aspects of a job."

What are some tips for success as a paralegal in your area of work?
"A successful paralegal knows what needs to be done and does it before he or she is asked. If you anticipate the needs of your attorneys and your clients, you will always be prepared to deal with matters more efficiently and effectively."

> "Bringing to your position all experiences that you have had will add to your value as a paralegal."

Paralegal Profiles

Every chapter has a profile of a paralegal who is currently working in a specific area of law. These profiles open with a short biography of the paralegal and then present the paralegal's own answers to questions asked by the interviewer. The paralegal tells of his or her greatest challenges on the job, gives suggestions about what he or she thinks students should concentrate on when studying to become a paralegal, and offers tips for being a successful paralegal in his or her line of work. This feature gives your students insights into various legal specialties and the diversity of paralegal working environments.

Featured-Guest Articles

Each chapter has a contributed article written by an educator or an expert in the field. These articles offer your students practical tips on some aspect of paralegal work relating to the topic covered in the chapter. Some examples are the following:

- "Paralegal Career Planning and Development," by Denise Templeton, president and chief executive officer of Templeton & Associates, a legal-support services firm, and one of the founders of the Minnesota Association of Legal Assistants, the American Association for Paralegal Education, and the National Federation of Paralegal Associations (Chapter 2).
- "Ten Tips on Ethics and the Paralegal," by Michael A. Pener, professor at Johnson County Community College, Overland Park, Kansas (Chapter 3).
- "Ten Tips for Drafting Interrogatories," by James W. H. McCord, director of paralegal programs at Eastern Kentucky University, Richmond, Kentucky (Chapter 6).
- "Keeping Current on Computer Technology," by Jan Richmond, instructor at St. Louis Community College, St. Louis, Missouri (Chapter 9).

From Chapter 1 . . .

FEATURED GUEST: WENDY B. EDSON

Ten Tips for Effective Communication

BIOGRAPHICAL NOTE

Wendy B. Edson received her master's degree in library science (M.L.S.) from the University of Rhode Island and served as law librarian at the Buffalo, New York, firm of Phillips, Lytle, Hitchcock, Blain and Huber. In 1978, she joined the Paralegal Studies faculty at Hilbert College, in Hamburg, New York, and helped to develop an ABA-approved bachelor's degree program in 1992. She teaches paralegalism and legal ethics, legal research and writing, law and literature, volunteerism, and alternate dispute resolution. She also developed and coordinates the internship program. Edson reviews and publishes on the topics of paralegal education, legal research and writing, and community service. She has lectured to legal professionals on legal research, teaching skills, internships, community service, environmental law, and ADR. Professor Edson is an AAfPE member and has presented papers at its national conferences and chaired model syllabi projects.

Words! They are the building blocks of human communication. Whether words are exchanged face-to-face—or by e-mail, phone, fax, or letter—communication is a two-way street. But how do we become skilled at maneuvering the *two-way* traffic of interpersonal communication? As in driving, we need to follow the "rules of the road." The rules of the road in regard to communication traffic are embodied in the following ten tips.

1. Establish Communication Equality. Communication equality does not require that individuals hold equal status in an office or organization but requires that each party believe in *equal rights* to speak and listen. Observe someone whom you consider to be a good communicator. You will note that he or she demonstrates equality by actively listening and responding appropriately to whoever is speaking. Workplace problems often reflect communication ailments rooted in inequality. A firm belief in communication equality, despite job titles, will help to create a cooperative, productive working environment.

2. Plan for Time and Space. Effective communication requires time. Imagine your reaction to a request to work overtime if your supervising attorney took thirty seconds to order you to do the work versus taking two minutes to explain the reason for the request and listening to your response. In the first situation, the attorney saved one and a half minutes but scored "zero" in terms of communication skills. In today's rushed world, it is easy to overlook the importance of communication skills in morale building and creating *Continued on next page*

a cooperative, efficient work force.

Effective communicators are aware of how the physical environment in which a conversation takes place can affect the communication process. Communication is always enhanced when the parties have reasonable privacy and are not continually interrupted. Another important factor is physical comfort. Choosing an inappropriate time and place for communication denies the importance of the matters being discussed and may send the wrong message to both the speaker and the listener.

3. Set the Agenda. Skilled communicators prepare an agenda—whether written or mental—of matters to be discussed in order of their priority. Frequently, both parties bring their respective agendas to a discussion, which means that priorities may need to be negotiated. A subordinate who brings up the topic of desired vacation time when the supervisor is preoccupied with a major project clearly demonstrates that his or her priorities are different from those of the supervisor.

Successful communication requires that the parties first negotiate a *common agenda*—that is, determine jointly the agenda for a particular discussion or meeting and what topics should take priority. Then, the topics can be dealt with one by one, in terms of their relative importance, to the satisfaction of both parties. Agenda *awareness* prevents parties from jumping from topic to topic without successfully resolving anything.

4. Fine-Tune Your Speaking Skills. Observe an individual whom you consider to be a good speaker, whether

---

FEATURED GUEST, *Continued*

before a group of persons or on a one-on-one basis. What skills does that individual demonstrate? Effective speakers work hard to express thoughts clearly; sometimes, they refer to notes or lists to refresh their memories. Skilled speakers also try to communicate accurately and to talk about matters that they know will interest their listeners. They cultivate *communication empathy*—the sincere effort to put themselves in their listeners' shoes. As you speak to others, pause occasionally and ask yourself: "Would I enjoy listening to what I am saying and how I am saying it?"

5. Cultivate Listening Skills. Listening is not just refraining from speaking while another person is talking but an *active* process—the other half of the communication partnership. An active listener does not interrupt the speaker. If you sense that the speaker is engaging in a monologue, responsive behavior—including body language, attentiveness, and appropriate remarks—can steer the conversation back to a dialogue without cutting off the speaker.

An active listener realizes that listening is an investment in effective communication. By truly responding to what is being said, rather than regarding listening time as insignificant or time to plan his or her own remarks, the skilled listener establishes a bond of trust with the speaker. Active listeners avoid preconceived ideas about topics being discussed and assume that they do not know all the answers.

6. Watch for Body Language. Body language is nonverbal communication that reflects our emotional state. Physical positions, such as

leaning forward or away from the speaker while listening, can reinforce or negate our spoken responses. Body attitudes, whether relaxed (comfortable posture, leaning forward, uncrossed arms and legs, relaxed neck and shoulders) or tense (stiff posture, backing away, crossed arms and legs, rigid neck and shoulders) vividly illustrate our responses before we utter a word. Eye contact is one of the most important tools in the body language tool kit for communication. Interviewers, social workers, and police officers have learned that steady and responsive eye contact means sincerity and credibility.

7. Put Note Taking in Perspective. Over involvement in note taking detracts from the communication process because opportunities to listen actively, speak responsively, and be sensitive to body language are reduced. The speaker may ramble while the listener records the ramblings in extensive notes.

When it is necessary to take notes, it is helpful to establish some rapport with the speaker or listener before launching the note-taking process. Alternatively, follow-up notes can be a workable solution to the problem. The note taker can devote the interview time to communication and, after the interview, record his or her general impressions of the interview and identify specific issues that need to be discussed further.

8. Recognize the Role of Criticism. *Constructive criticism* focuses on specific actions or behaviors rather than personalities. It is objective rather than subjective. Criticism that is stated calmly and objectively ("We need to rewrite the section on holo-

> "Eye contact is one of the most important tools in the body language tool kit for communication."

graphic wills.") is much more palatable for the person being criticized than is criticism in the form of a personal attack ("You did a terrible job"). By placing emphasis on actions instead of personalities, the parties can more easily work toward a satisfactory solution. If both the critic and the person being criticized can remain calm and can separate actions from personalities, then criticism will usually produce the desired result and *mutual* satisfaction.

9. Aim for Satisfactory Closure. Closure means "wrapping up" the communication. Successful communicators know that handling closure properly can leave a participant with a good feeling even if the solution was not exactly what he or she initially desired. Summarizing the discussion and checking for agreement or a need for further discussion will encourage all participants to follow the tenth tip.

10. Commit to Communicate. Excellent speakers and listeners have positive, self-confident attitudes that problems can be solved if the "rules of the road" are followed. Skilled communicators cultivate open minds, self-knowledge, and the ability to tolerate differences and empathize with others. They are committed to exercising their rights and responsibilities as speakers and listeners in the communication process.

Today's Professional Paralegal

Near the end of every chapter we have included a special feature entitled *Today's Professional Paralegal*. This important feature exposes your students to situations that they are likely to encounter on the job and offers guidance on how certain types of problems can be resolved. Some examples are the following:

- Managing Conflict (Chapter 4).
- Drafting *Voir Dire* Questions Like a Pro (Chapter 6).
- Accessing Government Information (Chapter 7).
- Preparing the Internal Memorandum (Chapter 8).

From Chapter 1 . . .

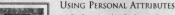

TODAY'S PROFESSIONAL PARALEGAL

A Winning Combination

Susan Latham is a legal secretary for Melinda Oakwood, a real-estate attorney who is a partner in the law firm of Morris, Crowther, Oakwood & Miller. The law firm is one of the largest in the state, employing over 300 attorneys, 75 paralegals, 130 secretaries, and many support staff members. Susan, who has become more of a legal assistant than a secretary to Melinda, has decided, at the age of forty, to return to the local university to obtain a paralegal degree. This way, Susan can be rewarded (in the form of higher wages) for the work that she actually does already and can seek advancement in the firm.

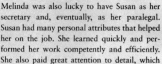

Susan has worked for Melinda for eleven years. She has been given increased responsibility because she has shown Melinda that she is dependable and reliable in handling her work assignments. Her work is always turned in on time, and it is always accurate.

LEARNING ON THE JOB

Susan was very lucky to have Melinda as a supervising attorney. Melinda, who had been a teacher for ten years before she went to law school, liked to teach Susan how to undertake new work assignments. When Susan had a new type of document to prepare at work, Melinda would give her a sample document and very good instructions. Now that Susan is studying to be a paralegal, Melinda has started assisting Susan with her school assignments by giving her sample documents and copies of the laws that require those documents. Melinda also points out the differences between the class assignments and the sample documents and discusses with Susan why the differences matter from a legal perspective.

Additionally, Melinda encourages Susan to ask questions about school assignments and to take her time completing them so that when they are turned in, they are accurate. Susan has a strong sense of commitment, so she always sees a project through even if it seems to take forever.

USING PERSONAL ATTRIBUTES

Melinda was also lucky to have Susan as her secretary and, eventually, as her paralegal. Susan had many personal attributes that helped her on the job. She learned quickly and performed her work competently and efficiently.

She also paid great attention to detail, which was one of the reasons Melinda encouraged Susan to get a paralegal degree. Unlike Melinda's former paralegal, who would send out letters and fail to include the documents that should have been enclosed, Susan was meticulous. And Melinda could always count on Susan to keep client information confidential.

Susan already had good computer and organizational skills when Melinda hired her. She did need to improve her analytical and listening skills, though. Susan's analytical skills are already improving as a result of a course she is taking in legal research, which requires case analysis. Over time, Susan learned to listen to Melinda's instructions and to question Melinda when Susan was not exactly certain about what Melinda wanted her to do.

THE RESULT: A WINNING TEAM

Melinda and Susan have developed a solid working relationship. It took time for Susan to develop some of the skills that she needed, but Melinda was a good and patient teacher. It also took time to develop a trusting relationship, but now Melinda can confidently delegate significant assignments to Susan, knowing that Susan will complete them accurately. Now that Susan is in a paralegal program, Melinda can also delegate more challenging work to Susan, and Susan can eventually be promoted to paralegal status. Melinda and Susan work productively and efficiently together. They like and rely on each other and enjoy their work. Theirs is a winning combination of talents and skills.

OTHER SPECIAL PEDAGOGICAL FEATURES

We have included in *West's Paralegal Today*, Second Edition, a number of additional pedagogical features, including those discussed below.

Chapter Outlines

On every chapter-opening page, a *Chapter Outline* lists the first-level headings within the chapter. These outlines allow you and your students to tell at a glance what topics are covered in the chapters.

Chapter Objectives

In every chapter, just following the *Chapter Outline*, we list five or six chapter objectives. Your students will know immediately what is expected of them as they read each chapter.

Margin Web Sites

As already mentioned, *On the Web* features appear in the page margins throughout the text. These features direct students to specific Web sites for further information on the topics being discussed.

Vocabulary and Margin Definitions

Legal terminology is often a major challenge for beginning paralegal students. We have used an important pedagogical device—margin definitions—to help your students understand legal terms. Whenever an important term is introduced, it is done so in boldface type and defined. In addition, the term is listed and defined in the margin of the page, alongside the paragraph in which the boldfaced term appears.

At the end of each chapter, all terms that have been boldfaced within the chapter are listed in alphabetical order in a section called *Key Terms and Concepts*. The page on which the term is defined is given after each term. Your students can briefly examine this list to make sure that they understand all of the important terms introduced in the chapter. If they do not understand a term completely, they can immediately refer to the page number given and review the term.

All boldfaced terms are again listed and defined in the *Glossary* at the end of the text. Spanish equivalents to many important legal terms in English are provided in a separate glossary.

Estate Administration
The process in which a decedent's personal representative settles the affairs of the decedent's estate (collects assets, pays debts and taxes, and distributes the remaining assets to heirs); the process is usually overseen by a probate court.

Joint Tenancy
The joint ownership of property by two or more co-owners in which each co-owner owns an undivided portion of the property. On the death of one of the joint tenants, his or her interest automatically passes to the surviving joint tenant or tenants.

Exhibits and Forms

When appropriate, we present exhibits illustrating important forms or concepts relating to paralegal work. Many exhibits are filled in with hypothetical data. Exhibits and forms in *West's Paralegal Today*, Second Edition, include those listed below:

- A Sample Retainer Agreement (Chapter 4).
- A Sample Complaint (Chapter 6).
- An Investigation Plan (Chapter 7).

In Chapter 8, we present a special exhibit (Exhibit 8.6), which shows the major components of a court case, including excerpts from the court's opinion. Important sections, terms, and phrases in the sample case are defined or discussed in margin annotations.

CHAPTER-ENDING MATERIALS FOR REVIEW AND STUDY

Every chapter contains numerous chapter-ending pedagogical materials. These materials are designed to provide a wide variety of assignments for your students.

The chapter-ending pedagogy begins with the *Key Terms and Concepts*, which we have already mentioned. Next are the materials described below.

Chapter Summary

Every chapter ends with a series of numbered paragraphs that summarize the major points made in the chapter. These summaries can be used by students to review and test their knowledge of the topics covered in the chapter.

Questions for Review

In every chapter, following the *Chapter Summary*, are ten relatively straightforward questions for review. These questions are designed to test the student's knowledge of the basic concepts discussed in the chapter.

Ethical Questions

Because of the importance of ethical issues in paralegal training, we have also included at the end of each chapter two or more ethical questions. Each question presents a hypothetical situation, which is followed by one or two questions about what the paralegal should do to solve the dilemma.

Practice Questions and Assignments

The "hands-on" approach to learning paralegal skills is emphasized in the practice questions and assignments. There are several of these questions and assignments at the end of each chapter. A particular situation is presented, and the student is asked to actually carry out an assignment.

Using Internet Resources

As already mentioned, concluding the chapter-ending materials in each chapter is a section titled *Using Internet Resources*. The Internet exercises presented in these sections are designed to familiarize students with useful Web sites and with the extensive array of resources now available online.

APPENDICES

To make this text a reference source for your students, we have included the appendices listed below:

A	NALA's Code of Ethics and Professional Responsibility
B	NALA's Model Standards and Guidelines for the Utilization of Legal Assistants, Annotated
C	NFPA's Model Code of Ethics and Professional Responsibility and Guidelines for Enforcement
D	The ABA's Model Guidelines for the Utilization of Legal Assistant Services
E	Paralegal Ethics and Regulation: How to Find State-Specific Information
F	Paralegal Associations
G	State and Major Local Bar Associations
H	Information on NALA's CLA and CLAS Examinations
I	Information on NFPA's PACE Examination
J	The Constitution of the United States
K	Spanish Equivalents for Important Legal Terms in English

NEW CHAPTERS AND SIGNIFICANT CHANGES TO THE SECOND EDITION

The authors have made a number of significant changes and additions to *West's Paralegal Today* for the Second Edition. We think that we have improved the text greatly, thanks in part to the many suggestions we have received from users of the First Edition as well as from other paralegal educators and legal professionals.

New Chapters, Features, and Other Changes

Generally, all elements in the book—including the text, exhibits, features, and end-of-chapter pedagogy—have been updated as necessary. Significant additions and changes to the Second Edition include the following:

- **An entirely new chapter on computer-assisted legal research (CALR)**—This chapter introduces the student to legal research using CD-ROMs, legal-research services such as Westlaw® and Lexis®, and the Internet.

- *Technology and Today's Paralegal*—This new feature, which appears in every chapter, explores ways in which paralegals can take advantage of new technology to simplify their tasks and enhance their efficiency.

- *On the Web*—This new feature, which appears in the page margins, highlights Web sites that are relevant to the topics being discussed and that students can access to obtain more information.

- *Using Internet Resources*—The Second Edition includes, at the end of every chapter, one or more Internet exercises to familiarize students with how to access and evaluate information available on the Web.

- New *Paralegal Profiles*—Most of these profiles are new to this edition.

- The *Developing Paralegal Skills* features have been modified—These features now include practical tips and checklists on the topics covered in the features.

- **NFPA's PACE examination and NALA's Online Campus**—These two recent developments are discussed in Chapter 1.

- **More information on paralegal practice areas**—Chapter 2 now includes descriptions of legal aid offices; freelance paralegals; and a number of emerging specialty areas, such as elder law and legal nurse consulting.

- **Coverage of the regulatory developments in New Jersey, Utah, and other states**—These developments are mentioned in Chapter 1 and discussed in more detail in Chapter 3.

- **New and updated appendices**—All appendices have been updated as necessary, and an entirely new appendix on NFPA's PACE examination has been added.

For Users of the First Edition

Those of you who have used the First Edition of this text will probably want to know of some other changes that have been made for the Second Edition. In addition to the changes and additions just mentioned, we have made the following changes to *West's Paralegal Today* for this edition:

- **Chapter 1** (Today's Professional Paralegal)—The chapter now includes a completely rewritten section on the definition of a paralegal and also includes the AAfPE's definition of a paralegal. Additionally, the AAfPE's role in paralegal education has been stressed, as has the growing importance of computer technology, including online communications, in the legal workplace.

- **Chapter 2** (Careers in the Legal Community)—The discussion of areas of paralegal practice now includes legal aid offices; freelance paralegals; and a number of emerging specialty areas, such as elder law and legal nurse consulting. The chapter also includes a section—and a special feature—on online job searching.
- **Appendix A of the First Edition**—The appendix formerly entitled "Mastering *West's Paralegal Today*: How to Study Legal Concepts and Procedures" has been moved to the front of the book. It now appears as an "Introduction to the Student" just before Chapter 1. A section entitled "Going Online" has been added to this introduction.

SUPPLEMENTAL TEACHING/LEARNING MATERIALS

West's Paralegal Today, Second Edition, is accompanied by what is arguably the largest number of teaching and learning supplements available for any text of its kind. We understand that instructors face a difficult task in finding the time necessary to teach the materials that they wish to cover during each term. In conjunction with a number of our colleagues, we have developed supplementary teaching materials that we believe are the best obtainable today. Each component of the supplements package is described below.

Instructor's Manual

Written by the authors of the text, the *Instructor's Manual* contains the following:

- A sample course syllabus.
- Chapter/lecture outlines.
- Teaching suggestions.
- Test Bank.
- Answers to text exercises and questions.
- Transparency masters.
- PowerPoint presentation slides.

Study Guide

Prepared by Celia Elwell of the University of Oklahoma, the *Study Guide* includes the following features:

- Chapter objectives are presented in checklist form so that students can review systematically the topics they have learned and determine which areas need more study.
- Chapter outlines provide succinct, easy-to-read summaries of the chapters and help students review the material. Study suggestions are included within the outlines, including tips on how to remember key information.
- Review questions in true-false, fill-in-the-blank, and multiple-choice formats provide students with an extensive review of the terminology and concepts presented in each chapter of the text. There are between thirty and fifty review questions for each chapter.
- Additional practice questions, questions for critical analysis, and ethical questions reinforce the concepts and procedures presented in the chapters.

Computerized Test Bank

The Test Bank found in the *Instructor's Manual* is also available in a computerized format on CD-ROM. The platforms supported include Windows™ 3.1 and 95, Windows™ NT, and Macintosh. Features include:

- Multiple methods of question selection.
- Multiple outputs—that is, print, ASCII, RTF.
- Graphic support (black and white).
- Random questioning output.
- Special character support.

State-Specific Supplements

State-specific supplements are available for California, Florida, New York, and Texas. These supplements are keyed to each chapter in the text and point out state-specific information when it differs from the text's discussion. These supplements will be made available online as a downloadable electronic supplement.

Citation-At-A-Glance

This handy reference card provides a quick, portable reference to the basic rules of citation for the most commonly cited legal sources, including judicial opinions, statutes, and secondary sources, such as legal encyclopedias and legal periodicals. *Citation-At-A-Glance* uses the rules set forth in *The Bluebook: A Uniform System of Citation*. A free copy of this valuable supplement is included with every student text.

Web Page

Come visit our Web site at **www.westlegalstudies.com**, where you will find a Web page specific to this book that includes the following:

- Sample materials.
- Hot links.
- State-specific materials.

Strategies for Paralegal Educators

Strategies and Tips for Paralegal Educators, a pamphlet by Anita Tebbe of Johnson County Community College, provides teaching strategies specifically designed for paralegal educators. It concentrates on how to teach and is organized in three parts: the WHO of paralegal education—students and teachers; the WHAT of paralegal education—goals and objectives; and the HOW of paralegal education—methods of instruction, methods of evaluation, and other aspects of teaching. A copy of this pamphlet is available to each adopter. Quantities for distribution to adjunct instructors are available for purchase at a minimal price. A coupon in the pamphlet provides ordering information.

Westlaw®

West's online computerized legal-research system offers students "hands-on" experience with a system commonly used in law offices. Qualified adopters can receive ten free hours of Westlaw®. Westlaw® can be accessed with Macintosh and IBM PCs and compatibles. A modem is required.

ACKNOWLEDGMENTS

We are grateful to the following paralegal educators, our featured guests in West's Paralegal Today, Second Edition, for enhancing the quality of our book with their tips and illuminating insights into paralegal practice:

Anna Durham Boling
Athens Area Technical Institute, GA

Audrey Casey
Andover College, ME

Andrea Nager Chasen
Private Law Practice

Wendy B. Edson
Hilbert College, NY

Thomas K. Jackson, Esquire
Norwalk Community-Technical
    College, CT

Nancy Johnson
Illinois Central College, IL

Gerald A. Loy
Broome County Community College, NY

James W. H. McCord
Eastern Kentucky University, KY

Michael A. Pener
Johnson County Community College, KS

Kathleen Mercer Reed
University of Toledo's Community
    and Technical College, OH

Jan Richmond
St. Louis Community College, MO

Denise Templeton
President and Chief Executive Officer
    of Templeton & Associates

Richard M. Terry
Baltimore City Community College, MD

Julia O. Tryk
Cuyahoga Community College, OH

Additionally, we extend our gratitude to those on-the-job paralegals who agreed to appear in the Paralegal Profiles of West's Paralegal Today, Second Edition.

In preparing West's Paralegal Today, Second Edition, we were also the beneficiaries of the expertise brought to the project by the editorial and production staff of the West Legal Studies program. Our editor, Joan Gill, successfully guided the project through each phase and put together a supplements package that is without parallel in the teaching and learning of paralegal skills. Rhonda Dearborn, our developmental editor, was also incredibly helpful in putting together the teaching/learning package. We sincerely appreciate the efforts of our project editor, Ann Borman, who designed what we feel is the most visually attractive paralegal text on the market, and of the production supervisor on the project, Bill Stryker. We also wish to thank our production manager, Wendy Troeger, and production editor, Laurie Boyce, for their assistance throughout the production process.

A number of other individuals contributed significantly to the quality of West's Paralegal Today, Second Edition. We wish to thank William Eric Hollowell for his assistance in creating what we believe is the best chapter on computer-assisted legal research in any paralegal text on the market today. We also thank Lavina Leed Miller and Roxie Lee for their help in coordinating the authors' work on the project and for their research and proofreading efforts. We are grateful to Suzie Franklin DeFazio, whose copyediting and proofreading skills will not go unnoticed, and to Suzanne Jasin for her assistance.

We know that we are not perfect. If you or your students have suggestions on how we can improve this book, write to us. That way, we can make West's Paralegal Today, Second Edition, an even better book in the future. We promise to answer every single letter that we receive.

Roger LeRoy Miller
Mary Meinzinger Urisko

INTRODUCTION TO THE STUDENT

The law sometimes is considered a difficult subject because it uses a specialized vocabulary and requires substantial time and effort to learn. Those who work with and teach law believe that the subject matter is exciting and definitely worth your efforts. Everything in *West's Paralegal Today: The Essentials,* Second Edition, has been written for the precise purpose of helping you learn the most important aspects of law and legal procedures.

Learning is a lifelong process. Your learning of legal concepts and procedures will not end when you finish your paralegal studies. On the contrary, the end of your paralegal studies marks the beginning of your learning process in regard to law and legal procedures. Just as valuable to you as the knowledge base you can acquire from mastering the legal concepts and terms in *West's Paralegal Today,* Second Edition, is a knowledge of *how to learn* those legal concepts and terms. The focus in this introduction, therefore, is on developing learning skills that you can apply to any subject matter and at any time throughout your career.

The suggestions and study tips offered in this introduction can help you "learn how to learn" law and procedures and maximize your chances of success as a paralegal student. They can also help you build lifelong learning habits that you can use in other classes and throughout your career as a paralegal.

MASTERING YOUR TEXT

A mistake commonly made by students is the assumption that the best way to understand the content of written material is to read and reread that material. True, if you read through a chapter ten times, you probably have acquired a knowledge of its contents, but think of the time you have spent in the process. What you want to strive for is using your time *effectively*. We offer here some suggestions on how to study the chapters of *West's Paralegal Today: The Essentials,* Second Edition most effectively.

Read One Section at a Time

A piano student once said to her teacher, "This piece is so complicated. How can I possibly learn it?" The teacher responded, "It's simple: measure by measure." That advice can be applied to any challenging task. As a paralegal student, you are faced with the task of learning complicated legal concepts and procedures. By dividing up your work into manageable units, you will find that before long, you have achieved your goal. Each chapter in *West's Paralegal Today,* Second Edition, is divided into several major sections. By concentrating on sections, rather than chapters, you will find it easier to master the chapter's contents.

Once you have read through a section, do not stop there. Go back through the section again and organize the material in your mind. Outlining the section is one way to mentally organize what you have read.

Make an Outline

An outline is simply a method for organizing information. The reason an outline can be helpful is that it illustrates visually how concepts relate to each other. Outlining can be done as part of your reading of each section, but your outline will be more accurate (and more helpful later on) if you have already read through a section and have a general understanding of the topics covered within that section.

THE BENEFITS OF OUTLINING. Although you may not believe that you need to outline, our experience has been that the act of *physically* writing an outline for a chapter helps most students to improve greatly their ability to retain and master the material being studied. Even if you make an outline that is no more than the headings in the text, you will be studying more efficiently than you otherwise would be.

Outlining is also a paralegal skill. As a paralegal, you will need to present legal concepts and fact patterns in an outline format. For example, paralegals frequently create legal memoranda to summarize their research results. The legal memorandum is usually presented in an outline format, which indicates how the topics covered in the memo relate to one another logically or sequentially. There is no better time to master the skill of outlining than the present, while you are a student. You can learn this skill by outlining sections and chapters of *West's Paralegal Today*, Second Edition.

IDENTIFY THE MAIN CONCEPTS IN EACH SECTION. You can use the chapter outlines at the beginning of each chapter as a starting point on your outlines for each section and chapter. The chapter-opening outlines include the headings of each major section within the chapter. You use these headings as a guide when creating a more thorough and detailed outline of each section. Be careful, though. To make an effective outline you have to be selective. Outlines that contain all the information in the text are not very useful. Your objective in outlining is to identify main concepts and to arrange more detailed concepts under those main concepts. Therefore, in outlining, your first goal is to *identify the main concepts in each section*. Often the large, first-level headings within your textbook and in the chapter-opening outlines are sufficient as identifiers of the major concepts within each section. You may decide, however, that you want to phrase an identifier in a way that is more meaningful to you.

OUTLINE FORMAT. Your outline should consist of several levels written in a standard outline format. The most important concepts are assigned an upper-case roman numeral; the second most important, a capital letter; the third most important, numbers; the fourth most important, lower-case letters; and the fifth most important, lower-case roman numerals. The number of levels you use in an outline varies, of course, with the complexity of the subject matter. In some outlines, or por-

tions of outlines, you may need to use only two levels. In others, you may need as many as five or more levels.

Consider Marking Your Text

From kindergarten through high school, you typically did not own your own textbooks. They were made available by the school system. You were told not to mark in them. Now that you own your own text for a course, your learning can be greatly improved by marking your text. There is a trade-off here. The more you mark up your textbook, the less you will receive from the bookstore when you sell it back at the end of the semester. The benefit is a better understanding of the subject matter, and the cost is the reduction in the price you receive for the resale of the text. Additionally, if you want a text that you can mark with your own notations, you necessarily have to buy a new one or a used one that has no markings. Both carry a higher price tag than a used textbook with markings.

THE BENEFITS OF MARKING. Marking is helpful because it assists you to become an *active* participant in the mastery of the material. Researchers have shown that the physical act of marking, just like the physical act of outlining, helps you better retain the material. The better the material is organized in your mind, the more you will remember. There are two types of readers—passive and active. The active reader outlines and/or marks. Active readers typically do better on exams. Perhaps one of the reasons that active readers retain more is because the physical act of outlining and/or marking requires greater concentration. It is through greater concentration that more is remembered.

DIFFERENT WAYS OF MARKING. The most commonly used form of marking is to underline important points. The second most commonly used method is to use a felt-tipped highlighter, or marker, in yellow or some other transparent color. Marking also includes circling, numbering, using arrows, making brief notes, or any other method that allows you to locate things when you go back to skim the pages in your textbook prior to an exam—or when creating your outline, if you mark your text first and then outline it.

POINTS TO REMEMBER WHEN MARKING. Here are two important points to remember when marking your text:

1. *Read through the entire section before you begin marking.* You cannot mark a section until you know what is important, and you cannot know what is important until you read through the whole section.

2. *Do not mark too extensively.* You should mark your text selectively. If you fill up each page with arrows, asterisks, circles, and underlines, marking will be of little use. When you go back to review the material, you will not be able to find what was important. The key is *selective* activity. Mark each page in a way that allows you to see the most important points at a glance.

Memory Devices

During the course of your study of *West's Paralegal Today,* Second Edition, you will encounter numerous legal terms that are most likely new to you. Your challenge will be to remember these terms and incorporate them into your own "working" vocabulary. You will also need to remember legal concepts and principles. We look here at some techniques for learning and retaining legal terms and concepts.

FLASH CARDS.   Using flash cards is a remarkably effective method of learning new terms or concepts. Through sheer repetition, or drilling, flash cards force you to recall certain ideas and repeat them. Although published flash cards are available in many bookstores, you should try to create your own by writing terms or concepts on index cards. Write the key term or concept on one side and the definition, process, or description on the other side.

There are several advantages to creating your own flash cards. First, the exercise of actually writing the information will help you insert the term into your permanent memory. Second, you do not need flash cards for terms that you already know or that you will not need to know for your particular course. Third, you can phrase the answer in a meaningful way, with unique cues that are designed just for your purposes. This personalizes the flash card, making the information easier to remember. Finally, you can modify the definition, if need be, so that it matches more closely the particular definition preferred by your instructor.

It is helpful to create your flash cards consistently and routinely at a given point in the learning process. One good moment is when you are reading or outlining your text. Make a flash card for each boldfaced term and write the margin definition on the flash card. Also include pronunciation instructions, if appropriate, on the card.

Take your flash cards with you everywhere. Review them at lunch, while you wait in line, or when you ride on the bus. When a flash card contains a term that is difficult to pronounce, say the term aloud, if possible, as often as you can. When you have a term memorized, set that card aside but save it as an exam-review device for later in the term. Prepare new cards as you cover new terms or concepts in class.

MNEMONICS.   One method that students commonly employ to remember legal concepts and principles is the use of mnemonic (pronounced "nee-*mahn*-ick") devices. Mnemonic devices are merely aids to memory. A mnemonic device can be a word, a formula, or a rhyme. As an aid to remembering the basic activities that paralegals may not legally undertake (see Chapter 3), for example, you might use the mnemonic FACt, in which the letters represent the following concepts:

F represents "fees"—paralegals may not set legal fees.

A represents "advice"—paralegals may not give legal advice.

Ct represents "court"—paralegals, with some exceptions, may not represent clients in court.

Whenever you want to memorize various components of a legal doctrine or concept, consider devising a mnemonic. Mnemonics need not make sense in themselves. The point is, if they help you remember something, then use them. Any association you can make with a difficult term to help you pronounce it, spell it, or define it more easily is a useful learning tool.

Identify What You Do Not Understand

One of the most important things you can do prior to class is clarify in your mind which terms, concepts, or procedures you *do not* understand. You can do this when marking your text by placing check marks or question marks by material that you find difficult to comprehend. Similarly, you can include queries in your outline.

Once you have outlined and marked your text, go back to any problem areas that you have encountered and *think about them.* You will find that it is very exciting to figure out difficult material on your own. If you still do not understand a concept thoroughly, make a note to follow up on this topic later in the classroom. Perhaps the instructor's lecture will clarify the issue. If not, make a point of asking for clarification.

As a paralegal, you may be frequently asked to undertake preliminary investigations of legal claims. Identifying what facts are *not known* is the starting point for any investigation and focuses investigatory efforts. As a student, you might think about class time as an opportunity to "investigate" further the subject matter of your course. Identifying before class what you do not know about a topic allows you to focus your "investigative" efforts, particularly your listening efforts, during class and to maximize classroom opportunities for learning.

LEARNING IN THE CLASSROOM

The classroom is the heart of your learning experience as a paralegal student. Each instructor develops an overall plan for a course that includes many elements, which are integrated, or brought together, during class sessions. A major element in your instructor's course plan will be, of course, the material presented in your textbook, *West's Paralegal Today,* Second Edition. As discussed in the preceding section, reading your textbook assignments thoroughly, before class, is one way to enhance your chances of truly mastering the subject matter of the course. Equally important to this goal, though, are listening carefully to your instructor and taking good notes.

Be an Active Listener

The ability to listen actively is a learned skill and one that will benefit you throughout your career as a paralegal. When your supervising attorney gives instructions, for example, it is crucial that you understand those instructions clearly. If you do not, you will need to ask the attorney to further clarify the instructions until you know exactly what your assignment is. Similarly, when you are interviewing clients or witnesses, you will need to be constantly interacting, mentally, with the information the client or witness is giving you so that you can follow up, immediately if necessary, on that information with further questions or actions.

As a paralegal student, you can practice listening skills in the classroom that you will need to exercise later on the job. The more immediate benefit of listening actively is, of course, a better chance of obtaining an excellent course grade.

In a nutshell, active listening as a student requires you to do the following:

1. *Listen attentively.* For anything to be communicated verbally by one person to another, the listener has to pay attention or no communication will take place. If you find your attention wandering in the classroom, make a conscious effort to become alert and focus on what is being said.
2. *Mentally interact with what is being said.* Active lis-

tening involves mentally "acting" on the information being conveyed by the speaker (your instructor). For example, if your instructor is discussing the elements required for a cause of action in negligence, you do not want simply to write down, word for word, what the instructor is saying. Rather, you first make sure that you *understand* the meaning of what is being said. This requires you to think about what is being said in the context of what else you know about the topic. Does the information make sense within that context? Does what you are hearing raise further questions in your mind? If so, make a note of them.

3. *Ask for clarification.* If you do not understand what the instructor is saying or if something is confusing, ask for clarification. How you do this will depend to some extent on the size of your class and the degree of classroom formality. In some classes, you might feel comfortable raising your hand and questioning the instructor at that point during the lecture or discussion. In other classes, you might make a note to talk to the instructor about the topic after class or later, during the instructor's office hours.

Take Good Notes

The ability to take good notes is another skill that will help you excel both in your paralegal studies and on the job as a paralegal. Ideally, you will understand clearly everything that is being said in the classroom, and note taking will simply consist of jotting down, in your own words, brief phrases and sentences to remind you of what was stated. Often, however, you may not understand fully what the instructor is talking about, or it may take half of the class period before it becomes clear to you where your instructor is going with a certain idea or topic. In the meantime, should you take notes?

The best answer to this question is, of course, "Ask for clarification." But in some situations, interrupting a lecturer may be awkward or perceived as discourteous. In these circumstances, the wiser choice might be to take notes. Write down, to the extent possible, what the instructor is saying, including brief summaries of any examples the instructor is presenting. Later, when you have more knowledge of the subject, what the instructor said during that period may fall into place. If not, find an opportunity to ask for clarification.

Two other suggestions for taking good notes and making effective use of them are the following: (1) develop and use a shorthand system and (2) review and summarize your notes as soon as possible after class.

DEVELOP AND USE A SHORTHAND SYSTEM. There may be times during a lecture when you want to take extensive notes. For example, your instructor may be discussing a hypothetical scenario to illustrate a legal concept. Because you know that hypothetical examples are very useful in understanding (and later reviewing) legal concepts, you want to include a description of the hypothetical example in your notes. Using abbreviations and symbols can help you include more information in your notes in less time.

In taking notes on a hypothetical example, consider designating a single letter as representative of each person or entity involved in the example. This eliminates the need to write and rewrite the names of each person or entity as they are used. For example, if a hypothetical involves three business firms, you could designate each firm by a letter: *A* could stand for Abel Electronics, *B* for Brentwood Manufacturing, and *C* for Crandall Industries.

Certain symbols and abbreviations, including those listed below, are fairly widely used as a kind of "shorthand" by legal professionals and others to designate certain concepts, parties, or procedures:

Δ	defendant
π	plaintiff
≈	similar to
≠	not equal to, not the same as
[	therefore
a/k/a	also known as
atty	attorney
b/c or b/cz	because
b/p	burden of proof
cert	*certiorari*
dely	delivery
dep	deposition
disc	discovery
JML	judgment as a matter of law
JOP	judgment on the pleadings
juris	jurisdiction
K	contract
mtg	mortgage
n/a	not applicable
neg	negligence
PL	paralegal
Q	as a consequence, consequently
re	regarding
§ or sec	section
s/b	should be

You will want to expand on this short list by creating and using other symbols or abbreviations. Once you develop a workable shorthand system, routinely use it in the classroom and then carry it over to your job. Most firms or corporations you will work for will also commonly use symbols and abbreviations, which you can add to your shorthand system later. It may also be helpful to become familiar with proofing symbols, which are listed under "proofreading" in the dictionary.

REVIEW AND REVISE YOUR NOTES AFTER EACH CLASS. An excellent habit to form is reviewing and revising your class notes as soon as possible after the class period ends. Often, at the moment you write certain notes, you are not sure of how they fit in the overall design of the lecture. After class, however, you usually have a better perspective and know how the "pieces of the puzzle" fit together. Reviewing and summarizing your notes while the topic is still fresh in your mind—at the end of each day, for example—gives you the opportunity to reorganize them in a logical manner.

If you have a computer available, consider also typing up your notes. That way, when you want to review them, you will be able to read them quickly. Using a basic outline format when typing your notes (or rewriting them, if you do not have a computer available) will be particularly helpful later. You can tell at a glance the logical relationships among the various statements made in class.

Although reviewing and summarizing your notes each day or at other frequent intervals may seem overly time consuming, in the long run it pays off. First, as with outlining and marking a text, reviewing your notes after class allows you to learn actively—you can think about what was covered during the class period, place various concepts in perspective, and decide what you do or do not understand after you complete your review. Second, you have probably already learned that memory is fickle. Even though we think we will not forget something we learned, in fact, we often do. When preparing for an exam, for example, you will want to remember what the instructor said in class about a particular topic. But, if you are like most people, your memory of that day and that class period may be rather fuzzy several weeks later. If you have taken good notes and summarized them legibly and logically, you will be able to review the topic quickly and effectively.

Networking in the Classroom

Several times in *West's Paralegal Today,* Second Edition, the authors, the featured-guest authors, and the paralegals profiled have all mentioned the importance of networking. The best time to begin networking is in the classroom. Consciously make an effort to get to know your instructor. Let him or her come to know you and your interests. Later, when looking for a job, you may want to ask that instructor for a reference.

Similarly, make an effort to become acquainted with other students in your class. Compared to students who are taking other college courses, such as math courses and history courses, there is a greater likelihood those of you in paralegal studies will be working in the same geographic area and may eventually belong to the same paralegal associations. Establishing connections with your classmates now may lead to networking possibilities later on the job, which offers many benefits for paralegals. One good way to establish long-term relationships with other students is by forming a study group.

FORMING AND ORGANIZING A STUDY GROUP

Many paralegal students join together in study groups to exchange ideas, to share the task of outlining subjects, to prepare for examinations, and to lend support to each other generally. If you want to start a study group, a good way to find potential members is to observe your classmates and decide which students participate actively and frequently in class. Then approach those individuals with your idea of forming a study group. The number of participants in a study group can vary. Ordinarily, three to five members is sufficient for a good discussion. A study group with more than six members may defeat the goal of having each member actively participate, to the greatest extent possible, in group discussions.

Some paralegal students form study groups that meet on an "as needed" basis. For example, any member could call a meeting when there is an upcoming exam or difficult subject matter to be learned. Other students establish ongoing study groups that meet throughout the year (and sometimes for the entire paralegal program). The group works as a team and as such is an excellent preparatory device for working as part of a legal team in a law firm. Study groups can also continue on after course work is completed to prepare for certification exams as paralegals. These groups are also a great way to build relationships with other future paralegals with whom you may want to network later, on the job.

MEETING TIMES AND PLACES.   It is helpful to set up a regular meeting time and hold that time sacred. The members must be committed to the meeting times and to completing their assignments, or the group will not serve its purpose. Study groups can meet anywhere. You might meet in a classroom, another school room, a member's home, a park, or a restaurant. Many paralegal schools and colleges have multipurpose rooms or study areas available to students who wish to meet in small groups. Some rooms are equipped with easels or drawing boards, which help facilitate discussions. Audiovisual equipment may also be available for the group's use, such as a television with a VCR for viewing videotaped lectures. The group should select a meeting place that has limited distractions and sufficient space to accommodate each member's opened books, notes, and other materials.

WORK ALLOCATION.   Teamwork is very important in the paralegal profession. Study groups can help you learn to function as a member of a team by distributing the workload among the group. Work (such as outlining chapters) should be allocated among the group members. It is important to define clearly who will be doing what work. It may be a good idea at the close of each meeting to have each member state out loud what work he or she will be responsible for completing prior to the next meeting. Whatever work one member does, he or she should make copies to distribute to the other members at the meeting.

EVALUATING YOUR GROUP.   You should realize from the outset that your study group will be of little help if you are doing most of the work. You need to make sure that everyone who joins the group is as committed to learning the material as you are and that you make this concern known to the others. The teamwork approach is only effective if everybody does his or her share. Teamwork involves trust and reliance. If you cannot trust one of the members to form an accurate outline of a topic, you will not be able to rely on that outline. You will end up doing the work yourself, just as a precaution. Therefore, be very selective about whom you invite to join the group. If you joined an already existing group, leave it if it turns out to be a waste of your time.

ORGANIZING YOUR WORK PRODUCT

A part of the learning experience takes place through special homework assignments, research projects, and possibly study-group meetings. For example, if you are studying pretrial litigation procedures, you will read about these procedures in Chapter 6 of *West's Paralegal Today,* Second Edition. Your instructor will also likely devote class time to a discussion of these procedures. Additionally, you may be asked to create a sample complaint or to check your state's rules governing the filing of complaints in state courts. You also might have notes on a study-group discussion of these procedures.

How can you best organize all the materials generated during the coverage of a given topic? Here are a few suggestions that you might find useful. If you follow these suggestions, you will find that reviewing your work prior to exams is relatively easy—most of the work will already have been done.

CONSIDER USING A THREE-RING BINDER. An excellent way to integrate what you have learned is by using a three-ring binder and divider sheets with tabs for the different topics you cover. As you begin studying *West's Paralegal Today,* Second Edition, for example, consider having a different section in your binder for each chapter. Within that section, you can place your chapter outline (formed while reading the text), notes taken in the classroom or during other reading assignments, samples of projects you have done relating to topics in that chapter, and so on.

INTEGRATE YOUR NOTES INTO ONE DOCUMENT, IF POSSIBLE. If you have used a computer to key in your chapter outlines and class notes, consider incorporating everything you have learned about a topic into one document—a master, detailed outline of the topic. This can be done relatively easily by using the "cut and paste" feature of word-processing programs. The result will be a comprehensive outline of a particular topic that will make reviewing the topic prior to an exam (and perhaps later, on the job) a simple matter.

THE BENEFITS OF USING A COMPUTER

Many of the paralegals profiled in *West's Paralegal Today,* Second Edition, mentioned that if they were students again, they would spend more time developing computer skills. You should consider acquiring a personal computer, if possible. If not, see if you can arrange with someone else to use his or her personal computer on a routine basis. If your school or college has computers available in the library or some other place for student use, you might also use one of those computers. Find out when there is usually a computer available—such as early in the morning—and use the computer routinely at this time.

Using a computer provides many benefits. First, you can practice your keyboarding and word-processing skills (essential paralegal skills) simultaneously as you take notes or work on research or other class projects. Second, if you have a computer available, you can type up and better organize your notes. Such time is well spent because it not only increases your knowledge of the topics but also makes it easy to review what you have learned prior to exams.

Finally, a key benefit of using a computer is the quality of any work product or homework assignment that you submit to your instructor. The editing and formatting features of word-processing programs allow you to correct misspelled words, reorganize your presentation, and generally revise your document with little effort. The spell-checker and grammar-checker features help you avoid glaring errors. The formatting features allow you to present your document in an attractive format. You can change margins and use different fonts (such as italics or boldface) to emphasize certain words or phrases. As a paralegal, you will be using a computer and a word-processing system to generate your work. You will also be expected to know how to use computers to create quality work products. The more you can learn about computers and word processing as a student, the easier it will be for you to perform your job as a paralegal.

GOING ONLINE

Another benefit of using a computer is, of course, the ability to go "online"—that is, connect to the Internet—and access the vast resources available on that worldwide computer network. In Chapter 9 of *West's Paralegal Today,* Second Edition, you will learn what the Internet is and how it can be used by legal professionals to obtain information on a variety of topics. A large number of colleges and universities offer free Internet access to their students. If you do not have a personal computer, check with your library to see if you can go online using one of the computers the library makes available to students.

You can obtain information online about most of the topics covered in this text. To help you learn how to find and evaluate specific online information, every chapter in this book ends with one or more Internet exercises in a section titled *Using Internet Resources.* Additionally, we have provided Internet addresses for numerous Web sites in the margins of the pages. If you go to these Web sites, you will find additional information about the topic being discussed in the text. In the *Technology and Today's Paralegal* features throughout this text, we have provided other Web sites when appropriate, and a good portion of Chapter 9 (titled "Computer-Assisted Legal Research") contains numerous references to specific Web sites that offer useful information for paralegals and other legal professionals.

Realize that Internet sites tend to come and go, and there is no guarantee that a site referred to in this text will be there by the time this book is in print. We have tried, though, to include sites that so far have proved to be fairly stable. If you do have difficulty reaching a site (that is, if your destination is "Not Found" or has "No DNS Entry"), do not immediately assume that the site does not exist. First, recheck the Web site address (Uniform Resource Locator, or URL) shown in your browser. Remember you have to type the URL exactly as written: upper case and lower case are important. If it appears that the URL has been keyed in correctly, then try the following technique: delete all of the information to the right of the forward slash that is farthest to the right and press enter.

For example, suppose that you are trying to reach the following Web site: lawlib.wuacc.edu/washlaw/washlaw.html. First, check the URL as you keyed it in. Then try deleting the final "washlaw.html" from the URL and press enter. If you still have problems, delete "washlaw," which is now the farthest to the right. Eventually, you will get back to the home page and can again start your search.

PREPARING FOR EXAMS

Being prepared for exams is crucial to doing well as a paralegal student. If you have followed the study tips and suggestions given in the preceding pages of this introduction, you will have little problem preparing for an exam. You will have at your fingertips detailed outlines of the topics covered, a marked textbook that allows you to review major concepts quickly and easily, and class notes. If you have integrated your outlines and class notes in one comprehensive, detailed outline, you will have an even easier task when it comes time to prepare for an examination.

In addition to mastering the material in *West's Paralegal Today,* Second Edition, and in the classroom, if you want to do well on an exam, you should develop an exam-taking strategy. For example, prior to any exam, you should find answers to the following questions:

- What type of exam are you going to take—essay, objective, or both?
- What reading materials and lectures will be covered on the exam?
- What materials should you bring to the exam? Will you need paper to write on, or will paper be provided?
- Will you be allowed to refer to your text or notes during the exam (as in an open-book exam)?
- Will the exam be computerized? If so, you will probably need to bring several number 2 pencils to the exam.

- How much time will be allowed for the exam?

The more you can find out in advance about an exam, the better you can prepare for it. For example, if you learn that there will be an essay question on the exam, one way to prepare for the question is to practice writing timed essays. In other words, find out in advance how much time you will have for each essay question, say fifteen minutes, and then practice writing an answer to a sample essay question during a fifteen-minute time period. This is the only way you will develop the skills needed to pace yourself for an essay exam. Because most essay exams are "closed book," do your timed essay practice without using the book.

Usually, you can anticipate certain essay exam questions. You do this by going over the major concept headings, either in your lecture notes or in your text. Search for the themes that tie the materials together, and then think about questions that your instructor might ask you. You might even list possible essay questions as a review device. Then write a short outline for each of the questions that will most likely be asked. Some instructors give their students a list of questions from which the essay questions on the exam will be drawn. This gives you an opportunity to prepare answers for each of the questions in advance. Even though you cannot take your sample essays to class and copy them there, you will have organized the material in your mind.

TAKING EXAMS

There are several strategies you can employ while taking exams to improve your grade, including those discussed below.

Following Instructions

Students are often in such a hurry to start an exam that they take little time to read the instructions. The instructions can be critical, however. In a multiple-choice exam, for example, if there is no indication that there is a penalty for guessing, then you should never leave a question unanswered. Even if there are only a few minutes remaining at the end of the exam, you should guess at the answers for those questions about which you are uncertain.

You also need to make sure that you are following the specific procedures required for the exam. Some exams require that you use a number 2 lead pencil to fill in the dots on a machine-graded answer sheet. Other exams require underlining or circling. In short, you have to look at the instructions carefully.

Finally, check to make sure that you have all the pages of the examination. If you are uncertain, ask the instructor or the exam proctor. It is hard to justify not having done your exam correctly because you failed to answer all of the questions. Simply stating that you did not have them will pose a problem for both you and your instructor. Do not take a chance. Double-check to make sure.

Use Exam Time Effectively

Examinations are often timed. This can make an otherwise straightforward question more difficult because of the *time pressure* that the student faces. Timed examinations require that a question or cluster of questions be answered within a specified period of time. If you must complete thirty multiple-choice questions in one hour, then you have two minutes to work on each individual question. If you finish fifteen of those questions in one minute instead of two, then you will have banked fifteen minutes that can be spent elsewhere on the examination or used to double-check your answers.

Consider the following example. Assume that you have ninety minutes for the entire exam: thirty minutes to answer the multiple-choice questions, fifteen minutes to answer the true-false questions, and forty-five minutes to answer a long essay question. If you could shave ten minutes off the time it takes to answer the multiple-choice section and five minutes off the time it takes to answer the true-false questions, you will have fifteen additional minutes to complete the long essay question.

Taking Objective Examinations

The most important point to discover initially with any objective test is if there is a penalty for guessing. If there is none, you have nothing to lose by guessing. In contrast, if a point or portion of a point will be subtracted for each incorrect answer, then you probably should not answer any question for which you are purely guessing.

Students usually commit one of two errors when they read objective-exam questions: (1) they read things into the questions that do not exist, or (2) they skip over certain words or phrases.

Most test questions include key words such as:

all
always
never
only

If you miss these key words you will be missing the "trick" part of the question. Also, you must look for questions that are only *partly* correct, particularly if you are answering true-false questions.

Never answer a question without reading all of the alternatives. More than one of them may be correct. If more than one of them seems correct, make sure you select the answer that seems the *most* correct.

Whenever the answer to an objective question is not obvious, start with the process of elimination. Throw out the answers that are clearly incorrect. Even with objective exams in which there is a penalty for guessing, if you can throw out several obviously incorrect answers, then you may wish to guess among the remaining ones because your probability of choosing the correct answer is relatively high. Typically, the easiest way to eliminate incorrect answers is to look for those that are meaningless, illogical, or inconsistent. Often, test authors put in choices that make perfect sense and are indeed true, but they are not the answer to the question you are to answer.

Writing Essay Exams

As with objective exams, you need to read the directions to the essay questions carefully. It is best to write out a brief outline *before* you start answering the question. The outline should present your conclusion in one or two sentences, then your supporting argument. You should take care not to include in your essay information that is irrelevant, even if you think it is interesting. It is important to stay on the subject. We can tell you from firsthand experience that no instructor likes to read answers to unasked questions.

Finally, write as legibly as possible. The authors can tell you that it is easier to be favorably inclined to a student's essay if we do not have to reread it several times to decipher the handwriting.

TODAY'S PROFESSIONAL PARALEGAL

Chapter Outline

⊞ INTRODUCTION ⊞ WHAT IS A PARALEGAL? ⊞ WHAT DO PARALEGALS DO?
⊞ HISTORY OF THE PARALEGAL PROFESSION ⊞ PARALEGAL EDUCATION
⊞ PARALEGAL SKILLS ⊞ PERSONAL ATTRIBUTES OF THE PROFESSIONAL PARALEGAL
⊞ THE FUTURE OF THE PROFESSION

After completing this chapter, you will know:

- What a paralegal is and does.

- How and why the paralegal profession developed.

- The professional organizations that exist for paralegals and the benefits of membership in them.

- The education and training available to paralegals.

- The skills that are useful for a paralegal to have.

- Some important personal attributes of the professional paralegal.

Introduction

If you are considering a career as a paralegal, be prepared to be part of an exciting profession. Among other things, you will find that paralegal work encompasses much, much more than drafting documents full of fine print and memorizing relevant legal procedures. As a paralegal, you will deal with real people and real problems. Even when you are doing legal research, the real world is not too far away. When locating and analyzing court cases, for example, you will find that each case tells a story of its own, involving specific people and circumstances. Generally, through your legal work you will learn much about human nature, the law, and how the law applies to real-life problems.

You will also find that the paralegal field offers a wide variety of opportunities for both personal and professional development. In the next chapter, you will read about career opportunities available for paralegals—and there are many. In fact, the paralegal profession is now one of the fastest-growing occupations in the United States. Jobs are available not only in law firms, large and small, but also in corporate enterprises, government offices and courts, real-estate firms, and numerous other organizations that use legal services, including public utilities, health insurers, and banks.

What is a paralegal? What do paralegals do? What kinds of educational training, job skills, and personal qualities must one have to become a successful paralegal? If you are contemplating a career as a professional paralegal, you will want to know the answers to these questions. In this introductory chapter, we provide those answers, as well as general background information on the evolution of the paralegal profession.

What Is a Paralegal?

One of the challenges of describing any emerging profession is defining with some precision what the members of that profession do. Certainly, since its beginnings in the 1960s and 1970s, it has been challenging to come up with a definition of the paralegal profession that is both broad enough to include the diverse types of services that paralegals perform and narrow enough to identify with some specificity who is and is not a member of this profession. As you will read in Chapter 3, if paralegal professionals are to be regulated—by licensing requirements, for example—then how paralegals are defined becomes a crucial issue and one with serious implications for the profession.

Generally, we can say that a **paralegal,** or a **legal assistant,** is a person sufficiently trained in law and legal procedures to assist attorneys in the delivery of legal services to the public or to perform legal work as otherwise authorized by law. If you aspire to be a paralegal, however, you will want to become familiar with the more specific definitions of a paralegal given by legal professionals. Look at Exhibit 1.1. There we show the definitions of a paralegal given by the **American Bar Association (ABA),** a national association of attorneys, and the two leading national paralegal associations, the **National Association of Legal Assistants (NALA)** and the **National Federation of Paralegal Associations (NFPA),** both of which will be discussed in more detail shortly. The final definition in the exhibit is that given by the **American Association for Paralegal Education (AAfPE),** an organization that plays a major role in developing paralegal educational programs and curriculum across the nation.

When reading through these definitions, note how the terms *paralegal* and *legal assistant* are used in the first three definitions (the definition given by AAfPE refers only to "paralegals"). The definitions given by the ABA and NFPA (usually

Paralegal (or Legal Assistant)
A person sufficiently trained or experienced in the law and legal procedures to assist attorneys in the delivery of legal services to the public or to perform legal work as otherwise authorized by law.

American Bar Association (ABA)
A voluntary national association of attorneys. The ABA plays an active role in developing educational and ethical standards for attorneys and in pursuing improvements in the administration of justice.

National Association of Legal Assistants (NALA)
One of the two largest national paralegal associations in the United States; formed in 1975. NALA is actively involved in paralegal professional development.

National Federation of Paralegal Associations (NFPA)
One of the two largest national paralegal associations in the United States; formed in 1974. NFPA is actively involved in paralegal professional development.

American Association for Paralegal Education (AAfPE)
A national organization of paralegal educators; the AAfPE was established in 1981 to promote high standards for paralegal education.

EXHIBIT 1.1
Four Definitions of a Paralegal, or Legal Assistant

The American Bar Association's definition:	The National Association of Legal Assistants' definition:	The National Federation of Paralegal Associations' definition:	The American Association for Paralegal Education's definition:
A legal assistant or paralegal is a person, qualified by education, training or work experience, who is employed or retained by a lawyer, law office, corporation, governmental agency or other entity and who performs specifically delegated substantive legal work for which a lawyer is responsible.	Legal assistants, also known as paralegals, are a distinguishable group of persons who assist attorneys in the delivery of legal services. Through formal education, training and experience, legal assistants have knowledge and expertise regarding the legal system and substantive and procedural law which qualify them to do work of a legal nature under the supervision of an attorney.	A paralegal/legal assistant is a person qualified through education, training or work experience to perform substantive legal work that requires knowledge of legal concepts and that is customarily, but not exclusively, performed by a lawyer. This person may be retained or employed by a lawyer, law office, governmental agency or other entity or may be authorized by administrative, statuory or court authority to perform this work.	Paralegals perform substantive and procedural legal work as authorized by law, which work, in the absence of the paralegal, would be performed by an attorney. Paralegals have knowledge of the law gained through education, or education and work experience, which qualifies them to perform legal work. Paralegals adhere to recognized ethical standards and rules of professional responsibility.

pronounced *nif*pah) imply that the terms may be used interchangeably. In this book, we follow this practice (as many attorneys do) and use the terms as if they were synonymous. NALA's definition, however, which states that legal assistants are "also known as paralegals," does not necessarily imply that the terms are interchangeable. In fact, NALA members generally prefer the term *legal assistant* over *paralegal* because it is more restrictive. Legal assistants work under the supervision of attorneys, whereas not all those who call themselves paralegals do so. As you will learn in Chapter 2, some paralegals—known as "independent paralegals" or "legal technicians"—work independently and provide certain types of legal help (such as obtaining or filling out legal forms for bankruptcy filings or other legal transactions) directly to the public.

Note also how the definitions use slightly different wording with respect to paralegal qualifications. Particularly notice how the terms *and* and *or* affect the definitions. For example, both the ABA and NFPA state that a paralegal (or legal assistant) is a person qualified by "education, training *or* work experience," whereas NALA uses the phrase "formal education, training *and* experience" and the AAfPE states that a paralegal's knowledge of the law is gained through "education, *or* education *and* work experience." [Emphasis added.] By using *and* instead of *or* before the word "experience," the latter two definitions place greater emphasis on education as a paralegal qualification.

Significantly, both the ABA and NALA define legal assistants, or paralegals, as those who do work "for which a lawyer is responsible" (see the ABA's definition) or "under the supervision of an attorney" (see NALA's definition). In contrast, NFPA's broad definition does not mention attorney supervision, and the AAfPE states that paralegals perform legal work "as authorized by law." All of these organizations, however, emphasize that there are certain types of legal work

On the Web
For more information on the definitions of a paralegal, or legal assistant, given by the ABA, NALA, NFPA, and AAfPE, go to the following Web sites:
ABA: www.abanet.org
NALA: www.nala.org
NFPA: www.paralegals.org
AAfPE: www.aafpe.org

ETHICAL CONCERN
Paralegal Expertise and Legal Advice

Paralegals often become very knowledgeable in a specific area of the law. If you specialize in environmental law, for example, you will become very knowledgeable about environmental claims. In working with a client on a matter involving an environmental agency, you might therefore be tempted to advise the client on which type of action would be most favorable to him or her. Never do so. As will be discussed in detail in Chapter 3, only attorneys may give legal advice, and paralegals who give legal advice risk penalties for the unauthorized practice of law. Whatever legal advice is given to the client must come either directly from the attorney or, if from you, must reflect exactly (or nearly exactly) what the attorney said with no embellishment on your part. After consulting with your supervising attorney, for example, you can say to the client that Mr. X (the attorney) "advises that you do all that you can to settle the claim as soon as possible."

---

that paralegals by law may not undertake. For example, a paralegal may not give legal advice, set legal fees, or (with rare exceptions) represent a client in court (see Chapter 3).

Finally, all four definitions indicate that paralegals perform "substantive" legal work. This is an important element of these definitions because it indicates that paralegals, although they are not attorneys, often perform work that was traditionally undertaken only by attorneys.

WHAT DO PARALEGALS DO?

Throughout this book, you will read about the different ways in which paralegals assist attorneys; it is impossible to list them all in this brief space. The following list is just a sampling of some of the tasks that paralegals typically perform in a traditional paralegal setting—a law office. Bear in mind, though, that today an increasing number of paralegals are finding work in nontraditional (non-law-office) settings, including corporations, government agencies, courts, insurance companies, real-estate firms, and virtually any other entity that uses legal services.

- *Draft legal documents*—such as legal correspondence, documents to be filed with the court, and interoffice memoranda.
- *Calendar and track important deadlines*—such as the dates when certain documents must be filed with the court.
- *Assist attorneys in preparing for trial*—by preparing exhibits, documents, and trial notebooks that the attorney will need to have on hand at trial. Some paralegals also assist attorneys during trials.
- *Interview clients and witnesses*—to gather relevant facts and information about a lawsuit, for example.
- *Conduct legal investigations*—to gather facts about cases by interviewing clients and witnesses and obtaining relevant records (such as medical records or the police report of an accident).
- *Organize and maintain client files*—or (as is often the situation) supervise the organization and maintenance of client files.

- *Conduct legal research*—to find, analyze, and summarize court decisions, statutes, or regulations applicable to a client's case.
- *Use computers and technology*—to carry out the above tasks.

The specific kinds of tasks that paralegals perform vary, of course, from office to office. If you work in a one-attorney office, for example, you will probably not have much secretarial or clerical assistance. In other words, your job might overlap to some extent with that of the legal secretary. Your tasks might range from conducting sophisticated legal research and investigations to performing nonbillable clerical activities, such as photocopying documents and answering the telephone while the secretary is out to lunch.

If you work in a larger law firm, you will have more support staff (secretaries, file clerks, and others) to whom you can delegate tasks. Your work might also be more specialized. Instead of dealing with a number of cases relating to different areas of the law, you might concentrate solely on certain types of cases. If you work in a law firm's real-estate department, for example, you will deal only with legal matters relating to that area of the law.

Typically, today's paralegal performs many tasks using various types of legal software, electronic communications systems, and online databases. For example, trial preparation (see Chapter 6) increasingly involves using document management systems to track and make readily accessible the various materials needed for trial. Also, when conducting legal investigations and research, paralegals can now access online much of the information that they need (see Chapters 8 and 9).

HISTORY OF THE PARALEGAL PROFESSION

The paralegal profession initially developed in response to the need for a legal professional to fill a position somewhere between that of an attorney and that of a legal secretary—so that legal services could be provided to the public at lower cost. The need for greater access to legal services, which became a significant issue in the 1960s, continues to propel developments in the legal arena, including the increased use of paralegals to make legal services more affordable.

To some extent, law clerks fill this need. A **law clerk** is a law student who gains practical experience in the law by working for a law firm. Law clerks are often hired on a temporary basis (for the summer, for example, when they are not attending school, or to assist on a specific project).[1]

The problem faced by law firms is that if they require permanent, full-time legal assistance, hiring a law student on a temporary or part-time basis will not fill this need. Another option is, of course, to hire a law-school graduate as a **staff attorney** (a hired attorney who, unlike a partner in a partnership, has no ownership rights in a firm) on a full-time basis; this, however, might be too great an expense for the firm.

Competent and experienced legal secretaries began to fill the need faced by many law firms to have full-time assistance at a lower cost. The first paralegals were legal secretaries who had become, through on-the-job experience, extremely competent and skilled in legal procedures. They learned how to do legal research and investigation, draft documents to be filed with the court, and perform other tasks that today's paralegals are trained to undertake. Eventually, legal assistants succeeded in defining themselves as a distinct professional group within the field of law. Paralegal professional associations and paralegal education programs

Law Clerk
In the context of law-office work, a law student who works as an apprentice, during the summer or part-time during the school year, with an attorney or a law firm to gain practical legal experience.

Staff Attorney
An attorney who is hired by a law firm as an employee and who has no ownership rights in the firm.

---

1. The term *law clerk* is also used to designate an attorney who does legal research and writing for a judge or a justice.

On the Web
The Web site
for the ABA's
Standing
Committee on Legal
Assistants is:
www.abanet.org/legalassts/
approval.html.
(*Note:* No Web address ever
ends in a comma, period, or
semicolon. Consequently,
you should ignore phrase-
ending punctuation
(commas or semicolons) and
sentence-ending punctuation
(periods) when using the
Web addresses cited in this
book.)

further advanced the professional status of paralegals. Today, individuals who want to become legal assistants can enter a paralegal program and receive specialized training.

In 1968, the ABA recognized, for the first time, the professional status of paralegals. In that same year, the ABA formed a special committee, now known as the ABA's Standing Committee on Legal Assistants, to study and discuss how lawyers could most effectively use nonlawyers in their practices. In the last thirty years, the committee has worked closely with paralegal organizations and other groups to achieve its goal of making legal services more affordable to the public by integrating legal assistants into the legal services delivery team. The ABA has played a significant role in approving paralegal education programs. The ABA has also created an "Associate Member" category for legal assistants. Membership allows legal assistants to become involved in the activities of the ABA and enhances the working relationship between lawyers and paralegals.

Paralegal Associations and Professional Growth

One feature that distinguishes a profession from other occupations is that the members of a profession form professional associations for the following purposes:

- To establish a forum (place) in which issues relating to their profession can be discussed, experiences can be shared, and communication networks can be established.
- To establish guidelines to regulate their activities, such as ethical codes of conduct.
- To determine the level of skills or educational preparation necessary to the type of work performed by the members of the profession.
- To establish or sponsor educational programs to train potential professional practitioners or provide continuing education for those members who are already practicing their profession.

The evolution of the *paralegal profession* is thus directly related to the formation of paralegal associations. The earliest paralegal associations were formed at the state and local levels. The formation of national paralegal associations in the mid-1970s significantly furthered the professional interests and goals of paralegals.

State Bar Association
An association of attorneys within a state. Membership in the state bar association is mandatory in over two-thirds of the states—that is, before an attorney can practice law in a state, he or she must be admitted to that state's bar association.

Affiliate
An entity that is connected (or affiliated) with another entity. State and local branches of national or regional paralegal associations are often referred to as affiliates.

STATE AND LOCAL PARALEGAL ASSOCIATIONS.   By the early 1970s, there were numerous local paralegal associations. If you look at Appendix F at the end of this book, you will see that today every state has a paralegal association, and several states have many regional or local organizations within their borders. Practicing paralegals typically belong to their local (and/or state) paralegal association, as well as one of the national paralegal associations discussed below. Most **state bar associations**—associations of attorneys at the state level—also allow paralegals to become associate members of their organizations.

THE NATIONAL FEDERATION OF PARALEGAL ASSOCIATIONS (**NFPA**). The National Federation of Paralegal Associations (NFPA), which was founded in 1974, was created to represent paralegals at U.S. Senate hearings that were considering the question of whether paralegals should be regulated. NFPA represented the few local paralegal organizations that existed in 1974. As of 1999, its membership consisted of about sixty paralegal associations from around the country, encompassing over 17,000 legal assistants. The member associations of NFPA are referred to as affiliated associations, or **affiliates**, of NFPA.

THE NATIONAL ASSOCIATION OF LEGAL ASSISTANTS (NALA).   The National Association of Legal Assistants (NALA) was formed in 1975. Unlike NFPA, NALA has individual members. As of 1999, NALA and its ninety affiliated associations reached over 18,000 legal assistants nationwide. While both NALA and NFPA encourage the growth of the profession, they differ on the direction that the profession should take, as you will learn in Chapter 3.

OTHER NATIONAL PARALEGAL ASSOCIATIONS.   As the profession developed, other national professional organizations were formed. Professional Legal Assistants, Inc. (PLA), was chartered in 1985. Other national paralegal professional associations include the Legal Assistant Management Association, the American Paralegal Association, and the National Association for Independent Paralegals. The names and addresses of these and other paralegal associations, including state associations, are given in Appendix F.

BENEFITS OF PROFESSIONAL MEMBERSHIP.   As a paralegal, you will find that membership in a paralegal association offers numerous benefits. Among other things, membership offers the following kinds of opportunities:

- To meet and network with others in your profession.
- To receive professional publications or access online databases that keep you up to date on the latest laws, court cases, and bar association opinions that affect the paralegal profession.
- To participate in meetings to develop policy relating to emerging issues concerning the profession.
- To continue your training and education through seminars, workshops, and other programs, including online Continuing Legal Education (CLE) programs.
- Depending on the association you join, to have access to group insurance plans or other special products and services offered by the association.

On the Web
You can find a detailed listing of national paralegal associations at the Web site of West Legal Studies, the West paralegal resource center. Go to www.WestLegalStudies.com.

Economics and the Paralegal Profession

In the modern competitive environment for legal services, clients shop around, and the cost of those services is an important factor in determining which lawyer or law firm will be hired. Lawyers can provide lower-cost legal services to their clients when they use paralegals because they can bill their clients at lower rates for paralegal work. As you will read in Chapter 4, in which this topic is explored more fully, the billable rate for a paralegal (the hourly rate charged to clients for work done on their behalf) is substantially less than that for an attorney.

Clients, then, benefit from the use of paralegals because the clients pay less for legal services. Lawyers who delegate substantive legal work to paralegals also benefit because it frees up their time and allows them to concentrate on the areas of legal work that demand their expertise. They can also take on more clients and thus increase the firm's profits.

PARALEGAL EDUCATION

One of the reasons for the growth of the paralegal profession has been the development of paralegal educational programs by paralegal educators. As mentioned earlier, the American Association for Paralegal Education (AAfPE) has played a leading role in this area. The AAfPE develops standards and competencies appropriate for paralegal training and promotes quality education programs generally.

ETHICAL CONCERN
Ethics and the Effective Utilization of Paralegals

As you will read in Chapter 3, the ethical codes and guidelines regulating attorneys urge attorneys to use paralegals effectively—because the effective use of paralegals in legal representation benefits the public by providing quality legal services at lower cost. Paralegal ethical codes and guidelines also reflect this commitment. As a paralegal, you will share in this ethical responsibility.

What can you do to promote the effective use of paralegal services? One thing you can do is to join a paralegal association and work together with other association members toward this goal. Another step you can take is to encourage your supervising attorney to delegate substantive work to you. For example, you might volunteer to take on certain tasks so that you can display your competence. Some attorneys do not yet realize how many tasks paralegals can competently perform and how beneficial it is for them (freeing up their time for other work and lowering clients' bills) to delegate substantive work to paralegals.

On the Web
You can download the entire one-hundred-page report submitted by the New Jersey Supreme Court Committee on Paralegal Education and Regulation from the following Web site: **www.state.nj.us/ judiciary/index.html.**

Although no law—as yet—requires paralegals to meet specific educational requirements, such laws may be just around the corner. In 1998, the New Jersey Supreme Court Committee on Paralegal Education and Regulation recommended that paralegals in the state of New Jersey be subject to a system of licensure. If the committee's recommendations are adopted by the New Jersey Supreme Court, paralegals in New Jersey will have to obtain licenses to practice their profession—and such licensing will involve educational requirements. Utah is also currently considering a proposal that paralegals be subject to licensing requirements, and a number of other states are evaluating similar plans. You will read more about this issue, which is of vital concern for paralegals, in Chapter 3.

Even in the absence of licensing requirements, however, you will find that the job market demands a certain amount of education and training. You will have difficulty finding employment as a paralegal without having completed a paralegal training course or having received a degree in the field. Depending on your educational background and experience, you can spend anywhere from several months to several years obtaining a paralegal certificate or a degree.

Educational Options

Educational options for paralegals include certificate programs and degree programs. These are available through colleges and universities, community colleges, business schools, and trade schools.

CERTIFICATE PROGRAMS.   Many paralegals choose the certificate program. Depending on the student's educational background, certificate programs can take up to eighteen months to complete. A student who already has a bachelor's degree can attend a program offered through a college or university. Normally, this type of program takes one year to finish. The certificate that is awarded to the student who successfully completes this type of program is referred to as a **postdegree certificate.**

Another option is to attend a certificate program offered by a private, for-profit business school, trade school, or college. Typically, this type of program

Postdegree Certificate
A certificate awarded by a college or university to an individual who, having already completed an associate's degree or bachelor's degree program, successfully completes a paralegal program of study.

requires a high school diploma for admission. The length of time to complete such a program ranges from three to eighteen months. After the program is completed, the student receives a **paralegal certificate.**

DEGREE PROGRAMS.   Degree options include an associate's degree or a bachelor's degree. The **associate's degree,** which normally is obtained from a community college, requires the completion of approximately sixty semester hours. The degree requirements are typically split evenly between general education courses (such as English, math, science, history, and social sciences) and law courses.

A **bachelor's degree** requires the completion of about 120 semester hours. From fifty to sixty of these hours are spent in general education courses similar to those required for the associate's degree. In addition, students take courses in their major area—legal-assistant studies—and may select a minor field (not all bachelor's programs require a minor). Minors that complement a legal-assistant major include computer information systems, business administration, communications, and public administration. These minors are helpful because they provide paralegals with useful skills and information relating to computer technology, business firms, and government agencies. Certain minors, particularly minors in environmental studies and computer information systems, help to boost the legal assistant's desirability in today's job market, which increasingly requires knowledge and skills in these areas. Additionally, paralegals who combine a bachelor's degree in a field such as nursing with a paralegal certificate are highly sought after.

ADVANCED DEGREES.   In addition to the degree programs discussed above, graduate programs offer degrees that may advance your career opportunities. For example, if you are interested in management or administration, a master's degree in business administration (MBA) or in legal administration would be of great help in attaining your career goals. A master's degree normally requires, at a minimum, an additional year of course work beyond the bachelor's degree.

A law degree, which all attorneys must obtain, requires extensive educational preparation. As you will read in Chapter 3, prospective attorneys must normally obtain a bachelor's degree from a four-year college or university and then attend law school for an additional three years.

Curriculum—A Blend of Substantive and Procedural Law

A legal assistant's education includes the study of both substantive law and procedural law. **Substantive law** includes all laws that define, describe, regulate, and create legal rights and obligations. For example, a law prohibiting employment discrimination on the basis of age falls into the category of substantive law. **Procedural law** establishes the methods of enforcing the rights established by substantive law. Questions about what documents need to be filed to begin a lawsuit, when the documents should be filed, which court will hear the case, which witnesses will be called, and so on are all questions of procedural law. In brief, substantive law defines our legal rights and obligations; procedural law specifies what methods, or procedures, must be employed to enforce those rights and obligations.

The ABA's Role in Paralegal Education

The ABA has played an active role in paralegal educational programs since the early 1970s. By 1973, the ABA had drafted and formally adopted a set of educational standards for paralegal training programs. Programs that meet these

Paralegal Certificate
A certificate awarded to an individual with a high school diploma or its equivalent who has successfully completed a paralegal program of study at a private, for-profit business school, trade school, or college.

Associate's Degree
An academic degree signifying the completion of a two-year course of study, normally at a community college.

Bachelor's Degree
An academic degree signifying the completion of a four-year course of study at a college or university.

 On the Web
Information on paralegal education programs is available on both the NALA and NFPA Web sites (www.nala.org and www.paralegals.org, respectively).

Substantive Law
Law that defines the rights and duties of individuals with respect to each other, as opposed to procedural law, which defines the manner in which these rights and duties may be enforced.

Procedural Law
Rules that define the manner in which the rights and duties of individuals may be enforced.

ABA-Approved Program
A legal or paralegal educational program that satisfies the standards for paralegal training set forth by the American Bar Association.

standards and that are approved by the ABA are usually referred to as **ABA-approved programs.** Today, the ABA approval commission consists of members of the ABA as well as representatives from NALA, NFPA, and the American Association for Paralegal Education. Of the paralegal education programs in existence today (about 650), the ABA has approved 218. Paralegal schools are not required to be ABA approved. ABA approval is a voluntary process that gives extra credibility to those schools that successfully apply for it.

Certification

Certification
Formal recognition by a private group or a state agency that an individual has satisfied the group's standards of proficiency, knowledge, and competence; ordinarily accomplished through the taking of an examination.

Certification involves recognition by a private professional group or a state agency that an individual has met specified standards of proficiency. Note that certification, as used here, is not the same as receiving a paralegal certificate. A paralegal certificate means that the paralegal has successfully completed a specific course of studies. A *certified paralegal,* in contrast, is one who has demonstrated his or her knowledge and competence in the field by taking and passing an examination administered by a private professional group or a state agency.

 On the Web
You can learn about upcoming CLAS exams on the NALA Web site at www.nala.org/educ.htm. For more information on NFPA's PACE program, go to www.paralegals.org/PACE/home.html.

NALA's CERTIFICATION PROGRAM.   NALA's certification program for paralegals is called the **Certified Legal Assistant (CLA)** Certification Program. Paralegals who wish to become certified by NALA may apply to take the CLA exam. The CLA exam provides recognition of the legal assistant's abilities and competence. This voluntary, comprehensive, two-day exam is given three times a year. The exam covers basic areas, such as communication skills (verbal and written), judgment and analytical skills, ethics, and human relations, as well as legal research and legal terminology. It also covers substantive and procedural law. Each person taking the exam must pass a section on the U.S. legal system, as well as four other areas of substantive law. The legal assistant can choose from nine sections: litigation, estate planning and probate, real estate, criminal law, bankruptcy, contracts, business organizations and corporations, administrative law, and family law.

In addition to the CLA exam, NALA offers exams for those who wish to become certified by NALA as specialists in certain areas of practice. To become a **Certified Legal Assistant Specialist (CLAS),** a legal assistant must demonstrate special competence in a particular field. Specialty exams are offered in the following areas: bankruptcy, civil litigation, probate and estate planning, corporate and business law, criminal law and procedure, real estate, and intellectual property. Appendix H offers further information on NALA certification procedures and requirements.

Certified Legal Assistant (CLA)
A legal assistant whose legal competency has been certified by the National Association of Legal Assistants (NALA) following an examination that tests the legal assistant's knowledge and skills.

Certified Legal Assistant Specialist (CLAS)
A legal assistant whose competency in a legal specialty has been certified by the National Association of Legal Assistants (NALA) following an examination of the legal assistant's knowledge and skills in the specialty area.

NFPA's CERTIFICATION PROGRAM.   In 1994, the members of NFPA voted to establish a certification program called the Paralegal Advanced Competency Exam, or PACE, which was implemented in 1996. This certification program is offered to paralegals who have a minimum of two years' experience and who meet specific educational requirements. The PACE is a four-hour, computer-generated examination designed to test the competency level of experienced paralegals. The exam has two tiers; each tier addresses different areas. The first tier deals with general legal issues, ethics, and state-specific laws. The second tier addresses specialty sections. A paralegal who passes the PACE exam may be designated as a "PACE-Registered Paralegal," or, more simply, an "RP." Information on NFPA's PACE program is included in Appendix I of this book.

DEVELOPING PARALEGAL SKILLS
Preparing for the CLA Exam

Rita Barron received her paralegal certificate over a year ago and has been working in a law office since graduation. She plans to take the Certified Legal Assistant (CLA) exam in a few months. Rita consults with Jill Sanderson, a CLA, about taking the exam. Jill advises Rita that forming a study group helped her to study for the test, when she was a student. Jill's group divided up topics, then met once a week to share outlines. It was a lot of work, but their efforts paid off; the entire group passed the exam with flying colors.

STUDY-GROUP TIPS

- Select committed group members.
- Devise a plan for sharing the work.
- Clearly assign topics to be outlined.
- Share outlines and assignments regularly.
- Evaluate the group members' efforts.
- Consult online resources or a CLA review guide.

STATE CERTIFICATION.   Many states are now considering the development of state-administered or statewide voluntary certification programs, and some states are beginning to implement such programs. In 1994, for example, the Texas Bar Association Board of Legal Specialization established a voluntary certification program that permits paralegals in Texas to become certified as specialists in the following three areas: civil trial law, personal-injury law, and family law. To become certified paralegal specialists in these areas, paralegals must meet minimum standards for certification.

In July 1994, the California Alliance of Paralegal Associations (CAPA) and NALA formally agreed to develop and administer a voluntary statewide certification program for paralegals in California. Under the program, launched in 1995, a paralegal may become certified as a California Advanced Specialist (CAS) in several specialty practice areas. These areas include civil litigation, business organizations and business law, real estate, estates and trusts, and family law. Other states, including Florida and Louisiana, have also implemented voluntary certification programs.

Keep in mind that certification is a *voluntary* procedure. Whether paralegals, like attorneys, should be regulated by state law through mandatory licensing requirements—which would involve meeting certain educational standards, just as certification does—is a separate issue. As mentioned earlier, New Jersey is in the process of evaluating whether to license paralegals in that state. In Utah, the state bar association has recommended a licensing program that includes passing the CLA exam. Other states are also considering some form of licensing procedures. We will discuss this issue further in Chapter 3, in the context of the regulation of legal professionals.

Continuing Legal Education

Paralegals can—and often do—extend their formal education after they begin employment through Continuing Legal Education (CLE) programs. CLE courses, which are offered by state bar associations and paralegal associations, often take the form of special seminars and workshops that focus on specific topics or areas.

On the Web
NALA is implementing an online campus for continuing legal education (CLE) at **www.nalacampus.com.** For information on NFPA's online CLE offerings, go to **www.paralegals.org/ CLE/home.html.**

Through CLE, attorneys and paralegals can learn more about specialized areas of law or keep up to date on the latest developments in the law and in technology. For example, if you work as a litigation paralegal, you might want to attend a seminar on computerized litigation support, or you might want to learn more about the rules of evidence or about how medical records can be used as litigation tools. Clearly, the more you learn about these or other topics relating to litigation, the more valuable you will become to your employer. For this reason, many employers today encourage their paralegals to take CLE courses and often pay some or all of the costs involved.

In most states, attorneys are required to take a specific number of hours of CLE each year to maintain their licenses to practice law. Some paralegal associations impose similar requirements on their members as a condition of membership renewal with full membership rights (including voting rights) in their organizations. Both NALA and NFPA require paralegals who are certified through their certification programs to take a designated number of CLE hours per year to maintain their status as certified paralegals. Each of these organizations now offers online CLE courses (see their Web sites for more information).

PARALEGAL SKILLS

Paralegals need and use a variety of skills on the job. Depending on your personality traits, some skills will be easier than others for you to learn. For example, if you tend to be an organized person, you will have little difficulty in acquiring and applying the required organizational skills. Throughout this book, you will read in detail about the specific skills that you will need in your work as a paralegal. Here, we describe the general types of skills that this profession requires.

Organizational Skills

Being a well-organized person is a plus for a legal assistant. Law offices are busy places. There are phone calls to be answered and returned, witnesses to get to court and on the witness stand on time, documents to be filed, and checklists and procedures to be followed. If you are able to organize files, create procedures and checklists, and keep things running smoothly, you will be doing a great service to the legal team and to clients.

If you work in a nontraditional setting, such as for a corporation or for the government, you will similarly find that good organizational skills are the key to success in your job. No matter where you work, you will need to organize files, certain types of data, and—most important—your time.

If organization comes naturally to you, you are ahead of the game. If not, now is the time to learn and practice organizational skills. You will find plenty of opportunities to do this as a paralegal student—by organizing your notebooks, devising an efficient tracking system for homework assignments, creating a study or work schedule and following it, and so on. Other suggestions for organizing your time and work, both as a student and as a paralegal on the job, are included at the beginning of this book. You will also find in any university or public library an abundance of books that offer guidelines on how to organize efficiently your work, your use of time, and your life generally.

Analytical Skills

Legal assistants also need analytical skills, especially when engaging in tasks relating to trials, legal investigations, legal research and writing, and certain other assignments. *Analysis* is usually defined as the separation of a whole into its parts. Legal professionals need to be able to take complex theories and fact patterns and break them down into smaller, more easily understandable components. As you will read in Chapter 8, an important aspect of legal research and writing involves analysis. Analysis is used to decipher the meaning of the law as set forth in the decisions handed down by the courts and in statutes passed by legislatures.

Analysis also involves, to some extent, the ability to synthesize—or put together—facts and legal concepts in such a way that they form a single unit, or "picture." For example, if you are conducting a legal investigation, you will uncover numerous facts and opinions about a certain event, such as an automobile accident. You will learn how the client believed the accident occurred, how any available witnesses described it, and what facts are indicated or implied by medical records or police reports. As a paralegal, you will want to discern how the facts and opinions you have gathered fit together into patterns or sequences. Further, you will want to determine how the facts fit into the legal strategy that your supervising attorney plans to pursue.

In any working environment, paralegals may be responsible for gathering and analyzing certain types of data. A corporate paralegal, for example, may be required to analyze new government regulations to see how they will affect the corporation. A paralegal working for the federal Environmental Protection Agency may be responsible for collecting and analyzing data on toxic waste disposal and drafting a memo setting forth his or her conclusions on the matter.

Computer Skills

In any workplace today, computer skills are essential. Advances in technology are virtually transforming the way in which law firms and other organizations operate. At a minimum, you will be expected to have experience with word processing (generating and revising documents using a computer) and to have some data-entry skills. Realize, though, that paralegals who are well versed in computer technology will increasingly have an edge over those who are not in the paralegal job market. Already, some of the best-paying paralegal positions are held by paralegal specialists who know how to use sophisticated computer equipment and software, such as database management systems, and how to adapt new technology to their workplace needs to improve efficiency.

We cannot stress enough that to become a successful paralegal, the best thing you can do during your paralegal training is to become as knowledgeable as possible about computer technology, including online communications. Throughout this book, you will read about how technology is now being applied to all areas of legal practice. You will also learn how you can use technology, particularly the Internet, to perform various paralegal tasks and to keep up to date on the law.

As computer technology continues to advance, high-tech paralegals will increasingly be in demand. (See this chapter's feature *Technology and Today's Paralegal: The Changing Paralegal Workplace*, on the next page, for a glimpse at how technology is not only transforming the paralegal workplace but also creating new types of paralegal positions.)

Interpersonal Skills

The ability to communicate and interact effectively with other people is an important asset for the paralegal. Paralegals work closely with their supervising attorneys, and the capacity to cultivate a positive working relationship helps get tasks done more efficiently. Paralegals also work with legal secretaries and other

TECHNOLOGY AND TODAY'S PARALEGAL

The Changing Paralegal Workplace

In many ways, technology has simplified the work of legal assistants. Documents can be easily drafted and revised on the computer. Mistakes can be eliminated with the stroke of a key, and changes can be made in a matter of just seconds. Computerized forms make generating the paperwork for routine legal transactions, such as bankruptcy filings or divorce petitions, a relatively simple matter. Database management systems allow paralegals to track or analyze hundreds—if not thousands—of documents without having to search through boxes filled with documents. E-mail messages can be created and sent in a fraction of the time it takes to create, reproduce, and distribute hard-copy memos or letters. Online databases have made it possible to conduct legal research and find information relevant to a legal investigation without leaving the office.

Indeed, it would seem that technology, by making legal work faster and easier to accomplish, might reduce the need for paralegals. That, however, is not true. Indeed, the opposite is occurring—technology is opening the door to new positions for paralegals. For example, some of today's paralegals are carving out a niche for themselves as Internet specialists. A paralegal who can conduct research efficiently, using online resources, is a valuable asset to any firm or agency. In a law office, efficient research saves

time and money—for the firm and clients alike. Other paralegals are becoming experts in electronic evidence—encoding documents relating to a particular legal matter so that those documents can easily be retrieved in the event of a lawsuit.

Another emerging field in which paralegals may play a significant role has to do with the types of documents that should be entered into, or retained on, electronic systems. Even documents that have been previously deleted from a hard drive may be retrieved and used as evidence in a lawsuit, and companies that want to prevent future problems with electronic evidence increasingly are turning to their lawyers for advice on this issue. A paralegal knowledgeable in this area is a valuable member of the legal team in such situations.

Finally, technology has made it possible for some paralegals to perform at least some of their work at home. The virtual workplace, made feasible by telephones, faxes, and modems, is now becoming a reality.

We cannot predict what the future may hold, but one thing seems certain: as technology advances, there will be an increasing need for creative adaptations of technology to the field of legal work. High-tech paralegals who can fill this need will very likely be the highest-paid—and the most valued—legal assistants in the future.

---

support staff in the law office, with attorneys and paralegals from other firms, with court personnel, and with numerous other people. Paralegals frequently interview clients and witnesses. As you will read in Chapter 7, if you can relate well to the person whom you are interviewing, your chances of obtaining useful information are increased.

There may be times when you will have to deal with clients who are experiencing difficulties in their lives, such as divorce or the death of a loved one. These people will need to be handled with sensitivity, tact, understanding, and courtesy. There will also be times when you will have to deal with people in your office who are under a great deal of stress or who for some other reason are demanding and less than courteous to you. You will need to know how to respond to these people in ways that promote positive working relationships.

Communication Skills

Good communication skills are critical when working in the legal area. In fact, it is sometimes said that the legal profession is a "communications profession" because effective legal representation depends to a great extent on how well a legal professional can communicate with clients, witnesses, court judges and juries, opposing attorneys, and others. Poor communication can damage a case, destroy a client relationship, and harm the legal professional's reputation. Good communication, in contrast, wins cases, clients, and sometimes promotions.

Communication skills include reading skills, speaking skills, listening skills, and writing skills. We look briefly at each of these skills here.

Although we focus on communication skills in the law-office setting, realize that good communication skills are essential to success in any work environment.

READING SKILLS.   Reading skills involve more than just being able to decipher the meaning of written letters and words. Reading skills also involve understanding the *meaning* of a sentence, paragraph, section, or page. As a legal professional, you will need to be able to read and understand many different types of written materials, including statutes and court decisions. You will therefore need to become familiar with legal terminology and concepts so that you grasp the meanings of these legal writings. You will also need to develop the ability to read documents *carefully* so that you do not miss important distinctions, such as the difference in meaning that can result from the use of *and* instead of *or*.

SPEAKING SKILLS.   Paralegals must also be able to speak well. In addition to using correct grammar, legal assistants need to be precise and clear in communicating ideas or facts to others. For example, when you discuss facts learned in an investigation with your supervising attorney, your oral report must communicate exactly what you found, or it could mislead the attorney. A miscommunication in this context could have serious consequences if it leads the attorney to take an action detrimental to the client's interests. Oral communication also has a nonverbal dimension—that is, we communicate our thoughts and feelings through gestures, facial expressions, and other "body language" as well as through words.

LISTENING SKILLS.   Good listening skills are extremely important in the context of paralegal work. Paralegals must follow instructions meticulously. To understand the instructions that you receive, you must listen carefully. Asking follow-up questions will help you to clarify anything that you do not understand. Also, repeating the instructions will not only ensure that you understand them but also give the attorney a chance to add anything that he or she may have forgotten to tell you initially. Listening skills are particularly important in the interviewing context. In Chapter 7, you will read in greater detail about different types of listening skills and techniques that will help you conduct effective interviews with clients or witnesses.

WRITING SKILLS.   Finally, it is important for paralegals to have excellent writing skills. Legal assistants draft letters, memoranda, and a variety of legal documents. Letters to clients, witnesses, court clerks, and others must be clear and well organized and must follow the rules of grammar and punctuation. Legal documents must also be free of errors. Lawyers are generally scrupulously attentive to detail in their work, and they expect legal assistants to be equally so. Remember, you represent your supervising attorney when you write. You will learn more about writing skills in Chapter 8.

PERSONAL ATTRIBUTES
OF THE PROFESSIONAL PARALEGAL

There are many different attributes that help paralegals succeed in their careers. The paralegal who is responsible, reliable, committed to hard work, objective,

FEATURED GUEST: WENDY B. EDSON

Ten Tips for Effective Communication

BIOGRAPHICAL NOTE

Wendy B. Edson received her master's degree in library science (M.L.S.) from the University of Rhode Island and served as law librarian at the Buffalo, New York, firm of Phillips, Lytle, Hitchcock, Blain and Huber. In 1978, she joined the Paralegal Studies faculty at Hilbert College, in Hamburg, New York, and helped to develop an ABA-approved bachelor's degree program in 1992. She teaches paralegalism and legal ethics, legal research and writing, law and literature, volunteerism, and alternative dispute resolution (ADR). She also developed and coordinates the internship program. Edson reviews and publishes on the topics of paralegal education, legal research and writing, and community service. She has lectured to legal professionals on legal research, teaching skills, internships, community service, environmental law, and ADR. Professor Edson is an AAfPE member and has presented papers at its national conferences and chaired model syllabi projects.

Words! They are the building blocks of human communication. Whether words are exchanged face to face—or by e-mail, phone, fax, or letter—communication is a two-way street. But how do we become skilled at maneuvering the *two-way* traffic of interpersonal communication? As in driving, we need to follow the "rules of the road." The rules of the road in regard to communication traffic are embodied in the following ten tips.

1. Establish Communication Equality. Communication equality does not require that individuals hold equal status in an office or organization but requires that each party believe in *equal rights* to speak and listen. Observe someone whom you consider to be a good communicator. You will note that he or she demonstrates equality by actively listening and responding appropriately to whoever is speaking. Workplace problems often reflect communication ailments rooted in inequality. A firm belief in communication equality, despite job titles, will help to create a cooperative, productive working environment.

2. Plan for Time and Space. Effective communication requires *time*. Imagine your reaction to a request to work overtime if your supervising attorney took thirty seconds to order you to do the work versus taking two minutes to explain the reason for the request and listening to your response. In the first situation, the attorney saved one and a half minutes but scored "zero" in terms of communication skills. In today's rushed world, it is easy to overlook the importance of communication skills in morale building and creating a cooperative, efficient work force.

Effective communicators are aware of how the physical environment in which a conversation takes place can affect the communication process. Communication is always enhanced when the parties have reasonable privacy and are not continually interrupted. Another important factor is physical comfort.

Choosing an inappropriate time and place for communication denies the importance of the matters being discussed and may send the wrong message to both the speaker and the listener.

3. Set the Agenda. Skilled communicators prepare an *agenda*—whether written or mental—of matters to be discussed in order of their priority. Frequently, both parties bring their respective agendas to a discussion, which means that priorities may need to be negotiated. A subordinate who brings up the topic of desired vacation time when the supervisor is preoccupied with a major project clearly demonstrates that his or her priorities are different from those of the supervisor.

Successful communication requires that the parties first negotiate a *common agenda*—that is, determine jointly the agenda for a particular discussion or meeting and what topics should take priority. Then, the topics can be dealt with one by one, in terms of their relative importance, to the satisfaction of both parties. *Agenda awareness* prevents parties from jumping from topic to topic without successfully resolving anything.

4. Fine-Tune Your Speaking Skills. Observe an individual whom you consider to be a good speaker, whether before a group of persons or on a one-on-one basis. What skills does that individual demonstrate? Effective

FEATURED GUEST, *Continued*

speakers work hard to express thoughts clearly; sometimes, they refer to notes or lists to refresh their memories. Skilled speakers also try to communicate accurately and to talk about matters that they know will interest their listeners. They cultivate *communication empathy*—the sincere effort to put themselves in their listeners' shoes. As you speak to others, pause occasionally and ask yourself: "Would I enjoy listening to what I am saying and how I am saying it?"

5. Cultivate Listening Skills.

Listening is not just refraining from speaking while another person is talking but an *active* process—the other half of the communication partnership. An active listener does not interrupt the speaker. If you sense that the speaker is engaging in a monologue, responsive behavior—including body language, attentiveness, and appropriate remarks—can steer the conversation back to a dialogue without cutting off the speaker.

An active listener realizes that listening is an investment in effective communication. By truly responding to what is being said, rather than regarding listening time as insignificant or time to plan his or her own remarks, the skilled listener establishes a bond of trust with the speaker. Active listeners avoid preconceived ideas about topics being discussed and assume that they do not know all the answers.

6. Watch for Body Language.

Body language is nonverbal communication that reflects our emotional state. Physical positions, such as leaning forward or away from the speaker while listening, can reinforce or negate our spoken responses.

Body attitudes, whether relaxed (comfortable posture, leaning forward, uncrossed arms and legs, relaxed neck and shoulders) or tense (stiff posture, backing away, crossed arms and legs, rigid neck and shoulders) vividly illustrate our responses before we utter a word. Eye contact is one of the most important tools in the body language tool kit for communication. Interviewers, social workers, and police officers have learned that steady and responsive eye contact means sincerity and credibility.

7. Put Note Taking in Perspective.

Overinvolvement in note taking detracts from the communication process because opportunities to listen actively, speak responsively, and be sensitive to body language are reduced. The speaker may ramble while the listener records the ramblings in extensive notes.

When it is necessary to take notes, it is helpful to establish some rapport with the speaker or listener before launching the note-taking process. Alternatively, follow-up notes can be a workable solution to the problem. The note taker can devote the interview time to communication and, after the interview, record his or her general impressions of the interview and identify specific issues that need to be discussed further.

8. Recognize the Role of Criticism.

Constructive criticism focuses on specific actions or behaviors rather than personalities. It is objective rather than subjective. Criticism that is stated calmly and objectively ("We need to rewrite the section on holographic wills.") is much more palatable for the person being criticized than is criticism in the form of a per-

> **"Eye contact is one of the most important tools in the body language tool kit for communication."**

sonal attack ("You did a terrible job."). By placing emphasis on actions instead of personalities, the parties can more easily work toward a satisfactory solution. If both the critic and the person being criticized can remain calm and can separate actions from personalities, then criticism will usually produce the desired result and *mutual* satisfaction.

9. Aim for Satisfactory Closure.

Closure means "wrapping up" the communication. Successful communicators know that handling closure properly can leave a participant with a good feeling even if the solution was not exactly what he or she initially desired. Summarizing the discussion and checking for agreement or a need for further discussion will encourage all participants to follow the tenth tip.

10. Commit to Communicate.

Excellent speakers and listeners have positive, self-confident attitudes that problems can be solved if the "rules of the road" are followed. Skilled communicators cultivate open minds, self-knowledge, and the ability to tolerate differences and empathize with others. They are committed to exercising their rights and responsibilities as speakers and listeners in the communication process.

DEVELOPING PARALEGAL SKILLS

Interviewing a Client

Brenda Lundquist is a paralegal in a one-attorney firm. Brenda has multiple responsibilities, including interviewing prospective divorce clients. Using a standard set of forms, Brenda meets with the prospective client and obtains information about the reasons for the divorce, finances and assets, and desired custody arrangements. This information is needed to assist her supervising attorney in determining whether she will take the case. The information also will help Brenda in preparing the documents to be filed with the court should the attorney decide to represent the client. Brenda enjoys the work because she likes helping people, and often people who are getting divorced need both emotional and legal support.

CHECKLIST FOR CLIENT INTERVIEWS

- Plan the interview in advance.
- Print out forms and checklists to use during the interview.
- Introduce yourself as a legal assistant.
- Explain the purpose of the interview to the client.
- Communicate your questions precisely.
- Listen carefully and be supportive, as necessary.
- Summarize the client's major concerns.
- Give the client a "time line" for what will happen next in the legal proceedings.

ethical, and generally considerate of others will have an easy time meeting the challenges presented by his or her work. These attributes define an individual's personality and character, and they are also important in paralegal practice.

Responsibility and Reliability

The paralegal must be responsible and reliable. The practice of law involves helping people with their legal problems. A paralegal's mistake, such as faxing a document to the wrong party or missing a deadline for filing a certain document with the court, could cause a client to lose his or her legal rights (and possibly cause a lawsuit to be brought against the attorney).

Attorneys frequently mention how they *rely* on their paralegals to perform certain tasks for them. The responsible paralegal is reliable. He or she completes tasks accurately and on time. Paralegals often mention how important trust is to efficient teamwork in the legal office. Each team member must be able to trust the other members of the legal team to do their share of the work—or the team effort may fail.

Commitment

Being committed to your work and the goals of your employer is important, too. Many tasks can take hours, days, weeks, or even months to perform, and you must be dedicated to giving your best effort until the job is completed. Commitment to your work involves persistence.

For example, if you are attempting to track down heirs to a will and you are having difficulty locating them, you must try everything possible to find them before you give up the search. You will need to review county birth and marriage records to try to locate them through their siblings and spouses. If that does not work, you will need to contact state agencies, such as the motor vehicle department, to try to obtain addresses from their driver's licenses or vehicle registration

PARALEGAL PROFILE

SUSAN J. MARTIN is a paralegal in the Trusts and Estates department of Devine, Millimet & Branch, a large law firm, and has offices in the firm's Manchester, New Hampshire, and Andover, Massachusetts, locations. She has been in the legal profession for over twenty-two years. She worked for nine years as a legal secretary before becoming a paralegal and has worked in both large and small law firms in New Hampshire, Maine, Florida, Colorado, and Montana. She has a certificate from the National Association of Legal Secretaries, a certificate in paralegal studies from the University of New Hampshire, and an associate's degree from Franklin Pierce College in New Hampshire, where she is currently a bachelor's degree candidate. Martin is a member of the PACE Development Committee of the National Federation of Paralegal Associations (NFPA) and was an item writer/content area expert for the PACE exam. She is president of the Paralegal Association of New Hampshire (1998–1999) and chairs its Committee on Paralegal Education; is editor of the association's bimonthly newsletter, The Annotator; *and is also an adjunct member of the Delivery of Legal Services Committee of the New Hampshire Bar Association and a member of the bar association's Technology Section.*

Trusts and Estates Paralegal

What do you like best about your work?

"One of the benefits of working in the trusts and estates field is that you are not involved in contentious lawsuits in which, in many cases, there is no winner and everyone is unhappy. Although estate clients are frequently dealing with grief and loss, they are not openly hostile or defensive. For the most part, clients view the trusts and estates team in a very positive way, and this makes the job very enjoyable."

What is the greatest challenge that you face in your area of work?

"Probably the greatest challenge of my job is keeping informed about the changes in federal and state tax law. The Internal Revenue Code is complex and convoluted, and new rules and regulations are promulgated daily. Also, it is not unusual to have an estate that is subject not only to federal tax laws but also to the tax laws of several states. Sorting out tax obligations and coordinating the timely filing of several tax returns can sometimes be a very difficult task."

What advice do you have for would-be paralegals in your area of work?

"To function well as a paralegal in the trusts and estates field, you must have a broad general knowledge of many other fields of law, including real estate, corporations, family law, and even civil litigation. You must also have some knowledge of basic accounting principles. People who function well as paralegals in this field usually have excellent quantitative skills, are extremely organized, are able to manage numerous files and deadlines simultaneously, can exercise sound independent judgment, and can work with a minimum of supervision. You must be computer literate and have proficient keyboarding skills."

"To be successful in this field, you must be bright and articulate, and have a passion for detail."

What are some tips for success as a paralegal in your area of work?

"To be successful in this field, you must be bright and articulate, and have a passion for detail. You should love working with people. Working with the elderly requires compassion, humility, and resourcefulness. In this field in particular, you will meet clients from every social strata, ethnic background, and cultural association, and that requires patience, tolerance, and good humor."

records. You might also have to advertise in newspapers. Being diligent in your search means that you keep going until you have exhausted virtually every possible information source.

Objectivity

Another personal attribute of professional behavior is objectivity. To the extent that personal emotions or biases interfere with the goal of serving the client's interest, the paralegal must set these emotions or biases aside. For example, your sympathy for a client's plight should not prevent you from acknowledging factual evidence that is harmful to the client's position.

Lawyers and paralegals sometimes find themselves working on behalf of clients whom, for one reason or another, they dislike or do not respect. You may dislike having to deal with one of your firm's overly aggressive business clients, for example, or with a criminal defendant charged with spousal abuse, which you find extremely offensive. But these feelings should not affect the quality of the services you render. The job of the attorney and the paralegal is to see that the client's interests are not harmed by their personal views or assumptions.

The Ability to Keep Confidences

One of the requirements of being a paralegal is the ability to keep client information confidential. The word *requirement* is used here because being able to keep confidences is not just a desirable attribute in a paralegal, but a mandatory one. As you will read in Chapter 3, attorneys are ethically and legally obligated to keep all information relating to the representation of a client strictly confidential unless the client consents to the disclosure of the information.[2] The attorney may disclose this information only to people who are also working on behalf of the client and who therefore need to know it. Paralegals share in this duty imposed on all attorneys. If a paralegal reveals confidential client information to anyone outside the group working on the client's case, the lawyer (and the paralegal) may face legal consequences (including being sued by the client) if the client suffers harm as a result.

Keeping client information confidential means that you, as a paralegal, cannot divulge such information even to your spouse, family members, or closest friends. You should not talk about a client's case in hallways, elevators, or other areas in which others may overhear your conversation. Keeping work-related information confidential is an important part of being a responsible and reliable paralegal.

Other Attributes

Other attributes of the professional paralegal include accuracy, efficiency, attentiveness to detail, discretion, diplomacy, and the ability to work under pressure. Each of these attributes is considered appropriate in a law office because it enhances the firm's ability to serve the client's needs most effectively.

When deadlines approach and the pace of office work becomes somewhat frantic, it may be difficult to meet the challenge of acting professionally. For example, you may have to complete a brief (a document filed with a court to support an attorney's argument) by noon. It is 11 A.M., and you still have a considerable portion of the brief to finish. When the pressure is on, it is important to remain calm and focus on completing your task quickly and accurately to ensure quality work.

THE FUTURE OF THE PROFESSION

Since its beginnings over thirty years ago, the paralegal profession has been in a state of constant change, and by all indications, it will continue to evolve as we enter the new century. Legal services are costly, and the public is demanding access to more affordable legal services. This means that the role of the paralegal in delivering lower-cost legal services will most likely continue to expand. According to

---

2. Exceptions to the confidentiality rule are made in certain circumstances, as will be discussed in Chapter 3.

TODAY'S PROFESSIONAL PARALEGAL
A Winning Combination

Susan Latham is a legal secretary for Melinda Oakwood, a real-estate attorney who is a partner in the law firm of Morris, Crowther, Oakwood & Miller. The law firm is one of the largest in the state, employing over 300 attorneys, 75 paralegals, 130 secretaries, and many support staff members. Susan, who has become more of a legal assistant than a secretary to Melinda, has decided, at the age of forty, to return to the local university to obtain a paralegal degree. This way, Susan can be rewarded (in the form of higher wages) for the work that she actually does already and can seek advancement in the firm.

Susan has worked for Melinda for eleven years. She has been given increased responsibility because she has shown Melinda that she is dependable and reliable in handling her work assignments. Her work is always turned in on time, and it is always accurate.

LEARNING ON THE JOB
Susan was very lucky to have Melinda as a supervising attorney. Melinda, who had been a teacher for ten years before she went to law school, liked to teach Susan how to undertake new work assignments. When Susan had a new type of document to prepare at work, Melinda would give her a sample document and very good instructions. Now that Susan is studying to be a paralegal, Melinda has started assisting Susan with her school assignments by giving her sample documents and copies of the laws that require those documents. Melinda also points out the differences between the class assignments and the sample documents and discusses with Susan why the differences matter from a legal perspective.

Additionally, Melinda encourages Susan to ask questions about school assignments and to take her time completing them so that when they are turned in, they are accurate. Susan has a strong sense of commitment, so she always sees a project through even if it seems to take forever.

USING PERSONAL ATTRIBUTES
Melinda was also lucky to have Susan as her secretary and, eventually, as her paralegal. Susan had many personal attributes that helped her on the job. She learned quickly and performed her work competently and efficiently. She also paid great attention to detail, which was one of the reasons Melinda encouraged Susan to get a paralegal degree. Unlike Melinda's former paralegal, who would send out letters and fail to include the documents that should have been enclosed, Susan was meticulous. And Melinda could always count on Susan to keep client information confidential.

Susan already had good computer and organizational skills when Melinda hired her. She did need to improve her analytical and listening skills, though. Susan's analytical skills are already improving as a result of a course she is taking in legal research, which requires case analysis. Over time, Susan learned to listen to Melinda's instructions and to question Melinda when Susan was not exactly certain about what Melinda wanted her to do.

THE RESULT: A WINNING TEAM
Melinda and Susan have developed a solid working relationship. It took time for Susan to develop some of the skills that she needed, but Melinda was a good and patient teacher. It also took time to develop a trusting relationship, but now Melinda can confidently delegate significant assignments to Susan, knowing that Susan will complete them accurately. Now that Susan is in a paralegal program, Melinda can also delegate more challenging work to Susan, and Susan can eventually be promoted to paralegal status. Melinda and Susan work productively and efficiently together. They like and rely on each other and enjoy their work. Theirs is a winning combination of talents and skills.

the U.S. Department of Labor's Bureau of Labor Statistics, paralegal employment is expected to grow much faster than the average for all occupations through the year 2005.

The paralegal profession is a dynamic, changing, and growing field within the legal arena. Although legal assistants initially worked only in the law-firm context, as mentioned, today's job opportunities for paralegals include working for corporations, government agencies, and other organizations. Those who enter the profession today will find not only a variety of career options but also the opportunity to help chart the course the profession will take in the future.

KEY TERMS AND CONCEPTS

ABA-approved program   10

affiliate   6

American Association for Paralegal Education (AAfPE)   2

American Bar Association (ABA)   2

associate's degree   9

bachelor's degree   9

certification   10

Certified Legal Assistant (CLA)   10

Certified Legal Assistant Specialist (CLAS)   10

law clerk   5

legal assistant   2

National Association of Legal Assistants (NALA)   2

National Federation of Paralegal Associations (NFPA)   2

paralegal   2

paralegal certificate   9

postdegree certificate   8

procedural law   9

staff attorney   5

state bar association   6

substantive law   9

CHAPTER SUMMARY

1. Many legal professionals use the terms *paralegal* and *legal assistant* interchangeably. A paralegal, or a legal assistant, can be defined as a person sufficiently trained in law and legal procedures to assist attorneys in the delivery of legal services to the public or to perform legal work as otherwise authorized by law. Paralegal expertise may be attained through on-the-job experience or through paralegal training programs, but paralegal training programs are increasingly important to success in the paralegal field (and may be required for paralegal practice in the future in states that adopt paralegal licensing programs). Paralegals are not attorneys but attorneys' assistants. Attorneys supervise paralegal work and assume ultimate responsibility for it. Paralegals perform many of the tasks involved in legal representation that have traditionally been handled by attorneys. Certain tasks, however (such as giving legal advice, setting fees for legal services, and representing clients in court), can only be handled by attorneys.

2. Typical tasks performed by paralegals who work in law offices include drafting legal documents, calendaring and tracking important deadlines, assisting attorneys in trial preparation and at trial, interviewing clients and witnesses, organizing and maintaining client files, conducting legal investigations, and conducting legal research.

3. The first paralegals were legal secretaries who, through on-the-job experience, developed the skills and expertise now taught in paralegal training programs. The paralegal profession evolved rapidly because paralegals filled the growing need for lower-cost, permanent, and competent legal assistance. In 1968, the American Bar Association recognized the professional status of paralegals.

4. The formation of paralegal associations was a significant step in the growth of the paralegal profession. By the early 1970s, numerous local paralegal organizations were in existence. By the mid-1970s, the National Federation of Paralegal Associations (NFPA) and the National Association of Legal

Assistants (NALA)—the two leading national paralegal associations—had been formed.

5. Paralegal professional associations provide a forum in which professional issues can be discussed, establish guidelines to regulate professional conduct, determine skill levels and educational requirements, and in some cases establish or sponsor educational programs. Professional membership provides numerous opportunities for paralegals.

6. The curriculum in paralegal programs focuses on both procedural law and substantive law. Paralegal educational options include certificate programs and degree programs. A person who has a bachelor's degree can receive a postdegree certificate by completing a program offered by a college or university, which usually takes one year. Paralegal certificates can be obtained through programs of varying lengths, offered by business schools, trade schools, and other for-profit occupational training centers. Degree options include an associate's degree and a bachelor's degree.

7. The American Bar Association has played an active role in paralegal education programs since the early 1970s. Paralegal programs that meet standards established by the ABA (currently, about one-third of all paralegal programs) are called ABA-approved programs.

8. Certification involves recognition by a private professional group or a state agency that a person has met specified standards of proficiency. The National Association of Legal Assistants (NALA) has developed a certification program for paralegals. After meeting specified requirements (including passing an examination), a paralegal can become certified by NALA as a Certified Legal Assistant (CLA) or a Certified Legal Assistant Specialist (CLAS). More recently, the National Federation of Paralegal Associations (NFPA) has developed a certification program called the Paralegal Advanced Competency Exam, or PACE. State certification programs now exist in several states, including Texas, California, Louisiana, and Florida.

9. Paralegals need to have a variety of skills. It is especially important for paralegals to have good organizational, analytical, computer, interpersonal, and communication skills.

10. Certain personal attributes are also important in paralegal practice. These attributes include responsibility, reliability, commitment to hard work, objectivity, the ability to keep confidences, accuracy, efficiency, attentiveness to detail, discretion, diplomacy, and the ability to work under pressure.

▓ QUESTIONS FOR REVIEW

1. What is a paralegal? What are some of the key elements in the four definitions of a legal assistant, or paralegal, given in Exhibit 1.1? Is there any difference between a paralegal and a legal assistant?

2. What kinds of tasks do paralegals perform?

3. Why did the paralegal profession evolve? What needs within the legal profession do paralegals meet? When and by which organization was the paralegal profession first recognized as a profession?

4. Name the two largest national paralegal associations in the United States. When and why were they formed? What are the benefits of belonging to a paralegal association?

5. What type of educational programs and training are available to paralegals? Must a person meet specific educational requirements to work as a paralegal?

6. What role does the American Bar Association play in paralegal education?

7. What does *certification* mean? What is a CLA? What is a CLAS? What does PACE stand for?

8. Name some states that have certification programs. Is state certification mandatory in those states?

9. List and describe the skills that are useful in paralegal practice. Do you have these skills?

10. List and describe some of the personal attributes of a professional paralegal. Do you feel that persons who do not have these attributes can cultivate them? If so, how?

❖ ETHICAL QUESTIONS

1. Richard attends a six-month paralegal course and earns a certificate. In the West Coast city where he lives, certified paralegals—those with a CLA designation—are in great demand in the job market. Richard responds to a newspaper advertisement for a certified paralegal, indicating that he is one. Has Richard done anything unethical? What is the difference between a certificate and certification?

2. Paula Abrams works as a paralegal for a small law firm that specializes in tax law. Recently, Paula purchased some new tax-return software and was trained in how to use it. Last week, Paula used the software to prepare tax returns for the Benedetto family. Paula saved the forms on a disk. She then retrieved the Benedetto forms and used them for the Marshalls' tax return. Paula entered much of the Marshalls' tax information into the computer. Mr. Marshall had not provided the children's Social Security numbers to Paula, though, so she only keyed in the information that she had available and decided to add the Social Security numbers later.

   In the tax-season rush, Paula inadvertently neglected to enter the children's Social Security numbers on the Marshalls' tax return. Several months later, the Marshalls received a letter from the Internal Revenue Service stating that their exemptions were denied because their children's Social Security numbers were claimed on someone else's tax return. How might this situation be resolved? What other kinds of ethical problems might result from using computer-generated forms?

❖ PRACTICE QUESTIONS AND ASSIGNMENTS

1. Refer to Appendix F and Appendix G at the end of this book (or, if you have access to the Internet, you can go to www.findlaw.com) and find the answers to the following questions:

   a. What is the street address, e-mail address, and telephone number of the state bar association in your state?

   b. Is there an affiliate of the National Association of Legal Assistants or the National Federation of Paralegal Associations in your city? Where is the nearest affiliate of either of these organizations located?

   c. Are there any regional or local paralegal associations in your area? If so, what are their names, street and e-mail addresses, and phone numbers?

2. Using the material on paralegal skills presented in the chapter, which of the following are skills that a paralegal should have? Explain why.

   a. Reading skills.   e. Math skills.

   b. Interpersonal skills.   f. Computer skills.

   c. Marketing skills.   g. Management skills.

   d. Oral communication skills.

3. Which of the following personal attributes, presented in the chapter, are helpful to a paralegal? Why?

   a. Insensitivity.   d. Unreliability.

   b. Commitment.   e. Objectivity.

   c. Integrity.   f. Inaccuracy.

❖ USING INTERNET RESOURCES

Browse through the materials on the Web sites of the National Association of Legal Assistants, or NALA (at www.nala.org), and the National Federation of Paralegal Associations, or NFPA (at www.paralegals.org). Then do the following:

1. Look closely at the benefits of membership listed by each of these organizations. How do they compare? Are there any significant differences?

2. Examine the information that is included on each site about the organization's certification program. For each program, summarize the requirements that a paralegal must meet to become certified.

3. Select an article about a current development or issue in the paralegal profession from either NALA's "News & Updates" or NFPA's "What's New?" pages. Write a one-paragraph summary of the article, indicating what the article is about and why the topic treated is significant.

4. Go to "What is a paralegal/legal assistant?" at the NALA Web site (at www.nala.org). Which of the following tasks might legal assistants perform, according to the information provided there?

   a. Draft legal documents.

   b. Try cases in court.

   c. Locate witnesses.

   d. Give legal advice.

   e. Set legal fees.

   f. Interview clients.

   g. Perform legal investigations.

CAREERS IN THE LEGAL COMMUNITY

Chapter Outline

☒ INTRODUCTION ☒ WHERE PARALEGALS WORK ☒ PARALEGAL SPECIALTIES
☒ PARALEGAL COMPENSATION ☒ PLANNING YOUR CAREER
☒ LOCATING POTENTIAL EMPLOYERS ☒ JOB-PLACEMENT SERVICES
☒ MARKETING YOUR SKILLS ☒ REEVALUATING YOUR CAREER

After completing this chapter, you will know:

- What types of firms and organizations hire paralegals.
- Some areas of law in which paralegals specialize.
- How much paralegals can expect to earn.
- How paralegals are compensated for overtime work.
- How to prepare a career plan and pursue it.
- What is involved in a job search and how to go about it.

On the Web
For helpful information on all aspects of paralegal careers, go to the National Association of Legal Assistants' Web site at **www.nala.org** and the National Federation of Paralegal Associations' Web site at **www.paralegals.org**

INTRODUCTION

As a paralegal, you will enjoy a broad spectrum of employment opportunities. In the past two decades, attorneys have begun to realize how the use of paralegals in the law office can help them achieve the goal of providing quality legal services at lower cost to clients. Paralegals perform a number of tasks that in the past only attorneys handled. By turning over these tasks to paralegals, whose hourly fees are lower than those of attorneys, law firms can represent more clients, and clients pay less for their services.

The fact that you are entering a growth profession presents further opportunities. As mentioned in Chapter 1, the first paralegals were legal secretaries who had acquired, through experience, the necessary skills and abilities to assist attorneys in substantive legal work within the law-firm environment. As the paralegal profession developed, so did opportunities for paralegals in other employment settings. Corporations began to realize how paralegals could be used effectively in their legal departments. Government agencies created positions for paralegals. Banks, insurance companies, and other firms and institutions began to hire paralegals to assist with work that required legal training. Today, most paralegals continue to work for law firms, as will be discussed shortly, but they are increasingly assuming greater responsibilities as attorneys realize the benefits of delegating substantive legal work to paralegals.

This chapter provides a point of departure for your career planning. In the pages that follow, you will read about where paralegals work, some special areas of paralegal practice, and how paralegals are compensated. You will also learn about the essential steps involved in planning for a successful career and how to go about finding a job.

WHERE PARALEGALS WORK

Paralegal employers fall into a number of categories. This section describes the general characteristics of each of the major types of working environments.

Law Firms

When paralegals first established themselves within the legal community in the 1960s, they assisted lawyers in a law-firm setting. Today, as indicated in Exhibit 2.1, law firms continue to hire more paralegals than do any other organizations. Law firms vary in size from the small, one-attorney office to the huge "megafirm" with hundreds of attorneys. As you can see in Exhibit 2.2, the majority of paralegals working for law firms are employed by firms having fewer than twenty attorneys, and over half (56 percent) are employed by firms having ten or fewer attorneys.[1]

WORKING FOR A SMALL FIRM.   Many paralegals begin their careers working for small law practices, such as one-attorney firms or firms with just a few attorneys. To some extent, this is because of the greater number of small law firms, relative to large ones. It may also be due to geographic location. For example, a

On the Web
You can obtain a host of information on specific law firms by going to their Web pages. For one example, go to Hale & Dorr's Web site at **www.haledorr.com**. (To find Web sites for law firms, check one of the legal directories discussed later in this chapter.)

---

1. One of the difficulties in describing law-firm environments is that the terms *small law firm* and *large law firm* mean different things to different people. In a large metropolitan city, for example, a firm with fifteen attorneys might qualify as a small law firm. In a smaller, more rural community, however, a firm with fifteen attorneys would be considered a very large law firm. In this text, we refer to law firms with fifteen or fewer attorneys as small law firms and firms with over fifteen attorneys as large firms.

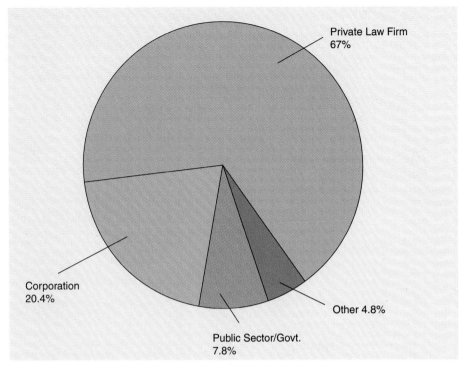

EXHIBIT 2.1
Where Paralegals Work

© 1999 James Publishing, Inc.
Reprinted courtesy of *Legal
Assistant Today* magazine. For
subscription information call
(800) 394-2626.

Source: "Are They Paying You What You're Worth? Legal Assistant Today's 1998–99 Salary Survey Results," *Legal Assistant Today,* January/February 1999, pp. 53–57.

paralegal who lives in a relatively rural environment, such as a small community, may find that his or her only option is to work for a small legal practice.

Working for a small firm offers many advantages to the beginning paralegal, and you should be aware of them. If the firm is a general law practice, you will have the opportunity to gain experience in many different areas of the law. You will be able to learn whether you enjoy working in one area (such as family law) more than another area (such as personal-injury law) in the event that you later decide to specialize. Some paralegals also prefer the often more personal and less formal environment of the small law office, as well as the variety of tasks and greater flexibility that frequently characterize this setting.

A characteristic of small firms that may prove challenging to you has to do with compensation. Small firms pay, on average, lower salaries than larger firms

NUMBER OF ATTORNEYS IN FIRM	PERCENTAGE OF ALL LAW-FIRM PARALEGALS EMPLOYED BY FIRM
0–5	40%
6–10	16%
11–20	15%
21–30	7%
31–40	4%
41–50	2%
Over 50	16%

EXHIBIT 2.2
**Paralegal Employment in
Law Firms by Size of Firm**

© 1999 James Publishing, Inc.
Reprinted courtesy of *Legal
Assistant Today* magazine. For
subscription information call
(800) 394-2626.

Source: "Legal Assistant Today's 1997–98 Salary Survey Results," *Legal Assistant Today,* March/April 1998, pp. 72–77. (These data were not included in the 1998–1999 salary survey results reported in *Legal Assistant Today,* January/February 1999, pp. 53–57.)

EXHIBIT 2.3
Paralegal Compensation

© 1999 James Publishing, Inc. Reprinted courtesy of *Legal Assistant Today* magazine. For subscription information call (800) 394-2626.

By Firm Size		By Type of Employer	
Number of Attorneys in Firm	**Average Salary**	**Employer**	**Average Salary**
1	$32,212	Private Law Firm	$33,880
2–5	$33,800	Corporation	$42,050
6–10	$34,109	Government	$31,370
11–25	$37,227		
26–50	$36,770		
51–100	$41,664		
101 plus	$41,232		

By Years of Experience			
Years of Experience	**Salary**		
	No Degree	**Associate's Degree**	**Bachelor's Degree**
Less than 1	$21,859	$23,640	$26,773
1–3	$30,505	$27,270	$31,328
3–5	$29,208	$30,319	$34,867
5–7	$38,325	$36,561	$32,765
7–10	$37,003	$35,786	$38,341
10–15	$37,209	$38,552	$38,577
15–20	$41,325	$45,301	$42,026
20 plus	$42,325	$44,550	$44,983

By Specialty			
Specialty	**Average Salary**	**Specialty**	**Average Salary**
Intellectual Property	$44,436	Employment	$33,445
Corporate	$39,758	Real Estate	$32,500
Environmental	$37,479	Family	$31,923
Litigation	$37,240	Personal Injury	$31,671
Bankruptcy	$35,884	Criminal	$31,645
Insurance Defense	$34,909	General	$29,169
Estate/Probate	$34,858	Workers' Compensation	$25,145
Regulatory	$33,890		

Source: "Are They Paying You What You're Worth? Legal Assistant Today's 1998–99 Salary Survey Results," *Legal Assistant Today,* January/February 1999, pp. 53–57.

do. As Exhibit 2.3 indicates, paralegal income is closely related to firm size. Generally, the larger the firm, the higher the paralegal salaries. Small firms also find it hard to afford the employee benefits packages, including insurance and pension plans, that large firms often provide for their employees.

Paralegals who work for small firms may also have less support staff to assist them. This means that if you work in a small law office, your job may involve a substantial amount of secretarial or clerical work.

WORKING FOR A LARGE FIRM.   In contrast to the (typically) more casual environment of the small law office, larger law firms usually are more formal. If you work for a larger firm, your responsibilities will probably be limited to specific, more well-defined types of tasks. For example, you may work for a department that handles (or for an attorney who handles) only certain types of cases, such as real-estate transactions. Office procedures and employment policies will also be more clearly defined and may be set forth in a written employment manual.

The advantages of the large firm include greater opportunities for promotions and career advancement, higher salaries and (typically) better benefits packages, more support staff for paralegals, and (often) more sophisticated computer technology and greater access to research resources.

You may view certain characteristics of large law firms as either advantages or disadvantages, depending on your personality and preferences. For example, if you favor the more specialized work and more formal working environment of the large law firm, then you will view these characteristics as advantages. If you prefer to handle a greater variety of tasks and enjoy the more personal, informal atmosphere of the small law office, then you might view the specialization and formality of the large law firm as disadvantages.

Corporations and Other Business Organizations

Over the past three decades, as mentioned earlier, paralegals have been given opportunities to work in business environments outside of law firms. Many of these businesses (such as insurance companies and banks) engage in activities that are highly regulated by government. Others (such as title insurance companies, law-book publishers, legal-software companies, and law schools) are in some way related to the practice of law. In addition, a vast number of businesses that need legal assistance hire paralegals.

An increasing number of paralegals work for corporate legal departments. Most major corporations hire in-house attorneys to handle corporate legal affairs. Some extremely large corporations have hundreds of attorneys on their payrolls. Paralegals who work for corporations ordinarily work under the supervision of in-house attorneys and assist them in such tasks as the following:

- Scheduling corporate meetings; drafting meeting notices, agendas, and minutes; and assembling documents necessary for meetings.
- Preparing case files, drafting documents, and doing other work related to lawsuits in which the corporation is involved.
- Collecting and interpreting technical information for corporate reports to a regulatory agency (such as the Environmental Protection Agency).
- Drafting documents necessary to register for patent, trademark, or copyright protection for a corporate product.
- Researching laws and regulations that might affect corporate actions or policies.
- Preparing and reviewing corporate contracts. (In large firms, some paralegals specialize in the area of contract analysis.)
- Working with outside counsel.

As noted in Exhibit 2.1, over 20 percent of paralegals are now working in corporate environments. On average, paralegals working for corporations receive higher salaries than those working for law firms, as indicated earlier in Exhibit 2.3. Paralegals who work for corporations normally work more regular hours and experience less stress than paralegals who work for law firms. For example, unlike in law firms, in the corporate environment paralegals are not required to generate a specific number of "billable hours" per year (hours billed to clients for paralegal services performed—discussed in Chapter 4) because there are no clients to bill—the corporation is the client.

Clerk @ Alphagraphics

Intellectual Property! — for many different kinds of businesses

DEVELOPING PARALEGAL SKILLS

Contracts Administrator

Martha Parnell, a legal assistant, works as a contracts administrator for the Best Engines Corporation. Martha's job is to take calls from buyers who want to negotiate contracts with Best Engines. The corporation uses preprinted forms containing provisions that Best Engines prefers to have in its contracts, terms that are advantageous to Best Engines. Some customers buy large quantities of engines to use in factories or to pump oil out of oil wells or through pipelines. These companies usually want to negotiate contract terms that provide them with more rights.

Martha has just received a telephone call from a buyer who wants to negotiate an indemnity provision, which in the preprinted form contract requires the buyer to pay Best Engines for any losses arising under the contract.

She discusses alternative indemnity provisions, such as splitting the indemnity or leaving it out entirely, with

the buyer. Martha then arranges to call the buyer back after discussing the various proposals with the general counsel (the attorney who heads the legal department).

TIPS FOR WORKING WITH CONTRACTS

- Know who—buyer or seller—holds the strongest bargaining position.
- Understand what the contract terms mean.
- Discuss all proposals with your client.
- Understand which terms your client will likely agree to and why.
- Determine which contract terms will be "deal busters."
- Set a timetable for finalizing the contract.

Government

A growing number of paralegals (around 8 percent) are employed by the government.

ADMINISTRATIVE AGENCIES.   Most paralegals who work for the government work for administrative agencies, such as the federal Environmental Protection Agency or a state environmental resources department. Paralegals who work for government agencies may be engaged in administrative appeals work, general or specialized legal research, welfare eligibility and claims, disability claims, the examination of documents (such as loan applications), and many other types of tasks. Your best source of information about employment positions in a particular administrative agency is the agency itself. You can find the names and telephone numbers of federal agencies, as well as a description of their functions, in the *United States Government Manual*, available in your public or college library.

Paralegals who work for government agencies normally work regular hours, tend to work fewer total hours per year (have more vacation time) than paralegals in other environments, and, like paralegals who work for corporations, do not have to worry about billable hours. Additionally, paralegals who work for the government usually enjoy comprehensive employment benefits. Salaries, however, are on average lower than those offered by traditional law firms and other employers in the private sector, as indicated earlier in Exhibit 2.3.

On the Web
You can locate information on government agencies at numerous Web sites, including that of FindLaw at **www.findlaw.com.**

LEGISLATIVE OFFICES.   Legislators in the U.S. Congress and in several state legislatures typically have staff members to help them with their various duties. These duties often include legal research and writing, and paralegals sometimes perform such services. For example, a senator who plans to propose an amendment to a law may ask a paralegal on his or her staff to research the legislative history of that law carefully (to discern the legislature's intention when passing the law) and write up a summary of that history.

LAW ENFORCEMENT OFFICES AND COURTS.   Many paralegals also work for government law enforcement offices and institutions. Some paralegals work for *public prosecutors.* Public prosecutors (such as district attorneys, state attorneys general, or U.S. attorneys) are government officials who are paid by the government. Accused persons may be defended by private attorneys, or, if they cannot afford to hire a lawyer, by *public defenders*—attorneys paid for by the state to ensure that criminal defendants are not deprived of their constitutional right to counsel. Both public prosecutors and public defenders rely on paralegals to handle much of their legal work.

Paralegals also find work in other government environments, such as federal or state court administrative offices. Court administrative work ranges from recording and filing court documents (such as the documents filed during a lawsuit—see Chapter 6) to handling collections for a regional tax authority for a local small claims court (courts that handle claims below a specified threshold amount—see Chapter 5). Paralegals may also work for bankruptcy courts (see page 35 for a discussion of bankruptcy law).

Legal Aid Offices

Legal aid offices provide legal services to those who find it difficult to pay for legal representation. During President Lyndon Johnson's "War on Poverty" in the 1960s, the government began to set aside funds for legal services organizations around the country to help less advantaged groups obtain needed legal assistance at low or no cost. Most legal aid continues to be government funded, although some support comes from private legal foundations.

Many paralegals who work in this type of setting find their jobs rewarding, even though they often receive lower salaries than they would in other areas. In part, this is because of the nature of the work—helping needy individuals. Additionally, paralegals in legal aid offices generally assume a wider array of responsibilities than they would in a traditional law office or one of the other environments described earlier. For example, some federal and state administrative agencies, including the Social Security Administration at the federal level, allow paralegals to represent clients in agency hearings and judicial proceedings. As you will read in Chapter 3, paralegals normally are not allowed to represent clients—only attorneys can do so. Exceptions to this rule exist when a court or agency permits nonlawyers to represent others in court or before administrative agency hearings.

Freelance Paralegals

A growing number of paralegals operate as freelancers. **Freelance paralegals** (also called *independent contractors* or *contract paralegals*) own their own businesses and perform specified types of legal work for attorneys on a contract basis.

Freelance Paralegal
A paralegal who operates his or her own business and provides services to attorneys on a contractual basis. A freelance paralegal works under the supervision of an attorney, who assumes responsibility for the paralegal's work product.

Attorneys who need temporary legal assistance sometimes contract with freelance paralegals to work on particular projects. Attorneys who need legal assistance but cannot afford to hire full-time paralegals might hire freelancers to work on a part-time basis. (The suggestions offered later in this chapter on how you can find work as a paralegal apply to freelance jobs as well.)

One of the benefits freelance paralegals enjoy about their services is the flexibility their jobs give them. Depending on the nature of the project, they may work at home or in an attorney's office. Some types of legal work, such as online legal research, can easily be conducted from a home office. Others, such as handling litigation documents or interviewing clients, require the paralegal to work in the attorney's office.

Realize that freelance paralegals work under attorney supervision. Freelancers are not to be confused with **independent paralegals**—often called *legal technicians,* who do *not* work under the supervision of an attorney and who provide (sell) legal services directly to the public. These services include helping members of the public obtain and fill out forms for certain types of legal transactions, such as bankruptcy filings and divorce petitions. As you will read in Chapter 3, independent paralegals run the risk of violating state statutes prohibiting the unauthorized practice of law.

PARALEGAL SPECIALTIES

While many paralegals work for small firms that offer a wide range of legal services, other paralegals have found it useful and satisfying to specialize in one area of law. There are numerous opportunities for the paralegal who wishes to concentrate his or her efforts on a particular area and become a specialist. Here we discuss just a few of these specialty areas.

Litigation Assistance

Working a lawsuit through the court system is called **litigation.** Paralegals who specialize in assisting attorneys in the litigation process are called **litigation paralegals.** Litigation paralegals work in general law practices, small litigation firms, litigation departments of larger law firms, or corporate legal departments. Litigation paralegals often specialize in a certain type of litigation, such as personal-injury litigation (which will be discussed shortly) or product-liability cases (which involve injuries caused by defective products). Some litigation paralegals may also work primarily on behalf of **plaintiffs** (those who bring lawsuits) or on behalf of **defendants** (those against whom lawsuits are brought). Lawyers in a personal-injury practice, for example, often represent plaintiffs. Lawyers in a criminal law practice represent criminal defendants—those accused of crimes.

You will read in detail about litigation procedures and the important role played by paralegals in the litigation process in Chapter 6. We indicate below just a sampling of the kinds of work that a paralegal might perform during the litigation process:

- Interview a client to obtain detailed information about a case.
- Locate and interview witnesses.
- Contact relevant medical personnel and institutions, employers, or other sources of factual information relating to a case. Prepare medical releases.
- Prepare documents to initiate (or defend against) a lawsuit and file them with the court, draft interrogatories (written questions to be answered under oath

---

Independent Paralegal
A paralegal who offers services directly to the public, normally for a fee, without attorney supervision. Independent paralegals assist consumers by supplying them with forms and procedural knowledge relating to simple or routine legal procedures.

Litigation
The process of working a lawsuit through the court system.

Litigation Paralegals
Paralegals who specialize in assisting attorneys in the litigation process.

Plaintiff
A party who initiates a lawsuit.

Defendant
A party against whom a lawsuit is brought.

by the opposing party), attend depositions (recorded question-and-answer sessions in which an attorney questions a party or a witness), and summarize deposition transcripts.

- Prepare exhibits for trial, arrange to have all needed equipment and supplies in the courtroom at the time of the trial, create a trial notebook for the attorney to refer to during the trial, and prepare the client and witnesses for trial.
- Assist at trial and in any posttrial procedures, such as those required for appealing the case to a higher court.

Personal-Injury Law

Much litigation involves claims brought by persons who have been injured in automobile accidents or other incidents as a result of the negligence of others. *Negligence* is a *tort*, or civil wrong, and someone who has been injured as a result of another's negligence is entitled under tort law to obtain compensation from the wrongdoer.

Paralegals who specialize in the area of personal-injury litigation often work for law firms that concentrate their efforts on this domain. Personal-injury paralegals are also hired by insurance companies to investigate claims. Defendants in personal-injury cases are typically insured by automobile or other insurance, and a defendant's insurance company will therefore have an interest in the outcome of the litigation.

A paralegal working on a personal-injury case would typically perform the following types of tasks:

- Interview a client (plaintiff) to obtain details about an accident and the injuries sustained by the client.
- Interview witnesses to the accident to gather as much information about the accident as possible.
- Obtain medical reports from physicians and hospitals describing the plaintiff's injuries.
- Obtain employment data to verify the amount of lost wages that should be claimed as damages—if the client's current or future employment is affected by the injury.
- Obtain a copy of the police report, and, if necessary, consult with police officers and investigators who worked on the case.
- Generally, provide litigation assistance.

Criminal Law

Law is sometimes classified into the two categories of civil law and criminal law. Civil law is concerned with the duties that exist between persons or between citizens and their governments, excluding the duty not to commit crimes. Contract law, for example, is part of civil law. The whole body of tort law, which has to do with the infringement by one person of the legally recognized rights of another, is an area of civil law.

Criminal law, in contrast, is concerned with wrongs committed against the public as a whole. Criminal acts are prohibited by federal, state, or local statutes. In a criminal case, the government seeks to impose a penalty on a person who has committed a crime. In a civil case, one party tries to make the other party comply with a duty or pay for the damage caused by the failure to so comply.

Civil Law
The branch of law dealing with the definition and enforcement of all private or public rights, as opposed to criminal matters.

Criminal Law
The branch of law that governs and defines those actions that are crimes and that subjects persons convicted of crimes to punishment imposed by the government.

DEVELOPING PARALEGAL SKILLS
Working for a Public Defender

Michele Sanchez works as a paralegal for the public defender's office in her county. Today, she has been assigned to go to the county jail to meet with a new client. The client has been jailed for child abuse and is very upset. She demands to be released from jail immediately. Michele notes her concerns and informs the client of the scheduling of the bail hearings.

TIPS FOR MEETING WITH A NEW CLIENT
- Review the case before meeting with the client.
- Listen carefully and supportively.
- Communicate with empathy.
- Minimize note taking.
- Do not appear to judge the client.

Paralegals who specialize in the area of criminal law may work for public prosecutors, public defenders, or criminal defense attorneys. Criminal litigation is similar to civil litigation in many respects, and the kinds of work performed by litigation paralegals (described previously) also apply in the criminal law context. In addition to providing general litigation assistance, a paralegal working in the area of criminal law might perform the following tasks:

- As a public prosecutor's legal assistant, draft search warrants, which authorize law enforcement officers to search a person or place.
- As a public prosecutor's legal assistant, draft arrest warrants, which authorize law enforcement officers to arrest and take into custody a criminal suspect.
- As a public prosecutor's legal assistant, act as a liaison between the police department and the public prosecutor's office.
- As a defense attorney's legal assistant, assist a criminal defendant in making arrangements to post bail (so that the defendant can be released from custody until further proceedings are held).
- Generally, help to make sure that a criminal defendant's constitutional rights are not violated by any action undertaken by police officers or attorneys handling the case.

On the Web
You can gain insight into criminal law and procedures by looking at some of the famous criminal law cases included on Court TV's Web site. Go to **www.courttv.com/ index.html**.

Corporate Law

Corporate law consists of the laws that govern the formation, financing, merger and acquisition, and termination of corporations, as well as the rights and duties of those who own and run the corporation.

Paralegals who specialize in corporate law may work for a corporation, in its legal department, or for a law firm that specializes in corporate law. The demand for paralegals who are experienced in the area of corporate law is expanding. If you refer back to Exhibit 2.3 on paralegal compensation, you will see that paralegals specializing in this area also receive, on average, higher salaries or wages than paralegals in most other specialty areas.

Here are just a few of the tasks that a paralegal working in the area of corporate law might be asked to undertake:

- Prepare articles of incorporation and file them with the appropriate state office (usually the secretary of state's office).
- Draft corporate bylaws (rules that govern the internal affairs of the corporation).

Corporate Law
Law that governs the formation, financing, merger and acquisition, and termination of corporations, as well as the rights and duties of those who own and run the corporation.

- Prepare minutes of corporate meetings and maintain a minutes binder.
- Draft shareholder proposals.
- Review or prepare documents relating to the sale of corporate securities (stocks and bonds); assist a supervising attorney in making sure that federal and state requirements relating to the sale of corporate securities are met.
- Assist with legal work relating to corporate mergers and acquisitions, such as researching a corporation's financial status.
- File the papers necessary to terminate a corporation's legal existence.

Bankruptcy Law

Bankruptcy law is a body of law that allows debtors to obtain relief from their debts. Bankruptcy law is federal law, and bankruptcy proceedings take place in federal courts (see the discussion of the federal court system in Chapter 5). The twin goals of bankruptcy law are (1) to protect a debtor by giving him or her a fresh start, free from creditors' claims; and (2) to ensure that creditors who are competing for a debtor's assets are treated fairly. Bankruptcy law provides for several types of relief, and both individuals and business firms may petition for bankruptcy.

Both large and small law firms practice bankruptcy law. A corporation undergoing bankruptcy proceedings (often in the form of a "reorganization," as provided for under bankruptcy law) may hire, on a temporary basis, a paralegal experienced in bankruptcy law to assist in the process. If you are working on behalf of a debtor who seeks bankruptcy relief, you might perform the following types of tasks:

- Interview the debtor (which may be an individual or a corporate representative) to obtain information relating to the debtor's income, debts, and assets.
- Review creditors' claims and verify their validity.
- Prepare the necessary documents for submission to the bankruptcy court.
- Attend bankruptcy proceedings.
- Assist in defending the debtor against any legal actions concerning the bankruptcy proceedings.

Bankruptcy Law
The body of federal law that governs bankruptcy proceedings. The twin goals of bankruptcy law are (1) to protect a debtor by giving him or her a fresh start, free from creditors' claims; and (2) to ensure that creditors who are competing for a debtor's assets are treated fairly.

On the Web
If you are interested in bankruptcy law, a good site for learning about current bankruptcy issues is that of the American Bankruptcy Institute at **www.abiworld.org**.

Employment and Labor Law

Laws governing employment relationships are referred to collectively as *employment and labor law*. Employment and labor law includes laws governing health and safety in the workplace, labor unions and union-management relations, employment discrimination, wrongful employment termination, pension plans, retirement and disability income (Social Security), employee privacy rights, the minimum wage that must be paid, and overtime wages.

Paralegals who are experienced in one or more of these areas of employment and labor law may work for law firms, corporations and other business entities, or government agencies. Often, paralegals specialize in just one area of employment law. For example, many paralegals work in the area of workers' compensation. Under state **workers' compensation statutes**, employees who are injured on the job are compensated from state funds (obtained from taxes paid by employers). Paralegals working in this area of employment law assist persons injured on the job in obtaining compensation from the state workers' compensation board. As mentioned earlier, some government agencies allow paralegals to represent clients during agency hearings, which are conducted by agencies to settle disputes,

Workers' Compensation Statutes
State laws establishing an administrative procedure for compensating workers for injuries that arise in the course of their employment.

On the Web
Several law firms that specialize in labor and employment issues have posted their newsletters on the Web. One such firm is Arent Fox, which you can access at **www.arentfox.com.**

or during negotiations with the agencies. Many state workers' compensation boards allow paralegals to represent clients in such hearings.

Numerous other areas of employment and labor law are regulated by administrative agencies, and paralegals working in those areas need to be familiar with the relevant agency's requirements and procedures. Here are just a few agencies involved in regulating the workplace and with which employment-law paralegals should be familiar:

- *National Labor Relations Board (NLRB)*—A federal agency that implements federal laws governing union organizational activities, union elections, and labor-management relations generally.

- *Occupational Safety and Health Administration (OSHA)*—A federal agency that implements federal laws governing safety in the workplace. OSHA establishes safety standards that employers must follow. State agencies also establish safety and health standards.

- *Equal Employment Opportunity Commission (EEOC)*—A federal agency that administers and enforces federal laws prohibiting employment discrimination on the basis of race, color, national origin, gender, religion, age, or disability. Before an employee can sue an employer for discrimination in violation of these federal laws, the employee must comply with EEOC procedures for handling such complaints.

- *Labor Management Services Administration (LMSA)*—A federal agency that implements the provisions of the federal Employee Retirement Income Security Act (ERISA), which imposes certain requirements on employers in regard to pension funds.

Paralegals working in the area of employment and labor law often have extensive contact with these and other administrative agencies. If you work as a paralegal in the law-firm or corporate environment, you might undertake the following types of tasks, each of which may involve rules and procedures established by government agencies:

- Conduct research on labor law to determine how the law applies to a labor-management contract or dispute.

- Draft a contract setting forth the terms of a labor-management agreement.

- Assist in informal negotiations to settle a dispute between an employee and an employer or between a labor union and a firm's managers.

- Assist in formal dispute-settlement proceedings before one of the above-mentioned government agencies.

- Act as a mediator to help parties involved in labor or employment conflicts settle their disputes out of court (see Chapter 5 for further information on mediation and other forms of alternative dispute resolution, or ADR).

- Inform a client of the procedures involved in submitting a claim of employment discrimination to the EEOC and assist the client in preparing the necessary documents.

- Prepare the documents needed to initiate (or defend against) a lawsuit for employment discrimination in violation of federal or state law and generally assist in the litigation process.

- Contact and work with the state workers' compensation board on behalf of a client who is seeking compensation for injuries incurred during the course of employment.

- Draft employment policies to make sure that a business client (or a corporate employer) complies with federal and state laws prohibiting discrimination in the workplace.

- Assist a business client (or a corporate employer) in benefits planning to ensure compliance with the requirements of ERISA and any other laws regulating employee benefits, such as health, life, or disability insurance.

Estate Planning and Probate Administration

Estate planning and probate administration both have to do with the transfer of an owner's property, or *estate*, on the owner's death. Through **estate planning**, the owner decides, *before* death, how his or her property will be transferred to others. The owner may make a **will,** for example, to designate the persons to whom his or her property shall be transferred. The formal requirements for a valid will are set forth in state statutes, and because these requirements may differ from state to state, paralegals working in this area should be familiar with their state's law governing wills. If the property passes by will, depending on the size of the estate and other factors, the genuineness of the will may have to be proved (**probated**) in **probate court** (a county or other court that handles probate procedures). Probate administration thus involves the procedures relating to the transfer of property *after* the owner's death.

The process of probate may take many months and, in some cases, more than a year. The *personal representative* (a person named in the will to handle the affairs of the deceased after his or her death) or an *administrator* (a person appointed by the court if no personal representative is named in the will) satisfies all obligations (pays debts, taxes, and so on) of the deceased. The personal representative or administrator also arranges to have the deceased's property distributed among the heirs in accordance with the will's provisions. Because the probate process can be time consuming, many people arrange to have at least some of their property transferred in ways other than by will.

One estate-planning possibility involves the establishment of a **trust,** a legal arrangement in which the property owner transfers legal title to his or her property to a *trustee*. The trustee (which may be a relative or trusted friend of the property owner, an attorney, a law firm, or a banking institution) has a duty imposed by law to hold the property for the use or benefit of another (the *beneficiary* of the trust). A trust created during the owner's life is called a living trust. A trust provided for in a will comes into existence on the owner's death. Estate planning often involves life insurance. A person who wants to provide for a spouse and children after his or her death, for example, may obtain a life insurance policy listing the spouse and children as beneficiaries. On the death of the insured person, the beneficiaries receive the amount specified in the policy.

Paralegals who specialize in the area of estate planning and probate frequently work for law firms, but they may also be employed by other firms or agencies, such as banks, as well as by probate courts. If you work in this area, these are some of the tasks that you might perform:

- Interview clients to obtain information relating to their assets, how and to whom they want to transfer their property on death, and what arrangements they want to have made for the guardianship of minor children.

- Draft wills and other documents required to set up a trust fund.

Estate Planning
Making arrangements, during a person's lifetime, for the transfer of that person's property or obligations to others on the person's death. Estate planning often involves executing a will, establishing a trust fund, or taking out a life insurance policy to provide for others, such as a spouse or children, on one's death.

Will
A document directing how and to whom the maker's property and obligations are to be transferred on his or her death.

Probate
The process of "proving" the validity of a will and ensuring that the instructions in a valid will are carried out.

Probate Court
A court that probates wills; usually a county court.

Trust
An arrangement in which title to property is held by one person (a trustee) for the benefit of another (a beneficiary).

On the Web
To find the wills of famous people (John Lennon, Jacqueline Kennedy Onassis, Elvis Presley, and dozens of others), go to **www.ca-probate.com/ wills.htm.**

> ### ETHICAL CONCERN
> ## Serving the Interests of Bereaved Clients
>
> One of the hardest events to cope with is the loss of a loved one, yet it is precisely at this time that bereaved persons must also cope with funeral arrangements and legal formalities. These formalities may include checking with an attorney, locating a will if one was made, tending to the decedent's financial affairs, and so on. Undertaking these activities can be costly, and financial needs may cause further stress.
>
> These are factors that paralegals should keep in mind when dealing with clients during the probate process. Probate proceedings always take time, but the duration may be reduced by the paralegal who files the necessary forms in a timely fashion and follows up on the status of the proceedings to make sure that there are no unnecessary delays. Your kind or sympathetic words may be appreciated by a bereaved client; but you can best serve his or her interests by doing your job efficiently and responsibly and by undertaking any action you can to speed up the probate process.

- Make sure that all procedural requirements are met during the probate process—that the proper documents are submitted to the court in a timely fashion, for example.
- Gather information relating to the debts and assets of the deceased, and assist in settling all financial and other obligations of the deceased.
- Locate heirs, if necessary.
- Explain probate procedures to family members or other heirs of the deceased and keep them informed of the status of the proceedings.

Intellectual-Property Law

Intellectual Property
Property that results from intellectual, creative processes. Copyrights, patents, and trademarks are examples of intellectual property.

Intellectual property consists of the products of individuals' minds—products that result from intellectual, creative processes. Those who create intellectual property acquire certain rights over the use of that property, and these rights are protected by law. Literary and artistic works are protected by *copyright law. Trademark law* protects business firms' distinctive marks or mottos. Inventions are protected by *patent law.*

Although it is an abstract term for an abstract concept, intellectual property is nonetheless wholly familiar to virtually everyone. The book you are reading is copyrighted. Undoubtedly, the personal computer you use is trademarked and patented. The software you use on that computer might be copyrighted. The primary benefit of intellectual-property rights to the owner is that he or she controls the commercial use of the property. The owner, for example, may sell the intellectual-property rights to another, may collect royalties on the use of the property (such as a popular song) by others, and may prevent all but one publisher from reproducing the property (such as a novel).

Many law firms (or special departments of large law firms) specialize in intellectual-property law, such as patent law, while other firms provide a spectrum of legal services to their clients, of which intellectual-property law is only a part. Corporate legal departments may be responsible for registering copyrights, patents, or trademarks with the federal government.[2] Paralegal specialists in the area of intellectual property frequently undertake the following kinds of work:

- Interview clients who want to register for copyright, trademark, or patent protection of certain intellectual property, such as a new computer program, a product name, or an invention.
- Conduct research to find out whether someone has already applied for patent or trademark protection of an invention or product that the firm's client (or a corporate employer) wants to develop or register.
- Draft the documents that are necessary to apply for patent, trademark, or copyright protection.
- Draft contracts or licensing agreements that provide for another's authorized use of a copyrighted, patented, or trademarked product.
- In the corporate environment, monitor others' uses of the corporation's intellectual property and others' compliance with licensing agreements.
- Assist in litigation resulting from the *infringement* (unlawful use of) copyright, trademark, or patent rights.

On the Web
If you are interested in how cyberspace is affecting the laws governing intellectual property, a good general site covering current issues is that offered by the Bureau of National Affairs at **www.bna.com/e-law**.

Environmental Law

Environmental law consists of all laws that have been created to protect the environment. Environmental law involves the regulation of air and water pollution, natural resource management, endangered species protection, hazardous waste disposal and the clean-up of hazardous waste sites, pesticide control, and nuclear power regulation.

Employers of paralegal specialists in environmental law include administrative agencies (such as the federal Environmental Protection Agency, the state's natural resource department, and the local zoning board), environmental law departments of large law firms, law firms that specialize in environmental law, and corporations. Corporations with legal departments often employ environmental specialists. For example, a corporation may employ a paralegal as an *environmental coordinator* to assist the corporation in proper compliance with environmental regulations.

Here are some of the types of tasks that paralegal specialists in the area of environmental law frequently perform:

- Coordinate a corporate employer's environmental programs and policies and ensure that the corporation is complying properly with environmental regulations.
- Obtain permits from local, state, or federal environmental agencies to use land in certain ways (such as clearing trees or filling wetlands).
- Prepare forms and documents relating to the disposal of hazardous waste created by a corporate client's (or corporate employer's) manufacturing plants.
- Assist in litigation or other legal actions relating to violations of environmental laws. Paralegals play an important role in coordinating different aspects of the litigation (which may involve multiple violators) and in managing case files, which are often voluminous.

Environmental Law
All state and federal laws or regulations enacted or issued to protect the environment and preserve environmental resources.

On the Web
For news articles on environmental topics and links to other sites that deal with environmental issues, go to the Environmental Law page of Law Journal EXTRA! at **www.ljx.com/practice/ environment/index.html**.

---

2. Copyrights are registered with the U.S. Copyright Office, Library of Congress, Washington, DC 20559. Patents and trademarks are registered with the Patent and Trademark Office, U.S. Department of Commerce, Washington, DC 20231.

- Attend conferences with administrative agency personnel or hearings conducted by an agency to assist in the settlement of a dispute.
- As an environmental agency employee, investigate and process claims of violations and assist in settling claims.

Real-Estate Law

Real Estate
Land and things permanently attached to the land, such as houses, buildings, and trees and foliage.

Real estate, or *real property*, consists of land and all things permanently attached to the land, such as houses, buildings, and trees and foliage. Because of the value of real estate (for most people, a home is the most expensive purchase they will ever make), attorneys frequently assist persons or business firms that buy or sell real property to make sure that nothing important is overlooked. Paralegals who specialize in the area of real estate may find employment in a number of environments, including small law firms that specialize in real-estate transactions, real-estate departments in large law firms, corporations or other business firms that frequently buy or sell real property, banking institutions (which finance real-estate purchases), title companies, or real-estate agencies. Here we list just a few of the tasks that paralegals working in this area might perform:

- Interview clients who want to buy or sell real property.
- Draft contracts for the sale of real estate.
- Conduct *title* examinations. (The title to real property represents the right to own and possess the property, and title examinations are conducted to see if there are any defects in the title.)
- Review title abstracts, which summarize the ownership history of real property.
- Draft mortgage agreements.
- Provide information to banking institutions involved in financing clients' real-estate purchases.
- Prepare *deeds* (a deed is a written document that transfers title from one person to another).
- Make sure that property transfers are recorded in the appropriate public office (usually the county register of deeds office).
- Schedule *closings* (the closing is the final step in the purchase of real estate).
- Attend closings (when permitted by state law to do so).

Family Law

Family Law
Law relating to family matters, such as marriage, divorce, child support, and child custody.

Family law, as the term implies, deals with family matters, such as marriage, divorce, alimony, child support, and child custody. Family law is governed primarily by state statutes. If you specialize in this area, you will need to become familiar with your state's requirements concerning marriage and divorce procedures, child support, and related issues.

As a family-law specialist, you might work for a small family-law practice, a family-law department in a large law firm, or with a state or local agency, such as a community services agency, that assists persons who need help with family-related problems. As a paralegal working in the area of family law, you might perform such tasks as the following:

- Interview a divorcing client to obtain information relating to the couple's assets and liabilities.
- Research state laws governing child custody and assist in making child-custody arrangements for a divorcing couple.

Real-Estate Paralegal

DORA DYE *earned a bachelor of arts degree in Spanish, with distinction in general scholarship, and a master of arts degree in Spanish from the University of California, Berkeley. In addition, Dye received a master of business administration degree in International Business, with distinction, from Armstrong University.*

Dye has been a real-estate and corporate paralegal since 1986. She has worked at several major San Francisco law firms and has transferred her skills in large real-estate and corporate transactions to the corporate environment. She is currently the Dispositions Closing Coordinator at the RREEF Funds.

Dye is a member of the San Francisco Paralegal Association (SFPA) and the National Federation of Paralegal Associations, Inc. (NFPA). She is an active member of the NFPA's PACE Development Committee and has taught the legal research and writing component of the PACE Review Seminar, as well as co-authored the chapter, "Factual and Legal Research" in the Paralegal Advanced Competency Exam Study Manual *with her husband, David Dye.*

Dye also teaches various courses in paralegal programs at the City College of San Francisco and California State University, Hayward. She has worked with members of the American Association for Paralegal Education to prepare model syllabi for real-estate law and introduction-to-paralegalism courses.

What do you like best about your work?

"I enjoy the field of real estate, because I am able to bring all of my experiences from the past to my current position. While working at various law firms, I became a senior paralegal specializing in multimillion-dollar real-estate closings. That experience has allowed me to transfer my knowledge and skills in real estate, business, and the law to a corporate environment and to work more effectively with internal and external legal counsel. Becoming a part-time paralegal instructor has enabled me to share my knowledge and skills with future paralegals. I have even used my Spanish skills when doing *pro bono* work."

What is the greatest challenge that you face in your area of work?

"Satisfying the twin goals of cost efficiency and the generation of a superior work product represents the greatest challenge. To meet these goals, it is important to 'get it right' the first time. Today, paralegals have a more personal relationship with clients. Clients call paralegals directly to handle issues that require the attorney's attention, thus improving the quality of legal services being delivered and keeping costs down."

What advice do you have for would-be paralegals in your area of work?

"Be as detail oriented as possible, and be the best that you can be in all things that you do. Bringing to your position all of the experiences that you have had will add to your value as a paralegal. Paralegal students should get work experience. Without work experience, students do not have an idea of office culture and environment, which are important aspects of a job."

What are some tips for success as a paralegal in your area of work?

"A successful paralegal knows what needs to be done and does it before he or she is asked. If you anticipate the needs of your attorneys and your clients, you will always be prepared to deal with matters more efficiently and effectively."

> **"A successful paralegal knows what needs to be done and does it before he or she is asked."**

ETHICAL CONCERN
Questions about Child Custody

Divorcing clients frequently ask whether they can take their children out of the state while the mediation or divorce proceedings are under way. For example, suppose that Kerry Lynn, a paralegal, receives a call from a client who wants to know if it would be all right to take her children to her mother's home in another state over the weekend. Kerry tells the client that there is no problem with that.

Normally, there would be no problem, but what Kerry doesn't know is that in this case, just two days ago, the court ordered that the children could not leave the state. The client, relying on Kerry's answer, violates the order. Kerry has both given legal advice to a client (which only attorneys may do) and has caused the client to suffer adverse legal consequences as a result of that advice.

In your work as a paralegal, you may face similar questions from divorcing parents. You should always let the client know that as a paralegal, you cannot give legal advice, which you would be doing if you answered such questions.

- Draft a settlement (separation) agreement.
- Prepare the necessary documents to be filed with the court in a divorce action and assist in the litigation process.
- Prepare a client for divorce proceedings.
- Assist a client—particularly a spouse who has never handled household financial affairs—in financial planning.
- Assist clients in adoption proceedings.
- Interact with mediators (see Chapter 5) and counselors who are dealing with family problems.

Emerging Specialty Areas

The above listing of specialty areas is by no means exhaustive. In addition to these domains, there are several emerging areas that offer opportunities for paralegals who wish to specialize. For example, as the U.S. population ages, more and more attorneys are focusing on servicing the needs of older clients. Elder law is the term used to describe this broad specialty. Paralegals who work in this practice area may be asked to assist in a variety of tasks, including those relating to estate planning (discussed earlier), age-discrimination claims, financial arrangements for long-term care, abuse suffered by elderly persons, and the visitation rights of grandparents.

An increasing number of paralegals are also finding work in the area of immigration law. In the 1990s, immigration rates climbed significantly from those of previous decades. As the number of immigrants increased, so did the need for legal services among immigrant groups. Today, a number of law firms specialize in immigration law, particularly in California, New York, and other states with large immigrant populations. If you specialize in this area, you might assist clients who need help in filling out applications for work permits or visas, or who need information on how to become U.S. citizens. You may help clients contact foreign

Elder Law
A term used to describe a relatively new legal specialty that involves servicing the needs of older clients, such as estate planning and making arrangements for long-term care.

Immigration Law
All laws that set forth the requirements that persons must meet if they wish to visit or immigrate to the United States.

government offices about their immigration status or assist clients who are involved in deportation proceedings.

Over the past decade, many nurses have found profitable and challenging work as paralegals. A paralegal who is also a trained nurse is particularly well equipped to evaluate legal claims involving injuries, such as those involved in personal-injury, medical malpractice, or product-liability lawsuits. A relatively new specialty area among nurses—and within the legal profession—is that of the legal nurse consultant (LNC). An LNC consults with legal professionals and others on medical aspects of legal claims or issues. LNCs usually work independently (offering their services on a contract basis) and are typically well paid for their services—up to $200 per hour, in some cases. The American Association of Legal Nurse Consultants now offers a certification program in which nurses who meet the eligibility criteria (including appropriate educational credentials and sufficient experience as a legal nurse) and pass an examination may become certified as LNCs.

As mentioned in the *Technology and Today's Paralegal* feature in Chapter 1, developments in technology are transforming the legal workplace. These developments are also opening doors to possible areas of specialization for paralegals. Paralegals who acquire expertise in high-tech equipment and software applications can perform valuable services for their employers and command high salaries.

Legal Nurse Consultant (LNC)
A nurse who consults with legal professionals and others about medical aspects of legal claims or issues. Legal nurse consultants normally must have at least a bachelor's degree in nursing and a significant amount of nursing experience.

On the Web
To learn more about the American Association of Legal Nurse Consultants and its certification programs, go to **www.aalnc.org.**

Paralegal Compensation

What do paralegals earn? This is an important question for anyone contemplating a career as a paralegal. You can get some idea of what paralegals make, on average, from paralegal compensation surveys. Following a discussion of these surveys, we look at some other components of paralegal compensation, including job benefits and how paralegals are compensated for overtime work.

Compensation Surveys

If you refer back to Exhibit 2.3, you can see that paralegal income is affected by a number of factors. We have already mentioned how the average income of paralegals is affected by firm size (smaller or larger) and the type of employer (law firm, corporation, or government). Other income-determining factors include years of experience working as a paralegal, as well as the area of practice. Note that the average salary of a paralegal working in the area of intellectual-property law is $44,436, approximately $19,291 more than that of a paralegal working in the area of workers' compensation. Average salaries are also affected by location.

Exhibit 2.3 indicates *national* averages. To have a clearer picture of what your potential future income will be, you need to look at the average paralegal income in the state where you live or plan to work. As you can see in Exhibit 2.4 on the next page, paralegals working in California earn, on average, over $16,706 more than paralegals working in Nebraska.

Keep in mind that salary statistics do not tell the whole story. Although paralegals earn more in California than in a midwestern state such as Nebraska, the cost of living is higher in California than in Nebraska. This means that your real income—the amount of goods and services that you can purchase with your income—may, in fact, be the same in both states despite the differences in salary. Salary statistics also do not reveal another important component of compensation—job benefits.

EXHIBIT 2.4
**Paralegal
Compensation by State**

© 1999 James Publishing, Inc. Reprinted courtesy of *Legal Assistant Today* magazine. For subscription information call (800) 394-2626.

State	Average Salary	State	Average Salary
Alabama	$36,225	Montana*	$26,742
Alaska	$26,800	Nebraska*	$24,440
Arizona	$37,268	Nevada*	$36,980
Arkansas	$33,592	New Hampshire*	$31,000
California	$41,146	New Jersey	$36,576
Colorado	$32,457	New Mexico*	$25,307
Connecticut	$37,364	New York	$39,123
Delaware	$39,500	North Carolina	$28,691
District of Columbia*	$39,750	North Dakota*	$33,491
Florida	$40,229	Ohio	$34,542
Georgia	$37,465	Oklahoma*	$32,400
Hawaii*	$39,400	Oregon	$38,196
Idaho*	$29,000	Pennsylvania	$35,557
Illinois	$31,851	Rhode Island*	$30,417
Indiana*	$29,674	South Carolina	$30,900
Iowa	$34,450	South Dakota*	$30,000
Kansas*	$30,840	Tennessee	$29,619
Kentucky	$27,183	Texas	$37,004
Louisiana*	$29,250	Utah*	$34,200
Maine*	$29,250	Vermont*	$32,750
Maryland*	$30,902	Virginia	$32,648
Massachusetts	$43,200	Washington	$33,851
Michigan	$34,651	West Virginia*	$33,500
Minnesota	$34,080	Wisconsin	$33,538
Mississippi*	$34,440	Wyoming*	$25,875
Missouri	$29,452		

*Based on less than ten verifiable submissions. This means that the salaries included here may not be representative of paralegal salaries in your state.

Source: "Are They Paying You What You're Worth? Legal Assistant Today's 1998–99 Salary Survey Results," *Legal Assistant Today,* January/February 1999, pp. 53–57.

Job Benefits

Part of your total compensation package as an employee will consist of various job benefits. These benefits may include paid holidays, sick leave, group insurance coverage (life, disability, medical, dental), pension plans, and possibly others. Benefits packages vary from firm to firm. For example, one employer may pay the entire premium for your life and health insurance, while another employer may require you to contribute part of the cost of the insurance. Usually, the larger the firm, the greater the value of the benefits package.

> **When evaluating any job offer, you need to consider the benefits that you will receive and what these benefits are worth to you.**

You will read more about the importance of job benefits later in this chapter, in the context of evaluating a job offer.

Salaries versus Hourly Wages

Most paralegals are salaried employees. In other words, they receive a specified annual salary regardless of the number of hours they actually work. Other paralegals are paid an hourly wage rate for every hour worked. Paralegals are frequently asked to work overtime, and how they are compensated for overtime work usually depends on whether they are salaried employees or are paid hourly wages. Many firms compensate their salaried paralegals for overtime work through year-end **bonuses,** which are special payments made to employees in recognition of their devotion to the firm and the high quality of their work. Paralegals often receive annual bonuses ranging from $1,200 to nearly $3,000, depending on years of experience, firm size, and so on. Some firms allow salaried employees to take compensatory time off work (for example, an hour off for every hour worked beyond usual working hours). Employees who are paid an hourly wage rate are normally paid overtime wages.

Bonus
An end-of-the-year payment to a salaried employee in appreciation for that employee's overtime work, work quality, diligence, or dedication to the firm.

Federal Law and Overtime Pay

A major issue in the paralegal profession in regard to compensation has to do with overtime pay. Some paralegals who receive year-end bonuses question whether their bonuses sufficiently compensate them for the amount of overtime they have worked. The debate over overtime pay is complicated by the fact that the Fair Labor Standards Act (Wage-Hour Law) of 1938 requires employers to pay employees **overtime wages**—one and a half times their normal hourly rate for all hours worked beyond forty hours per week. The act exempts certain types of employees from this overtime-pay requirement, however. *Exempt employees* include those who qualify under the terms of the act as holding "administrative," "executive," or "professional" positions.

The issue, then, is whether paralegals are exempt or nonexempt employees under the Fair Labor Standards Act. If they are exempt, they need not be paid an hourly overtime rate. If they are nonexempt, by law they must be paid overtime wages. Many firms argue that their paralegals are professionals and thus exempt from the act. Other firms, fearing possible liability for unfair labor practices, are beginning to pay overtime wages to their paralegals. Paralegals seem to be split fairly evenly on the issue, as are their employers. According to the 1998–99 paralegal compensation survey conducted by the National Association of Legal Assistants (NALA), 56.1 percent of paralegals are classified by their employers as exempt employees, while 43.9 percent are classified as nonexempt.[3]

In early 1994, a federal court addressed this issue for the first time. The case arose when twenty-three paralegals who worked for Page & Addison, a law firm in Dallas, Texas, sought $40,000 in back wages for overtime hours that they had worked. The Department of Labor, which enforces the Fair Labor Standards Act, had concluded that the paralegals were nonexempt employees and thus subject to the act's overtime provisions. The federal court, however, disagreed, finding that paralegals could be classified as exempt (or professional) employees because they perform important work and exercise discretion and independent judgment.[4] Although the court decision in the *Page & Addison* case is significant, it does not mean that all paralegals are now classified as exempt employees. Rather, the issue is decided on the basis of the specific facts of a given case. The question of how paralegals should be classified for labor-law purposes continues to divide the profession.

Overtime Wages
Wages paid to workers who are paid an hourly wage rate to compensate them for overtime work (hours worked beyond forty hours per week). Under federal law, overtime wages are at least one and a half times the regular hourly wage rate.

---

3. *Legal Assistant Today,* January/February, 1999, p. 55.
4. *U.S. Department of Labor v. Page & Addison, P.C.,* U.S. District Court, Dallas, Texas, No. 91-2655, March 15, 1994.

PLANNING YOUR CAREER

Career planning involves essentially three steps. The first step is defining your long-term goals. The second step involves devising short-term goals and adjusting these goals to meet the realities of the job market. We look at these two steps of career planning in this section. Later in this chapter, we discuss the third step: reevaluating your career after you have had some on-the-job experience as a paralegal.

Defining Your Long-Term Goals

From the outset, you will want to define, as clearly as possible, your career goals, and this requires some personal reflection and self-assessment. What are you looking for in a career? Why do you want to become a paralegal? Is income the most important factor? Is job satisfaction (doing the kind of work you like) the most important factor? Is the environment in which you work the most important factor? What profession could best utilize your special talents or skills? Asking yourself these and other broad questions about your personal preferences and values will help you define more clearly your overall professional goals.

Do not be surprised to find that your long-term goals change over time. As you gain more experience as a paralegal and your life circumstances change, you may decide that your former long-term goals are no longer appropriate. For example, you may desire a level of career involvement as a single person that may not be appropriate to your situation should you marry and have children. Similarly, later in life, when your children leave home and you are faced with an "empty nest," you may have different goals with respect to your work.

Also, at the outset of your career, you cannot know what opportunities might present themselves in the future. Career planning is an ongoing challenge for paralegals, just as it is for everyone. Throughout your career as a paralegal, you will probably meet other paralegals who have made career changes. A high percentage of paralegals in today's work force, for example, decided to become paralegals after several years of working in another profession, such as nursing, law enforcement, business administration, or accounting. Changes within the profession, your own experiences, and new opportunities constantly affect the career choices before you. The realities you face during your career may play a significant role in modifying your long-term goals.

Short-Term Goals and Job Realities

Long-term goals are just that—goals that we hope to achieve over the long run. It may take many years or even a lifetime to attain certain long-term goals that we set for ourselves. Short-term goals are the steps that we take to realize our long-term goals. As an entry-level paralegal, one of your short-term goals is simply to find a job.

Ideally, you will find a job that provides you with a salary commensurate with your training and abilities, a level of responsibility that is comfortable (or challenging) for you, and excellent job benefits. The realities of the job market are not always what we wish them to be, however. You should be prepared for the possibility that you might not find the "right" employer or the "perfect" job for you when you first start your job search. You may be lucky from the outset, but then again, it may take several attempts before you find the employer and the job that best suits your needs, skills, and talents. Remember, though, that even if you do not find the perfect job right away, you can gain valuable skills and experience in *any* job environment—skills and experience that can help you achieve long-term goals in the future. In fact, you might want to "try on" jobs at different-sized firms and in different specialty areas to see how they "fit" with your particular needs.

LOCATING POTENTIAL EMPLOYERS

Looking for a job is time consuming and requires attention to detail, persistence, and creativity. Your paralegal education is preparing you, among other things, to do investigative research. The investigative skills that you will use on the job as a paralegal are the ones that you should apply when looking for a job.

Where do you begin your investigation? How can you find out what paralegal jobs are available in your area or elsewhere? How do you know which law firms practice the type of law that interests you? The following suggestions will help you find answers to all of these questions.

Networking

Career opportunities often go unpublished. Many firms post notices within their own organizations before publishing online or in the "Help Wanted" section of a newspaper or periodical. This opens doors to their own employees before the general public. It also spares employers from having to wade through hundreds of employment applications for a vacant position. If you have connections within an organization, you may be told that a position is opening before other candidates are aware that an opportunity exists.

Paralegals looking for jobs often learn of available positions through networking. For paralegals, **networking** is the process of making personal connections with other paralegals, paralegal instructors, attorneys, and others who are involved in (or who know someone who is involved in) the paralegal or legal profession. You should begin networking while you are still attending your paralegal program. Cultivate relationships with your instructors. Let them know your career interests, and ask them for their advice. See if your local paralegal association allows students to be members. If it does, attend meetings and become acquainted with other paralegals, who may know of job opportunities.

Networking
Making personal connections and cultivating relationships with people in a certain field, profession, or area of interest.

Cultivate connections during your internship as a paralegal, as well. One of the benefits of internships or of working part-time in a law firm while studying to be a paralegal is that it allows you to establish connections that may be useful in your job search, and the firm itself may offer you a full-time job when you graduate. According to the 1998–99 survey of paralegal compensation conducted by the National Association of Legal Assistants (NALA), over 28 percent of paralegals found entry-level jobs or new jobs through networking.[5] Throughout your career, you will find that networking can provide valuable job leads.

Finding Available Jobs

Your next effort should be to locate sources that list paralegal job openings. A good place to start is with the classified ads in your local newspaper. **Trade journals** and similar publications, such as your local or state bar association's

Trade Journal
A newsletter, magazine, or other periodical that provides a certain trade or profession with information (products, trends, or developments) relating to that trade or profession.

---

5. "Are They Paying You What You're Worth? Legal Assistant Today's 1998–99 Salary Survey Results," *Legal Assistant Today,* January/February 1999, pp. 53–57.

journal or newsletter, usually list openings for legal professionals, including paralegals. Increasingly, employers advertise job openings in online publications and turn to online databases to find prospective employees. In fact, today probably the best starting point when launching your job search is the Internet. (For more information on how you can use the Internet to search for jobs, see the feature *Technology and Today's Paralegal: Online Job Searching.*)

Identifying Possible Employers

You should also identify firms and organizations for which you might like to work and submit an employment application to them. In a well-organized job search, you will locate and contact those organizations that offer the benefits, salary, opportunities for advancement, work environment, and legal specialty of your choice. Even though one of these organizations may not have vacancies in your field at the moment, you want your job application to be immediately available to the potential employer when an opening does occur. Most firms, if they are interested in your qualifications, will keep your application on file for six months or so and may contact you if a position becomes available.

It is a good idea to begin compiling employer information for your job search while you are still completing your paralegal studies. Many of the resources you will need are available at the college or university that you attend or through your paralegal program (or, increasingly, online).

THE YELLOW PAGES. An obvious source of information is the Yellow Pages of your local telephone directory. Look under "Attorneys" for the names of attorneys and law firms in your locale. If you want to work in a special area, such as real estate, you might look under other listings, such as "Title Companies." Many libraries have the Yellow Pages for major cities across the country, which allows you to broaden the geographic scope of your search. You may be able to find similar information in online "Yellow Pages" listings.

LEGAL DIRECTORIES. There are numerous legal directories that provide lists of attorneys, their locations, and their areas of practice. The *Martindale-Hubbell Law Directory,* which you can find at most law libraries (or online at **www.martindale.com**), lists the names, addresses, telephone numbers, areas of legal practice, and other data for many lawyers and law firms throughout the United States. It is an excellent resource for paralegals interested in working for law firms or corporate legal departments. *West's Legal Directory* is another valuable source of information. It is now on the Internet at **www.wld.com**. The directory contains a detailed listing of U.S. and Canadian attorneys and law firms, state and federal attorneys and offices, and corporate legal departments and general counsel. You can find links to more than one hundred other directories listing attorneys and legal professionals at the following government Web site: **www.house.gov**.

JOB-PLACEMENT SERVICES

Throughout your job search, make full use of your school's placement service. Many paralegal programs provide job-placement services, and ABA-approved schools are required to provide ongoing placement services for students. Placement offices are staffed with personnel trained to assist you in finding a job, as well as in preparing job-search tools, such as your résumé and a list of potential employers.

On the Web
You can search the Yellow Pages online at a number of Web sites, including Yahoo's Yellow Pages at yp.yahoo.com.

On the Web
If you are looking for a job in a corporate legal department, CompanyLink offers information on more than 45,000 U.S. companies. Go to **www.companylink.com**. Hoovers Online offers 10,000 "company capsules" and links to even more Web sites at **www.hoovers.com**.

TECHNOLOGY AND TODAY'S PARALEGAL

Online Job Searching

Given how the Internet has affected all aspects of business and professional life, it is not surprising that it has also become an invaluable device for both employers looking for job candidates and those seeking jobs. Today's paralegal can take advantage of this tool to make job searches much easier than in the past.

ONLINE EMPLOYMENT ADS

Paralegals looking for employment can access an increasing number of online sources to find out what positions are available in their field. A good starting point is the Hieros Gamos Employment Center's Web site (at www.hg.org/employment.html), which calls itself "the largest source of jobs on the Internet." At this site, in addition to finding job vacancies in your field, you can indicate the type of position you are interested in and ask to be notified by e-mail when a position in that area is posted. If you go to jobs.findlaw.com, you will find a state-by-state list of job openings for paralegals.

A site sponsored by Cornell University and *Human Resource Executive* magazine (at www.workindex.com) allows you to search for listings in your area and also provides links to numerous other job-information sites and search engines. You can find links to multiple state employment offices, federal jobs, and employment ads from publications in various areas of the country at Job Bank USA's site (go to www.jobbankusa.com/jobs.html).

Many states now publish job openings for state government positions on their Web pages, and some include application forms on their sites as well. For example, Vermont publishes its biweekly job notices on its Web site (at www.state.vt.us/pers/recruit/bulletin.htm).

These sites and the links they offer will help get you started on your job search. To find other sites, check with your paralegal program director, your school's placement office, or your local paralegal association. All of these sources will have information on current Web sites that you can access for job information. You might also check NFPA's Internet marketing page (at www.paralegals.org/Marketing/Internet.html) to obtain information on how you can include your ad or résumé on its site.

POST YOUR RÉSUMÉ ONLINE

Increasingly, employers are recruiting new employees by using online résumé banks. These sites allow employers to search through databases of job seekers to find job candidates whose skills and qualifications most closely correlate with the employers' needs. In a sense, résumé banks are the online world's version of the traditional "Positions Wanted" ads in newspapers. A key difference for job seekers is that, unlike ads in newspapers and other publications, there is little or no cost involved in posting a résumé online—or keeping it there for some time.

One of the oldest résumé sites is that offered by LAWMATCH (at www.lawmatch.com). LAWMATCH, like many other sites now offering such services, has both public and confidential sections. In a public listing, the identity of the candidate is revealed online. In a confidential listing, the identity of the candidate is not revealed; rather, interested employers are directed to call LAWMATCH, which then notifies the candidate of the employment opportunity. Confidential listings typically are sought by people who may not want their current employers to know that they are interested in other employment. This kind of site may be useful to you later in your career, when you are looking for greater opportunities. The Legal Employment Search Site (at www.legalemploy.com) has links to numerous sites where you can post your résumé online; this site also gives helpful suggestions on how to use the Internet in your job search.

WEB HOME PAGES

Virtually all large firms (and increasingly, many small firms) have Web pages, as do federal and state government agencies. Once you have the name of a firm or agency that interests you, you can go online to see if that organization has a Web page. The Web page of a firm or agency may contain much useful information for job seekers, including, in some cases, available positions and the name of the person you should contact about employment.

To find home pages of law firms, a good starting point is FindLaw's site at www.findlaw.com/14firms/index.html. Just keying in the name of the firm on a search engine may lead you to the firm's home page. You can locate the home pages for federal government agencies by accessing Federal World's site at www.fedworld.gov. To locate information on state governments, including state agencies, try www.law.cornell.edu/states/index.html and www.findlaw.com/11stategov/index.html.

FEATURED GUEST: DENISE TEMPLETON

Paralegal Career Planning and Development

BIOGRAPHICAL NOTE

Denise Templeton is the president and chief executive officer of Templeton & Associates, a legal support services firm based in Minneapolis, Minnesota. She has been involved with the paralegal profession since she graduated from the Institute for Paralegal Training in Philadelphia in 1972. Her professional career has included work as a legal assistant in both the public and private sectors, as well as seven years as the director of the legal-assistant program at the University of Minnesota. In 1985, she founded the Minnesota Legal Assistant Institute, a private, postsecondary certificate program.

Templeton is also a founder of the Minnesota Association of Legal Assistants, the American Association for Paralegal Education, and the National Federation of Paralegal Associations (NFPA). She is currently on the NFPA Advisory Council.

In the early 1970s, the paralegal field was just beginning to be officially recognized, and its parameters were undefined. The larger law firms and corporate legal departments were the first to grasp the concept that legal assistants could free busy attorneys by taking over the more routine legal tasks. This enabled law firms to get more work done in the same amount of time and at a constant level of quality. Because paralegals were a less expensive resource than attorneys, clients were able to pay less for legal services without sacrificing quality.

Then, as now, the majority of paralegals were employed in the litigation area [relating to lawsuits]. Over time, more specialty areas have opened up, and today's paralegal can be involved in anything from real estate to environmental law. Many opportunities are available now, and many more will be created in the future. People are entering the paralegal field in greater numbers each year. The successful legal assistant knows the importance of adopting a career-development strategy. My strategy includes six basic components: (1) self-awareness, (2) knowledge of the field, (3) openness to opportunity, (4) professional development, (5) support systems, and (6) periodic review.

SELF-AWARENESS

Self-awareness involves creating a vision. You must envision what you want and expect from a paralegal career based on your knowledge of yourself and what is important to you in your work. As you develop your career path, think about where you want to start and where you want to be in the long run. There are many possibilities in terms of both work environments and types of work. As a beginner, you may seek a large, structured office and a position that is clearly defined. One of the larger law firms or a corporate legal department may provide you with this framework. You may, however, sense that a smaller, less structured environment would be more comfortable for you. Your duties may be more varied. In any event, analyze your previous experience and prioritize your goals. Decide which goal is most important for you.

KNOWLEDGE OF THE FIELD

In tandem with self-assessment, consider the realities of the paralegal field itself. Again, because of the many options available in terms of legal specialties and work environments, the paralegal field can accommodate many types of people.

Another option is to contact a local paralegal association (or the state bar association's paralegal division, if one exists) to learn the names of any legal-placement services in your area. (The names and addresses of paralegal associations and bar associations in each state are listed in Appendix F and Appendix G, respectively, at the end of this book.) If you use the services of a legal-placement agency, be sure that you make it clear to the agency that you are looking for work as a paralegal, not as a legal secretary. Also, find out whether you or the employer will pay the agency's placement fee. In some agencies and for some jobs, you may be required to pay part or all of the fee.

FEATURED GUEST, *Continued*

Some areas of law require more intensity, time, and dedication than others. If you are already juggling the demands of a job and a family, for example, overtime may be a serious problem. Talk to people working in the area that interests you. Learn about the advantages and disadvantages of working in that area. The more you learn about that area, the more accurate and complete will be your picture of what to expect and how the position fits in with your vision.

OPENNESS TO OPPORTUNITY

By keeping an open mind and being aware of changing interests, you will be able to create new opportunities for yourself and take advantage of opportunities that arise as your career develops. Even if you have already created your vision of the ideal paralegal career path, stay open to possibilities that may present themselves. If you are trained in probate practice (which deals with the transfer of property on a person's death), for example, you may find that real estate is a compatible specialty. By making your interest in real-estate practice known to your supervisor, you demonstrate a willingness to expand your legal knowledge. Ultimately, you may work for a corporation in its real-estate management or development division. The idea of cross-training becomes increasingly more acceptable as

firms develop a more flexible work force. When the economy takes a turn for the worse, those who have multiple skills can be reassigned rather than laid off.

PROFESSIONAL DEVELOPMENT

Closely aligned with openness to opportunity is staying aware of developments in your profession. Developing and maintaining professional contacts and reading paralegal publications regularly are great ways to keep up with trends in your field. This knowledge can help you decide when and how to make turns in your career path. Also, the critical skill of networking plays an important role for any professional, including the paralegal. From the beginning, keep a current list of the people you meet and the areas in which they work. Become an active member of your local paralegal association. If there is no paralegal association in your community, then start one. Read the periodicals published by national paralegal associations and bar associations, and read materials that will keep you up to date on what is happening locally and nationally with paralegals. Ask paralegals and attorneys what they read, and attend continuing-education seminars to expand your knowledge base.

SUPPORT SYSTEMS

The value of having people give you encouragement and constructive crit-

> **"Today's paralegal can be involved in anything from real estate to environmental law."**

icism cannot be overstated. When you share ideas and concerns with others involved in your work, you will have a more balanced perspective on your work. Balance is an important ingredient in life. When you are working in a very intense, deadline-oriented atmosphere, balance can be painfully elusive. That is why having friends and participating in activities both inside and outside the legal profession is important to your well-being. Promise yourself that you will take regular vacations with family and friends and keep yourself healthy, happy, and productive.

PERIODIC REVIEW

Remember, change is the only constant in life. Many opportunities exist now that were not possible when the paralegal field was beginning. Many new opportunities will arise in the future. By taking the time periodically to take stock of your own changing needs and desires, as well as the evolution of the field, you can decide which career step to take next and when to take it. For those paralegals who take charge of their own destinies, there are many ways to grow and prosper as legal professionals.

MARKETING YOUR SKILLS

Once you have located potential employers, the next step in your job search is to market your skills and yourself effectively to those employers. Marketing your skills involves three stages: the application process, interviewing for jobs, and following up on job interviews.

You should keep in mind throughout your job search that each personal contact you make, whether it results in employment or not, has potential for your future. A firm may not hire you today, for example, because you lack experience.

DEVELOPING PARALEGAL SKILLS

A Career Plan

Rob Johnson, a paralegal student who is working toward a bachelor's degree with a major in legal assistance, needs to find a job for the internship class that is required for graduation. Rob, however, does not want to take just any job. Rob wants his internship to be the springboard for his career as a paralegal. Rob thus begins to implement some career-planning strategies.

CHECKLIST FOR CAREER PLANNING

- Establish long-term goals.
- Review the current job market and establish short-term goals.
- Locate available jobs and employers.
- Network.
- Reevaluate your job every few years.

But it may hire you a year from now if by then you have the experience that it is seeking. Therefore, always keep track of the contacts you make during your search, be patient, and be professional. You may be surprised how many doors will open for you, if not today, then tomorrow.

The Application Process

As a paralegal looking for professional employment, you will need to assemble and present professional application materials. The basic materials you should create are a résumé, a cover letter, a list of professional references, and a portfolio. The following discussion explains each of these documents and gives some practical tips on how to create them.

THE RÉSUMÉ.   For almost all job applications, you must submit a personal *résumé*, which summarizes your employment and educational background. Your résumé is an advertisement, and you should invest the time to make that advertisement effective. Because personnel officers in law firms, corporations, and government agencies may receive a hundred or more résumés for each position they advertise, your résumé should create the best possible impression if you want to gain a competitive edge over other job seekers.

Either generate your résumé yourself, using a computer and a laser printer, or have a professional résumé-preparation service do it for you. Format each page so that the reader is able to scan it quickly and catch the highlights. You might vary the type size, but never use a type size or style that is difficult to read.

What to Include in Your Résumé.   Your name, address, telephone number, e-mail address, and fax number belong at the beginning of your résumé. The résumé should be simple, brief, and clear. As a general rule, it should contain only information that is relevant to the job that you are seeking. A one-page résumé is usually sufficient, unless two pages are required to list relevant educational background and work experience. Exhibit 2.5 shows a sample résumé. Note that you should avoid placing your name and address in the upper left-hand corner, as this area is often stapled.

Divide your résumé into logical sections with headings, such as those shown in Exhibit 2.5. Whenever you list dates, such as educational and employment

EXHIBIT 2.5
A Sample Résumé

ELENA LOPEZ

1131 North Shore Drive
Nita City, NI 48804
Telephone: (616) 555-0102 • Fax: (616) 555-2103 • E-mail: elopez@nitanet.net

---

EMPLOYMENT OBJECTIVE

A position as a paralegal in a private law firm that specializes in personal-injury practice.

EDUCATION

1998   Postbaccalaureate Certificate
Midwestern Professional School for Paralegals, Green Bay, WI
Focus: Litigation Procedures; Legal Investigation, Research, Writing.
GPA 3.8.

1993   Bachelor of Arts degree
University of Wisconsin, Madison, WI 53706.
Political Science major. GPA 3.5.

PARALEGAL EXPERIENCE

- Paralegal with the Caldwell Legal Clinic,
  3189 Plainview, Nita City, Nita 48801. June 1998 to the present.
  Responsibilities: General legal research and writing, and trial preparation in personal-injury cases.

- Paralegal with the Free Legal Aid Society,
  122 W. Fourth St., Green Bay, WI 54311. June 1997 to May 1998.
  Responsibilities: Part-time assistance to legal aid attorneys in their representation of indigent clients in matters such as divorce, abuse, child custody, paternity, and landlord/tenant disputes.

- Research Assistant,
  Political Science Department, University of Wisconsin. January 1994 to May 1997.
  Responsibilities: Research on the effectiveness of federal welfare programs in reducing poverty in the United States.

AFFILIATIONS

Paralegal Association of Wisconsin
National Association of Legal Assistants

---

dates, list them chronologically, in reverse order. In other words, list your most recent educational or work history first. When discussing your education, list the names, cities, and states of the colleges or universities that you have attended and the degrees that you have received. You may want to indicate your major and minor concentrations and those courses that are most related to your professional goal, such as "Major: Paralegal Studies" or "Minor: Political Science." When listing your work experience, specify what your responsibilities have been in each position that you have held. Also, include any volunteer work that you have done.

Scholarships or honors should also be indicated. If you have a high grade point average (GPA), you should include it in your résumé. Under the heading "Selected Accomplishments," you might indicate your ability to speak a foreign language or other special skill, such as online research skills.

What if you are an entry-level paralegal and have no work experience to list? What can you include on your résumé to fill out the page? If you are facing this situation, add more information on your educational background and experience. You can list specific courses that you took, particular skills—such as computer skills—that you acquired during your paralegal training, and student affiliations.

Do Not Include Personal Data.   Avoid including personal data (such as age, marital status, number of children, gender, or hobbies) in your résumé. Employers are prohibited by law from discriminating against employees or job candidates on the basis of race, color, gender, national origin, religion, age, or disability. You can help them fulfill this legal obligation by not including in your résumé any information that could serve as a basis for discrimination. For the same reason, you would be wise not to include a photograph of yourself with your résumé. Also, most prospective employers are not interested in such information as personal preferences, pastimes, or hobbies.

Proofread Your Results.   Carefully proofread your résumé. Use the spelling checker and grammar checker on your computer, but do not rely on them totally. Have a friend or teacher review your résumé for punctuation, syntax, grammar, spelling, and content. If you find an error, you need to fix it, even if it means having new résumés printed. A mistake on your résumé tells the potential employer that you are a careless worker, and this message may ruin your chances of landing a job.

THE COVER LETTER.   To encourage the recruiter to review your résumé, you need to capture his or her attention with a *cover letter* that accompanies the résumé. Because the cover letter often represents your first contact with an employer, it should be written carefully and precisely. It should be brief, perhaps only two or three paragraphs in length. Exhibit 2.6 shows a sample cover letter. Whenever possible, you should learn the name of the individual in charge of hiring (by phone or e-mail, if necessary) and direct your letter to that person. If you do not know the name of the individual responsible for reviewing résumés, use a generic title, such as "Human Resources Manager" or "Legal-Assistant Manager."

Your cover letter should point out a few things about yourself and your qualifications for the position that might persuade a recruiter to examine your résumé. As a recently graduated paralegal, for example, you might draw attention to your high academic standing at school, your eagerness to specialize in the same area of law as the employer (perhaps listing some courses relating to that specialty), and your willingness to relocate to the employer's city. Your job is to convince the recruiter that you are a close match to the mental picture that he or she has of the perfect candidate for the job. Make sure that the reader knows when and where you can be reached. Often this is best indicated in the closing paragraph of the letter, as shown in Exhibit 2.6.

As with your résumé, you should read through your letter several times and have someone else read it also to make sure that it is free from mistakes and easily understood. You should use the same type of paper for your cover letter as you use for your résumé.

ELENA LOPEZ

1131 North Shore Drive
Nita City, NI 48804
Telephone: (616) 555-0102 • Fax: (616) 555-2103 • E-mail: elopez@nitanet.net

August 22, 1999

Mr. Allen P. Gilmore
Jeffers, Gilmore & Dunn
553 Fifth Avenue, Suite 101
Nita City, NI 48801

Dear Mr. Gilmore:

I am responding to your advertisement in the *University of Nita
Law Journal* for a paralegal to assist you in personal-injury
litigation.

My bachelor of arts degree is from the University of Wisconsin.
I am a recent graduate of the Midwestern Professional School for
Paralegals. My paralegal courses included litigation procedures,
legal research, legal investigation, and legal writing. I hope to
specialize in the area of personal-injury law.

I would like very much to meet with you or your representative to
learn more about the position that you have available. I am enclosing a copy of my résumé and a list of professional references.

If you wish to contact me, I can be reached at the telephone number
and e-mail address given above.

Sincerely yours,

Elena Lopez

Elena Lopez

Enclosures

EXHIBIT 2.6
A Sample Cover Letter

What about e-mailing your cover letter and résumé to prospective employers?
This is a difficult question. On the one hand, e-mail is much faster than regular
mail or express delivery services. On the other hand, an e-mail résumé does not
look as nice. Furthermore, while some firms are accustomed to receiving applications by e-mail, others are not. Generally, you need to use your own judgment. If
the job you are applying for was advertised online or if the employer provided an

e-mail address for interested job candidates to use, then e-mail is probably appropriate. Job candidates who submit applications via e-mail should also send, via regular mail, printed copies of their letters and résumés as well.

LIST OF PROFESSIONAL REFERENCES.   If a firm is interested in your application, you will probably be asked to provide a list of references—people whom the firm can contact to obtain information about you and your abilities. A paralegal instructor who has worked closely with you on an academic project, an internship supervisor who has firsthand knowledge of your work, or a past employer who has observed your problem-solving ability would all make excellent references. You should have at least three professionally relevant references, but no more than five references are necessary (if an interviewer needs additional references, he or she will ask for them). Never include the names of family members, friends, or others who will be clearly biased in your favor.

You should list your references on a separate sheet of paper, making sure to include your name, address, telephone number, and so on at the top of the page, in the same format as on your résumé. For each person included on your list of references, include his or her current institutional affiliation or business firm, address, telephone number, fax number, and, if you know it, e-mail address. Generally, try to make it easy for prospective employers to contact and communicate with your references.

When creating your list of references, always remember the following rule:

> **Never list a person's name as a reference unless you have first obtained that person's permission to do so.**

After all, it will not help you win the position if one of your references is surprised by the call or is unavailable, such as a paralegal instructor who is out of the country for the year. Such events raise a red flag to the interviewer and indicate that you are not concerned with details.

Obtaining permission from legal professionals to use their names as references also gives you an opportunity to discuss your plans and goals with them, and they may be able to advise you and assist you in your networking. Additionally, it gives you a chance to discuss with them the kinds of experience and skills in which a prospective employer may be interested.

Professional Portfolio
A job applicant's collection of selected personal documents (such as school transcripts, writing samples, and certificates) for presentation to a potential employer.

YOUR PROFESSIONAL PORTFOLIO.   When a potential employer asks you for an interview, have your **professional portfolio** of selected documents ready to give to the interviewer. The professional portfolio should contain another copy of your résumé, a list of references, letters of recommendation written by previous employers or instructors, samples of legal documents that you have composed, college or university transcripts, and any other relevant professional information, such as proof of professional certification or achievement. This collection of documents should be well organized and professionally presented. Depending on the size of your portfolio, a cover sheet, a table of contents, and a commercial binder may be appropriate.

The interviewer may be very interested in your research and writing skills. Therefore, your professional portfolio should contain several brief samples of legal writing. If you are looking for your first legal position, go through your paralegal drafting assignments and pull out those that reflect your best work and that relate to the job skills you wish to demonstrate. Then, working with an instructor or other mentor, revise and improve those samples for inclusion in the portfolio. Documents that you have drafted while an intern or when working as a part-time or full-time paralegal might also be used. These documents make excellent writing samples because they involve real-life circumstances. Be careful, however, and always remember to do the following:

 On any sample document, completely blacken out (or "white out") any identifying reference to the client unless you have the client's permission to disclose his or her identity or the information is not confidential.

Always include a résumé, as well as a list of references, in your professional portfolio, even though you already sent your résumé to the prospective employer with your cover letter. Interviewers may not have the résumé at hand at the time of the interview, and providing a second copy with your professional portfolio is a thoughtful gesture on your part.

Some interviewers may examine your professional portfolio carefully. Others may retain it to examine later, after the interview has concluded. Still others may not be interested in it at all. If there is a particular item in your portfolio that you would like the interviewer to see, make sure you point this out before leaving the interview.

The Interview

Interviews with potential employers may be the most challenging (and most stressful) aspect of your search for employment. The interview ordinarily takes place after the employer has reviewed your cover letter and résumé. Often, if the employer is interested in your application, a secretary or legal assistant will contact you to schedule an interview.

Every interview will be a unique experience. Some interviews will go very well, but you may still lose out to another candidate. Nonetheless, you have made a good contact, and you may be able to use this interviewer as a resource for information about other jobs. Remember what went right about the interview, and try to use that information at the next one. Other interviews may go poorly. There are good lessons to be learned from poor interviews, however.

You will also find that some interviewers are more skilled at interviewing than others. Some have a talent for getting applicants to open up and discuss candidly their work and backgrounds. Others are confrontational and put the already nervous candidate on the defensive. Still others may be unprepared for the interview. They may not have had time to check the job requirements, for example, or when the position is available. Unfortunately, as the person being interviewed, you have no control over who will interview you. The following discussion will help you prepare for a first paralegal job interview and will also serve as a refresher for you when seeking a career change.

BEFORE THE INTERVIEW.   You can do many things prior to the interview to enhance your chances of getting the job. First of all, you should do your "homework." Learn as much about the employer as possible. Check with your instructors or other legal professionals to find out if they are familiar with the firm or the interviewer. Check the employer's Web site, if there is one, and consult relevant directories, such as legal and company directories, as well as business publications, to see what you can learn about the firm and its members. When you are called for an interview, learn the full name of the interviewer, so that you will be able to address him or her by name during the interview and properly address a follow-up letter. During the interview, use Mr. or Ms. unless directed by the interviewer to be less formal.

ETHICAL CONCERN
"Gilding the Lily"

When applying and interviewing for a job, be honest about your skills and job qualifications. Even though you are trying to impress a prospective employer, never succumb to the temptation to "gild the lily" by exaggerating your experience and qualifications.

Suppose that you are interviewing for a job and the interviewer asks you about your GPA. Wanting to impress the interviewer, you say that your GPA was 3.8 when in fact it was 3.4. This "little white lie" may cost you the job. Prospective employers usually check your credentials, including your transcripts. Any misrepresentation, no matter how minor it may seem, will create a negative impression. Professional responsibility requires, among other things, that you be honest and pay scrupulous attention to detail—not only on the job but also during the job-application process.

Anticipate and review in your mind the possible questions that you might be asked during the interview. Then prepare (and possibly rehearse with a friend) your answers to these questions. For example, if you did not graduate from high school with your class but later fulfilled the requirements to graduate and received a general equivalency diploma (GED), you might well be asked why you dropped out of school. If you have already prepared an answer for this question, it may save you the embarrassment of having to decide, on the spot, how to reduce a complicated story to a brief sentence or two.

You should also prepare yourself to be interviewed by a "team" of legal professionals, such as an attorney and another paralegal or perhaps two or more attorneys and/or paralegals. Many prospective employers today invite others who will be working with a new paralegal to participate in the interviewing process.

Promptness is an extremely important factor. When preparing for an interview, you should therefore do the following:

 Arrive for the interview at least ten minutes early and allow plenty of extra time to get there. If the firm is located in an area that is unfamiliar to you, make sure that you know how to get there, how long it will take, and, if you are driving, whether parking space is available nearby.

Appearance is also important. Wear a relatively conservative suit or dress to the interview, and limit your use of jewelry or other flashy accents. You can find further tips on how to prepare for a job interview by checking online career sites or by looking at books dealing with careers and job hunting at a local bookstore or the library.

AT THE INTERVIEW.   During the interview, pay attention and listen closely to the interviewer's questions, observations, and comments. The interviewer asks questions to learn whether the candidate will fit comfortably into the firm, whether the candidate is organized and competent and will satisfactorily perform the job, and whether the candidate is reliable and will apply himself or herself to mastering the tasks presented. Your answers should be directly related to the questions, and you should not stray from the point. If you are unsure of what the interviewer means by a certain question, ask for clarification.

EXHIBIT 2.7
**Objectionable or
Illegal Questions**

Q. Are you married?

A. If you are concerned about my social life interfering with work, I can assure you that I keep the two very distinct.

Q. Do you have any children yet?

A. That question leads me to believe that you would be concerned about my ability to prioritize my job and other responsibilities. Is that something that you are worried about?

Q. Are you or your husband a member of the Republican Party?

A. That is a private matter. Please realize that my family and political life will not interfere with my ability to do excellent work for your firm.

Q. You're quite a bit more mature than other applicants. Will you be thinking of retiring in the next ten years?

A. I don't understand how my age relates to my ability to perform this job.

Interviewers use certain question formats to elicit certain types of responses. Four typical formats for questions are the following:

- *Closed-ended questions*—to elicit simple "Yes" or "No" answers.
- *Open-ended questions*—which invite you to discuss, in some detail, a specific topic or experience.
- *Hypothetical questions*—to learn how you might respond to situations that could arise during the course of your employment.
- *Pressure questions*—to see how you deal with uncomfortable situations or unpleasant discussions.

You will learn more about these question formats in Chapter 7, when we discuss some techniques that paralegals use when interviewing clients.

Be aware that certain types of questions are illegal, or at least objectionable. These include questions directed at your marital status, family, religion, race, color, national origin, age, health or disability, or arrest record. You do not have to answer such questions unless you choose to do so. Exhibit 2.7 shows some examples of how you might respond to these types of questions.

As odd as it may seem, one of the most difficult moments is when the interviewer turns the questioning around by asking, "Now then, do you have any questions?" Be prepared for this query. Before the interview, take time to list your concerns. Bring the list to the interview with you. Questioning the interviewer gives you an opportunity to learn more about the firm and how it uses paralegal services. Questioning the interviewer also may also give the interviewer an opportunity to see how you might interview a client on behalf of the firm. Exhibit 2.8 on the next page lists some sample questions that you might ask the interviewer. Note that you should not raise the issue of salary at the first interview unless you are offered the job.

AFTER THE INTERVIEW.   You should not expect to be hired as the result of a single interview, although occasionally this does happen. Often, two and maybe three interviews take place before you are offered a job. After leaving the interview, jot down a few notes to provide a refresher for your memory should you be called back for a second (or third) interview. You will impress the interviewer if

EXHIBIT 2.8
Questioning the Interviewer

Questions that you might want to ask the interviewer include the following:

- What is the method by which the firm assigns duties to paralegals?
- How do paralegals function within the organization?
- What clerical support staff is available for paralegals?
- Does the job involve travel? How will travel expenses be covered?
- What computer technology is used by the firm?
- Does the firm support paralegal continuing-education and training programs?
- Will client contact be direct or indirect?
- Does the firm have an in-house library and access to computerized research services that paralegals can use?
- Will the paralegal be assigned work in a given specialty, such as real-estate or family law?
- When does the job begin?
- What method is used to review and evaluate paralegal performance?
- How are paralegals supervised and by whom?
- Are paralegals classified as exempt employees by this firm?

you are able to "pick up where you left off" from a discussion initiated several weeks earlier. Also, list the names and positions of the people you met during the interview or just before or after it.

The Follow-Up Letter

A day or two after the interview, but not longer than a week later, you should send a *follow-up letter* to the interviewer. In this brief letter, you can reiterate your availability and interest in the position, thank the interviewer for his or her time in interviewing you, and perhaps refer to a discussion that took place during the interview.

You may have left the interview with the impression that the meeting went poorly. But the interviewer may have a different sense of what happened at the meeting. Interviewers have different styles, and what you interpreted to be a bad interview may just have been a reflection of that interviewer's particular approach or style. You simply have no way of being certain, so follow through and make yourself available for the job or at least for another meeting. For an example of a follow-up letter, see Exhibit 2.9.

Maintain Job-Hunting Files

In addition to keeping your professional portfolio materials up to date, you need to create a filing system to stay abreast of your job-search activities. You should create a separate file for each potential employer and keep copies of your letters, including e-mail messages, and any responses to that employer in your file. You might also want to keep lists or notes on addresses, telephone numbers, e-mail addresses, dates of contacts, advantages and disadvantages of employment with the various firms that you have contacted or by which you have been interviewed, topics discussed at interviews, and so on. Then, when you are called for an interview, you will have information on the firm at your fingertips. Always keep in mind that when looking for paralegal employment, your "job" is finding work as a paralegal—and it pays to be efficient.

EXHIBIT 2.9
A Sample Follow-Up Letter

E LENA L OPEZ

1131 North Shore Drive
Nita City, NI 48804
Telephone: (616) 555-0102 • Fax: (616) 555-2103 • E-mail: elopez@nitanet.net

September 3, 1999

Mr. Allen P. Gilmore
Jeffers, Gilmore & Dunn
553 Fifth Avenue, Suite 101
Nita City, NI 48801

Dear Mr. Gilmore:

Thank you for taking time out of your busy schedule to meet with
me last Thursday about your firm's entry-level paralegal position. I
very much enjoyed our discussion, as well as the opportunity to
meet some of your firm's employees.

I am extremely interested in the possibility of becoming a member
of your legal team and look forward to the prospect of meeting
with you again in the near future.

Sincerely yours,

Elena Lopez

Elena Lopez

Your files will also provide you with an excellent resource for networking
even after you have a permanent position. The files may also provide useful information for a career change in the future.

Salary Negotiations

Sometimes a firm states a salary or a salary range in its advertisement for a paralegal. During a first interview, a prospective employer may offer that information
as well. In other situations, an applicant does not know what the salary for a certain position will be until he or she is offered the job.

When you are offered a job, be prepared for the prospective employer to indicate a salary figure and ask you if that figure is acceptable to you. If it is acceptable, then you have no problem. If you think it is too low, then the situation
becomes more delicate. If you have no other job offer and really need a job, you
may not want to foreclose this job opportunity by saying that the salary is too low.
You might instead tell the prospective employer that the job interests you and that

BENEFITS

What benefits are included? • Will the benefits package include medical insurance? • Life insurance? • Disability insurance? • Dental insurance? • What portion, if any, of the insurance premium will be deducted from your wages? • Is there an employee pension plan? • How many paid vacation days will you have? • Will the firm cover your paralegal association fees? • Will the firm assist you in tuition and other costs associated with continuing paralegal education? • Will the firm assist in day-care arrangements and/or costs? • Will you have access to a company automobile? • Does the firm help with parking expenses (important in major cities)?

CAREER OPPORTUNITIES

Does the position offer you opportunities for advancement? You may be willing to accept a lower salary now if you know that it will increase as you move up the career ladder.

COMPENSATION

Will you receive an annual salary or be paid by the hour? • If you will receive an annual salary, will you receive annual bonuses? • How are bonuses determined? • Is the salary negotiable? (In some large firms and in government agencies, it may not be.)

COMPETITION

How stiff is the competition for this job? If you really want the job and are competing with numerous other candidates for the position, you might want to accept a lower salary just to land the job.

JOB DESCRIPTION

What are the paralegal's duties within the organization? Do you have sufficient training and experience to handle these duties? • Are you under- or overqualified for the job? • Will your skills as a paralegal be utilized effectively? • How hard will you be expected to work? • How much overtime work will likely be required? • How stressful will the job be?

JOB FLEXIBILITY

How flexible are the working hours? • If you work eight hours overtime one week, can you take a (paid) day off the following week? • Can you take time off during periods when the workload is less?

LOCATION

Do you want to live in this community? • What is the cost of living in this area? Remember, a $40,000 salary in New York City, where housing and taxes are very expensive, may not give you as much real income as a $30,000 salary in a smaller, midsized community in the Midwest.

PERMANENCE

Is the job a permanent or temporary position? Usually, hourly rates for temporary assistance are higher than for permanent employees.

TRAVEL

Will you be required to travel? • If so, how often or extensively? • How will travel expenses be handled? Will you pay them up front and then be reimbursed by the employer?

EXHIBIT 2.10
Salary Negotiations:
What Is This Job Worth to You?

you will consider the offer seriously. Also, remember that salary is just one factor in deciding what a job is worth to you. In addition to salary, you need to consider job benefits and other factors, including those listed in Exhibit 2.10.

Some prospective employers do not suggest a salary or a salary range but rather ask the job applicant what kind of salary he or she had in mind. You should be prepared for this question and should have researched paralegal salaries in the area.

 Unless you are already familiar with the firm's salary structure, you should research the compensation given to paralegals in similar job situations in your community before you discuss salary with a prospective employer.

You can find information on salaries by checking local, state, and national paralegal compensation surveys. Check first with your local paralegal association to see if it has collected data on local paralegal salaries. You might also find helpful information in your school's placement office.

Suppose that you have found in your research that paralegals in the community usually start at $29,000 but that many with your education and training start at $33,000. If you ask for an annual salary of $35,000, then you may be unrealistically expensive—and the job offer may be lost. If you ask for $33,000, then you are still "in the ballpark"—and you may win the job.

Negotiating salaries can be difficult. On the one hand, you want to obtain a good salary and do not want to underprice your services. On the other hand, overpricing your services may extinguish an employment opportunity or eliminate the possibility of working for an otherwise suitable employer. Your best option might be to state a salary range that is acceptable to you. That way, you are not pinned down to a specific figure. Note, though, that if you indicate an acceptable salary range, you invite an offer of the lowest salary—so the low end of the salary range should be the threshold amount that you will accept.

REEVALUATING YOUR CAREER

Once you have gained experience working as a paralegal, you can undertake the third step in career planning: reevaluation. Assume that you have worked for a long enough period (two to four years, for example) to have acquired experience in certain types of paralegal work. At this point, you should reevaluate your career goals and reassess your abilities based on your accumulated experience.

Paralegals who want to advance in their careers normally have three options: (1) being promoted or transferring to another department or branch office of the firm, (2) moving to another firm—and perhaps another specialty, and (3) going back to school for additional education.

Career Paths

Larger firms often provide career paths for their paralegal employees. Moving from the entry-level position of *legal-assistant clerk* to the position of *legal-assistant manager*, for example, may be one career track within a large law firm. A career track with a state government agency might begin at a *legal-technician* level and advance to a *legal-specialist* level.

Creating Opportunities

Smaller firms, in contrast, usually have no predetermined career path or opportunities for promotion and career advancement. If you are the only paralegal in a small law firm, there will be no specified career path within the firm for you to follow. If you find yourself in this situation, you might consider staying with the firm and creating your own position or career ladder. Moving up the ladder is often a matter of bringing in someone new to assist you with your paralegal responsibilities. Are you prevented from taking on more complicated tasks (which you are capable of performing) because of your heavy workload, much of which could be handled by a paralegal with less experience? Suggest a plan to your employer that shows how you can provide more complex legal services if you delegate many of your existing responsibilities to a new paralegal employee. One of the advantages of working for a small firm is the lack of any set, formal structure for promotions. If the firm is expanding, the paralegal may have significant input into how and to whom responsibilities will be assigned as new people are hired.

You can also create opportunities by acquiring additional education. If you are interested in a particular specialty area, course work in that area, in addition

TODAY'S PROFESSIONAL PARALEGAL

Conducting a Title Exam

Kim Murphy is a paralegal working for the real-estate law firm of Clark & Clark. Today, Kim is going to the Winston County Register of Deeds office to examine the title to the Spartan Shopping Center, located in Winston County. The owner of the shopping center, one of Clark & Clark's clients, has received an offer to sell the center, which has recently become very valuable. Kim's supervising attorney must prepare an abstract of title, which is a history of who owned the property, when past transfers were made, and other significant events. The abstract will be used to assure the buyer that he or she will receive clear and marketable title to the property.

Kim arrives at the county offices. She takes the elevator to the third floor, where the Register of Deeds Office is located. As Kim approaches the counter, a clerk asks her, "What do you need today?" Kim recognizes the clerk, Sam McGrath, who has worked there for as long as Kim has worked for Clark & Clark. He often assists Kim and is very helpful.

"Sam, I need to run a title search and then I need copies of the deeds for the Spartan Shopping Center," responds Kim. "Okay, fill out this form, and I'll run the title search for you on the computer," says Sam. Kim writes down the name and address of the shopping center and hands the form to Sam.

EXAMINING OWNERSHIP RECORDS

Sam leaves the counter and goes to a room behind it, which contains computers. He runs the search through the computer that contains all of the records that were originally held in a book called the *Liber*. This is where all of the deeds, liens, and other documents affecting title to real estate are filed. Sam returns with a computerized list and copies of the deeds that show who has owned the property.

Kim thanks Sam and sits down at a nearby table to review the information that Sam has given her. Kim reads through each deed. She checks to see that each deed contains the same description of the property—to ensure that the entire parcel of land was conveyed (transferred) with

each sale. Kim sees that it was. She also checks to make sure that the seller of the Spartan Shopping Center is the legal owner of the property.

CHECKING FOR LIENS

Next, Kim reviews the computer printout for any *liens* (rights of creditors against the property for payment of debts) that might have been filed against the property. Kim notes the mortgage lien, which is normal and expected. Typically, when the purchase of real property is financed by a mortgage loan, the lending institution places a lien on the property until the buyer has made all payments due under the terms of the loan contract. She also notes that the Internal Revenue Service (IRS) has placed a tax lien on the property. A tax lien means that the current owner is behind in the payment of taxes and that the IRS has the right to *foreclose on* (take temporary ownership of) the shopping center and sell it, using the proceeds to pay the overdue taxes. Any remaining proceeds would be returned to the shopping center's owner. If the IRS is not paid at the time of the new mortgage, the IRS will have priority over the new lender. Most lenders will not grant a loan under these circumstances.

THE CONSEQUENCES OF THE TAX LIEN FOR THE CLIENT

Kim realizes that the tax lien creates serious problems for Clark & Clark's client. Once the abstract is prepared, the buyer's attorney will learn about the lien and warn the buyer of the obvious risk. This tax lien must be resolved before Clark & Clark's client can sell the property.

Kim makes a copy of the computer printout and walks over to the cashier to pay for the title search and the copies of the deeds. The cost is $5.00 for the title search and $1.00 for each deed. She makes certain to get a receipt so that she can be reimbursed by the firm for the expense. Kim then returns to the office to inform her supervising attorney of the tax lien.

to your existing paralegal training and experience, may help land a job that can advance your career ambitions. Alternatively, you might decide to work toward an advanced degree, such as a master's in business administration (MBA), to create new career opportunities. Some paralegals opt to go to law school and become attorneys.

Other Options

There are many other alternatives. You may apply for a job with another firm that offers you a better position or more advancement opportunities. You might apply for a position that has become available in a branch office of your firm. You might volunteer to speak to paralegal classes and seminars and, in so doing, establish new contacts and contribute to paralegal professional development. Researching and writing law-related articles for your paralegal association's newsletter or trade magazine improves your professional stature in the legal community as well. Any of these activities will increase your visibility both inside and outside the firm. In a broad sense, these activities are part of networking. The people you meet when engaging in these activities may offer you employment opportunities that you did not even know existed but that are perfect for you.

KEY TERMS AND CONCEPTS

bankruptcy law 35	freelance paralegal 31	professional portfolio 56
bonus 45	immigration law 42	probate 37
civil law 33	independent paralegal 32	probate court 37
corporate law 34	intellectual property 38	real estate 40
criminal law 33	legal nurse consultant (LNC) 43	trade journal 47
defendant 32	litigation 32	trust 37
elder law 42	litigation paralegal 32	will 37
environmental law 39	networking 47	workers' compensation statutes 35
estate planning 37	overtime wages 45	
family law 40	plaintiff 32	

CHAPTER SUMMARY

1. The job opportunities available in today's paralegal employment market are extraordinarily varied. Traditionally, paralegals worked for law firms, and most paralegals continue to work in the law-firm environment. Increasingly, however, paralegals are finding employment in corporate legal departments, as well as other business institutions, such as banks and insurance companies. A growing number of paralegals work for government agencies at the federal or state level. Paralegals also work in law enforcement offices, in courts, in legal aid offices, or in their own businesses, as freelancers.

2. Paralegals often specialize in particular areas of law, including the following areas: litigation assistance, personal-injury law, criminal law, corporate law, bankruptcy law, employment and labor law, estate planning and probate administration, intellectual-property law, environmental law, real-estate law, and family law. Emerging specialty areas include elder law, immigration law, and legal nurse consulting.

3. Salaries and wage rates for paralegal employees vary substantially. Factors affecting compensation include geographical location, firm size, and type of employer (law firm, corporation, or government agency). Many paralegals are salaried—that is, they are paid a specified amount per year, regardless of the number of hours worked. Overtime work is compensated through year-end bonuses or in some other way, such as equivalent time off work. Other paralegals are paid hourly wages for all regular hours worked and overtime wages for all hours worked exceeding forty hours per week.

4. Career planning involves three steps: defining your long-term career goals, devising short-term goals and adjusting those goals to fit job realities, and reevaluating your career and career goals after you have had some on-the-job experience.

5. When looking for employment, you should apply the investigative skills that you learned in your paralegal training. Many paralegals learn of jobs through networking with other professionals. You can begin networking while you are still a paralegal student. You can locate potential employers by reviewing published and posted information about law firms and other possible employers, including information contained in legal trade journals, newspapers, and directories. Using Internet resources is increasingly an efficient means of finding useful information about prospective employers. You should also stay in contact with your school's placement service.

6. In marketing your skills as a paralegal, you will need to submit an application to potential employers. The application documents you create should include a résumé, a cover letter, a list of professional references, and a professional portfolio. The résumé presents a clear and concise summary of your employment and educational history. The cover letter briefly mentions some of your most important qualifications and draws attention to the résumé. The pro-

fessional portfolio, which you provide at the job interview, contains an additional copy of the résumé, letters of recommendation, brief samples of legal writing, transcripts, and other relevant documents.

7. In preparing for a job interview, you should learn as much about the firm as possible. You should also anticipate questions that might be asked and prepare answers in advance. Make sure that you know how to get to the prospective employer's office, and arrive about ten minutes early. During the interview, listen closely to the questions that are asked. Illegal questions need not be answered, but you should phrase your responses carefully. After the interview, send a follow-up letter to the interviewer. The letter should thank the interviewer for his or her time and reaffirm your interest in the position.

8. Career goals change over time, as do job opportunities. Advancing in your career may mean educating your employer about your abilities so that you can take on more responsibility, looking for a job in a different department or branch office of the same firm or with another firm, or acquiring further education. Active participation in paralegal professional organizations or in paralegal education is a way to achieve higher visibility in the profession and to learn of new professional opportunities.

QUESTIONS FOR REVIEW

1. Name and describe five types of organizations that hire paralegals. What percentage of paralegals work in law firms?

2. From your perspective, what would be the advantages and disadvantages of working for each of the following organizations?

   a. A small law firm.

   b. A large law firm.

   c. A corporation.

   d. A government agency or organization.

3. List and briefly describe each of the paralegal specialties discussed in this chapter. Which specialty area or areas interest you the most? Why?

4. How are paralegals compensated? What is the average paralegal salary in your state? On average, in what specialty area do paralegals receive the highest salaries?

5. What are the advantages of being paid a salary? List some advantages of being paid an hourly wage.

What are the disadvantages of each type of paralegal compensation?

6. How can paralegals locate potential employers? Of the methods suggested in this chapter for locating potential employers, which method do you think would be most effective in finding a job? Why?

7. List and describe the materials that are needed for the job-application process.

8. What should you do before a job interview? What types of questions may be asked during a job interview? What steps should you take after a job interview?

9. When are salary arrangements discussed during the job-application process? What factors other than salary should you consider when determining what a job is worth?

10. What are some ways in which you can advance in your paralegal career?

⊞ ETHICAL QUESTIONS

1. Tom Brown is a legal assistant in a busy litigation firm. As Tom is walking in the door at 8:30 A.M., he passes Mike Walker, his supervising attorney, who is on his way to court to begin a trial. As they pass, Mike says to Tom, "I need a motion and a brief for the *Jones* case. I've left the file on your desk." Mike walks out the door and down the street to court. Tom becomes very anxious because he knows very little about the case and the law involved. Can Tom competently prepare the motion and brief? Why or why not? What should Tom do?

2. Laura Bronson has just started her first job with the firm of Thompson & Smith, a general law practice. Laura is asked to prepare articles of incorporation for one of the firm's corporate clients. Laura did not take corporate law while studying to be a paralegal and has never prepared articles of incorporation before. Should Laura accept the assignment? If she does accept it, what obligations does she have?

3. Dennis Walker works at a very busy law firm. On each side of his desk, there are one-foot-high stacks of work, leaving only enough room for a small work space in the center of the desk and a spot for the telephone. His floor is likewise stacked high with legal documents. Dennis constantly misses deadlines and is often in trouble for turning work in late or doing work incorrectly. Dennis has tried to get organized but feels that it is impossible to do so because he has such a heavy workload. What are Dennis's ethical obligations in this situation?

⊞ PRACTICE QUESTIONS AND ASSIGNMENTS

1. Outside of the traditional law firm, for what types of employers do paralegals work?

2. Using Exhibit 2.5, *A Sample Résumé,* prepare a résumé. If access to word-processing software with a variety of fonts and graphics is available, try creating a highly professional résumé using this type of software or other technology to which you have access.

3. Which of the following factors affect paralegal compensation?

   a. Geographical location.

   b. Job-interview preparation.

   c. Type of employer.

   d. Short-term goals.

   e. Firm size.

⊞ USING INTERNET RESOURCES

1. Go on the Internet and access LAWMATCH at **www.lawmatch.com,** an online résumé bank. How do you use it? Would you post your résumé there? Why or why not? If you are currently looking for a position, try posting your résumé on that site.

2. Visit the Web site of CareerPath, located at **www. careerpath.com.** Browse through the site and write a one-page description of its offerings with respect to paralegal careers. Next, click on the box titled "Find Jobs by Newspaper." Conduct a search for jobs in the "legal" category (entering "paralegal" as a key word) that were listed in the most recent Sunday editions of three newspapers in your region. Then answer the following questions:

   a. What were the names and dates of the three newspapers you selected? How many ads for paralegals did you find in these papers?

   b. Were any of the ads for entry-level positions?

   c. What percentage of the ads were for work in law offices? List the other types of firms or organizations that advertised job openings, if there were any.

   d. Select two of the ads that most interest you and write a brief summary of the paralegal responsibilities involved in each job.

   e. Generally, how were interested paralegals directed to respond to the ads? Did any firms invite responses by e-mail?

CHAPTER 3

ETHICS AND PROFESSIONAL RESPONSIBILITY

Chapter Outline

⊞ INTRODUCTION ⊞ THE REGULATION OF ATTORNEYS ⊞ ATTORNEY ETHICS AND PARALEGAL PRACTICE ⊞ THE INDIRECT REGULATION OF PARALEGALS ⊞ THE UNAUTHORIZED PRACTICE OF LAW ⊞ SHOULD PARALEGALS BE LICENSED? ⊞ A FINAL NOTE

After completing this chapter, you will know:

- Why and how legal professionals are regulated.

- Some important ethical rules governing the conduct of attorneys.

- How the rules governing attorneys affect paralegal practice.

- The kinds of activities that paralegals are and are not legally permitted to perform.

- Some of the pros and cons of regulation, including the debate over paralegal licensing.

INTRODUCTION

As discussed in the previous chapter, paralegals preparing for a career in today's legal arena have a variety of career options. Regardless of which career path you choose to follow, you should have a firm grasp of your state's ethical rules governing the legal profession. When you work under the supervision of an attorney, as most paralegals do, you and the attorney become team members. You will work together on behalf of clients and share in the ethical and legal responsibilities arising as a result of the attorney-client relationship.

In preparing for a career as a paralegal, you must know what these responsibilities are, why they exist, and how they affect you. The first part of this chapter is devoted to the regulation of attorneys because the ethical duties imposed on attorneys by state law affect paralegals as well. If a paralegal violates one of the rules governing attorneys, that violation may result in serious consequences for the client, for the attorney, and for the paralegal. As you read through the rules governing attorney conduct that are discussed in this chapter, keep in mind that these rules also govern paralegal practice, if indirectly.

Although attorneys are subject to direct regulation by the state, paralegals are not—although they may be in the near future, in the form of licensing requirements. Paralegals are regulated indirectly, however, both by attorney ethical codes and by state laws that prohibit nonlawyers from practicing law.[1] As the paralegal profession develops, professional paralegal organizations, the American Bar Association, and state bar associations of attorneys continue to issue guidelines that also serve to indirectly regulate paralegals.

THE REGULATION OF ATTORNEYS

The term *regulate* derives from the Latin term *regula*, meaning "rule." According to Webster's dictionary, to regulate means "to control or direct in agreement with a rule." To a significant extent, attorneys engage in **self-regulation** because they themselves establish the majority of the rules governing their profession. One of the hallmarks of a profession is the establishment of minimum standards and levels of competence that its members should follow. The accounting profession, for example, has established such standards, as have physicians, engineers, and members of virtually every other profession.

Attorneys are also regulated externally by the state, because the rules of behavior established by the legal profession are adopted and enforced by state authorities. The purpose of regulating attorney behavior is to protect the public interest. By establishing educational and licensing requirements, state authorities ensure that anyone practicing law is competent to do so. Second, by defining specific ethical requirements for attorneys, the states protect the public against unethical attorney behavior that may affect clients' welfare. We will discuss these requirements and rules shortly. First, however, you should know how these rules are created and enforced.

Self-Regulation
The regulation of the conduct of a professional group by members of the group themselves. Self-regulation usually involves the establishment of ethical or professional standards of behavior with which members of the group must comply.

---

1. Some legal professionals maintain that statutes that prohibit nonlawyers from practicing law constitute a form of direct regulation, because paralegals who violate such statutes may be directly sanctioned (in the form of criminal penalties) under those laws. In this chapter, we use the term *direct regulation* to mean state regulation of a specified professional group, particularly through state licensing requirements.

Who Are the Regulators?

Key participants in determining what rules should govern attorneys and the practice of law, as well as how these rules should be enforced, are bar associations, state supreme courts, state legislatures, and, in some cases, the United States Supreme Court. Procedures for regulating attorneys vary, of course, from state to state. What follows is a general discussion of some of the possible regulators.

BAR ASSOCIATIONS.   Lawyers themselves determine the requirements for entering the legal profession and the rules of conduct they will follow. Traditionally, lawyers have joined together in professional groups, or bar associations, at the local, state, and national levels to discuss issues affecting the legal profession and to decide on standards of professional conduct.

Although membership in local and national bar associations is always voluntary, membership in the state bar association is mandatory in over two-thirds of the states. In these states, before an attorney can practice law, he or she must be admitted to the state's bar association. Approximately half of the lawyers in the United States are members of the American Bar Association (ABA), the voluntary national bar association discussed in Chapter 1. As you will read shortly, the ABA plays a key regulatory role by proposing model (uniform) codes, or rules of conduct, for adoption by the various states.

STATE SUPREME COURTS.   Typically, the state's highest court, often called the state supreme court, is the ultimate regulatory authority in that state.[2] The court's judges decide what conditions (such as licensing requirements, discussed below) must be met before an attorney can practice law within the state and under what conditions that privilege will be suspended or revoked. In many states, the state supreme court works closely with the state bar association. The state bar association may recommend rules and requirements to the court. If the court so orders, these rules and requirements become state law. Under the authority of the courts, state bar associations often perform routine regulatory functions, including the initiation of disciplinary proceedings against attorneys who fail to comply with professional requirements.

STATE LEGISLATURES.   State legislatures regulate the legal profession by enacting legislation affecting attorneys—statutes prohibiting the unauthorized practice of law, for example. In a few states, the states' highest courts delegate significant regulatory responsibilities to the state legislatures, which may include the power to bring disciplinary proceedings against attorneys.

THE UNITED STATES SUPREME COURT.   Occasionally, the United States Supreme Court decides issues relating to attorney conduct. For example, until a few decades ago, state ethical codes, or rules governing attorney conduct, prohibited lawyers from advertising their services to the public. These restrictions on advertising were challenged as an unconstitutional limitation on attorneys' rights to free speech, and ultimately, the United States Supreme Court decided the issue. In a case decided in 1977, *Bates v. State Bar of Arizona,*[3] the Supreme Court ruled that truthful advertising of the availability and price of routine legal services was protected speech

On the Web
You can access information on state bar associations, legislatures, and courts, including the United States Supreme Court, at www.findlaw.com. The American Bar Association is online at www.abanet.org.

---

2. There are exceptions, however. In some states, a lower state appellate court performs this function.
3. 433 U.S. 350, 97 S.Ct. 2691, 53 L.Ed.2d 810 (1977). (See Chapter 8 for a discussion of how to read case citations.)

under the First Amendment to the U.S. Constitution and that provisions of state ethical codes forbidding such advertising were therefore unconstitutional.

Licensing Requirements

The licensing of attorneys, which gives them the right to practice law, is accomplished at the state level. Each state has different requirements that individuals must meet before they are allowed to practice law and give legal advice. Generally, however, there are three basic requirements:

1. In most states, prospective attorneys must have obtained a bachelor's degree from a university or college[4] and must have graduated from an accredited law school (in many states, the school must be accredited by the ABA), which requires an additional three years of study.

2. In all states, a prospective attorney must pass a state bar examination—a very rigorous and thorough examination that tests the candidate's knowledge of the law and (in some states) the state's ethical rules governing attorneys. The examination covers both state law (law applicable to the particular state in which the attorney is taking the exam and wishes to practice) and multistate law (law applicable in most states, including federal law).[5]

3. The candidate must pass an extensive personal background investigation to verify that he or she is a responsible individual and otherwise qualifies to engage in an ethical profession. An illegal act committed by the candidate in the past, for example, might disqualify the individual from being permitted to practice law.

Only when these requirements have been met can an individual be admitted to the state bar and legally practice law within the state.

Licensing requirements for attorneys are the result of a long history of attempts to restrict entry into the legal profession. The earliest of these restrictions date to the colonial era. During the 1700s, local bar associations began to form agreements to restrict membership to those who fulfilled certain educational and apprenticeship requirements. At the same time, to curb unnecessary litigation and the detrimental effects of incompetent legal practitioners, courts began to require that individuals representing clients in court proceedings had to be licensed by the court to do so.

Beginning in the mid-1850s, restrictions on who could (or could not) practice law were given statewide effect by state statutes prohibiting the **unauthorized practice of law (UPL).** Court decisions relating to unauthorized legal practice also date to this period. By the 1930s, virtually all states had enacted legislation prohibiting anyone but licensed attorneys from practicing law. As you will see in subsequent sections, many of the regulatory issues facing the legal profession—and particularly paralegals—are directly related to these UPL statutes.

Ethical Codes and Rules

The legal profession is also regulated through ethical codes and rules adopted by each state—in most states, by order of the state supreme court. These codes of professional

Licensing
A government's official act of granting permission to an individual, such as an attorney, to do something that would be illegal in the absence of such permission.

Unauthorized Practice of Law (UPL)
The act of engaging in actions defined by a legal authority, such as a state legislature, as constituting the "practice of law" without legal authorization to do so.

---

4. In some states, including Vermont, one need not have completed a bachelor's degree but must have completed a specified number of credits toward a degree.

5. Note that a few states allow individuals who have not attended law school but who have undertaken a form of independent study and practice (usually as paralegals) to take the bar exam and be admitted to the practice of law.

On the Web
To find out which code of ethics your state has adopted, go to **www.legalethics.com/ states.htm.**

conduct—the names of the codes vary from state to state—evolved over a long period of time. A major step toward ethical regulation was taken in 1908, when the ABA approved the Canons of Ethics, which consisted of thirty-two ethical principles. In the following decades, various states adopted these canons as law.

Today's state ethical codes are based, for the most part, on two subsequent revisions of the ABA canons: the Model Code of Professional Responsibility (published in 1969) and the Model Rules of Professional Conduct (published in 1983 to replace the Model Code). Although most of the states have now adopted the 1983 revision, the 1969 code is still in effect in some states, so you should be familiar with the basic format and content of both the Model Code and the Model Rules.

THE MODEL CODE OF PROFESSIONAL RESPONSIBILITY.   The ABA Model Code of Professional Responsibility, often referred to simply as the Model Code, consists of nine canons. In the Model Code, each canon is followed by sections entitled "Ethical Considerations" (ECs) and "Disciplinary Rules" (DRs). The ethical considerations are "aspirational" in character—that is, they suggest ideal conduct, not behavior that is necessarily required by law. For example, Canon 6 ("A lawyer should represent a client competently") is followed by EC 6–1, which states (in part) that a lawyer "should strive to become and remain proficient in his practice." In contrast, disciplinary rules are mandatory in character—an attorney may be subject to disciplinary action for breaking one of the rules. For example, DR 6–101 (which follows Canon 6) states that a lawyer "shall not . . . [n]eglect a legal matter entrusted to him."

THE MODEL RULES OF PROFESSIONAL CONDUCT.   The 1983 revision of the Model Code—referred to as the Model Rules of Professional Conduct or, more simply, as the Model Rules—represented a thorough revamping of the code. The Model Rules replaced the canons, ethical considerations, and disciplinary rules of the Model Code with a set of rules organized under eight general headings, as outlined in Exhibit 3.1. Each rule is followed by comments shedding additional light on the rule's application and how it compares with the Model Code's treatment of the same issue.

Reprimand
A disciplinary sanction in which an attorney is rebuked for his or her misbehavior. Although a reprimand is the mildest sanction for attorney misconduct, it is nonetheless a serious one and may significantly damage the attorney's reputation in the legal community.

Suspension
A serious disciplinary sanction in which an attorney who has violated an ethical rule or a law is prohibited from practicing law in the state for a specified or an indefinite period of time.

Disbarment
A severe disciplinary sanction in which an attorney's license to practice law in the state is revoked because of unethical or illegal conduct.

Sanctions for Violations

Attorneys who violate the rules governing professional conduct are subject to disciplinary proceedings brought by the state bar association, state supreme court, or state legislature—depending on the state's regulatory scheme. In most states, unethical attorney actions are reported (by clients, legal professionals, or others) to the ethics committee of the state bar association, which is obligated to investigate each complaint thoroughly. For serious violations, the state bar association or the court initiates disciplinary proceedings against the attorney.

Sanctions range from a **reprimand** (a formal "scolding" of the attorney—the mildest sanction[6]) to **suspension** (a more serious sanction by which the attorney is prohibited from practicing law in the state for a given period of time, such as one month or one year, or for an indefinite period of time) to **disbarment** (revocation of the attorney's license to practice law in the state—the most serious sanction).

---

6. Even this mildest sanction can seriously damage an attorney's reputation within the legal community. In some states, state bar associations publish in their monthly journals the names of violators and details of the violations for all members of the bar to read (see the discussion of attorney disciplinary proceedings in the feature *Today's Professional Paralegal* at the end of this chapter).

EXHIBIT 3.1
The ABA Model Rules of Professional Conduct (Headings Only)

CLIENT-LAWYER RELATIONSHIP

1.1	Competence
1.2	Scope of Representation
1.3	Diligence
1.4	Communication
1.5	Fees *Rule 5.4*
1.6	Confidentiality of Information *Rule 1.6*
1.7	Conflict of Interest: General Rule
1.8	Conflict of Interest: Prohibited Transactions
1.9	Conflict of Interest: Former Client
1.10	Imputed Disqualification: General Rule
1.11	Successive Government and Private Employment
1.12	Former Judge or Arbitrator
1.13	Organization as Client
1.14	Client under a Disability
1.15	Safekeeping Property
1.16	Declining or Terminating Representation

COUNSELOR

2.1	Advisor
2.2	Intermediary
2.3	Evaluation for Use by Third Persons

ADVOCATE

3.1	Meritorious Claims and Contentions
3.2	Expediting Litigation
3.3	Candor toward the Tribunal
3.4	Fairness to Opposing Party and Counsel
3.5	Impartiality and Decorum of the Tribunal
3.6	Trial Publicity
3.7	Lawyer as Witness
3.8	Special Responsibilities of a Prosecutor
3.9	Advocate in Nonadjudicative Proceedings

TRANSACTIONS WITH PERSONS OTHER THAN CLIENTS

4.1	Truthfulness in Statements to Others
4.2	Communication with Person Represented by Counsel
4.3	Dealing with Unrepresented Person
4.4	Respect for Rights of Third Persons

LAW FIRMS AND ASSOCIATIONS

5.1	Responsibilities of a Partner or Supervisory Lawyer
5.2	Responsibilities of a Subordinate Lawyer
5.3	Responsibilities Regarding Nonlawyer Assistants
5.4	Professional Independence of a Lawyer
5.5	Unauthorized Practice of Law
5.6	Restrictions on Right to Practice

PUBLIC SERVICE

6.1	*Pro Bono Publico* Service *for the good*
6.2	Accepting Appointments
6.3	Membership in Legal Services Organization
6.4	Law Reform Activities Affecting Client Interests

INFORMATION ABOUT LEGAL SERVICES

7.1	Communications Concerning a Lawyer's Services
7.2	Advertising
7.3	Direct Contact with Prospective Clients
7.4	Communication of Fields of Practice
7.5	Firm Names and Letterheads

MAINTAINING THE INTEGRITY OF THE PROFESSION

8.1	Bar Admission and Disciplinary Matters
8.2	Judicial and Legal Officials
8.3	Reporting Professional Misconduct
8.4	Misconduct
8.5	Jurisdiction

© 1999. Reprinted by permission of the American Bar Association. Copies of the ABA Model Rules of Professional Conduct (1999) are available from Service Center, American Bar Association, 750 North Lake Shore Drive, Chicago, IL 60611, 312-988-5522. Courtesy: National Federation of Paralegal Associations, Inc.

Malpractice
Professional misconduct or negligence—the failure to exercise due care—on the part of a professional, such as an attorney or a physician.

Damages
Money sought as a remedy for a civil wrong, such as a breach of contract or a tortious act.

In addition to these sanctions, attorneys may be subject to civil liability for negligence. As discussed in Chapter 2, *negligence* (called **malpractice** when committed by a professional, such as an attorney) is a tort (a wrongful act). Tort law allows one who is injured by another's wrongful or careless act to bring a civil lawsuit against the wrongdoer for **damages** (compensation in the form of money). Of course, a client is permitted to bring a lawsuit against an attorney only if the client has suffered harm because of the attorney's failure to perform a legal duty.

If a paralegal's breach of a professional duty causes a client to suffer substantial harm, the client may sue not only the attorney but also the paralegal. Although law firms' liability insurance policies typically cover paralegals as well as attorneys, if the paralegal is working on a contract (freelance) basis, he or she will not be covered under a liability policy covering the firm's employees. Just one lawsuit could ruin a freelance paralegal financially—as well as destroy that paralegal's reputation in the legal community. (Note that liability insurance is especially important for independent paralegals, or legal technicians, as well.)

Attorneys and paralegals are also subject to potential criminal liability under criminal statutes prohibiting fraud, theft, and other crimes.

ATTORNEY ETHICS AND PARALEGAL PRACTICE

The state ethical codes are fairly uniform because they are patterned after either the Model Code or the Model Rules (except in California and Florida, whose codes depart significantly from the ABA's models). Because most state codes are guided by the Model Rules of Professional Conduct, the rules discussed in this section are drawn from the Model Rules. Keep in mind, though, the following important guideline:

 Your own state's code of conduct is the governing authority on attorney conduct in your state.

As a paralegal, one of your foremost professional responsibilities is to meticulously follow the rules set forth in your state's ethical code. You will thus want to obtain a copy of your state's ethical code and become familiar with its contents. A good practice is to keep the code near at hand in your office (or on your desk).

Professional duties—and the possibility of violating them—are involved in virtually every task you will perform as a paralegal. Even if you memorize every one of the rules governing the legal profession, you can still quite easily unintentionally violate a rule (you should realize that paralegals rarely breach professional duties intentionally). To minimize the chances that you will unintentionally violate a rule, you need to know not only what the rules are but also how they apply to the day-to-day realities of your job.

The rules relating to competence, confidentiality, and conflict of interest deserve special attention here because they pose particularly difficult ethical problems for paralegals. Other important rules that affect paralegal performance—including the duty to charge reasonable fees, the duty to protect clients' property, and the duty to keep the client reasonably informed—will be discussed elsewhere in this text as they relate to special topics.

The Duty of Competence

The first of the Model Rules states one of the most fundamental duties of attorneys—the duty of competence. Rule 1.1 of the Model Rules reads as follows:

A lawyer shall provide competent representation to a client. Competent representation requires the legal knowledge, skill, thoroughness and preparation reasonably necessary for representation.

Competent legal representation is a basic requirement of the profession, and breaching (failing to perform) this duty may subject attorneys to one or more of the sanctions discussed earlier. As a paralegal, you should realize that when you undertake work on an attorney's behalf, you share in this duty. If your supervising attorney asks you to research a particular legal issue for a client, for example, you must make sure that your research is careful and thorough—because the attorney's reputation (and the client's welfare) may depend on your performance. You should also realize that careless conduct of the research, if it results in substantial injury to the client's interests, may subject you personally to liability for negligence, not to mention the loss of a job or career opportunities.

Breach
To violate a legal duty by an act or a failure to act.

HOW THE DUTY OF COMPETENCE CAN BE BREACHED.   Most breaches of the duty of competence are inadvertent. Often, breaches of the duty of competence have to do with missed deadlines. Paralegals frequently work on several cases simultaneously, and keeping track of every deadline in every case can be challenging—especially for paralegals who are pressed for time.

Organization is the key to making sure that all deadlines are met. All important dates relating to every case or client should be entered on a calendar. Larger firms typically use computerized calendaring and "tickler" (reminder) systems. Even the smallest firm normally has calendaring procedures and tickler systems in place. In addition to making sure that all deadlines are entered into the appropriate systems, you may want to have your own personal calendar for tracking dates that are relevant to the cases on which you are working—and then make sure that you consistently use it. You should develop a habit of checking your calendar every morning when you arrive at work or some other convenient time. Also, you should check frequently with your attorney about deadlines that he or she may not have mentioned to you.

The duty of competence can also be breached in numerous other ways. For example, erroneous information might be included (or crucial information omitted) in a legal document to be filed with the court. If the attorney fails to notice the error before signing the document, and the document is delivered to the court containing the erroneous information, a breach of the duty of competence has occurred. Depending on its legal effect, this breach may expose the attorney and the paralegal to liability for negligence. To prevent these kinds of violations, you need to be especially careful in drafting and proofreading documents.

Generally, if you are ever unsure about what to include in a document, when it must be completed or filed with the court, how extensively you should research a legal issue, or any other aspect of an assignment, you should ask your supervising attorney for special instructions. You should also make sure that your work is adequately overseen by your attorney, to reduce the chances that it will contain costly mistakes or errors.

INADEQUATE SUPERVISION.   Rule 5.3 of the Model Rules defines the responsibilities of attorneys in regard to nonlawyer assistants. This rule states, in part, that "A lawyer should give . . . assistants appropriate instruction and supervision. . . . The measures employed in supervising nonlawyers should take account of the fact that they do not have legal training and are not subject to professional discipline." The rule also states that "a lawyer shall be responsible for the conduct of [a nonlawyer] that would be a violation of the rules of professional conduct if engaged in by a lawyer."

On the Web
The Web sites of the two national paralegal associations, the National Association of Legal Assistants (NALA) and the National Federation of Paralegal Associations (NFPA), are good sources for information on the ethical responsibilities of paralegals, including new, technology-related ethical challenges. You can access NALA's site at www.nala.org. The URL for NFPA'S site is www.paralegals.org.

ETHICAL CONCERN
Missed Deadlines

As a paralegal, you will find that one of your most useful allies is a calendar. Consistently entering important deadlines on a calendaring system (computerized or otherwise) will help to ensure that you and your supervising attorney do not breach the duty of competence simply because a document was not filed with the court on time. For example, if a *complaint* (the document that initiates a lawsuit—see Chapter 6) is served on one of your firm's clients, you must file with the court the client's *answer* to the complaint within a specified number of days. If you fail to file the answer during that time period, the court could enter a judgment in favor of the party bringing the lawsuit. As you might imagine, the consequences of this judgment—called a *default judgment*—can be extremely detrimental to the client. As a paralegal, you need to be aware of the seriousness of the consequences of missed deadlines for your clients, especially the consequences of failing to file an answer on time.

Because attorneys have a duty to supervise nonlawyer assistants and are held legally responsible for their assistants' work, it may seem logical to assume that attorneys will take time to direct that work carefully. In fact, paralegals may find it difficult to ensure that their work is adequately supervised. For one thing, most paralegals are kept very busy, and making sure that all their tasks are properly overseen can be time consuming. Similarly, an attorney often does not want to take the time to read through every document drafted by his or her paralegal—particularly if the attorney knows that the paralegal is competent. Nonetheless, as a paralegal, you have a duty to assist your supervising attorney in fulfilling his or her ethical obligations, including the attorney's obligation to supervise your work.

If you ever feel that your attorney is not adequately supervising your work, there are several things you can do. You can try to improve communications with the attorney—generally, the more you communicate with your supervising attorney, the more likely it is that the attorney will take an active role in directing your activities. You can also ask the attorney for feedback on your work. Sometimes, it helps to place reminders on your personal calendar to discuss particular issues or questions with the attorney. Then, when an opportunity to talk to him or her arises, these issues or questions will be fresh in your mind. Another tactic is to attach a note to a document that you have prepared for the attorney, requesting him or her to review the document (or revised sections of the document) carefully before signing it.

Confidentiality of Information

Rule 1.6 of the Model Rules concerns attorney-client confidentiality. The rule of confidentiality is one of the oldest and most important rules of the legal profession, primarily because it would be difficult for a lawyer to properly represent a client without such a rule. A client must be able to confide in his or her attorney so that the attorney can best represent the client's interest. Because confidentiality is one of the easiest rules to violate, a thorough understanding of the rule is essential.

The general rule of confidentiality, as stated in the first paragraph of Rule 1.6, is that all information relating to the representation of a client must be kept confidential

---

DEVELOPING PARALEGAL SKILLS
Inadequate Supervision

Michael Patton is a paralegal in a small, busy, general practice law firm. His supervising attorney, Muriel Chapman, answers his question about the amount of temporary alimony to be inserted into the judgment of divorce that he is preparing. She tells Michael that the $5,000 figure is the total amount, not the annual amount.

Next, Michael requests that Muriel review the judgment before it is signed by the parties and filed with the court. Muriel tells Michael that she does not need to review his work—she is confident that he has prepared the document correctly because he always asks questions when he is uncertain. Michael remembers the adequate supervision rule and asks Muriel again to review his work. She finally agrees, stating, "You know, Michael, you are rather persistent in making me do 'the right thing.'"

TIPS FOR OBTAINING ADEQUATE SUPERVISION

- Request your supervising attorneys to review your work.
- Use notes or ticklers as reminders to ask for a review.
- Make the review as convenient as possible for your supervising attorney.
- Discuss your ethical concerns with the attorney.
- Be persistent.

---

unless the client consents to disclosure. Note that the rule does not make any qualifications about what kind of information is confidential. It simply states that a lawyer may not reveal "information relating to representation of a client." ⸺ *Confidentiality*

Does this mean that if a client tells you that he is the president of a local company, you have to keep that information confidential, even when the whole community knows that fact? For example, could you tell your spouse, "Mr. X is the president of XYZ Corporation"? It may seem permissible, because that fact is, after all, public knowledge. But in so doing, you must not indicate, by words or conduct, that Mr. X is a client of your firm. In such a situation, it is hard to know just what assumptions might be made based on what you have said. Consider another example. Suppose that one evening at dinner you told your spouse that you had met Mr. X that day. Your spouse might reasonably assume that your firm was handling some legal matter involving Mr. X. Because it may be difficult to decide what information is or is not confidential, a good rule of thumb is the following:

> **Paralegals should regard all information about a client or a client's case as confidential information.**

EXCEPTIONS TO THE RULE.   Rule 1.6 provides for certain exceptions, each of which we look at here.

Client Consents to the Disclosure.   Paragraph (a) of the rule indicates that an attorney may reveal confidential information if the client consents to the disclosure. For example, suppose that an attorney is drawing up a will for a client, and the client is making his only son the sole beneficiary under the will and leaving nothing to his daughter. The daughter calls and wants to know how her father's will reads. The attorney cannot divulge this confidential information to the daughter because the client has not consented to such disclosure. Now suppose that the client told the attorney that if his daughter calls the attorney to find out if she inherited anything under the will, the attorney is to "go ahead and tell her that she gets nothing." In this situation, the attorney could disclose the information because the client consented to the disclosure.

Impliedly Authorized Disclosures.   Paragraph (a) of Rule 1.6 also states that an attorney may make "disclosures that are impliedly authorized in order to carry out the representation." The latter exception is clearly necessary. Legal representation of clients necessarily involves the attorney's assistants, and they must have access to the confidential information to do their jobs. If a paralegal is working on the client's case, for example, he or she must know what the client told the attorney about the legal matter and must have access to information in the client's file concerning the case.

Client Intends a Harmful Act.   Paragraph (b) of Rule 1.6 provides for two other exceptions. The first exception applies when a client reveals that he or she intends to commit a criminal act that may cause bodily harm or death to another. In this situation, the policy underlying the rule of confidentiality (protection of the client's legal rights) is outweighed by the policy of protecting another from imminent bodily harm or death.

The problem with this exception is that it is sometimes difficult to determine whether the client really intends to do what he or she threatens. Also, it is not always clear whether a client's intended behavior is in fact a criminal act that will result in bodily harm or death to another. If you are ever confronted with a situation in which you suspect that a client is about to harm another, discuss the matter immediately with your supervising attorney; he or she will decide what should be done.

Defending against a Client's Legal Action.   The second exception in paragraph (b) of Rule 1.6 is particularly important for attorneys and paralegals. The classic example of this exception is a client's malpractice suit against an attorney. In this situation, it is essential for the lawyer to reveal confidential information to prove that he or she was not negligent. Note, though, that the attorney is permitted to disclose confidential information only to the extent that it is essential to defend against the lawsuit.

VIOLATIONS OF THE CONFIDENTIALITY RULE.   Paralegals, like other professionals, spend a good part of their lives engaged in their work. Naturally, they are tempted to discuss their work at home, with spouses and family members, or with others, such as co-workers and good friends. As a paralegal, perhaps one of the greatest temptations you will face is the desire to discuss a particularly interesting case, or some aspect of a case, with someone you know. You can deal with this temptation in two ways: you can decide, as a matter of policy, never to discuss anything concerning your work; or you can limit your discussion to issues and comments that will not reveal the identity of your client. The latter approach is, for many paralegals, a more realistic solution, but it requires great care. Something you say may reveal a client's identity, even though you are not aware of it.

Conversations Overheard by Others.   Violations of the confidentiality rule may happen simply by oversight. For example, suppose that you and the legal secretary in your office are both working on the same case and continue, as you walk down the hallway toward the elevator, a conversation about the case that you started in the office. You pause in front of the elevator, not realizing that your

DEVELOPING PARALEGAL SKILLS

Client Intends to Commit a Crime

Samantha Serles, a legal assistant with a degree in psychology, is meeting with a client whom her firm is defending. The client, Jim Storming, has been charged with the murder of his mother-in-law. Samantha's job is to assess the client's mental state and consider whether he needs further evaluation. Samantha begins talking to Jim. She asks him how things are going and how he feels. He rolls his eyes at her questions and says, "How do you think I feel, being locked up in this place?" She decides to try to talk to him about the crime. "Jim," she says, "have you thought any more about how your mother-in-law died and about what happened that night?" "Yeah," he says. "I've thought about it plenty. I killed her, you know. But they aren't going to be able prove that I did it."

Samantha just listens as he continues. "I hated her. She talked my wife into divorcing me, and then she and

my ex-wife turned my kids against me. I'm going to get even with my ex-wife for that, too. I've been talking to some guys in here. They told me how I can have her taken care of while I'm in here. Then I won't have to take the rap for that one either." Samantha has seen enough to know that Jim needs psychiatric evaluation.

CHECKLIST FOR DETERMINING WHETHER A CLIENT INTENDS A HARMFUL ACT

- Is the threat one of a criminal act?
- If so, is it one that would cause bodily harm or death to another?
- Is the threat real?
- Always inform your supervising attorney of the threat.

---

conversation is being overheard by someone around the corner from you. You have no way of knowing the person is there, and you have no way of knowing whether the confidential information that you inadvertently revealed will have any adverse effect on your client's interests. One way to avoid the possibility of unwittingly revealing confidential information to **third parties** is to follow this rule of thumb:

 Never discuss confidential information when you are in a common area, such as a hallway, an elevator, or a cafeteria, where a conversation might be overheard.

Electronic Communications and Confidentiality.   Whenever you talk to or about a client on the telephone, make sure that your conversation will not be overheard by a third party. You may be sitting in your private office, but if your door is open, someone may overhear the conversation. Paralegals should take special care when using cellular phones. Cellular phones are not secure; conversations on such phones can be picked up by anyone in the vicinity with a scanner. As a precaution, you should thus never disclose confidential information when talking on a cellular phone. Because of the widespread use of mobile phones, paralegals today often, as a routine precaution, ask a client who is calling whether he or she is calling from a mobile unit. If the client is using a mobile phone, the paralegal can caution the client that confidential information should not be discussed.

Even such a simple operation as sending a fax can pose ethical pitfalls. Generally, you should exercise great care to make sure that you (1) send the fax to the right person (for example, when a letter is addressed to an opposing party in a lawsuit but is supposed to be sent to the client for his or her approval) and (2) dial the correct fax number.

Third Parties
Persons or entities that are not directly involved in an agreement (such as a contract), legal proceeding (such as a lawsuit), or relationship (such as an attorney-client relationship).

ETHICAL CONCERN
Social Events and Confidentiality

Assume that you are at a party with some other paralegals. You tell a paralegal whom you know quite well of some startling news—that a client of your firm, a prominent city official, is being investigated for drug dealing. Although your friend promises to keep this information strictly confidential, she nonetheless relays it to her husband, who in turn tells a co-worker, who in turn tells a friend, and so on. Within a few days, the news has reached the press, and the resulting media coverage results in irreparable harm to the official's reputation and standing in the community. If it can be proved that the harm is the direct result of your breach of the duty of confidentiality, the official could sue both you and the attorney for whom you work for damages.

You also need to be cautious when sending e-mail messages. For example, suppose that you are asked by your supervising attorney to send an e-mail message to a client and to attach a document containing the attorney's analysis of confidential information submitted by the client. The client's e-mail address is in your e-mail "address book," along with other numbers. You click on the client's name, type a brief message, attach the document, and click "send." Too late, you realize that you accidentally clicked on the opposing counsel's name instead of your client's. By a click of the mouse, you have disclosed important confidential information. To avoid this kind of problem, before you click "send," you should take a minute to review not only the message—grammar, sentence structure, and spelling—but also to verify the recipient's name and/or address. (For a further discussion of confidentiality problems posed by the use of e-mail, see the feature *Technology and Today's Paralegal: Is E-Mail "Confidential"?*)

Other Ways of Violating the Confidentiality Rule.   There are numerous other ways in which you can reveal confidential information without intending to do so. A file or document sitting on your desk, if observed by a third party, may reveal the identity of a client or enough information to suggest the client's identity. A computer screen, if visible to those passing by your desk, could convey information to someone who is not authorized to know that information.

On the Web
A good site for updates on how technology affects the responsibilities of legal professionals is the Web site of Law Journal EXTRA! at **www.ljx.com/practice/professionalresponsibility.**

Confidentiality and the Attorney-Client Privilege

All information relating to a client's representation is considered confidential information. Some confidential information also qualifies as privileged information, or information subject to the **attorney-client privilege.**

The attorney-client privilege can be vitally important during the litigation process. As you will read in Chapter 6, prior to a trial each attorney is permitted to obtain information relating to the case from the opposing attorney and other persons, such as witnesses. This means that attorneys must exchange a certain amount of information relating to their clients. An attorney need not divulge privileged information, however—unless the client consents to the disclosure or a court orders the disclosure. Similarly, if an attorney is called to the witness stand

Attorney-Client Privilege
A rule of evidence requiring that confidential communications between a client and his or her attorney (relating to their professional relationship) be kept confidential, unless the client consents to disclosure.

TECHNOLOGY AND TODAY'S PARALEGAL

Is E-Mail "Confidential"?

The widespread use of the Internet by lawyers and paralegals has raised a host of ethical issues, many of which you will read about in later chapters of this book. Here we look at a question of particular importance to all legal professionals, including paralegals: Does communicating with a client via e-mail constitute a violation of the confidentiality rule?

Although the courts have not yet addressed this question, bar associations in several states have rendered ethical opinions on the subject. Among the first to do so was South Carolina, which concluded in 1994 that lawyers should not use e-mail for sensitive client communications because it is possible for e-mail to be intercepted. For the next few years, there seemed to be a growing consensus that only encrypted communications (encoded messages, using encryption software) with clients could be considered confidential.

Since 1997, however, several states have reached the opposite conclusion. For example, when the Vermont state bar's ethics panel considered the issue recently, it reasoned that since "(a) e-mail privacy is no less to be expected than in ordinary phone calls, and (b) unauthorized interception is illegal, a lawyer does not violate [the confidentiality rule] by communicating with a client by e-mail . . . without encryption." The panel went on to say that in various instances "of a very sensitive nature, encryption might be prudent, in which case ordinary phone calls would obviously be deemed inadequate." This reasoning is typical of state bar ethics committees in some other states, including Illinois, Arizona, and even South Carolina—which reversed its earlier opinion when it revisited the issue in 1997.

Despite this trend toward acknowledging e-mail as a confidential medium, as a paralegal you should be very cautious when communicating with clients over the Internet. In one of its two cyberspace ethics opinions, the National Federation of Paralegal Associations (NFPA) advised paralegals that the best way to avoid possible confidentiality problems is to simply not put any confidential information on the Internet. NFPA also suggested that legal professionals take other steps, such as considering encryption for e-mail with clients, establishing procedures and policies on the topic for all office personnel to follow, and using disclaimers in e-mail messages to indicate that the communications may not be secure.

during a trial, the attorney may not disclose privileged information unless the court orders him or her to do so.

WHAT KIND OF INFORMATION IS PRIVILEGED?   State statutes and court cases define what constitutes privileged information. Generally, any communications concerning a client's legal rights or problem fall under the attorney-client privilege. For example, suppose that an attorney's client is a criminal defendant. The client tells the attorney that she was actually in the vicinity of the crime site at the time of the crime, but to her knowledge, no one noticed her presence there. This is privileged information that the attorney may only disclose with the client's consent or on a court's order to do so.

Other types of information, although confidential, are not necessarily privileged. For example, information relating to a client's identity is usually not privileged. Nor, as a rule, is information concerning client fees. Furthermore, information concerning the client's personal or business affairs is not privileged unless it is related to the legal claim. For example, suppose that a client who is bringing a malpractice suit against a physician mentions to the attorney that he is divorcing his wife. Unless the client's divorce is related in some way to the malpractice suit being handled by the attorney, the information about the divorce normally is not considered privileged.

ETHICAL CONCERN
Personal versus Professional Ethics

What happens when a paralegal's personal ethical standards come into conflict with a professional duty, such as the duty of confidentiality? When this dilemma faced Merrell Williams, a paralegal with the Kentucky law firm of Wyatt, Tarrant & Combs, he decided to violate the duty of confidentiality to satisfy his conscience. From 1988 to 1992, he took over 4,000 pages of confidential documents belonging to his firm's client, tobacco manufacturer Brown & Williamson (B&W), and gave them to the press and others. The documents immediately became a "smoking gun" for antismoking forces involved in litigation against the tobacco industry.

To some, Williams is a hero. After all, he sacrificed his job and faced a lawsuit by his former employer (which was settled in 1997) to help protect the public against the dangers of smoking. To others, Williams's actions were wrongful. Essentially, the question boils down to this: Is it ever in the public interest for a legal professional to violate an ethical duty, particularly when that duty was established by the legal profession to further its goal of protecting the public?

Work Product
An attorney's mental impressions, conclusions, and legal theories regarding a case being prepared on behalf of a client. Work product normally is regarded as privileged information.

Certain materials relating to an attorney's preparation of a client's case for trial are protected as privileged information under what is known as the **work product** doctrine. Usually, information concerning an attorney's legal strategy for conducting a case is classified as work product and, as such, may be subject to the attorney-client privilege. Legal strategy includes the legal theories that the attorney plans to use in support of the client's claim, how the attorney interprets the evidence relating to the claim, and so on. Certain evidence gathered by the attorney to support the client's claim, however, such as financial statements relating to the client's business firm, would probably not be classified as work product. Because it is often difficult to tell what types of information (including work product) qualify as privileged, paralegals should consult closely with their supervising attorneys whenever issues arise that may require that such a distinction be made.

WHEN THE ATTORNEY-CLIENT PRIVILEGE ARISES.   The attorney-client privilege comes into existence the moment a client communicates with an attorney concerning a legal matter. People sometimes mistakenly assume that there is no duty to keep client information confidential unless an attorney agrees to represent a client and the client signs a retainer agreement. This is not so.

 The privilege—and thus the duty of confidentiality—arises even if the lawyer decides not to represent the client and even when the client is not charged any fee.

DURATION OF THE PRIVILEGE.   The client is the holder, or "owner," of the privilege, and only the client can waive (set aside) the privilege. Unless waived by the client, the privilege lasts indefinitely. In other words, the privilege continues even though an attorney has completed the client's legal matter and is no longer working on the case. As with all confidential information relating to a client's case, privileged information is subject to the exceptions to the confidentiality rule discussed above.

Additionally, always keep in mind that privileged information is *confidential* information. If confidential information is disclosed to others, it is no longer "confidential" and can no longer be considered privileged information. This is another reason why it is so important to guard against accidental violations of the confidentiality rule: if the rule is violated, information that otherwise might have been protected by the attorney-client privilege can be used in court, which may be harmful to the the client's interests. To illustrate, consider the e-mail example given earlier, in which the paralegal inadvertently sent a confidential document to opposing counsel instead of the client. The document, because it contained the attorney's analysis of confidential client information, might be classified as privileged information under the work product doctrine. The disclosure of the information to the opposing counsel destroyed its confidential character—and therefore any possibility that it might be protected as privileged information.

Conflict of Interest

If an attorney engages in an activity that adversely affects a client's interests (such as simultaneously representing opposing parties in a legal proceeding), the attorney faces a **conflict of interest**. Model Rules 1.7, 1.8, 1.9, and 1.10 all pertain to conflict-of-interest situations. Rule 1.7 states the general rule: "A lawyer shall not represent a client if the representation of the client will be directly adverse to another client."

A classic example of a conflict of interest exists when an attorney simultaneously represents two adverse parties in a legal proceeding. Clearly, in such a situation, the attorney's loyalties must be divided. It would be as if a football player agreed to play on both teams during a game—half of the time with one team and half with the other.

Conflict of Interest
A situation in which two or more duties or interests come into conflict, as when an attorney attempts to represent opposing parties in a legal dispute.

SIMULTANEOUS REPRESENTATION.   If an attorney decides that representing two parties in a legal proceeding will not adversely affect either party's interest, then the attorney is permitted to do so—but only if both parties agree. Normally, attorneys avoid this kind of situation because what might start out as a simple, uncontested proceeding may evolve into a legal battle. Divorce proceedings, for example, may begin amicably but end up in heated disputes over child-custody arrangements or property division. The attorney then faces a conflict of interest: assisting one party will necessarily be adverse to the interests of the other. Note that because of the potential for a conflict of interest in divorce proceedings, some courts do not permit attorneys to represent both spouses, even if the spouses consented to such an arrangement.

Similar conflicts arise when the "family attorney" is asked to handle a family matter and the family members eventually disagree on what the outcome should be. For example, consider a situation in which two adult children request the family lawyer to handle the procedures required to settle their deceased parent's estate. The parent's will favors one of the children, and the other child decides to challenge the will's validity. The attorney cannot represent both sides in this dispute without facing a conflict of interest.

Attorneys representing corporate clients may face conflicts of interest when corporate personnel become divided on an issue. For example, assume that ABC Corporation has retained Carl Finn, an attorney, to represent the corporation. Finn typically deals with the corporation's president, Julie Johnson, when rendering legal assistance and advice. At times, however, Finn deals with other corporate personnel, including Seth Harrison, the corporation's accountant. Harrison and Johnson disagree with each other on several major issues, and eventually

Johnson arranges to have Harrison fired. Harrison wants attorney Finn to represent him in a lawsuit against the corporation for wrongful termination of his employment. Finn now faces a conflict of interest.

FORMER CLIENTS.   A conflict of interest may also involve former clients. Model Rule 1.9 states that "[a] lawyer who has formerly represented a client in a matter shall not thereafter represent another person in the same or substantially related matter in which that person's interests are materially adverse to the interests of the former client unless the former client consents after consultation." The rule regarding former clients is closely related to the rule on preserving the confidentiality of a client. The rationale behind the rule is that an attorney, in representing a client, is entrusted with certain information that may be unknown to others, and that information should not be used against the client—even after the represention has ended.

For example, assume that a year ago an attorney defended a company against a lawsuit for employment discrimination brought by one of the company's employees. During the course of the representation, the attorney learned a great deal about the company. Now, someone who was injured while using one of that same company's products consults with the attorney about the possibility of bringing a product-liability lawsuit against the company. The attorney normally must refuse to represent this person. Because the attorney has confidential information about the company that could be used to harm the company's interest, a conflict of interest exists.

Job Changes and Former Clients.   The rule concerning former clients does not prohibit an individual from working at a firm or agency that may represent interests contrary to those of a former client. If that were the situation, many of those who have worked for very large firms would be unable ever to change jobs. Generally, the rules vary, depending on the specific circumstances. In some situations, when a conflict of interest results from a job change, the new employer can avoid violating the rules governing conflict of interest through the use of screening procedures. The new employer can erect an impenetrable screen, referred to as an **ethical wall,** around the new employee so that the new employee remains ignorant about the case giving rise to the conflict of interest.

Ethical Wall
A term that refers to the procedures used to create a screen around a legal employee to shield him or her from information about a case in which there is a conflict of interest.

Walling-Off Procedures.   Law offices usually have special procedures for "walling off" an attorney or other legal professional from a case when a conflict of interest exists. The firm may announce in a written memo to all employees that a certain attorney or paralegal should not have access to specific files, for example, and may set out procedures to be followed to ensure that access to those files is restricted. Computer documents relating to the case may be protected by warning messages or in some other way. Commonly, any hard-copy files relating to the case are flagged with a sticker to indicate that access to the files is restricted.

Firms normally take great care to establish such procedures and observe them carefully, because if confidential information is used in a way harmful to a former client, the firm may be sued by the client and have to pay steep damages. In defending against such a suit, the firm will need to demonstrate that it took reasonable precautions to protect that client's interests.

OTHER CONFLICT-OF-INTEREST SITUATIONS.   There are several other types of situations that may give rise to conflicts of interest. Gifts from clients may create conflicts of interest, because they tend to bias the judgment of the attorney or paralegal. Some types of gifts are specifically prohibited. For example, Rule 1.8(c)

DEVELOPING PARALEGAL SKILLS

Building an Ethical Wall

Lana Smith, a paralegal, has been asked by her supervising attorney to set up an ethical wall because a new attorney, Sandra Piper, has been hired from the law firm of Nunn & Bush. While employed by Nunn & Bush, Piper represented the defendant, Seski Manufacturing, in the ongoing case of *Tymes v. Seski Manufacturing Co.* Lana's firm represents the plaintiff, Joseph Tymes, in that same case, so Piper's work for Nunn & Bush creates a conflict of interest. Lana makes a list of the walling-off procedures to use to ensure that the firm cannot be accused of violating the rules on conflict of interest.

CHECKLIST FOR BUILDING AN ETHICAL WALL

- Prepare a memo to the office manager regarding the conflict and the need for special arrangements.

- Prepare a memo to the team representing Tymes to inform them of the conflict of interest and the special procedures to be used.

- Prepare a memo to the firm, giving the case name, the nature of the conflict, the parties involved, and instructions to maintain a blanket of silence with respect to Sandra Piper.

- Arrange for Piper's office to be on a different floor from the team to demonstrate, if necessary, that the firm took steps to prevent Piper and the team from having access to one another or each other's files.

- Arrange with the office manager for special computer passwords to be issued to the team members so that access to computer files on the *Tymes* case is restricted to team members only.

- Place "ACCESS RESTRICTED" stickers on the files for the *Tymes* case.

- Develop a security procedure for signing out and tracking the case files in the *Tymes* case—to prevent inadvertent disclosure of the files to Piper or her staff members.

---

of the Model Rules of Professional Conduct prohibits an attorney from preparing documents (such as wills) for a client that gives the attorney or a member of the attorney's family a gift. (An exception to this rule exists, of course, when the attorney is a relative of the client.) Note that as a paralegal, you may be offered gifts from appreciative clients at Christmas or other times. Generally, such gifts pose no ethical problems. If a client offers you a gift that has substantial value, however, you should discuss the issue with your supervising attorney.

Attorneys also need to be careful about taking on a client whose case may create an "issue conflict" for the attorney. Generally, an attorney cannot represent a client with respect to a substantive legal issue if the client's position is directly contrary to that of another client being represented by the lawyer—or the lawyer's firm—in a case being brought within the same jurisdiction (the geographic area or subject matter over which a specific court has authority to decide legal disputes). The reason for this rule, which is set forth in Model Rule 1.7 and has been clarified by an opinion on the matter issued by the American Bar Association (ABA),[7] is that courts are obligated to follow precedents—earlier decisions on cases involving similar facts and issues (see Chapter 5). The court's ruling in one of the attorney's cases could therefore alter the outcome of the other case.

Occasionally, conflicts of interest may arise when two family members who are both attorneys or paralegals are involved in the representation of adverse parties in a legal proceeding. Model Rule 1.8(i) prohibits an attorney from representing a client if the adverse party to the dispute is being represented by a member of the attorney's family (such as a spouse, parent, child, or sibling). If you, as a

---

7. American Bar Association Formal Opinion 93–377, October 16, 1993.

paralegal, are married to or living with another paralegal or an attorney, you should inform your firm of this fact if you ever suspect that a conflict of interest might result from your relationship.

CONFLICTS CHECKS.　　Whenever a potential client consults with an attorney, the attorney will want to make sure that no potential conflict of interest exists before deciding whether to represent the client. Running a **conflicts check** is a standard procedure in the law office and one that is frequently undertaken by paralegals. Before you can run a conflicts check, you need to know the name of the prospective client, the other party or parties that may be involved in the client's legal matter, and the legal issue involved. Normally, every law firm has some established procedure for conflicts checks, and in larger firms there is usually a computerized database containing the names of former clients and the other information you will need in checking for conflicts of interest.

Conflicts Check
A procedure for determining whether an agreement to represent a potential client will result in a conflict of interest.

THE INDIRECT REGULATION OF PARALEGALS

Paralegals are regulated *indirectly* in several ways. Clearly, the ethical codes for attorneys just discussed indirectly regulate the conduct of paralegals. Additionally, paralegal conduct is regulated indirectly by standards and guidelines created by paralegal professional groups as well as guidelines for the utilization of paralegals developed by the American Bar Association and various states.

Paralegal Ethical Codes

In addition to indirect regulation through attorney ethical codes, paralegals are becoming increasingly self-regulated. Recall from Chapter 1 that the two major national paralegal associations in the United States—the National Federation of Paralegal Associations, or NFPA, and the National Association of Legal Assistants, or NALA—were formed to define and represent paralegal professional interests on a national level. Shortly after they were formed, both of these associations adopted codes of ethics defining the ethical responsibilities of paralegals.

NFPA'S CODE OF ETHICS.　　In 1977, NFPA adopted its first code of ethics, called the Affirmation of Responsibility, which has since been revised several times and, in 1993, was renamed the Model Code of Ethics and Professional Responsibility. In 1997, NFPA revised the code, particularly its format, and took the bold step of appending to its code a set of enforcement guidelines setting forth recommendations on how to discipline paralegals who violate ethical standards promulgated by the code. The full title of NFPA's current code is "Model Code of Ethics and Professional Responsibility and Guidelines for Enforcement."

Exhibit 3.2, beginning on page 89, presents the preamble to the revised document as well as Section 1, which contains the ethical standards under the title, "NFPA Model Disciplinary Rules and Ethical Considerations." (For the full text of the code, including Section 2, which consists of the enforcement guidelines, see Appendix C at the end of this text.)

NALA'S CODE OF ETHICS.　　In 1975, NALA issued its Code of Ethics and Professional Responsibility, which, like NFPA's code, has since undergone several revisions. Exhibit 3.3 on page 92 presents NALA's code in its entirety. Note that NALA's code, like the Model Code of Professional Responsibility discussed earlier in this chapter, presents ethical precepts as a series of "canons." (Prior to the 1997 revision of its code, NFPA also listed its ethical standards as "canons.")

On the Web
You can find NALA'S Code of Ethics and Professional Responsibility online at **www.nala.org/stand.htm**.

FEATURED GUEST: MICHAEL A. PENER

Ten Tips for Ethics and the Paralegal

BIOGRAPHICAL NOTE

Michael A. Pener developed the Paralegal Program at Johnson County Community College in 1977. It was approved by the American Bar Association (ABA) in 1980. He was the program's first director and continued in that capacity until 1987, when he became one of its full-time professors. Pener is one of the founders of the American Association for Paralegal Education (AAfPE). He served on its initial board of directors and, in 1985 and 1986, as its president. He is a long-time member of the Ethics Advisory Services Committee and Legal Assistant Committee of the Kansas Bar Association

(KBA). Starting in 1992, he served for three years as one of the AAfPE's representatives on the Approval Commission of the ABA Standing Committee on Legal Assistants.

As a legal-assistant educator and practicing attorney, I have developed several ethics-related "truths" for my students that I think are essential for their professional survival as working legal assistants. Each of these truths is important, and the legal assistant must adhere to all of them if he or she wants to avoid, or lessen the impact of, situations involving ethical problems. While I believe the following tips will keep you out of trouble, no list of this type is ever complete without your own input—so use it to develop ethical "rules" appropriate for your work and legal practice area.

1. Obtain Copies of State and Local Ethical Rules. Keep up with current state ethical rules for attorneys and paralegals and continually review their application in cases, disciplinary proceedings, and ethical opinions of local, state, and national lawyer associations. Specifically, there are now many guidelines on major areas of concern to the legal profession, including the use of legal assistants by lawyers, con-

fidentiality, the unauthorized practice of law, conflicts of interest, and legal competence.

2. Attend Continuing Legal Education (CLE) Programs on Legal Ethics. In many states, lawyers are required to have CLE hours on legal ethics. Attending CLE programs not only reminds you of what the rules require but also helps you remain current in ethical developments within the profession.

3. Network with Other Legal Assistants. Network with other legal assistants through local paralegal organizations and education programs and through the National Federation of Paralegal Associations and the National Association of Legal Assistants. Both of the national organizations have professional ethical codes and are involved in court cases affecting paralegals.

4. Make No Assumptions about Others. In an ideal world, all legal professionals would act ethically at all times. In such a world, there would be no need for rules to govern attorney behavior and no need for disciplinary actions. As a paralegal, you may encounter situations in which you suspect unethical behavior on the part of someone with whom you work.

COMPLIANCE WITH PARALEGAL CODES OF ETHICS.   Paralegal codes of ethics state the ethical responsibilities of paralegals generally, but they particularly apply to members of paralegal organizations that have adopted the codes. Any paralegal who is a member of an organization that has adopted one of these codes is expected to comply with the code's requirements. Note that compliance with these codes is not legally mandatory. In other words, if a paralegal does not abide by a particular ethical standard of a paralegal association's code of ethics, the association cannot initiate state-sanctioned disciplinary proceedings against the paralegal. The association can, however, expel the paralegal from the association, which may have significant implications for the paralegal's future career opportunities.

On the Web
You can find NFPA's Model Code of Ethics and Professional Responsibility and Guidelines for Enforcement on the Web at **www.paralegals.org/ Development/ modelcode.html.**

FEATURED GUEST, *Continued*

Ignoring unethical behavior will not necessarily make it go away. Always keep your professional ethical requirements in mind; at times, this may mean you need to discuss the matter with someone in authority.

5. **Double-Check Your Work.** Expect the unexpected, especially when dealing with unfamiliar matters or with strangers. Don't assume that the documents you produce will be checked for accuracy by others. As a legal assistant, you will need to pay the utmost attention to detail and double-check everything that you do to make sure it is accurate. Also, make sure that all written communications are sent to the proper person.

6. **Review All Documents That You Receive.** When documents are being exchanged in the drafting stage with opposing counsel or during negotiations, always review the documents that you receive in their entirety.

7. **Anticipate and Prepare for Ethical Problems.** Anticipate and prepare for situations in your work and professional relationships that may give rise to ethical problems. In this chapter, you will encounter a number of "real-life" situations that will test your understanding and application of legal ethics. Study them carefully, because they most likely will happen to you. Also, note that clients want to know how their legal matters are progressing, but lawyers are sometimes too busy to attend to their clients' needs in this respect. Legal assistants may end up communicating more frequently with clients than attorneys do. If the lawyer for whom you work puts you in this role, you should feel complimented by the lawyer's confidence in you. Watch out, however, for a client who becomes overly dependent on you and your judgment. Very soon he or she may be asking you for your "legal opinion" and guidance in dealing with the lawyer. If you respond to this, you will get into trouble very quickly.

8. **Use Caution When Notarizing Documents or Signing Documents as a Witness.** If you are a notary public, only notarize those documents that were signed in your presence. As a notary public, you have a statutory requirement to perform the duties of your appointed office. Failure to act as required may subject you to personal liability. This means that you must refuse a lawyer's request to notarize a document that was not signed in your presence. Similarly, never sign any

> **"Ignoring unethical behavior will not necessarily make it go away."**

document as a witness without first reviewing it to make sure that your signature is properly requested.

9. **Maintain a Balance between Personal and Legal Ethics.** Try to maintain a proper balance between your personal ethics and legal ethics. This may be the most difficult thing for you to do. You may be a party to confidential communications by clients that concern unethical, and even immoral, behavior on their part. Your law firm may have a policy or engage in an activity that is acceptable by legal ethical standards but that you personally consider to be unethical. Professionally, you must accept this. If you personally cannot, then you may have no other choice but to seek employment elsewhere.

10. **Rely on Your Common Sense and Intuition.** Use your common sense and intuition. Develop an awareness of what is right and wrong behavior in any given situation and then seek the answer to any legal ethical problem that you encounter.

Guidelines for the Utilization of Paralegals

As mentioned earlier in this chapter, the reason attorneys are regulated by the state is to protect the public from the harms that could result from incompetent legal advice and representation. Licensing requirements for attorneys thus serve the public interest. At the same time, they give lawyers something of a monopoly over the delivery of legal services—a monopoly that, in turn, may have detrimental effects on those who cannot afford to pay attorneys for their services. The increased use of paralegals stems, in part, from the legal profession's need to reduce the cost of legal services. The use of paralegals to do substantive legal work

EXHIBIT 3.2

NFPA's Code of Ethics and Professional Responsibility and Guidelines for Enforcement (Preamble and Section 1 Only)

Courtesy: National Federation of Paralegal Associations, Inc.

MODEL CODE OF ETHICS AND PROFESSIONAL RESPONSIBILITY AND GUIDELINES FOR ENFORCEMENT

PREAMBLE

The National Federation of Paralegal Associations, Inc. ("NFPA") is a professional organization comprised of paralegal associations and individual paralegals throughout the United States and Canada. Members of NFPA have varying backgrounds, experiences, education and job responsibilities that reflect the diversity of the paralegal profession. NFPA promotes the growth, development and recognition of the paralegal profession as an integral partner in the delivery of legal services.

In May 1993 NFPA adopted its Model Code of Ethics and Professional Responsibility ("Model Code") to delineate the principles for ethics and conduct to which every paralegal should aspire.

Many paralegal associations throughout the United States have endorsed the concept and content of NFPA's Model Code through the adoption of their own ethical codes. In doing so, paralegals have confirmed the profession's commitment to increase the quality and efficiency of legal services, as well as recognized its responsibilities to the public, the legal community, and colleagues.

Paralegals have recognized, and will continue to recognize, that the profession must continue to evolve to enhance their roles in the delivery of legal services. With increased levels of responsibility comes the need to define and enforce mandatory rules of professional conduct. Enforcement of codes of paralegal conduct is a logical and necessary step to enhance and ensure the confidence of the legal community and the public in the integrity and professional responsibility of paralegals.

In April 1997 NFPA adopted the Model Disciplinary Rules ("Model Rules") to make possible the enforcement of the Canons and Ethical Considerations contained in the NFPA Model Code. A concurrent determination was made that the Model Code of Ethics and Professional Responsibility, formerly aspirational in nature, should be recognized as setting forth the enforceable obligations of all paralegals.

The Model Code and Model Rules offer a framework for professional discipline, either voluntarily or through formal regulatory programs.

§1. NFPA MODEL DISCIPLINARY RULES AND ETHICAL CONSIDERATIONS

1.1 A PARALEGAL SHALL ACHIEVE AND MAINTAIN A HIGH LEVEL OF COMPETENCE.

Ethical Considerations

EC-1.1(a) A paralegal shall achieve competency through education, training, and work experience.

EC-1.1(b) A paralegal shall participate in continuing education in order to keep informed of current legal, technical and general developments.

EC-1.1(c) A paralegal shall perform all assignments promptly and efficiently.

1.2 A PARALEGAL SHALL MAINTAIN A HIGH LEVEL OF PERSONAL AND PROFESSIONAL INTEGRITY.

Ethical Considerations

EC-1.2(a) A paralegal shall not engage in any ex parte communications involving the courts or any other adjudicatory body in an attempt to exert undue influence or to obtain advantage or the benefit of only one party.

EC-1.2(b) A paralegal shall not communicate, or cause another to communicate, with a party the paralegal knows to be represented by a lawyer in a pending matter without the prior consent of the lawyer representing such other party.

EC-1.2(c) A paralegal shall ensure that all timekeeping and billing records prepared by the paralegal are thorough, accurate, honest, and complete.

EC-1.2(d) A paralegal shall not knowingly engage in fraudulent billing practices. Such practices may include, but are not limited to: inflation of hours billed to a client or employer; misrepresentation of the nature of tasks performed; and/or submission of fraudulent expense and disbursement documentation.

EC-1.2(e) A paralegal shall be scrupulous, thorough and honest in the identification and maintenance of all funds, securities, and other assets of a client and shall provide accurate accounting as appropriate.

EXHIBIT 3.2
**NFPA's Code of Ethics and
Professional Responsibility and
Guidelines for Enforcement
(Preamble and Section 1
Only)—Continued**

EC-1.2(f) A paralegal shall advise the proper authority of non-confidential knowledge of any dishonest or fraudulent acts by any person pertaining to the handling of the funds, securities or other assets of a client. The authority to whom the report is made shall depend on the nature and circumstances of the possible misconduct (e.g., ethics committees of law firms, corporations and/or paralegal associations, local or state bar associations, local prosecutors, administrative agencies, etc.). Failure to report such knowledge is in itself misconduct and shall be treated as such under these rules.

1.3   A PARALEGAL SHALL MAINTAIN A HIGH STANDARD OF PROFESSIONAL CONDUCT.

Ethical Considerations

EC-1.3(a) A paralegal shall refrain from engaging in any conduct that offends the dignity and decorum of proceedings before a court or other adjudicatory body and shall be respectful of all rules and procedures.

EC-1.3(b) A paralegal shall avoid impropriety and the appearance of impropriety and shall not engage in any conduct that would adversely affect his/her fitness to practice. Such conduct may include, but is not limited to: violence, dishonesty, interference with the administration of justice, and/or abuse of a professional position or public office.

EC-1.3(c) Should a paralegal's fitness to practice be compromised by physical or mental illness, causing that paralegal to commit an act that is in direct violation of the Model Code/Model Rules and/or the rules and/or laws governing the jurisdiction in which the paralegal practices, that paralegal may be protected from sanction upon review of the nature and circumstances of that illness.

EC-1.3(d) A paralegal shall advise the proper authority of non-confidential knowledge of any action of another legal professional that clearly demonstrates fraud, deceit, dishonesty, or misrepresentation. The authority to whom the report is made shall depend on the nature and circumstances of the possible misconduct, (e.g., ethics committees of law firms, corporations and/or paralegal associations, local or state bar associations, local prosecutors, administrative agencies, etc.). Failure to report such knowledge is in itself misconduct and shall be treated as such under these rules.

EC-1.3(e) A paralegal shall not knowingly assist any individual with the commission of an act that is in direct violation of the Model Code/Model Rules and/or the rules and/or laws governing the jurisdiction in which the paralegal practices.

EC-1.3(f) If a paralegal possesses knowledge of future criminal activity, that knowledge must be reported to the appropriate authority immediately.

1.4   A PARALEGAL SHALL SERVE THE PUBLIC INTEREST BY CONTRIBUTING TO THE DELIVERY OF QUALITY LEGAL SERVICES AND THE IMPROVEMENT OF THE LEGAL SYSTEM.

Ethical Considerations

EC-1.4(a) A paralegal shall be sensitive to the legal needs of the public and shall promote the development and implementation of programs that address those needs.

EC-1.4(b) A paralegal shall support bona fide efforts to meet the need for legal services by those unable to pay reasonable or customary fees; for example, participation in pro bono projects and volunteer work.

EC-1.4(c) A paralegal shall support efforts to improve the legal system and access thereto and shall assist in making changes.

1.5   A PARALEGAL SHALL PRESERVE ALL CONFIDENTIAL INFORMATION PROVIDED BY THE CLIENT OR ACQUIRED FROM OTHER SOURCES BEFORE, DURING, AND AFTER THE COURSE OF THE PROFESSIONAL RELATIONSHIP.

Ethical Considerations

EC-1.5(a) A paralegal shall be aware of and abide by all legal authority governing confidential information in the jurisdiction in which the paralegal practices.

EC-1.5(b) A paralegal shall not use confidential information to the disadvantage of the client.

EC-1.5(c) A paralegal shall not use confidential information to the advantage of the paralegal or of a third person.

EC-1.5(d) A paralegal may reveal confidential information only after full disclosure and with the client's written consent; or, when required by law or court order; or, when necessary to prevent the client from committing an act that could result in death or serious bodily harm.

EC-1.5(e) A paralegal shall keep those individuals responsible for the legal representation of a client fully informed of any confidential information the paralegal may have pertaining to that client.

EC-1.5(f) A paralegal shall not engage in any indiscreet communications concerning clients.

1.6 A PARALEGAL SHALL AVOID CONFLICTS OF INTEREST AND SHALL DISCLOSE ANY POSSIBLE CONFLICT TO THE EMPLOYER OR CLIENT, AS WELL AS TO THE PROSPECTIVE EMPLOYERS OR CLIENTS.

Ethical Considerations

EC-1.6(a) A paralegal shall act within the bounds of the law, solely for the benefit of the client, and shall be free of compromising influences and loyalties. Neither the paralegal's personal or business interest, nor those of other clients or third persons, should compromise the paralegal's professional judgment and loyalty to the client.

EC-1.6(b) A paralegal shall avoid conflicts of interest that may arise from previous assignments, whether for a present or past employer or client.

EC-1.6(c) A paralegal shall avoid conflicts of interest that may arise from family relationships and from personal and business interests.

EC-1.6(d) In order to be able to determine whether an actual or potential conflict of interest exists a paralegal shall create and maintain an effective recordkeeping system that identifies clients, matters, and parties with which the paralegal has worked.

EC-1.6(e) A paralegal shall reveal sufficient non-confidential information about a client or former client to reasonably ascertain if an actual or potential conflict of interest exists.

EC-1.6(f) A paralegal shall not participate in or conduct work on any matter where a conflict of interest has been identified.

EC-1.6(g) In matters where a conflict of interest has been identified and the client consents to continued representation, a paralegal shall comply fully with the implementation and maintenance of an Ethical Wall.

1.7 A PARALEGAL'S TITLE SHALL BE FULLY DISCLOSED.

Ethical Considerations

EC-1.7(a) A paralegal's title shall clearly indicate the individual's status and shall be disclosed in all business and professional communications to avoid misunderstandings and misconceptions about the paralegal's role and responsibilities.

EC-1.7(b) A paralegal's title shall be included if the paralegal's name appears on business cards, letterhead, brochures, directories, and advertisements.

EC-1.7(c) A paralegal shall not use letterhead, business cards or other promotional materials to create a fraudulent impression of his/her status or ability to practice in the jurisdiction in which the paralegal practices.

EC-1.7(d) A paralegal shall not practice under color of any record, diploma, or certificate that has been illegally or fraudulently obtained or issued or which is misrepresentative in any way.

EC-1.7(e) A paralegal shall not participate in the creation, issuance, or dissemination of fraudulent records, diplomas, or certificates.

1.8 A PARALEGAL SHALL NOT ENGAGE IN THE UNAUTHORIZED PRACTICE OF LAW.

Ethical Considerations

EC-1.8(a) A paralegal shall comply with the applicable legal authority governing the unauthorized practice of law in the jurisdiction in which the paralegal practices.

EXHIBIT 3.2

NFPA's Code of Ethics and Professional Responsibility and Guidelines for Enforcement (Preamble and Section 1 Only)—Continued

EXHIBIT 3.3
**NALA's Code of Ethics and
Professional Responsibility**

© 1975, 1977, 1994 National
Association of Legal Assistants, Inc.
Reprinted with permission.

A legal assistant must adhere strictly to the accepted standards of legal ethics and to the general principles of proper conduct. The performance of the duties of the legal assistant shall be governed by specific canons as defined herein so justice will be served and goals of the profession attained. (See Model Standards and Guidelines for Utilization of Legal Assistants, Section II.)

The canons of ethics set forth hereafter are adopted by the National Association of Legal Assistants, Inc., as a general guide intended to aid legal assistants and attorneys. The enumeration of these rules does not mean there are not others of equal importance although not specifically mentioned. Court rules, agency rules and statutes must be taken into consideration when interpreting the canons.

Definition: Legal assistants, also known as paralegals, are a distinguishable group of persons who assist attorneys in the delivery of legal services. Through formal education, training and experience, legal assistants have knowledge and expertise regarding the legal system and substantive and procedural law which qualify them to do work of a legal nature under the supervision of an attorney.

Canon 1.
A legal assistant must not perform any of the duties that attorneys only may perform nor take any actions that attorneys may not take.

Canon 2.
A legal assistant may perform any task which is properly delegated and supervised by an attorney, as long as the attorney is ultimately responsible to the client, maintains a direct relationship with the client, and assumes professional responsibility for the work product.

Canon 3.
A legal assistant must not: (a) engage in, encourage, or contribute to any act which could constitute the unauthorized practice of law; and (b) establish attorney-client relationships, set fees, give legal opinions or advice or represent a client before a court or agency unless so authorized by that court or agency; and (c) engage in conduct or take any action which would assist or involve the attorney in a violation of professional ethics or give the appearance of professional impropriety.

Canon 4.
A legal assistant must use discretion and professional judgment commensurate with knowledge and experience but must not render independent legal judgment in place of an attorney. The services of an attorney are essential in the public interest whenever such legal judgment is required.

Canon 5.
A legal assistant must disclose his or her status as a legal assistant at the outset of any professional relationship with a client, attorney, a court or administrative agency or personnel thereof, or a member of the general public. A legal assistant must act prudently in determining the extent to which a client may be assisted without the presence of an attorney.

Canon 6.
A legal assistant must strive to maintain integrity and a high degree of competency through education and training with respect to professional responsibility, local rules and practice, and through continuing education in substantive areas of law to better assist the legal profession in fulfilling its duty to provide legal service.

Canon 7.
A legal assistant must protect the confidences of a client and must not violate any rule or statute now in effect or hereafter enacted controlling privileged communications.

Canon 8.
A legal assistant must do all other things incidental, necessary, or expedient for the attainment of the ethics and responsibilities as defined by statute or rule of court.

Canon 9.
A legal assistant's conduct is guided by bar associations' codes of professional responsibility and rules of professional conduct.

benefits clients because the hourly rate for paralegals is, of course, substantially lower than that for attorneys.

For this reason, bar associations (and courts, when approving fees) encourage attorneys to delegate work to paralegals whenever feasible to lower the costs of legal services for clients—and thus provide the public with greater access to legal services. In fact, some courts, when determining awards of attorneys' fees, have refused to approve fees at the attorney's hourly rate for work that could have been performed by a paralegal at a lower rate.

NALA, the ABA, and many of the states have adopted guidelines for the utilization of paralegal services. These guidelines were created in response to a variety of questions concerning the role and function of paralegals within the legal arena that had arisen during the 1970s and 1980s, including the following: What are paralegals? What kinds of tasks do they perform? What are their professional responsibilities? How can attorneys best utilize paralegal services? What responsibilities should attorneys assume with respect to their assistants' work?

NALA'S MODEL STANDARDS AND GUIDELINES.   In 1984, NALA adopted its Model Standards and Guidelines for the Utilization of Legal Assistants. This document addresses and provides guidance on several issues of paramount importance to legal assistants today. It begins by listing the minimum qualifications that legal assistants should have and then, in a series of guidelines, indicates what legal assistants may and may not do. We will examine these guidelines in more detail shortly. (See Appendix B for the complete text of the annotated version of NALA's Model Standards and Guidelines, as revised in 1997.)

On the Web
NALA'S Model Standards and Guidelines are online at www.nala.org/stand.htm.

THE ABA'S MODEL GUIDELINES.   The ABA adopted its Model Guidelines for the Utilization of Legal Assistant Services in 1991. The ABA Standing Committee on Legal Assistants, which drafted the guidelines, based them on the NALA guidelines, various state codes and guidelines on the use of paralegals, and relevant state court decisions. The document consists of ten guidelines, each of which is followed by a lengthy comment on the derivation, scope, and application of the guideline. The ten guidelines are presented in Exhibit 3.4 on the next page. (For reasons of space, Exhibit 3.4 presents only the guidelines; for the comments, refer to the version of the Model Guidelines in Appendix D of this text.)

STATE GUIDELINES.   Over two-thirds of the states have adopted some form of guidelines concerning the use of legal assistants by attorneys, the respective responsibilities of attorneys and legal assistants in performing legal work, the types of tasks paralegals may perform, and other ethically challenging areas of legal practice. Although the guidelines of some states reflect the influence of NALA's standards and guidelines, the state guidelines focus largely on state statutory definitions of the practice of law, state codes of ethics regulating the responsibilities of attorneys, and state court decisions. As a paralegal, you should make sure that you become familiar with your state's guidelines.

The Increasing Scope of Paralegal Responsibilities

The ethical standards and guidelines just discussed, as well as court decisions concerning paralegals, all support the goal of increasing the use of paralegals in the delivery of legal services. Today, paralegals can perform virtually any legal task as long as the work is supervised by an attorney and does not constitute the unauthorized practice of law (to be discussed shortly). Guideline 2 of the ABA's Model Guidelines indicates the breadth of paralegal responsibilities:

EXHIBIT 3.4
**The ABA's Model Guidelines
for the Utilization of Legal
Assistant Services
(Comments Not Included)**

© 1999. Reprinted by permission of
the American Bar Association.
Annotations and commentary to
the Guidelines are not included in
this Exhibit. A copy of the
Guidelines with annotations and
commentary is available through
the ABA Legal Assistants
Department staff office.
Phone: (312) 988-5616;
Fax: (312) 988-5677;
E-mail: legalassts@abanet.org.

Guideline 1: A lawyer is responsible for all of the professional actions of a legal assistant performing legal assistant services at the lawyer's direction and should take reasonable measures to ensure that the legal assistant's conduct is consistent with the lawyer's obligations under the ABA Model Rules of Professional Conduct.

Guideline 2: Provided the lawyer maintains responsibility for the work product, a lawyer may delegate to a legal assistant any task normally performed by the lawyer except those tasks proscribed to one not licensed as a lawyer by statute, court rule, administrative rule or regulation, controlling authority, the ABA Model Rules of Professional Conduct, or these Guidelines.

Guideline 3: A lawyer may not delegate to a legal assistant:

(a) Responsibility for establishing an attorney-client relationship.
(b) Responsibility for establishing the amount of a fee to be charged for a legal service.
(c) Responsibility for a legal opinion rendered to a client.

Guideline 4: It is the lawyer's responsibility to take reasonable measures to ensure that clients, courts, and other lawyers are aware that a legal assistant, whose services are utilized by the lawyer in performing legal services, is not licensed to practice law.

Guideline 5: A lawyer may identify legal assistants by name and title on the lawyer's letterhead and on business cards identifying the lawyer's firm.

Guideline 6: It is the responsibility of a lawyer to take reasonable measures to ensure that all client confidences are preserved by a legal assistant.

Guideline 7: A lawyer should take reasonable measures to prevent conflicts of interest resulting from a legal assistant's other employment or interests insofar as such other employment or interests would present a conflict of interest if it were that of the lawyer.

Guideline 8: A lawyer may include a charge for the work performed by a legal assistant in setting a charge for legal services.

Guideline 9: A lawyer may not split legal fees with a legal assistant nor pay a legal assistant for the referral of legal business. A lawyer may compensate a legal assistant based on the quantity and quality of the legal assistant's work and the value of that work to a law practice, but the legal assistant's compensation may not be contingent, by advance agreement, upon the profitability of the lawyer's practice.

Guideline 10: A lawyer who employs a legal assistant should facilitate the legal assistant's participation in appropriate continuing education and *pro bono publico* activities.

Provided the lawyer maintains responsibility for the work product, a lawyer may delegate to a legal assistant any task normally performed by the lawyer except those tasks proscribed to one not licensed as a lawyer by statute, court rule, administrative rule or regulation, controlling authority, the ABA Model Rules of Professional Conduct, or these Guidelines.

Paralegals working for attorneys may interview clients and witnesses, investigate legal claims, draft legal documents for attorneys' signatures, attend will executions (in some states), appear at real-estate closings (in some states), and undertake numerous other types of legal work, as long as the work is supervised by attorneys. When state or federal law allows them to do so, paralegals can also represent clients before government agencies. Paralegals are allowed to perform freelance services for attorneys and, depending on state law and the type of service, perform limited independent services for the public.

Legal assistants are also permitted to give information to clients on many types of matters relating to a case or other legal matter. When arranging for client interviews, they let clients know what kind of information is needed and what documents to bring to the office. They inform clients about legal procedures and what the client should expect to experience during the progress of a legal proceeding. For example, in preparing for trial, legal assistants instruct clients on trial procedures, what they should wear to the trial, and so on. Clearly, as a legal assistant, you will be permitted to give clients all kinds of information. Nonetheless, you must make sure that you know where to draw the line between giving permissible types of advice and giving "legal advice"—advice that only attorneys are licensed to give under state laws.

The specific types of tasks that paralegals are legally permitted to undertake are described throughout this book; it would be impossible to list them all here. Generally, Guideline 2 of the ABA's Model Guidelines makes it clear that paralegals can engage in a wide spectrum of legal activities.

> **Apart from tasks that only attorneys can legally perform, paralegals may perform almost any type of legal work as long as the attorney authorizes the work and assumes responsibility for the paralegal's work product.**

As you can see from the ABA's guidelines, paralegals may not perform "tasks that only attorneys can legally perform." If they do so, they risk liability for the unauthorized practice of law—an important topic to which we now turn.

THE UNAUTHORIZED PRACTICE OF LAW

An awareness of what kinds of activities constitute the unauthorized practice of law (UPL) is vitally important for practicing paralegals. Paralegals judged to have engaged in the UPL may be subject to fines and possibly imprisonment. UPL actions are complicated by the fact that state statutes stipulating that only licensed attorneys can engage in the practice of law rarely indicate with any specificity what constitutes the "practice of law." For example, Ethical Consideration (EC) 3–5 to Canon 3 of the ABA's Model Code reads as follows:

> Functionally, the practice of law relates to the rendition of services for others that call for the professional judgment of a lawyer. The essence of the professional judgment of the lawyer is his educated ability to relate the general body and philosophy of law to a specific legal problem of a client.

Model Rule 5.5 is also vague on this issue. It essentially states that the practice of law varies from state to state, that restricting the practice of law to attorneys benefits the public interest, and that attorneys can delegate functions to paralegals as long as attorneys supervise the work and retain responsibility for it. Both the Model Code and the Model Rules also specifically prohibit lawyers from assisting in the "unauthorized practice of law."

Because of this lack of specificity with respect to what constitutes the practice of law, it is difficult to predict with certainty what type of action may constitute the "unauthorized" practice of law. Generally, though, state statutes regulating the practice of law, as well as court decisions concerning the authorized (and unauthorized) practice of law, indicate that certain types of activities, because they lie at the heart of the attorney-client relationship, can be performed *only* by attorneys. Otherwise stated, paralegals are prohibited from performing such activities. NALA's Model Standards and Guidelines summarize these prohibited activities in Guideline 2, which states that legal assistants should not perform any of the following actions:

- Establish attorney-client relationships.
- Set legal fees.
- Give legal opinions or advice.
- Represent a client before a court, unless authorized to do so by the court.
- Engage in, encourage, or contribute to any act which could constitute the unauthorized practice of law.

The first two activities in that list—establishing attorney-client relationships and setting legal fees—are fairly straightforward. The others, however, are less so and merit further discussion.

Giving Legal Opinions and Advice

Clearly, giving legal advice goes to the essence of legal practice. After all, a person would not seek out a legal expert if he or she did not want legal advice on some matter. Although a paralegal may communicate an attorney's legal advice to a client, the paralegal may not give legal advice.

You need to be extremely careful to avoid giving legal advice even when discussing matters with friends and relatives. Although other nonlawyers often give advice affecting others' legal rights or obligations, paralegals may not do so. For example, when an individual receives a speeding ticket, a friend or relative who is a nonlawyer might suggest that the person should argue the case before a judge and explain his or her side of the story. When a paralegal gives such advice, however, he or she may be accused of engaging in the unauthorized practice of law. Legal assistants are prohibited from giving even simple, common-sense advice because of the understandably greater weight given to the advice of someone who has legal training.

Similarly, you need to be cautious in the workplace. Although you may have developed great expertise in a certain area of law, you must refrain from advising clients with respect to their legal obligations or rights. For example, suppose that you are a bankruptcy specialist and know that a client who wants to petition for bankruptcy has two realistic options to pursue under bankruptcy law. Should you tell the client about these options and their consequences? No, you should not. In effect, advising someone of his or her legal options is very close to advising a person of his or her legal rights and may therefore—in the view of many courts, at least—constitute the practice of law. Also, even though you may qualify what you say by telling the client that he or she needs to check with an attorney, this does not alter the fact that you are giving advice on which the client might rely.

What constitutes the giving of legal advice is difficult to pin down. As you read earlier, paralegals are permitted to advise clients on a number of matters, and drawing the line between permissible and impermissible advice may at times be difficult. To be on the safe side (and avoid potential liability for the unauthorized practice of law), a good rule of thumb is the following:

    Never advise a client or other person on any matter if the advice may alter the legal position or legal rights of the one to whom the advice is given.

Whenever you are pressured to render legal advice—as you surely will be at one time or another, by your firm's clients or others—simply say that you cannot

On the Web
A good starting point for locating your state's UPL statute and UPL court cases is FindLaw's Web site at **www.findlaw. com/casecode/state.html.**

On the Web
For some tips on how to avoid the UPL, go to **www.paralegals.org/ Development/upl.html.**

give legal advice because it is against the law to do so. Paralegals usually find that this frank and honest statement provides an easy solution to the problem.

Representing Clients in Court

The rule that only attorneys—with limited exceptions—can represent others in court has a long history. Recall from the discussion of attorney regulation earlier in this chapter that attorney licensing was initially required only for court representation. In the last few decades, the ethical reasoning underlying this rule has been called into question by two developments.

First, in 1975 the United States Supreme Court held that people have a constitutional right to represent themselves in court.[8] Some people have questioned why a person can represent himself or herself in court but cannot hire a person more educated in the law to do so unless that person is a licensed attorney. Second, the fact that paralegals are allowed to represent clients before some federal and state government agencies, such as the federal Social Security Administration and state welfare departments, has called into question the ethical underpinnings of this rule. Nonetheless, as a paralegal you should know that you are not allowed to appear in court on behalf of your supervising attorney—although local courts in some states are carving out exceptions to this rule for limited purposes.

Disclosure of Paralegal Status

Because of the close working relationship between an attorney and a paralegal, a client may have difficulty perceiving that the paralegal is not also an attorney. For example, a client's call to an attorney may be transferred to the attorney's paralegal if the attorney is not in the office. The paralegal may assume that the client knows that he or she is not an attorney and may speak freely with the client about a legal matter, advising the client that the attorney will be in touch with the client shortly. The client, however, may assume that the paralegal is an attorney and may make inferences based on the paralegal's comments that result in actions with harmful consequences—in which event the paralegal might be charged with the unauthorized practice of law.

To avoid such problems, you should always do the following:

> **When dealing with clients or potential clients, disclose your paralegal status to ensure that they realize that you are a paralegal and not an attorney.**

Similarly, in correspondence with clients or others, you should indicate your nonattorney status by adding "Paralegal" or "Legal Assistant" after your name. If you have printed business cards or if your name is included in the firm's letterhead or other literature, also make sure that your nonlawyer status is clearly indicated.

Guideline 1 of NALA's Model Standards and Guidelines emphasizes the importance of the disclosure of paralegal status by stating that all legal assistants have an ethical responsibility to "[d]isclose their status as legal assistants at the outset of any professional relationship with a client, other attorneys, a court or administrative agency or personnel thereof, or members of the general public." Disciplinary Rule 1.7 of NPFA's Model Code of Ethics and Professional Responsibility also stresses the importance of disclosing paralegal status. Guideline 4 of the ABA's

---

8. *Faretta v. California,* 422 U.S. 806, 95 S.Ct. 2525, 45 L.Ed.2d 562 (1975).

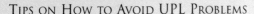

DEVELOPING PARALEGAL SKILLS
Avoiding UPL Problems

Jenna Martin, a paralegal, is attending a client's holiday party. She is the first person from her firm to arrive at the party. As she enters the room, Mr. Holbrook, the president of the company, introduces himself to Jenna. She responds, saying, "It's nice to meet you. I'm Jenna Martin, with the firm of Atkins & White." Assuming that Jenna is an attorney, Holbrook begins to ask her for legal advice about a tax problem that the company is having. Jenna now needs to take action to avoid the unauthorized practice of law.

TIPS ON HOW TO AVOID UPL PROBLEMS

• Always introduce yourself as a paralegal, or legal assistant.

• Always include your title when signing letters or other documents.

• Make sure that your nonattorney status is clearly indicated on business cards and company letterhead.

• Always disclose your status to a court or other tribunal.

• If a client does not understand your role, explain it. Make it clear that paralegals may not give legal advice.

• Refer the client to an attorney for legal advice.

Model Guidelines places on attorneys the responsibility for disclosing the nonattorney status of paralegals:

> It is the lawyer's responsibility to take reasonable measures to ensure that clients, courts, and other lawyers are aware that a legal assistant, whose services are utilized by the lawyer in performing legal services, is not licensed to practice law.

Paralegals Freelancing for Attorneys

Some paralegals have their own businesses and work as freelance paralegals for attorneys, as you learned in the previous chapter. In the early 1990s, there was some concern over whether freelance paralegals were, by definition, sufficiently supervised by attorneys to avoid liability for the unauthorized practice of law. In a landmark decision in 1992, the New Jersey Supreme Court stated that it could find no reason why freelance paralegals could not be just as adequately supervised by the attorneys for whom they worked as those paralegals working in attorneys' offices. Since that decision, courts in several other states and ethical opinions issued by various state bar associations have held that freelance paralegals who are adequately supervised by attorneys are not engaging in the unauthorized practice of law.

In its opinion, the New Jersey Supreme Court also called for the establishment of a Committee on Paralegal Education and Regulation to study the practice of paralegals and make recommendations to the court. The committee's report, submitted to the court in 1998, recommended that paralegals in New Jersey should be subject to state licensing requirements. This recommendation has caused widespread debate among legal professionals in New Jersey and elsewhere—as you will read shortly.

Freelance Paralegal

DOROTHY SECOL *has worked in the legal profession for over thirty years and has been a freelance paralegal since 1982. She maintains an office in Allenhurst, New Jersey. Secol is a graduate of Monmouth University, West Long Branch, New Jersey.*

Secol is a member of the National Association of Legal Assistants (NALA) and received her CLA status in 1978. In addition, she is a former trustee of the Central Jersey Paralegal Association and a former vice president and trustee of the Legal Assistants Association of New Jersey. She is also an associate member of the New Jersey State Bar Association and serves on its Paralegal Committee and Foreclosure Committee. She is also on the Paralegal Advisory Boards of Brookdale Community College and Ocean County College. Secol is also a mediator for three courts in her area.

Secol is the author of Starting and Managing Your Own Business: A Freelancing Guide for Paralegals, *published by Aspen Publishing Company, and has written articles for the* New Jersey Law Journal *and* New Jersey Lawyer. *In addition, Secol was a petitioner in the case of* In re Opinion 24 of the Committee on the Unauthorized Practice of Law, *128 N.J. 114 (1992). In that case, the court held that "there is no distinguishable difference between an in-house and freelance paralegal working under the direct supervision of an attorney."*

What do you like best about your work?

"The aspect I like most about my work is the creativity. Whether it's defining an issue and then researching it, writing an argument to oppose or support your position, drafting a contract or a pleading, or working up a file, I am using my intellect and judgment. I love the fact that the law changes constantly—no day is ever the same. There is never any boredom to contend with, and you constantly have to be on your toes to keep up with the changes.

"I love the excitement of running a business. The entrepreneurial aspect of being a freelance paralegal has allowed me the opportunity to grow and to learn how to be a businessperson as well as a paralegal. I have to deal with employees, vendors, clients, and suppliers, as well as provide for insurance, office equipment, advertising, marketing, technology, and much, much more. The flexibility of being in business has allowed me to spend time with my family when needed. I have had a chance to meet people from all over, to learn how different attorneys tackle problems, and to learn from different experiences. Working for many attorneys at one time gives you a different perspective than you would have if you worked for one attorney or for attorneys in one firm with a specific ideology."

What is the greatest challenge that you face in your area of work?

"The greatest challenge I have is consistently providing excellent services, maintaining professionalism at all times, and producing a product for the attorney that is as near perfect as it can get. Attorneys use the services of a freelance paralegal because they are short staffed, they do not have personnel with knowledge in a certain area of substantive law, or someone on their staff is on vacation or taking sick leave. It is up to me to ensure that the product they receive is perfect; otherwise, they don't need us. We must provide a better service than they are used to. Our services are our marketing tools."

What advice do you have for would-be paralegals in your area of work?

"Freelancing is not for the recent college graduate or someone with one or two years of experience; it is for the seasoned, experienced paralegal. To freelance, you must have a certain business acumen. Freelancing is more than just being a paralegal; it means running a business, whether it is out of your house or out of an office. You must have a certain temperament and personality. Some of the necessary characteristics are: (1) you must be a perfectionist—you are committed to be the very best you can be and you are not afraid of meeting change or of being different; (2) you must be a risk taker—you have to look for opportunities where your services are needed, and you also must learn to create a need where there was none before; (3) you must have a positive attitude and a good self-image, and you must know that you can do the job; and (4) you must have the necessary skills in order to be successful, which means being up to date on your market areas and

PARALEGAL PROFILE   # Freelance Paralegal *Continued*

> **"Freelancing is more than just being a paralegal; it means running a business . . . . "**

your areas of substantive law, as well as having the very latest knowledge on which to base your business decisions (including knowledge of new technology, equipment, and so forth)."

What are some tips for success as a paralegal in your area of work?

"You must have a quality program for your services. Offer services above and beyond that which are required, and make your service indispensable. You should also know your market and your competition. If you are a real-estate paralegal, be sure you are in an area where there is a need for those services. Choose your areas of substantive law based on your expertise, and then market them to those attorneys that will need your services. Additionally, you should establish goals. Be sure to have a business plan in place. Know where you want to be and how you expect to get there. You also need to plan your finances carefully. You will not have a weekly paycheck. Be sure you have enough capitalization to tide you over until your business picks up enough for you to meet all your financial obligations. Remember, you are now in business and will have certain responsibilities to meet, such as buying and maintaining equipment, supplies, rent, insurance, and subscriptions."

Independent Paralegals and the UPL

As mentioned in Chapter 2, independent paralegals (also called legal technicians) provide "self-help" legal services directly to the public. Since the 1970s, when these types of services began to spring up around the country, the courts have had to wrestle with questions such as the following: If an independent paralegal advises a customer on what forms are necessary to obtain a simple, uncontested divorce, how those forms should be filed with the court, how the court hearing should be scheduled, and so on, do those activities constitute the practice of law?

Generally, the mere dissemination of legal information does not constitute the unauthorized practice of law. There is a fine line, however, between the dissemination of legal information (by providing legal forms to a customer, for example) and giving legal advice (which may consist of merely selecting the forms that best suit the customer's needs)—and the courts do not always agree on just where this line should be drawn.

EARLY CASES.   An early case on this issue was *The Florida Bar v. Brumbaugh,*[9] which was decided in 1978 by the Florida Supreme Court. The case was brought by The Florida Bar against Ms. Brumbaugh, who prepared legal documents for people who sought a simple, uncontested divorce. Brumbaugh prepared all the necessary court documents and told her customers how to file the documents with the court, how to schedule the court hearings, and—in a conference the day before the hearing—what would occur at the hearing.

---

9. 355 So.2d 1186 (Fla. 1978).

The Florida Bar claimed that Brumbaugh was engaging in the practice of law in violation of the state's UPL statute. The Florida Supreme Court held that Brumbaugh could sell legal forms and other printed information regarding divorces and other legal procedures, that she could fill in the forms as long as the customer provided the information in writing, and that she could advertise her services. She could not, however, advise customers of their legal rights; tell them which forms should be used, how they should be filled out, and where to file them; or tell them how to present their cases in court.

A year later, the same court decided *The Florida Bar v. Furman*,[10] which involved a woman who performed legal services very similar to those performed by Brumbaugh. The court held that the woman, Ms. Furman, had engaged in the unauthorized practice of law by failing to comply with the decision in *Brumbaugh*. The *Furman* case received substantial publicity when Ms. Furman disobeyed a later *injunction* (a court order to cease engaging in the prohibited activities) and was sentenced to prison for **contempt of court** (failing to cooperate with a court order).

AN ONGOING PROBLEM.   Independent paralegals continue to face UPL allegations against them brought by bar associations and others. In 1995, an Oregon independent paralegal, Robin Smith, was taken to court by the Oregon State Bar for engaging in the UPL. The trial court agreed with the bar association that Smith's activities constituted the practice of law and thus violated the state's UPL statute. The court stated that "the practice of law includes the drafting or selection of documents and the giving of advice in regard thereto any time an informed or trained discretion must be exercised in the selection or drafting of a document to meet the needs of the persons being served." The court ordered Smith to cease conducting her business activities, and the decision was upheld on appeal.[11]

In 1998, a UPL case was under way in California against a number of independent paralegals. The case was settled after the California legislature passed Senate Bill 1418, which provided that independent paralegals—referred to as "Legal Document Assistants" in the bill—could perform only certain types of services (generally, assist clients in filling out legal forms) and not others. The settlement incorporated the restrictions set forth in Senate Bill 1418.

Notably, even Nolo Press, the well-known publisher of self-help law books, has been under attack for the UPL. An official Texas UPL committee, acting on behalf of the Texas Supreme Court, claimed that Nolo Press, merely by publishing self-help law publications in Texas, violated the Texas UPL statute. (Texas is the only state that prohibits publishers of such books from selling them in its state.) The committee would not disclose which Nolo books were involved—or any other information Nolo asked for—because of an apparent requirement that the committee keep all information confidential. Nolo requested the Texas Supreme Court to order the committee to open up the process. As of early 1999, the Texas Supreme Court had not yet ruled on this matter. According to Nolo Press, the Texas state bar association was also planning to create a committee to review the methods used by the Texas UPL committee.

Generally, unless a state statute or rule specifically allows paralegals to directly assist the public without the supervision of an attorney, paralegals should be wary of engaging in such practices. Because the consequences of violating state UPL statutes can be so serious, we cannot emphasize enough the following advice:

Contempt of Court
The intentional obstruction or frustration of the court's attempt to administer justice. A party to a lawsuit may be held in contempt of court (punishable by a fine or jail sentence) for refusing to comply with a court's order.

On the Web
Nolo Press has placed all of the documents it has produced in response to the Texas UPL Committee's charges on its Web site. If you are interested in reading this information, go to **www.nolo.com/texas**.

---

10. 376 So.2d 378 (Fla. 1979).
11. *Oregon State Bar v. Smith*, 149 Or.App. 171, 942 P.2d 793 (1997).

ETHICAL CONCERN

Saying "If I were you . . ." and the UPL

Any time that a paralegal, in responding to someone concerned about legal rights, says, "If I were you, I would . . . ," the paralegal is, in effect, giving legal advice—and engaging in the unauthorized practice of law. For example, assume that a client calls your law office, and you take the call. The client, Mrs. Rabe, is an older woman who is very upset about the fact that an insurance company did not pay on a $1,000 life insurance policy that she had purchased covering the life of her grandson, who had just died. Mrs. Rabe tells you all of the details, and even though you feel she might win a lawsuit against the insurance company, it would probably cost her a lot more than $1,000 in the process. Mrs. Rabe wants to know if your supervising attorney will see her about the case, and when you tell her the attorney is out of town, she presses you for advice. Finally, you say, "Well, if I were you, I'd take the case to small claims court. You would not have to hire an attorney, it would be less costly, and you might recover some of the money." What the paralegal did not tell Mrs. Rabe is that if she sues the insurance company, she might win not just the $1,000 payment but also substantial punitive damages for the insurance company's wrongful behavior—and possibly have benefited by other penalties imposed under the state's insurance statute.

 Any paralegal who contemplates working as an independent paralegal must thoroughly investigate the relevant state laws and court decisions on UPL before offering any services directly to the public and must rigorously abide by the letter of the law.

SHOULD PARALEGALS BE LICENSED?

One of the major issues facing legal professionals and other interested groups today is whether paralegals should be subject to direct regulation by the state through licensing requirements. Unlike certification, which was discussed in Chapter 1, licensing involves direct and mandatory regulation, by the state, of an occupational or professional group. When licensing requirements are established for a professional group, such as for attorneys, a license is required before a member of the group can practice his or her profession.

Much of the impetus toward paralegal regulation has been fueled by the activities of independent paralegals, or legal technicians—those who provide legal services directly to the public without attorney supervision. Many independents call themselves paralegals even though they have little, if any, legal training, background, or experience. Yet at the same time, those who cannot afford to hire an attorney can benefit by the self-help services provided by paralegals who do have training and experience.

General versus Limited Licensing

A number of states—most prominently, New Jersey, Utah, Wisconsin, California, New York, Texas, and Minnesota—have considered implementing a **general licensing** program. A general licensing program would require all paralegals to

General Licensing
A type of licensing in which all individuals within a specific profession or group (such as paralegals) must meet licensing requirements imposed by the state before they may legally practice their profession.

meet certain educational requirements and other specified criteria before being allowed to practice their profession.

For example, New Jersey is considering recommendations by the New Jersey Supreme Court Committee on Paralegal Education and Regulation that would require paralegals to be licensed to practice their profession. The committee's report and its recommendations, which are the most detailed ever devised by a state body on the topic, propose that paralegals be subject to state licensure based on demonstrated educational requirements and knowledge of the ethical rules governing the legal profession. If these recommendations are adopted by the New Jersey Supreme Court, they will become law in that state, and other states may look to the New Jersey scheme for guidance. In other words, what happens in New Jersey could have a significant impact on paralegal practice throughout the country.

The Utah state bar association has issued a report recommending mandatory licensure that includes passing the CLA exam. A number of other states, including Wisconsin, are also recommending licensing programs for paralegals.

As an alternative to general licensing, over half the states are considering **limited licensing**, which would limit licensing requirements to those paralegals (independent paralegals, or legal technicians) who wish to provide specified legal services directly to the public. With limited licensing, qualified paralegals would be authorized to handle routine legal services traditionally rendered only by attorneys, such as advising clients on simple divorces, will executions, bankruptcy petitions, incorporation, real-estate transactions, selected tax matters, and other specified services as designated by the state licensing body. Already, at least twenty-two states allow some form of limited nonlawyer practice, and some states would like to establish a regulatory mechanism—such as a limited licensing program—to protect the consumers of these services.

On the Web
The entire report issued by the New Jersey Supreme Court Committee on Paralegal Education and Regulation, including its recommendations for the licensure of New Jersey paralegals, can be downloaded from the following Web site: **www.state.nj.us/judiciary/ index.html.**

Limited Licensing
A type of licensing in which a limited number of individuals within a specific profession or group (such as independent paralegals within the paralegal profession) must meet licensing requirements imposed by the state before those individuals may legally practice their profession.

Direct Regulation—The Pros and Cons

A significant part of the debate over direct regulation has to do with the issue of who should do the regulating. Certainly, state bar associations and government authorities would want to have a say in the matter. Yet paralegal organizations and educators, such as NALA, NFPA, and the American Association for Paralegal Education (AAfPE), would also want to play a leading role in developing the education requirements, ethical standards, and disciplinary procedures required by a licensing program.

The problem is, NALA, NFPA, and the AAfPE have different views on these matters. Furthermore, as you learned in Chapter 1, these organizations have not adopted a uniform definition of a paralegal—the definitions vary from one organization to another. Until legal professionals can agree on a definition of the term *paralegal,* it will be difficult to regulate the paralegal profession in a way that is acceptable to the majority of the group being regulated—paralegals.

NFPA's Position.   NFPA endorses the regulation of the paralegal profession on a state-by-state basis insofar as regulation expands the utilization of paralegals to deliver cost-efficient legal services. If it can be demonstrated that there is a public need for lower-cost legal services, NFPA is in favor of the regulation of paralegals, providing the paralegals meet certain minimum criteria.

NFPA contends that the licensing of paralegals would accomplish several goals. First, attorneys and the public would benefit because only demonstrably qualified paralegals would be licensed to practice the profession. Second, attorneys' search costs in finding competent assistance would be reduced. Third, the licensing of paralegals would be a step forward in the development of the paralegal profession. Fourth, licensing would permit paralegals to legally perform specified tasks, and therefore they would not be at risk for the unauthorized practice of law to the extent they are today. And finally, the licensing of paralegals would give consumers greater access to low-cost legal assistance for routine legal matters. NFPA argues that the latter issue (access to legal services) provides a compelling reason to expand the role of paralegals.

NFPA proposes a two-tiered system of licensing: general licensing and specialty licensing. General licensing by a state board or agency would require all paralegals within the state to satisfy stipulated requirements in regard to education, experience, and continuing education; it would also subject practicing paralegals to disciplinary procedures by the licensing body. (As mentioned, NFPA has already developed a set of model enforcement guidelines, which were appended to its code of ethics in 1997—see Appendix C.) Specialty licensing would require paralegals who wish to practice in a specialized area to demonstrate, by an examination (see the discussion of the PACE examination in Chapter 1), their proficiency in that area.

As to the regulatory developments in New Jersey, NFPA has taken the position that the requirements suggested by the New Jersey Supreme Court Committee on Paralegal Education and Regulation are a positive development for the paralegal profession. The requirements will help to weed out the "bad apples" in the profession—including those who call themselves paralegals but do not have the necessary education or experience to practice competently and those who violate UPL statutes. According to Laurel Bielec, a past vice president of NFPA, the New Jersey requirements have "the potential to fulfill the hopes of those in the profession that paralegal regulation will finally allow paralegals to provide the legal services they are competent to perform."[12]

NALA'S POSITION.   While NALA supports voluntary certification, it believes that imposing licensing requirements on paralegals would be premature. Currently, paralegals perform a wide range of tasks and work in a variety of settings. In NALA's opinion, to impose mandatory, uniform requirements on a group of professionals whose function is not yet sufficiently defined would limit paralegal opportunities, closing the door to those paralegals who could not meet the requirements for licensing and prohibiting activities that paralegals are currently authorized to undertake.

NALA looks at certification and the development of paralegal education programs as being, at least at this point in time, a reasonable alternative to licensing. NALA emphasizes that most paralegals work under the supervision of attorneys and are thus already subject to regulation via attorney codes. NALA takes the position that the licensure recommendations issued by the New Jersey Supreme Court Committee on Paralegal Education and Regulation, if adopted by the New Jersey Supreme Court, would be harmful to the growth of the profession. The regulatory scheme would not allow paralegals to qualify for employment in New Jersey based on experience alone. Rather, under the proposed rules, only those who completed an ABA-approved educational program would be able to obtain a

---

12. Laurel Bielec, "A Giant Leap towards Regulation: What's Going on in New Jersey, and How Could It Affect You?" *Legal Assistant Today,* November/December 1998, pp. 12–15.

license to practice their profession in New Jersey. According to NALA, this would curb competition in paralegal education as well.[13]

NALA's objections to specific limited licensing proposals for independent paralegals (legal technicians) do not reflect opposition to the idea of limited licensing for independent paralegals so much as disagreement with specific aspects of the proposed regulatory schemes.

THE AAFPE'S POSITION.   The major concern of the American Association for Paralegal Education (AAfPE) is that paralegals and paralegal educators should have some kind of a voice in determining the educational and ethical requirements that would be required for a licensing program. This prospect is dimmed by the competition between NALA and NFPA, which have conflicting views on significant issues facing the profession, ranging from the definition of a paralegal to the educational standards that paralegals should meet. According to Diane Petropulos, a former president of the AAfPE, these competing paralegal organizations need to put forth a unified front if paralegals are to have any influence over the future regulation of the profession. Otherwise, by default, the decision will not be theirs to make. In an article published in *Legal Assistant Today,* Petropulos stated, "We have our own profession to craft and significant contributions to make, but we must close the gap between NALA and NFPA to effectively set standards."[14]

On the Web
For updates on the positions taken by NFPA, NALA, and the AAfPE on regulation, as well as regulatory developments, check their Web sites: for NFPA, www.paralegals.org; for NALA, www.nala.org; for the AAfPE: www.aafpe.org.

Other Considerations

While the positions taken by NFPA, NALA, and the AAfPE outline the main contours of the debate over regulation, other groups emphasize some different considerations. For example, one of the concerns of lawyers is that if independent paralegals are licensed—through limited licensing programs—to deliver low-cost services directly to the public, this would cut into the business (and profits) of law firms. Many lawyers are also concerned that if paralegals are subject to mandatory licensing requirements, law firms will not be able to hire and train persons of their choice to become paralegals.

Some paralegals and paralegal associations are concerned that mandatory licensing would require all paralegals to be "generalists." As it is, a large number of paralegals specialize in particular areas, such as bankruptcy or family law, and do not need to have the broad knowledge of all areas of paralegal practice that licensing might require.

A FINAL NOTE

As a professional paralegal, you will have an opportunity to voice your opinion on whether paralegals should be directly regulated by state governments and, if so, what qualifications should be required before a license to practice your profession will be granted. Keep in mind, though, that all of the issues discussed in this chapter are directly relevant to your paralegal career. The most important

---

13. For further details on NALA's response to the New Jersey proposed regulatory scheme, see "Special Report: Executive Summary: NALA Statement re Report of the New Jersey Supreme Court Committee on Paralegal Education and Regulation," *NALA Newsletter,* Fall 1998, pp. 4–7.
14. "Who's in Charge?" *Legal Assistant Today,* January/February 1999, pp. 14–15.

TODAY'S PROFESSIONAL PARALEGAL

Working for the Attorney Discipline Board

Denise James is a legal assistant who works for the Attorney Discipline Board in her state. She has an interesting job that entails a variety of responsibilities. One of Denise's job responsibilities is to contact attorneys to sit on the Attorney Discipline Board's hearing panel. She consults the list of attorneys who have volunteered to sit on the panel and calls them to make arrangements for the hearing panels. She forwards to them background information and briefs on the cases that they will hear. On the day of the hearing, she meets the attorneys, escorts them to the hearing room, provides them with hearing examiners' robes, and assists them in getting the hearing started.

PREPARING "NOTICES OF DISCIPLINE"

Another of Denise's duties is to prepare the "Notices of Discipline" that are published every month in the state bar association journal, which is a monthly publication that is sent to all licensed attorneys in the state. These notices identify which attorneys have been subject to disciplinary actions and for what reasons. To prepare this month's notices, Denise pulls out all of the "final orders of discipline" that were entered this month. Then she reads through and summarizes each order.

SUMMARIZING DISCIPLINARY PROCEEDINGS

Denise reads through a final order sanctioning an attorney. The attorney, who commingled a client's funds with her own personal funds, was suspended. The funds involved consisted of a check in the settlement of a personal-injury lawsuit. The attorney deposited the check to her personal checking account and then used the money to pay her monthly bills. She did not issue a check to the client for the money until three months later. The client continually called the attorney's office and demanded the settlement check. The attorney kept stalling and then simply refused to return the client's phone calls.

Denise then summarized the disciplinary proceedings against the attorney as follows: "[attorney's name], P12345, Binghamton, by Attorney Discipline Board, Binghamton County, Hearing Panel #6, effective June 3, 2000. Respondent commingled client's funds by using the client's money, received in a settlement, to pay her personal bills, then paid the client three months later. The hearing panel found respondent's conduct to be in violation of Court Rule 1.15 and the state Rules of Professional Conduct. A suspension was issued and costs were assessed in the amount of $751.53."

There is never a dull moment working for the Attorney Discipline Board. The unfortunate part is that Denise sees many cases in which clients have lost legal rights because their cases were neglected for a variety of reasons.

---

point to remember as you embark on a paralegal career is that you need to think and act in a professionally responsible manner in your particular workplace. Although this takes time and practice, in the legal arena there is little room for learning ethics by "trial and error." Therefore, you need to be especially attentive to the ethical rules governing attorneys and paralegal practice discussed in this chapter.

The *Ethical Concerns* throughout this book will offer further insights into some of the ethical problems that can arise in various areas of paralegal performance. Understanding how violations can occur will help you anticipate and guard against them as you begin your paralegal career. Once on the job, you can continue your preventive tactics by asking questions whenever you are in doubt and by making sure that your work is adequately supervised.

⬚ KEY TERMS AND CONCEPTS

attorney-client privilege   80

breach   75

conflict of interest   83

conflicts check   86

contempt of court   101

damages   74

disbarment   72

ethical wall   84

general licensing   102

licensing   71

limited licensing   103

malpractice   74

reprimand   72

self-regulation   69

suspension   72

third parties   79

unauthorized practice of
    law (UPL)   71

work product   82

⬚ CHAPTER SUMMARY

1. The legal profession is regulated by licensing requirements and ethical rules adopted and enforced by state authorities. The purpose of attorney regulation is to protect the public against incompetent legal professionals and unethical attorney behavior. Key participants in the regulation of attorneys are state bar associations, state supreme courts, state legislatures, the United States Supreme Court (occasionally), and the American Bar Association, which establishes model rules and guidelines relating to attorney conduct to be adopted by the various states.

2. Most states have adopted a version of either the 1969 Model Code of Professional Responsibility or the 1983 revision of the Model Code, called the Model Rules of Professional Conduct, both of which were published by the American Bar Association. The majority of the states have adopted the Model Rules. The Model Code and Model Rules spell out the ethical and professional duties governing attorneys and the practice of law. Attorneys who violate the duties imposed by these rules may be subject to sanctions in the form of a reprimand, a suspension, or a disbarment. Additionally, attorneys (as well as paralegals) are subject to potential liability for malpractice or for violations of criminal statutes.

3. Some of the ethical rules governing attorney behavior pose particularly difficult problems for paralegals. One of the most frequently violated rules is the duty of competence. This duty is violated whenever a client suffers harm as a result of the attorney's incompetent action or inaction. Breaching the duty of competence may lead to a lawsuit against the attorney (and perhaps the paralegal) for negligence.

4. Another ethical pitfall for paralegals is inadvertently breaching the rule of confidentiality. The confidentiality rule requires that all information relating to a client's representation must be kept in confidence and not revealed to third parties who are not authorized to know the information. Some client information is regarded as privileged information. An attorney may reveal privileged information only if the client consents, if a court orders the attorney to reveal the information, or in special circumstances, as when revealing the information is necessary to protect another from bodily harm or death. Paralegals need to constantly guard against revealing confidential information to third parties both on and off the job.

5. Attorneys are prohibited from representing a client if the attorney's representation of that client will adversely affect the interests of another client, including former clients. An attorney may represent both sides in a legal proceeding only if the attorney feels that neither party's rights will be adversely affected and only if both clients are aware of the conflict of interest and consent to the representation. Paralegals also fall under this rule. If a firm is handling a case that one of the firm's attorneys or paralegals cannot work on, owing to a conflict of interest, that attorney or paralegal must be "walled off" from the case—that is, prevented from having any access to files or other information relating to the case. Normally, whenever a prospective client consults with an attorney, a conflicts check is done to ensure that if the attorney or firm accepts the case, no conflict of interest will exist.

6. Paralegals are regulated indirectly by attorney ethical rules, by ethical codes created by paralegal professional associations, and by guidelines on the utilization of paralegals, which define the status and function of paralegals and the scope of their

authorized activities. The American Bar Association and several states have also adopted guidelines on the utilization of paralegals. These codes and guidelines provide paralegals, attorneys, and the courts with guidance on the paralegal's role in the practice of law.

7. Court decisions, state attorney ethical rules, paralegal ethical codes and guidelines, and the guidelines on the use of legal assistants that have been adopted by the American Bar Association and several states all express a general consensus that paralegals, under attorneys' supervision, may perform virtually any legal task that attorneys can, with five exceptions. A paralegal may not (1) establish an attorney-client relationship, (2) set the fees to be charged for an attorney's services, (3) give legal advice or opinions, (4) represent a client in court (with some exceptions), or (5) engage in the unauthorized practice of law.

8. The fact that both paralegals working for attorneys and independent paralegals engage in work that traditionally only attorneys have performed raises concerns about the unauthorized practice of law. Lawsuits against independent paralegals, particularly,

focused attention on the unauthorized practice of law. Determining what constitutes the unauthorized practice of law is complicated by the fact that state UPL statutes generally offer only vague or very broad definitions of what constitutes the practice of law. Generally, the paralegal must be extremely cautious when contemplating the possibility of working without attorney supervision.

9. A major concern today for both legal professionals and the public is whether paralegals should be directly regulated by the state through licensing requirements. General licensing would establish minimum standards that every paralegal would have to meet in order to practice as a paralegal in the state. Limited licensing would require paralegals wishing to offer routine legal services directly to the public in certain areas, such as family law and bankruptcy law, to demonstrate their proficiency in that area. The pros and cons of direct regulation through licensing are being debated vigorously by the leading paralegal and paralegal education associations, state bar associations, state courts, state legislatures, and public-interest groups.

QUESTIONS FOR REVIEW

1. Why is the legal profession regulated? Who are the regulators? How is regulation accomplished?

2. What are the two primary sets of ethical rules that guide the legal profession in the United States? Who created these rules?

3. How is the paralegal profession regulated by attorney ethical codes?

4. What does the duty of competence involve? How can violations of the duty of competence be avoided?

5. What is the attorney-client privilege? What is its relationship to the rule of confidentiality? What are some potential consequences of violating the confidentiality rule?

6. What is a conflict of interest? How do law firms "wall off" an attorney or a paralegal when a conflict of interest exists?

7. How is the paralegal profession regulated by paralegal codes of ethics? Why have model guidelines been established on the utilization of paralegals?

8. What types of tasks may legally be performed by paralegals? What types of tasks may normally be performed only by attorneys?

9. What is the practice of law? What is the unauthorized practice of law (UPL)? How might paralegals violate state statutes prohibiting the UPL?

10. What would the general licensing of paralegals involve? What is limited licensing? What are some of the pros and cons in the debate over paralegal licensing?

ETHICAL QUESTIONS

1. Anton Snow, a paralegal, has been asked to research the cases decided by courts in his state to see if he can find a case in which a landlord was held liable for crimes caused by a third party (someone other than

the landlord or the tenant) on leased premises. Anton finds a case in which the trial court held that a landlord was liable for harms suffered by a plaintiff when she was mugged and robbed in an apartment complex's parking lot. Anton does not take the time to update the case. He therefore fails to find out that the state court of appeals later reversed the trial court's decision. Thus, the trial court's decision, which Anton gives to his supervising attorney, is no longer "good law." The supervising attorney, relying on Anton's research, advises the client accordingly. Discuss the potential problems that the client, the attorney, and Anton might face as a result of Anton's failure to update the trial court's decision.

2. Norma Sollers works as a paralegal for a small law firm. She is a trusted, experienced employee who has worked for the firm for twelve years. One morning, Linda Lowenstein, one of the attorneys, calls in from her home and asks Norma to sign Linda's name to a document that must be filed with the court that day. Norma had just prepared the final draft of the docu-

ment and placed it on Linda's desk for her review and signature. Linda explains to Norma that because her child is sick, she does not want to leave home to come into the office. Norma knows that she should not sign Linda's name—only the client's attorney can sign the document. She mentions this to Linda, but Linda says, "Don't worry. No one will ever know that you signed it instead of me." How should Norma handle this situation?

3. Matthew Hinson is an independent paralegal. He provides divorce forms and typing and filing services to the public at very low rates. Samantha Eggleston uses his services. She returns with the forms filled out, but she has one question: How much in monthly child-support payments will she be entitled to receive? How may Matthew legally respond to this question?

PRACTICE QUESTIONS AND ASSIGNMENTS

1. Kathryn Borstein works as a legal assistant for the legal department of a large manufacturing corporation. In the process of interviewing a middle-management accountant with the company relating to an employment discrimination lawsuit, Kathryn discovers that a few of the top executives cheat on their income tax returns by not declaring a portion of their bonuses. Kathryn becomes disenchanted with her job with the corporation for these and other reasons and finds a new job with a law firm. Her supervising attorney in the new law firm is involved in a case against her former employer. The attorney tells Kathryn that the only way to deal with these big corporations is to get whatever dirt you can on them and then threaten to go to the press. He wants to know if she can give him any such information. Can she tell him the "dirt" about the executives who cheat on their income taxes? Why or why not? What ethical rules are involved in her decision?

2. Peter Smith, a paralegal, is using the Internet to find property tax records for a client. The client has come to the firm because he wants to buy a parcel of property, but he also wants to make sure that the property taxes have been paid. Peter finds a Web site for the county register of deeds. He locates the property and notes that, according to the information given on the Web page, the taxes have been paid. He prints the page and writes a brief memo to the attorney. The attorney then advises the client that the taxes have been paid and that it is okay to go ahead and purchase the property. The client does so, but several

weeks later he receives a notice that he owes $6,500 in back taxes. The client, who is understandably upset, complains to Peter's boss. Peter is sent to the county register of deeds to look up the records relating to the property. Peter finds that the correct information was in the county's records but was not on the Web site. He makes a copy of what he finds and returns to the office. What ethical rule has been violated here? What do these "facts" reveal about the reliability of information posted on the Internet?

3. In which of the following instances may confidential client information be disclosed?

   a. During an emotional divorce trial, the client suffers a nervous breakdown and admits herself to the psychiatric ward of the local hospital. Her nervous breakdown will strengthen her case.

   b. A client's daughter calls to find out whether her mother has left her certain property in her will. The mother does not want the daughter to know that the daughter has been disinherited until the will is read after the mother's death.

   c. The client in a divorce case threatens to hire a hit man to kill her husband because she perceives that killing her husband is the only way that she can stop him from stalking her. It is clear that the client intends to do this.

   d. A former client sues her attorney for legal malpractice in the handling of a breach of contract case involving her cosmetics home-sale business.

The attorney discloses that the client is having an affair with her next-door neighbor, a fact that is unrelated to the malpractice or breach of contract case.

4. According to this chapter's text, which of the following tasks may a paralegal legally perform?

   a. Draft a complaint at an attorney's request.

   b. Interview a witness to a car accident.

   c. Represent a client before an administrative agency.

   d. Investigate the facts of a car-accident case.

   e. Work as a freelance paralegal for attorneys.

   f. Work as an independent paralegal providing legal services directly to the public.

5. Review the facts in Ethical Question 3. What do the following ethical codes say about the unauthorized practice of law, and how would these statements apply to Hinson's situation? Could Hinson be disciplined if he gives Samantha the information she requested?

   a. NFPA's Model Code of Ethics and Professional Responsibility (see Appendix C or visit NFPA's Web site at **www.paralegals.org**).

   b. NALA's Code of Ethics and Professional Responsibility (see Appendix A or visit NALA's Web site at **www.nala.org**).

   Do your answers differ? If so, how?

▣ USING INTERNET RESOURCES

1. Go to **www.paralegals.org**, the home page for the National Federation of Paralegal Associations (NFPA). Click on the box titled "Professional Development," which will take you to a page that lists, among other things, "NFPA Informal Ethics and Disciplinary Opinions" on various issues. Then do the following:

   a. List five issues that NFPA has addressed in these opinions.

   b. Choose one opinion and write a paragraph explaining why the issue dealt with in the opinion is important for paralegals.

   c. Choose the same or a different opinion, read completely through it, and write a paragraph summarizing NFPA's "advice" on the issue being addressed in the opinion.

2. Go online and find the case *Oregon State Bar Association v. Smith,* 149 Or.App. 171, 942 P.2d 793 (1997). It can be accessed through the FindLaw Web site at **www.findlaw.com**. Click on "State Law Resources," scroll down to "Oregon," and when the Oregon page appears, select "Primary Materials, Cases, Codes, and Regulations." When that page appears, scroll down to "Archived since 1997," and click on it. This should retrieve a query box. Enter "paralegals & UPL" (do not include quote marks). Scroll through the cases found through this search until you see *Oregon State Bar Association v. Smith.* Read through the first four paragraphs of the decision and then answer the following questions.

   a. Who is Robin Smith, and what was she accused of?

   b. What is an injunction? Why, and against whom, was an injunction issued in this case?

   c. What does "enjoined" mean? What was the People's Paralegal Service, Inc., enjoined from doing?

   d. Did these activities constitute the unauthorized practice of law?

   e. How did People's Paralegal Service, Inc., argue against the injunction?

3. Go online to **www.findlaw.com** to access information on state bar associations, membership rules, ethics rules, and attorney discipline. Then answer the following questions:

   a. What are the requirements for an attorney to become licensed to practice law in your state? (Hint: The way that these requirements are listed varies from state to state. You may find these requirements under such listings as "Admissions," "Board of Law Examiners," "Supreme Court Rules," or "Court of Appeals Rules.") Do they differ from the requirements described in this chapter? If so, how?

   b. How are attorneys disciplined in your state? What are the various sanctions that may be imposed? Are disciplinary hearings open to the public? If so, try to attend one.

   c. Look up your state's ethical rules on competence,

confidentiality, and conflict of interest. Are those rules the same as the rules discussed in this chapter? If not, what are the differences? Are the rules in your state stricter or more lenient?

d. Look for rules on the admission of paralegals to the state bar association in your state. Also look for your state's guidelines on the utilization of legal assistants. What did you find?

4. Go to **www.legalethics.com**, which covers ethical issues related to the use of the Internet, and answer the following questions:

a. Click on "Ethics Sites." Which version of the ABA's ethical rules has your state enacted? Has your state enacted a non-ABA version? Click on your state. Summarize the ethical rules or opinions that have been issued by your state regarding the use of the Internet.

b. Click on "E-Mail." Does your state have an ethical opinion or rule regarding the use of e-mail? If so, summarize the opinion or rule.

c. Click on "Other Issues (UPL/Referral Services)." Locate articles discussing practicing law across state boundaries by participating in listservs and discussion groups. Are such activities considered to be the unauthorized practice of law? Explain.

CHAPTER 4

THE LEGAL WORKPLACE

Chapter Outline

▨ INTRODUCTION ▨ THE ORGANIZATIONAL STRUCTURE OF LAW FIRMS ▨ LAW-OFFICE MANAGEMENT AND PERSONNEL ▨ EMPLOYMENT POLICIES ▨ FILING PROCEDURES ▨ FINANCIAL PROCEDURES ▨ COMMUNICATING WITH CLIENTS ▨ LAW-OFFICE CULTURE AND POLITICS

After completing this chapter, you will know:

- How law firms may be organized and managed.
- Some typical policies and procedures governing paralegal employment.
- The importance of an efficient filing system in legal practice and some typical filing procedures.
- How clients are billed for legal services.
- How law-office culture and politics affect the paralegal's working environment.

INTRODUCTION

The wide variety of environments in which paralegals work makes it impossible to describe in any detail how the particular firm with which you find employment will be run. Typically, though, the way in which that firm operates will relate, at least in part, to the firm's specific form of business organization. Because most paralegals are employed by private law firms, this chapter focuses on the organization, management, and procedures characteristic of these firms.

In the beginning of the chapter, we look at how the size and organizational structure of a law firm affects the paralegal's working environment. As you might imagine, the working environment in a firm owned and operated by one attorney is significantly different from that in a large law firm with two or three hundred attorneys or a large corporate enterprise—or even a government agency.

We then look at other aspects of the working environment of paralegals. Typically, the firm you work for will have specific policies and procedures relating to employment conditions, filing systems, billing and timekeeping procedures, and financial procedures. We conclude the chapter with a brief discussion of law-office culture and politics.

THE ORGANIZATIONAL STRUCTURE OF LAW FIRMS

Law firms range in size from the small, one-attorney firm to the huge megafirm that consists of hundreds of attorneys. Regardless of their size differences, though, in terms of business organization, law firms typically organize their businesses as sole proprietorships, partnerships, or professional corporations. Because the way in which a business is organized affects the law-office environment, we look briefly at each of the three major organizational forms here.

Sole Proprietorships

Many law firms, particularly smaller firms, are **sole proprietorships**. Sole proprietorships are the simplest business form and are often used by attorneys when they first set up legal practices. In a sole proprietorship, one individual—the sole proprietor—owns the business. The sole proprietor is entitled to any profits made by the firm but is also personally liable for all of the firm's debts or obligations. **Personal liability** means that the business owner's personal assets (such as a home, automobile, savings or investment accounts, and other property) may have to be sacrificed to pay business obligations if the business fails.

An attorney who practices law as a sole proprietor is often called a *sole (solo) practitioner*. Although a sole practitioner may at times hire a staff attorney to help with the legal work, the attorney will be paid a specific sum for his or her time and will not share in the profits or losses of the firm itself.

Working for a sole practitioner is a good way for a paralegal to learn about law-office procedures because the paralegal will typically perform a wide variety of tasks. Many sole practitioners hire one person to perform the functions of secretary, paralegal, administrator, and manager. Paralegals holding this kind of position would probably handle the following kinds of tasks: receiving and date-stamping the mail, organizing and maintaining the filing system, interviewing clients and witnesses, bookkeeping (receiving payments from clients, preparing and sending bills to clients, and so on), conducting investigations and legal research, drafting legal documents, assisting the attorney in trial preparation

Sole Proprietorship
The simplest form of business, in which the owner is the business. Anyone who does business without creating a formal business entity has a sole proprietorship.

Personal Liability
An individual's personal responsibility for debts or obligations. The owners of sole proprietorships and partnerships are personally liable for the debts and obligations incurred by their business firms. If their firms go bankrupt or cannot meet debts as they become due, the owners will be personally responsible for paying the debts.

and perhaps in the courtroom, and numerous other tasks, including office administration.

Working for a sole practitioner is also a good way to find out which area of law you most enjoy because the paralegal will learn about procedures relating to many different areas of legal work. Alternatively, if you work for a sole practitioner who specializes in one area of law, you will have an opportunity to develop expertise in that area. In sum, working in a small law firm gives you a broad overview of law-office procedures and legal practice. This knowledge will help you throughout your career.

Partnerships

Partnership
An association of two or more persons to carry on, as co-owners, a business for profit.

Partner
A person who has undertaken to operate a business jointly with one or more other persons. Each partner is a co-owner of the business firm.

Managing Partner
The partner in a law firm who makes decisions relating to the firm's policies and procedures and who generally oversees the business operations of the firm.

The majority of law firms are either partnerships or professional corporations. In a **partnership**, two or more individuals undertake to do business jointly as **partners**. A partnership may consist of just a few attorneys or over a hundred attorneys. In a partnership, each partner owns a share of the business and shares jointly in the firm's profits or losses. Like sole proprietors, partners are personally liable for the debts and obligations of the business if the business fails.

In smaller partnerships, the partners may participate equally in managing the partnership. They will likely meet periodically to make decisions relating to clients, policies, procedures, and other matters of importance to the firm. In larger partnerships, managerial decisions are usually made by a committee consisting of some of the partners, one of whom may be designated as the **managing partner.**

The partnership may hire associate attorneys, but, as in a sole proprietorship, the associates will not have ownership rights in the firm. Normally, an associate hopes to become a partner, and if the associate's performance is satisfactory, the partners may invite the associate to become a partner in the firm.

Professional Corporations

Professional Corporation (P.C.)
A firm that is owned by shareholders, who purchase the corporations stock, or shares. The liability of shareholders is often limited to the amount of their investments.

Shareholder
One who purchases corporate stock, or shares, and who thus becomes an owner of the corporation.

A **professional corporation** (P.C.) is owned by **shareholders,** so called because they purchase the corporation's stock, or shares, and thus own a share of the business. The shareholders share in the profits and losses of the firm in proportion to how many shares they own. Their personal liability, unlike that of partners, may or may not be limited to the amount of their investments, depending on the circumstances and on state law. Limited personal liability is one of the key advantages of the corporate form of business.

In many respects, the professional corporation is run like a partnership, and the distinction between these two forms of business organization is often more a legal formality than an operational reality. Because of this, attorneys who organize their business as a professional corporation are nonetheless sometimes referred to as partners. For the sake of simplicity, in this chapter we will refer to anyone who has ownership rights in the firm as a partner.

LAW-OFFICE MANAGEMENT AND PERSONNEL

When you take a job as a paralegal, one of the first things you will want to learn is the relative status of the office personnel. Particularly, you will want to know who has authority over you and to whom you are accountable. You also want to know who will be accountable to you—whether you have an assistant or a secretary (or share an assistant or a secretary with another paralegal), for example. In a small firm, you will have no problem learning this information. If you work for

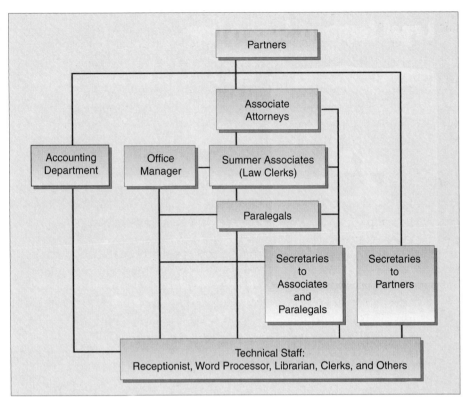

EXHIBIT 4.1
**A Sample Organizational
Chart for a Law Partnership**

a larger law firm, however, the lines of authority may be more difficult to perceive. Your supervisor will probably instruct you, either orally or in writing, on the relative status of the firm's personnel. If you are not sure about who has authority over whom and what kinds of tasks are performed by various employees, you should ask your supervisor.

The lines of authority and accountability vary from firm to firm, depending on the firm's size and its organizational and management preferences. A sample organizational chart for a relatively small law partnership is shown in Exhibit 4.1. The ultimate decision makers in the hypothetical firm represented by that chart are the partners. Next in authority are the associate attorneys and summer associates (law clerks—see Chapter 1). The paralegals in this firm are supervised by both the attorneys (in regard to legal work) and the office manager (in regard to office procedural and paralegal staffing matters). In larger firms, there may be a **legal-assistant manager,** who coordinates and oversees paralegal staffing and various programs relating to paralegal educational and professional development.

In addition to attorneys and paralegals, law-firm employees include administrative personnel. In large firms, the partners may hire a **legal administrator** to run the business end of the firm. The legal administrator might delegate some of his or her authority to an office manager and other supervisory employees. In small firms, such as that represented by the chart in Exhibit 4.1, an **office manager** handles the administrative aspects of the firm. The legal administrator or office manager typically is in charge of docketing (calendaring) legal work undertaken by the attorneys; establishing and overseeing filing procedures; implementing new legal technology, such as new docketing software; ordering and monitoring supplies; and generally making sure that the office runs smoothly and that office procedures are established and followed. In a small firm, the office manager might also handle

Legal-Assistant Manager
An employee in a law firm who is responsible for overseeing the paralegal staff and paralegal professional development.

Legal Administrator
An administrative employee of a law firm who manages the day-to-day operations of the firm. In smaller law firms, legal administrators are usually called office managers.

Office Manager
An administrative employee who manages the day-to-day operations of a business firm. In larger law firms, office managers are usually called legal administrators.

Legal Support Supervisor

ANITA HONG *graduated from the paralegal program of St. Mary's College in 1984. She has worked as a paralegal since 1985. Her first paralegal job was with the Oakland city attorney's office, where she started out as one of two paralegals in a pilot program. The program was a success. Since then, Hong has gone on to supervise a paralegal staff for that office and subsequently became the legal support supervisor for the Oakland city attorney's office. Today, in addition to her supervisory duties, she also provides paralegal and administrative assistance to the city attorney's office's executive management team. Hong is currently serving as a primary representative in the National Federation of Paralegal Associations (NFPA) on behalf of the San Francisco Paralegal Association.*

What do you like best about your work?

"Challenge! From day one, I've been challenged to succeed in various tasks given to me since I began my career as a paralegal in 1985. From there, I was promoted to a legal-assistant supervisor in 1989, and I went on to supervising a staff of paralegals and legal secretaries in 1994. This eventually evolved into a legal support supervisor position in 1997. What I enjoy most is the camaraderie among legal secretaries, paralegals, and attorneys."

What is the greatest challenge that you face in your area of work?

"Communication and customer service. When problems arise, I am one of the problem solvers and troubleshooters for my staff and the office as a whole. The types of problem solving range from customer service, to discovery issues, to staff issues. I have to be fast on my feet and resolve issues as quickly as possible. As a supervisor, I work very hard to stay on top of my work and deal with staff and office issues as they come up."

What advice do you have for would-be paralegals in your area of work?

"Be a mentor to paralegals new to the field. Give back what you've gained. As with any profession, it's okay to be the 'new kid on the block.' Look for mentors to guide you. I was very blessed to have a mentor to guide me as a paralegal and, eventually, as a supervisor. Also, I am fortunate to have a supervisor to help me to become a better supervisor."

"As paralegals, we must hold ourselves to the same level of professional and ethical standards as the attorneys in the legal profession."

What are some tips for success as a paralegal in your area of work?

"Besides having excellent analytical skills and common sense, you must have good people skills. It is important to have good relationships with your clients and your co-workers. Be a quick learner and be a team player. Show a 'can do' attitude, and be flexible about new tasks given to you. Show that you are 'in control.' Be ready to ask for guidance. If you make a mistake, be accountable for your actions without being defensive. Otherwise, people will lose confidence in your credibility and professional ability. As paralegals, we must hold ourselves to the same level of professional and ethical standards as the attorneys in the legal profession."

client billing procedures. The hypothetical firm represented in Exhibit 4.1 has an accounting department to perform this function.

The **support personnel** in a large law office may include secretaries, receptionists, bookkeepers, file clerks, messengers, and others. Depending on their functions and specific jobs, support personnel may fall under the supervision of any number of other personnel in the firm. In a very small firm, just one person—the legal secretary, for example—may perform all of the above-mentioned functions.

Support Personnel
Those employees who provide clerical, secretarial, or other support to the legal, paralegal, and administrative staff of a law firm.

EMPLOYMENT POLICIES

Employees of a law firm, which include all personnel other than the firm's owners or freelance paralegals who work for the firm on a contract basis, are subject to the firm's specific employment policies and procedures. A firm's basic rules or policies governing employment relationships may be set forth in an **employment manual** in larger firms. In smaller firms, these rules and policies are often unwritten. In either situation, when you take a job as a paralegal, or perhaps before you accept a position, you will want to become familiar with the firm's basic conditions of employment. There will be an established policy, for example, on how much vacation time you are entitled to during the first year, second year, and so on. There will also be a policy governing which holidays are observed by the firm, how much sick leave you can take, when you are expected to arrive at the workplace, and what will serve as grounds for the employer to terminate your employment.

Employment Manual
A firm's handbook or written statement that specifies the policies and procedures that govern the firm's employees and employer-employee relationships.

Employment policies and benefits packages vary from firm to firm. A foremost concern of paralegals (and employees generally) is how much they will be paid for their work, how they will be paid (that is, whether they will receive salaries or hourly wages), and what job benefits they will receive. These issues were discussed in detail in Chapter 2, so we will not examine them here. Rather, we look at some other areas of concern to paralegals in regard to employment policies, including performance evaluations and termination procedures.

Performance Evaluations

Many law firms have a policy of conducting periodic performance evaluations. Usually, performance is evaluated annually, but some firms conduct evaluations every six months.

Because paralegal responsibilities vary from firm to firm, no one evaluation checklist applies to every paralegal. Some of the factors that may be considered during a performance evaluation are indicated in Exhibit 4.2 on the next page. Note, though, that performance evaluations are much longer and more detailed than the list shown in the exhibit. For example, each major item in that list may have several subheadings and perhaps further subheadings under those subheadings. Normally, under each item listed on a performance evaluation is a series of options—ranging from "very good" to "unsatisfactory" or something similar—for the supervisor or attorney to check.

When you begin work as a paralegal, you should learn at the outset what exactly your duties will be and what performance is expected of you. This way, you will be able to prepare for your first evaluation from the moment you begin working. You will not have to wait six months or a year before you learn that you were supposed to be doing something that you failed to do.

In the busy workplace, you will probably not have much time available to discuss issues with your supervisor that do not relate to immediate needs. And even

EXHIBIT 4.2

Factors That May Be Considered in a Performance Evaluation

1. RESPONSIBILITY
Making sure that all tasks are performed on time and following up on all pending matters.

2. EFFICIENCY
Obtaining good results in the least amount of time.

3. PRODUCTIVITY
Producing a sufficient quantity of work in a given time period.

4. COMPETENCE
Knowledge level and skills.

5. INITIATIVE
Applying intelligence and creativity to tasks and making appropriate recommendations.

6. COOPERATION
Getting along well with others on the legal team.

7. PERSONAL FACTORS
Appearance, grooming habits, friendliness, poise, and so forth.

8. DEPENDABILITY
Arriving at work consistently on time and being available when needed.

if you do find a moment, you may feel awkward in broaching a discussion about your performance or about workplace problems. Performance evaluations are designed specifically to allow both the employer and the employee to exchange their views on such issues.

During performance reviews, you can learn how the firm rates your performance. You can gain valuable feedback from your supervisor, learn more about your strengths and weaknesses, and identify the areas in which you need to improve your skills or work habits. You can also give feedback to your supervisor on how you feel about the workplace. For example, if you think that your expertise is not being fully utilized, this would be a good time to discuss that issue and perhaps suggest some ways in which your knowledge and experience could be put to better use.

Some paralegals, particularly in smaller firms, have found that their busy supervising attorneys sometimes put off conducting "promised" evaluations. If you ever find yourself in this situation, consider preparing your own evaluation and presenting it to your supervising attorney for review.

Employment Termination

Virtually all policy manuals deal with the subject of employment termination. If you work for a firm that has prepared such a manual for its employees, the manual will likely specify what kind of conduct serves as a basis for firing employees. For example, the manual might specify that if an employee is absent more than twelve days a year for two consecutive years, the employer has grounds to terminate the employment relationship. The manual will also probably describe employment-termination procedures. For example, the firm might require that it be notified one month in advance if an employee decides to leave the firm; if the employee fails to give one month's notice, he or she may forfeit accumulated vacation time or other benefits on termination.

Employment Discrimination

Traditionally, employment relationships have been governed by the common law doctrine of employment at will. Under this doctrine, employers may hire and fire employees "at will"—that is, for any reason or no reason. Today, courts have created several exceptions to this doctrine, and state and federal statutes now regulate numerous aspects of the employment relationship. Under federal law (and many state statutes), employers may not refuse to hire job applicants, refuse to promote employees, or fire employees for discriminatory reasons—because of the employee's age, gender, or race, for example. Virtually every large law firm today has special policies and procedures that must be followed with respect to claims of employment discrimination.

> **On the Web**
> For information on federal laws governing employment discrimination, access the Equal Employment Opportunity Commission's Web site at **www.eeoc.gov.**

For example, an employee who experiences sexual harassment—a form of gender-based discrimination that is prohibited by federal law and most state laws—may be required by the firm's harassment policy to follow formal complaint channels to resolve the issue. If an employee fails to follow the required procedures, the firm may be able to avoid legal responsibility for the harassment. Similarly, if an employer does not have established procedures in place for dealing with harassment or other forms of discrimination, the employer may find it difficult to avoid liability for the harassment or discriminatory treatment initiated by supervisors or others against a particular employee.

FILING PROCEDURES

Every law firm, regardless of its size or organizational structure, has some kind of established filing procedures. Efficient filing procedures are important in any law firm, because the paperwork generated by even a small firm can be substantial. Efficient filing procedures are particularly necessary in law offices because important and confidential documents must be safeguarded yet be readily retrievable when they are needed. If a client file is misplaced or lost, the client may suffer irreparable harm.

Additionally, documents must be filed in such a way as to protect client confidentiality. The duty of confidentiality was discussed at length in Chapter 3, but it deserves special mention here because of the extent to which it frames all legal work and procedures. This is particularly true of filing procedures. All information received from or about clients, including client files and documents, is considered confidential.

> **A breach of confidentiality by a paralegal or other employee can cause the firm to incur potentially extensive liability.**

If you work for a small firm, filing procedures may be rather informal, and you may even assume the responsibility for organizing and developing an efficient filing system. Larger firms normally have specific procedures concerning the creation, maintenance, use, and storage of office files. If you take a job with a large firm, a supervisor will probably spend some time training you in routine office procedures, including filing procedures. Although the trend today, particularly in larger firms, is toward computerized filing systems, firms routinely create "hard copies" to ensure that files are not lost if a computer system crashes.

Generally, law offices maintain several types of files. Typically, a law firm's filing system will include client files, work-product files and reference materials, and forms files (as well as personnel files, which we do not discuss here).

Client Files

To illustrate client filing procedures, we present below the phases in the "life cycle" of a hypothetical client's file. The name of the client is Katherine Baranski; she has just retained one of your firm's attorneys to represent her in a lawsuit that

DEVELOPING PARALEGAL SKILLS
Client File Confidentiality

Robert James, a paralegal with the law firm of Jenkins & Fitzgerald, takes a client's file with him to the law library to do some legal research. While he walks several aisles away to look for a particular legal reference book, Lori Sanger, an attorney from another firm, walks by and notices the file. She can see on the file the law firm's name, the client's name (Purdy Contracting, Inc.), the court's docket number, and the firm's file number. Because she recognizes the client's name, she writes down the docket number, goes to the court clerk's office, and requests the court's file, which is public information. She reads through the file and sees that Purdy Contracting, Inc., a construction company, is being sued for a substantial amount of damages.

Lori has a client who is about to award a big construction project to Purdy Contracting. She calls her client and warns the client that this lawsuit could bankrupt Purdy. As a result, Purdy Contracting does not get the job and complains to Jenkins & Fitzgerald. The firm changes

its policy so that client names no longer appear on the outside of client files.

CHECKLIST FOR CLIENT FILE CONFIDENTIALITY

- Create a confidential name for the client file, using alphabetical and/or numerical sequences.
- Do not leave files out in the open in public places, such as libraries or courts, where their contents can be observed by others.
- Do not leave files in areas within the law firm where other clients might observe the file and its contents.
- Follow the law firm's procedures for closing a file to ensure that extra copies of the documents and letters are destroyed.
- Destroy old files that no longer need to be retained by shredding them.

she is bringing against Tony Peretto. Because Baranski is initiating the lawsuit, she is referred to as the *plaintiff*. Peretto, because he has to defend against Baranski's claims, is the *defendant*. The name of the case is *Baranski v. Peretto*. Assume that you will be working on the case and that your supervising attorney has just asked you to open a new case file. Assume also that you have already verified, through a "conflicts check" (discussed in Chapter 3), that no conflict of interest exists.

OPENING A NEW CLIENT FILE.   The first step that you (or a secretary, at your request) will take in opening a new file is to assign the case a file number. For reasons of both efficiency and confidentiality, many firms identify their client files by numbers or some kind of numerical and/or alphabetical sequence instead of the clients' names, as mentioned earlier. The *Baranski v. Peretto* case file might be identified by the letters BARAPE—the first four letters of the plaintiff's name followed by the first two letters of the defendant's name. Increasingly, law firms are using computerized databases to record and track case titles and files. For example, some firms have file labels containing bar codes in which are embedded attorney codes, subject-matter codes, the client's name and file number, and so on.

Typically, law firms maintain a master client list on which clients' names are entered alphabetically and cross-referenced to the clients' case numbers. If file numbers consist of numerical sequences, there is also a master list on which the file numbers are listed in numerical order and cross-referenced to the clients' names.

ADDING SUBFILES.   As the work on the *Baranski* case progresses and more documents are generated or received, the file will expand. To ensure that documents will be easy to locate, you will create subfiles. A special subfile might be created for client documents (such as a contract, will, stock certificate, or photograph) that the firm needs for reference or for evidence at trial. As correspondence relating to the *Baranski* case is generated, you will probably add a correspondence subfile. You will also want a subfile for your or the attorney's notes on the case, including research results.

As you will read in Chapter 6, litigation involves several stages. As the *Baranski* litigation progresses through these various stages, subfiles for documents relating to each stage will be added to the *Baranski* file. Many firms find it useful to color-code or add tabs to subfiles so that they can be readily identified. Often, in large files, an index of each subfile's contents is created and attached to the inside cover of the subfile.

Documents are typically filed within each subfile in reverse chronological order, with the most recently dated document on the top. Usually, to safeguard the documents, they are punched at the top with a two-hole puncher so that they can be secured within the file with a clip. Note, though, that original client documents should not be punched or altered in any way. They should always be left loose within the file. For example, if you were holding in the file a property deed belonging to a client, you would not want to alter that document in any way.

FILE USE AND STORAGE.   Typically, files are stored in a central file room or area. Most firms have some kind of procedure for employees to follow when removing files from the storage area. For example, a firm might require the office staff to replace a removed file with an "out card" indicating the date, the name of the file, and the name or initials of the person who removed it.

Note that documents should never be removed from a client file or subfile. Rather, the entire file or subfile should be removed for use. This ensures that important documents will not be separated from the file and possibly mislaid or lost. Many paralegals and other users make copies of documents in the file for their use. For example, if you are working on the *Baranski* case and need to review certain documents in the file, you might remove those documents from the file temporarily, copy them, and immediately return the file to storage.

CLOSING A FILE.   Assume that the *Baranski* case has been settled out of court and that no further legal work on Baranski's behalf needs to be done. For a time, her file will be retained in the inactive files, but when it is fairly certain that no one will need to refer to it very often, if ever, it will be closed. Closed files are often stored in a separate area of the building or even off-site. Traditionally, many larger law firms stored the contents of old files on microfilm. Today, firms can use scanning technology to scan file contents for storage on CD-ROMs, Zip disks, magnetic tapes, or other data-storage devices.

Specific procedures for closing files vary from firm to firm. Typically, when a case is closed, original documents provided by the client (for example, a deed to property) are returned to the client, and extraneous materials, such as extra copies of documents or cover letters, are destroyed.

DESTROYING OLD FILES.   Law firms do not have to retain client files forever, and at some point, the *Baranski* case file will be destroyed. Old files are normally destroyed by shredding them so that confidentiality is preserved. Law firms exercise great care when destroying client files because a court or government agency

FEATURED GUEST: KATHLEEN MERCER REED

Ten Tips for Creating and Maintaining an Efficient File System

BIOGRAPHICAL NOTE

Kathleen Mercer Reed holds a bachelor of science degree in legal administration from the University of Toledo and has a law degree. She currently works as an associate professor and as the director of Legal Assistant Technology at the University of Toledo's Community and Technical College, the same program from which she received her associate's degree in 1985. A member of many legal-assistant advisory committees, Reed is a former president of the Toledo Association of Legal Assistants. She is active in national paralegal education issues and a frequent speaker on the paralegal profession.

File maintenance is one of the most important aspects of legal work. Without an organized case file, the attorney is unable to make sure that the case is on track and deadlines are being met. This can mean unhappy clients and a resulting loss of business. Generally, attorneys rely on their paralegals to assume responsibility for the essential task of maintaining (or supervising the maintenance of) the files. Filing systems vary. In some firms, they are highly structured and efficient; in other firms, they may be virtually nonexistent. If you are ever faced with the challenge of setting up (or reorganizing) a file system, here are some tips to consider.

1. Set Aside Time for Planning.
The major problem relating to filing systems is the time factor. Law offices are extremely busy places. Time is money in the law firm. Everyone wants to get on with the important job of performing work for the client. But filing systems must be planned. You need to recognize this fact and allow time for the planning process.

2. Create a System That Is Simple, Yet Effective.
Remember that you and the attorney will not be the only ones working with the file. Secretaries, receptionists, and file clerks may also need to use client files. Don't create a system that generates confusion about where certain documents are to be

filed or where they can be found. Try to establish a simple, logical system that can be readily understood by everybody.

3. Make Sure That the Files Are Clearly Labeled.
Each file should be clearly labeled so that it can be easily located. Files are more easily recognized when the labels are consistently placed on files and consistently typed, printed, or handwritten.

4. Don't Be Afraid to Create as Many Files as You Need.
Don't hesitate to create additional files, especially subfiles, if you think that they are necessary. Generally, the more subfiles you create, the better organized your file will be—and the easier it will be to retrieve specific documents.

5. Make Sure That the Filing System Ensures Client Confidentiality.
When setting up your file system, make sure that the system protects client confidentiality to the greatest possible extent. Some law firms are eliminating alphabetical systems (files in which the client's name is clearly identified on the file folder) and are using numeric filing systems instead. Numeric file systems eliminate the risk of one client seeing another client's name when the file is opened. Remember, a firm can breach a client's right to confidentiality simply

Statute of Limitations
A statute setting the maximum time period within which certain actions can be brought or rights enforced. After the period of time has run, no legal action can be brought.

may impose a heavy fine on a law firm that destroys a file that should have been retained for a longer period of time. How long a particular file must be retained depends on many factors, including the nature of the client's legal matters and governing statutes, such as the statute of limitations.

State **statutes of limitations** limit the time period during which specific types of legal actions may be brought. Statutes of limitations for legal-malpractice actions vary from state to state—from six months to ten years after the attorney's last contact with the client. When the statute of limitations in your state expires is thus an important factor in determining how long to retain a client file, because an attorney or law firm will need the information contained in the client's file to

---

FEATURED GUEST, *Continued*

by divulging (inadvertently or otherwise) the fact that the client consulted the firm, even as a potential client.

6. Set Up Efficient Case-Opening Procedures. A client file should be set up within twenty-four hours of the initial client interview and sent back to the attorney assigned to the file. This means that conflict-of-interest checks and initial file organization must be done quickly. A thorough conflicts check must be done to prevent the necessity of spending hours on a plaintiff's case only to find out that another attorney in the law firm is representing the defendant in that same case. At the same time, the file must be given to the attorney promptly so that he or she can begin working for the client and avoid missing any deadlines.

7. Establish an Efficient Check-Out System. No matter how well organized your file is, you can't work on the file if you can't find it! In a very small law office, this may not be a great concern. But the larger the firm, the more difficult it becomes to locate files—because more people have access to them. A file that you or an attorney needs

urgently may be sitting on a partner's desk, but you do not know this. You need to establish and enforce some kind of sign-out system, such as placing "out cards" or "sign-out cards" in the file whenever a file folder is removed.

8. Establish Proper Procedures for Closing and Storing Files. Closed files must be properly stored and maintained for several reasons. First, a client may contact the firm—sometimes months after his or her case has been closed—to obtain documents or information from the client's file. Second, work that you did on past cases can be a great resource when working on current cases, and if old files are easily accessible, you will not have to "reinvent the wheel" whenever you work on a case that is similar to a case already in the firm's files. Third, and most important, there are state and national standards governing file retention. Find out how long your law firm is legally required to store and maintain closed files. For all of these reasons, closed files must be maintained with as much integrity as active files.

9. Establish Proper Procedures for Destroying Files. Client confi-

> "[B]y getting involved in file organization, your job as a paralegal is made easier."

dentiality must be maintained even when destroying very old closed files. One lawyer was shocked to find out that the paper from his closed files had been made into note pads and donated to a local school! There are a number of companies nationwide that deal exclusively with the destruction of confidential files. Use one of them or encourage your firm to invest in a paper shredder.

10. Keep in Mind the Ultimate Goal of Your Filing System. When setting up and maintaining a filing system, you should always keep in mind your primary goal—to help the firm deliver legal services more efficiently and economically. With an organized case file, the attorney can make sure that the case is on track and that deadlines are being met. Clients are happier, and malpractice actions are avoided. Additionally, by getting involved in file organization, your job as a paralegal is made easier. You not only stay well informed on file contents but also don't have to waste time searching for needed files or documents.

---

defend against a malpractice action. If the file has been destroyed, the firm will not be able to produce any documents or other evidence to refute the plaintiff's claim.

Work-Product Files and Reference Materials

Many law firms keep copies of research projects, legal memoranda, and various case-related documents prepared by the firm's attorneys and paralegals so that these documents can be referred to in future projects. In this way, legal personnel do not have to start all over again when working on a claim similar to one dealt with in the past.

Traditionally, hard copies of work-product files, or legal-information files, were filed in the firm's law library with other reference materials and publications. Today, work-product documents and research materials are often generated on computers and stored on diskettes, Zip disks, CD-ROMs, or other data-storage devices. Often, in large firms, these materials will be kept in a central data bank that is readily accessible by the firm's personnel.

Forms Files

Forms File
A reference file containing copies of the firm's commonly used legal documents and informational forms. The documents in the forms file serve as a model for drafting new documents.

Every law firm keeps on hand various forms that it commonly uses. These forms may be kept in various files or, as is often the case, stored in a **forms file**. A forms file might include forms for retainer agreements (to be discussed shortly), for filing lawsuits in specific courts, for bankruptcy petitions, for real-estate matters, and for numerous other types of legal matters. Often, to save time, copies of documents relating to specific types of cases are kept for future reference. Then, when the attorney or paralegal works on a similar case, those documents can serve as models, or guides. (These forms may be kept in a work-product file, as just mentioned.)

Increasingly, forms files are being computerized. Computerized forms have simplified legal practice by allowing legal personnel to generate customized documents within minutes. Forms for many standard legal transactions are now available from legal-software companies on disk or CD-ROM. They are also available online at an increasing number of Web sites, as you will read in Chapter 9.

On the Web
For a sampling of the types of legal forms available on the Web, check the following sites: www.lectlaw.com/form.html and www.legaldocs.com.

FINANCIAL PROCEDURES

Like any other business firm, a law firm needs to at least cover its expenses or it will fail. In the business of law, the product is legal services, which are sold to clients for a price. A foremost concern of any law firm is therefore to establish a clear policy on fee arrangements and efficient procedures to ensure that each client is billed appropriately for the time and costs associated with serving that client. Efficient billing procedures require, in turn, that attorneys and paralegals keep accurate records of the time that they spend working on a given client's case or other legal matter.

Fee Arrangements

A major ethical concern of the legal profession has to do with the reasonableness of attorneys' fees and the ways in which clients are billed for legal services. Among other things, state ethical codes governing attorneys require legal fees to be reasonable. For example, Rule 1.5 of the Model Rules of Professional Conduct states, "A lawyer's fees shall be reasonable." The rule then lists the factors that should be considered in determining the reasonableness of a fee. The factors include the time and labor required to perform the legal work, the fee customarily charged in the locality for similar legal services, and the experience and ability of the lawyer performing the services.

Retainer Agreement
A signed document stating that the attorney or the law firm has been hired by the client to provide certain legal services and that the client agrees to pay for those services in accordance with the terms set forth in the retainer agreement.

Normally, fee arrangements are discussed and agreed on at the outset of any attorney-client relationship. Most law firms require each client to agree, in a signed writing called a **retainer agreement**, to whatever fee arrangements have been made. (Some states also require, by law, that fee arrangements be stated in writing.) The agreement specifies that the client is retaining (hiring) the attorney and/or firm to represent the client in a legal matter and states that the client agrees

EXHIBIT 4.3
A Sample Retainer Agreement

RETAINER AGREEMENT

I, Katherine Baranski, agree to employ Allen P. Gilmore and his law firm, Jeffers, Gilmore & Dunn, as my attorneys to prosecute all claims for damages against Tony Peretto and all other persons or entities that may be liable on account of an automobile accident that caused me to sustain serious injuries. The accident occurred on August 4, 1999, at 7:45 A.M., when Tony Peretto ran a stop sign on Thirty-eighth Street at Mattis Avenue and, as a result, his car collided with mine.

I agree to pay my lawyers a fee that will be one-fourth (25 percent) of any sum recovered in this case, regardless of whether the sum is received through settlement, lawsuit, arbitration, or any other way. The fee will be calculated on the sum recovered, after costs and expenses have been deducted. The fee will be paid when any money is actually received in this case. I agree that Allen P. Gilmore and his law firm have an express attorney's lien on any recovery to ensure that their fee is paid.

I agree to pay all necessary costs and expenses, such as court filing fees, court reporter fees, expert witness fees and expenses, travel expenses, long-distance telephone and facsimile costs, and photocopying charges. I understand that these costs and expenses will be billed to me by my attorney on a monthly basis and that I am responsible for paying these costs and expenses, even if no recovery is received.

I agree that this agreement does not cover matters other than those described above. It does not cover an appeal from any judgment entered, any efforts necessary to collect money due because of a judgment entered by a court, or any efforts necessary to obtain other benefits, such as insurance.

I agree to pay a carrying charge amounting to the greater of two dollars ($2.00) or two percent (2%) per month on the average daily balance of bills on my account that are thirty days overdue. If my account is outstanding by more than sixty (60) days, all work by the attorney shall cease until the account is paid in full or a monthly payment plan is agreed on.

This contract is governed by the law of the state of Nita.*

I AGREE TO THE TERMS AND CONDITIONS STATED ABOVE:

Date: ___2 / 4 / 2000___   *Katherine Baranski*

                                Katherine Baranski

I agree to represent Katherine Baranski in the matter described above. I will receive no fee unless a recovery is obtained. If a recovery is obtained, I will receive a fee as described above.

I agree to notify Katherine Baranski of all developments in this matter promptly, and I will make no settlement of this matter without her consent.

I AGREE TO THE TERMS AND CONDITIONS STATED ABOVE:

Date: ___2 / 4 / 2000___   *Allen P. Gilmore*

                                Allen P. Gilmore
                                Jeffers, Gilmore & Dunn
                                553 Fifth Avenue
                                Suite 101
                                Nita City, Nita 48801

*A hypothetical state.

to the fee arrangements set forth in the agreement. Exhibit 4.3 shows a sample retainer agreement.

Basically, there are three types of fee arrangements: fixed fees, hourly fees, and contingency fees. We examine here each of these types of fees, as well as some alternative fee arrangements that have recently come into use.

ETHICAL CONCERN

Handling Clients' Questions about Fees

Suppose that you work as a paralegal for a sole practitioner, Marina Tesner, who is just setting up practice. You know that the attorney is soliciting new clients and that she relies on you, when she is out of the office, to make sure that potential clients are not turned away for any reason. One day, while Tesner is out of town, a man named Henry Roth calls the office. He is purchasing a home and wants to consult with an attorney before signing the final papers four days from now. You explain that Ms. Tesner is out of the office but will return in two days and could see him then. Roth says that he would wait for a couple of days if he knew what Tesner would charge for her services. Should you tell him that Ms. Tesner usually bills clients $125 an hour for her services, which is a low billable rate for your community? No, you should not. As discussed in Chapter 3, professional ethical codes prohibit anyone but an attorney from setting legal fees. If you told Roth what he wanted to know, you may be engaging in the unauthorized practice of law.

Fixed Fee
A fee paid to the attorney by his or her client for having rendered a specified legal service, such as the creation of a simple will.

FIXED FEES. The client may agree to pay a **fixed fee** for a specified legal service. Certain procedures, such as incorporation and simple divorce filings, are often handled on a fixed-fee basis because the attorney can estimate fairly closely how much time will be involved in completing the work. Charging fixed fees is increasingly becoming a preferred method of billing. This is because it helps attorneys avoid lawsuits and other problems that can result when clients allege that their legal fees were excessive.

HOURLY FEES. Traditionally, with the exception of litigation work done on a contingency-fee basis (discussed below), most law firms have charged clients hourly rates for legal services. Hourly rates vary widely from firm to firm. Some litigation firms, for example, can charge extremely high hourly rates ($500 an hour or more) for their services because of their reputation for obtaining favorable settlements or court judgments for their clients. In contrast, an attorney just starting up a practice as a sole practitioner will have to charge a lower, more competitive rate (which may be as low as $75 per hour) to attract clients.

Today, law firms also bill clients for hourly rates for paralegal services. Because the hourly rate for paralegals is lower than that for attorneys, clients benefit from attorneys' use of paralegal services. Generally, the billing rate for paralegal services depends on the size of the firm. According to the compensation survey conducted by the National Federation of Paralegal Associations (NFPA) in 1997, in firms with less than ten attorneys, the range of billing rates for paralegals was from $61 to $71 per hour; in firms with over two hundred attorneys, the range was from $81 to $90 per hour. The average billing rate, according to the 1997 survey conducted by the National Association of Legal Assistants (NALA), was $64.

Note that although your services might be billed to the client at a certain rate, say $70, that does not mean that the firm will actually pay you $70 an hour as wages. The billable rate for paralegal services, as for attorney services, has to take into account the firm's expenses for overhead (rent, utilities, employee benefits, supplies, and so on).

CONTINGENCY FEES.   A common practice among litigation attorneys, especially those representing plaintiffs in certain types of cases (such as personal-injury or negligence cases) is to charge the client on a contingency-fee basis. A **contingency fee** is contingent (dependent) on the outcome of the case. If the plaintiff wins the lawsuit and recovers damages or settles out of court, the attorney will be entitled to a certain percentage of the amount recovered. If the plaintiff loses the lawsuit, the attorney gets nothing—although the client normally will reimburse the attorney for the costs and expenses involved in preparing for trial (costs and expenses are discussed below, in regard to billing procedures).

Often, the attorney's contingency fee is one-fourth or one-third of the amount recovered. The agreement may provide for modification of the amount depending on how and when the dispute is settled. For example, an agreement that provides for a contingency fee of 25 percent of the amount recovered for a plaintiff may state that the amount will be reduced to a lower percentage if the case is settled out of court. In this situation, the agreement might provide that if the case is settled before trial, the attorney's fee will be one-tenth of the amount recovered in the settlement.

While some people maintain that the use of contingency fees is ethically questionable (because it may motivate attorneys to resort to aggressive tactics just to win a case), the legal profession deems it ethical because it allows the public to have broader access to legal services. Contingency-fee arrangements allow clients who otherwise could not afford legal services to have their claims settled, in or out of court, by competent attorneys.

Note that contingency-fee agreements only apply if an attorney represents the client in a civil lawsuit. In a civil case, the plaintiff frequently seeks money damages from the defendant to compensate the plaintiff for harms suffered. If the plaintiff "wins" the case, the attorney's fee will be a percentage of the amount awarded. Criminal cases, in contrast, are brought by the state (through the district attorney, county attorney, or other attorney working for the government). If the court finds the defendant guilty, the state imposes a penalty (a fine and/or imprisonment) on him or her. If the defendant is deemed innocent in the eyes of the court, no money is awarded to the defendant. In criminal cases, contingency fees are thus not an option.

ALTERNATIVE FEE ARRANGEMENTS.   Recently, some attorneys have been creating alternative fee arrangements with their clients. One relatively new billing practice, called "task-based billing," is similar to a fixed-fee arrangement: a fixed fee is charged for specific types of tasks that are involved in a legal matter. For example, the attorney might charge a flat fee for conducting a pretrial deposition (in which a party in a lawsuit or a witness gives sworn testimony—see Chapter 6). Another alternative billing practice is sometimes referred to as "value billing." When this arrangement is used, the fees charged to the client vary, depending on the results of the representation—if a lawsuit is lost, won, or settled, for example.

Client Trust Accounts

Law firms often require new clients to pay a **retainer**—an initial advance payment to the firm to cover part of the fee and various costs that will be incurred on the client's behalf (such as mileage or other travel expenses, phone and fax charges, and so on). Funds received as retainers, as well as any funds received on behalf of the client (such as a payment to a client to settle a lawsuit), are placed in a special bank account. This account is usually referred to as a client **trust account** (or escrow account).

Contingency Fee
A legal fee that consists of a specified percentage (such as 30 percent) of the amount the plaintiff recovers in a civil lawsuit. The fee must be paid only if the plaintiff prevails in the lawsuit (recovers damages).

Retainer
An advance payment made by a client to a law firm to cover part of the legal fees and/or costs that will need to be incurred on that client's behalf.

Trust Account
A bank or escrow account in which one party (the trustee, such as an attorney) holds funds belonging to another person (such as a client); a bank account into which funds advanced to a law firm by a client are deposited.

ETHICAL CONCERN

Trust Accounts

Suppose that a legal professional who has access to funds held in trust for clients borrows money from those funds for temporary personal use. Would such borrowing be unethical? Would it be illegal? The answer to both questions is a resounding "Yes!" By law, anyone who takes for personal use any property (including money) that is legally entrusted to his or her care commits a form of theft called embezzlement. It does not matter whether the person who used the funds intended to replace them the next day, week, or month. The fact is, a crime has been committed.

It is extremely important that the funds held in a trust account be used *only* for expenses relating to the costs of serving that client's needs.

Misuse of client funds constitutes a breach of the firm's duty to its client. An attorney's personal use of the funds, for example, can lead to disciplinary action and possible disbarment, as well as criminal penalties. *Commingling* (mixing together) a client's funds with the firm's funds also constitutes abuse and is one of the most common ways in which attorneys breach their professional obligations. If you handle a client's trust account, you should be especially careful to document fully your use of the funds to protect yourself and your firm against the serious problems that may arise if there are any discrepancies in the account.

The Prohibition against Fee Splitting

An important ethical rule with which paralegals should be familiar is Rule 5.4 of the Model Rules of Professional Conduct. That rule states, "A lawyer or law firm shall not share legal fees with a nonlawyer." For this reason, paralegals cannot become partners in a law partnership (because the partners share the firm's income), nor can they have a fee-sharing arrangement with an attorney in any way.

One of the reasons for this rule is that it protects the attorney's independent judgment concerning legal matters. For example, if an attorney became partners with two or three nonattorneys, the nonattorneys would have a significant voice in determining the firm's policies. In this situation, a conflict might arise between a policy of the firm and the attorney's duty to exercise independent professional judgment in regard to a client's case. The rule against fee splitting also protects against the possibility that nonlawyers would, indirectly through attorneys, be able to engage in the practice of law, which no one but an attorney can do.

Billing and Timekeeping Procedures

As a general rule, a law firm bills its clients monthly. Each client's bill reflects the amount of time spent on the client's matter by the attorney or other legal personnel. In the context of legal work, client billing serves an obvious financial function (collecting payment for services rendered). It also serves a communicative function, as you will learn later in this chapter.

DEVELOPING PARALEGAL SKILLS
Creating a Trust Account

Louise Larson has been hired to work for Don Jones. Don is just starting his own sole practice of law after many years of working with a medium-sized law firm in which he had nothing to do with the firm's financial management. Louise's first assignment is to establish a client trust account. Don and Louise review the ethical rules regarding client property and funds. These rules require that client funds not be commingled with the lawyer's funds. "It's too easy to 'borrow' from a client's funds when they are in the lawyer's own bank account," explains Don.

CHECKLIST FOR CREATING
A CLIENT TRUST ACCOUNT

• Obtain and prepare the necessary forms from the bank in which the account will be maintained.

• Devise a bookkeeping method for tracking all fees and expenses for a particular case and/or client.

• Retain all deposit slips and canceled checks.

• Keep a record of payments made to clients.

• Decide who will have access to the account.

Generally, client bills are prepared by a legal secretary or a bookkeeper or, in larger firms, by someone in the accounting department. The bills are based on the fee arrangements made with the client and the time slips collected from the firm's attorneys and paralegals. The time slips (discussed below) indicate how many hours are to be charged to each client at what hourly rate.

The *legal fees* billed to clients will be based on the number of billable hours generated for work requiring legal expertise. **Billable hours** are the hours or fractions of hours that attorneys and paralegals spend in client-related work that requires legal expertise and that can be billed directly to clients. The *costs* billed to clients will include expenses incurred by the firm (such as court fees, travel expenses, phone and fax charges, express-delivery charges, and copying costs) on the client's behalf. If an attorney is retained on a contingency-fee basis, the client is not billed monthly for legal fees. The client is normally billed monthly for any costs incurred on the client's behalf, however.

Typically, a preliminary draft of the client's bill will be given to the attorney responsible for that client's account. After the attorney reviews and possibly modifies the bill, the final draft of the bill is generated and sent to the client. Exhibit 4.4 on page 130 illustrates a sample client bill in its final form.

Most law firms today have computerized their billing procedures, using time-and-billing software designed specifically for law-office use. Because it would be impossible to describe in this section each of the hundreds of such programs that are used, we look here at traditional timekeeping and billing procedures. A knowledge of these procedures, which illustrate the basic principles involved in client billing, will help you understand whatever type of time-and-billing software your employer may use.

DOCUMENTING TIME AND EXPENSES.   Accurate timekeeping by attorneys and paralegals is crucial because clients cannot be billed for time spent on their behalf unless that time is documented. Attorneys and paralegals normally keep track of the time they spend on each client's work. Traditionally, **time slips** have been used for this purpose. Each time slip documents in hours and fractions of hours (commonly in tenths or quarters of an hour) the amount of time spent on a particular day on a particular task for a particular client. Usually, an attorney or a paralegal

Billable Hours
Hours or fractions of hours that attorneys and paralegals spend in work that requires legal expertise and that can be billed directly to clients.

On the Web
You can obtain information on selected time-and-billing software at the following Web sites: www.pclaw.com/ pclawjr.htm, www.timeslips.com, and www.intuit.com.

Time Slip
A record documenting, for billing purposes, the hours (or fractions of hours) that an attorney or a paralegal worked for each client, the date on which the work was done, and the type of work that was undertaken.

EXHIBIT 4.4
A Sample Client Bill

Jeffers, Gilmore & Dunn
553 Fifth Avenue
Suite 101
Nita City, NI 48801

BILLING DATE: February 28, 2000

Thomas Jones, M.D.
508 Oak Avenue
Nita City, Nita 48802

RE: Medical-Malpractice Action Brought against Dr. Jones,
         File No. 15789

DATE	SERVICES RENDERED	PROVIDED BY	HOURS SPENT	TOTAL
1/30/00	Initial client consultation	APG (attorney)	1.00	$150.00
1/30/00	Client interview	EML (paralegal)	1.00	74.00
1/30/00	Document preparation	EML (paralegal)	1.00	74.00
2/5/00	Interview: Susanne Mathews (nurse)	EML (paralegal)	1.50	111.00
	TOTAL FOR LEGAL SERVICES			$409.00

DATE	EXPENSES			
2/5/00	Hospital charges for a copy of the medical documents			$75.00
	TOTAL FOR EXPENSES			$75.00
	TOTAL BILL TO CLIENT			$484.00

---

includes on the time slip his or her initials, the date, the client number, and a description of the type of legal services performed. (This description will appear on the client's bill.) Exhibit 4.5 shows a sample time slip. Any costs incurred on behalf of clients are entered on **expense slips**. Exhibit 4.6 shows a sample expense slip.

BILLABLE VERSUS NONBILLABLE HOURS.   The time recorded on time slips is charged either to a client (billable hours) or to the firm (nonbillable hours). As mentioned, billable time generally includes the hours or fractions of hours that attorneys and paralegals spend in client-related work that requires legal expertise. For example, the time you spend researching or investigating a client's claim is billable time. So is the time spent in conferences with or about a client, drafting documents on behalf of a client, interviewing clients or witnesses, and traveling (to and from the courthouse to file documents, for example).

    Time spent on other tasks, such as administrative work, staff meetings, or performance reviews, is nonbillable time. For example, suppose that you spend thirty

Expense Slip
A slip of paper on which any expense, or cost, that is incurred on behalf of a client (such as the payment of court fees or long-distance telephone charges) is recorded.

EXHIBIT 4.5
A Sample Time Slip

TIME SLIP

Name of timekeeper_____   Client name/number_____

File number_____   Time allocated_____

Hourly rate_____   Billable/nonbillable_____

Date service rendered_____

Brief description of legal service:_____

_____

_____

---

minutes photocopying forms for the forms file, time sheets, or a procedures manual for the office. That thirty minutes would not be considered billable time.

Generally, law firms have a legitimate reason for wanting to maximize their billable hours:

> **The financial well-being of a law firm depends to a great extent on how many billable hours are generated by its employees.**

Nonbillable time ultimately cuts into the firm's profits. Of course, as mentioned earlier, nonbillable time is factored into the hourly rate charged for legal services. But to remain competitive, a law firm cannot charge too high an hourly rate. Therefore, the more billable hours generated by the firm's legal professionals, the more profitable the business will be.

Law firms normally tell their paralegals and associate attorneys how many billable hours they are expected to produce and the consequences of not being able to meet that number. Some firms expect associate attorneys to produce a minimum of 2,200 billable hours per year; other firms require fewer or more hours. Depending on the firm, a paralegal may be expected to generate between 1,250 and 2,000 billable hours per year.

Attorneys and paralegals face substantial pressure to produce billable hours for the firm. As a paralegal, you may be subject to this pressure and must learn how to handle it. For example, suppose that your employer expects you to produce 1,800 billable hours per year. Discounting vacation time and holidays (assuming a two-week vacation and ten paid holidays), this equates to 37.5 hours

EXHIBIT 4.6
A Sample Expense Slip

EXPENSE SLIP

Name_____

Client name and file number_____

Billable/nonbillable_____

Date of expense_____

Brief description of expense incurred:_____

_____

_____

Quantity and rate (if applicable)_____

ETHICAL CONCERN

Back Up Your Work

Even a person who uses computers on a routine basis can easily forget—while the computer system is working—that a power failure or other problem can occur at any time. Should this happen, you may lose all current work that has not been saved to your hard disk. Surge protectors help to protect against "computer meltdown," but you should have, in addition, back-up copies of all of your work as well as a contingency plan—such as a second computer available to use.

Backing up your work frequently on a diskette or other external storage device is particularly important and can "save the day" if the computer system crashes or fails to the extent that data on the hard drive cannot be retrieved. If you routinely back up documents, you may save yourself the hours of valuable time that could be required to recreate a document or file. You will also save yourself and the firm from the problem of deciding who will pay—the client or the law firm—for the extra time you had to spend to complete the work. Moreover, with back-up copies available, your employer will never have to be without a crucial document when it's needed. Another important precaution you can take to prevent loss of work is to have a crash-saving program, such as Norton Utilities, available to recover lost data.

---

weekly. Assuming that you work 40 hours a week, you will have 2.5 hours a week for such nonbillable activities as interoffice meetings, performance reviews, coffee breaks, tidying up your desk, reorganizing your work area, or chatting with others in the office. As you can imagine, unless you are willing to work more than eight hours a day, you may have difficulty meeting the billable-hours requirement.

Ethics and Client Billing Practices

Because attorneys have a duty to charge their clients "reasonable" fees, legal professionals must be careful in their billing practices. They must not "pad" their clients' bills by including more billable hours than actually worked on behalf of those clients. They also must avoid **double billing**—billing more than one client for the same time.

Double Billing
Billing more than one client for the same billable time period.

DOUBLE BILLING.   Sometimes, situations arise in which it is difficult to determine which client should be billed for a particular segment of time. For example, suppose that you are asked to travel to another city to interview a witness in a case for Client A. You spend three hours traveling in an airplane, travel time that is necessary in working on behalf of Client A. You spend two hours in the airplane summarizing a document relating to a case for Client B. Who should pay for those two hours, Client A, Client B, or both? In this situation, you could argue—as many attorneys do in similar circumstances—that you generated five billable hours, three on Client A's work and two on Client B's case. This is an example of how double billing can occur.

Double billing also occurs when a firm bills a new client for work that was done for a previous client. For example, suppose that an attorney is working on a case for Client B that is very similar to a case handled by the firm a year ago for Client A. The firm charged Client A $2,000 for the legal services. Because much of the research, writing, and other work done on Client A's case can transfer over

DEVELOPING PARALEGAL SKILLS

A Client Complains about a Bill

Joni Winston takes a phone call for her supervising attorney, Mary Perkins. The caller, Joe Hendry, wants to leave a message regarding the bill for settling his father's estate. Joni tells Mr. Hendry that she worked with him on the estate matter and identifies herself as Mary's legal assistant. She asks Mr. Hendry for the details of the billing problem. He tells her that he was "double-billed" for the filing of the letters of authority with the probate court and threatens to file a grievance against Mary with the bar association if the matter is not resolved by 5:00 P.M. that day.

Joni sympathizes with Mr. Hendry and promises to look into the problem and call him back by the end of the day. Joni and Mary review the bill and determine that a temporary secretary had mislabeled the second billing entry. The entry should have read "Preparing estate tax return" instead of "Filing letters of authority with the probate court." The amount billed remains the same. Joni returns Mr. Hendry's call, as promised, and explains to him what happened.

TIPS FOR AVOIDING BILLING ERRORS

- Select a billing system that is "user friendly."
- Carefully record your time.
- Establish procedures for regularly turning in time sheets and for recording your time.
- Assign billing tasks to one reliable staff member.
- Have attorneys review bills before they are sent to clients.

to Client B's case, the firm is able to complete the work for Client B in half the time. In this situation, would it be fair to bill Client B $2,000 also? After all, $1,000 of that amount represents hours spent on Client A's case (and for which Client A has already been billed). At the same time, would it be fair to Client A to bill Client B less for essentially the same services? Would it be fair to the firm if it was not allowed to profit from cost efficiencies generated by overlapping work?

Some firms today are tackling this ethical problem by splitting the benefits derived from cost efficiencies between the client and the firm. For example, the attorney in the above example might split the savings created by the overlapping research ($1,000) with Client B by billing Client B $1,500 instead of $2,000. Other firms still bill their clients for the time spent on previous work that transfers over to new clients' cases.

THE AMERICAN BAR ASSOCIATION'S RESPONSE TO DOUBLE BILLING.   The American Bar Association (ABA) addressed this ethical "gray area" in the legal profession—double billing—in an ethical opinion issued in 1993. In its first formal opinion on the issue, the ABA stated that attorneys are prohibited from charging more than one client for the same hours of work. Additionally, the ABA rejected the notion that the firm, and not the client, should benefit from cost efficiencies created by the firm's work for previous clients. "The lawyer who has agreed to bill solely on the basis of time spent is obliged to pass the benefit of these economies on to the client." Although ABA opinions do not become legally binding on attorneys until they are adopted by the states as law, they do carry much weight in the legal profession.

COMMUNICATING WITH CLIENTS

Sending monthly bills to clients is one way to keep attorney-client communication channels open. Such communication is important because attorneys have a duty

TECHNOLOGY AND TODAY'S PARALEGAL

Cyberspace Communications

In the past few years, e-mail has become a standard communication tool used by business and professional firms, including law firms. The reason why e-mail is among the fastest-growing technologies is simple: it is a quick, easy-to-use, and inexpensive way to communicate. In large law firms or corporate enterprises, as well as in government agencies, e-mail messages are rapidly replacing the printed "interoffice memos" of the past. E-mail is also becoming a standard way for attorneys and paralegals to communicate with clients, opposing counsel, witnesses, and others.

Because e-mail is transmitted through an electronic medium—computer networks—it is difficult to remember that it is also a *written communication*. In other words, writing skills still apply. If you want to convey a written message to someone, you need to make sure that you use clear and effective language. Also, e-mail messages frequently are printed out and retained in client or correspondence files, so that a record exists of the communication. This means that any typos, misspellings, and incorrect usage in a message may be more permanent than you realize at the time you send the message.

One thing you can do to ensure that your e-mail messages are professional in tone and quality is to make sure that your e-mail program has a spell checker. Additionally, before you send important e-mail messages, you should print them out first and read them carefully to confirm that the grammar, spelling, and punctuation are correct—just as you would review and proofread a written letter. It often helps to print out important messages, let them sit a while, and review and proofread them later when your "eye" is fresher.

There are several other things that you can do to enhance e-mail communications and ward off potential problems. One is to request feedback for important messages. For example, if you send a message to a client informing him or her of an important court date or other matter, request the client to verify that the message was received. Similarly, you should respond immediately to incoming e-mail whenever possible so that the sender knows the message has been received and (perhaps) what actions are being taken on it. Finally, as in all other communications, such as phone calls and face-to-face encounters, you should remember to disclose your paralegal status in your e-mail communications. This is important to avoid potential liability for the unauthorized practice of law (discussed in Chapter 3).

to keep a client reasonably informed. Rule 1.4 of the Model Rules of Professional Conduct reads as follows:

> (a) A lawyer shall keep a client reasonably informed about the status of a matter and promptly comply with reasonable requests for information.
> (b) A lawyer shall explain a matter to the extent reasonably necessary to permit the client to make informed decisions regarding the representation.

As a paralegal, you need to be aware that keeping clients reasonably informed about the progress being made on their cases goes beyond courtesy and the cultivation of a client's goodwill—it is a legal duty of attorneys. The meaning of "reasonably informed" varies, of course, depending on the client and on the nature of the work being done by the attorney. In some cases, a phone call every week or two will suffice to keep the client informed. In other cases, the attorney may ask the paralegal to draft a letter to a client explaining the status of the client's legal matter. Some firms institute a regular monthly mailing to update clients on the status of their claims or cases. Generally, as a paralegal, you should discuss with your supervising attorney how each client should be kept informed of the status of his or her case.

Copies of all letters to a client should, of course, be placed in the client's file. Additionally, the client's file should contain a written record of each phone call

TODAY'S PROFESSIONAL PARALEGAL

Managing Conflict in the Legal Workplace

On Cheryl Hardy's first day at her new job as a legal assistant at Comp-Lease, Inc., a computer leasing corporation, Cheryl is introduced to the department staff by her boss, Dennis Hoyt. Dennis then takes her to meet the legal team. When she meets Jackie, the team secretary, Jackie gives her a frosty "Hello," without a handshake or smile, and then looks down at the desk. Cheryl does not understand why Jackie seems hostile. She has just met Jackie and has not done or said anything to offend her.

After her lunch break, Cheryl is given her first lease package to prepare. The work consists of drafting a lease (rental) agreement and giving it to the secretary to input into the computer and print out the agreement form. Cheryl prepares the draft and gives it to Jackie. Cheryl is very polite and tells Jackie not to rush because the agreement does not have to be sent out for two days. When Cheryl asks Jackie for the lease two days later, it is not done. Jackie tells Cheryl to check with her after lunch to see how it is coming. "Great," thinks Cheryl to herself, as she walks back to her desk. "My first week on the job and I'll be in trouble because of Jackie."

ANALYZING THE PROBLEM

Cheryl decides to talk to a co-worker, Sandy, about the problem. At lunch, Cheryl explains the situation to Sandy. "She probably resents you," says Sandy. "You see, Jackie has always wanted to be a paralegal. The company has a policy that you have to have a degree or a certificate, even if you have experience, and so she cannot move into a paralegal position without some education. She has not been able to attend a paralegal training program because of family obligations and the expense involved. I'm sure that she knows that you were a legal secretary and that you worked your way through school. When Dennis told us that he had hired a new paralegal, he made your experience and education quite clear."

"Thanks, Sandy," says Cheryl. "That clears up the situation a lot. Now I can understand why she reacted the way she did to me."

SOLVING THE PROBLEM

Cheryl has an idea. She invites Jackie to lunch. Jackie talks about her interest in becoming a paralegal, her frustration with the company's policy, and her inability to get a certificate or degree because of family obligations and the cost of going back to school. Cheryl tells Jackie that she was in a similar situation and that she got a scholarship from her school to pay for most of her education. She tells Jackie that she might be able to get one, too. She encourages Jackie by telling her, truthfully, that she is obviously bright enough to be a paralegal. Cheryl gives Jackie the name and phone number of Lois Allison, the director of the program that Cheryl attended. "Why don't you call her and tell her that I referred you? Explain that you are in the same situation that I was in when I started. She can tell you what might be available," suggested Cheryl.

When Cheryl returns to her office from lunch, she calls Lois Allison. She explains Jackie's situation and tells Lois that Jackie might be calling to get information on the program and scholarships. Lois replies that she will be happy to talk to Jackie and to help her if she can.

Later that afternoon, when Cheryl gives Jackie a lease package to prepare, Jackie prepares it right away. She even brings it into Cheryl's office, which she does not have to do. "I just want to thank you for going out of your way for me," says Jackie. "I called Lois Allison, and she wants me to come in and fill out some application forms. She thinks that I might qualify for a scholarship. So I might get to go to school after all." Cheryl smiles and replies, "I am glad that Lois could help you."

---

made to or received from a client. That way, there is a "paper trail" in the event it is ever necessary to provide evidence of communication with the client. (Actually, this is a good practice for all phone calls relating to a client's matter.) You will learn about the various forms of letters that attorneys send to clients in Chapter 8. Increasingly, attorneys and paralegals communicate with clients via e-mail, which can pose special problems—as discussed in this chapter's *Technology and Today's Paralegal: Cyberspace Communications.*

Law-Office Culture and Politics

As a paralegal, you will find that each law firm you work for is unique. Even though two firms may be the same size and have similar organizational structures, they will have different cultures, or "personalities." The culture of a given legal workplace is ultimately determined by the attitudes of the firm's owners (the partners, for example) in regard to the fundamental goals of the firm.

Additionally, you will find that each firm has a political infrastructure that may have little to do with the lines of authority and accountability that are spelled out in the firm's employment manual or other formal policy statement. An up-and-coming younger partner in the firm, for example, may in fact exercise more authority than one of the firm's older partners who is about to retire. There may be rivalry between associate attorneys for promotion to partnership status, and you may be caught in the middle of it. If you are aware (and you may not be) of the rivalry and your position relative to it, you may find yourself tempted to take sides—which could jeopardize your own future with the firm.

Unfortunately, paralegals have little way of knowing about the culture and politics of a given firm until they have worked for the firm a while. Of course, if you know someone who works for or who has worked for a firm and value that employee's opinion, you might gain some advance knowledge about the firm's environment from that source. Otherwise, when you start to work for a firm, you will need to learn for yourself about interoffice politics. One way to do this is to listen carefully whenever a co-worker discusses the firm's staff and ask discreet questions to elicit information from co-workers about office politics and unwritten policies. This way, you can both prepare yourself to deal with these issues and protect your own interests. Ultimately, after you've worked for the firm for a time, you will be in a position to judge whether the firm you have chosen is really the "right firm" for you.

Key Terms and Concepts

billable hours 129	legal-assistant manager 115	retainer 127
contingency fee 127	managing partner 114	retainer agreement 124
double billing 132	office manager 115	shareholder 114
employment manual 117	partner 114	sole proprietorship 113
expense slip 130	partnership 114	statute of limitations 122
fixed fee 126	personal liability 113	support personnel 117
forms file 124	professional	time slip 129
legal administrator 115	corporation (P.C.) 114	trust account 127

Chapter Summary

1. In terms of business organization, a law firm may take the form of a sole proprietorship, in which one individual owns the business; a partnership, in which two or more individuals—called partners—jointly own the business; or a professional corporation, in which two or more individuals—called shareholders—own the business. The sole proprietor is entitled to all the firm's profits, bears the burden of any losses, and is personally liable for the firm's debts or other obligations. Partners share jointly the profits or losses of the firm and are subject to personal liability for all of the firm's debts or other obligations. The owner-shareholders of a professional corporation, like partners, share the firm's profits or losses but, unlike partners, are normally not liable for the firm's debts or other obligations beyond the amount they invested in the corporation.

2. Law-firm personnel include the owners of the firm (partners, for example); associate attorneys, who are hired as employees and do not have ownership rights in the business; summer associates, or temporary law clerks; paralegals; administrative personnel, who are supervised by the legal administrator or office manager; and support personnel, including receptionists, secretaries, clerks, and others. Paralegals should learn, on first taking a job in a law firm, the relative status of law-firm personnel. Particularly, they should learn to whom they are accountable and who, in turn, is accountable to them.

3. Employment policies relate to compensation and employee benefits, performance evaluations, employment termination, and other rules of the workplace, such as office hours. Usually (particularly in larger firms), these policies are spelled out in an employment manual or other writing. Most large firms today have policies and procedures governing discrimination in the workplace.

4. Confidentiality is a major concern and a fundamental policy of every law firm. A breach of confidentiality by anyone in the law office can subject the firm to extensive legal liability. The requirement of confidentiality lends a unique character to the law-office experience and shapes, to a significant extent, law-office procedures.

5. Every law firm follows certain procedures in regard to its filing system. In larger firms, these procedures may be written up in a procedural book. In smaller firms, procedures may be more casual and based on habit or tradition. A typical law firm has client files, work-product files and reference materials, forms files, and personnel files. Proper file maintenance is crucial to a smoothly functioning firm. An efficient filing system helps to ensure that important documents will not be lost or misplaced and will be available when needed. Filing procedures in a law office must also maximize client confidentiality and the safekeeping of documents and other evidence.

6. A foremost concern of any law firm is to establish a clear policy on fee arrangements and efficient billing procedures, so that each client is billed appropriately. Types of fee arrangements include fixed fees, hourly fees, and contingency fees. Clients who pay hourly fees are billed monthly for the time spent by attorneys or other legal personnel on the clients' cases or projects, as well as all costs incurred on behalf of the clients.

7. Firms require attorneys and paralegals to document how they use their time. Because the firm's income depends on the number of billable hours produced by the firm's legal personnel, firms usually require attorneys and paralegals to generate a certain number of billable hours per year. This requirement subjects legal personnel to significant pressure. Double billing presents a major ethical problem for law firms.

8. Attorneys have a duty to keep their clients reasonably informed of the matters being handled by the attorneys for the clients. Paralegals should be aware that this is a legal duty and that they can play a significant role in keeping attorney-client communication channels open. Billing statements to clients serve as a method of communicating with clients, as do periodic phone calls, letters, or e-mail messages.

9. Each office has its own culture, or personality, which is largely shaped by the attitudes of the firm's owners and the qualities they look for when hiring personnel. Each firm also has a political infrastructure that is not apparent to outsiders. Office culture and politics make a great difference in terms of job satisfaction and comfort. Wise paralegals will learn as soon as possible after taking a job, from co-workers or others, about these aspects of the legal workplace.

QUESTIONS FOR REVIEW

1. What are the three basic organizational structures of law firms?

2. What is the difference between an associate and a partner?

3. Who handles the administrative tasks of a law firm? Who supervises the work performed by paralegals in a law firm?

4. Name some of the topics that might be included in an employment policy manual. How do firms evaluate paralegal performance?

5. Why is maintaining confidentiality so important in law offices? How does the confidentiality requirement affect law-office procedures and practices?

6. What kinds of files do law firms maintain? What general procedures are typically followed in regard to client files?

7. How does a law firm arrange its fees with its clients? What ethical obligations do attorneys have with respect to legal fees?

8. How do lawyers and legal assistants keep track of their time? What is the difference between billable and nonbillable hours? What is a client trust account?

9. Describe some of the ways that attorneys communicate with clients. Why is communicating with clients important?

10. What is meant by the phrase, "law-office culture and politics"? How might law-office culture and politics affect a paralegal?

ETHICAL QUESTIONS

1. Catherine works as a paralegal for a sole practitioner. Catherine and the legal secretary both work in a large reception area. A client is waiting in the reception area to see the attorney. The legal secretary brings a fax of a real-estate contract that she just received from a client, Mrs. Henley. Then she transfers the client to Catherine. Mrs. Henley tells her that her supervising attorney had promised to review the real-estate contract prior to the *closing* (the final step in the sale of real estate) and that the closing will take place at 4 P.M. today. Before becoming a paralegal, Catherine worked as a Realtor and is very experienced in real-estate closings. Mrs. Henley knows this and insists that Catherine review and approve the contract if the attorney does not have time to review it. With what ethical problem is Catherine faced? How can these problems be resolved in a sole practitioner's office?

2. Carla Seegen is an experienced legal assistant who is also a licensed Realtor. She sold real estate for eight years before becoming a paralegal. Carla works in a small law firm and has recently been assigned to work for Mike McAllister, who is a new attorney and the son of one of the firm's founding partners, John McAllister. Mike is asked to handle a real-estate closing for the firm's biggest client. Mike is unfamiliar with the client's business. Furthermore, he studied property law only briefly in law school and has no experience in real-estate transactions. Carla soon learns of Mike's lack of knowledge and experience because he does not ask her to draft the appropriate documents and undertake the kinds of tasks that are necessary for the closing. Whenever she mentions these things to Mike, however, or offers to show him what must be done, Mike becomes annoyed. Carla likes her job and knows that if she continues to annoy Mike, she may be fired. At the same time, she is concerned about the client's welfare and legal protection. Should she talk to one of the partners about the problem? Should she discuss the issue with John McAllister, Mike's father? How would you handle the situation?

3. Roberta Miller works as a paralegal, secretary, and receptionist for a sole practitioner. She is working on a bankruptcy file for a client, Gina Thomas. Because Roberta is running late for a meeting with a client, James Archer, she leaves the file—which is clearly marked, "Gina Thomas/Bankruptcy"—on her desk. Mr. Archer comes into her office for the meeting. During the meeting, Roberta turns to her computer to print a document for Mr. Archer to sign. While her back is turned, Mr. Archer notices the Gina Thomas file on Roberta's desk. Gina Thomas is his neighbor. When Roberta turns around, Mr. Archer begins to ask her questions about the file. Has an ethical violation occurred? If so, by whom and of what rule, and how could the violation have been avoided?

4. Attorney Smith represents Mrs. White in a divorce and custody action against Mr. White. At the outset of the representation, Mrs. Smith makes it clear that all that she is interested in is obtaining custody of her children. She even suggests that they propose trading the house for custody of the children in the settlement of the dispute. Attorney Smith tells Mrs. White, "Don't worry, I can get your kids. I don't suggest offering to trade the house for the children, though, because custody rights can always change, and once you give away the house, it's gone and you have nothing." The case drags on for over three years. Mrs. White pays attorney Smith $30,000. At the end of the

trial, which lasted for three months, the outstanding bill is over $100,000, and, while Mrs. White lost custody of the children, she is awarded the house. The house has enough equity to pay attorney Smith's bill, including significant fees for his legal assistant's time. The attorney demands that Mrs. White give him a lien against her house. She refuses to do so, and they are thrown into a fee dispute. Mrs. White discovers that attorney Smith's fees for his services are significantly higher than what other family-law attorneys in her area normally charge. What ethical rule comes into play here? What arguments would Mrs. White make against attorney Smith? What would be his counterarguments?

5. Sam Martin, an attorney, receives a settlement check for a client's case. It is made out jointly to Sam and his client. Sam signs it and instructs his paralegal to deposit it into his law firm's bank account, instead of the client's trust account, because he wants to take out his fee before he gives the client his portion of the money. May Sam do this? Why or why not?

6. Tom Baker, a paralegal, has been doing research for a client using Westlaw® (a computerized research service discussed in Chapter 9). Tom's supervising attorney tells him to bill the Westlaw® charges that he just incurred on behalf of one client to both that client's and another client's account. The second client to be billed is a large and prosperous corporation, and the research Tom conducted applies to the second client as well. What ethical violation has occurred? What should Tom do?

PRACTICE QUESTIONS AND ASSIGNMENTS

1. Using the material presented in the chapter, identify the following law practices by their organizational structure:

   a. Bill James is an attorney who practices law on his own. He owns his legal practice, the building in which he works, and most of the office furniture. He leases his office equipment. Bill has one secretary and one paralegal who work for him.

   b. Roberta Wagner owns a law firm with Joe Rosen. They own equal interests in the firm, participate equally in the firm's management, and share jointly in its profits and losses. Wagner & Rosen has three associates, six secretaries, and three paralegals who work for the firm.

   c. Randall Smith and Susan Street own a law firm together as shareholders. They employ eight associate attorneys, twelve secretaries, and five legal assistants.

2. Using the material presented in the chapter, identify the following law-office personnel:

   a. Martha Marsh works as a paralegal in a large law firm. After thirteen years with the firm, Martha is promoted. She now oversees paralegal staffing, assignments, and professional development.

   b. Mark James was hired by the partners of a large law firm, Smith & Smith, to manage the day-to-day operations of the firm.

   c. Rhonda Allen is an attorney who works as an employee for Marsh & Martin, a law firm with 250 attorneys.

   d. Tom is a file clerk for Jepp & Allen, P.C.

   e. Michael O'Dowd is a lawyer. He owns O'Dowd & O'Dowd, P.C., with his sister, Jane.

3. Henry Hampton III, a senior partner in the all-male law firm of Willette, Hampton & Kohl, hired Karla Black, the first woman attorney in the history of the firm. She was a top graduate from the number one law school in the country. After six months, the "boys" decided they did not like having a woman in their "club," and they fired Karla, claiming this was legitimate under the employment-at-will doctrine. Write one paragraph explaining the employment-at-will doctrine; then write a second paragraph analyzing this situation and explaining whether Willette, Hampton & Kohl could legally fire Karla Black under this doctrine.

4. Mary Anne is a paralegal student who has taken a job with a sole practitioner. The attorney has a general practice and handles legal matters relating to family law, real estate, estate planning and probate, and general civil litigation. He is very busy and, consequently, very disorganized. Mary Anne's first task is to help him organize his office, especially his client files. When Mary Anne arrives for her first day of work, she finds that he does not keep his files in the filing

cabinets in the office. Rather, they are on his desk, credenza, piled up on the floor, and anywhere else that he happens to leave them. Using the material in this chapter, how would you create a filing system for the attorney's office? Be sure to include a discussion of how you would store, maintain, and destroy files.

5. Identify the type of billing that is being used in each of the following examples:

   a. The client is billed $150 per hour for a partner's time, $100 per hour for an associate attorney's time, and $70 per hour for a legal assistant's time.

   b. The attorney's fee is one-third of the amount that the attorney recovers for the client, either through a pretrial settlement or through a trial.

   c. The client is charged $175 to change the name of the client's business firm.

6. Louise Lanham hires John J. Roberts, an attorney with the law firm of Sands, Roberts & Simpson, located at 1000 Plymouth Road, Phoenix, Arizona, to represent her in a divorce. She agrees to pay attorney Roberts a rate of $150 per hour and to pay a legal-assistant rate of $75 per hour. She also agrees to pay all costs and expenses, such as filing fees, expert-witness fees, court-reporter fees, and other fees incurred in the course of her representation. Using Exhibit 4.3, *A Sample Retainer Agreement*, draft a retainer agreement between Louise Lanham and John J. Roberts.

USING INTERNET RESOURCES

1. Go online and access the following site: www.bizfilings.com. Select the link to "frequently asked questions" (FAQs) about incorporation. Summarize in writing the answers given to the following questions:

   a. What are the advantages of incorporation?

   b. What are the disadvantages of incorporation?

   c. How many directors must a corporation have?

   d. What factors should be considered when deciding on a corporate name?

2. Find legal forms on the Internet by going to the following Web site: www.legaldocs.com. Make a list of the types of forms that are available. Are they free? If not, how much do the forms cost? How can they be purchased? What methods of payment are accepted?

3. Research time-and-billing software on the Internet by going to the following Web site: www.timeslips.com. Click on the brochure and read about the software. Is it limited to one type of billing arrangement, or is it flexible? Can it create reports? What else can it do?

CHAPTER 5

THE AMERICAN LEGAL SYSTEM

Chapter Outline

⊠ INTRODUCTION ⊠ WHAT IS LAW? ⊠ CONSTITUTIONAL LAW
⊠ STATUTORY LAW ⊠ ADMINISTRATIVE LAW ⊠ CASE LAW AND THE
COMMON LAW TRADITION ⊠ THE AMERICAN SYSTEM OF JUSTICE
⊠ STATE COURT SYSTEMS ⊠ THE FEDERAL COURT SYSTEM
⊠ ALTERNATIVE DISPUTE RESOLUTION

After completing this chapter, you will know:

- The meaning and relative importance in the American legal system of constitutional law, statutory law, administrative law, and case law.

- What the common law tradition is and how English law influenced the development of the American legal system.

- The requirements that must be met before a lawsuit can be brought in a particular court by a particular party.

- The types of courts that make up a typical state court system and the different functions of trial courts and appellate courts.

- The organization of the federal court system and the relationship between state and federal jurisdiction.

- The various ways in which disputes can be resolved outside the court system.

INTRODUCTION

Like the legal systems of many other countries, the American legal system is based on tradition. For the most part, the colonists who first came to America were governed by English law. As a result, the law of England continued to be the paramount model for American jurists and legislators after the colonists declared their independence from England in 1776. English common law from medieval times onward thus became part of the American legal tradition as well, modified as necessary to suit conditions unique to America.

This chapter opens with a discussion of the nature of law and then focuses on the sources of American law, including constitutional law, statutory law, administrative law, and case law. We then examine the common law tradition and its significance in the American legal system. You will also read about another component of the American legal structure—the court system and alternative methods of dispute settlement.

WHAT IS LAW?

Paralegals spend their entire careers dealing with legal matters. But even the most experienced paralegal might be hard pressed to give you a useful definition of *law*. What is law? There is no one answer to this question because how law is defined depends on the speaker's personal philosophy about such matters as morality, ethics, and truth. As a result, there have been and will continue to be different definitions of *law*. Although the various definitions differ in their particulars, they all are based on the following general observation concerning the nature of **law:**

Law
A body of rules of conduct with legal force and effect, prescribed by the controlling authority (the government) of a society.

> **Law consists of a body of rules of conduct with legal force and effect, prescribed by the controlling authority (the government) of a society.**

In the United States, these "rules of conduct" are embodied in numerous sources, including constitutions, statutes, administrative law, case law, and the common law tradition.

CONSTITUTIONAL LAW

Courts have numerous sources of law to consider when making their decisions, including constitutional law. The federal government and the states have separate constitutions that set forth the general organization, powers, and limits of their respective governments.

The Federal Constitution

Supremacy Clause
The provision in Article VI of the U.S. Constitution that provides that the Constitution, laws, and treaties of the United States are "the supreme Law of the Land." Under this clause, state and local laws that directly conflict with federal law will be rendered invalid.

The U.S. Constitution, as amended, is the supreme law of the land. This principle is set forth in Article VI of the Constitution, which provides that the Constitution, laws, and treaties of the United States are "the supreme Law of the Land." This provision is commonly referred to as the **supremacy clause.** A law in violation of the Constitution (including its amendments), no matter what its source, will be declared unconstitutional if it is challenged. For example, if a state legislature enacts a law that conflicts with the federal Constitution, a person or business firm that is subject to that law may challenge its validity in a court action. If the court agrees with the complaining party that the law is unconstitutional, it will declare the law invalid and refuse to enforce it.

The U.S. Constitution sets forth the powers of the three branches of the federal government and the relationship between the three branches. The need for a written declaration of the rights of individuals eventually caused the first Congress of the United States to submit twelve amendments to the Constitution to the states for approval. Ten of these amendments, commonly known as the **Bill of Rights,** were adopted in 1791 and embody a series of protections for the individual—and in some cases, business entities—against various types of interference by the federal government.[1]

Bill of Rights
The first ten amendments to the Constitution.

CONSTITUTIONAL RIGHTS.   Summarized below are the protections guaranteed by the Bill of Rights. The full text of the Constitution, including its amendments, is presented in Appendix J at the end of this book.

1. The First Amendment guarantees the freedoms of religion, speech, and the press and the rights to assemble peaceably and to petition the government.
2. The Second Amendment guarantees the right to keep and bear arms.
3. The Third Amendment prohibits, in peacetime, the lodging of soldiers in any house without the owner's consent.
4. The Fourth Amendment prohibits unreasonable searches and seizures of persons or property.
5. The Fifth Amendment guarantees the rights to indictment by grand jury and to due process of law, and prohibits compulsory self-incrimination and double jeopardy. The Fifth Amendment also prohibits the taking of private property for public use without just compensation.
6. The Sixth Amendment guarantees the accused in a criminal case the right to a speedy and public trial by an impartial jury and the right to counsel. The accused has the right to cross-examine witnesses against him or her and to solicit testimony from witnesses in his or her favor.
7. The Seventh Amendment guarantees the right to a trial by jury in a civil case involving at least twenty dollars.[2]
8. The Eighth Amendment prohibits excessive bail and fines, as well as cruel and unusual punishment.
9. The Ninth Amendment establishes that the people have rights in addition to those specified in the Constitution.
10. The Tenth Amendment establishes that those powers neither delegated to the federal government nor denied to the states are reserved for the states.

THE COURTS AND CONSTITUTIONAL LAW.   You should realize that the rights secured by the Bill of Rights are not absolute. The broad principles enunciated in the Constitution are given form and substance by the courts. For example, even though the First Amendment guarantees the freedom of speech, we are not, in fact, free to say anything we want. In interpreting the meaning of the First Amendment's guarantee of free speech, the United States Supreme Court has made it clear that certain types of speech will not be protected. For example, speech that harms the

On the Web
For information on the role of the United States Supreme Court in interpreting the Constitution, go to www.usscplus.com.

---

1. One of these proposed amendments was ratified 203 years later (in 1992) and became the Twenty-seventh Amendment to the Constitution. See Appendix J.
2. Twenty dollars was forty days' pay for the average person when the Bill of Rights was written.

good reputation of another is deemed a tort, or civil wrong. If the speaker is sued, he or she may be ordered by a court to pay damages to the harmed person.

Courts often have to balance the rights and freedoms enunciated in the Bill of Rights against other rights, such as the right to be free from the harmful actions of others. Ultimately, it is the United States Supreme Court, as the final interpreter of the Constitution, that both gives meaning to our constitutional rights and determines their boundaries.

State Constitutions

Each state also has a constitution that sets forth the general organization, powers, and limits of the state government. The Tenth Amendment to the U.S. Constitution, which defines the powers and limitations of the federal government, reserves all powers not granted to the federal government to the states. Unless they conflict with the U.S. Constitution, state constitutions are supreme within the states' respective borders. State constitutions are thus important sources of law.

Constitutional Law and the Paralegal

Many paralegals assist attorneys in handling cases that involve constitutional provisions or rights. For example, a corporate client might claim that a regulation issued by a state administrative agency, such as the state department of natural resources, is invalid because it conflicts with a federal law or regulation. (Administrative agencies are discussed later in this chapter.) You may be assigned the task of finding out which regulation takes priority. Many cases arise in which the plaintiff claims that his or her First Amendment rights have been violated. Suppose that a plaintiff's religious beliefs forbid working on a certain day of the week. If he or she is required to work on that day, the plaintiff may claim that the employer's requirement violates the First Amendment, which guarantees the free exercise of religion.

No matter what kind of work you do as a paralegal, you will find that a knowledge of constitutional law will be beneficial. This is because the authority and underlying rationale for the substantive and procedural laws governing many areas of law are ultimately based on the Constitution. For example, a knowledge of constitutional law is helpful to paralegals working in the area of criminal law, because criminal procedures are essentially designed to protect the constitutional rights of accused persons.

STATUTORY LAW

Laws passed by the federal Congress and the various state legislatures are called **statutes**. These statutes make up another source of law, which, as mentioned earlier, is generally referred to as **statutory law**. When a legislature passes a statute, that statute is ultimately included in the federal code of laws or the relevant state code of laws. The California Code, for example, contains the statutory law of the state of California.

Statutory law also includes local ordinances. An **ordinance** is a statute (law, rule, or order) passed by a municipal or county government unit to govern matters not covered by federal or state law. Ordinances commonly have to do with city or county land use (zoning ordinances), building and safety codes, and other matters affecting the local unit. Persons who violate ordinances may be fined or jailed, or both. No state statute or local ordinance may violate the U.S. Constitution—due to the supremacy clause, as mentioned earlier—or the state constitution.

On the Web

If you are interested in looking at state constitutions, including the one for your state, go to www.findlaw.com/casecode/state.html.

Statute
A written law enacted by a legislature under its constitutional law-making authority.

Statutory Law
Laws enacted by a legislative body.

Ordinance
An order, rule, or law enacted by a municipal or county government to govern a local matter unaddressed by state or federal legislation.

DEVELOPING PARALEGAL SKILLS

State versus Federal Regulation

Stephanie Wilson works as a paralegal in the legal department of National Pipeline, Inc., whose business is transporting natural gas to local utilities, factories, and other sites throughout the country. Last month, a pipeline running under a suburban street in Minneapolis, Minnesota, exploded, resulting in several severe injuries and one death.

The federal government has regulated pipeline safety and maintenance since 1968, under the Natural Gas Pipeline Safety Act. As a result of the explosion, the state of Minnesota wants to regulate pipeline safety as well. Stephanie's boss, the general counsel, and several other executives believe that the federal act preempts, or occupies, this field of law, preventing the state from enacting another layer of safety legislation. Stephanie is assigned the task of researching the statute and relevant case law to determine if the federal law does in fact preempt the state's regulation.

TIPS FOR DETERMINING FEDERAL PREEMPTION

- Read through the statute to see if it expressly states that Congress intended to preempt the field.
- Look for an actual conflict between a federal and state law.
- Look for indications that Congress has impliedly occupied the field: Is the federal regulatory scheme pervasive? Is federal occupation of the field necessitated by the need for national uniformity? Is there a danger of conflict between state laws and the administration of the federal program?
- Locate and read through cases discussing the issue of federal preemption in this area.

The Expanding Scope of Statutory Law

Today, legislative bodies and administrative agencies assume an ever-increasing share of lawmaking. Much of the work of modern courts consists of interpreting what the rulemakers intended to accomplish when a particular law was drafted and enacted and deciding how the law applies to a specific set of facts.

Statutory Law and the Paralegal

As a paralegal, you may often be dealing with cases that involve violations of statutory law. If you work for a small law firm, you may become familiar with the statutory law governing a wide spectrum of activities. If you specialize in one area, such as bankruptcy law, you will become very familiar with the federal statutory law governing bankruptcy and bankruptcy procedures. Here are just a few examples of the areas in which you might work that are governed extensively by statutory law:

- *Corporate law*—governed by state statutes.
- *Patent, copyright, and trademark law*—governed by federal statutes.
- *Employment law*—governed to an increasing extent by federal statutes concerning discrimination in employment, workplace safety, labor unions, pension plans, Social Security, and other aspects of employment. Each state also has statutes governing certain areas of employment, such as safety standards in the workplace and employment discrimination.
- *Antitrust law*—governed by federal statutes prohibiting specific types of anti-competitive business practices.

On the Web
A good starting point to access federal statutes, as well as state statutes that are now online, is **www.findlaw.com**.

- *Consumer law*—governed by state and federal statutes protecting consumers against deceptive trade practices (such as misleading advertising), unsafe products, and generally any activities that threaten consumer health and welfare.
- *Wills and probate administration* (relating to the transfer of property on the property owner's death)—governed by state statutes.

A paralegal working in an area (or on a case) governed by statutory law needs to know how to both locate and interpret the relevant state or federal statutes. You will learn how to find and analyze statutory law in Chapter 8.

ADMINISTRATIVE LAW

There is virtually no way that the federal Congress or a state legislature can oversee the actual implementation of all the laws that it enacts. To assist them in their governing responsibilities, legislatures at all levels of government often delegate such tasks to **administrative agencies**, particularly when the issues relate to highly technical areas. By creating and delegating some of its authority to an administrative agency, a legislature may indirectly monitor a particular area in which it has passed legislation without becoming bogged down in the details relating to enforcement—details that are best left to specialists.

Agency Creation and Function

To create an administrative agency at the federal level, Congress passes **enabling legislation**, which specifies the name, purpose, composition, and powers of the agency being created. The Occupational Safety and Health Act of 1970, for example, provided for the creation of the Occupational Safety and Health Administration to administer and implement the provisions of the act, to issue rules as necessary to protect employees from dangerous conditions in the workplace, and to enforce the act's provisions and the agency's rules.

There are dozens of federal administrative agencies, each of which has been established to perform specific governing tasks. For example, the federal Environmental Protection Agency coordinates and enforces federal environmental laws. The Food and Drug Administration enforces federal laws relating to the safety of foods and drugs. The Federal Trade Commission issues and enforces rules relating to unfair advertising or sales practices. Each state also has a number of administrative agencies, many of which parallel agencies at the federal level. For example, state environmental laws are implemented by state environmental agencies, such as a state's department of natural resources. The rules, orders, and decisions of administrative agencies at all levels of government constitute what is known as **administrative law**.

Administrative Law and the Paralegal

Paralegals frequently deal with administrative agencies. If you work for a law firm that has many corporate clients, you may be involved extensively in researching and analyzing agency regulations and their applicability to certain business activities. If you work for a corporate legal department, you will probably assist the attorneys in the department in a vital task—determining which agency regulations apply to the corporation and whether the corporation is complying with those regulations. If you work for an administrative agency, you may be involved in drafting new rules, in analyzing survey results to see if a new rule is necessary, in mediating disputes

Administrative Agency
A federal or state government agency established to perform a specific function. Administrative agencies are authorized by legislative acts to make and enforce rules relating to the purpose for which they were established.

Enabling Legislation
A statute enacted by a legislature that authorizes the creation of an administrative agency and specifies the name, purpose, composition, and powers of the agency being created.

Administrative Law
A body of law created by administrative agencies in the form of rules, regulations, orders, and decisions in order to carry out their duties and responsibilities.

On the Web
The *United States Government Manual* describes the origins, purposes, and administrators of every federal department and agency. You can access this publication online at **www.gpo.ucop.edu.**

between a private party and an agency, in investigations to gather facts about compliance with agency rules, and numerous other tasks. In any law practice, you may be asked to assist clients who are involved in disputes with administrative agencies.

Paralegals often become very familiar with administrative process when helping clients obtain needed benefits from state or federal administrative agencies. You may work with local agencies in helping the homeless obtain medical assistance, for example. As noted in Chapter 2, some administrative agencies, including the Social Security Administration, allow paralegals to represent clients at administrative agency hearings and other procedures. We list below a few federal government agencies and describe how paralegals may be involved with administrative law and procedures relating to those agencies.

- *Equal Employment Opportunity Commission (EEOC).* If a client wants to pursue a claim against his or her employer for employment discrimination, the client must first contact the EEOC. The EEOC may investigate and try to settle the claim. If the problem cannot be resolved by the EEOC or if the EEOC decides not to take action on the matter, the client will be entitled to sue the employer directly. You may be involved in contacting the EEOC and assisting the client in complying with procedures required by the EEOC for handling complaints of employment discrimination.

- *Internal Revenue Service (IRS).* If you work for a corporate law department, you might be asked to assist corporate counsel in handling corporate taxes and related IRS requirements. If you work in a law firm, a corporate client may request legal assistance in settling a dispute with the IRS or in complying with tax laws.

- *Securities and Exchange Commission (SEC).* If you work for a corporation that sells shares of stock in its company to the public, you may be asked to assist in drafting the documents necessary to fulfill registration requirements under federal securities law. If you work for a law firm, you may perform similar tasks for corporate clients. You may also assist in the defense of a client who has been charged with "insider trading" in violation of securities law (which prohibits the purchase or sale of securities for personal gain based on knowledge available only to corporate officers or employees and not to the general public).

- *Food and Drug Administration (FDA).* Any firm that places foods or drugs on the market must make sure that those products are safe and properly labeled. If you work for a corporation or on behalf of a corporate client that markets food or drug products, you may be involved in procedures required by the FDA for product testing and labeling or for seeking FDA approval to market a firm's product.

On the Web
Links to federal government administrative agencies can be found at FedWorld's Web site. Go to www.fedworld.gov.

CASE LAW AND THE COMMON LAW TRADITION

Another important source of law consists of the decisions rendered by judges in cases that come before the courts. This body of law is called **case law.** To understand the importance of case law in the United States, you need to first understand what is meant by the common law tradition, which originated in medieval England.

As mentioned earlier, because of our colonial heritage much of American law is based on the English legal system. After the United States declared its independence from England, American jurists continued to be greatly influenced by English law and English legal writers. Indeed, much of American law in such areas as contracts, torts (types of civil wrongs), property law, and criminal law derives in large part from the English legal system.

Case Law
Rules of law announced in court decisions.

The Origins and Nature of the Common Law

In 1066, the Normans conquered England, and William the Conqueror and his successors began the process of unifying the country under their rule. One of the means they used to this end was the establishment of the king's courts, or *curiae regis*. Before the Norman Conquest, disputes had been settled according to the local legal customs and traditions in various regions of the country. The king's courts sought to establish a uniform set of customs for the country as a whole. What evolved in these courts was the beginning of the **common law**—a body of general rules that prescribed social conduct and applied throughout the entire English realm.

Courts developed the common law rules from the principles underlying judges' decisions in actual legal controversies. Judges attempted to be consistent. When possible, they based their decisions on the principles suggested by earlier cases. They sought to decide similar cases in a similar way and considered new cases with care because they knew that their decisions would make new law. Each interpretation became part of the law on the subject and served as a legal **precedent**. Later cases that involved similar legal principles or facts could be decided with reference to that precedent. The courts were thus guided by traditions and legal doctrines that evolved over time.

The practice of deciding new cases with reference to former decisions, or precedents, eventually became a cornerstone of the English and American judicial systems. It forms a doctrine called *stare decisis*[3] ("to stand on decided cases"). Under this doctrine, judges are obligated to follow the precedents established by their own courts or by higher courts within their jurisdictions. Sometimes a court will depart from the rule of precedent if it decides that the precedent is simply incorrect or that technological or social changes have rendered the precedent inapplicable.

The Common Law Today

The common law developed in England and still used in the United States consists of the rules of law announced in court decisions, or case law. These rules of law include interpretations of constitutional provisions, of statutes enacted by legislatures, and of regulations created by administrative agencies, such as the federal Environmental Protection Agency. The common law governs all areas not covered by *statutory law,* which (as discussed previously) generally consists of those laws enacted by state legislatures and by the federal Congress.

Common Law and the Paralegal

As a paralegal, you will find that a basic understanding of the common law tradition will serve you well whenever you need to research and analyze case law. The doctrine of *stare decisis* and the distinction between different types of remedies are critical concepts when applied to real-life situations faced by clients.

For example, suppose that a client wants to sue another party for breaching a contract to perform computer consulting services. In this situation, the common law of *contracts* would apply to the case. If you were asked to research the case, you would search for previous cases dealing with similar issues to see how those cases were decided. You would want to know of any precedents set by a higher court in your jurisdiction—and, of course, by the United States Supreme Court—on that issue.

Common Law
A body of law developed from custom or judicial decisions in English and U.S. courts and not attributable to a legislature.

Precedent
A court decision that furnishes an example or authority for deciding subsequent cases in which identical or similar facts are presented.

Stare Decisis
A flexible doctrine of the courts, recognizing the value of following prior decisions (precedents) in cases similar to the one before the court; the courts' practice of being consistent with prior decisions based on similar facts.

On the Web
To learn how the Supreme Court justified its departure from precedent in the 1954 *Brown* decision, you can access the Court's opinion online at www.findlaw.com.

---

3. Pronounced *ster*-ay dih-*si*-ses.

ETHICAL CONCERN
Legal Research and *Stare Decisis*

One of the challenges faced by legal professionals is keeping up with the ever-changing law. For example, suppose that you are asked to do research on a case involving issues similar to those in a case you researched just three months ago. If you apply your previous research results to the current client's case, you need to verify that your earlier research still applies—that is, that previous case decisions are still "good law." In three months' time, an appeals court might have created a new precedent, and failure to update your research (how to do this is explained in Chapters 8 and 9) can lead to serious consequences for the client—and for you and the attorney, if the client decides to sue the attorney for negligence (specifically, for breaching the duty of competence).

In addition to lawsuits involving contract law, the common law also applies to *tort law* (the law governing civil wrongs, such as negligence or assault and battery, as opposed to criminal wrongs). As a paralegal, you may be working on behalf of clients bringing or defending against the following types of actions, all of which involve tort law:

- *Personal-injury lawsuits*—actions brought by plaintiffs to obtain compensation for injuries allegedly caused by the wrongful acts of others, either intentionally or through negligence.
- *Malpractice lawsuits*—actions brought by plaintiffs against professionals, such as physicians and attorneys, to obtain compensation for injuries allegedly caused by professional negligence (breach of professional duties).
- *Product-liability lawsuits*—actions brought by plaintiffs to obtain compensation for injuries allegedly caused by defective products.

Numerous other areas, such as property law and employment law, are also still governed to some extent by the common law. Depending on the nature of your job as a paralegal, you may be dealing with many cases that are governed by the common law.

THE AMERICAN SYSTEM OF JUSTICE

Before a lawsuit can be brought before a court, certain requirements must be met. We examine here these important requirements and some of the basic features of the American system of justice.

Types of Jurisdiction

In Latin, *juris* means "law," and *diction* means "to speak." Thus, "the power to speak the law" is the literal meaning of the term **jurisdiction.** Before any court can hear a case, it must have jurisdiction over the person against whom the suit is brought or over the property involved in the suit. The court must also have jurisdiction over the subject matter.

Jurisdiction
The authority of a court to hear and decide a specific action.

JURISDICTION OVER PERSONS.   Generally, a court can exercise personal jurisdiction (*in personam* jurisdiction) over residents of a certain geographical area. A state trial court, for example, normally has jurisdictional authority over residents within the state or within a particular area of the state, such as a county or district. A state's highest court (often called the state supreme court[4]) has jurisdictional authority over all residents within the state.

In some cases, under the authority of a long arm statute, a court can exercise personal jurisdiction over nonresidents as well. A **long arm statute** is a state law permitting courts to exercise jurisdiction over nonresident defendants. Before a court can exercise jurisdiction over a nonresident under a long arm statute, though, it must be demonstrated that the nonresident had sufficient contacts (*minimum contacts*) with the state to justify the jurisdiction. For example, if a California citizen committed a wrong within the state of Arizona, such as causing an automobile injury or selling defective goods, an Arizona state court usually could exercise jurisdiction over the California citizen. Similarly, a state may exercise personal jurisdiction over a nonresident defendant who is sued for breaching a contract that was formed within the state.

In regard to corporations, the minimum-contacts requirement is usually met if the corporation does business within the state. A Maine corporation that has a branch office or manufacturing plant in Georgia, for example, has sufficient minimum contacts with the state of Georgia to allow a Georgia court to exercise jurisdiction over the Maine corporation. If the Maine corporation advertises and sells its products in Georgia, those activities may also suffice to meet the minimum-contacts requirements. A state court may also be able to exercise jurisdiction over a corporation in another country if it can be demonstrated that the foreign corporation has met the "minimum-contacts" test. For example, consider an Italian corporation that markets its products through an American distributor. If the corporation knew that its products would be distributed to local markets throughout the United States, it could be sued in any state by a plaintiff who was injured by the corporation's product.

JURISDICTION OVER PROPERTY.   A court can also exercise jurisdiction over property that is located within its boundaries. This kind of jurisdiction is known as *in rem* jurisdiction, or "jurisdiction over the thing." For example, suppose that a dispute arises over the ownership of a boat in dry dock in Fort Lauderdale, Florida. The boat is owned by an Ohio resident, over whom a Florida court cannot normally exercise personal jurisdiction. The other party to the dispute is a resident of Nebraska. In this situation, a lawsuit concerning the boat could be brought in a Florida state court on the basis of the court's *in rem* jurisdiction.

JURISDICTION OVER SUBJECT MATTER.   Jurisdiction over subject matter is a limitation on the types of cases a court can hear. In both the state and federal court systems, there are courts of *general jurisdiction* and courts of *limited jurisdiction*. The basis for the distinction lies in the subject matter of cases heard. For example, **probate courts**—state courts that handle only matters relating to the transfer of a person's assets and obligations on that person's death, including matters relating to the custody and guardianship of children—have limited subject-matter jurisdiction. A common example of a federal court of limited subject-matter jurisdiction is a bankruptcy court. **Bankruptcy courts** handle only bankruptcy proceedings, which are governed by federal bankruptcy law (bankruptcy law allows debtors to obtain

Long Arm Statute
A state statute that permits a state to obtain jurisdiction over nonresident individuals and corporations. Individuals or corporations, however, must have certain "minimum contacts" with that state for the statute to apply.

Probate Court
A court having jurisdiction over proceedings concerning the settlement of a person's estate.

Bankruptcy Court
A federal court of limited jurisdiction that hears only bankruptcy proceedings.

---

4. As will be discussed shortly, a state's highest court is often referred to as the state supreme court, but there are exceptions. For example, in New York the supreme court is a trial court.

relief from their debts when they cannot make ends meet). In contrast, a court of general jurisdiction can decide virtually any type of case.

The subject-matter jurisdiction of a court is usually defined in the statute or constitution creating the court. In both the state and federal court systems, a court's subject-matter jurisdiction can be limited not only by the subject of the lawsuit, but also by the amount of money in controversy, by whether a case is a felony (a more serious type of crime) or a misdemeanor (a less serious type of crime), or by whether the proceeding is a trial or an appeal.

ORIGINAL AND APPELLATE JURISDICTION.   The distinction between courts of original jurisdiction and courts of appellate jurisdiction normally lies in whether the case is being heard for the first time. Courts having **original jurisdiction** are courts of the first instance, or **trial courts**—that is, courts in which lawsuits begin, trials take place, and evidence is presented. In the federal court system, the *district courts* are trial courts. In the various state court systems, the trial courts are known by different names. The key point here is that normally, any court having original jurisdiction is known as a trial court. Courts having **appellate jurisdiction** act as reviewing courts, or **appellate courts.** In general, cases can be brought before them only on appeal from an order or a judgment of a trial court or other lower court. State and federal trial and appellate courts will be discussed more fully later in this chapter.

Jurisdiction of the Federal Courts

Because the federal government is a government of limited powers, the jurisdiction of the federal courts is limited. Article III of the U.S. Constitution established the boundaries of federal judicial power. Section 2 of Article III states that "[t]he judicial Power shall extend to all Cases, in Law and Equity, arising under this Constitution, the Laws of the United States, and Treaties made, or which shall be made, under their Authority."

FEDERAL QUESTIONS.   Whenever a plaintiff's cause of action is based, at least in part, on the U.S. Constitution, a treaty, or a federal law, then a **federal question** arises, and the case comes under the judicial power of federal courts. Any lawsuit involving a federal question can originate in a federal court. People who claim that their constitutional rights have been violated can begin their suits in a federal court.

DIVERSITY JURISDICTION.   Federal district courts can also exercise original jurisdiction over cases involving **diversity of citizenship.** Such cases may arise between (1) citizens of different states, (2) a foreign country and citizens of a state or of different states, or (3) citizens of a state and citizens or subjects of a foreign country. The amount in controversy must be more than $75,000 before a federal court can take jurisdiction in such cases. For purposes of diversity-of-citizenship jurisdiction, a corporation is a citizen of the state in which it is incorporated and of the state in which its principal place of business is located. A case involving diversity of citizenship can be filed in the appropriate federal district court.

As an example of diversity jurisdiction, assume that the following events have taken place. Maria Ramirez, a citizen of Florida, was walking near a busy street in Tallahassee, Florida, one day when a large crate flew off a passing truck and hit and seriously injured her. She incurred numerous medical expenses and could not work for six months. She now wants to sue the trucking firm for $500,000 in damages. The trucking firm's headquarters are in Georgia, although the company does business in Florida.

Original Jurisdiction
The power of a court to take a case, try it, and decide it.

Trial Court
A court in which most cases usually begin and in which questions of fact are examined.

Appellate Jurisdiction
The power of a court to hear and decide an appeal; that is, the power and authority of a court to review cases that already have been tried in a lower court and the power to make decisions about them without actually holding a trial. This process is called appellate review.

Appellate Court
A court that reviews decisions made by lower courts, such as trial courts; a court of appeals.

Federal Question
A question that pertains to the U.S. Constitution, acts of Congress, or treaties. A federal question provides a basis for jurisdiction by the federal courts. This jurisdiction is authorized by Article III, Section 2, of the Constitution.

Diversity of Citizenship
Under Article III, Section 2, of the Constitution, a basis for federal court jurisdiction over certain disputes, including disputes between citizens of different states.

A basis for Fed. Court jurisdiction over disputes including those between citizens of diff. states.

In this situation, Maria could bring suit in a Florida court because she is a resident of Florida, the trucking firm does business in Florida, and that is where the accident occurred. She could also bring suit in a Georgia court, because a Georgia court could exercise jurisdiction over the trucking firm, which is headquartered in that state. As a third alternative, Maria could bring suit in a federal court because the requirements of diversity jurisdiction have been met—the lawsuit involves parties from different states, Florida and Georgia, and the amount in controversy (the damages Maria is seeking) exceeds $75,000.

Note that in a case based on a federal question, a federal court will apply federal law. In a case based on diversity of citizenship, however, a federal court will normally apply the law of the state in which the court sits. This is because cases based on diversity of citizenship normally do not involve activities that are regulated by the federal government. Therefore, federal laws do not apply, and state law will govern the issue.

EXCLUSIVE VERSUS CONCURRENT JURISDICTION.   When both federal and state courts have the power to hear a case, as is true in suits involving diversity of citizenship (such as Maria's case described above), **concurrent jurisdiction** exists. When cases can be tried only in federal courts or only in state courts, **exclusive jurisdiction** exists. Federal courts have exclusive jurisdiction in cases involving federal crimes, bankruptcy, patents, trademarks, and copyrights; in suits against the United States; and in some areas of admiralty law (law governing transportation on the seas and ocean waters). States also have exclusive jurisdiction in certain subject matters—for example, in divorce and adoptions.

When concurrent jurisdiction exists, a plaintiff bringing a lawsuit has a choice: he or she may bring the case in either a state court or a federal court. Normally, an attorney will look at several factors before advising a client on which court would be more advantageous. These factors include convenience (the physical location of the court), how long it would take in either type of court to get the case to trial (state courts often have heavier caseloads, and thus the wait may be longer), and the temperaments and judicial philosophies of the judges of the courts.

Venue

Jurisdiction has to do with whether a court has authority to hear a case involving specific persons, property, or subject matter. **Venue**[5] is concerned with the most appropriate location for a trial. For example, two state courts may have the authority to exercise jurisdiction over a case, but it may be more appropriate or convenient to hear the case in one court than in the other.

Basically, the concept of venue reflects the policy that a court trying a suit should be in the geographic neighborhood (usually the county) in which the incident leading to the lawsuit occurred or in which the parties involved in the lawsuit reside. Pretrial publicity or other factors, though, may require a change of venue to another community, especially in criminal cases in which the defendant's right to a fair and impartial jury has been impaired. For example, a change of venue from Oklahoma City to Denver, Colorado, was ordered for the trials of Timothy McVeigh and Terry Nichols after they had been indicted in connection with the 1995 bombing of the Alfred P. Murrah Federal Building in Oklahoma City. The bombing killed more than 160 persons and injured hundreds of others. In view of these circumstances, it was thought that to hold the trial in Oklahoma City would prejudice the rights of the defendants to a fair trial.

Concurrent Jurisdiction
Jurisdiction that exists when two different courts have the power to hear a case. For example, some cases can be heard in either a federal or a state court.

Exclusive Jurisdiction
Jurisdiction that exists when a case can be heard only in a particular court, such as a federal court.

Venue
The geographical district in which an action is tried and from which the jury is selected.

---

5. Pronounced *ven*-yoo.

DEVELOPING PARALEGAL SKILLS
Choice of Courts: State or Federal?

Susan Radtke, a lawyer specializing in the area of employment discrimination, and her legal assistant, Joan Dunbar, are meeting with a new client. The client wants to sue her former employer for gender discrimination. The client complained to her employer when she was passed over for a promotion. She was fired, she claims, as a result of her complaint. The client appears to have a strong case, because several of her former co-workers have agreed to testify that they heard the employer say on many occasions that he would never promote a woman to a managerial position.

Since both state and federal laws prohibit gender discrimination, the case could be brought in either state or federal court. The client tells Susan that because of Susan's experience, she wants her to decide whether the case

should be filed in a state or federal court. Joan will be drafting the complaint, so Susan and Joan discuss the pros and cons of filing the case in each court. Joan reviews a list of considerations with Susan.

TIPS FOR CHOOSING A COURT

- Review the jurisdiction of each court.
- Evaluate the strengths and weaknesses of the case.
- Evaluate the remedy sought.
- Evaluate the jury pool available for each court.
- Evaluate the likelihood of winning in each court.
- Evaluate the length of time it will take each court to decide the case.

Judicial Procedures

Litigation in court, from the moment a lawsuit is initiated until the final resolution of the case, must follow specifically designated procedural rules. The procedural rules for federal court cases are set forth in the Federal Rules of Civil Procedure. State rules, which are often similar to the federal rules, vary from state to state—and even from court to court within a given state. Rules of procedure also differ in criminal and civil cases. Paralegals who work for trial lawyers need to be familiar with the procedural rules of the relevant courts. Because judicial procedures will be examined in detail in Chapter 6, we do not discuss them here.

On the Web
The Federal Rules of Civil Procedure are now available online at www.cornell.edu.

The American System of Justice and the Paralegal

Paralegals should be familiar with such concepts as jurisdiction and venue, because these concepts affect pretrial litigation procedures. For example, a defendant in a lawsuit may claim that the court in which the plaintiff filed the lawsuit cannot exercise jurisdiction over the matter—or over the defendant or the defendant's property. If you are working on behalf of the defendant, you may be asked to draft a motion to dismiss the case on this ground. You may also be asked to draft a legal memorandum in support of the motion, outlining the legal reasons why the court cannot exercise jurisdiction over the case. (Motions to dismiss and supporting documents are discussed in Chapter 6.) Additionally, a party to a lawsuit may request that a case filed in a state court should be "removed" to a federal court (if there is a basis for federal jurisdiction) or vice versa. You may also be asked to draft a document requesting a change of venue (or objecting to an opponent's request for a change of venue) or to dismiss the case because the plaintiff lacks standing to sue.

If you work for a plaintiff's attorney, you might be asked to draft a complaint to initiate a lawsuit. Once the attorney reviews the facts with you, he or she may

---

ETHICAL CONCERN
Meeting Procedural Deadlines

One of the paralegal's most important responsibilities is making sure that court deadlines are met. For example, suppose that your supervising attorney asks you to file with the court a motion to dismiss (a document requesting the court to dismiss a lawsuit for a specific reason). You know that the deadline for filing the motion is three days away. You plan to deliver the motion to the court the next day, so you don't place a reminder note on your calendar. In the meantime, you place the motion in the client's file. The next morning, you arrive at work and immediately are called to help your supervising attorney with last-minute trial preparations on another case. You are busy all afternoon interviewing witnesses in still another case. You have totally forgotten about the motion to dismiss and do not think of it again until a week later—when the deadline for filing the motion has passed. Because you forgot to file the motion, your supervising attorney has breached the duty of competence. How can you make sure that you remember important deadlines? The answer is simple: *always* enter deadlines on the office calendaring system and *always* check your calendar several times a day. Also, realize that missed deadlines provide the basis for many malpractice suits against attorneys.

---

expect you to know whether concurrent jurisdiction exists. If concurrent jurisdiction exists, the attorney may expect you to ask whether the suit should be filed in a state or a federal court. If concurrent jurisdiction does not exist, the attorney may assume that you know in which court the case will be filed and that you know how to prepare the complaint for the appropriate court.

Recall from Chapter 1 that paralegal education and training emphasizes both substantive and procedural law. A paralegal can be a valuable member of a legal team if he or she has adequate knowledge of the procedural requirements relating to litigation and to different types of legal proceedings. You will read in detail about litigation procedures in Chapter 6.

STATE COURT SYSTEMS

Each state has its own system of courts, and no two state systems are the same. As Exhibit 5.1 indicates, there may be several levels, or tiers, of courts within a state court system: (1) state trial courts of limited jurisdiction, (2) state trial courts of general jurisdiction, (3) appellate courts, and (4) the state's highest court (often called the state supreme court). Judges in the state court system are usually elected by the voters for a specified term.

Generally, any person who is a party to a lawsuit has the opportunity to plead the case before a trial court and then, if he or she loses, before at least one level of appellate court. Finally, if a federal statute or federal constitutional issue is involved in the decision of a state supreme court, that decision may be further appealed to the United States Supreme Court.

Trial Courts

Trial courts are exactly what their name implies—courts in which trials are held and testimony taken. You will read in detail about trial procedures in Chapter 6.

On the Web
State court systems vary widely from state to state. To learn about your state's court system, go to the Center for Information Law and Policy's Web site at **www.cilp.org/tblhome.html**.

On the Web
The Web site of the National Center for State Courts offers links to the Web pages of all state courts. Go to **www.ncsc.dni.us/court/ sites/courts.htm**.

EXHIBIT 5.1
State Court Systems

State court systems vary widely from state to state, and it is therefore impossible to show one "typical" state court system. This exhibit is typical of the court systems in several states, however, including Texas, California, Arizona, and Nevada.

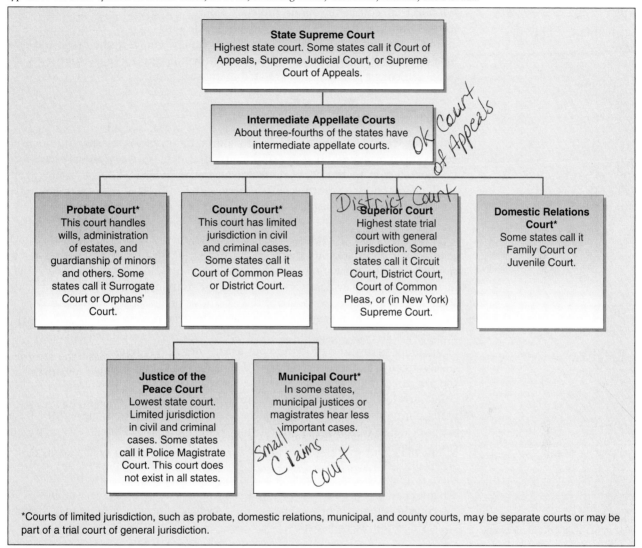

*Courts of limited jurisdiction, such as probate, domestic relations, municipal, and county courts, may be separate courts or may be part of a trial court of general jurisdiction.

In that chapter, we follow a hypothetical case through the various stages of a trial. Briefly, a trial court is presided over by a judge, who issues a decision on the matter before the court. If the trial is a jury trial (many trials are held without juries), the jury will decide the outcome of factual disputes, and the judge will issue a judgment based on the jury's conclusion. During the trial, the attorney for each side introduces evidence (such as relevant documents, exhibits, and testimony of witnesses) in support of his or her client's position. Each attorney is given an opportunity to cross-examine witnesses for the opposing party and challenge evidence introduced by the opposing party.

State trial courts have either general or limited jurisdiction. Trial courts that have general jurisdiction as to subject matter may be called county, district, superior, or circuit courts.[6] The jurisdiction of these courts is often determined by the

---

6. The name in Ohio is Court of Common Pleas; the name in New York is Supreme Court.

size of the county in which the court sits. State trial courts of general jurisdiction have jurisdiction over a wide variety of subjects, including both civil disputes (such as landlord-tenant matters or contract claims) and criminal prosecutions.

Courts with limited jurisdiction as to subject matter are often called special inferior trial courts or minor judiciary courts. Courts of limited jurisdiction include domestic relations courts, which handle only divorce actions and child-custody cases; local municipal courts, which mainly handle traffic cases; and probate courts, which, as previously mentioned, handle the administration of wills, estate-settlement problems, and related matters.

Courts of Appeals

Generally, courts of appeals (appellate courts, or reviewing courts) are not trial courts. In some states, however, trial courts of general jurisdiction may have limited jurisdiction to hear appeals from the minor judiciary—for example, from small claims courts or traffic courts. Every state has at least one court of appeals, which may be an intermediate appellate court or a state supreme court.

INTERMEDIATE APPELLATE COURTS. About three-fourths of the states have intermediate appellate courts. The subject-matter jurisdiction of these courts is substantially limited to hearing appeals. Appellate courts do not retry cases (conduct new trials, in which evidence is submitted to the court and witnesses are examined). Rather, an appellate court panel of three or more judges reviews the record of the case on appeal, which includes a transcript of the trial proceedings, and determines whether the trial court committed a prejudicial error of law. Appellate courts look at questions of law and procedure but usually not at questions of fact.

Normally, an appellate court will defer to a trial court's finding of fact because the trial court judge and jury were in a better position to evaluate testimony; they could directly observe witnesses' gestures, demeanor, and nonverbal behavior generally during the trial. At the appellate level, the judges review the written transcript of the trial, which does not include these nonverbal elements. An appellate court will challenge a trial court's finding of fact only when the finding is clearly erroneous (that is, when it is contrary to the evidence presented at trial) or when there is no evidence to support the finding. For example, if a jury concluded that a manufacturer's product harmed the plaintiff but no evidence was submitted to the court to support that conclusion, the appellate court would hold that the trial court's decision was erroneous.

HIGHEST STATE COURTS. The highest appellate court in a state is usually called the supreme court but may be called by some other name. For example, in both New York and Maryland, the highest state court is called the Court of Appeals. The decisions of each state's highest court on all questions of state law are final. Only when issues of federal law are involved can a decision made by a state's highest court be overruled by the United States Supreme Court.

State Court Systems and the Paralegal

Because each state has its own unique system of courts, you will need to become familiar with the court system of your particular state. What is the official name of your state's highest court, or supreme court? How many intermediate state appellate courts are in your state, and to which of these courts should appeals from your local trial court or courts be appealed? What courts in your area have jurisdiction over what kinds of disputes?

In addition to knowing the names of your state's courts and their jurisdictional authority, you will also need to become familiar with the procedural requirements of specific courts. Paralegals frequently assist their attorneys in drafting legal documents to be filed in state courts, and the required procedures for filing these documents may vary from court to court. You will read more about court procedures in Chapter 6.

As indicated earlier, state courts exercise exclusive jurisdiction over all matters that are not subject to federal jurisdiction. Family law and probate law (discussed in Chapter 2), for example, are two areas in which state courts exercise exclusive jurisdiction. If you work in these or other areas of the law over which state courts exercise jurisdiction, you will need to be familiar with procedural requirements established by state (or local) courts relating to those areas.

Realize also that many paralegals work within the court system, both in state courts and county courts (which are part of the state court system). Some paralegals work as assistants to court clerks. A knowledge of state courts and procedures can thus be a valuable tool in your career as a paralegal. In addition, many paralegals work for bankruptcy courts, which are part of the federal court system—a topic to which we now turn.

On the Web
The Web site for the federal courts offers information on the federal court system and links to all federal courts at **www.uscourts.gov**.

THE FEDERAL COURT SYSTEM

The federal court system is basically a three-tiered model consisting of (1) U.S. district courts (trial courts of general jurisdiction) and various courts of limited jurisdiction, (2) U.S. courts of appeals (intermediate courts of appeals), and (3) the United States Supreme Court. Exhibit 5.2 on the next page shows the organization of the federal court system.

According to the language of Article III of the U.S. Constitution, there is only one national Supreme Court. All other courts in the federal system are considered "inferior." Congress is empowered to create other inferior courts as it deems necessary. The inferior courts that Congress has created include those on the first and second tiers in our model—the district courts and various courts of limited jurisdiction, as well as the U.S. courts of appeals.

Unlike state court judges, who are usually elected, federal court judges are appointed by the president of the United States, subject to the approval of the U.S. Senate. Federal judges receive lifetime appointments (because under Article III they "hold their Offices during good Behavior").

U.S. District Courts

At the federal level, the equivalent of a state trial court of general jurisdiction is the district court. There is at least one federal district court in every state. The number of judicial districts can vary over time, primarily owing to population changes and corresponding caseloads. Currently, there are ninety-four judicial districts.

U.S. district courts have original jurisdiction in federal matters. Federal cases typically originate in district courts. There are other trial courts with original, but special (or limited) jurisdiction, such as the federal bankruptcy courts and others shown in Exhibit 5.2.

On the Web
Superior Information Services, a Michigan Internet consulting company, provides a single site from which you can access Web pages for trial courts. Go to **www.courts.net**.

U.S. Courts of Appeals

In the federal court system, there are thirteen U.S. courts of appeals—also referred to as U.S. circuit courts of appeals. The federal courts of appeals for twelve of the

EXHIBIT 5.2
The Organization of the Federal Court System

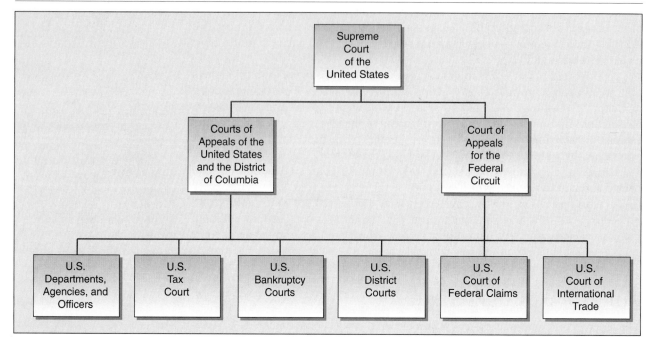

circuits (including the District of Columbia Circuit) hear appeals from the federal district courts located within their respective judicial circuits. The court of appeals for the thirteenth circuit, called the Federal Circuit, has national appellate jurisdiction over certain types of cases, such as cases involving patent law and cases in which the U.S. government is a defendant.

A party who is dissatisfied with a federal district court's decision on an issue may appeal that decision to a federal circuit court of appeals. As in state courts of appeals, the decisions of the circuit courts are made by a panel of three or more judges. The judges review decisions made by trial courts to see if any errors of law were made, and the judges generally defer to a district court's findings of fact. The decisions of the circuit courts of appeals are final in most cases, but appeal to the United States Supreme Court is possible. Exhibit 5.3 shows the geographical boundaries of U.S. circuit courts of appeals and the boundaries of the U.S. district courts within each circuit.

The United States Supreme Court

The United States Supreme Court consists of nine justices. These justices, like all federal judges, are nominated by the president of the United States and confirmed by the Senate.

The Supreme Court is given original, or trial court, jurisdiction in a small number of situations. Under Article III, Section 2, of the U.S. Constitution, the Supreme Court can exercise original jurisdiction in all cases "affecting Ambassadors, other public Ministers and Consuls, and those in which a State shall be a Party." In all other cases, the Supreme Court may exercise only appellate jurisdiction "with such Exceptions, and under such Regulations as the Congress shall make." Most of the Supreme Court's work is as an appellate court. The Supreme Court can review any

EXHIBIT 5.3
U.S. Courts of Appeals and U.S. District Courts

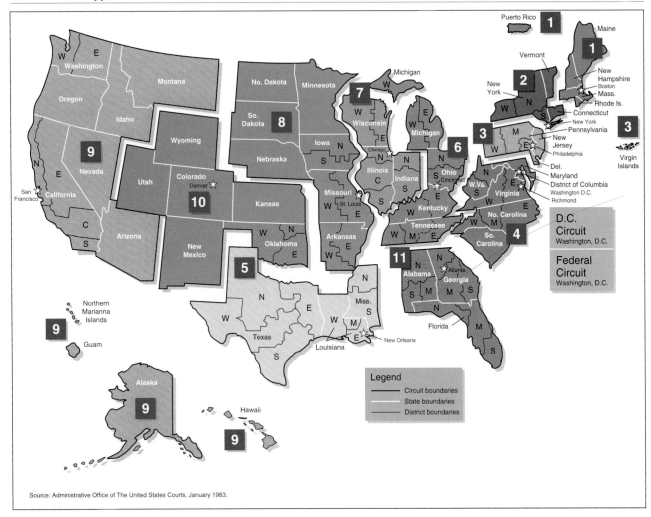

Source: Administrative Office of The United States Courts, January 1983.

case decided by any of the federal courts of appeals, and it also has appellate authority over some cases decided in the state courts.

Many people are surprised to learn that there is no absolute right of appeal to the United States Supreme Court. Thousands of cases are filed with the Supreme Court each year, yet in recent years, it has heard fewer than one hundred cases each year. To bring a case before the Supreme Court, a party requests the Court to issue a writ of *certiorari*. A **writ of *certiorari*[7]** is an order issued by the Supreme Court to a lower court requiring the latter to send it the record of the case for review. Parties can petition the Supreme Court to issue a writ of *certiorari*, but whether the Court will issue one is entirely within its discretion. The Court will not issue a writ unless at least four of the nine justices approve of it. This is called the **rule of four**. The Court is not required to issue a writ of *certiorari*, and most petitions for writs are denied. A denial is not a decision on the merits of a case, nor does it indicate agreement with the lower court's opinion. It simply means that the Supreme Court declines to grant the request (petition) for appeal. Furthermore, denial of the writ has no value as a precedent.

Writ of *Certiorari*
A writ from a higher court asking the lower court for the record of a case for review.

Rule of Four
A rule of the United States Supreme Court under which the Court will not issue a writ of *certiorari* unless at least four justices approve of the decision to issue the writ.

7. Pronounced sur-shee-uh-*rah*-ree.

Typically, the petitions granted by the Court involve cases that raise important constitutional questions or that conflict with other state or federal court decisions. Similarly, if federal appellate courts are rendering inconsistent opinions on an important issue, the Supreme Court may review a case involving that issue and generate a decision to define the law on the matter.

The Federal Court System and the Paralegal

In your work as a paralegal, you will probably be dealing occasionally with the federal court system. As discussed above, certain cases involving diversity of citizenship may be brought in either a state or a federal court. Many litigants who could sue in a state court will opt for a federal court if diversity of citizenship exists for the reasons mentioned earlier.

You may also be working on behalf of plaintiffs whose claims concern a federal question. An increasing number of cases in federal courts are brought by plaintiffs who allege employment discrimination in violation of federal laws, such as Title VII of the Civil Rights Act of 1964, which prohibits employment discrimination based on race, color, national origin, gender, or religion. Other federal laws prohibit discrimination based on age or disability. Sexual harassment and pregnancy discrimination are considered by the courts to fall under the protective umbrella of Title VII's prohibition against gender discrimination, and such cases frequently come before federal courts.

Federal courts exercise exclusive jurisdiction over cases relating to bankruptcy, patents, copyrights, trademarks, federal crimes, and certain other claims. If you work on such cases, you will be dealing with the federal court system and the court procedures set forth in the Federal Rules of Civil Procedure. As with state courts, you should make sure that you know the specific requirements of the particular federal court in which a client's lawsuit is to be filed, because each federal court has some discretionary authority over its procedural rules. (Among other things, you will need to know whether you can file documents with the relevant federal court electronically. For more information on electronic filing, see this chapter's feature *Technology and Today's Paralegal: Filing Court Documents Electronically,* on page 162.) You will read in detail about the procedural rules governing litigation proceedings in federal courts in Chapter 6.

On the Web
United States Supreme Court cases since 1893 can be accessed online at **www.findlaw.com.**

ALTERNATIVE DISPUTE RESOLUTION

Litigation in court is generally a last resort because of the high costs associated with litigating even the simplest complaint. In addition, because of the growing backlog of cases pending in the courts, it may sometimes be several years before a case is actually tried. Finally, the legal process is beset with uncertainties. One cannot know in advance how effectively the opposing side will argue its case or how the personal views and perceptions of judges and jurors may affect the outcome of the trial.

For these and other reasons, more and more individuals and business firms are turning to **alternative dispute resolution (ADR)** instead of resolving their disputes in court. Approximately 95 percent of all civil lawsuits are settled without a trial. Sometimes, a claim is settled before a lawsuit has been initiated. Most frequently, a settlement is achieved after the lawsuit is filed but before a trial takes place. In such situations, pretrial investigations give the parties and their attorneys an opportunity to assess the plaintiff's damages realistically and determine the relative strengths and weaknesses of the disputants' cases. Because so many cases are

Alternative Dispute Resolution (ADR)
The resolution of disputes in ways other than those involved in the traditional judicial process. Mediation and arbitration are forms of ADR.

DEVELOPING PARALEGAL SKILLS

Federal Court Jurisdiction

Mona, a new client, comes to the law offices of Henry, Jacobs & Miller in Detroit, Michigan. She wants to file a lawsuit against a New York hospital where she had emergency gallbladder surgery. Mona contracted an infection as a result of the surgery and nearly died. She was so sick that she missed several months of work and lost wages of $18,000. She also has medical expenses exceeding $60,000. Jane Doyle, a paralegal, is asked to review the case to determine if it can be filed in federal court.

CHECKLIST FOR DETERMINING FEDERAL COURT JURISDICTION

- Is the case based, at least in part, on the U.S. Constitution, a treaty, or other question of federal law?

- If the case does not involve a question of federal law, does it involve more than $75,000 and one of the following:
  - ✓ Citizens of different states?
  - ✓ A foreign country and citizens of a state or different states?
  - ✓ Citizens of a state and a foreign country?

- If it involves a combination of more than $75,000 and one of the citizenship requirements above, then diversity jurisdiction exists.

---

settled before they reach trial, attorneys and paralegals usually devote as much attention to these possibilities as to trial preparations.

As a paralegal, you may find that expertise in the area of ADR will serve you well in terms of career possibilities and advancement. Indeed, paralegals can play a significant role in many of the ADR options discussed in the following pages.

We now look at the various methods employed for settling disputes outside the court system. We begin by discussing the three basic (and traditional) forms of ADR—negotiation, mediation, and arbitration.

Negotiation and Mediation

Negotiation is one alternative means of resolving disputes. Attorneys frequently advise their clients to try to negotiate a settlement of their disputes voluntarily before they proceed to trial. During pretrial negotiation, the parties and/or their attorneys may meet informally one or more times to see if a mutually satisfactory agreement can be worked out. As a result of these negotiations, a **settlement agreement** may be reached.

Another alternative method of resolving disputes is to enlist the aid of a mediator. A mediator is expected to propose solutions, but he or she does not *impose* any solution or decision on the parties. In the **mediation** process, the parties themselves must reach agreement; the role of the mediator is to help the parties view their dispute more objectively and find common grounds for agreement.

The parties may select a mediator on the basis of his or her expertise in a particular field or reputation for fairness and impartiality. The mediator does not need to be a lawyer. The mediator may be one person, such as a paralegal, an attorney, or a volunteer from the community, or a panel of mediators may be used. Usually, a mediator charges a fee, which can be split between the parties. Many state and federal courts now require that parties mediate their disputes before

Negotiation
A method of alternative dispute resolution in which disputing parties, with or without the assistance of their attorneys, meet informally to resolve the dispute out of court.

Settlement Agreement
An out-of-court resolution to a legal dispute, which is agreed to by the parties in writing. A settlement agreement may be reached at any time prior to or during a trial.

Mediation
A method of settling disputes outside of court by using the services of a neutral third party, who acts as a communicating agent between the parties; a method of dispute settlement that is less formal than arbitration.

TECHNOLOGY AND TODAY'S PARALEGAL

Filing Court Documents Electronically

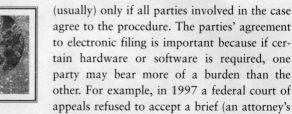

During the course of a lawsuit, many documents are filed with the court. Typically, paralegals or their support staff are the persons who make sure that the necessary paperwork reaches the relevant court in a timely fashion. The cumbersome task of physically delivering litigation documents to courthouses may be eased considerably in the future, however, depending on the success of current experiments with electronic filing, such as by e-mail or by CD-ROM.

The federal court system first experimented with an electronic filing system in January 1996 (in an asbestos case heard by the U.S. District Court for the Northern District of Ohio). Since that time, the project has been expanded, and currently at least nine federal courts allow attorneys to file documents electronically in certain types of cases. At last count, more than 130,000 documents in approximately 10,000 cases had been filed electronically in federal courts.

A number of state courts have also undertaken pilot projects to see whether electronic filing systems are feasible. For example, since late 1997 the Pima County, Arizona, court system has been accepting pleadings (documents filed at the beginning of a lawsuit) via e-mail. In early 1998, the supreme court of the state of Washington also began to accept online filings of litigation documents. (For a list of the courts experimenting with electronic filing, go to the Web site sponsored by Maryland Judge Arthur Ahalt, at www.mdlaw.net/efile.htm.)

To date, electronic filing typically has been permissible only in cases specifically approved by the court and (usually) only if all parties involved in the case agree to the procedure. The parties' agreement to electronic filing is important because if certain hardware or software is required, one party may bear more of a burden than the other. For example, in 1997 a federal court of appeals refused to accept a brief (an attorney's written argument supporting his or her client's position in a case) filed on a CD-ROM because the other party to the lawsuit did not have the equipment to "read" the brief and access the hypertext links included on the CD-ROM.

For paralegals, electronic filing—if and when it is fully implemented—will be a boon. As you might imagine, generating legal documents, filing them with the court, and making the documents available to all parties involved in the litigation are time-consuming responsibilities (see Chapter 6 for more details on pretrial litigation procedures). With electronic filing, tasks that now take hours to complete may require only minutes in the future. Because of the reduced time and paperwork involved, electronic filing will also mean substantial savings for attorneys, their clients, and the courts.

Although electronic filing creates many benefits, there are numerous hurdles to overcome on the road to this "paperless" future. Many of these hurdles are, of course, technological in nature. Some of them, though, are human. In fact, probably the most important factor in determining the success of electronic filing is the commitment of the legal community, including paralegals, to using new technology to make traditional legal procedures simpler and less costly to perform.

On the Web
You can find publications pertaining to ADR by accessing the Federal Judicial Center at www.fjc.gov.

being allowed to resolve the disputes through trials. When mediation is required by a court before the parties can have the court hear their dispute, the mediators may be appointed by the court. Mediation usually results in the quick settlement of disputes.

Because a mediator need not be a lawyer, this field is open to paralegals who acquire training and expertise in this area. Generally, any paralegal aspiring to work as a mediator must have excellent communication skills. This is because, as a mediator, it will be your job to listen carefully to each party's complaints and communicate possible solutions to a dispute in a way that is not offensive to either party. (See this chapter's featured-guest article entitled "Mediation and the Paralegal" beginning on page 164 for further details on the functions performed by mediators and the role played by paralegals in the mediation process.)

Arbitration

A more formal method of alternative dispute resolution is **arbitration.** The key difference between arbitration and the forms of ADR just discussed, negotiation and mediation, is that in those forms of ADR, the parties themselves settle their dispute—although a third party may assist them in doing so. In arbitration, the third party hearing the dispute normally makes the decision for the parties. In a sense, the arbitrator becomes a private judge, even though the arbitrator does not have to be a lawyer. Frequently, a panel of experts arbitrates the dispute.

Depending on the parties' circumstances and preferences, the arbitrator's decision may be legally binding or nonbinding on the parties. In nonbinding arbitration, the parties submit their dispute to a third party but remain free to reject the third party's decision. Nonbinding arbitration is more similar to mediation than to binding arbitration. Arbitration that is mandated by the courts is often not binding on the parties. If, after mandatory arbitration, the parties are not satisfied with the results of arbitration, they may then ignore the arbitrator's decision and have the dispute litigated in court. Even if the arbitrator's decision is legally binding, a party may be able to appeal the decision to a court for judicial review.

Frequently disputes are arbitrated because of an arbitration clause in a contract entered into before the dispute arose. An **arbitration clause** provides that any disputes arising under the contract will be resolved by arbitration. For example, an arbitration clause in a contract for the sale of goods might provide that "any controversy or claim arising under this contract will be referred to arbitration before the American Arbitration Association."[8]

If parties enter into a contract containing an arbitration clause, it is likely that either a state or a federal statute will compel them to arbitrate any dispute arising under the contract. Most states have statutes under which arbitration clauses are enforced, and some state statutes compel arbitration of certain types of disputes, such as those involving public employees. At the federal level, the Federal Arbitration Act (FAA) of 1925 enforces arbitration clauses in contracts relating to certain types of activities, such as those involving interstate commerce (commerce between two or more states).

Other ADR Forms

The three forms of ADR just discussed are the oldest and traditionally the most commonly used forms. In recent years, a variety of new types of ADR have emerged. Some of them combine elements of mediation and arbitration. For example, in *binding mediation,* a neutral mediator tries to facilitate agreement between the parties, but if no agreement is reached the mediator issues a legally binding decision on the matter. In *mediation arbitration (med-arb),* an arbitrator attempts first to help the parties reach an agreement, just as a mediator would. If no agreement is reached, then formal arbitration is undertaken, and the arbitrator issues a legally binding decision.

Other ADR forms are sometimes referred to as "assisted negotiation" because they involve a third party in what is essentially a negotiation process. For example, in *early neutral case evaluation,* the parties select a neutral third party (generally an expert in the subject matter of the dispute) to evaluate their respective positions. The parties explain their positions to the case evaluator however they

Arbitration
The settling of a dispute by submitting it to a disinterested third party (other than a court), who renders a decision that may or may not be legally binding.

Arbitration Clause
A clause in a contract that provides that, in case of a dispute, the parties will determine their rights by arbitration rather than through the judicial system.

On the Web
The Virtual Magistrate Project, which is sponsored by several ADR organizations (including the American Arbitration Association), offers a forum for online dispute resolution at **vmag.vcilp.org.**

---

8. As will be discussed shortly, the American Arbitration Association is a leading provider of arbitration services in the United States.

FEATURED GUEST: ANDREA NAGER CHASEN

Mediation and the Paralegal

BIOGRAPHICAL NOTE

Andrea Nager Chasen received her master's degree in public administration, specializing in the theory and practice of decision-making processes, from New York University. Four years later, she earned her law degree at the American University School of Law. Following graduation from law school, through her work as a litigator, she became interested in alternative methods of dispute resolution. Her interest led her to an in-depth exploration of mediation as one method of resolving disputes out of court. As a consequence, she has developed and taught courses in mediation and has served as a mediator. Currently, she mediates and arbitrates disputes on a full-time basis in her private practice.

With all of the attention on alternative dispute resolution (ADR) methods as tools for conflict resolution, how is the traditional law firm to respond? Will the availability of ADR result in the end of the trial as

we know it and the exhaustive amount of work that goes into preparing for trial? Rest assured, there is still work (and lots of it) to be done. But the type of work will differ from what the average attorney and paralegal are used to doing. This feature focuses on just one method of ADR—mediation—and the paralegal's role in this process.[a]

WHAT DOES A MEDIATOR DO?

Before considering the paralegal's role in the mediation process, it is important to know how mediators help parties in settling their conflicts. Generally, the mediator undertakes to do the following:

1. Learn what the parties' real interests are (as opposed to the positions that the parties have put forward).

2. Assess realistically the alternative ways in which the dispute might be resolved.

3. Deal with the differences between the parties' perceptions of the issues involved in the dispute.

4. Learn (in private sessions with each party) what information the parties are unwilling to disclose to each other.

5. Devise options and solutions that meet the interests of all parties involved in the dispute.

Throughout the proceedings, the mediator maintains a neutral position

a. *Editor's Note*: The author of this article describes some of the general features of the mediation process and the paralegal's role in mediation. Realize, however, that the mediation process may be voluntary or mandated by a court, and different states (and different courts within a state) may have different mediation procedures.

and focuses on the parties' feelings and statements that can be used productively. The mediator never imposes a judgment but acts as a facilitator to help the parties reach their own agreement.

THE PARALEGAL'S ROLE IN THE MEDIATION PROCESS

What tasks does the paralegal perform in relation to the mediation process? Perhaps the best way to answer this question is to divide the mediation process into various stages and examine the role of the paralegal during each stage. Generally, as with cases that go to trial, a good deal of the paralegal's efforts will be involved in overall case management.

Stage One: Premediation.   The first stage of the mediation process consists of finding out the facts about a client's claim against another party and determining whether mediation might be appropriate at this point. In divorce or custody matters, if the couple has retained attorneys but negotiations appear to be failing, then an attempt to mediate the dispute may be useful. Sometimes, the client's case will already be in the initial stages of litigation, and pretrial investigations will be underway. Mediation may also be forced on the parties by a court or other authority at almost the "eleventh hour" prior to trial—after both parties are fully prepared to present their respective cases to the court.

Paralegals play an important role during the premediation stage by investigating the factual background of the dispute. Preliminary investigations should also include, where appropriate, valuations and appraisals of personal and real property, damages, and

FEATURED GUEST, *Continued*

compensatory payments. Finally, the paralegal should make necessary contacts with the parties and continue to generally manage the case.

Stage Two: Selecting Mediation. Certain factors should be considered in reviewing the available tools (including litigation) for conflict resolution. If the disputing parties have a continuing relationship—as business partners, for example—court-imposed decisions may alienate the parties and intensify the conflict. Also, having the conflict resolved by a court can be costly and time consuming.

Generally, mediation can be arranged to meet the scheduling demands of the parties and is far less costly than litigation. Furthermore, because the mediator does not impose the decision, the parties control how the agreement is shaped. Unlike litigation, mediation is not adversarial in nature; rather, it seeks to find common grounds on which an agreement can be based. Therefore, the process tends to reduce the antagonism between the disputants and to allow them to resume their former relationship more easily.

The paralegal's role during this preliminary stage is to develop a clear understanding of the client's needs and interests so that the attorney can better assess whether mediation would be a desirable alternative for resolving the dispute. The paralegal can also provide the attorney with a list of prescreened, qualified mediators. (Such lists can be obtained from numerous organizations, including the American Arbitration Association, the federal

Mediation and Conciliation Service, local courts, bar associations, and chambers of commerce.) Once the lists are obtained, then a further screening of potential mediators may be desirable. Each mediator brings a specific style to mediation. Some mediators may act more as case evaluators, while others may use certain techniques to help the parties carefully examine their relationship issues. The kind of case for which mediation is sought may indicate the type of mediation style that is desirable. For example, if the matter is a straightforward negligence case where the relationship between the parties is secondary, the selection of a mediator who provides case evaluation may be appropriate. If the relationship issues require more attention, as with business partners, employers and employees, or a divorcing couple, this calls for the selection of a mediator who is skilled in assisting the parties in recognizing their relationship issues in addition to the other matters involved in the case.

Stage Three: Mediation Sessions. During the mediation sessions, the mediator allows both sides to present their views and spends time with the parties, either jointly or in private meetings with each party, to uncover the real interests and needs of the disputants. Sometimes, the parties may reach agreement after just one mediation session, but commonly several sessions are held so that the parties have the time and opportunity to obtain information on issues that need to be addressed. It may be necessary, for example, to obtain financial data relating to one or both of the parties. And, of

> **"The mediator never imposes a judgment but acts as a facilitator to help the parties reach their own agreement."**

course, several sessions may be required simply to reach a satisfactory agreement.

The paralegal can play a crucial role during this stage of the mediation process by helping to provide additional information for the sessions as they progress. The paralegal can also help in the drafting of any preliminary responses that are required during the course of the mediation. The paralegal may also draft the final agreement—unless that duty is assumed by the mediator.

CONCLUSION

Mediation can be useful at many stages of a dispute between parties. Mediation may help to resolve the entire dispute or just one aspect of it. Case management within the legal office is as important for the cases that are to be mediated as it is for the cases that will be tried in court. The paralegal can play a significant role in overall case management by doing the following:

1. Maintaining good methods of tracking and organizing data during the premediation stage.

2. Assisting the parties in selecting an appropriate mediator.

3. Providing necessary data and information during mediation sessions.

ETHICAL CONCERN
Potential Arbitration Problems

Many individuals and business firms prefer to arbitrate disputes rather than take them to court. For that reason, they often include arbitration clauses in their contracts. These clauses normally specify who or what organization will arbitrate the dispute and where the arbitration will take place. To safeguard a client's interests, when drafting and reviewing arbitration clauses in contracts, the careful paralegal will be alert to the possibility that those who arbitrate the dispute might not be totally neutral or that the designated place of arbitration is so geographically distant from the client's location that it may pose a great inconvenience and expense for the client should an arbitrable dispute arise. The paralegal should call any such problems to his or her supervising attorney's attention. The attorney can then discuss the problem with the client and help the client negotiate an arbitration clause that is more favorable to the client's position.

---

wish. The case evaluator then assesses the strengths and weaknesses of the parties' positions, and this evaluation forms the basis of negotiating a settlement.

The mini-trial is a form of assisted negotiation that is often used by business parties. In a *mini-trial,* each party's attorney briefly argues the party's case before representatives of each firm who have the authority to settle the dispute. Typically, a neutral third party (usually an expert in the area being disputed) acts as an adviser. If the parties fail to reach an agreement, the adviser renders an opinion as to how a court would likely decide the issue. The proceeding assists the parties in determining whether they should negotiate a settlement of the dispute or take it to court.

Court-Referred ADR

Today, the majority of states either require or encourage parties to undergo mediation or arbitration prior to trial. Generally, when a trial court refers a case for arbitration, the arbitrator's decision is not binding on the parties. If the parties do not agree with the arbitrator's decision, they can go forward with the lawsuit.

The types of court-related ADR programs in use vary widely. In some states, such as Missouri, ADR is voluntary. In other states, such as Minnesota, parties are required to undertake ADR before they can have their cases heard in court. Some states, such as Minnesota, offer a menu of options. Other states, including Florida (which has a statewide, comprehensive mediation program), offer only one alternative.

Several federal courts have also instituted ADR programs. Courts in several federal districts require arbitration prior to trial in cases involving less than $100,000, and a number of other federal courts provide for voluntary arbitration. Additionally, numerous federal courts hold summary jury trials. In a *summary jury trial (SJT),* the parties present their arguments and supporting evidence (other than witness testimony—witnesses are not called in an SJT), and the jury then renders a verdict. Unlike in an actual trial, the jury's verdict is not binding. The verdict does, however, act as a guide to both sides in reaching an agreement during the mandatory negotiations that immediately follow the SJT. The SJT is much speedier than a regular trial, and frequently the parties are able to settle their dispute without resorting to an actual trial. If no settlement is reached, both sides have the right to a full trial later.

Today's courts are experimenting with a variety of other alternatives to speed up (and reduce the cost of) justice. These alternatives include summary procedures for commercial litigation, the appointment of special masters to assist judges in deciding complex issues, and permitting an expanded use of paralegals in the handling of routine legal matters.

Providers of ADR Services

ADR services are provided by both government agencies and private organizations. A major provider of ADR services is the **American Arbitration Association (AAA)**. Most of the nation's largest law firms are members of this nonprofit association. Founded in 1926, the AAA now settles about seventy thousand disputes a year in its numerous offices around the country. Cases brought before the AAA are heard by an expert or a panel of experts in the area relating to the dispute and are usually settled quickly. Generally, about half of the panel members are lawyers. To cover its costs, the AAA charges a fee, paid by the party filing the claim. In addition, each party to the dispute pays a specified amount for each hearing day, as well as a special additional fee for cases involving personal injuries or property loss.

Hundreds of for-profit firms around the country also provide ADR services. Typically, these firms hire retired judges to conduct arbitration hearings or otherwise assist parties in settling their disputes. The leading firm in this relatively new private system of justice is JAMS/Endispute, which is based in Santa Ana, California. Private ADR firms normally allow the parties to decide on the date of the hearing, the presiding judge, whether the judge's decision will be legally binding, and the site of the hearing—which may be a conference room, a law-school office, or a leased courtroom. The judges follow procedures similar to those of the federal courts and use similar rules. Usually, each party to the dispute pays a filing fee and a designated fee for a hearing session or conference.

As mentioned, courts also have ADR programs in which disputes are resolved by court-appointed attorneys or paralegals who are qualified to act as arbitrators or mediators in certain types of disputes. Many paralegals have found that becoming a mediator or an arbitrator is an especially rewarding career option.

American Arbitration Association (AAA)
The major organization offering arbitration services in the United States.

ETHICAL CONCERN
Private Justice

The use of for-profit arbitration providers has been controversial. Critics raise the ethical question as to whether it is fair to put a "price tag" on justice by making dispute-settlement forums more available to those who can afford them than to those who cannot. Supporters of private ADR services maintain that any alternative that can help reduce the heavy caseload of the courts ultimately helps everybody. As a concerned citizen, you may have strong views on the matter. In your capacity as a paralegal, however, you should not let your personal ethical standards prevent you from implementing whatever (legal) course of action the client, in consultation with your supervising attorney, chooses to undertake.

TODAY'S PROFESSIONAL PARALEGAL

Arbitrating Commercial Contracts

Julia Lorenz has worked as a legal assistant for International Airlines (IA) for ten years. She works in the legal department on the staff of the general counsel. Her job has been to work with Jim Manning, senior attorney. This attorney is responsible for all of the corporation's contracts, including the following: major contracts with jet manufacturers for the purchase of aircraft, contracts with catering companies to supply food during flights, fuel contracts, employment and labor contracts, and many small contracts for the purchase and lease of equipment and supplies for the numerous airline offices and ticket counters.

REVIEWING PROPOSED CONTRACTS

Julia's job is to review the provisions of proposed major contracts, such as the contracts to purchase jet aircraft, and to provide Jim with an article-by-article summary of the contracts' provisions. Jim then negotiates these contracts to obtain the most favorable terms possible for the airline. Once he has negotiated a contract, Julia makes the final changes and forwards it to the appropriate IA corporate official to review and sign.

ATTENDING ARBITRATION PROCEEDINGS

All of the airline's major contracts contain arbitration clauses that require all contract disputes to be resolved through binding arbitration services provided by the American Arbitration Association (AAA). On numerous occasions, Julia has attended arbitration proceedings with Jim. In preparing for arbitration, Julia obtains affidavits, prepares subpoenas, and arranges for witnesses to be present to testify. During the arbitration proceedings, she assists in presenting material into evidence. She and Jim have developed a good rapport with several arbitrators at the local AAA office, and they usually request these arbitrators when they have a case that must be arbitrated.

BECOMING AN ARBITRATOR

Julia's knowledge of arbitration procedures and her outstanding work in preparing for arbitration, as well as during the proceedings, won her significant recognition from this group of arbitrators. One of the arbitrators eventually approached Julia and suggested that she apply for approval as an arbitrator. She said that she would consider it.

Julia later mentioned the arbitrator's suggestion to Jim. He thought that Julia had been paid quite a compliment. He encouraged her to contact the AAA to inquire about the possibility of being approved as an arbitrator. When Julia called the AAA, she learned that arbitrators in the area of commercial arbitration are not required to be attorneys. She would need eight years of experience in her field and would have to meet certain educational requirements. When Julia realized that she had the necessary qualifications, she submitted an application. About two months later, she was approved as an arbitrator.

ADR and the Paralegal

The time and money costs associated with litigating disputes in court continue to rise, and, as a result, disputing parties are increasingly turning to ADR as a means of settling their disagreements. As a way to reduce their caseloads, state and federal courts are also increasingly requiring litigants to undergo arbitration prior to bringing their suits before the courts. Although paralegals have always assisted attorneys in work relating to the negotiation of out-of-court settlements for clients, they may play an even greater role in the future. Some paralegals are qualified mediators and directly assist parties in reaching a mutually satisfactory agreement. Some paralegals serve as arbitrators. As more and more parties utilize ADR, paralegals will have increasing opportunities in this area of legal work.

If you are interested in becoming a mediator, you need to be thoroughly familiar with ADR law in the state in which you work. Some states do not require

PARALEGAL PROFILE

Litigation Paralegal

LEE A. PAIGE graduated from the University of West Los Angeles School of Paralegal Studies with an ABA-approved paralegal certificate. He holds paralegal specialist certificates in litigation, real estate, environmental law, and intellectual-property law. His experience includes state and federal litigation, copyrights, patent and trademark prosecution, assignments, and licensing. He is currently employed as a senior paralegal in the Los Angeles office of the Seattle-based law firm of Preston, Gates & Ellis, where he assists attorneys with railroad litigation and environmental-law research.

In 1998 Paige served as president of the Los Angeles Paralegal Association, the largest association of paralegals in the nation. For the past ten years he has been extremely active in the promotion and development of the paralegal profession both in California and nationally. He is frequently called on to serve as a motivational speaker and paralegal expert by high schools, colleges, paralegal schools, and paralegal and legal associations. As a representative of the California Alliance of Paralegal Associations, he has lobbied the state bar association and the state legislature in an effort to codify a legal definition of the term paralegal *and specific educational standards for traditional paralegals. He has authored several articles on the paralegal profession and is a contributing writer to* Legal Assistant Today *magazine.*

What do you like best about your work?

"I very much enjoy research! To some paralegals, such a statement might sound a little crazy, but I really do enjoy researching more than any other part of my job. As a former news writer, my natural penchant for 'digging' for a story comes in quite handy. It is very gratifying to me for an attorney to give me a problem and rely on me to find the answer. I get quite an adrenaline rush from 'fact-finding' missions and a wealth of satisfaction from 'delivering the goods' that are the result of my computerized or manual research."

What is the greatest challenge that you face in your area of work?

"The greatest challenge I currently face is keeping ahead of our ever-mounting litigation schedule. I primarily assist a partner in my firm who represents a major railway company and juggles a huge caseload. My boss is an excellent attorney, but, as is the case with many litigators, he is frequently overloaded. His secretary and I must be constantly vigilant with his weekly calendar and daily schedule to prevent time conflicts and make sure that he does not miss any crucial dates or court appearances."

What advice do you have for would-be paralegals in your area of work?

"I frequently lecture at local paralegal schools, and the advice I normally give paralegal students is to focus their studies on areas of law that are of interest to them. This will give them an idea of where their real strengths are. I work in litigation, but it is not for everyone. Litigation is very complex and demanding, and if students go into it blindly they may be disappointed. Many people enter into the paralegal profession as a second career, perhaps as a result of a layoff, forced relocation, or downsizing. Other people see becoming a paralegal as a way of getting a "foot in the door" of the legal profession, and still

"One success tip that I always give to students and working paralegals is to never stop learning."

others use it as a proving ground in anticipation of going on to law school and becoming an attorney. Whatever their reasons for becoming paralegals, I always advise would-be paralegals to investigate the profession before they jump in, and to only attend an ABA-approved school."

What are some tips for success as a paralegal in your area of work?

"One success tip that I always give to students and working paralegals is to never stop learning. Paralegals should voluntarily take additional classes and seminars beyond their paralegal certificates. Such classes will keep them abreast of new developments in law and procedure that can affect their ability to assist their attorneys in the representation of their clients and increase their value to their employers."

mediators to meet any special training requirements. For example, Florida law requires that a family mediator "shall be a person with the appropriate attributes who can demonstrate sensitivity toward the parties involved and facilitate solutions to the problem." Other states require mediators to have up to sixty hours of training in certain fields, such as family law, child development, or family dynamics.

KEY TERMS AND CONCEPTS

administrative agency   146

administrative law   146

alternative dispute resolution (ADR)   160

American Arbitration Association (AAA)   167

appellate court   151

appellate jurisdiction   151

arbitration   163

arbitration clause   163

bankruptcy court   150

Bill of Rights   143

case law   147

common law   148

concurrent jurisdiction   152

diversity of citizenship   151

enabling legislation   146

exclusive jurisdiction   152

federal question   151

jurisdiction   149

law   142

long arm statute   150

mediation   161

negotiation   161

ordinance   144

original jurisdiction   151

precedent   148

probate court   150

rule of four   159

settlement agreement   161

stare decisis   148

statute   144

statutory law   144

supremacy clause   142

trial court   151

venue   152

writ of *certiorari*   159

CHAPTER SUMMARY

1. Law has been defined variously over the ages, yet all definitions of law rest on the following assumption about the nature of law: law consists of a body of rules of conduct with legal force and effect, prescribed by the controlling authority (the government) of a society.

2. Important sources of American law are constitutional law (the law established by the U.S. Constitution and the constitutions of the various states), statutory law (which consists of statutes enacted by the U.S. Congress and state legislatures, as well as ordinances passed by local governing bodies), and administrative law (which consists of the rules and regulations issued and enforced by administrative agencies at both the state and federal levels).

3. A major source of American law is case law—the decisions embodied in court cases—and the common law. The common law tradition originated in medieval England with the creation of the king's courts and was established in America during the colonial era. A cornerstone of the common law tradition is the doctrine of *stare decisis*, under which judges are expected to abide by the law as established by previous court decisions. Today, the common law governs all areas not covered by statutory law.

4. Before a court can hear a case, the court must have jurisdiction over the person against whom the suit is brought or over the property involved in the suit. It must also have jurisdiction over the subject matter of the dispute. Courts of general jurisdiction can hear

most types of disputes. Courts of limited jurisdiction are restricted in the types of actions they can decide. Courts having original jurisdiction are courts in which the trial of a case begins. Courts having appellate jurisdiction are reviewing courts. They do not try cases anew but review the decisions of trial courts.

5. Federal courts can exercise jurisdiction over claims involving (1) a federal question, which arises when the plaintiff's claim is based at least in part on the U.S. Constitution, a treaty, or a federal law; or (2) diversity of citizenship, which arises when the case involves citizens of different states, a foreign country and citizens of a state or different states, or citizens of a state and citizens or subjects of a foreign country. The amount in controversy must exceed $75,000 for jurisdiction based on diversity of citizenship to arise.

6. Venue has to do with the appropriate geographical area in which a case should be brought. The concept of venue reflects the policy that a court trying a suit should be in the geographic neighborhood (usually the county) in which the incident leading to the suit occurred or in which the parties involved in the suit reside.

7. Paralegals should become familiar with the procedural rules of the specific court in which a case is filed. Federal court procedures are set forth in the Federal Rules of Civil Procedure. States rules vary from state to state—and even from court to court within a given state. Also, court procedural rules are different for civil cases than for criminal cases.

8. The structure of state court systems varies from state to state. A typical state court system may consist of several tiers. On the bottom tier are courts of limited jurisdiction. On the next tier are usually the trial courts of general jurisdiction. Trial courts are courts of original jurisdiction—in other words, courts in which lawsuits are initiated, trials are held, and evidence is presented. The upper tier consists of appellate courts, to which trial court decisions can be appealed. Appellate courts are reviewing courts; their function is to review the trial court's decision in cases that are appealed. The highest state appellate court is typically called the state supreme court, although there are exceptions. Cases can be appealed from a state's highest court to the United States Supreme Court only if a federal question is involved.

9. The federal court system consists of U.S. district courts (trial courts), U.S. courts of appeals (intermediate appellate courts), and the United States Supreme Court. Decisions from a district court can be appealed to the court of appeals of the circuit (geographical area) in which the district court is located. There are thirteen circuit courts of appeals. Decisions rendered by these circuit courts may be appealed to the United States Supreme Court.

10. The United States Supreme Court is the highest court in the land. There is no absolute right of appeal to the Supreme Court, and the Court hears only a fraction of the cases that are filed with it each year. If the Court decides to review a case, it will issue a writ of *certiorari,* which is an order by the Supreme Court to a lower court requiring the latter to send it the record of the case for review. As a rule, only those petitions that raise the possibility of important constitutional questions are granted.

11. The costs and time-consuming character of litigation, as well as the adversarial nature of court proceedings, have caused many to turn to various forms of alternative dispute resolution (ADR) for settling their disagreements. Out-of-court settlements are reached in the majority of lawsuits, usually before the trial begins.

12. Negotiation, the simplest method of ADR, may or may not involve a third party; the parties to the dispute simply try to work out their problems to avoid going to court. Mediation is a form of ADR in which the parties attempt to reach agreement with the help of a neutral third party, called a mediator (or a panel of mediators), who helps the disputants explore alternative possibilities for settling their differences as amicably as possible. The mediator proposes various solutions for the parties to consider.

13. Arbitration is the most formal method of ADR. In arbitration, a neutral third party (a lawyer, expert, panel of specialists, or other party) renders a decision after the parties present their cases and evidence in a hearing. Normally, in voluntary arbitration (as opposed to court-mandated ADR), the parties agree at the outset to be legally bound by the arbitrator's decision. Increasingly, parties are including in their contracts arbitration clauses—provisions by which the parties agree to arbitrate any disputes that may arise under the contract.

14. Other forms of ADR include binding mediation, mediation arbitration (med-arb), early neutral case evaluation, and mini-trials.

15. To ease their heavy caseloads, numerous state and federal courts today encourage or require parties to disputes to mediate or arbitrate their disputes before they can be heard in court. If a party is not satisfied

with the results of mediation or arbitration, however, that party normally can take the issue to court.

16. Both government agencies and private organizations provide ADR services. The leading provider of such services is the American Arbitration Association (AAA). Numerous for-profit firms in the nation also provide ADR services. For-profit firms usually hire retired judges to conduct ADR procedures.

◈ QUESTIONS FOR REVIEW

1. What is law? Why are there so many different definitions of law?

2. What is constitutional law? If a state constitution conflicts with the U.S. Constitution, which constitution takes priority?

3. What is a statute? How is statutory law created?

4. What is an administrative agency? How are such agencies created?

5. Where, when, and how did the common law tradition begin? What does *stare decisis* mean? Why is it said that the doctrine of *stare decisis* became the cornerstone of English and American law?

6. Define *jurisdiction* and explain why jurisdiction is important. What is the difference between venue and jurisdiction?

7. Over what types of cases may federal courts exercise jurisdiction? What is the relationship between state and federal jurisdiction?

8. Describe the functions of a trial court. How do they differ from the functions of an appellate court?

9. What are the typical courts in a state court system? What are the three basic tiers, or levels, of courts in the federal court system? How do cases reach the United States Supreme Court?

10. List and explain the various methods of alternative dispute resolution.

◈ ETHICAL QUESTIONS

1. John Scott, an attorney, has asked his legal assistant, Nanette Lynch, to do some research. Nanette is to research the state statutes to find out how many persons are required to witness a will. Nanette looks up the relevant state statute and finds it difficult to understand because it is so poorly written. After studying the statute for a while, Nanette decides that two witnesses are required and conveys this information to John. Actually, the statute requires that three persons witness a will or it will not be valid. John, relying on Nanette's conclusion, has two persons witness a client's will the next day. Have John and Nanette violated any ethical rules? Explain.

2. A legal assistant in your law firm is working on a case law research project for a class that she is taking. She spends two hours doing personal case law research for her project on a computerized legal-research service that charges the firm several dollars per minute of online time. The legal assistant bills the two hours to a major client's file, assuming that no one will ever learn what she has done. You happen to be sitting at the terminal next to her, and you notice that she bills the time to one of the firm's clients. What should you do? What would you do if you learned that your supervising attorney had billed personal research time to a client's file?

3. Larry Simpson is working on a lawsuit that was recently filed in a federal district court on the basis of diversity-of-citizenship jurisdiction. Larry, a legal assistant, just received the plaintiff's answers to interrogatories (attorneys' written questions to the parties in a lawsuit), which he has been assigned by his supervising attorney to summarize. Larry discovers that the plaintiff's damages are nowhere near the $75,000 required for diversity jurisdiction. What should Larry do?

4. Suzanne Andersen's supervising attorney, Amy Lynch, works occasionally as a mediator for family-law cases in the local courts. Amy has mediated a divorce case today involving the property settlement of a wealthy businessperson, who happens also to be a defendant in another lawsuit in which Amy represents the plaintiff. As a result of her mediation today, Amy has learned some confidential financial information about this man. She now has come to Suzanne, her paralegal, and asked her to use this information to his disadvantage in the lawsuit. How should Suzanne handle this situation?

▨ PRACTICE QUESTIONS AND ASSIGNMENTS

1. Identify the constitutional amendment being violated in the following hypothetical situations:

   a. Jeremy's boss threatens to fire him if he does not work on Saturday nights, even though that is when he attends worship services.

   b. The city proposes an ordinance requiring that anyone caught stealing be punished by having his or her hand cut off for the first offense and the other hand cut off for the second offense.

   c. Because Robert's house is located in a poor neighborhood, the police decided that he must be a drug dealer. The police burst in and tear the place apart searching for drugs. They find nothing.

   d. The federal government bans all advertising of cigarettes.

2. Identify the type of law (common law, constitutional law, statutory law, or administrative law) that applies in each of the following scenarios:

   a. Jean Gorman strongly disagrees with the U.S. government's decision to declare war on a foreign country. She places an antiwar sign in the window of her home. The city passes an ordinance that bans all such signs.

   b. An official of the state department of natural resources learns that the Ferris Widget Company has violated the state's Hazardous Waste Management Act. The official issues a complaint against the company for not properly handling and labeling its toxic waste.

   c. Mrs. Sams was walking down a busy street when two teenagers on Rollerblades crashed into her because they weren't watching where they were going. As a result of the teenagers' conduct, Mrs. Sams broke her hip, and according to her doctor, she will never walk normally again. She sues the teenagers for damages.

   d. Joseph Barnes is arrested and charged with the crime of murder.

3. A plaintiff and defendant are involved in an auto accident. Both are residents of the county and state in which the accident took place. The plaintiff files an auto negligence lawsuit in the county circuit court where the trial will occur. What types of jurisdiction does the court have? Compare it to the other types of jurisdiction discussed in the chapter.

4. Marcia, who is from Toledo, Ohio, drives to Troy, Michigan, and shops at a popular mall. When leaving the parking lot, Marcia causes a car accident to occur when she runs a stop sign. On what basis could a Michigan court obtain jurisdiction over Marcia?

5. Identify each of the following courts:

   a. This state court takes testimony from witnesses and receives evidence. It may have either general or limited subject-matter jurisdiction.

   b. This court has appellate jurisdiction and is part of a court system that is divided into geographical units called *circuits*.

   c. This state court usually has a panel of three or more judges who review the record of a case for errors of law and procedure. It does not have original jurisdiction.

   d. This court can exercise diversity-of-citizenship jurisdiction and receives testimony and other evidence.

   e. The decisions of this court are usually final. It is the highest appellate court in its geographical area.

   f. This federal court has nine justices. It has original jurisdiction over a few types of cases but functions primarily as an appellate court. There is no automatic right to appeal cases to this court.

6. Look at Exhibit 5.3. In which federal circuit is your state located? How many federal judicial districts are located in your state? In which federal district is your community located?

▨ USING INTERNET RESOURCES

1. Go to FindLaw's home page at **www.findlaw.com**. This site offers links to many of the federal and state sources of law that you have read about in this chapter. In this exercise, you will be examining state laws, so click on "U.S. State Resources." The page you reach will list all of the states in alphabetical order. Open the site for your state, and then select "Primary Materials." Browse through the state sources of law that can be accessed online, and then answer the following questions:

a. Were you able to access the text of your state's constitution?

b. Did the site include your state's code (compilation of statutes) and administrative regulations?

c. What other primary materials were included in the site?

d. Now browse through the "Primary Materials" sites for three other states. How did your state's site compare to those of other states in terms of comprehensiveness and ease of use?

2. Paralegals frequently assist in ADR proceedings or even, in some cases, serve as mediators or arbitrators. To learn more about ADR procedures, go to **www.adr.org**, the home page for the American Arbitration Association (AAA). Browse through the site's offerings and find the answers to the following questions:

a. Where on the AAA's site is the "Demand for Arbitration" form located? How long is the form? In what circumstances would it be used? What procedure is involved in filing the document (for example, who should receive copies of the form, how many copies must be sent, and so on)? Under AAA rules, within how many days must an answering statement be filed?

b. Where on the site is the "Submission to Dispute Resolution" form located? What kind of information is required to fill out the form? How does this form differ from the "Demand for Arbitration" form? What ADR options are listed on the form? How many copies of the form must be filed with the AAA?

3. The United States Supreme Court Web site contains useful information on the United States Supreme Court. Go to its Web site at **www.usscplus.com**.

a. Click on "Current Term." What are the names of the cases and subjects included in this term?

b. Click on "The Court," and then select "Justices." How many justices are on the Supreme Court? What are their names? What law schools did they attend? Who appointed each justice?

4. Go to the Web site, **www.courts.net**. This useful Web site provides a directory to courts throughout the country. This information is helpful for learning about the court system in a particular state, as well as locating the court. Click on your state. What information is available about the courts in your state? Make a list of the courts that are included. Click on the various courts, and make a list of the type of information that is available, such as judges' names, telephone numbers, court addresses, and so on.

CHAPTER 6

THE CIVIL LITIGATION PROCESS

Chapter Outline

⊠ INTRODUCTION ⊠ CIVIL LITIGATION—AN OVERVIEW
⊠ THE PRELIMINARIES ⊠ THE PLEADINGS ⊠ PRETRIAL MOTIONS
⊠ DISCOVERY ⊠ PREPARING FOR TRIAL ⊠ THE TRIAL
⊠ POSTTRIAL MOTIONS AND PROCEDURES

After completing this chapter, you will know:

- The basic steps involved in the civil litigation process and the types of tasks that may be required of paralegals during each step of the process.

- How a lawsuit is initiated and what documents are filed during the pleadings stage of the civil litigation process.

- What discovery is and the kind of information that attorneys and their paralegals obtain from parties to the lawsuit and from witnesses when preparing for trial.

- How attorneys prepare for trial and the ways in which paralegals assist in this task.

- The various phases of a trial and the kinds of trial-related tasks that paralegals often perform.

- The options available to the losing party after the verdict is in.

175

INTRODUCTION

The paralegal plays a particularly important role in helping the trial attorney prepare for and conduct a civil trial. Popular television shows and movies tend to glamorize courtroom trials as semantic battles between quick-witted litigators, but the success of any trial depends primarily on how well the attorney and the paralegal have prepared for it.

Preparation for trial involves a variety of tasks. The law relating to the client's case must be carefully researched. Evidence must be gathered and documented. The litigation file must be created and carefully organized. Procedural requirements and deadlines for filing certain documents with the court must be met. **Witnesses**—persons asked to testify at trial—must be prepared in advance and be available to testify at the appropriate time during the trial. Any exhibits, such as charts, photographs, or videotapes, to be used at the trial must be properly prepared, mounted, scanned into the computer, or filmed. Arrangements must be made to have any necessary equipment, such as a VCR, videodisc, or CD-ROM player and projector, available for use at the trial. The paralegal's efforts are critically important in preparing for trial, and attorneys usually rely on paralegals to ensure that nothing has been overlooked during trial preparation.

Attorneys may request that their paralegals assist them during the trial as well. In the courtroom, the paralegal can perform numerous tasks. For example, the paralegal can locate documents or exhibits as they are needed. The paralegal can also observe jurors' reactions to statements made by attorneys or witnesses, check to see if a witness's testimony is consistent with sworn statements made by the witness before the trial, and perhaps give witnesses some last-minute instructions outside the courtroom before they are called to testify.

The complexity of even the simplest civil trial requires that the paralegal have some familiarity with the litigation process and the applicable courtroom procedures. Much of this expertise, of course, can only be acquired through hands-on experience. Yet every paralegal should be acquainted with the basic phases of civil litigation and the forms and terminology commonly used in the process. In this chapter, you will learn about the stages of a civil lawsuit, from the initial attorney-client meeting to the time of trial, as well as about trial and posttrial procedures.

CIVIL LITIGATION—AN OVERVIEW

Although civil trials vary greatly in terms of complexity, cost, and detail, they all share similar structural characteristics. They begin with an event that gives rise to the legal action, and (provided the case is not settled by the parties at some point during the litigation process—as most cases are) they end with the issuance of a **judgment,** the court's decision on the matter. In the interim, the litigation itself may involve all sorts of twists and turns. Even though each case has its own "story line," most civil lawsuits follow some version of the course charted in Exhibit 6.1.

Understanding and meeting procedural requirements is essential in the litigation process. These requirements are spelled out in the procedural rules of the court in which a lawsuit is brought. All civil trials held in federal district courts are governed by the **Federal Rules of Civil Procedure (FRCP).**[1] These rules specify what must be done during the various stages of the federal civil litigation process. For example, FRCP 4 (Rule 4 of the FRCP) describes the procedures that

Witness
A person who is asked to testify under oath at a trial.

On the Web
For a summary of the step-by-step procedures followed during a civil law case in one state court (Arizona), go to www.supreme.state.az.us/ courts/guide.htm#How.

Judgment
The court's final decision regarding the rights and claims of the parties to a lawsuit.

Federal Rules of Civil Procedure (FRCP)
The rules controlling all procedural matters in civil trials brought before the federal district courts.

---

1. Some practitioners use the abbreviation FRCivP to distinguish the Federal Rules of Civil Procedure from the Federal Rules of Criminal Procedure.

EXHIBIT 6.1
A Typical Case Flow Chart

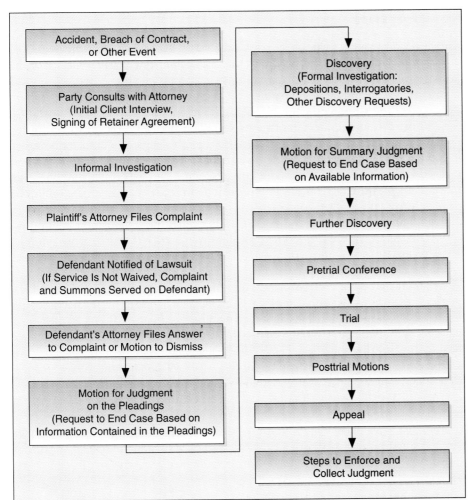

must be followed in notifying the defendant of the lawsuit. Each state also has its own rules of civil procedure (which in many states are similar to the FRCP). In addition, many courts have their own local rules of procedures that supplement the federal or state rules. The attorney and the paralegal must comply with the rules of procedure that apply to the specific court in which the trial will take place.

To illustrate the procedures involved in litigation, we present a hypothetical civil lawsuit. The case involves an automobile accident in which a car driven by Tony Peretto collided with a car driven by Katherine Baranski. Baranski suffered numerous injuries and incurred substantial medical and hospital costs. She also lost wages for the five months that she was unable to work. Baranski has decided to sue Peretto for damages. Because Baranski is the person initiating the lawsuit, she is the plaintiff. Peretto, because he must defend against Baranski's claims, is the defendant. The plaintiff and the defendant are referred to as the *parties* to the lawsuit. (Some cases involve several plaintiffs and/or defendants.)

The attorney for the plaintiff (Baranski) is Allen P. Gilmore. Gilmore is assisted by paralegal Elena Lopez. The attorney for the defendant (Peretto) is Elizabeth A. Cameron. Cameron is assisted by paralegal Gordon McVay. Throughout this chapter, *Case at a Glance* features in the page margins will remind you of the names of the players in this lawsuit.

▓ **Case at a Glance**

The Plaintiff—
Plaintiff: Katherine Baranski
Attorney: Allen P. Gilmore
Paralegal: Elena Lopez

The Defendant—
Defendant: Tony Peretto
Attorney: Elizabeth A. Cameron
Paralegal: Gordon McVay

THE PRELIMINARIES

Katherine Baranski arranges to meet with Allen P. Gilmore, an attorney with the law firm of Jeffers, Gilmore & Dunn, to see if Gilmore will represent her in the lawsuit. Gilmore asks paralegal Elena Lopez to prepare the usual forms and information sheets, including a retainer agreement and a statement of the firm's billing procedures, and to bring them with her to the initial interview with Baranski.

During the initial client interview, Katherine Baranski explains to attorney Gilmore and paralegal Lopez the facts of her case as she perceives them. Baranski tells them that Tony Peretto, who was driving a Dodge van, ran a stop sign and crashed into the driver's side of her Ford Escort as she was driving through the intersection of Mattis Avenue and Thirty-eighth Street in Nita City, Nita. The accident occurred at 7:45 A.M. on August 4, 1998. Baranski has misplaced Peretto's address, but she knows that he lives in another state, the state of Zero.[2] Baranski claims that as a result of the accident, she has been unable to work for five months and has lost approximately $15,000 in wages. Her medical and hospital expenses total $85,000, and the property damage to her car is estimated to be $10,000.

Gilmore agrees to represent Baranski in the lawsuit against Peretto. He explains the fee structure to Baranski, and she signs the retainer agreement.[3] He also has Baranski sign forms authorizing Gilmore to obtain relevant medical, employment, and other records relating to the claim. (These forms, which are called *release forms,* will be discussed in Chapter 7.) At the end of the interview, Gilmore also asks Lopez to schedule a follow-up interview with Baranski. Lopez will conduct the follow-up interview and obtain more details from Baranski about the accident and its consequences.

After Baranski leaves the office, attorney Gilmore asks paralegal Lopez to undertake a preliminary investigation to glean as much information as possible concerning the factual circumstances of Baranski's accident. You will read in Chapter 7 about the steps that a paralegal can take when investigating the facts of a client's case, and therefore we will not discuss investigation here.

THE PLEADINGS

Complaint
The pleading made by a plaintiff or a charge made by the state alleging wrongdoing on the part of the defendant.

The next step will be for plaintiff Baranski's attorney (Gilmore) to file a complaint in the appropriate court. The **complaint**[4] is a document that states the claims the plaintiff is making against the defendant. The complaint also contains a statement regarding the court's jurisdiction over the dispute and a demand for a remedy (such as money damages).

Pleadings
Statements by the plaintiff and the defendant that detail the facts, charges, and defenses involved in the litigation.

The filing of the complaint is the initial step that begins the legal action against the defendant, Peretto. The plaintiff's complaint and the defendant's answer—both of which are discussed below—are **pleadings**. The pleadings inform each party of the claims of the other and specify the issues (disputed questions) involved in the case. We examine here the complaint and answer, two basic pleadings. Exhibit 6.2 includes other types of pleadings that, under the FRCP, may also be filed with the court during this stage of the litigation.

Drafting the Complaint

The complaint itself may be no more than a few paragraphs long, or it may be many pages in length, depending on the complexity of the case. In the Baranski

---

2. Nita and Zero are fictitious states invented for the purpose of this hypothetical.
3. See Chapter 4 for a discussion of legal fees and the form and function of the retainer agreement.
4. In state courts, this document may be called a *petition.*

EXHIBIT 6.2
Types of Pleadings

Initial Pleadings

Complaint Filed by the plaintiff to initiate the lawsuit.
Answer Filed by the defendant in response to the plaintiff s complaint.

Counterclaim and Reply

Counterclaim Filed by the defendant against the plaintiff, asserting a claim for an injury arising from the same incident that forms the basis for the plaintiff s claim. There are two types of counterclaims:

1. A *compulsory* counterclaim must be asserted if it arises out of the same transaction or event that gave rise to the plaintiff s complaint or the right to assert the claim will be waived (forgone). Example: Defendant Peretto claims that plaintiff Baranski s negligence caused him to suffer injuries for which he should be compensated.

2. A *permissive* counterclaim arises from a separate transaction than the one forming the basis for the original lawsuit. Example: Defendant Peretto claims that plaintiff Baranski, prior to the accident had purchased a used Rolls-Royce from him, and Baranski s check bounced. Peretto has the option of either bringing a separate lawsuit against Baranski to collect the amount of the bounced check or filing a permissive counterclaim for that amount in this lawsuit.

Reply Filed by the plaintiff in response to the defendant s counterclaim.

Cross-Claim and Answer

Cross-claim Filed by a defendant against another defendant or a plaintiff against another plaintiff. When cross-claims are made, the defendants are suing one another (or the plaintiffs are suing one another). Example: Assume that plaintiff Baranski had been struck by two vehicles, one belonging to defendant Peretto and one belonging to Leon Balfour. If Peretto and Balfour had been named as co-defendants in Baranski s complaint, then Peretto s attorney could also file a cross-claim on behalf of Peretto against Balfour.

Answer Filed by the party against whom a cross-claim is brought.

Third Party Complaint and Answer

Third Party Complaint Filed by the defendant (in response to the plaintiff s complaint) or by the plaintiff (in response to the defendant s counterclaim) to bring into the litigation a third party who could be liable. Example: Defendant Peretto files a third party complaint against the manufacturer of the van that he was driving. Peretto asserts that the manufacturer should be liable for Baranski s injuries because the van s brakes were defective and therefore Peretto was unable to stop at the stop sign.

Answer Filed by the third party in response to the third party complaint.

case, the complaint will probably be only a few pages long unless special circumstances justify additional details. The complaint will include the following sections, each of which we discuss below:

- Caption.
- Jurisdictional allegations.
- General allegations (the body of the complaint).
- Prayer for relief.
- Signature.
- Demand for a jury trial.

Exhibit 6.3 shows a sample complaint. The sections of the complaint are indicated in the marginal annotations.

Baranski's case is being filed in a federal court, so the Federal Rules of Civil Procedure (FRCP) apply. If Baranski's case were filed in a state court, paralegal Lopez might need to review the appropriate state rules of civil procedure. The rules for drafting pleadings in state courts differ from the FRCP. The rules also differ from state to state and even from court to court within the same state. Lopez could obtain pleading forms, either from "form books" available in the law firm's files or library (or on computer disk or online) or from pleadings drafted previously in similar cases litigated by the firm in the court in which the Baranski case will be filed.

THE CAPTION.   All documents submitted to the court or other parties during the litigation process begin with a caption. The caption of the complaint identifies the court in which the action is being filed, the names of the parties, and the designation of the document as a "Complaint." The caption leaves a space for the court to insert the name of the judge who will be hearing the case. The caption also leaves a space for the court to insert the file number, or case number, that it assigns to the case. (The court's file number may also be referred to as the *docket number*. A **docket** is the list of cases entered on a court's calendar and thus scheduled to be heard.) Exhibit 6.3 shows how the caption will read in the case of *Baranski v. Peretto.*

Docket
The list of cases entered on a court's calendar and thus scheduled to be heard by the court.

JURISDICTIONAL ALLEGATIONS.   Because attorney Gilmore is filing the lawsuit in a federal district court, he will have to include in the complaint an allegation that the federal court has jurisdiction to hear the dispute. (An **allegation** is an assertion, claim, or statement made by one party in a pleading that sets out what the party expects to prove to the court.) Recall from Chapter 5 that federal courts can exercise jurisdiction over disputes involving either a *federal question* or *diversity of citizenship.* A federal question arises whenever a claim in a civil lawsuit relates to a federal law, the U.S. Constitution, or a treaty executed by the U.S. government. Diversity of citizenship exists when the parties involved in the lawsuit are citizens of different states and the amount in controversy exceeds $75,000. Because Baranski and Peretto are citizens of different states (Nita and Zero, respectively) and because the amount in controversy exceeds $75,000, the case meets the requirements for diversity-of-citizenship jurisdiction. Gilmore thus asserts that the federal court has jurisdiction on this basis, as illustrated in Exhibit 6.3.

Allegation
A party's statement, claim, or assertion made in a pleading to the court. The allegation sets forth the issue that the party expects to prove.

GENERAL ALLEGATIONS (THE BODY OF THE COMPLAINT).   The body of the complaint contains a series of allegations, stated in numbered paragraphs. In plaintiff Baranski's complaint, the allegations outline the factual events that gave rise to Baranski's claims.[5] The events are described in a series of chronologically arranged, numbered allegations so that the reader can understand them easily. As Exhibit 6.3 shows, the numbers of the paragraphs in the body of the complaint continue the sequence begun in the section on jurisdictional allegations.

---

5. The body of the complaint described in this section is a *fact pleading,* in which sufficient factual circumstances must be alleged to convince the court that the plaintiff has a cause of action. State courts often require fact pleadings, whereas federal courts only require *notice pleading.* FRCP 8(a) requires only that the complaint have "a short and plain statement of the claim showing that the pleader is entitled to relief." Fact pleading and notice pleading are not totally different—that is, the same allegation of facts could be in the body of a complaint submitted to either a federal or a state court. Federal courts simply have fewer requirements in this respect, and therefore they are often more attractive to litigants.

EXHIBIT 6.3
The Complaint

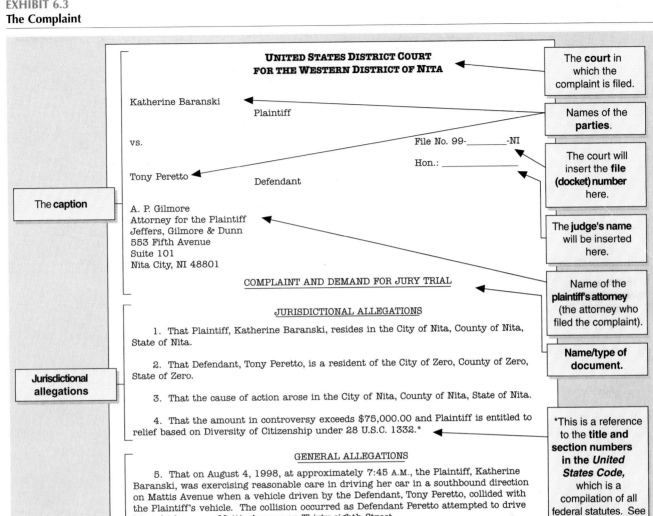

UNITED STATES DISTRICT COURT
FOR THE WESTERN DISTRICT OF NITA

The **court** in which the complaint is filed.

Katherine Baranski

Plaintiff

Names of the **parties**.

vs.   File No. 99-_____-NI

Hon.: _____

The court will insert the **file (docket) number** here.

Tony Peretto   Defendant

The **judge's name** will be inserted here.

The **caption**

A. P. Gilmore
Attorney for the Plaintiff
Jeffers, Gilmore & Dunn
553 Fifth Avenue
Suite 101
Nita City, NI 48801

Name of the **plaintiff's attorney** (the attorney who filed the complaint).

COMPLAINT AND DEMAND FOR JURY TRIAL

Name/type of document.

JURISDICTIONAL ALLEGATIONS

1. That Plaintiff, Katherine Baranski, resides in the City of Nita, County of Nita, State of Nita.

Jurisdictional allegations

2. That Defendant, Tony Peretto, is a resident of the City of Zero, County of Zero, State of Zero.

3. That the cause of action arose in the City of Nita, County of Nita, State of Nita.

4. That the amount in controversy exceeds $75,000.00 and Plaintiff is entitled to relief based on Diversity of Citizenship under 28 U.S.C. 1332.*

*This is a reference to the **title and section numbers in the *United States Code,*** which is a compilation of all federal statutes. See Chapter 14 for a further discussion of how to understand citations (references) to statutory law.

GENERAL ALLEGATIONS

5. That on August 4, 1998, at approximately 7:45 A.M., the Plaintiff, Katherine Baranski, was exercising reasonable care in driving her car in a southbound direction on Mattis Avenue when a vehicle driven by the Defendant, Tony Peretto, collided with the Plaintiff's vehicle. The collision occurred as Defendant Peretto attempted to drive his vehicle across Mattis Avenue on Thirty-eighth Street.

6. That the Defendant, Tony Peretto, owed the Plaintiff, Katherine Baranski, the following duties of care:

A. Duty to stop at the stop sign on Thirty-eighth Street before crossing Mattis Avenue.
B. Duty to make reasonable observations of vehicles in plain view before crossing Mattis Avenue.
C. Duty not to drive his motor vehicle in a reckless, careless, or heedless manner with willful and wanton disregard for the safety and rights of others, within the meaning of Section 9.2326(2) of the Nita Statutes Annotated.

General allegations

7. That the Defendant, Tony Peretto, breached each of the above duties and violated the following statutes of the State of Nita:

A. That he was guilty of reckless driving within the meaning of Section 9.2326 of the Nita Statutes Annotated.
B. That he was guilty of careless and negligent driving within the meaning of Section 9.2326(2) of the Nita Statutes Annotated.

8. That at the time of the collision, the weather conditions were clear and it was daylight.

EXHIBIT 6.3
The Complaint—Continued

9. That at the time of the collision, the Plaintiff, Katherine Baranski, was a generally healthy female, twenty-five years of age.

10. That as a result of the collision, the Plaintiff, Katherine Baranski, suffered severe physical injuries, which prevented her from working for five months, and property damage to her vehicle. The costs that the Plaintiff, Katherine Baranski, incurred as a result of the collision included $85,000 in medical bills, $15,000 in lost wages, and $10,000 in automobile-repair costs.

11. That the injuries sustained by the Plaintiff as a result of the collision were solely caused by the negligence of the Defendant, Tony Peretto.

WHEREFORE, the Plaintiff prays for the following relief:

A. That the Plaintiff be awarded appropriate compensatory damages;

B. That the Plaintiff be awarded an amount deemed fair and just by a Jury to compensate the Plaintiff for damages sustained as presented by the evidence in this case;

C. That the Plaintiff be awarded such other further relief as the Court deems proper. Plaintiff Katherine Baranski claims judgment against the Defendant in an amount in excess of $75,000 in actual, compensatory, and exemplary damages together with attorneys' fees, court costs, and other costs as provided by law.

> **The prayer for relief.**

Date: 2/10/99

Jeffers, Gilmore & Dunn

Allen P. Gilmore

Allen P. Gilmore
Attorney for Plaintiff
553 Fifth Avenue
Suite 101
Nita City, NI 48801

> **The signature of the plaintiff's attorney.**

Katherine Baranski, being first duly sworn, states that she has read the foregoing Complaint by her subscribed and that she knows the contents thereof, and the same is true, except those matters therein stated to be upon information and belief, and as to those matters, she believes to be true.

Katherine Baranski

Plaintiff

Sworn and subscribed before me this 10th day of February, 1999.

Leela M Shay

Notary Public, Nita County,
State of Nita

My Commission Expires:

March 10, 2003

> **Affidavit (and plaintiff's signature).**

DEMAND FOR A JURY TRIAL

The Plaintiff demands a trial by jury.

Date: 2/10/99

Jeffers, Gilmore & Dunn

Allen P. Gilmore

Allen P. Gilmore
Attorney for the Plaintiff
553 Fifth Avenue
Suite 101
Nita City, Nita 48801

> **Demand for a jury trial.**

When drafting the complaint, paralegal Lopez will present the facts forcefully and in a way that supports and strengthens the client's claim. Lopez must be careful, however, not to exaggerate the facts or make false statements. Rather, she must present the facts in such a way that the reader could reasonably infer that defendant Peretto was negligent and that Peretto's negligence caused Baranski's injuries and losses.

What if her research into the case had given Lopez reason to believe that a fact was probably true even though she could not be certain as to its validity? She could still include the statement in the complaint by prefacing it with the phrase, "On information and belief . . . ." This language would indicate to the court that the plaintiff, Baranski, had good reason to believe the truth of the statement but that the evidence for it either had not yet been obtained or might not hold up under close scrutiny.

After telling plaintiff Baranski's story, paralegal Lopez will add one or more paragraphs outlining the harms suffered by the plaintiff and the remedy (in money damages) that the plaintiff seeks.

PRAYER FOR RELIEF AND SIGNATURE.   Paralegal Lopez will include at the end of the complaint a paragraph, similar to that shown in Exhibit 6.3, asking that judgment be entered for the plaintiff and appropriate relief be granted. This *prayer for relief* will indicate that plaintiff Baranski is seeking money damages to compensate her for the harms that she suffered. In federal practice, the signature following the prayer for relief certifies that the plaintiff's attorney (or the plaintiff, if he or she is not represented by an attorney) has read the complaint and that the facts alleged are true to the best of his or her knowledge. In addition to the attorney's signature, some courts require an affidavit signed by the plaintiff verifying that the complaint is true to the best of the plaintiff's knowledge. **Affidavits** are sworn statements attesting to the existence of certain facts. They are acknowledged by a notary public or another official authorized to administer such oaths or affirmations. Exhibit 6.3 illustrates an affidavit for the Baranski complaint.

Affidavit
A written statement of facts, confirmed by the oath or affirmation of the party making it and made before a person having the authority to administer the oath or affirmation.

DEMAND FOR A JURY TRIAL.   A trial can be held with or without a jury. If there is no jury, the judge determines the truth of the facts alleged in the case. The Seventh Amendment to the U.S. Constitution guarantees the right to a jury trial in federal courts in all "suits at common law" when the amount in controversy exceeds $20. Most states have similar guarantees in their own constitutions, although many states put a higher minimum dollar restriction on the guarantee (for example, in Iowa the minimum amount is $1,000). If this threshold requirement is met, either party may request a jury trial. The right to a trial by jury does not have to be exercised, and many cases are tried without one. If plaintiff Baranski wants a jury trial, Gilmore will ask paralegal Lopez to include a demand for jury trial (similar to the one illustrated in Exhibit 6.3) with the complaint.

Filing the Complaint

Once the complaint has been prepared, carefully checked for accuracy, and signed by attorney Gilmore, paralegal Lopez will file the complaint with the court in which the action is being brought. To file the complaint, Lopez will deliver it to the clerk of the court, together with a check payable to the court in the amount of the required filing fee. (If Lopez is not aware of the court's specific procedures for filing the complaint, she should call the court clerk to verify the amount of the filing fee and how many copies of the complaint need to be filed.) The court clerk

DEVELOPING PARALEGAL SKILLS
Federal Court Rules—Creating a Complaint Checklist

Ann Marston is a paralegal who works in a firm with a federal court practice. A new paralegal, Brian Blake, is joining the firm, and Ann has been asked to train Brian. Her supervising attorney suggested that she create a checklist for drafting federal court complaints. The checklist could be used to train not only Brian but also new associates in the firm.

Before she begins drafting a complaint, Ann meets with Brian and explains what she does. Ann tells Brian that she starts by getting the file and reviewing her notes, memos from the client interview, and any reports, such as police reports, that are in the file. She explains that these sources will assist her in describing how, for example, a personal injury occurred in an accident case. She also checks to see if she made any notes, during her meeting with the attorney who will handle the case, regarding the court in which the case will be filed, because in some cases the state and federal courts have concurrent jurisdiction. Next, she finds out the plaintiff's and the defendant's correct legal names. If necessary, she contacts the secretary of state to obtain the legal name of a corporation. Lastly, she takes out her copy of the Federal Rules of Civil Procedure and reviews Rules 8, 10, and 11, which specify the kind of information that should be included in complaints filed in a federal court.

CHECKLIST FOR DRAFTING A COMPLAINT

- Determine when the statute of limitations expires by checking the file for the relevant dates.
- Locate a previously drafted complaint form for the types of cases involved.
- Determine the court's basis for jurisdiction in the case, and draft an allegation explaining it.
- Determine the facts that create the cause of action, or the legal basis for the lawsuit.
- Draft the "general allegations," or the body of the complaint. If the plaintiff has more than one legal basis for the relief sought, draft as many "counts" as the plaintiff has.
- Determine the specific type of relief, such as money damages, that the plaintiff is seeking, and draft a prayer for relief.
- Insert a signature block for an attorney's signature after a reasonable inquiry into the facts that support the claim.
- Determine if a jury trial is desired, and draft a demand for a jury trial if needed.

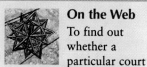

On the Web
To find out whether a particular court permits documents to be filed electronically and, for some courts, to obtain the appropriate forms, visit that court's Web page (or the home page for the state court system). You can find links to federal and state courts at www.findlaw.com.

files the complaint by stamping the date on the document; assigning the case a file number, or docket number; and assigning the case to a particular judge. (In state courts, the file number may not be assigned until later.)

Although traditionally a complaint or other litigation-related document has been delivered personally to the court clerk, the 1993 revision of Rule 5(a) of the FRCP provides that federal courts may permit filing by fax or "other electronic means." As you read in Chapter 5, several jurisdictions now permit electronic filing. In the future, filing court documents electronically will likely become a common method of filing.

After the complaint has been filed, the court will consult with the attorneys for both sides, often through a scheduling conference. Following this meeting, the judge will enter a *scheduling order* that sets out the time limits within which pretrial events (such as the pleadings, discovery, and the final pretrial conference) must be completed and the date of the trial. Under FRCP 16(b), the scheduling order should be entered "as soon as practicable and in no event more than 120 days after the complaint is filed."

EXHIBIT 6.4
A Summons in a Civil Action

United States District Court

WESTERN ———— DISTRICT OF ———— NITA

Katherine Baranski

v.

Tony Peretto

SUMMONS IN A CIVIL ACTION

CASE NUMBER:

TO:

Tony Peretto
1708 Johnston Drive
Zero City, ZE 59806

YOU ARE HEREBY SUMMONED and required to file with the Clerk of this Court and serve upon

PLAINTIFF'S ATTORNEY
    Allen P. Gilmore
    Jeffers, Gilmore & Dunn
    553 Fifth Avenue
    Suite 101
    Nita City, NI 48801

an answer to the complaint which is herewith served upon you, within _____20_____ days after service of this summons upon you, exclusive of the day of service. If you fail to do so, judgment by default will be taken against you for the relief demanded in the complaint.

C. H. Hynek

CLERK

John Dolan

BY DEPUTY CLERK

February 10, 1999

DATE

Service of Process

Before the court can exercise jurisdiction over the defendant—in effect, before the lawsuit can begin—the court must have proof that the defendant was notified of the lawsuit. If defendant Peretto did not agree to *waive* service of process (waiver of service will be discussed later) or if the case against Peretto had been filed in a state court, Peretto would be served with a summons. Serving the summons and complaint—that is, the delivery of these documents to the defendant in a lawsuit—is referred to as **service of process**.

THE SUMMONS.   The **summons** identifies the parties to the lawsuit, as well as the court in which the case will be heard, and directs the defendant to respond to the complaint within a specified period of time. In the Baranski case, paralegal Lopez will prepare a summons by filling out a form similar to that shown in Exhibit 6.4.

Service of Process
The delivery of the summons and the complaint to a defendant.

Summons
A document served on a defendant in a lawsuit informing the defendant that a legal action has been commenced against him or her and that the defendant must appear in court on a certain date to answer the plaintiff's complaint.

If the case were being brought in a state court, paralegal Lopez would deliver the summons to the court clerk at the same time she delivered the complaint. (In federal court cases, as will be discussed below, the complaint may already have been filed under the new FRCP provisions relating to waiver of notice.) After the clerk files the complaint and signs, seals, and issues the summons, attorney Gilmore will be responsible for making sure that the documents are served on defendant Peretto. The service of the complaint and summons must be effected within a specified time—120 days under FRCP 4(m)—after the complaint has been filed.

SERVING THE COMPLAINT AND SUMMONS.   How service of process occurs depends on the rules of the court or jurisdiction in which the lawsuit is brought. Under FRCP 4(c)(2), service of process in federal court cases may be effected "by any person who is not a party and who is at least 18 years of age." Paralegal Lopez, for example, could serve the summons by personally delivering it to defendant Peretto or to someone living in his home. Alternatively, she could make arrangements for someone else to do so, subject to the approval of attorney Gilmore. In some types of cases, Gilmore might request that the court have a U.S. marshal or other federal official serve the summons.

Under FRCP 4(e)(1), service of process in federal court cases may also be effected "pursuant to the law of the state in which the district court is located." Many state courts require that the complaint and summons be served by a public officer, such as a sheriff.

Regardless of how the summons is served, attorney Gilmore will need some kind of proof that defendant Peretto actually received the summons. In federal court cases, unless service is made by a U.S. marshal or other official, proof of service can be established by having the process server fill out and sign a form similar to the **return-of-service form** shown in Exhibit 6.5. This form can then be submitted to the court as evidence that service has been effected.

Paralegal Lopez must be very careful to comply with the service requirements of the court in which plaintiff Baranski's suit has been filed. If service is not properly made, defendant Peretto will have a legal ground (basis) for asking the court to dismiss the case against him, thus delaying the litigation. As mentioned earlier, the court will not be able to exercise jurisdiction over Peretto until he has been properly notified of the lawsuit being brought against him.

SERVING CORPORATE DEFENDANTS.   In cases involving corporate defendants, the summons and complaint may be served on an officer or a *registered agent* (representative) of the corporation. The name of a corporation's registered agent is usually obtainable from the secretary of state's office in the state in which the company incorporated its business (and, usually, the secretary of state's office in any state in which the corporation does business).

Notice and Waiver of Service—FRCP 4(d)

The 1993 revision of the FRCP added Rule 4(d), which allows for a simpler and less costly alternative to service of process. Under this rule, a plaintiff's attorney is permitted to notify the defendant directly, through the mails or "other reliable means," of the lawsuit. After the complaint has been filed, attorney Gilmore will thus probably ask paralegal Lopez to follow the procedures outlined in FRCP 4(d).

To comply with FRCP 4(d), Lopez will need to fill out two forms. Form 1A, which is shown in Exhibit 6.6 on page 188, is entitled "Notice of Lawsuit and Request for Waiver of Service of Summons." This form, which must be signed by

Return-of-Service Form
A document signed by a process server and submitted to the court to prove that a defendant received a summons.

EXHIBIT 6.5
A Return-of-Service Form

RETURN OF SERVICE		
Service of the Summons and Complaint was made by me	DATE	2/11/99
NAME OF SERVER Elena Lopez	TITLE	Paralegal

Check one box below to indicate appropriate method of service

☒ Served personally upon the defendant. Place where served: Defendant Peretto's Home: 1708 Johnston Drive, Zero City, Zero 59806

☐ Left copies thereof at the defendant's dwelling house or usual place of abode with a person of suitable age and discretion then residing therein.
    Name of person with whom the summons and complaint were left:

☐ Returned unexecuted:

☐ Other (specifiy):

STATEMENT OF SERVICE FEES

TRAVEL 40 miles @ 33¢/mile	SERVICES 1 hour @ $56/hour	TOTAL $69.20

DECLARATION OF SERVER

I declare under penalty of perjury under the laws of the United States of America that the foregoing information contained in the Return of Service and Statement of Service Fees is true and correct.

Executed on ____2/11/99____   *Elena Lopez*
                    Date   *Signature of Server*

                    308 University Avenue, Nita City, Nita 48804
                    Address of Server

attorney Gilmore, requests defendant Peretto to waive the requirement that he be notified of the lawsuit by having a summons served on him. Next, Lopez will fill out Form 1B, entitled "Waiver of Service of Summons." Exhibit 6.7 on page 189 indicates the information that must be included in this form. Once these forms are filled out and attorney Gilmore has reviewed and signed them, paralegal Lopez will send to defendant Peretto a packet containing the following contents:

- Two copies each of Form 1A and Form 1B.

EXHIBIT 6.6
Form 1A—Notice of Lawsuit and Request for Waiver of Service of Summons

TO:_____ (A) _____
[as_____ (B) _____ of _____ (C) _____]

    A lawsuit has been commenced against you (or the entity on whose behalf you are addressed). A copy of the complaint is attached to this notice. It has been filed in the United States District Court for the_____ (D) _____ and has been assigned docket number_____ (E) _____.

    This is not a formal summons or notification from the court, but rather my request that you sign and return the enclosed waiver of service in order to save the cost of serving you with a judicial summons and an additional copy of the complaint. The cost of service will be avoided if I receive a signed copy of the waiver within_____ (F) _____ days after the date designated below as the date on which this Notice and Request is sent. I enclose a stamped and addressed envelope [or other means of cost-free return] for your use. An extra copy of the waiver is also attached for your records.

    If you comply with this request and return the signed waiver, it will be filed with the court and no summons will be served on you. The action will then proceed as if you had been served on the date the waiver is filed, except that you will not be obligated to answer the complaint before 60 days from the date designated below as the date on which this notice is sent (or before 90 days from that date if your address is not in any judicial district of the United States).

    If you do not return the signed waiver within the time indicated, I will take appropriate steps to effect formal service in a manner authorized by the Federal Rules of Civil Procedure and will then, to the extent authorized by those Rules, ask the court to require you (or the party on whose behalf you are addressed) to pay the full costs of such service. In that connection please read the statement concerning the duty of parties to waive the service of the summons, which is set forth on the reverse side [or at the foot] of the waiver form.

    I affirm that this request is being sent to you on behalf of the plaintiff, this_____ day of_____ ,___ .

                  _____
                   Signature of Plaintiff's Attorney or
                   Unrepresented Plaintiff

Notes:
    A–Name of individual (or name of officer or agent of corporate defendant)
    B–Title, or other relationship of individual to corporate defendant
    C–Name of corporate defendant, if any
    D–District
    E–Docket number of action
    F–Addressee must be given at least 30 days (60 days if located in foreign country) in which to return waiver

- A copy of the complaint.
- An addressed, stamped envelope for defendant Peretto to use when returning Form 1B.

    If defendant Peretto agrees to waive service of process, he will need to sign and return the waiver to attorney Gilmore within thirty days after the waiver form was sent by Gilmore. (For defendants located in a foreign country, the time period is extended to sixty days.)

    The aim of FRCP 4(d) is to eliminate the costs associated with service of process and to foster cooperation among adversaries. To encourage defendants to agree to the waiver of service, FRCP 4(d)(3) provides that defendants who return the required waiver are not required to respond to the complaint for sixty days (ninety days for defendants outside the United States) after the date on which the request for waiver of service was sent. In contrast, if a defendant does not agree to waive service and a complaint and summons must be served, then (under FRCP 12)

EXHIBIT 6.7
Form 1B—Waiver of
Service of Summons

TO: _____ (name of plaintiff's attorney or unrepresented plaintiff) _____

    I acknowledge receipt of your request that I waive service of a summons in the action of (caption of action) , which is case number ____ (docket number) ____ in the United States District Court for the _____ (district) ____. I have also received a copy of the complaint in the action, two copies of this instrument, and a means by which I can return the signed waiver to you without cost to me.

    I agree to save the cost of service of a summons and an additional copy of the complaint in this lawsuit by not requiring that I (or the entity on whose behalf I am acting) be served with judicial process in the manner provided by Rule 4.

    I (or the entity on whose behalf I am acting) will retain all defenses or objections to the lawsuit or to the jurisdiction or venue of the court except for objections based on a defect in the summons or in the service of the summons.

    I understand that a judgment may be entered against me (or the party on whose behalf I am acting) if an answer or motion under Rule 12 is not served upon you within 60 days after (date request was sent) , or within 90 days after that date if the request was sent outside the United States.

_____

Date

Signature _____
Printed/typed name: _____
      [as_____]
      [of_____]

[To be printed on foot of or on reverse side of form:]

DUTY TO AVOID UNNECESSARY COSTS OF SERVICE OF SUMMONS

    Rule 4 of the Federal Rules of Civil Procedure requires parties to cooperate in saving unnecessary costs of service of the summons and complaint. A defendant located in the United States, who, after being notified of an action and asked by a plaintiff located in the United States to waive service of a summons, fails to do so will be required to bear the cost of such service unless good cause be shown for its failure to sign and return the waiver.

    It is not good cause for a failure to waive service that a party believes that the complaint is unfounded, or that the action has been brought in an improper place or in a court that lacks jurisdiction over the subject matter of the action or over its person or property. A party who waives service of the summons retains all defenses and objections (except any relating to the summons or to the service of the summons), and may later object to the jurisdiction of the court or to the place where the action has been brought.

    A defendant who waives service must within the time specified on the waiver form serve on the plaintiff's attorney (or unrepresented plaintiff) a response to the complaint and must also file a signed copy of the response with the court. If the answer or motion is not served within this time, a default judgment may be taken against that defendant. By waiving service, a defendant is allowed more time to answer than if the summons had been actually served when the request for waiver of service was received.

the defendant must respond to the complaint within twenty days after process is served.

The Defendant's Response

Once a defendant receives the plaintiff's complaint, either via mail or through service of process, the defendant must respond to the complaint within a specified time period (in federal cases, within the time periods specified above). If the defendant fails to respond within that time period, the court, on the plaintiff's motion, will enter a **default judgment** against the defendant. The defendant will then be liable for the entire amount of damages that the plaintiff is claiming and will lose the opportunity to either defend against the claim in court or settle the issue with the plaintiff out of court.

Default Judgment
A judgment entered by a clerk or court against a party who has failed to appear in court to answer or defend against a claim that has been brought against him or her by another party.

In the Baranski case, assume that defendant Peretto consults with an attorney, Elizabeth A. Cameron, to decide on a course of action. Before Cameron advises Peretto on the matter, she will want to investigate plaintiff Baranski's claim and obtain evidence of what happened at the time of the accident. She may ask her paralegal, Gordon McVay, to call anyone who may have witnessed the accident and any police officers who were at the scene. Attorney Cameron will also ask McVay to gather relevant documents, including the traffic ticket that Peretto received at the time of the accident and any reports that might have been filed by the police. If all goes well, attorney Cameron and paralegal McVay will complete their investigation in a few days and then meet to assess the results. In deciding how best to respond to the complaint, Peretto's attorney, Cameron, must consider whether to file an answer or a motion to dismiss the case.

Answer
A defendant's response to a plaintiff's complaint.

THE ANSWER.   A defendant's **answer** must respond to each allegation in the plaintiff's complaint. FRCP 8(b) permits the defendant to admit or deny the truth of each allegation. Defendant Peretto's attorney may advise Peretto to admit to some of the allegations in plaintiff Baranski's complaint, because doing so narrows the number of issues in dispute.

For example, paragraph 5 of Peretto's answer might read "Defendant admits the allegations contained in paragraph 5 of the Plaintiff's complaint." If Peretto wishes to deny an allegation, such as the plaintiff's allegation in paragraph 11, he may state in his answer, "Defendant denies the allegation of negligence contained in paragraph 11 of the Plaintiff's complaint." Another option for the defendant is to state in the answer that he or she does not have sufficient information on which to base an admission or a denial. For example, paragraph 9 of the answer might state that the defendant "lacks sufficient information to form a belief as to the truth of the allegation contained in paragraph 9 of the Plaintiff's complaint."

Like the complaint, the answer begins with a caption and ends with the attorney's signature. It may also include, following the attorney's signature an affidavit signed by the defendant, as well as a demand for a jury trial.

A defendant may assert, in the answer, a reason why he or she should not be held liable for the plaintiff's injuries even if the facts, as alleged by the plaintiff, are true. This is called raising an **affirmative defense**. For example, Peretto might claim that someone else was driving his Dodge van when it crashed into Baranski's car. Although affirmative defenses are directed toward the plaintiff, the plaintiff is not required to file additional pleadings in response to these defenses.

Case at a Glance

The Plaintiff—
   Plaintiff: Katherine
      Baranski
   Attorney: Allen P.
      Gilmore
   Paralegal: Elena Lopez

The Defendant—
   Defendant: Tony Peretto
   Attorney: Elizabeth A.
      Cameron
   Paralegal: Gordon
      McVay

Affirmative Defense
A response to a plaintiff's claim that does not deny the plaintiff's facts but attacks the plaintiff's legal right to bring an action.

Motion
A procedural request or application presented by an attorney to the court on behalf of a client.

MOTION TO DISMISS.   A **motion** is a procedural request submitted to the court by an attorney on behalf of his or her client. When one party files a motion with the court, it must also send to, or serve on, the opposing party a *notice of motion*. The notice of motion informs the opposing party that the motion has been filed and indicates when the court will hear the motion. The notice of motion gives the opposing party an opportunity to prepare for the hearing and argue before the court why the motion should not be granted.

The **motion to dismiss,** as the phrase implies, requests the court to dismiss the case for reasons provided in the motion. Defendant Peretto's attorney, for example, could file a motion to dismiss if she believed that Peretto had not been properly served, that the complaint had been filed in the wrong court, that the statute of limitations for that type of lawsuit had expired, or that the complaint did not state a claim for which relief (a remedy) could be granted. See Exhibit 6.8 for an example of a motion to dismiss.

Motion to Dismiss
A pleading in which a defendant admits the facts as alleged by the plaintiff but asserts that the plaintiff's claim fails to state a cause of action (that is, has no basis in law) or that there are other grounds on which a suit should be dismissed.

EXHIBIT 6.8
A Motion to Dismiss

```
              UNITED STATES DISTRICT COURT
            FOR THE WESTERN DISTRICT OF NITA


   Katherine Baranski
                        Plaintiff

                                              File No. 99-14335-NI
   vs.
                                              Hon. Harley M. LaRue

   Tony Peretto
                        Defendant



   Elizabeth A. Cameron
   Attorney for the Defendant
   Cameron & Strauss, P.C.
   310 Lake Drive
   Zero City, ZE 59802


                     MOTION TO DISMISS


      The Defendant, Tony Peretto, by his attorney, moves the court to dismiss
   the above-named action because the statute of limitations governing the
   Plaintiff's claim has expired, as demonstrated in the memorandum of law
   that is being submitted with this motion.  The Plaintiff therefore has no
   cause of action against the Defendant.

                              Cameron & Strauss, P.C.

                              *Elizabeth A Cameron*
   Date:  2/20/99            Elizabeth A. Cameron
                              Attorney for the Defendant
                              310 Lake Drive
                              Zero City, ZE 59802
```

If defendant Peretto's attorney decides to file a motion to dismiss plaintiff Baranski's claim, she may want to attach one or more *supporting affidavits*—sworn statements as to certain facts that may contradict the allegations made in the complaint. Peretto's attorney may also have her paralegal draft a **memorandum of law** (which is called a *brief* in some states) to be submitted along with the motion to dismiss and the accompanying affidavits. The memorandum of law will present the legal basis for the motion, citing any statutes and cases that support it. A supporting affidavit gives factual support to the motion to dismiss, while the memorandum of law provides the court with the legal grounds for the dismissal of the claim.[6]

Memorandum of Law
A document (known as a brief in some states) that delineates the legal theories, statutes, and cases on which a motion is based.

PRETRIAL MOTIONS

Many motions may be made during the pretrial litigation process, including those listed and described in Exhibit 6.9 on the next page. Some pretrial motions, if granted by the court, will end a case before trial. These motions include the

---

6. The memorandum of law described here should not be confused with the legal memorandum discussed in Chapter 8. The latter is an internal memorandum (that is, a memo submitted— usually by the paralegal—to an attorney).

EXHIBIT 6.9
Pretrial Motions

MOTION TO DISMISS: A motion filed by the defendant in which the defendant asks the court to dismiss the case for a specified reason, such as improper service, lack of personal jurisdiction, or the plaintiff's failure to state a claim for which relief can be granted.

MOTION TO STRIKE: A motion filed by the defendant in which the defendant asks the court to strike (delete from) the complaint certain of the paragraphs contained in the complaint. Motions to strike help to clarify the underlying issues that form the basis for the complaint by removing paragraphs that are redundant or irrelevant to the action.

MOTION TO MAKE MORE DEFINITE AND CERTAIN: A motion filed by the defendant to compel the plaintiff to clarify the basis of the plaintiff's cause of action. The motion is filed when the defendant believes that the complaint is too vague or ambiguous for the defendant to respond to it in a meaningful way.

MOTION FOR JUDGMENT ON THE PLEADINGS: A motion that may be filed by either party in which the party asks the court to enter judgment in its favor based on information contained in the pleadings. A judgment on the pleadings will only be made if there are no facts in dispute and the only question is how the law applies to a set of undisputed facts.

MOTION TO COMPEL DISCOVERY: A motion that may be filed by either party in which the party asks the court to compel the other party to comply with a discovery request. If a party refuses to allow the opponent to inspect and copy certain documents, for example, the party requesting the documents may make a motion to compel production of documents.

MOTION FOR SUMMARY JUDGMENT: A motion that may be filed by either party in which the party asks the court to enter judgment in its favor without a trial. Unlike a motion for judgment on the pleadings, a motion for summary judgment can be supported by evidence outside the pleadings, such as witnesses' affidavits, answers to interrogatories, or other evidence obtained prior to or during discovery.

EXHIBIT 6.9
Pretrial Motions

Motion for Judgment on the Pleadings
A motion, which can be brought by either party to a lawsuit after the pleadings are closed, for the court to decide the issue without proceeding to trial. The motion will be granted only if no facts are in dispute and the only issue concerns how the law applies to a set of undisputed facts.

Motion for Summary Judgment
A motion requesting the court to enter a judgment without proceeding to trial. The motion can be based on evidence outside the pleadings and will be granted only if no facts are in dispute and the only issue concerns how the law applies to a set of undisputed facts.

motion to dismiss (which has already been discussed), the motion for judgment on the pleadings, and the motion for summary judgment.

Once the two attorneys in the Baranski case, Gilmore and Cameron, have finished filing their respective pleadings and amendments, either one of them may file a **motion for judgment on the pleadings.** Motions for judgment on the pleadings are often filed when it appears from the pleadings that the plaintiff has failed to state a cause of action for which relief may be granted. They may also be filed when the pleadings indicate that no facts are in dispute and the only question is how the law applies to a set of undisputed facts. For example, assume for a moment that in the Baranski case, defendant Peretto admitted to all of plaintiff Baranski's allegations in his answer and raised no affirmative defenses. In this situation, Baranski's attorney, Gilmore, would file a motion for judgment on the pleadings in Baranski's favor.

A **motion for summary judgment** is similar to a motion for judgment on the pleadings in that the party filing the motion is asking the court to grant a judgment in its favor without a trial. As with a motion for judgment on the pleadings,

PARALEGAL PROFILE

Litigation Paralegal

CHARISSE A. CHARLES-HAMPTON *received her bachelor of arts degree,* cum laude, *in legal administration in December 1993 from the University of West Florida. Her first paralegal job was as an intern for a judge. After graduation, she was hired by a small law firm as a workers' compensation litigation paralegal and is currently working as a litigation paralegal, primarily in the area of personal injury.*

She is an active member of the Pensacola Legal Assistants Association and serves as chairperson for the Scholarship Awards Committee.

What do you like best about your work?

"What I like best about my work is being able to communicate with people in various offices to assist our clients in defending their claims. I have met a lot of people via the telephone and in so doing, have established great working relationships with many doctors' offices, judges' offices, clerks at the courthouse, and adjusters at various insurance companies, to list just a few. My working relationships with these people make my job much easier when I need to call on their assistance for our clients."

What is the greatest challenge that you face in your area of work?

"The greatest challenge for me is playing the role of both a plaintiff's paralegal and a defense paralegal. Some days it is very hard to empathize with clients who I know in my heart are not seriously injured and are only looking for a handout. On the flip side, it is sometimes very difficult to not allow my emotions to come into play when defending a matter for an insurance company regarding an individual who has been seriously injured."

"Communication can help you or destroy you."

What advice do you have for would-be paralegals in your area of work?

"I suggest that they focus heavily on their communication skills. Communication can help you or destroy you. I encourage them to attend workshops that focus on communicating with clients who are both difficult and not so difficult. I also encourage would-be paralegals to be detail oriented. Lastly, I suggest that they welcome challenges, big or small."

What are some tips for success as a paralegal in your area of work?

"Tips for success as a personal-injury paralegal include good communication skills, organizational skills, computer skills, timeliness, a willingness to accept changes, and a willingness to make changes that will benefit all parties involved."

a court will only grant a motion for summary judgment if it determines that no facts are in dispute and the only question is how the law applies to a set of facts agreed on by both parties.

When the court considers a <u>motion for summary judgment,</u> it can take into account *evidence outside the pleadings.* This distinguishes the motion for summary judgment from the motion to dismiss and the motion for judgment on the pleadings. To support a motion for summary judgment, one party can submit evidence obtained at any point prior to trial (including during the discovery stage of litigation—to be discussed shortly) that refutes the other party's factual claim. In the Baranski case, for example, suppose that Peretto was in another state at the time of the accident. Defendant Peretto's attorney could make a motion for

ETHICAL CONCERN
Keeping Client Information Confidential

As it happens, attorney Gilmore's legal assistant, Lopez, is a good friend of plaintiff Baranski's daughter. Lopez learns from the results of Baranski's medical examination that Baranski has a terminal illness. Lopez is sure that the daughter, who quarreled with her mother two months ago and hasn't spoken to her since, is unaware of the illness and would probably be very hurt if she learned that Lopez knew of it and didn't tell her. Should Lopez tell her friend about the illness? No. This is confidential information at this point, which Lopez only became aware of by virtue of her job. Should the information be revealed publicly during the course of the trial, then Lopez would be free to disclose it to her friend if the friend still remained unaware of it. In the meantime, Lopez is ethically (and legally) obligated not to disclose the information to anyone who is not working on the case, including her friend.

▨ Case at a Glance

The Plaintiff—
   Plaintiff: Katherine Baranski
   Attorney: Allen P. Gilmore
   Paralegal: Elena Lopez

The Defendant—
   Defendant: Tony Peretto
   Attorney: Elizabeth A. Cameron
   Paralegal: Gordon McVay

Discovery
Formal investigation prior to trial. During discovery, opposing parties use various methods, such as interrogatories and depositions, to obtain information from each other and from witnesses to prepare for trial.

Privileged Information
Confidential communications between certain individuals, such as an attorney and his or her client, that are protected from disclosure except under court order.

Interrogatories
A series of written questions for which written answers are prepared and then signed under oath by a party to a lawsuit (the plaintiff or the defendant).

summary judgment in Peretto's favor and attach to the motion a witness's sworn statement that Peretto was in the other state at the time of the accident. Unless plaintiff Baranski's attorney could bring in sworn statements by other witnesses to show that Peretto was at the scene of the accident, Peretto would normally be granted his motion for summary judgment.

DISCOVERY

Before a trial begins, the parties can use a number of procedural devices to obtain information and gather evidence about the case. Plaintiff Baranski's attorney, for example, will want to know how fast defendant Peretto was driving, whether he had been drinking, whether he saw the stop sign, and so on. The process of obtaining information from the opposing party or from other witnesses is known as **discovery**.

The FRCP and similar rules in the states set forth the guidelines for discovery activity. Discovery includes gaining access to witnesses, documents, records, and other types of evidence. The rules governing discovery are designed to make sure that a witness or a party is not unduly harassed, that **privileged information** (communications that may not be disclosed in court) is safeguarded, and that only matters relevant to the case at hand are discoverable. Currently, the trend is toward allowing more discovery and thus fewer surprises. The 1993 revision of the FRCP significantly changed the rules governing discovery in federal court cases. To the extent that state courts decide to follow the new federal rules, discovery in such cases will also be affected. You will learn how the revised rules affect the traditional discovery process in the next section.

Traditional discovery devices include interrogatories, depositions, requests for documents, requests for admissions, and requests for examinations. Each of these discovery tools is examined below.

Interrogatories

Interrogatories are written questions that must be answered, in writing, by the parties to the lawsuit and then signed by the parties under oath. Typically, the

FEATURED GUEST: JAMES W. H. McCORD

Ten Tips for Drafting Interrogatories

BIOGRAPHICAL NOTE

Since 1978, James McCord has been active in paralegal education as the director of paralegal programs at Eastern Kentucky University. He has served as president of the American Association for Paralegal Education, as a member of the American Bar Association Legal Assistant Program Approval Commission, and as chair of the Kentucky Bar Association Committee on Paralegals. He received his law degree from the University of Wisconsin and practiced law before taking the position at Eastern Kentucky University. McCord is the author of The Litigation Paralegal: A Systems Approach, *which is now in its third edition;* ABA Approval: An Educator's Guide; *and (as co-author)* Criminal Law and Procedure for the Paralegal.

Interrogatories that are well thought out and carefully phrased can help to clarify the factual circumstances of the case, the types of evidence that can be obtained, and the issues in dispute. Because they help to define and shape a lawsuit, your ability to draft good interrogatories will make you a valued member of the litigation team. Here are some tips that you might find useful when you are asked to draft interrogatories.

1. Know the Limits of Interrogatories. Interrogatories have limits. The questions must seek information that is relevant to the issues or that will lead to relevant facts. The number of questions may be limited by the relevant rules or by the judge. Ethical standards explicitly forbid using interrogatories to harass a party or for the primary purpose of swamping the opponent with paperwork. Objections to interrogatories cause unwanted delay and possible loss of valuable information. Opponents usually object to questions that are irrelevant, vague or ambiguous, unduly burdensome, too numerous, or too broad in scope (covering too great a time span, for example). An attorney will also object to questions that seek protected information (such as the privileged communication between spouses or between an attorney and his or her client) or the ideas and strategies that make up the attorney's work product.

2. Develop Objectives for the Interrogatories. Review the case file to familiarize yourself with its contents. Meet with your supervising attorney to discuss the attorney's approach to the case. Identification of the key issues in the case, as well as the strategies and directions the attorney intends to pursue at trial, will help you streamline your work. With your attention focused on only the pertinent matters, reread the complaint, answer, and any other pleadings. Identify the elements to be proved and the defenses to be asserted, then list possible evidence that would support or disprove those elements or defenses. Divide the list into three parts: the information you already possess, information you have that needs to be clarified, and information that you need but do not yet possess. For items in the last two groups, indicate likely persons, files, documents, or other sources that will provide the information or give you leads to the information.

3. Refer to Form Books or Previous Interrogatories. Collections of commonly used interrogatories can be found in the firm's library, a law library, or practice manuals. These are frequently categorized by the type of case—personal injury, contract, antitrust, and so on. Check interrogatories from similar cases in the firm's files to locate pertinent questions. Local examples keyed to local practice are especially helpful. Use the gathered examples as a guide only, then shape your questions to the unique needs of your case. Input useful examples into your computer and edit them to your satisfaction. Add your own questions to fully address the elements of the case at hand.

4. Use Preliminary Sections to Define and Instruct. Following the desired case caption, draft an introductory paragraph stating the name of the person to whom the questions are directed, that answers to the questions are requested, the date answers are due, and the applicable rule or rules of procedure. A subsequent section should define any terms or identify any acronyms that will be

FEATURED GUEST, *Continued*

repeated in the questions. This promotes clarity and avoids repetitious language. It reduces evasiveness by giving you the power to define the terms as broadly or as narrowly as needed. Interrogatories from previous cases define commonly repeated terms, such as *document, identify, you,* and *corporate officer,* and thus are good sources for the definitions section. Review your proposed definitions in light of your case to make sure that they do not exclude a particularly valuable area of information. The definition and instruction sections should not be so long that they are difficult to read.

5. **Cover the "Who, What, Why, When, Where, and How."** When planning your interrogatories, try to cover the "who, what, why, when, where, and how." Focus on the pleadings. Include in the interrogatories questions that will elicit the basis for each allegation and each denial made in the pleadings. Also include questions that will help you locate evidence that goes beyond the allegations and denials in the pleadings. You might draft questions that ask, for example, for the address and custodian of certain documents, physical evidence, exhibits and witnesses to be relied on, and other items. (Under the revised FRCP, much of the information will already have been disclosed by the parties.)

6. **Phrase Your Questions Simply, Concisely, and Accurately.** The questions should be written simply and concisely. Try to eliminate all unnecessary adjectives and adverbs. Break complex questions into shorter and simpler components.

Avoid giving the defendant options that allow the defendant to select the easiest and least informative answer. Be reasonable in the scope of your requests. For example, you should limit the time span for which records or other kinds of information are sought.

Also, make sure that no words are misspelled. Misspellings create an impression of incompetence and may allow respondents to answer legitimately that they have no knowledge of the whereabouts of "Mr. Fones" when you need information about "Mr. Jones."

7. **Avoid Questions Calling for a "Yes" or "No" Answer.** Questions that permit a "yes" or "no" response are of little value unless you include follow-up questions. Questions should determine if the person's statement is based on personal observation or secondhand knowledge. "Why" questions are easily circumvented with such responses as "That is what he wanted to do," or "He believed he should."

8. **Make Effective Use of Opinion and Contention Questions.** Opinion and contention questions are permitted by federal and most state rules. They identify where the opponent stands on key factual questions. For example, "Do you contend that the intersection light was red before the defendant entered the intersection? If so, on what do you base your contention? What persons have knowledge of these facts?" and so forth. The answers to these types of questions identify the facts in contention and the evidence on which the con-

> **"Your ability to draft good interrogatories will make you a valued member of the litigation team."**

tention is based. This is extremely useful because other discovery devices do not get at the reasons or evidence that forms the basis for a contention or opinion. It is best to reserve this kind of question for a time later in the discovery process when previous discovery has revealed the contentions and most of the investigation in the case is completed. Otherwise, "I do not know yet" is a likely response.

9. **Add Concluding or Summary Interrogatories.** Include one or more questions to provide some protection for anything you forgot to address. This may prevent the opponent from using evidence at trial that you should have learned about earlier. A concluding request might be, "Identify any additional information pertinent to this lawsuit but not set out in your previous answers."

10. **Employ the Evasiveness Test and Submit the Document to Your Supervising Attorney.** Proofread the drafted interrogatories. Test your questions by placing yourself in the position of the other party and seeing if you can weasel your way around and out of providing such information. Redraft questions if necessary. Once this is done, give the document to your supervising attorney for any final review and signature. Have the interrogatories served on defendant.

paralegal drafts the interrogatories for the attorney's review and approval. In the Baranski case, for example, attorney Gilmore will probably ask paralegal Lopez to draft interrogatories to be sent to defendant Peretto.

All discovery documents, including interrogatories, normally begin with a caption similar to the complaint caption illustrated earlier in this chapter. Following the caption, Lopez will add the name of the party who must answer the interrogatories, instructions to be followed by the party, and definitions of certain terms that are used in the interrogatories. The body of the document consists of the interrogatories themselves—that is, the questions that the opposing party must answer. The interrogatories should end with a signature line for the attorney below which appears the attorney's name and address.

Before drafting the questions, Lopez will want to review carefully the contents of the case file (including the pleadings and the evidence and other information that she obtained during her preliminary investigation into plaintiff Baranski's claim) and consult with attorney Gilmore on what litigation strategy should be pursued. For further guidance, she might consult form books containing sample interrogatories as well as interrogatories used in similar cases previously handled by the firm. (For tips on how to draft effective interrogatories, see this chapter's earlier featured-guest article on that topic beginning on page 195.)

Depending on the complexity of the case, interrogatories may be few in number, or they may run into the hundreds. Exhibit 6.10 on the next page illustrates the first page of a sample set of interrogatories that have traditionally been used in cases similar to the Baranski-Peretto case. Realize that some state courts now limit the number of interrogatories that can be used, and the 1993 revision of FRCP 33 limits the number of interrogatories in federal court cases to twenty-five (unless a greater number is allowed by stipulation of the parties or by court order). Therefore:

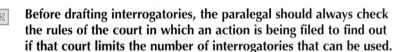

Before drafting interrogatories, the paralegal should always check the rules of the court in which an action is being filed to find out if that court limits the number of interrogatories that can be used.

After receiving the interrogatories, defendant Peretto must answer them within a specified time period (thirty days under FRCP 33) in writing and under oath, as mentioned above. Very likely, he will have substantial guidance from his attorney and his attorney's paralegal in forming his answers. Peretto must answer each question truthfully, of course, because he is under oath. His attorney and her paralegal would counsel him, though, on how to phrase his answers so that they are both truthful and strategically sound. For example, they would advise Peretto on how to limit his answers to prevent disclosing more information than is necessary.

Depositions

Like interrogatories, **depositions** are given under oath. Unlike interrogatories, however, depositions are usually conducted orally (except in certain circumstances, such as when the party being deposed is at a great distance and cannot be deposed via telephone). Furthermore, they may be taken from nonparty witnesses. As indicated earlier, interrogatories can only be taken from the parties to the lawsuit. The attorney wishing to depose a party must give that party's attorney reasonable notice in writing.

When an attorney takes the deposition of a party or witness, the attorney is able to question the person being deposed (the **deponent**) in person and then follow up with any other questions that come to mind. Even though the deposition is usually taken at the offices of one of the party's attorneys, the fact that the

On the Web

The first set of interrogatories submitted by Paula Jones to President Bill Clinton in Jones's lawsuit against Clinton for sexual harassment are included in Court TV's online library at **www.courttv.com/library/ government/jones/ questions.html.**

Deposition

A pretrial question-and-answer proceeding, usually conducted orally, in which a party or witness answers an attorney's questions. The answers are given under oath, and the session is recorded.

Deponent

A party or witness who testifies under oath during a deposition.

EXHIBIT 6.10
Sample Interrogatories (Excerpt)

UNITED STATES DISTRICT COURT
FOR THE WESTERN DISTRICT OF NITA

Katherine Baranski
        Plaintiff

vs.

Tony Peretto   Defendant

File No. 99-14335-NI

Hon. Harley M. LaRue

A. P. Gilmore
Attorney for the Plaintiff
Jeffers, Gilmore & Dunn
553 Fifth Avenue
Suite 101
Nita City, NI 48801

PLAINTIFF'S FIRST INTERROGATORIES TO DEFENDANT

    PLEASE TAKE NOTICE that the following Interrogatories are directed to you under the provisions of Rule 26(a)(5) and Rule 33 of the Federal Rules of Civil Procedure. You are requested to answer these Interrogatories and to furnish such information in answer to the Interrogatories as is available to you.

    You are required to serve integrated Interrogatories and Answers to these Interrogatories under oath, within thirty (30) days after service of them upon you. The original answers are to be retained in your attorney's possession and a copy of the answers are to be served upon Plaintiff's counsel.

    The answers should be signed and sworn to by the person making answer to the Interrogatories.

    When used in these Interrogatories the term "Defendant," or any synonym thereof, is intended to and shall embrace and include, in addition to said Defendant, all agents, servants and employees, representatives, attorneys, private investigators, or others who are in possession or who may have obtained information for or on behalf of the Defendant.

    These Interrogatories shall be deemed continuing and supplemental answers shall be required immediately upon receipt thereof if Defendant, directly or indirectly, obtains further or different information from the time answers are served until the time of trial.

1. Were you the driver of an automobile involved in an accident with plaintiff on the _____ day of _____, 19 ___, at about _____ o'clock _____ A.M. at the intersection of _____ and _____, in the city of _____ in the county of _____, state of_____? If so, please state the following:

   (a) Whether your name is correctly spelled in the complaint in this cause of action;
   (b) Any other names by which you have been known, including the dates during which you have used those names;
   (c) Your Social Security number and place and date of birth;
   (d) Your height, weight, and eye and hair color;
   (e) Your address at the time of the accident;
   (f) The names, addresses, and phone numbers of your present and former spouses (if any) and all of your children, whether natural or adopted, who were residing with you at the time of the accident (if any).

2. Please list your places of residence for the last five years prior to your current residence, including complete addresses and dates of residence as well as the names of owners or managers.

deponent has sworn to tell the truth necessitates that both the attorney and the deponent treat the deposition proceedings as seriously as they would if the deponent were on the witness stand in court.

FRCP 30, as revised in 1993, prohibits the taking of any depositions in federal court cases before the parties have made the disclosures required under revised Rule 26 (these rules will be discussed shortly). Revised Rule 30 also states that the court's approval is required if, without written agreement by the parties, either attorney wants to take more than one deposition from the same party or witness, or more than a total of ten depositions.

THE ROLE OF THE DEPONENT'S ATTORNEY.   The deponent's attorney will attend the deposition, but the attorney's role will be limited. The attorney may make occasional objections to the opposing attorney's questions if the questions appear to be irrelevant to the case or ask for privileged information. If plaintiff Baranski were to be deposed by defendant Peretto's attorney, Cameron, then Baranski's attorney, Gilmore, would object to any of Cameron's questions that were misleading or ambiguous or that wandered too far from the issues relating to the claim.

Gilmore would also caution Baranski to limit her responses to the questions and not to engage in speculative answers that might prejudice her claim. If plaintiff Baranski was asked whether she had ever been involved in an automobile accident before, for example, Gilmore would probably caution her to use a simple (but truthful) "yes" or "no" answer. Attorney Gilmore normally would permit Baranski to volunteer additional information only in response to precisely phrased questions.

As will be discussed below, deposition proceedings are recorded. If both attorneys agree to do so, however, they can go "off the record" to clarify a point or discuss a disputed issue. Depositions are stressful events, and tempers often flare. In the event that the deposition can no longer be pursued in an orderly fashion, the attorney conducting the deposition may have to terminate it.

The above description of the role of the deponent's attorney at a deposition is typical for cases filed in state courts and, until the 1993 revision of the FRCP, in federal courts as well. The revised FRCP, however, imposes strict limitations on an attorney's right to object to questions asked of his or her client during a deposition. Rule 30(d)(1) now requires that an attorney may instruct a deponent not to answer only "when necessary to preserve a privilege, to enforce a limitation on evidence directed by the court, or to present a motion [to terminate the deposition]." The revised rule also states that all objections during a deposition must be stated concisely and in a nonargumentative, nonsuggestive manner. This rule is consistent with the revised FRCP 26, which imposes an ongoing duty on each party to disclose relevant information to the other party in the lawsuit.

THE DEPOSITION TRANSCRIPT.   Every utterance made during a deposition is recorded. A court reporter will usually record the deposition proceedings and create an official **deposition transcript**. Methods of recording a deposition include stenographic recording (a traditional method that involves the use of a shorthand machine), tape recording, videotape recording, or some combination of these methods. Revised Rule 30(b)(2) of the FRCP states that unless the court orders otherwise, a deposition "may be recorded by sound, sound-and-visual, or stenographic means."

The deposition transcript may be used by either party during the trial to prove a particular point or to **impeach** (call into question) the credibility of a witness who says something during the trial that is different from what he or she stated during the deposition. For example, a witness in the Baranski case might state during the

---

Case at a Glance

The Plaintiff—
Plaintiff: Katherine Baranski
Attorney: Allen P. Gilmore
Paralegal: Elena Lopez

The Defendant—
Defendant: Tony Peretto
Attorney: Elizabeth A. Cameron
Paralegal: Gordon McVay

Deposition Transcript
The official transcription of the recording taken during a deposition.

Impeach
To call into question the credibility of a witness by challenging the truth or accuracy of his or her trial statement.

On the Web

If you are interested in the history of court reporting, visit the Web site of the National Court Reporters Association at www.vervbatimreports.com.

deposition that defendant Peretto *did not* stop at the stop sign before proceeding to cross Mattis Avenue. If at trial, the witness states that Peretto *did* stop at the stop sign before crossing Mattis Avenue, plaintiff Baranski's attorney (Gilmore) could challenge the witness's credibility on the basis of the deposition transcript. Exhibit 6.11 shows a page from a transcript of a deposition conducted by attorney Gilmore in the Baranski case. The deponent was Julia Williams, an eyewitness to the accident. On the transcript, the letter "Q" precedes each question asked by Gilmore, and the letter "A" precedes each of Williams's answers.

SUMMARIZING AND INDEXING THE DEPOSITION TRANSCRIPT.   Typically, the paralegal will summarize the deposition transcript. The summary, which along with the transcript will become part of the litigation file, allows the members of the litigation team to review quickly the information obtained from the deponent during the deposition.

In the Baranski case, assume that paralegal Lopez is asked to summarize the deposition transcript of Julia Williams. A commonly used format for deposition summaries is to summarize the information sequentially—that is, in the order that

EXHIBIT 6.11
A Deposition Transcript (Excerpt)

67	Q: Where were you at the time of the accident?
68	A: I was on the southwest corner of the intersection.
69	Q: Are you referring to the intersection where Thirty-eighth Street crosses Mattis Avenue?
70	A: Yes.
71	Q: Why were you there at the time of the accident?
72	A: Well, I was on my way to work. I usually walk down Mattis Avenue to the hospital.
73	Q: So you were walking to work down Mattis Avenue and you saw the accident?
74	A: Yes.
75	Q: What did you see?
76	A: Well, as I was about to cross the street, a dark green van passed within three feet of me and ran the
77	stop sign and crashed into another car.
78	Q: Can you remember if the driver of the van was a male or a female?
79	A: Yes. It was a man.
80	Q: I am showing you a picture. Can you identify the man in the picture?
81	A: Yes. That is the man who was driving the van.
82	Q: Do you wear glasses?
83	A: I need glasses only for reading. I have excellent distance vision.
84	Q: How long has it been since your last eye exam with a doctor?
85	A: Oh, just a month ago, with Dr. Sullivan.

DEVELOPING PARALEGAL SKILLS
Deposition Summaries

After a deposition is taken, each attorney orders a copy of the deposition transcript. Copies may be obtained in printed form or on a computer disk. When the transcript is received, the legal assistant's job is to prepare a summary of the testimony that was given. The summary is typically only a few pages in length.

The legal assistant must be very familiar with the lawsuit and the legal theories that are being pursued so that he or she can point out inconsistencies in the testimony and how the testimony varies from the pleadings. The paralegal might also give special emphasis to any testimony given by deponents that will help to prove the client's case in court.

After the deposition summary has been created, the paralegal places the summary in the litigation file, usually in a special discovery folder or binder within the larger

file. The deposition summary will be used to prepare for future depositions, to prepare pretrial motions, and to impeach witnesses at the trial, should they give contradictory testimony.

TIPS FOR SUMMARIZING A DEPOSITION

- Find out how the deposition is to be summarized—by chronology, by legal issue, by factual issues, or otherwise.
- Read through the deposition transcript and mark important pages.
- Using a dictaphone or dictation software, dictate a summary of the information on the marked pages.
- Be sure to include a reference to the page and line that is being summarized.
- Take advantage of software that will assist in summarizing the deposition transcript.

it was given during the deposition—as shown in Exhibit 6.12 on the next page. Notice that the summary includes the page and line numbers in the deposition transcript where the full text of the information can be found.

Often, in addition to summarizing the transcript, the paralegal provides an index to the document. The index consists of a list of topics (such as education, employment status, injuries, medical costs, and so on) followed by the relevant page and line numbers of the deposition transcript. Together, the summary and the index allow anyone involved in the case to locate information quickly. Today, key-word indexes allow attorneys and paralegals to locate within seconds deposition testimony on a particular topic. Often, court reporters will provide key-word indexes on request. (For a discussion of the services offered by today's court reporters, see the feature *Technology and Today's Paralegal: Indexing the Deposition Transcript* on page 203.)

Other Discovery Requests

During the discovery phase of litigation, attorneys often request documents so that they may familiarize themselves with specific facts or events that were earlier disclosed by the parties or learned on investigation. In federal court cases, the revised FRCP 34 authorizes each party to request documents and other forms of evidence held by other parties and witnesses, but such requests cannot be made until after the initial prediscovery meeting of the parties (discussed below) has taken place. In most state courts, and depending on the nature of the case, the inspection of documents may be the first step in the discovery process if document inspection will facilitate the widest possible scope of discovery.

During discovery, a party can also request that the opposing party admit the truth of matters relating to the case. For example, plaintiff Baranski's attorney can

---

▨ Case at a Glance

The Plaintiff—
Plaintiff: Katherine Baranski
Attorney: Allen P. Gilmore
Paralegal: Elena Lopez

The Defendant—
Defendant: Tony Peretto
Attorney: Elizabeth A. Cameron
Paralegal: Gordon McVay

EXHIBIT 6.12
**A Deposition
Summary (Excerpt)**

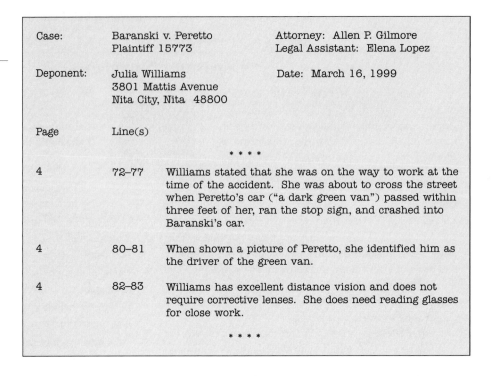

Case:	Baranski v. Peretto Plaintiff 15773	Attorney: Allen P. Gilmore Legal Assistant: Elena Lopez
Deponent:	Julia Williams 3801 Mattis Avenue Nita City, Nita 48800	Date: March 16, 1999

Page	Line(s)	
		* * * *
4	72–77	Williams stated that she was on the way to work at the time of the accident. She was about to cross the street when Peretto's car ("a dark green van") passed within three feet of her, ran the stop sign, and crashed into Baranski's car.
4	80–81	When shown a picture of Peretto, she identified him as the driver of the green van.
4	82–83	Williams has excellent distance vision and does not require corrective lenses. She does need reading glasses for close work.
		* * * *

request that defendant Peretto admit that he did not stop at the stop sign before crossing Mattis Avenue at Thirty-eighth Street. Such admissions save time at trial because the parties will not have to spend time proving facts on which they already agree. Any matter admitted under such a request is conclusively established as true for the trial. FRCP 36 permits requests for admission, but the 1993 revision of this rule stipulates that a request for admission cannot be made, without the court's permission, prior to the prediscovery meeting of the attorneys. In view of the limitations on the number of interrogatories under the revised FRCP (and under some state procedural rules that impose similar limitations), requests for admissions are a particularly useful discovery tool.

During discovery, the defendant's attorney may also want to verify the nature and extent of any injuries alleged by the plaintiff. If a defendant has genuine doubts as to the nature of the plaintiff's injuries the defendant may petition the court to order that the plaintiff submit to a medical examination. Although a medical examination may appear to be overly intrusive, FRCP 35(a) permits such an examination when the existence of the plaintiff's claimed injuries is in dispute. The examination, however, must be preceded by a court order. Because plaintiff Baranski is suing defendant Peretto for injuries arising from the accident, the existence, nature, and extent of her injuries is vitally important in calculating the damages that she might be able to recover from Peretto. Consequently, Baranski will probably be ordered by the court to undergo a physical examination if Peretto's attorney submits such a request.

Revised Discovery Procedures under FRCP 26

The 1993 amendments to the FRCP significantly changed discovery procedures in the federal courts. Under the revised rules, each party to a lawsuit has a duty to disclose to the other party specified types of information prior to the discovery stage of litigation. Under revised Rule 26(f), once a lawsuit is brought, the parties

Indexing the Deposition Transcript

Depositions have always played a key role in the litigation process. In the pretrial phase, they enable the parties' attorneys to gain information about the case. In the trial phase, they are often used as a weapon in the legal battle. An attorney can impeach (call into question) a witness's credibility during cross-examination by pointing to discrepancies between what a witness said during a deposition and what that witness has just said on the stand at trial.

As you might imagine, using deposition testimony in this way requires that the attorney and his legal assistant be able to access quickly the relevant portion of the deposition transcript. This is why carefully prepared deposition indexes are so important to the litigation process and its outcome. Typically, it is the paralegal's responsibility to index the deposition, and this can be a time-consuming task.

What many attorneys and paralegals do not realize is that technological advances have allowed court-reporting firms to offer a variety of services for just a nominal fee—and sometimes for free. For example, a court reporter can generate a concordant index of each word in the deposition transcript by both page and line number, as well as a key-word index of referenced terms. Searches for a key word can be designed so that they call up not only the key word but also a specified number of transcript lines above and below the word. Key-word indexes make it easy for the paralegal, during trial, to instantly retrieve deposition testimony on a particular topic. For example, in the Baranski case, if a witness is testifying that Peretto stopped at a stop sign, the paralegal could search that witness's deposition testimony for the word "stop sign" to verify whether the witness's testimony on the stand was consistent with that given during the deposition.

When depositions are videotaped, as they often are, the court reporter can synchronize his or her computer clock with the videographer's time stamps. When concordant indexing is combined with video time stamps, every word in the videotape is also indexed. This means that, using a splitscreen monitor, a particular portion of the transcript can be viewed simultaneously with the corresponding portion of the videotape. Many attorneys are finding that presenting at trial such synchronized text-video presentations of deposition testimony is far more effective than simply reading the witness's words.

As a paralegal, you will benefit by being aware of the variety of services that today's court reporters offer. To learn more about court-reporting technology and services, visit the Web site of the National Court Reporters Association at **www.verbatimreporters.com**. You can also locate court reporters in your area and learn what services they offer by doing a "Geo search" at that site.

(the plaintiff and defendant and/or their attorneys, if the parties are represented by counsel) must schedule a prediscovery meeting to discuss the nature of the lawsuit, any defenses that may be raised against the claims being brought, and possibilities for promptly settling or otherwise resolving the dispute. The meeting should take place as soon as practicable but at least fourteen days before a scheduling conference is held or a scheduling order issued. Either at this meeting or within ten days after it, the parties must also make the initial disclosures described below and submit to the court a plan for discovery. As the trial date approaches, the attorneys must make subsequent disclosures relating to witnesses, documents, and other information that is relevant to the case.

The new discovery rules do not replace the traditional methods of discovery discussed in the preceding section. Rather, the revised rules impose a duty on attorneys to disclose specified information automatically to opposing counsel early in the litigation process so that the time and costs of traditional discovery methods can be reduced. Under the revised rules, attorneys may still use the traditional discovery tools (depositions, interrogatories, and so on) to obtain information, but they cannot use these methods until the prediscovery meeting has been held and initial disclosures have been made. Also, to save the court's time,

---

ETHICAL CONCERN
Why Subpoena Friendly Witnesses?

The beginning paralegal might logically ask why it is necessary to subpoena friendly witnesses (those favorable to the client's position). The answer to this question is twofold. First, subpoenas make it easier for witnesses to be excused from their jobs and any other obligations on the date that they are to appear in court. Second, attorneys must take reasonable steps (and serving witnesses with subpoenas is a reasonable measure) to ensure that the clients' interests are best served. If a witness had not been subpoenaed and for some reason failed to appear at trial, the lack of his or her crucial testimony could jeopardize the client's chances of winning the case. By serving the witness with a subpoena, the attorney has proof that he or she has not breached the duty of competence to the client.

▓ Case at a Glance

The Plaintiff—
    Plaintiff: Katherine
    Baranski
    Attorney: Allen P.
    Gilmore
    Paralegal: Elena Lopez

The Defendant—
    Defendant: Tony Peretto
    Attorney: Elizabeth A.
    Cameron
    Paralegal: Gordon
    McVay

---

the revised rules give attorneys a freer hand in crafting a discovery plan that is appropriate to the nature of the claim, the parties' needs, and so on.[7]

PREPARING FOR TRIAL

As the trial date approaches, the attorneys for the plaintiff and the defendant and their respective paralegals complete their preparations for the trial. The paralegals collect and organize all of the documents and other evidence relating to the dispute. Plaintiff Baranski's attorney, Gilmore, will focus on legal strategy and how he can best use the information learned during the pleadings and discovery stages when presenting Baranski's case to the court. He will meet with his client and with his key witnesses to make last-minute preparations for trial. He might also meet with defendant Peretto's attorney to try once more to settle the dispute. Gilmore's legal assistant, Elena Lopez, will be notifying witnesses of the trial date and helping Gilmore prepare for trial. For example, she will make sure that all exhibits to be used during the trial are ready and verify that the trial notebook (to be discussed shortly) is in order.

Contacting and Preparing Witnesses

Typically, the paralegal is responsible for ensuring that witnesses are available and in court on the day of the trial. In the Baranski case, attorney Gilmore and paralegal Lopez will have lined up witnesses to testify on behalf of their client, plaintiff Baranski. In preparing for the trial, Lopez will inform each of the witnesses that the trial date has been set and that they will be expected to appear at the trial to testify. A **subpoena**—an order issued by the court clerk directing a person to appear in court—will be served on each of the witnesses to ensure their presence in court. A subpoena to appear in a federal court is shown in Exhibit 6.13. (Although not shown in the exhibit, a return-of-service form, similar to the one illustrated earlier in this chapter in Exhibit 6.5, will be attached to the subpoena to verify that the witness received it.)

Subpoena
A document commanding a person to appear at a certain time and place to give testimony concerning a certain matter.

---

7. The 1993 revision of the FRCP, including the revision of Rule 26 governing discovery requirements, allows federal district courts to modify, or opt not to follow, these rules requiring early disclosures. About one-fourth of the existing ninety-four U.S. federal districts have opted not to follow these rules.

EXHIBIT 6.13
A Subpoena

𝔘𝔫𝔦𝔱𝔢𝔡 𝔖𝔱𝔞𝔱𝔢𝔰 𝔇𝔦𝔰𝔱𝔯𝔦𝔠𝔱 𝔠𝔬𝔲𝔯𝔱	DISTRICT Nita

Katherine Baranski

DOCKET NO. 99-14335-NI

v.

TYPE OF CASE
☒ CIVIL   ☐ CRIMINAL

Tony Peretto

SUBPOENA FOR
☒ PERSON   ☐ DOCUMENT(S) or OBJECT(S)

TO: Julia Williams
3765 Mattis Avenue
Nita City, NI 48803

YOU ARE HEREBY COMMANDED to appear in the United States District Court at the place, date, and time specified below to testify in the above-entitled case.

PLACE	COURTROOM
4th and Main Nita City, NI	B
	DATE AND TIME 8/4/99 10:00 A.M.

YOU ARE ALSO COMMANDED to bring with you the following document(s) or Object(s): (1)

☐ *See additional information on reverse*

This subpoena shall remain in effect until you are granted leave to depart by the court or by an officer acting on behalf of the court.

U.S. MAGISTRATE (2) OR CLERK OF COURT C. H. Hynek	DATE
(BY) DEPUTY CLERK *John Dolan*	July 13, 1999

This subpoena is issued upon application of the:	ATTORNEY'S NAME AND ADDRESS
☒ Plantiff ☐ Defendant ☐ U.S. Attorney	Allen P. Gilmore Jeffers, Gilmore & Dunn 553 Fifth Avenue, Suite 101 Nita City, NI 48801

(1) If not applicable, enter "none"
(2) A subpoena shall be issued by a magistrate in a proceeding before him, but need not be under the seal of the court. (Rule 17(a). Federal Rules of Criminal Procedure.)

Unless she is already familiar with the court's requirements, paralegal Lopez will want to check with the court clerk to find out about what fees and documents she needs to take to the court to obtain the subpoena. The subpoena will then be served on the witness. Most subpoenas to appear in federal court can be served by anyone who is eighteen years of age or older, including paralegals, who often serve subpoenas. Subpoenas to appear in state court are often served by the sheriff or other process server.

No prudent attorney ever puts a party or a witness on the stand unless the attorney has discussed the testimony beforehand with the party or witness. Prior to the trial, attorney Gilmore and paralegal Lopez will meet with each witness and prepare him or her for trial. Gilmore will prepare the witness for the types of questions to expect from himself and from opposing counsel during the trial. He might do some role-playing with the witness to help the witness understand how the questioning will proceed during the trial and to prepare him or her for the opposing attorney's questions. Gilmore will also review with the witness any sworn statements made during discovery (during a deposition, for example). Additionally, Gilmore will review the substantive legal issues involved in the case and how the witness's testimony will affect the outcome of those issues.

Lopez will handle other aspects of witness preparation. She will advise the witness on trial procedures, when and where the witness will testify, and so on. Lopez might take the witness to the courtroom in which the trial will take place (if the courtroom is not in use) and familiarize the witness with the courtroom environment. She will show the witness where he or she will sit while giving testimony, where the judge and jurors will be, and where the attorneys will be seated.

Exhibits and Displays

Paralegals are frequently asked to prepare exhibits or displays that will be presented at trial. Attorney Gilmore may wish to present to the court a photograph of plaintiff Baranski's car taken after the accident occurred, a diagram of the intersection, an enlarged document (such as a police report), or other relevant evidence. Paralegal Lopez will be responsible for making sure that all exhibits are properly prepared and ready to introduce at trial. If any exhibits require special equipment, such as an easel or a VCR, Lopez must also make sure that these will be available in the courtroom and properly set up when they are needed. Increasingly, attorneys are using high-tech equipment to prepare their trial presentations.

Today, advances in technology have made it possible for documents and exhibits to be presented to the court on computer monitors. As you might imagine, presentation technology has significantly changed the ways in which paralegals prepare for trial. Instead of making sure that an easel is in the courtroom for displaying an enlargement of a particular document, the paralegal may be asked to rent and use a digital camera to photograph key exhibits so that they can be incorporated into the computerized presentation. Instead of preparing copies of photos to hand out to the judge and jury, paralegals may be asked to scan the photos into a computerized presentation system. When witnesses are testifying at trial, instead of looking at a hard copy of the witness's pretrial deposition, the paralegal may be requested to compare the witness's trial testimony with what he or she said during the deposition, using key-word searches (see the *Technology and Today's Paralegal* feature earlier in this chapter).

The Trial Notebook

To present plaintiff Baranski's case effectively, attorney Gilmore will need to have in the courtroom all of the relevant documents; he will also need to be able to locate them quickly. To accomplish both of these goals, Lopez will prepare a **trial notebook**. The notebook will contain copies of the pleadings, interrogatories, deposition transcripts and summaries, pretrial motions, a list of exhibits and when they will be used, a witness list and the order in which the witnesses will testify, relevant cases or statutes that Gilmore plans to cite, and generally any document or information that will be important to have close at hand during the trial.

> ▦   **Unless the paralegal knows from prior experience what his or her supervising attorney wants to include in the trial notebook and how it should be organized, the paralegal should discuss these matters with the attorney.**

Typically, the trial notebook is a three-ring binder (or several binders, depending on the complexity of the case). The contents of the notebook are separated by divider sheets with tabs on them. Paralegal Lopez will create a general index to the

---

▦ **Case at a Glance**

The Plaintiff—
    Plaintiff: Katherine
    Baranski
    Attorney: Allen P.
    Gilmore
    Paralegal: Elena Lopez

The Defendant—
    Defendant: Tony Peretto
    Attorney: Elizabeth A.
    Cameron
    Paralegal: Gordon
    McVay

Trial Notebook
A binder that contains copies of all of the documents and information that an attorney will need to have at hand during the trial.

DEVELOPING PARALEGAL SKILLS
Trial Support

Scott Greer, a paralegal with the firm of Dewey & Stone, is helping an attorney prepare for a trial in a personal-injury lawsuit. The client was injured in an automobile accident and is now a paraplegic. Scott has received a memo from his supervising attorney requesting that he prepare a diagram of the accident and arrange to have a "day in the life" videotape created for presentation to the jury. The video will show what a typical day in the life of the plaintiff is like as a result of the injuries sustained in the accident. Scott contacts Trial Support Services, Inc., a firm that specializes in litigation support, to make the video. Scott also obtains permission

to have Trial Support Services, Inc., create the diagram as well.

TIPS FOR CREATING TRIAL VIDEOS

- Use a reliable trial-support services provider or vendor.
- Arrange to meet the vendor at the location where the videotape will be made.
- Make sure that the videotape is realistic, so that the court will allow its use.
- Preview the video before giving it to the attorney.
- Make sure that the vendor is timely paid.

---

notebook's contents and place this index at the front of the notebook. She may also create an index for each section of the binder and place those indexes at the beginnings of the sections. Some paralegals use a computer notebook and a software retrieval system to help them quickly locate documents, especially in complicated cases involving thousands of documents.

When preparing the trial notebook, always remember the following:

 The documents in the trial notebook should not be the original documents but rather copies of them.

The original documents (unless they are needed as evidence at trial) should always remain in the firm's files, both for reasons of security (should the trial notebook be misplaced) and to ensure that Lopez or others in the office will have access to the documents while the notebook is in court with the attorney.

Pretrial Conference

Before the trial begins, the attorneys usually meet with the trial judge in a **pretrial conference** to explore the possibility of resolving the case and, if a settlement is not possible, at least agree on the manner in which the trial will be conducted. In particular, the parties may attempt to clarify the issues in dispute and establish ground rules to restrict such matters as the admissibility of certain types of evidence. Once the pretrial conference has concluded, both parties turn their attention to the trial itself. Assuming that the trial will be heard by a jury, however, one more step is necessary before the trial begins: selecting the jurors who will hear the trial and render a verdict on the dispute.

Jury Selection

Before the trial gets under way, a panel of jurors must be assembled. The clerk of the court usually notifies local residents by mail that they have been selected for jury duty. The process of selecting the names of these prospective jurors varies,

Pretrial Conference
A conference prior to trial in which the judge and the attorneys litigating the suit discuss settlement possibilities, clarify the issues in dispute, and schedule forthcoming trial-related events.

On the Web
Numerous firms offer trial consulting services, including assistance in jury selection. You can access the Web site of one such firm, Jury Research Institute, at **www.jri-inc.com.**

depending on the court, but often they are randomly selected by the court clerk from lists of registered voters or those within a state to whom driver's licenses have been issued. The persons selected then report to the courthouse on the date specified in the notice. At the courthouse, they are gathered into a single pool of jurors, and the process of selecting those jurors who will actually hear the case begins. Although some types of trials require twelve-person juries, most civil matters can be heard by a jury of six persons.

Each attorney will question prospective jurors in a proceeding known as ***voir dire***.[8] Legal assistants often work with their attorneys to write up the questions that will be asked of jurors during *voir dire*. Because all of the jurors will have previously filled out forms giving basic information about themselves, the attorneys and their paralegals can tailor their questions accordingly. They fashion the questions in such a way as to uncover any biases on the part of prospective jurors and to find persons who might identify with the plights of their respective clients. When large numbers of jurors are involved, during the *voir dire* process the attorneys may direct their questions to groups of jurors, as opposed to individual jurors, to minimize the amount of time needed to choose the jurors who will sit on the jury. Note that in some courts, judges may question the jurors, using questions prepared by the attorneys.

During *voir dire*, the attorney for each side may exercise a certain number of **challenges** to prevent particular persons from being allowed to serve on the jury. Both attorneys can exercise two types of challenges: challenges "for cause" and peremptory challenges. If attorney Gilmore concludes that a particular prospective juror is biased against Baranski for some reason, he may exercise a **challenge for cause** and request that the prospective juror not be included in the jury. Each attorney may also exercise a limited number of peremptory challenges. Attorneys may exercise **peremptory challenges** without giving any reason for their desire to exclude a particular juror. Peremptory challenges based on racial criteria or gender, however, are illegal.[9]

After both sides have completed their challenges, those jurors who have been excused are permitted to leave. The remaining jurors, those found to be acceptable by both attorneys, will be seated in the jury box.

Voir Dire

A proceeding in which attorneys for the plaintiff and the defendant ask prospective jurors questions to determine whether potential jury members are biased or have any connection with a party to the action or with a prospective witness.

Challenge

An attorney's objection, during *voir dire,* to the inclusion of a particular person on the jury.

Challenge for Cause

A *voir dire* challenge for which an attorney states the reason why a prospective juror should not be included in the jury.

Peremptory Challenge

A *voir dire* challenge to exclude a potential juror from serving on the jury without any supporting reason or cause. Peremptory challenges based on racial or gender criteria are illegal.

On the Web

If you want to try your hand at being a juror, go to www.cyberjury.com. This interactive Web site allows visitors to act as jurors in deciding cases.

THE TRIAL

During the trial, the attorneys, Allen Gilmore and Elizabeth Cameron, will present their cases to the jury. Because the attorneys will be concentrating on the trial, it will fall to their paralegals to coordinate the logistical aspects of the trial and observe as closely as possible the trial proceedings. Because paralegal Lopez is thoroughly familiar with the case and Gilmore's legal strategy, she will be a valuable ally during the trial. She will be able to anticipate Gilmore's needs and provide appropriate reminders or documents as Gilmore needs them. She will also

---

8. Pronounced vwahr *deehr.* Literally, these French verbs mean "to see, to speak." During the *voir dire* phase of litigation, attorneys do in fact see the jurors speak. In legal language, however, the phrase refers to the process of interrogating jurors to learn about their backgrounds, attitudes, and so on.

9. Discriminating against prospective jurors on the basis of race was prohibited by the United States Supreme Court in *Batson v. Kentucky,* 476 U.S. 79, 106 S.Ct. 1712, 90 L.Ed.2d 69 (1986). Discriminating against prospective jurors on the basis of gender was prohibited by the Supreme Court in *J.E.B. v. Alabama ex rel. T.B.,* 511 U.S 127, 114 S. Ct. 1419, 128 L.Ed.2d 89 (1994). See Chapter 8 for an explanation of how to read court citations.

ETHICAL CONCERN
Should You Tell Your Supervising Attorney What You Know about a Prospective Juror?

During *voir dire*, paralegal Lopez notices one of her neighbors among the prospective jurors. Lopez knows that her neighbor is strongly biased against foreigners and will probably not be an impartial juror in the case against Tony Peretto, who has a slight foreign accent. Lopez also knows that she and attorney Gilmore want their client, plaintiff Baranski, to win the case, and a juror biased against Peretto would definitely help them achieve this goal. Should Lopez tell Gilmore what she knows about this prospective juror? Yes. It is to Gilmore's—and his client's—advantage to know all he can about the prospective jurors, and it is up to Gilmore to decide how to use whatever information he obtains. Furthermore, Lopez has no duty to keep confidential any information that she has learned about her neighbor.

---

monitor each witness's testimony to ensure that it is consistent with previous statements made by the witness.

Generally, Lopez will act as a second pair of eyes and ears during the trial. She will observe how the jury is responding to various witnesses and their testimony or to the attorneys' demeanor and questions. She will take notes during the trial on these observations as well as on the points being stressed and the types of evidence introduced by the opposing counsel, Cameron. At the end of the day, Lopez and Gilmore may review the day's events, and Lopez's "trial journal" will provide a ready reference to the major events that transpired in the courtroom.

Opening Statements

The trial both opens and closes with attorneys' statements to the jury. In their **opening statements,** the attorneys will give a brief version of the facts and the supporting evidence that they will use during the trial. Because some trials can drag on for weeks or even months, it is extremely helpful for jurors to hear a summary of the story that will unfold during the trial. Otherwise, they may be left wondering how a particular piece of evidence fits into the dispute. In short, the opening statement is a kind of "road map" that describes the destination that each attorney hopes to reach and outlines how he or she plans to reach it.

The Plaintiff's Case

Once the opening statements have been made, Gilmore will present the plaintiff's case first. Because he is the plaintiff's attorney, he has the burden of proving that defendant Peretto was negligent. Attorney Gilmore will call several eyewitnesses to the stand and ask them to tell the court about the sequence of events that led to the accident. This form of questioning is known as **direct examination.** After attorney Gilmore has finished questioning a witness on direct examination, defendant Peretto's attorney, Cameron, will begin her **cross-examination** of that witness. During her cross-examination, Cameron will be primarily concerned with reducing the witness's credibility in the eyes of the jury and the judge. Cameron

---

▨ Case at a Glance

The Plaintiff—
 Plaintiff: Katherine Baranski
 Attorney: Allen P. Gilmore
 Paralegal: Elena Lopez

The Defendant—
 Defendant: Tony Peretto
 Attorney: Elizabeth A. Cameron
 Paralegal: Gordon McVay

Opening Statement
An attorney's statement to the jury at the beginning of the trial. The attorney briefly outlines the evidence that will be offered during the trial and the legal theory that will be pursued.

Direct Examination
The examination of a witness by the attorney who calls the witness to the stand to testify on behalf of the attorney's client.

Cross-Examination
The questioning of an opposing witness during the trial.

Redirect Examination
The questioning of a witness
following the adverse party's
cross-examination.

Recross-Examination
The questioning of an opposing
witness following the adverse
party's redirect examination.

**Motion for a Directed Verdict
(Motion for Judgment as a Matter
of Law)**
A motion requesting that the court
grant a judgment in favor of the
party making the motion on the
ground that the other party has not
produced sufficient evidence to
support his or her claim.

On the Web
For an example
of how
witnesses are
examined at trial, you can
read through one or more
of the trial transcripts from
O. J. Simpson's trial, which
are online at
**www.courttv.com/old/
casefiles/simpson/
transcripts.**

Closing Argument
An argument made by each side's
attorney after the cases for the
plaintiff and defendant have been
presented. Closing arguments are
made prior to the jury charge.

must confine her cross-examination to matters that were—or could have been—brought up during direct examination and those that relate to a witness's credibility.

After Cameron has finished cross-examining each witness, plaintiff Baranski's attorney, Gilmore, will need to repair any damage done to the credibility of the witness's testimony—or, indeed, to the case itself. Gilmore will do this by again questioning the witness and allowing the witness to explain his or her answer. This process is known as **redirect examination**. Following Gilmore's redirect examination, defendant Peretto's attorney, Cameron, will be given an opportunity for **recross-examination**. When both attorneys have finished with the first witness, Gilmore will call the succeeding witnesses in plaintiff Baranski's case, each of whom will be subject to cross-examination (and redirect and recross, if necessary).

After attorney Gilmore has presented his case for plaintiff Baranski, then Cameron, as counsel for defendant Peretto, may decide to make a **motion for a directed verdict** (now also known as a **motion for judgment as a matter of law** in federal courts). Through this motion, attorney Cameron will be saying to the court that the plaintiff's attorney, Gilmore, has not offered enough evidence to support a claim against defendant Peretto. If the judge agrees to grant the motion, then a judgment will be entered for defendant Peretto, plaintiff Baranski's case against him will be dismissed, and the trial will be over.

The motion for a directed verdict (judgment as a matter of law) is seldom granted. If the judge had believed that Baranski's case was that weak before the trial started, then the judge would probably have granted a pretrial motion to dismiss the case, thereby avoiding the expense of a trial. Occasionally, however, the occurrence of certain events—such as the death of a key witness—might mean the plaintiff has no evidence at all to support his or her allegations. In that event, the court may grant the defendant's motion for a directed verdict, or judgment as a matter of law.

The Defendant's Case

Assuming that the motion for directed verdict (motion for judgment as a matter of law) is denied by the court, the two attorneys, Gilmore and Cameron, will now reverse their roles. Attorney Cameron will now begin to present evidence demonstrating the weaknesses of plaintiff Baranski's claims against defendant Peretto. She will essentially follow the same procedure used by Gilmore when he presented plaintiff Baranski's side of the story. Cameron will call witnesses to the stand and question them. After Cameron's direct examination of each witness, that witness will be subject to possible cross-examination by Gilmore, redirect examination by Cameron, and recross-examination by Gilmore.

Once Cameron has finished presenting her case on behalf of defendant Peretto, Gilmore will be permitted to offer evidence to *rebut* (refute) evidence introduced by Cameron in Peretto's behalf. After Gilmore's rebuttal, if any, both attorneys will make their closing arguments to the jury.

Closing Arguments

In their **closing arguments**, the attorneys summarize their presentations and argue in their clients' favor. A closing argument should include all of the major points that support the client's case. Both attorneys will want to organize their presentations so they can explain to the jury their respective arguments and show how their arguments are supported by the evidence. Once both attorneys have completed their remarks, the case will be submitted to the jury and the attorneys' role in the trial will be finished.

ETHICAL CONCERN
Communicating with Jurors

Suppose that you are the paralegal working on the Baranski case with attorney Allen Gilmore, and one of your neighbors is a juror in the case. One evening, while you are gardening in your back yard, your neighbor approaches you and says, "You know, I didn't really understand what that witness, Williams, was saying. Did she really see the accident? Also, is it true that Mrs. Baranski will never be able to walk normally again?" You know the answers to these questions, and you would like the juror to know the truth. You also know that it would enhance Baranski's chances of winning the case if this juror were as familiar with the factual background as you are. What should you do? First, you should inform your neighbor that as a paralegal, you have an ethical duty to abide by the professional rules of conduct governing the legal profession. One of these rules prohibits *ex parte* (private) communications with jurors about a case being tried. Second, you should remind your neighbor that jurors are not permitted to discuss a case they are hearing with anyone.

The Verdict

Before the jurors begin their deliberations, the judge gives the jury a **charge**, in which the judge sums up the case and instructs the jurors on the rules of law that apply to the issues involved in the case. Following its receipt of the charge, the jury begins its deliberations. Once it has reached a decision, the jury issues a **verdict** in favor of one of the parties. If the verdict is in favor of the plaintiff, the jury will specify the amount of damages to be paid by the defendant. Following the announcement of the verdict, the jurors are discharged. Usually, immediately after the verdict has been announced and the jurors discharged, the party in whose favor the verdict was issued makes a motion asking the judge to issue a *judgment*—which is the court's final word on the matter—consistent with the jury's verdict. For example, if the jury in the Baranski case finds that defendant Peretto was negligent and awards plaintiff Baranski damages in the amount of $75,000, the judge will order defendant Peretto to pay the plaintiff that amount.

POSTTRIAL MOTIONS AND PROCEDURES

Every trial must have a winner and a loser. Although civil litigation is an expensive and cumbersome process, the losing party may wish to pursue the matter further after the verdict has been rendered. Assume that plaintiff Baranski wins at trial and is awarded $75,000 in damages. Also assume that defendant Peretto's attorney, Cameron, believes that the verdict for plaintiff Baranski is not supported by the evidence. In this situation, she may file a **motion for judgment notwithstanding the verdict** (also known as a *motion for judgment as a matter of law* in the federal courts).[10] By filing this motion, attorney Cameron asks the judge to enter a

Charge
The judge's instruction to the jury, following the attorneys' closing arguments, setting forth the rules of law that the jury must apply in reaching its decision, or verdict.

Verdict
A formal decision made by a jury.

Motion for Judgment Notwithstanding the Verdict
A motion (also referred to as a motion for judgment as a matter of law in federal courts) requesting that the court grant judgment in favor of the party making the motion on the ground that the jury verdict against him or her was unreasonable or erroneous.

 On the Web
To find information on jury verdicts in assorted trials throughout the country, including the amount of damages awarded in each case, go to www.morelaw.com.

---

10. Amendments to the FRCP in 1991 designated both the motion for a directed verdict and the motion for judgment notwithstanding the verdict as motions for judgment as a matter of law. One of the reasons for the change was to allow both the preverdict and postverdict motions to be referred to with a terminology that does not conceal their common identity (both motions claim, at different times during the proceedings, that there is insufficient evidence against the defendant to justify a claim—or a verdict—against the defendant). Many judges and attorneys continue to use the former names of these motions, however, so we include them in our discussion.

TODAY'S PROFESSIONAL PARALEGAL

Drafting *Voir Dire* Questions Like a Pro

Andrea Leed, a legal assistant, is preparing for trial. Her boss is a famous trial attorney, Mary Marshall. Mary rarely loses a case. One of her many secrets to success is that she always draws up a jury profile and prepares carefully for *voir dire*.

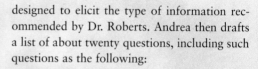

Mary is defending a corporation in an environmental liability case. The case involves many complex engineering and scientific issues that the jury will need to understand in order to reach its verdict. It is a common practice in these types of cases to select a "blue ribbon" jury—a jury consisting of persons who are very well educated. Mary has suggested that Andrea locate and hire a psychologist to prepare a jury profile.

CONSULTING WITH AN EXPERT

Andrea contacts TrialPsych, Inc., a consulting firm headed by Dr. Linda Robertson, who specializes in jury selection. Dr. Robertson would be delighted to work on the case, but her services are very expensive, and Andrea must find out whether the client is willing to pay Dr. Robertson's fee. The client agrees to pay the fee, so Andrea meets with Dr. Robertson to discuss the case. Andrea explains that the client is a corporation and that the case involves complex scientific and engineering issues. Dr. Robertson consults her files for statistical information on these types of cases. She finds that the ideal jury would be made up of white-collar professionals holding advanced degrees in engineering or another applied science. Also, the prospective jurors would ideally be against extensive government regulation of the corporate world.

DRAFTING *VOIR DIRE* QUESTIONS

Andrea returns to the office and discusses with Mary the results of her consultation with Dr. Roberts. Mary and Andrea decide to draft questions for *voir dire* that are designed to elicit the type of information recommended by Dr. Roberts. Andrea then drafts a list of about twenty questions, including such questions as the following:

1. Please state your name and address.
2. Where are you employed, and how long have you been employed there?
3. What is the highest level of education that you have attained: high school diploma, some college but no degree, college degree, advanced degree (please specify)?
4. If you have attended college or received a college degree, what was your field of study?
5. Have you ever been fired by a corporate employer in a way that you believed was unfair?
6. Have you ever worked for a government regulatory agency, and, if so, what were your responsibilities in that position?
7. Have you, or persons or business firms with whom you are or have been associated, ever been sued for violating environmental statutes or regulations? If so, what were the violations?
8. In your opinion, what should be the government's role in regulating a company's operations?

REVIEWING THE *VOIR DIRE* QUESTIONS

Andrea faxes the list of questions to Dr. Robertson, who reviews them and faxes back some suggested changes, which Andrea incorporates. When the final list of questions is drawn up, Andrea presents it to Mary and places a copy of the list in the trial notebook. Mary asks Andrea to call Dr. Robertson and ask her if she is available to sit in on the actual *voir dire* process to ensure that jury selection goes smoothly.

Motion for a New Trial
A motion asserting that the trial was so fundamentally flawed (because of error, newly discovered evidence, prejudice, or other reason) that a new trial is needed to prevent a miscarriage of justice.

judgment in favor of defendant Peretto on the ground (basis) that the jury verdict in favor of plaintiff Baranski was unreasonable and erroneous. Cameron may file this motion only if she previously filed a motion for a directed verdict (or judgment as a matter of law) during the trial and the motion was denied at that time.

Rule 50 of the Federal Rules of Civil Procedure permits either party to file a **motion for a new trial**. Such a motion may be submitted along with a motion for a judgment notwithstanding the verdict. A motion for a new trial is a far more drastic tactic because it asserts that the trial was so pervaded by error or otherwise fundamentally flawed that a new trial should be held. Because such a motion reflects adversely on the way in which the judge conducted the trial, it should only be filed if the attorney truly believes that a miscarriage of justice will otherwise result. For a motion for a new trial to have a reasonable chance of being granted, the motion must allege such serious problems as jury misconduct, prejudicial jury instructions, excessive or inadequate damages, or the existence of newly discovered evidence (but not if the evidence could have been discovered earlier through the use of reasonable care).

If attorney Cameron's posttrial motions are unsuccessful or if she decides not to file them, she may still file an **appeal**. The purpose of an appeal is to have the trial court's decision either reversed or modified by an appellate court. The appellate court will review the trial court's proceedings to decide whether the trial court erred in applying the law to the facts of the case, in instructing the jury, or in administering the trial generally. Appellate courts rarely tamper with a trial court's findings of fact because the judge and jury were in a better position than the appellate court to evaluate the credibility of witnesses, the nature of the evidence, and so on.

Appeal
The process of seeking a higher court's review of a lower court's decision for the purpose of correcting or changing the lower court's judgment or decision.

When a case is appealed, the attorneys for both parties submit written *briefs* that present their positions regarding the issues to be reviewed by the appellate court. The briefs outline each party's view of the proper application of the law to the facts. After the appellate court has had an opportunity to review the briefs, the court sets aside a time for both attorneys to argue their positions before the panel of judges. Following the oral arguments, the judges will decide the matter and then issue a formal written opinion, which normally will be published in the relevant reporter (see Chapter 8 for a detailed discussion of how court opinions are published).

 On the Web
The Federal Rules of Appellate Procedure are online at **www.law.cornell.edu/ topics/archive/ appellate_procedure.html.**

▦ KEY TERMS AND CONCEPTS

❖ CHAPTER SUMMARY

1. Although civil lawsuits vary from case to case in terms of their complexity, cost, and detail, all civil litigation involves similar procedural steps, as described in Exhibit 6.1.

2. The first step in the civil litigation process occurs when the attorney initially meets with a client who wishes to bring a lawsuit against another party or parties. Once the attorney agrees to represent the client in the lawsuit and the client has signed the retainer agreement, the attorney and the paralegal undertake a preliminary investigation into the matter to ascertain the facts alleged by the client and gain other factual information relating to the case. A litigation file is also created for the case.

3. The pleadings—which consist of the plaintiff's complaint, the defendant's answer, and any counterclaim or other pleadings listed in Exhibit 6.2—inform each party of the claims of the other and delineate the details of the dispute. The complaint, which initiates the lawsuit, is filed with the appropriate court. Typically, the defendant is notified of a lawsuit by the delivery of the complaint and a summons (service of process). In federal court cases, revised FRCP 4 permits the plaintiff's attorney to notify the defendant, by first-class mail or other reliable means, of the lawsuit and enclose with the notice a form that the defendant can sign to waive the requirement of service of process. If the defendant does not sign and return the form, then the plaintiff's attorney will arrange to have the defendant served with the complaint and summons.

4. On receiving the complaint (and summons, if process is served), the defendant has several options. The defendant may submit an answer. The answer may deny any wrongdoing, or it might assert an affirmative defense against the plaintiff's claim. Alternatively or simultaneously, the defendant might make a motion to dismiss the case, perhaps on the ground that the relevant statute of limitations has expired.

5. A motion for judgment on the pleadings is a pretrial motion that may be filed by either party after all pleadings have been filed. The motion may be granted if it can be shown that no factual dispute exists. A motion for summary judgment may be filed by either party during or after the discovery stage of litigation. In determining whether to grant the latter motion, the judge can consider evidence apart from the pleadings—such as evidence contained in affidavits, depositions, and interrogatories. The motion for summary judgment will not be granted if any facts are in dispute.

6. In preparing for trial, the attorney for each party undertakes a formal investigative process called discovery to obtain evidence helpful to his or her client's case. Traditional discovery tools include interrogatories and depositions as well as various requests, including a request for documents in the possession of the other party or opposing counsel (or a third party), a request for admission (of the truth of certain statements) by the opposing party, and a request for a physical examination (to establish the truth of claimed injuries or health status).

7. In federal court cases, revised FRCP 26 requires that the attorneys cooperate in forming a discovery plan early in the litigation process. The rule also requires attorneys to automatically disclose relevant information. Under FRCP 26, only after initial disclosures have been made can attorneys resort to the use of traditional discovery tools.

8. Before the trial begins, attorneys for both sides and their paralegals gather and organize all evidence, documents, and other materials relating to the case. Paralegals often assist in contacting and issuing subpoenas to witnesses, as well as making sure that all exhibits and displays are ready by the trial date and that the trial notebook is prepared. The attorneys for both sides meet with the trial judge in a pretrial conference to decide whether a settlement is possible or, if not, to decide how the trial will be conducted and what types of evidence will be admissible.

9. The jury-selection process is called *voir dire*. During this process, the attorneys can exclude certain persons in the jury pool from sitting on the jury through the exercise of challenges for cause and a limited number of peremptory challenges.

10. Once the jury has been selected and seated, the trial begins. The paralegal, if he or she attends the trial, coordinates witnesses' appearances, tracks the testimony of witnesses and compares it with sworn statements that the witnesses made prior to the trial, and provides the attorney with appropriate reminders or documents when necessary. The paralegal generally acts as a second set of eyes and ears for the attorney during the trial.

11. The trial begins with opening statements in which both attorneys briefly give their versions of the facts

of the case and the evidence supporting their views. The plaintiff's attorney then presents evidence supporting the plaintiff's claim, including the testimony of witnesses. The attorney's questioning of the witnesses whom he or she calls is referred to as direct examination. The defendant's attorney may then cross-examine the witness, after which the plaintiff's attorney may question the witness on redirect examination, followed by possible recross-examination by the defendant's attorney.

12. After the plaintiff's attorney has presented his or her client's case, the defendant's attorney may make a motion for a directed verdict, also called a motion for judgment as a matter of law. This motion asserts that the plaintiff has not offered enough evidence to support the validity of the plaintiff's claim against the defendant. If the judge grants the motion, the case will be dismissed. The attorneys then reverse their roles, and the defendant's attorney presents evidence and testimony to refute the plaintiff's claims. Any witnesses called to the stand by the defendant's attorney will be subject to direct examination by that attorney, cross-examination by the plaintiff's attorney, and possibly redirect examination and recross-examination.

13. After the defendant's attorney has finished his or her presentation, both attorneys give their closing arguments, and then the judge instructs the jury in a charge—a document that includes statements of the applicable law and a review of the facts as they were presented during the trial. The jury then begins its deliberations. When the jury has reached a decision, it issues a verdict in favor of one party or the other.

14. The losing party's attorney may file a motion for judgment notwithstanding the verdict (motion for judgment as a matter of law), alleging that the judge should enter a judgment in favor of the losing party in spite of the verdict because the verdict was not supported by the evidence or was otherwise erroneous. In conjunction with the motion, or in the alternative, the attorney may also file a motion for a new trial, asserting that the trial was so flawed—by judge or juror misconduct or by other pervasive errors—that a new trial should be held. Finally, the attorney may, depending on the client's wishes, appeal the decision to an appellate court for further review and decision.

QUESTIONS FOR REVIEW

1. What are the basic steps in the litigation process prior to the trial? How does the paralegal assist the attorney in each of these steps?

2. What documents constitute the pleadings in a civil lawsuit? How are defendants notified of lawsuits that have been brought against them? What new procedures are required under revised FRCP 4 for notifying the defendant in a lawsuit?

3. Name three pretrial motions and state the purpose of each.

4. What is discovery? When does it take place? List three discovery devices that can be used to obtain information prior to trial.

5. How have the 1993 amendments to the FRCP affected the discovery process in federal court cases?

6. What role does the paralegal play in preparing witnesses, exhibits, and displays for trial? How can the paralegal assist the attorney in preparing the trial notebook?

7. What is a pretrial conference? What issues are likely to be raised and decided at a pretrial conference?

8. How are jurors selected? What is the difference between a peremptory challenge and a challenge for cause?

9. Describe the basic procedures involved in a trial. What role might the paralegal play during the trial? What types of trial-related tasks may the paralegal perform?

10. Name the posttrial motions that are available. In what situation is each of them used? Describe the procedure for filing an appeal. What factors are considered by an attorney when deciding whether a case should be appealed?

✦ ETHICAL QUESTIONS

1. Pamela Hodges has just started working as a paralegal for Lawyers, Inc., a high-volume, low-overhead law firm that handles mostly simple and routine litigation. Her supervising attorney, Carol Levine, has two initial client meetings scheduled at the same time. Carol tells Pam to handle one, and she (Carol) will come in to sign the retainer agreement. After one and a half hours, Carol is still tied up, and the client is demanding that Pam sign the retainer agreement or he will find another attorney. Should Pam let the client leave and risk losing his business, or should Pam sign the retainer agreement? Does she have other options?

2. Scott Emerson takes a job as a paralegal with a large law firm that specializes in defending clients against product-liability claims. The firm's clients are some of the largest manufacturing companies in the country. Mark Jones, an associate attorney, assigns Scott the job of drafting and sending out interrogatories to the plaintiff in a case brought against one of the firm's clients. Specifically, Scott is told to send out a standard set of one hundred interrogatories, each with five parts. Scott eventually learns that one of the favorite discovery tactics of the firm is to inundate plaintiffs with discovery requests, interrogatories, and depositions to cause continuous delays and to outspend the plaintiffs. Scott knows that the relevant state court rules do not limit the number of interrogatories that can be used, but he suspects that the firm's tactics are ethically questionable. Are they? What should Scott do?

3. A client claiming to have severely injured his back at work comes into the office of a law firm. The client, in a wheelchair, seeks legal advice about filing a lawsuit, and the attorney decides to take the case. Two days later, Alvin Kerrigan, the attorney's paralegal, sees the new client on the roof of a building installing shingles. What should Alvin do?

4. During a lunch break in the course of a trial, Louise Lanham, a paralegal, was washing her hands in the rest room. One of the members of the trial jury came up to her and said, "I don't understand what negligence is. Can you explain it to me?" How should Louise answer this question?

✦ PRACTICE QUESTIONS AND ASSIGNMENTS

1. Assume that you work for attorney Tara Jolans of Adams & Tate, 1000 Town Center, Suite 500, White Tower, Michigan. Jolans has decided to represent Sandra Nelson in her lawsuit against David Namisch. Based on the following information, draft a complaint to be filed in the U.S. District Court for the Eastern District of Michigan.

   Sandra Nelson is a plaintiff in a lawsuit resulting from an automobile accident. Sandra was turning left at a traffic light at the intersection of Jefferson and Mack Streets, while the left-turn arrow was green, when she was hit from the side by a car driven by David Namisch, who failed to stop at the light. The accident occurred on Friday, June 3, 1999, at 11:30 P.M. David lives in New York, was visiting his family in Michigan, and just prior to the accident had been out drinking with his brothers. Several witnesses saw the accident. One of the witnesses called the police.

   Sandra was not wearing her seat belt at the time of the accident, and she was thrown against the windshield, sustaining massive head injuries. When the police and ambulance arrived, they did not think that she would make it to the hospital alive, but she survived. She wants to claim damages of $500,000 for medical expenses, $65,000 for lost wages, and $35,000 for property damage to her Rolls Royce. The accident was reported in the local newspaper, complete with photographs.

2. Draft the first ten questions for a set of interrogatories to be directed to the plaintiff, Sandra Nelson, based on the facts given in Question 1 above.

3. Using the material presented in the chapter on pretrial motions, identify each of the following motions:

   a. Tom Smith is a defendant in an auto-negligence case. His attorney files a motion requesting that a judgment be granted in Tom's favor without a trial. He attaches to the motion an affidavit of an eyewitness, who saw the plaintiff run a stop sign.

   b. Dr. Higgins is sued for medical malpractice. The plaintiff recovered completely and has no damages. Dr. Higgins's attorney files a motion asking that the case against his client be dismissed for failure to state a claim on which relief can be granted.

c. After the answer is filed in a case brought by a plaintiff who slipped and fell on a broken egg on a grocery store floor, her attorney files a motion requesting that the court enter a judgment in the plaintiff's favor based on the undisputed facts contained in both the answer and the complaint.

d. Dr. Higgins's attorney loses the motion discussed above. When the plaintiff's attorney requests medical records, Dr. Higgins instructs his attorney to refuse to provide the records. The plaintiff's attorney files a motion to obtain the records.

4. Draft a series of questions for the plaintiff's attorney and for the two defendants' attorneys (the attorneys representing the doctor and the pharmaceutical company, respectively) to use during *voir dire* in a case involving the following facts:

> The plaintiff's daughter died five days after starting on a regimen of taking weight-control pills. The daughter died because the pills were incompatible with her blood type. Prior to taking the pills, she was a perfectly healthy, twenty-five-year-old law student. The mother is bringing a medical-malpractice suit against the doctor for prescribing the wrong type of pill. The mother is also suing the pharmaceutical company that manufactured the pill on the ground that it failed to warn of the dangers of its pill for those persons, including her daughter, whose blood types were incompatible with the pill.

▨ USING INTERNET RESOURCES

1. Access the Web site of the National Court Reporters Association at **www.verbatimreporters.com**.

   a.   Click on "Site Map" and then go to the "About Court Reporting" page. Read about the history of court reporting, and then answer the following questions:

   - When was the stenotype first invented? How does this machine work?

   - What is computer-aided transcription (CAT)? What is "realtime" translation?

   b.   Now go to the "Geo search" page, and do a search for your city (if you live in a smaller community, enter the name of a large city in your area or state) and answer these questions:

   - How many court reporters or court-reporting firms offer services in that area?

   - List five types of services that one (or more) of these court reporters or firms offer.

2. The Court TV Web site contains the transcripts of O. J. Simpson and others involved in his trial. Access the Web site at: **www.courttv.com/old/casefiles/ simpson**. Click on "transcripts." Click on "Read excerpts from the three-day direct examination of O. J. Simpson." Read the transcripts and then answer the following questions:

   a. What is the date of the first transcript?

   b. What subject is addressed in the first transcript?

   c. What type of question is the first question asked of O. J. Simpson?

   d. What types of questions are included in the third and fifth questions?

   e. Why were these types of questions being asked during direct examination?

   f. Compare the first, third, and fifth questions to the second, fourth, and sixth questions. How do they differ?

CHAPTER 7

CONDUCTING INTERVIEWS AND INVESTIGATIONS

Chapter Outline

⊞ INTRODUCTION ⊞ PLANNING THE INTERVIEW ⊞ INTERVIEWING SKILLS
⊞ INTERVIEWING CLIENTS ⊞ INTERVIEWING WITNESSES
⊞ PLANNING AND CONDUCTING INVESTIGATIONS

After completing this chapter, you will know:

- How to prepare for an interview and the kinds of skills employed during the interviewing process.

- The common types of client interviews paralegals may conduct and the different types of witnesses paralegals may need to interview during a preliminary investigation.

- How to create an investigation plan.

- The variety of sources that you can use when trying to locate information or witnesses.

- Rules governing the types of evidence that are admissible in court.

- How to summarize your investigation results.

INTRODUCTION

Paralegals frequently interview clients. After the initial client interview (which is usually conducted by the supervising attorney), the paralegal may conduct one or more subsequent interviews to obtain detailed information from the client. How the paralegal relates to the client has an important effect on the client's attitude toward the firm and the attorney or legal team handling the case.

Additionally, paralegals often conduct pretrial investigations to learn as much as possible about the case. As part of a preliminary investigation into a client's claim, the paralegal may interview one or more witnesses to gain as much information as possible. The more factual evidence that can be gathered in support of a client's claim, the better the client's chances in court—or in any other dispute-settlement proceeding.

Learning how to conduct interviews and investigations is thus an important part of preparing for your career as a paralegal. In this chapter, you will read about the basic skills and concepts that you can apply when interviewing clients or witnesses, and when conducting investigations.

PLANNING THE INTERVIEW

Planning an interview involves organizing many details. As a paralegal, you may be responsible for locating a witness, scheduling the interview, determining where the interview should take place, arranging for the use of one of the firm's conference rooms or other office space for the interview, and additional related details. Crucial to the success of any interview is how well you prepare for it.

Know What Information You Want to Obtain

Prior to any interview, you should have clearly in mind the kind of information you want to obtain from the client or witness being interviewed—the **interviewee**. You should know what questions you want to ask and have them prepared in advance. Advance preparation for an interview depends, of course, on the type of interview being conducted. In many situations, the paralegal (or the firm) will already have created specific preprinted or computerized forms indicating what kind of information should be gathered during client interviews relating to particular types of claims. Using preprinted forms ensures that all essential information will be obtained.

> **Interviewee**
> The person who is being interviewed.

If you are interviewing a client who is petitioning for bankruptcy, for example, you will need to obtain from the client the types of information that must be included on the bankruptcy forms to be submitted to the court. The bankruptcy forms will serve as a checklist for you to follow during the client interview. Similarly, if your firm frequently handles personal-injury cases, you will probably have available a preprinted or computerized personal-injury intake sheet, such as that shown in Exhibit 7.1 on the next page, to use as a guide when obtaining client information during the initial client interview.

Recording the Interview

Some interviewers tape-record their interviews. Before you tape-record an interview, you should always do the following:

 Obtain permission to tape-record the interview from both your supervising attorney and the person being interviewed.

EXHIBIT 7.1
Personal-Injury Intake Sheet

PERSONAL-INJURY INTAKE SHEET

Prepared for Clients of
Jeffers, Gilmore & Dunn

1. Client Information:

Name: Katherine Baranski

Address: 335 Natural Blvd.

Nita City, NI   48802

Social Security No.: 206-15-9858

Marital Status: Married   Years Married: 3

Spouse's Name: Peter Baranski

Children: None

Phone Numbers: Home (473) 555-2211   Work (473) 555-4849

Employer: Nita State University

Mathematics Department

Position: Associate Professor of Mathematics

Responsibilities: Teaching

Salary: $ 46,000

2. Related Information:

Client at Scene: Yes

Lost Work Time: 5 months

Client's Habits: Normally drives south on Mattis Avenue on way to university each morning at about the same time.

When you are using a tape recorder, you should state or include at the beginning of the tape the following identifying information:

- The name of the person being interviewed and any other relevant information about the interviewee.
- The name of the person conducting the interview.
- The names of other persons present at the interview, if any.
- The date, time, and place of the interview.
- On the record, the interviewee's consent to having the interview tape-recorded.

If more than one tape is used, you should indicate at the end of each tape that the interview will be continued on the next tape in the series, and each subsequent tape should contain identifying information.

EXHIBIT 7.1
**Personal-Injury Intake Sheet—
Continued**

3. Incident/Accident:

Date: August 4, 1998   Time: 7:45 A.M.

Place: Mattis Avenue and 38th Street, Nita City, Nita

Description: Mrs. Baranski was driving south on Mattis Avenue

when a car driven by Tony Peretto, who was

attempting to cross Mattis at 38th Street, collided

with Mrs. Baranski's vehicle.

Witnesses: None known by Mrs. Baranski

Defendant: Tony Peretto

Police: Nita City

Action Taken: Mrs. Baranski was taken to City Hospital

by ambulance (Nita City Ambulance Co.).

4. Injuries Sustained:

Nature: Multiple fractures to left hip and leg; lacerations

to left eye and left side of face; multiple contusions

and abrasions

Medical History: No significant medical problems prior to the

accident

Treating Hospital: Nita City Hospital

Treating Physician: Dr. Swanson

Hospital Stay: August 4, 1998   to November 20, 1998

Insurance: Southwestern Insurance Co. of America

Policy No: 00631150962 -B

Interview Conducted by:

Allen P. Gilmore   January 30, 1999
Attorney   Date

Elena Lopez   January 30, 1999
Paralegal/Witness   Date

There are several advantages to tape-recording an interview. For one thing, having a record of the interview on tape reduces the need to take extensive notes during the interview. You can either have the tape transcribed for future reference, or you can listen to the tape later (when creating an interview summary, for example—discussed later) to refresh your memory of how the interviewee responded to certain questions. You may also want to have other members of the legal team read the transcript or listen to the tape. Sometimes, what might not have seemed significant to you may seem significant to someone else working on the case. Also, as a case progresses, a remark made by the interviewee that did not seem important at the time of the interview may take on added importance in view of evidence gathered after the interview was held.

DEVELOPING PARALEGAL SKILLS

The Tape-Recorded Interview

Justin Hooper is preparing for an interview that will be tape-recorded. He takes the tape recorder to the conference room where the interview will take place and sets up the tape recorder. The witness arrives and is shown into the conference room by the receptionist. Justin takes a prepared statement from a file folder containing the introductory remarks used in a tape-recorded interview. He reads it into the tape recorder:

"My name is Justin Hooper. I am a paralegal at the law firm of Smith & Howard. The firm is representing Mr. Barry Buckner, the defendant in *Jones v. Buckner*. This tape-recorded interview is taking place in the law offices of Smith & Howard on January 6, 1999. The time is two o'clock P.M."

Justin then turns to the witness and asks the witness to state and spell her name into the tape recorder. Justin also asks the witness for her consent to have the interview tape-recorded, so that the witness's consent will be on the record. Then the interview begins.

TIPS FOR CONDUCTING A TAPE-RECORDED INTERVIEW

- Test the tape-recorder before the interview to ensure that it is working properly.
- Create a prepared introductory statement that gives the name of the interviewer; the date, time, and location of the interview; the case name; and other relevant information.
- Ask the witness to state and spell his or her name into the tape recorder.
- Ask the witness for permission to tape-record the interview—be certain the witness's answer is tape-recorded.
- Ask all others present during the interview to state and spell their names.
- Have additional tapes available, and immediately label additional tapes as they are used.
- If more than one tape is used, be certain to state on each tape which number the tape is and state how many tapes were used.

There are also some disadvantages to tape-recording interviews. A major disadvantage is that some clients and witnesses may be uncomfortable and less willing to disclose information freely if they know everything they are saying is being recorded. Such reluctance is understandable in view of the fact that the interviewee cannot know in advance what exactly will transpire during the course of the interview or how the tape may later be used. When asking an interviewee for his or her permission to tape-record an interview, you should therefore evaluate carefully how the interviewee responds to this question. Depending on the interviewee's response, you might consider taking notes instead of tape-recording the session.

INTERVIEWING SKILLS

Interviewing skills are essentially any skills—particularly interpersonal and communication skills—that help you to conduct a successful interview. In this section, you will learn how the use of interpersonal and communication skills can help you establish a comfortable relationship with the interviewee. Then, you will read about specific questioning and listening techniques that can help you control the interview and elicit various types of information.

Interpersonal Skills

At the outset of any interview, remember that your primary goal is to obtain information from the client or witness being interviewed. Although some people communicate information and ideas readily and effectively, others may need considerable coaching and encouragement. If they feel comfortable in your presence and in the interviewing environment, they will generally be more willing to disclose information.

As you begin an interview, you should remember that the interviewee may be very nervous or at least uncomfortable. Because the time you have to talk with a client or witness will be limited, you should put that individual at ease as quickly as possible. A minute or two spent chatting casually with the client or witness is time well spent. Also, saying or doing something that shows your concern for the interviewee's physical comfort helps to make the interviewee feel more relaxed. For example, you might offer the individual a cup of coffee or other beverage.

Using language that the interviewee will understand is essential in establishing a good working relationship with that person. If you are interviewing a client with only a grade school education, for example, do not use the phrase "facial lacerations" when talking about "cuts on the face." If you are interviewing a witness who does not speak English very well, arrange to have an interpreter present unless you are fluent in the witness's native language. Because most clients and witnesses are not familiar with legal terminology, you should always abide by the following rule of thumb when conducting interviews:

> **Avoid using legal terms that will not be clearly understood by the interviewee.**

If you must use a specific legal term to express an idea, be sure that you define the term and that it is clearly understood.

Questioning Skills

When questioning witnesses or clients, you should remember to remain objective at all times and gather as much relevant factual information as possible. Sometimes, you may have difficulty remaining objective when questioning witnesses because you sympathize with the client and may not want to hear about facts that are contrary to the client's position. But relevant factual information includes those details that adversely affect the client's case as well as those that support his or her position. Indeed, your supervising attorney must know *all* of the facts, especially any that might damage the client's case in court.

The experienced legal interviewer uses certain questioning techniques to prompt interviewees to communicate the information needed. There are several types of questions, including open-ended, closed-ended, hypothetical, pressure, and leading questions.

OPEN-ENDED QUESTIONS.   The **open-ended question** is a broad, exploratory question that invites any number of possible responses. The open-ended question can be used when you want to give the interviewee an opportunity to talk at some length about a given subject. "What happened on the night of October 28—the night of the murder?" is an open-ended question. Other examples of open-ended questions are "And what happened next?" and "What did you see as you approached the intersection?" When you ask a question of this kind, be prepared

Open-Ended Question
A question that is phrased in such a way that it elicits a relatively detailed discussion of an experience or event.

for a lengthy response. If a witness has difficulty narrating the events he or she observed or if a lull develops during the explanation, you will need to encourage the witness to continue through the use of various prompting responses (which will be discussed shortly in the context of listening skills).

Open-ended questions are useful in interviewing clients or friendly witnesses (witnesses who favor the client's position). This is because these kinds of interviewees are usually forthcoming, and you will be able to gain information from them by indicating in broad terms what you want them to describe.

Closed-Ended Question
A question that is phrased in such a way that it elicits a simple "yes" or "no" answer.

CLOSED-ENDED QUESTIONS.   The **closed-ended question,** in contrast, is intended to elicit a "yes" or "no" response from the interviewee. "Did you see the murder weapon?" is an example of a closed-ended question. Although closed-ended questions tend to curb communication, they are useful in some situations. For example, if an interviewee tends to digress frequently from the topic being discussed, using closed-ended questions can help keep him or her on track. Closed-ended questions, because they invite specific answers, also may be useful in relaxing the interviewee in preparation for more difficult questions that may follow later in the interview. In addition, closed-ended questions may help to elicit information from adverse witnesses (those who are not favorable to the client's position) who may be reluctant to volunteer information.

Hypothetical Question
A question based on hypothesis, conjecture, or fiction.

HYPOTHETICAL QUESTIONS.   As a paralegal, you may be asked to interview an expert witness either to gather information about a case or to evaluate whether that person would be an effective expert witness at trial (expert witnesses will be discussed later in this chapter). The **hypothetical question** is frequently used with expert witnesses. Hypothetical questions allow you to obtain an answer to an important question without giving away the facts (and confidences) of a client's case. For example, you might invent a hypothetical situation involving a certain type of knee injury (the same kind of injury as that sustained by a client) and then ask an orthopedic surgeon what kind of follow-up care would ordinarily be undertaken for that type of injury.

Pressure Question
A question intended to make the interviewee feel uncomfortable and respond emotionally. Pressure questions are sometimes used by interviewers to elicit answers from interviewees who may otherwise be unresponsive.

PRESSURE QUESTIONS.   Sometimes interviewers use a type of question known as a pressure question. **Pressure questions** are intended to make the interviewee feel uncomfortable and to induce him or her to respond emotionally. The pressure question may be useful in eliciting a response from an interviewee who is reluctant to discuss a matter with you. If an eyewitness, for example, refuses to state whether he or she saw the murderer, an interviewer might pressure him or her into responding by asking a question such as the following: "The murder weapon—a heavy board—was found a mile from the victim's body. Did you know that the board was traced to the construction site right next door to your store?"

Note that pressure questions should be used only as a last resort, and then used very carefully. As an interviewer, you want to enlist the interviewee's cooperation, not alienate him or her.

Leading Question
A question that suggests, or "leads to," a desired answer. Interviewers may use leading questions to elicit responses from witnesses who otherwise would not be forthcoming.

LEADING QUESTIONS.   The **leading question** is one that suggests to the listener the answer to the question. "Isn't it true that you were only ten feet away from where the murder took place?" is a leading question. This question, of course, invites a "yes" answer. Leading questions are very effective for drawing information out of eyewitnesses or clients, particularly when they are reluctant to disclose information. They are also useful when interviewing adverse witnesses who are hesitant to communicate information that may be helpful to the client's

Q:	You were drinking beer in the parking lot during lunch and then got behind the wheel to drive anyway, didn't you?
A:	Yes.
Q:	You saw the driver of the green van run the stop sign, right?
A:	Yes.
Q:	Isn't it true that you were so intoxicated at the time of the accident that you can't remember what happened?
A:	Yes.

EXHIBIT 7.2
Leading Questions

position. When used with clients and friendly witnesses, however, leading questions have a major drawback:

> **Leading questions may lead to distorted answers because the client or witness may tailor the answer to fit his or her perception of what the interviewer wants to know.**

For this reason, in the interviewing context, leading questions should be used cautiously and only when the interviewer is fully aware of the possible distortions that might result. For other examples of leading questions, see Exhibit 7.2 above.

intended to elicit a yes or no response

Listening Skills

The interviewer's ability to listen is perhaps the most important communication skill used during the interviewing process. Whenever you conduct an interview, you will want to absorb fully the interviewee's verbal answers, as well as his or her nonverbal messages. Prior to the interview, you should make sure that the room in which it is to be held will be free of noises, phone calls, visitors, and other interruptions or distractions. During the interview itself, you can use several listening techniques to maximize communication and guide the interviewee toward the fullest disclosure of needed information.

For communication to be truly an interactive process, the listener must engage in active listening. **Active listening** requires the listener to pay close attention to what the speaker is saying. Active listening is critical to a productive interview. A paralegal's lack of attention during the interview may mean important details could be missed, and ultimately, the client could suffer.

Active Listening
The act of listening attentively to the speaker's verbal or nonverbal messages and responding to those messages by giving appropriate feedback.

> **If you ever find your attention wandering during an interview, have the interviewee repeat what he or she just said to make sure that you have not missed anything.**

You do not have to admit that your attention was wandering, of course. Simply say that you want to make sure that your impression of what the interviewee said is accurate.

Active listening also involves feedback. As a listener, you can give feedback, in the form of both verbal and nonverbal cues, to encourage the speaker to continue discussing a topic. An example of a verbal cue is "I'm listening, please go on" or "And then what happened?" Verbal feedback can also be given by simply murmuring an "uh huh" or a "hmm" here and there to let the speaker know you are attentive. A nonverbal cue can be any facial expression or body language that

suggests to the listener the answer to the question

shows you are interested in what is being said. Nodding positively, for example, is an effective way to convey, nonverbally, your interest. Maintaining eye contact is another nonverbal cue to indicate your interest in what is being said.

Finally, active listening involves the ability to analyze on the spot the interviewee's comments in the context of the larger picture. Often, something that the interviewee says opens a door to another area that should be explored. When this happens, you need to decide whether to explore that area now or later (perhaps at a subsequent interview).

 In general, you need to be constantly analyzing your interviewee's responses and deciding how those responses should direct your further questioning.

INTERVIEWING CLIENTS

Typically, the paralegal interviews either clients or witnesses. Here we look at client interviews. (We will discuss witness interviews shortly.) The various types of client interviews include the initial client interview, subsequent client interviews to obtain further information, and informational interviews, or meetings, to inform the client of the status of his or her case and to prepare the client for trial or other legal proceedings. We look next at each of these types of interviews.

The Initial Client Interview

As discussed in Chapter 4, when a client seeks legal advice from an attorney, the attorney normally holds an initial interview with the client. During this interview, the client explains his or her legal problem so that the attorney can advise the client on possible legal options and the legal fees that may be involved. Either then or at a later time, the client and the attorney will agree on the terms of the representation, if the attorney decides to take the case.

Paralegals often attend initial client interviews. Although the attorney normally conducts this first interview, the paralegal plays an important role. Usually, you will observe the client, take notes on what the client is saying, and provide the client with forms, statements explaining the firm's fees, and other prepared information normally given to new clients. Following the interview, you and the attorney may compare your impressions of the client and of what the client said during the interview.

All of the people present at the interview should be introduced to the client, their titles given, and the reason for their presence at the interview made known to the client. In introducing you, the paralegal, to the potential client, the attorney will probably stress that you are not a lawyer.

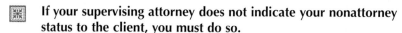 **If your supervising attorney does not indicate your nonattorney status to the client, you must do so.**

If a firm decides to take a client's case, the client should be introduced to every member of the legal team who will be working on the case.

A follow-up letter, such as the one shown in Exhibit 7.3, will be sent to the client after the interview. The letter will state whether or not the attorney has decided to accept the case or, if the attorney orally agreed during the initial client interview to represent the client, will confirm the oral agreement in writing.

Subsequent Client Interviews

Paralegals are often asked to conduct additional interviews with clients whose cases have been accepted. For example, assume that a client wants to obtain a

EXHIBIT 7.3
**A Sample Follow-Up
Letter to a Client**

Jeffers, Gilmore & Dunn
553 Fifth Avenue
Suite 101
Nita City, NI 48801

Telephone: (616) 555-9690
Fax: (616) 555-9679
e-mail: jgd@nitanet.net

February 2, 1999

Ms. Katherine Baranski
335 Natural Boulevard
Nita City, Nita 48802

Dear Ms. Baranski:

It was a pleasure to meet and talk with you on January 30. Jeffers, Gilmore & Dunn will be pleased to act as your representative in your action against Tony Peretto to obtain compensation for your injuries.

I am enclosing a fee agreement for your review. If you wish this firm to act as your legal counsel, please sign and date the agreement and return it to me as soon as possible. A self-addressed, stamped enveloped is enclosed for your convenience. As soon as I receive the completed agreement, we will begin investigating your case.

As I advised during our meeting, to protect your rights, please refrain from speaking with the driver of the vehicle, his lawyer, or his insurance company. If they attempt to contact you, simply tell them that you have retained counsel and refer them directly to me. I will handle any questions that they may have.

If you have any questions, please do not hesitate to call me or my paralegal, Ms. Elena Lopez.

Sincerely,

Allen P. Gilmore

Allen P. Gilmore
Attorney at Law

APG/db

Encs.

divorce. After the initial interview, your supervising attorney may ask you to arrange for a subsequent interview with the client to obtain all the information necessary to prepare the divorce pleadings. When scheduling the interview, you should tell the client what kinds of documents or other data he or she should bring to the interview. During the interview, you will fill out the form that the firm uses to record client information in divorce cases. Paralegals often assume responsibility for gathering most of the information needed to file for a divorce or to begin child-custody proceedings.

When conducting a client interview, the paralegal should always disclose his or her nonlawyer status if this fact was not made clear at an earlier session. Remember, even if you had been introduced to the client as a "legal assistant," the client may not realize that a legal assistant is not an attorney. To protect yourself against potential claims that you have engaged in the unauthorized practice of law, you should clearly state to the client that you are "not an attorney."

FEATURED GUEST: ANNA DURHAM BOLING

Ten Tips for More Effective Interviewing

BIOGRAPHICAL NOTE

Anna Durham Boling graduated from the University of Georgia School of Law in 1984 and is licensed to practice law in the state of Georgia. Following graduation from law school, Boling practiced real-estate law for four years. She then accepted a position as an instructor in the paralegal studies program at Athens Area Technical Institute in Athens, Georgia. She was named director of the program in July 1989. Under her direction, the program was approved by the American Bar Association in February 1992. Boling currently works for the Institute of Government at the University of Georgia.

Interviewing clients and witnesses is a learned skill. Interviewers, whether they are lawyers, legal assistants, or others, become more effective over time as they acquire more interviewing experience. There are many interviewing "tips" that can enhance the abilities of even the novice interviewer, however. The following suggestions are ones I have found to be particularly helpful. As you develop your interviewing skills, you may find that the tips that serve you best are the ones you develop yourself. In the meantime, you can learn from the experiences of others.

1. **Verify Information.** When interviewing clients and witnesses, realize that every bit of information obtained must be verified. I do not mean to suggest that all clients or all witnesses lie (although, unfortunately, some do). On the contrary, each individual client or witness will describe his or her perception of what happened, and you will find that no two people ever perceive the same factual occurrence in exactly the same way. A good method to verify information is therefore to interview several people about the event or issue under investigation. Another way to verify information is to use additional sources, such as documentary evidence.

2. **Let the Interviewee Vent His or Her Emotions.** Sometimes, clients or witnesses come to interviews with heightened emotions regarding the matters about which they are to be questioned. In such situations, they may need an opportunity to vent their feelings before they can relax enough to discuss a subject that is painful or bothersome to them. When this happens, it is often helpful to put the time clock aside and interact with the interviewee on a personal level. Showing compassion for the interviewee's emotional needs will help you establish a rapport with that person, which will enhance the possibility of effective communication.

3. **Keep an Open Mind.** Be careful not to categorize a client's problem. Both the interviewer and the person being interviewed can fall prey to this trap, particularly during the initial interview. For example, a client in financial distress might say that he wants to declare bankruptcy. All he knows is that his financial situation is worsening and that he wants to obtain some relief. He thinks that bankruptcy is the only answer, but there may be other answers to the client's dilemma, and other legal issues may be involved. Explore the client's entire situation. In this example, find out what caused the financial distress so that you can better understand the client's specific circumstances. In this way, the legal team will be better able to offer the best and most complete service possible.

4. **Listen Carefully.** Listen carefully to the person being interviewed. Do not make assumptions about the inter-

The Informational Interview

The informational interview, or meeting, is an interview in which the client is brought in to discuss upcoming legal proceedings. Most clients know very little about the procedures involved in litigation, and firms often have their paralegals

FEATURED GUEST, *Continued*

viewee or anticipate a particular answer before asking the question. An interviewer taking this approach may miss important or even critical information. Learn to listen to the interviewee's answers and "digest" the information objectively—without letting any assumptions interfere with the listening process. In this way, you may discern valuable pieces of information that could significantly affect the outcome of the case.

5. **Record Information.** Write down everything that is learned in the course of an interview. Recording the information on paper, on a computer, or with a tape recorder is especially important for the beginner because of the level of detail that must be reported. You may think, "I could never forget that piece of information." But in a busy practice full of distractions, you may have forgotten that information by the end of the interview.

6. **Engage in Interactive Communication.** Interviewing should be interactive. It should involve a meaningful exchange between the interviewer and the interviewee. When listening to the answers to your questions, ask yourself, "In light of this response, what else would I like to know?" By posing this question to yourself, you will be able to carry each line of questioning to its logical extreme and, in doing so, arrive at the most complete picture possible.

7. **Be Prepared for the Interview.** Be thoroughly prepared for your interview. Preparation is particularly important for the inexperienced interviewer. Reviewing closed files in your law firm that are similar to the case at hand is often very helpful. Determine what information in those files is significant. Notice which questions recur from file to file. This will enable you to construct a line of questioning that will elicit the desired information. Interview preparation is time consuming, but the benefits can be enormous. As your interviewing skills develop, the preparation time for subsequent interviews will decrease significantly.

8. **Learn the Chronology of the Factual Circumstances.** If possible, have the person being interviewed relate what he or she knows about the subject matter of your investigation in the order in which the events occurred. If the interviewee can relay his or her story in this manner, then the risk of omitting important facts is lessened substantially. Encourage your interviewee to supply as complete a description as possible and to avoid omitting any details. Although this request may elicit some useless information, it is better to have too much, rather than too little, information. You will be able to weed out unimportant or irrelevant information after the interview.

> "Interviewing clients and witnesses is a learned skill."

9. **Remain Objective.** It is important to have an objective understanding of the client's problem. When assisting in the representation of a client, it is quite natural to feel sympathy for that person, particularly if he or she has suffered a substantial hardship. But too much sympathy may prevent you from objectively evaluating the factual circumstances of the client's case. Remember that your supervising attorney will be in a better position to defend the client's interests if the attorney is aware of all information relating to the case, including information that appears to be unfavorable to the client.

10. **Evaluate the Results.** Just as it is important to prepare for interviews, it is important to review your work once the case has been resolved. In retrospect, you can determine whether any information that turned out to be important to the case was missed and if so, how or why it was missed. You can also learn how important information was successfully obtained. This evaluation exercise will enhance your effectiveness as an interviewer and help you prepare for interviews in future cases.

explain these procedures to clients and prepare clients for the trial experience. For example, the paralegal can describe to clients what will take place during the trial, how to groom themselves appropriately for trial, where to look when they testify, and so on. The informational interview helps the client understand why certain proceedings are taking place and his or her role in those proceedings.

ETHICAL CONCERN
Handling Client Documents

Clients frequently give paralegals important documents relating to their cases during interviews. State codes of ethics impose strict requirements on attorneys in regard to the safekeeping of clients' funds and other property, including documents. Suppose, for example, that a client gives you the only copy she has of her divorce agreement. You should never rely on memory when it comes to client documents. Instead, immediately after the conclusion of the interview, you should record the receipt of any documents or other items received from the client. The information may be recorded in an evidence log (discussed later in this chapter) or in some other way, depending on the procedures established by your firm to govern the receipt and storage of such property. An evidence log or other method of recording documents and items received from clients provides you with evidence—should it be necessary—of what you did (or did not) receive from a client.

Summarizing the Interview

The interviewing process does not end with the close of the interview. A final and crucial step in the process involves summarizing the results of the interview for the legal team working on the case. As a paralegal, you will create an intake memorandum following each initial client interview. If the firm has a prepared intake form for particular types of cases, such as the personal-injury intake sheet referred to earlier and illustrated in Exhibit 7.1, the completed form might constitute the interview summary. Information obtained during any subsequent interviews with a client should be analyzed and summarized in a memo for your supervising attorney or other team members to review and for later inclusion in the client's file.

Your interview summary should be created immediately after the interview, while the session is still fresh in your mind. When summarizing the results of a client interview, you should carefully review your notes and, if the session was tape-recorded, review the tape. You should never rely totally on your memory of the statements made during the interview. It is very easy to forget the client's specific words, and it may be very important later to know exactly how the client phrased a certain comment or response. Relying on memory is also risky because, as mentioned earlier, sometimes a statement that seemed irrelevant at the time of the interview may turn out to be very important to the case. You should thus make sure that the facts are accurately recorded and are as reliable as possible.

On the Web
You can find databases containing numerous expert witnesses at various Web sites, including **www.experts.com**, **www.hg.org/expert-serv. html**, and **www.claims.com**.

INTERVIEWING WITNESSES

Witnesses play a key role in establishing the facts of an event. As a legal investigator, your goal is to elicit as much relevant and reliable information as possible from each witness about the event that you are investigating. Interviewing witnesses is in many ways similar to interviewing clients, and many of the interviewing skills, such as listening skills, that we have already discussed apply to interviews of witnesses. A major difference between clients and witnesses, however, is that the latter may not always be friendly to the client's position. Here we

ETHICAL CONCERN
The Unauthorized Practice of Law

Paralegals must be especially careful not to give legal advice when interviewing clients. Suppose that you are conducting a follow-up interview of a client, Sue Collins. Collins was injured in a car accident and is suing the driver of the other car involved for negligence. During the initial client interview, Collins told you and your supervising attorney that the accident was totally the result of the other driver's negligence. During the course of your follow-up interview, however, Collins presents you with an interesting hypothetical. She says to you, "What would happen, in a lawsuit such as mine, if the plaintiff was not watching the road when the accident occurred? What if the plaintiff was looking in the back seat to see why her baby was crying? Could the plaintiff still expect to win in court?" Under the laws of your state, contributory negligence (when a person's own negligence contributed to or caused his or her injuries) on the part of the plaintiff is an absolute bar to the recovery of damages. Should you explain this to Collins? No. Even though the question is phrased as a hypothetical, it is possible that your answer could affect Collins's future actions. Your best option is to tell Collins that you are not permitted to give legal advice but that you will relay the "hypothetical" question to your supervising attorney.

describe the various types of witnesses as well as some basic skills and principles that are particularly relevant to investigative interviews.

Types of Witnesses

Witnesses include expert witnesses, lay witnesses, and eyewitnesses. Witnesses are also sometimes classified as friendly witnesses or hostile (or adverse) witnesses.

EXPERT WITNESSES.   An **expert witness** is an individual who has professional training, advanced knowledge, or substantial experience in a specialized area, such as medicine, computer technology, ballistics, or construction techniques. Paralegals often arrange to hire expert witnesses either to testify in court or to render an opinion on some matter relating to the client's case. Expert witnesses are often used in cases involving medical malpractice and product liability to establish the duty, or standard of care, that the defendant owed to the plaintiff. For example, if a client of your firm is suing a physician for malpractice, your supervising attorney might arrange to have another physician testify as to the standard of care owed by a physician to a patient in similar circumstances.

Expert Witness
A witness with professional training or substantial experience qualifying him or her to testify on a particular subject.

LAY WITNESSES.   Most witnesses in court are lay witnesses. In contrast to expert witnesses, **lay witnesses** do not possess any particular skill or expertise relating to the matter before the court. They are people who happened to observe or otherwise have factual knowledge about an event. A professional or expert in one field may be a lay witness in regard to another field about which he or she does not have expert knowledge. A physician involved in a fraud claim, for example, might give testimony about the fraud as a lay witness but not as an expert witness.

Lay Witness
A witness who can truthfully and accurately testify on a fact in question without having specialized training or knowledge; an ordinary witness.

EYEWITNESSES.   In attempting to gain more information about an event relating to a client's legal claim, paralegals may be required to interview eyewitnesses.

ETHICAL CONCERN
Keeping the Client Informed

Attorneys have a duty to keep their clients reasonably informed about their cases or claims. As a paralegal, you should assume the responsibility for making sure that the attorney does not breach this duty. Periodic notes or phone calls to the client not only keep the client informed about progress on the case but also keep you in touch with the case status—and you and your supervising attorney will be less likely to miss important deadlines relating to the litigation. Frequent communications with clients also cultivate goodwill. Clients generally welcome any news from their attorneys' offices. Even a letter saying "nothing is happening" is usually appreciated. To make sure that the client is kept informed, you will want to have some kind of a tickler system to remind you to contact the client at periodic intervals.

Eyewitness
A witness who testifies about an event that he or she observed or has experienced firsthand.

Eyewitnesses are lay witnesses who have witnessed an event and who may testify in court as to what they observed. The term *eyewitness* is deceiving, and perhaps a better term might be "sense" witness. This is because an eyewitness may have firsthand knowledge of an event, but this knowledge need not have been derived from the sense of sight—that is, from actually seeing the event. An eyewitness may be someone who listened in on a telephone conversation between an accused murderer and his or her accomplice. A blind man may have been an eyewitness to a car crash, because he heard it.

In interviews, eyewitnesses are ordinarily asked to describe an event, in their own words and as they recall it, that relates to the client's case. Eyewitness accounts may be lengthy, and the paralegal may want to tape-record the interview session to ensure accuracy. The experienced paralegal may also find that different eyewitnesses to the same event have contradictory views on what actually took place. People's perceptions of reality differ, as paralegals often find when comparing eyewitness reports.

FRIENDLY WITNESSES.   Some witnesses to an event may be the client's family, friends, co-workers, neighbors, or other persons who know the client and who want to be helpful in volunteering information. These witnesses are regarded as **friendly witnesses.** You may think that friendly witnesses are the best kind to interview, and they often are. They may also be biased in the client's favor, however, so the paralegal should look closely for the actual facts (and not the witness's interpretation of the facts) when interviewing friendly witnesses.

Friendly Witness
A witness who gives voluntary testimony at an attorney's request on behalf of the attorney's client; a witness who is prejudiced against the client's adversary.

Hostile Witness
A witness for the opposing side in a lawsuit or other legal proceeding; an adverse witness.

HOSTILE WITNESSES.   Witnesses who may be prejudiced against your client or friendly to your client's adversary are regarded as **hostile witnesses** (or *adverse witnesses*). Interviewing hostile witnesses can be challenging. Sometimes the witness has an interest in the outcome of the case and would be in a better position if your client lost in court. For example, if the client is a tenant who refuses to pay rent until the landlord makes a structural repair to the roof, then the paralegal interviewing the landlord's manager should be prepared to deal with that person as a potentially hostile witness.

Sometimes, hostile witnesses refuse to be interviewed. On learning that the alternative might be a subpoena, however, a hostile witness may consent to at least a limited interview. If you plan to interview hostile witnesses, keep in mind the following rule of thumb:

> **Contact and interview hostile witnesses in the early stages of your investigation. The longer you wait, the greater the chance that they may be influenced by the opposing party's attorney or the opinions of persons sympathetic to the opposing party.**

When interviewing hostile witnesses, you need to be especially careful to be objective, fair, and unbiased in your approach. This does not mean that you have to ignore your client's interests. On the contrary, you will best serve those interests by doing all you can to keep from further alienating a witness whose information might ultimately help your client's case.

Questioning Witnesses

When you are asking questions as a legal investigator, you should follow this rule of thumb:

> **Phrase your questions so that they lead to the most complete answer possible.**

Investigative questions should be open ended. Compare, for example, the following two questions:

1. "Did you see the driver of the green van run the stop sign?"
2. "What did you see at the time of the accident?"

The first question calls for a "yes" or "no" answer. The second question, in contrast, invites the witness to explain fully what he or she actually saw. Something else that the witness saw could be important to the case—but unless you allow room for the witness's full description, you will not learn about this information.

Notice that the first question also assumes a fact—that the driver of the green van ran the stop sign. The second question, however, makes no assumptions and conveys no information to the witness that may influence his or her answer. Generally, the less the witness knows about other witnesses' descriptions, the better, because those other descriptions could influence the witness's perception of the event. You want to find out exactly what the witness observed, in his or her own words.

Checking the Witness's Qualifications

When you are interviewing a witness during the course of an investigation, you often will not know whether the testimony of that witness will be needed in court or even whether the claim you are investigating will be litigated. Nonetheless, you should operate under the assumption that each witness is a potential court witness. Thus, you should make sure that the witness is competent to testify and reliable. Is there any indication that the witness has a physical or mental disability that might interfere with the accuracy of his or her perception of the witnessed event? Has the witness ever been convicted of a crime? Does he or she abuse drugs or have a reputation in the community as a troublemaker? If it can be shown that a witness is unreliable or incompetent to testify, the witness's testimony normally will not be admitted in court.

Also investigate the witness's possible biases. Does the witness have an interest in the claim being investigated that would tend to make his or her testimony prejudicial? Is the witness a relative or close friend of one of the parties involved

EXHIBIT 7.4
**Information Contained
in a Witness Statement**

1. **Information about the Witness**
   —Name, address, and phone number
   —Name, address, and phone number of the witness's employer or
     place of business
   —Interest, if any, in the outcome of the claim being investigated

2. **Information about the Interview**
   —Name of the interviewer
   —Name of the attorney or law firm for which the claim is
     being investigated
   —Date, time, and place of the interview

3. **Identification of the Event Witnessed**
   —Nature of the action or event observed by the witness
   —Date of the action or event

4. **Witness's Description of the Event**

5. **Attestation Clause**
   —Provision or clause at the end of the statement affirming the truth of the witness's
     description as written in the statement.

[Witness's Signature]

in the claim? Does the witness hold a grudge against one of the parties? If the answer to any of these questions is yes, the witness's testimony may be discredited in court. In any event, it will probably not be as convincing as testimony given by a neutral, unbiased witness.

Witness Statements

Witness Statement
The written transcription of a statement made by the witness during an interview and signed by the witness.

Whenever you interview a witness, you should take notes and prepare a memorandum of the interview. Depending on the procedures followed by your firm, you may want to have the witness—particularly if he or she is a hostile witness—sign a statement. A **witness statement** is a written statement setting forth what the witness said during the interview. Exhibit 7.4 shows the type of information normally contained in a witness statement, and Exhibit 7.5 presents an excerpt from a sample witness statement.

Statutes and court rules vary as to the value of witness statements as evidence. Usually, statements made by witnesses during interviews cannot be introduced as evidence in court, but they can be used for other purposes. For example, if a hostile witness's testimony in court contradicts something he or she said during your interview, the witness statement may be used to impeach the witness—that is, to call into question the witness's testimony or demonstrate that the witness is unreliable. Witness statements also can be used to refresh a witness's memory.

PLANNING AND CONDUCTING INVESTIGATIONS

Because factual evidence is crucial to the outcome of a legal problem, investigation is necessarily an important part of legal work. Attorneys often rely on paralegals to conduct investigations, and you should be prepared to accept the

EXHIBIT 7.5

A Sample Witness Statement (Excerpt)

STATEMENT OF JULIA WILLIAMS

I, Julia Williams, am a thirty-five-year-old female. I reside at 3801 Mattis Avenue, Nita City, Nita 48800, and my home telephone number is (408) 555-8989. I work as a nurse at the Nita City Hospital & Clinic, 412 Hospital Way, Nita City, Nita 48802. My work telephone number is (408) 555-9898. I am making this statement in my home on the afternoon of February 8, 1999. The statement is being made to Elena Lopez, a paralegal with the law firm of Jeffers, Gilmore & Dunn.

In regard to the accident on the corner of Mattis Avenue and Thirty-eighth Street on August 4, 1999, at approximately 7:45 A.M. on that date, I was standing at the southwest corner of that intersection, waiting to cross the street, when I observed . . .

* * * *

I affirm that the information given in this statement is accurate and true to the best of my knowledge.

Julia Williams

Julia Williams

responsibility for making sure that an investigation is conducted thoroughly and professionally. In the following pages, you will read about the basics of legal investigation—how to plan and undertake an investigation, how the rules of evidence shape the investigative process, and the importance of carefully documenting the results of your investigation.

Of course, you have already read about one aspect of investigations—interviewing witnesses. A preliminary investigation, however, can involve much more. For one thing, before witnesses can be interviewed, they must be located. Information relating to the case may also have to be obtained from a police department, weather bureau, or other source.

Where Do You Start?

Assume that you work for Allen Gilmore, the attorney who represented the plaintiff in the hypothetical case discussed in Chapter 6. Recall that the plaintiff in that case, Katherine Baranski, sued Tony Peretto for negligence. Peretto had run a stop sign at an intersection and as a result, his car collided with Baranski's. Further assume that the case is still in its initial stages. Attorney Gilmore has just met with Katherine Baranski for the initial client interview. You sat in on the interview, listened carefully to Baranski's description of the accident and of the damages she sustained as a result (medical expenses, lost wages, and so on), and took thorough notes.

After the interview, Gilmore asks you to do a preliminary investigation into Baranski's claim. It is now your responsibility to find the answers to a number of questions. Did the accident really occur in the way perceived by the client, Katherine Baranski? Exactly where and when did it happen? How does the police report describe the accident? Were there any witnesses? Was Tony Peretto insured and, if so, by what insurance company? What other circumstances (such as weather) are relevant? Your supervising attorney will want to know the answers to these and other questions before advising Baranski as to what legal action should be pursued.

In undertaking any legal investigation, your logical point of departure is the information you have already acquired about the legal claim or problem. In the

EXHIBIT 7.6
An Investigation Plan

INVESTIGATION PLAN
File No. 15773

	Date Requested	Date Received

1. Contact Police Department
 —To obtain police report
 —To ask for photographs of accident scene
 —To talk with investigating officer

 —SOURCE: Nita City Police Dept.
 —METHOD: Request in person or by mail

2. Contact Known Witnesses
 —Tony Peretto, van driver
 —Michael Young, police officer at accident scene
 —Julia Williams, witness at accident scene
 —Dwight Kelly, witness at accident scene

 —SOURCE: Police report
 —METHOD: Contact witnesses by initial phone
 call and personal interview when possible

3. Obtain Employment Records
 —To learn employment status and income of
 Mrs. Baranski

 —SOURCE: Nita State University
 —METHOD: Written request by mail with
 Mrs. Baranski's release enclosed

4. Obtain Hospital Records
 —To learn necessary information about
 Mrs. Baranski's medical treatment and costs

 —SOURCE: Nita City Hospital
 —METHOD: Written request by mail with
 Mrs. Baranski's release enclosed

Baranski case, this information consists of the statements made by Baranski during the initial client interview and summarized in your notes. Baranski had described what she remembered about the accident, including the date and time it occurred. She said she thought that the police investigator had the names of some persons who had witnessed the accident. She also stated that she was employed as an assistant professor in the math department at Nita State University, earning approximately $46,000 a year. By using common sense and a little imagination, you can map out a fairly thorough investigation plan based on this information.

Creating an Investigation Plan

Investigation Plan
A plan that lists each step involved in obtaining and verifying the facts and information that are relevant to the legal problem being investigated.

An **investigation plan** is simply a step-by-step list of the tasks that you plan to undertake to verify or obtain factual information relating to a legal problem. In the Baranski case, the steps in your investigation plan would include those summarized in Exhibit 7.6 and discussed in the following pages. The paralegal should make sure that his or her supervising attorney approves the investigation plan. Generally, throughout the investigation, it is important to keep in close touch with your supervising attorney about progress being made.

EXHIBIT 7.6
An Investigation Plan—
Continued

	Date Requested	Date Received
5. Contact National Weather Service —To learn what the weather conditions were on the day of the accident	_____	_____
—SOURCE: National Weather Service or newspaper —METHOD: Phone call or written request		
6. Obtain Title and Registration Records —To verify Tony Peretto's ownership of the vehicle	_____	_____
—SOURCE: Department of Motor Vehicles —METHOD: Order by mail		
7. Contact Tony Peretto's Insurance Company —To find out about insurance coverage —To check liability limits	_____	_____
—SOURCE: Insurance company —METHOD: Written request by mail		

8. Use a Professional Investigator
—To contact such witnesses as
  –ambulance attendants
  –doctors
  –residents in neighborhood of accident scene
—To inspect vehicle
—To take photos of accident site
—To investigate accident scene, etc.
	_____
	
	_____
	_____
	_____
		_____
		
		_____
		_____
		_____

—SOURCE: Regular law-firm investigator —METHOD: In person		

CONTACTING THE POLICE DEPARTMENT.   The initial step in your plan should be to contact the police department. You will want to look at a copy of the police report of the accident, view any photographs that were taken at the scene, obtain the names of persons who may have witnessed the accident, and, if possible, talk to the investigating officer.

CONTACTING AND INTERVIEWING WITNESSES.   Next, you will want to contact and interview any known witnesses and document their descriptions of what took place at the time of the accident. Known witnesses include the driver (Tony Peretto) of the vehicle that hit Katherine Baranski, the police officer at the scene, and the other witnesses noted in the police investigation report. Keep in mind that if Tony Peretto is aware of Baranski's intention to sue him, he will probably have retained an attorney. If he has, then you are not permitted to contact him directly—all communications with him will have to be through his attorney.

OBTAINING MEDICAL AND EMPLOYMENT RECORDS.   To justify a claim for damages, you will need to ascertain the nature of the injuries sustained by Baranski as a result of the accident, the medical expenses that she incurred, and her annual or monthly income (to determine the amount of wages she lost as a

DEVELOPING PARALEGAL SKILLS
Keeping an Evidence Log

Steve Fessler works as a paralegal for Marty Melman, a sole practitioner. Marty is representing June Linden, the plaintiff in a personal-injury case. Marty asked Steve to obtain X-rays of the plaintiff's fractured ankle. The fracture occurred as a result of an auto accident.

Steve receives a phone call from the hospital indicating that the X-rays are ready to be picked up. Steve drives to the hospital, picks up the X-rays, and brings them back to the office. He places them in a special folder and applies an exhibit label to the folder, which contains a thorough description of the X-rays for purposes of identification. The special folder will preserve the X-rays. Next, he places the folder in the evidence cabinet, which is kept locked so that access to the cabinet is controlled. He takes out a notebook entitled "Evidence Log" and places a clean log sheet in it.

TIPS FOR CREATING AN EVIDENCE LOG

- The form should contain blanks for the file name, a description of the evidence, and information about its acquisition, such as the date and by whom and how it was acquired.

- Additionally, the form should contain information blanks for identifying marks on the evidence, where the evidence is kept within the firm, and the name of the evidence custodian.

- The form should include columns that show the chain of custody of the evidence, such as columns for the name, date, and purpose of each release of the evidence.

- There should be a prominent statement on the form that the evidence must be safeguarded and returned in the same condition. Anyone removing the evidence should be required to sign this statement.

- Consider taking a Polaroid snapshot before and after each transfer of the evidence.

This way, if the evidence needs to be removed and reviewed by someone, such as an expert witness, there will be a record of the evidence and who has or had custody of it. Maintaining an evidence log also helps to protect against claims that the evidence is not authentic or has been altered while in the law firm's possession.

---

result of the accident). To obtain this information, you will need copies of her medical and employment records.

Note that the institutions holding these records will not release them to you unless Katherine Baranski authorizes them to do so. Therefore, you will also need to arrange with Baranski to sign release forms to include with your requests for copies. A sample authorization form to release medical records is shown in Exhibit 7.7. You should make sure that Baranski signs these forms before she leaves the office after the initial interview. Otherwise, waiting for her to return the signed forms may delay your investigation.

In addition to obtaining medical records, you may be asked to do some research on the type of injury sustained by Baranski and related statistical or other information. Some helpful online sources for medical information are discussed in the feature *Technology and Today's Paralegal: Online Medical Research* on page 240.

CONTACTING THE NATIONAL WEATHER SERVICE.   Weather conditions at the time of the accident may have an important bearing on the case. If it was snowing heavily at the time of the Baranski-Peretto accident, for example, Peretto's attorney may argue that Peretto did not see the stop sign or that ice on the road prevented him from stopping. You will therefore want to ascertain what the weather conditions were at the time of the accident by contacting the National Weather Service. Also, when you interview eyewitnesses, you should ask them about weather conditions at the place and time of the accident.

On the Web
The National Weather Service is online at www.nws.noaa.gov.

EXHIBIT 7.7
**Authorization to
Release Medical Records**

TO: Nita City Hospital & Clinic   PATIENT: Katherine Baranski
Nita City, NI 48803   335 Natural Boulevard
Nita City, NI 48802

You are hereby authorized to furnish and release to my attorney, Allen P. Gilmore of Jeffers, Gilmore & Dunn, all information and records relating to my treatment for injuries incurred on August 4, 1998. Please do not disclose information to insurance adjusters or to other persons without written authority from me. The forgoing authority shall continue in force until revoked by me in writing, but for no longer than one year following the date given below.

Date: January 30, 1999.   *Katherine Baranski*
                                   Katherine Baranski

Please attach your invoice for any fee or photostatic costs and send it with the information requested above to my office.

Thank you,

Allen P. Gilmore
Allen P. Gilmore
Jeffers, Gilmore & Dunn
Attorneys at Law
553 Fifth Avenue
Suite 101
Nita City, NI 48801

Helena Moritz
Helena Moritz
Notary Public State of Nita
Nita County
My Commission Expires November 12, 2002

OBTAINING VEHICLE TITLE AND REGISTRATION RECORDS.   To verify that Tony Peretto owns the vehicle that he was driving at the time of the accident, you will need to obtain title and registration records. Usually, these can be acquired from the state department of motor vehicles, although in some states the secretary of state's office handles such records. The requirements for obtaining such information vary from state to state and may include the submission of special forms and fees. Therefore, you should call the relevant state department or office in advance to find out what procedures should be followed.

CONTACTING THE INSURANCE COMPANY.   If you learned the name of Peretto's insurance company from Baranski or from the police report, you will want to contact that company to find out what kind of insurance coverage Peretto has and the limits of his liability under the insurance policy. Insurance companies usually are reluctant give this information to anyone other than the policyholder. They sometimes cooperate with such requests, however, because

On the Web
Relevant driving and vehicle-registration records may be on the Web. See, for example, the list of licensed drivers in the state of Texas at www.publicdata.com. To find the home pages of your state's government agencies, go to www.findlaw.com.

TECHNOLOGY AND TODAY'S PARALEGAL

Online Medical Research

Attorneys and paralegals frequently deal with cases involving personal injuries, medical malpractice, product liability, or other health-related problems. In such cases, paralegals may be asked to do some research on a particular medical topic, procedure, or device. (A paralegal may also be asked to locate  an expert witness in the medical field; you will read about online databases of expert witnesses in Chapter 9.)

You might want to begin your research by familiarizing yourself with the relevant medical terminology. To do this, you can access medical dictionaries and glossaries online. For example, you can find the "Online Medical Dictionary" maintained by CancerWEB at **www.graylab. ac.uk/omd/index.html**. To find online medical glossaries, you can go to **www.va-business.com/electro/hmos/gloss. html** or **www.hmri.com/onthehealthcareteam/index.html**.

Some medical journals are also available online if what you need is an article on a particular medical subject. For example, the *Journal of the American Medical Association* can be found at **www.ama-assn.org/public/journals/ jama/jamahome.htm**. Reuters Health Information Services provides current news on medical topics for both health professionals and the general public (see **www.reutershealth.com**). There are also many medical texts on the Web. Good, comprehensive sources include Martindale's Health Science Guide at **www.sci.lib.uci.edu/~martindaleHSGuide.html** and the Multimedia Medical Reference Library at **www.med-library.com/medlibrary**.

Information about medical devices, drugs, and medical procedures can be found at the Food and Drug Administration's site (at **www.fda.gov**) or at Yahoo's medical site (at **www.yahoo.com/Health/Medicine**). Links to other medical sites are available on the American Medical Association's Web pages at **www.ama-assn.org/med_link/ med_link.html**.

Other useful medical-research sites include HealthGate's site at **www.healthgate.com/index.shtml**, which gives you free access to MEDLINE and other medical databases, and the Web site of the National Institutes of Health at **www.nih.gov**. The latter site has a wealth of information and offers links to a number of other sites, including the National Library of Medicine and MEDLINE.

---

they know that if they do not, the information can be obtained during discovery, should a lawsuit be initiated.

USING A PROFESSIONAL INVESTIGATOR'S SERVICES.   Some law firms routinely use the services of professional investigators. Depending on the circumstances, your supervising attorney may decide to use a professional investigator for certain tasks, including those described above. You might be responsible for working with the investigator. For example, you might arrange for the investigator to inspect and take photographs of the accident scene.

Locating certain witnesses (witnesses who have moved, for example) may be difficult and time consuming. This is another task that your supervising attorney may prefer the professional investigator to handle, particularly if the attorney needs your assistance in the office. The investigator might also be asked to locate other witnesses, such as the ambulance driver or attendants, physicians who treated Baranski, or residents in the area who might have observed the accident.

Locating Witnesses

Perhaps one of the most challenging tasks for the legal investigator is locating a witness whose address is unknown or who has moved from a previous, known address. Suppose, for example, that in the Baranski case the police investigation report lists the name, address, and telephone number of Edna Ball, a witness to the accident. When you call her number, a recording informs you that the phone has been disconnected. You go to her address, and the house appears to be vacant. What is your next step?

At this point, many paralegals suggest to their supervising attorneys that a professional investigator take over the search. But if you alone must locate the witness, there are several sources to which you can turn. A good starting point is to visit other homes in the neighborhood. Perhaps someone living nearby knows Edna Ball and can give you some leads as to where she is or what happened to her. Other sources are discussed below.

TELEPHONE AND CITY DIRECTORIES.   The telephone directory can sometimes be a valuable source of information for the investigator. In trying to locate Edna Ball, for example, you might check to see if her name is still listed in the current directory and, if so, whether it is listed jointly with someone, such as her husband. Your local telephone information service might have a new number listed for her. If the information-service operator indicates that the number is unlisted, you can explain the nature of your concern and request that the operator phone Edna Ball at that number to see if she is willing to call you.

City directories are also good potential sources of information. Such directories may be available in the local library or the law firm's library. A city directory generally contains more information than a phone book. For example, some city directories list places of employment and spouses' names in addition to addresses and telephone numbers. Typically, city directories provide a listing of names and phone numbers by street address. In the Baranski case, if you wanted to obtain the telephone numbers of persons who live in the area of the Baranski-Peretto accident, you could consult a city directory for addresses near the intersection where the accident occurred.

On the Web
To find telephone book Web sites, you can do a broad search using a search engine, such as that of Infoseek at **www.infoseek.com**.

OTHER INFORMATION SOURCES.   Other sources of information are media reports (newspaper and magazine articles and television videos covering the event being investigated); court records (probate proceedings, lawsuits, and so on); deeds to property (usually located in the county courthouse); birth, marriage, and death certificates; voter registration lists; the post office (to see if the witness left a forwarding address); credit bureaus; the tax assessor's office; and city utilities, such as the local electric or water company.

Professional organizations may be useful sources as well. For example, if you have learned from one of Edna Ball's neighbors that she is a paralegal, you can check with state and local paralegal associations to see if they have current information on her. You might also check with federal, state, or local governmental agencies or bureaus (discussed in the following section) to see if the information contained in public records will be helpful in locating Edna Ball.

Accessing Government Information

Records and files acquired and stored by government offices and agencies can be a tremendous resource for the legal investigator. Public records available at local government buildings or offices (such as the county courthouse or post office) were mentioned above. Additionally, it is possible to obtain information from federal agencies, such as the Social Security Administration, and from state departments or agencies, such as the state revenue department or the secretary of state's office. If you wish to obtain information from any government files or records, you should check with the specific agency or department to see what rules apply.

On the Web
You can access the home pages of federal agencies by going to **www.findlaw.com**.

PARALEGAL PROFILE

Insurance Paralegal

KIRTRENA S. DEEN *received her bachelor of arts degree in legal administration from the University of West Florida in Pensacola, Florida, in 1996. On graduation, she worked at a large law firm as a legal assistant for approximately a year and a half in the area of personal-injury and employment law. Currently, she is employed as a claims representative for a national automobile insurance company. In September 1998, she received her Florida Department of Insurance Adjusters license. Additionally, she serves on the University of West Florida Legal Administration Program Advisory Board as a paralegal representative in the corporate/public sector.*

What do you like best about your work?

"I enjoy the responsibility and exposure of investigating, evaluating, and negotiating a variety of automobile claims as opposed to adjusting only specific types of automobile claims. Some examples of the claims I am assigned to adjust include property, bodily-injury, arson, theft, vandalism, and weather-related claims. I also enjoy the investigative process of meeting the parties involved, securing recorded statements, conducting scene investigations, and canvassing for witnesses."

What is the greatest challenge that you face in your area of work?

"Once a claim has been reported, the claims representative must investigate to establish coverage, finalize legal liability, and inspect the reported damage. Once the claim has been thoroughly investigated, it must be evaluated to determine a fair settlement and negotiated accordingly. Therefore, the greatest challenge of adjusting claims is completing the investigation, evaluation, and negotiation process promptly and fairly while complying with the terms of the insurance policy and governing statutory laws."

What advice do you have for would-be paralegals in your area of work?

"My advice is to possess strong interpersonal skills, as well as superior writing and oral communication skills. Due to the variety of claims assigned, claims representatives in my area daily communicate and negotiate with insureds, claimants, and other claims representatives, as well as attorneys, regarding the settlement of claims. Additionally, regular meetings and communication with paint and body shop managers is needed regarding the assessment of automobile damage. Thus, the ability to communicate effectively with all kinds of people is a great asset to possess in my area of work."

What are some tips for success as a paralegal in your area of work?

"Know the terms and conditions of the insurance policy and regularly refer to the policy to substantiate them. The insurance policy is the contract between the insurance company and the insured to which they must adhere. Know the statutory laws governing claims handling in your area and keep abreast of changes. Be detail oriented and analytical in the investigation process. Feel passionate about your work. Passion for your work will enable you to go that extra mile to handle claims promptly and fairly."

> "[T]he ability to communicate effectively with all kinds of people is a great asset to possess in my area of work."

EXHIBIT 7.8
**Freedom of Information
Act Request Form**

Agency Head or FOIA Officer
Title
Name of Agency
Address of Agency
City, State, Zip

Re: Freedom of Information Act Request.

Dear_____:

Under the provisions of the Freedom of Information Act,
5 U.S.C. 552, I am requesting access to [identify the records as clearly
and specifically as possible].

If there are any fees for searching for, or copying, the records I have requested, please
inform me before you fill the request. [Or: . . . please supply the records without informing
me if the fees do not exceed $_____.]

[Optional] I am requesting this information [state the reason for your request if you think
it will assist you in obtaining the information].

[Optional] As you know, the act permits you to reduce or waive fees
when the release of the information is considered as "primarily benefiting
the public." I believe that this request fits that category and I therefore
ask that you waive any fees.

If all or any part of this request is denied, please cite the specific
exemption(s) that you think justifies your refusal to release the information,
and inform me of the appeal procedures available to me under the law.

I would appreciate your handling this request as quickly as possible,
and I look foward to hearing from you within ten days, as the law stipulates.

Sincerely,

Signature
Name
Address
City, State, Zip

The Freedom of Information Act (FOIA), which was enacted by Congress in 1966, requires the federal government to disclose certain records to any person on request. A request that complies with the FOIA procedures need only contain a reasonable description of the information sought. Exhibit 7.8 illustrates the proper format for a letter requesting information under the FOIA. Note that the FOIA exempts some types of information from the disclosure requirement, including classified information (information concerning national security), confidential material dealing with trade secrets, government personnel rules, and personal medical files.

Investigation and the Rules of Evidence

Because an investigation is conducted to obtain information and verify facts that may eventually be introduced as evidence at trial, you should know what kind of evidence will be admissible in court before undertaking your investigation.

Evidence is anything that is used to prove the existence or nonexistence of a fact. Whether evidence will be admitted in court is determined by the **rules of evidence**—rules that have been created by the courts to ensure that any evidence presented in court is fair and reliable. The Federal Rules of Evidence govern the admissibility of evidence in federal courts. For cases brought in state courts, state rules of evidence apply. (Many states have adopted evidence rules patterned on the

Evidence
Anything that is used to prove the existence or nonexistence of a fact.

Rules of Evidence
Rules governing the admissibility of evidence in trial courts.

Accessing Government Information

Ellen Simmons has started a new job as a paralegal for Smith & Case, a law firm that handles Superfund cases. Ellen is about to request copies of documents from the EPA. Ellen calls and speaks to Christopher Peter, a paralegal with the EPA. She identifies herself as a paralegal from Smith & Chase, which is representing a client involved at the Suburban Landfill Superfund site. Ellen is greeted with an icy silence and wonders what she might have said to offend Christopher. She asks if the EPA has the waste-in/waste-out report that gives the total volume of hazardous waste at the site and lists the potentially responsible parties.

Christopher responds, in a surprised voice, that the EPA does have the documents. "Are you new?" asks Christopher. "Is it that obvious?" jokes Ellen. Christopher responds that it's not really that obvious and explains that her predecessor always just sent in a FOIA request for everything that the EPA had in its files and that it took weeks to respond to requests from her firm. "Believe me, your firm has quite a reputation around here," says Christopher.

Ellen knows that she is off to a good start in her new job and with an important legal assistant at the EPA. She smiles to herself as she promises to submit the FOIA request for only the waste-in/waste-out report.

TIPS FOR WORKING WITH GOVERNMENT AGENCIES

- Review the file to familiarize yourself with the case before calling the agency.
- Review the agency's regulations to ascertain which documents the agency prepares in specific types of cases, such as Superfund cases.
- Make a list of the various documents.
- Determine in advance (from the list) which documents you will be requesting.
- Develop a list of alternatives to use in the event that the documents that you request have not been prepared or are not available.
- Make reasonable requests from the agency.
- Cultivate good working relationships with agency staff members.

---

federal rules.) Of course, you will not need to become an expert in evidentiary rules, but a basic knowledge of how evidence is classified and what types of evidence are admissible in court will greatly assist your investigative efforts.

DIRECT VERSUS CIRCUMSTANTIAL EVIDENCE.   Two types of evidence may be brought into court—direct evidence and circumstantial evidence. **Direct evidence** is any evidence that, if believed, establishes the truth of the fact in question. For example, bullets found in the body of a shooting victim provide direct evidence of the type of gun that fired them. **Circumstantial evidence** is indirect evidence that, even if believed, does not establish the fact in question but only the degree of likelihood of the fact. In other words, circumstantial evidence can create an inference that a fact exists.

For example, suppose that your firm's client owns the type of gun that shot the bullets found in the victim's body. This circumstantial evidence does not establish that the client committed the crime. Combined with other circumstantial evidence, however, it is possible that a jury could be convinced that the client committed the crime. For instance, if other circumstantial evidence indicates that your firm's client had a motive for harming the victim and that the client was at the scene of the crime at the time the crime was committed, a jury might conclude that the client committed the crime.

Direct Evidence
Evidence establishing the existence of a fact that is in question without relying on inferences.

Circumstantial Evidence
Indirect evidence that is offered to establish, by inference, the likelihood of a fact that is in question.

RELEVANCE.   Evidence will not be admitted in court unless it is relevant to the matter in question. **Relevant evidence** is evidence that tends to prove or disprove the fact in question. For example, evidence that the gun belonging to your firm's client was in the home of another person when the victim was shot would be relevant, because it would tend to prove that the client did not shoot the victim.

Even relevant evidence may not be admitted in court if its probative (proving) value is substantially outweighed by other important considerations. For example, even though evidence is relevant, it may not be necessary—the fact at issue may already have been sufficiently proved or disproved by previous evidence. In that situation, the introduction of further evidence would be a waste of time and would cause undue delay in the trial proceedings. Relevant evidence may also be excluded if it would tend to distract the jury from the main issues of the case, mislead the jury, or cause the jury to decide the issue on an emotional basis.

Relevant Evidence
Evidence tending to make a fact in question more or less probable than it would be without the evidence. Only relevant evidence is admissible in court.

AUTHENTICATION OF EVIDENCE.   At trial, an attorney must lay the proper foundation for the introduction of certain evidence, such as documents, exhibits, and other objects, and must demonstrate to the court that the evidence is what the attorney claims. The process by which this is accomplished is referred to as **authentication.** The authentication requirement relates to relevance, because something offered in evidence becomes relevant to the case only if it is authentic, or genuine.

Authentication
Establishing the genuineness of an item that is to be introduced as evidence in a trial.

 As a legal investigator, you therefore need to make sure that the evidence you obtain is not only relevant but also capable of being authenticated if introduced at trial.

Commonly, evidence is authenticated by the testimony of witnesses. For example, if an attorney wants to introduce an autopsy report as evidence in a case, he or she can have the report authenticated by the testimony of the medical examiner who signed it. Generally, an attorney must offer enough proof of authenticity to convince the court that the evidence is, in fact, what it is purported to be.

The rules of evidence require authentication because certain types of evidence, such as exhibits and objects, cannot be cross-examined by opposing counsel, as witnesses can, yet such evidence may have a significant effect on the jury. The authentication requirement provides a safeguard against the introduction of non-verified evidence that may strongly influence the outcome of the case.

The Federal Rules of Evidence provide for the self-authentication of specific types of evidence. In other words, certain documents or records need not be authenticated by testimony. Certified copies of public records, for example, are automatically deemed authentic. Other self-authenticating evidentiary documents include official publications (such as a report issued by the federal Environmental Protection Agency), documents containing a notary public's seal or the seal of a public official, newspaper or magazine articles, and manufacturers' trademarks or labels.

HEARSAY.   When interviewing witnesses, you need to make sure that a witness's statements are based on the witness's own knowledge and not hearsay. **Hearsay** is defined as any testimony given in court about a statement made by someone else. Literally, it is what someone heard someone else say. For example, if a witness in the Baranski case testified in court as to what he or she heard another observer say about the accident, that testimony would be hearsay. Generally, hearsay is not admissible as evidence. To a great extent, this is because the listener may have misunderstood what another person said, and without the opportunity of cross-examining the originator of the statement, the misperception cannot be challenged.

Exceptions to the hearsay rule are made in certain circumstances. Generally, these exceptions allow hearsay to be considered as evidence when the hearsay

Hearsay
An oral or written statement made by an out-of-court declarant that is later offered in court by a witness (not the declarant) concerning a matter before the court. Hearsay is generally not admissible as evidence.

Interviewing a Client

Amanda Blake, a paralegal, works for John Kerrigan, a sole practitioner. A new client, Joel Sontag, calls for an appointment to make his will. The attorney has to go out of town for a court hearing. Because Sontag seems to be anxious to get the will done, the attorney asks Amanda to meet with Sontag and interview him to obtain some basic information. The attorney will review the information when he returns from his trip and then call Sontag to advise him on the will and other estate-planning possibilities.

PREPARING FOR THE INTERVIEW

Amanda reserves the conference room. On the day of Sontag's visit, she has it set up for the interview. She has already made a copy of the will and estate-planning checklist that she will use to ensure that she gets all of the essential information from Sontag. The secretary shows Sontag into the conference room when he arrives.

MEETING THE CLIENT

Amanda introduces herself, saying, "Hello, Mr. Sontag, I'm Amanda Blake, John Kerrigan's legal assistant. I'll be meeting with you today to obtain the estate-planning information that Mr. Kerrigan needs if he is to advise you. Sontag responds, "Mr. Kerrigan told me that we would be meeting today. He also told me how capable you are." Amanda smiles and says, "Thanks. And did Mr. Kerrigan explain to you that I'm not an attorney?" Sontag responds, "Yes, he did." Amanda then removes her checklist and note pad from her file.

OBTAINING INFORMATION ABOUT THE CLIENT

"I'll be reviewing this checklist to make sure that we obtain all of the information that we need for your will," Amanda informs Joel. "First, I need you to fill out the client information form," instructs Amanda. "As you can see, it requires you to give us personal information, such as your name, legal residence, date of birth, and other data." Joel takes the form and fills it out. When he is finished, he hands it to Amanda.

"Now I need some other information. First, I need to know if you're married," states Amanda. "Yes, I am," responds Joel. "Your wife's name is?" asks Amanda. "Nicole Lynn Sontag," answers Joel. "And your wife resides with you at the address that you've given on the client information form?" asks Amanda. "Yes, she does,"

Joel states. "When was she born, and what's her Social Security number?" asks Amanda. "She was born on January 17, 1958, and her Social Security number is 363-46-2350," says Joel.

"Now, Joel, do you have any children?" asks Amanda. "Yes, we have one son, Joel, Jr., age four," answers Joel. "Do you want to provide for both of them in your will?" asks Amanda. "Yes," responds Joel. "Do you have any other relatives for whom you want to provide?" asks Amanda. "Yes, I have a brother, Alfred Sontag, who lives in a home for autistic people," answers Joel. "I'll need the address for the home," responds Amanda. Joel takes an address book out of his briefcase and gives her the address. "Is there anyone else whom you want to provide for in your will?" asks Amanda. "No," responds Joel.

OBTAINING INFORMATION ABOUT THE CLIENT'S PROPERTY

"Now we need to discuss property," Amanda informs Joel. "Do you own a home?" she asks. "Yes," he answers. Amanda says, "I need to know if the home is located at the address you gave on the form, when you bought it, what it cost, what its present approximate market value is, whether you own it jointly with your wife, and the balance on your mortgage." Joel gives her all of the requested information. Amanda continues questioning Joel about his property holdings until she has covered all the items on her checklist.

CONCLUDING THE INTERVIEW

"Well," says Amanda, "we've covered everything on the checklist. Now we need to set up a time for you to meet with Mr. Kerrigan to discuss estate-planning procedures and your will. Because you jointly own property with your wife, Mr. Kerrigan may want both of you to meet with him. Would two o'clock next Tuesday afternoon be a good time for you both to come in to meet with Mr. Kerrigan?" Joel tells Amanda that he thinks that both he and his wife could arrange to meet with the attorney at that time. They tentatively schedule an appointment for that date. Joel will call Amanda if the appointment must be changed. Joel gets up to leave the office, saying that he'll probably see her again next Tuesday. "I'll look forward to that," says Amanda. Amanda then begins to prepare a detailed summary of the interview to give to her supervising attorney on his return.

consists of statements that are highly reliable or believable, such as a dying person's statement on the cause or circumstances of his or her impending death. Statements made by persons in a moment of excitement caused by a startling event or condition may be admissible.

Summarizing Your Results

The final step in any investigation is summarizing the results. Generally, your investigation report should provide an overall summary of your findings, a summary of the facts and information gathered from each source that you investigated, and your general conclusions and recommendations based on the information obtained during the investigation.

OVERALL SUMMARY.   The overall summary of the investigation should thoroughly describe for the reader all of the facts you have gathered about the case. This section should be written in such a way that someone not familiar with the case could read it and become adequately informed of the case's factual background.

SOURCE-BY-SOURCE SUMMARIES.   You should also create a list of your information sources, including witnesses, and summarize the facts gleaned from each of these sources. Each "source section" should contain all of the information gathered from that source, including direct quotes from witnesses. Each source section should also contain a subsection giving your personal comments on that particular source. You might comment on a witness's demeanor, for example, or on whether the witness's version of the facts was consistent or inconsistent with that of other witnesses. Your impressions of the witness's competence or reliability could be noted. If the witness provided you with further leads to be explored, this information could also be included.

GENERAL CONCLUSIONS AND RECOMMENDATIONS.   In the final section, you will present your overall conclusions about the investigation, as well as any suggestions that you have on the development of the case. Attorneys rely heavily on their investigators' impressions of witnesses and evaluations of investigative results because the investigators have firsthand knowledge of the sources. Your impression of a potentially important witness, for example, may help the attorney decide whether to arrange for a follow-up interview with the witness. Usually, the attorney will want to interview only the most promising witnesses, and your impressions and comments will serve as a screening device. Based on your findings during the investigation, you might also suggest to the attorney what further information can be obtained during discovery, if necessary, and what additional research needs to be done.

⊠ KEY TERMS AND CONCEPTS

active listening 225	eyewitness 232	lay witness 231
authentication 245	friendly witness 232	leading question 224
circumstantial evidence 244	hearsay 245	open-ended question 223
closed-ended question 224	hostile witness 232	pressure question 224
direct evidence 244	hypothetical question 224	relevant evidence 245
evidence 243	interviewee 219	rules of evidence 243
expert witness 231	investigation plan 236	witness statement 234

❖ CHAPTER SUMMARY

1. Paralegals often interview clients and witnesses. Interviewing skills include interpersonal skills, questioning skills, and communication skills, particularly listening skills.

2. Paralegals can use several types of questions during the interviewing process, including open-ended, closed-ended, hypothetical, pressure, and leading questions.

3. Prior to the interview, the paralegal should prepare the interview environment to ensure that interruptions, noises, and delays will be minimized, that the client will be comfortable, and that any necessary supplies, forms, and equipment are at hand. If an interview is to be tape-recorded, the paralegal must obtain permission from both his or her supervising attorney and the interviewee to tape the session.

4. There are basically three types of client interviews: the initial interview (usually conducted by the attorney but often attended by the paralegal), the subsequent interview (often conducted by the paralegal), and the informational interview (or meeting, also typically handled by the paralegal). As soon as possible after an interview is concluded, the paralegal should summarize in a written memorandum the information gathered in the interview.

5. Witnesses interviewed by paralegals include expert witnesses (who have specialized training in a given area), lay witnesses (ordinary witnesses who have factual information about the matter being investigated), eyewitnesses (who have firsthand knowledge of an event—because they saw it happen, for example), friendly witnesses (who are favorable to the client's position), and hostile witnesses (who are prejudiced against the client or resent being interviewed for other reasons). Following an interview of a witness, the paralegal should create a witness statement that identifies the witness, discloses what was discovered during the interview, and is signed by the witness.

6. Factual evidence is crucial to the outcome of a legal problem, and paralegals are often asked to conduct investigations to discover any factual evidence that supports (or contradicts) a client's claims. Before starting an investigation, the paralegal should create an investigation plan—a step-by-step list of what sources will be investigated to obtain specific types of information. The paralegal should discuss the plan with his or her supervising attorney before embarking on the investigation.

7. There are several information sources available to paralegals who wish to locate factual information regarding witnesses or other persons involved in a lawsuit. These sources include telephone and city directories, media reports, court records, utility companies, professional organizations, and information recorded, compiled, or prepared by federal, state, and local government entities. The Freedom of Information Act of 1966 requires that federal agencies disclose certain of their records to any person on request, providing that the form of the request complies with the procedures mandated by the act.

8. Evidence is anything that is used to prove the existence or nonexistence of a fact. Direct evidence is any evidence that, if believed, establishes the truth of the fact in question. Circumstantial evidence is evidence that does not directly establish the fact in question but that indicates the degree of likelihood of the fact's existence. Because an investigation is undertaken to verify or uncover factual information that may eventually be used at trial, the paralegal should be familiar with what kind of evidence is admissible in court. Rules of evidence established by the federal and state courts spell out what types of evidence may or may not be admitted in court.

9. To be admissible in court, evidence must be relevant. Evidence must also be authenticated by a demonstration (usually by the testimony of a witness) that the evidence is what the attorney claims it to be. Some forms of evidence, such as certified copies of public records, are automatically deemed to be authentic and need not be authenticated by testimony. Hearsay (secondhand knowledge) is generally not admissible, although there are certain exceptions to this rule.

10. When the investigation is complete, the paralegal should summarize the results. The summary should include an overall summary, a source-by-source summary, and a final section giving the paralegal's conclusions and recommendations.

⬚ QUESTIONS FOR REVIEW

1. What kinds of skills do interviewers employ during interviews?

2. What are the different types of questions that can be used in an interview? When would you use each type?

3. What takes place during the initial client interview? What is the paralegal's role at this interview? What other types of client interviews are commonly conducted by paralegals? What is the purpose of each type?

4. List and describe the various types of witnesses. In what kinds of situations might each of these types of witnesses be used?

5. What is a witness statement? How is it used?

6. Why and how do you create an investigation plan? What types of actions might be included in an investigation plan?

7. List five sources that you would consult in attempting to locate a witness. Which would be the most useful? Which would be the least useful? Why?

8. What is evidence? How are the rules of evidence used?

9. Define and give examples of the following types of evidence: direct evidence, circumstantial evidence, relevant evidence, authenticated evidence, and hearsay.

10. What is included in an investigation summary? Why should one be prepared?

⬚ ETHICAL QUESTIONS

1. Leah Fox, a legal assistant, has been asked by the attorney for whom she works to contact several potential witnesses to see what they know about an event. The first witness that Leah calls says, "I don't know if I should get involved. I don't want to get in trouble. You see, I was supposed to be at work, but I called in sick. If I get involved and my employer finds about where I really was, I might get fired. You're a lawyer, what do you think?" How should Leah respond?

2. Leah Fox, a legal assistant, is conducting a follow-up interview with a new client, who is seeking a divorce. Leah is asking the client about the couple's marital property. According to the client, the couple wants to divide the property evenly on their divorce. When Leah asks the client about checking or savings accounts, the client says to Leah, "You know, Leah, I have this 'secret' savings account, but I don't want anybody to know about it. Please don't tell Mr. Harcourt [Leah's supervising attorney] what I've just told you." What should Leah do in this situation?

3. Jeffrey Jones starts a new job as a paralegal. He reviews a file and notices that the client has not been contacted and updated on the status of the case in three months. He also notices that there is a settlement conference scheduled for tomorrow and that the client needs to be in court. What should Jeffrey do?

4. Jeffrey is asked to review the *Clemmons v. Auto Manufacturer of America* file and to continue the investigation in the case. His boss represents the auto manufacturer in this product-liability case and believes, based on the evidence uncovered so far, that he has an open-and-shut case against the plaintiff, who claims that her husband was killed when the car exploded on impact during an auto accident. Jeffrey begins interviewing witnesses, including an engineer who works for the company. The engineer states that he knew the car was defective and would explode on impact. Jeffrey is worried that his boss will be upset about this fact, because it damages his "open-and-shut" case. What should Jeffrey do?

5. Thomas Lent is a new legal assistant with a law firm that specializes in personal-injury cases. He is reviewing a "Request to Produce Documents" that was recently received in a case that his supervising attorney is handling for the plaintiff. The document requests the plaintiff's medical records, but it does not state specifically which records or for what injuries. Thomas's supervising attorney instructs Thomas to obtain copies of all of the plaintiff's medical records. The plaintiff's medical-records file is several inches thick because the plaintiff is an elderly person and has various medical problems. Thomas is instructed to bury the relevant medical records in the stack and not to make them obvious to the defendant's attorney. If she wants these records, she will have to sort through the file, says the attorney. What should Thomas do? Can the attorney be disciplined for this kind of behavior?

6. In response to a discovery request, Lynnette Banks, a paralegal in a corporate law firm, receives a package of documents in the mail. She opens the package and begins to read through the documents. As she does so, she discovers some that have the words "Privileged and Confidential" stamped on them. She scans a document and realizes that it is a letter from the opposing counsel to his client. The letter reveals the opposing attorney's legal strategy for the case on which Lynette is now working. What should Lynnette do?

❖ PRACTICE QUESTIONS AND ASSIGNMENTS

1. Review the Baranski-Peretto hypothetical case discussed earlier in this text (see Chapter 6). Then write sample questions that you would ask the interviewee when interviewing eyewitnesses to the accident. Phrase at least one question in each of the question formats discussed in this chapter.

2. Using the information in this chapter on questioning skills, identify the following types of questions:

   a. "From January 10 through January 17, 1999, you were on a cruise in the Bahamas, Mr. Johnson. Your credit-card records, which were subpoenaed, indicate that you purchased two tickets. If your wife did not accompany you on that cruise, who did?"

   b. "Did you go on a cruise in the Bahamas with another woman, Mr. Johnson?"

   c. "Isn't it true, Mr. Johnson, that someone other than your wife accompanied you on a cruise in the Bahamas?"

   d. "Mr. Johnson, will you please describe your whereabouts between January 10 and January 17, 1999?"

3. Lena Phillips, a fifty-two-year-old, self-employed seamstress, fell down the three steps in front of her house and fractured her right wrist. She was treated in the emergency room at the Neighborhood Hospital by Dr. Ralph Dean on the day that she fell, January 10, 1999, and released. On January 17, January 25, and February 11, 1999, she visited Dr. Dean's office for follow-up care to make sure that the wrist was healing properly. It appeared that the wrist was healing properly during the month in which she was treated by Dr. Dean. She noticed, however, that even though she had a full range of motion in her wrist, the wrist angled inward somewhat. When she queried Dr. Dean about this, he told her that some angling of the wrist was inevitable.

   Over the course of the following year her wrist became increasingly crooked and bent inward. She went to an orthopedist, Dr. Alicia Byerly, on March 30, 2000. Dr. Byerly tried a splint, but without success. She eventually performed surgery on the wrist at the Neighborhood Hospital on May 3, 2000, but was unable to correct the problem. Dr. Byerly told Ms. Phillips that she should have had surgery on the wrist during the first three weeks after it was broken to correct the angling problem.

   Lena Phillips has come to the firm for which you work, the law firm of Samson & Gore, 5000 West Avenue, Northville, NH 12345, because she wants to sue Dr. Dean for medical malpractice. On May 15, 2000, you are asked to investigate her case. Draft an investigation plan.

4. Using Exhibit 7.3, *A Sample Follow-Up Letter to a Client*, as an example, draft a follow-up letter to Lena Phillips based on the facts from question 3. The attorney that gave you the assignment is Alan Samson. You will need to include a retainer agreement and instruct the client not to talk to Dr. Dean.

5. Using the factual background presented in question 3, draft an "Authorization to Release Medical Information" letter for Lena Phillips to sign. Her name and address are Lena A. Phillips, 150 North Street, Northville, NH, 12345.

6. Using the information in Exhibit 7.4, *Information Contained in a Witness Statement*, and Exhibit 7.5, *A Sample Witness Statement (Excerpt)*, draft a witness statement based on the following facts.

   You work for the law firm of Thomas & Snyder and on April 1, 2000, you are interviewing a witness to a car-train accident that happened a few hours earlier. The interview takes place at the police station. The witness's name is Henry Black. Henry is retired and lives at 2002 Stephens Road, Clinton Township, Pennsylvania. His telephone number is (123) 456–7890.

   Henry was in his Cadillac, stopped in front of the railroad tracks on Jefferson Avenue in Clinton Township, Pennsylvania, at approximately 10:00 A.M., when a red 1999 Mercury Villager sped past him and across the tracks. He was very surprised that a car would not stop at the tracks because the train was only about thirty feet away and was blowing its whistle. There were no gates or guard rails in front of the tracks. Henry looked over at the driver of the Villager and saw that she was talking on a cellular phone as she was driving. She did not appear to hear the train. As her Villager crossed the tracks, the train struck the passenger side of her vehicle. Fortunately, there appeared to be no one else in the vehicle.

7. Assume that a witness is being questioned about statements that she heard a third party make. Determine which of the following statements would qualify as exceptions to the hearsay rule:

   a. The third party exclaimed, "Watch out, he's not stopping at the red light!"

   b. The third party apologized, "Are you all right? I am so sorry. I didn't mean to hurt you."

   c. The third party uttered just before he died, "Make sure you find Joe. He is the one who shot me. Tom didn't have anything to do with this."

   d. The third party exclaimed, "I smell gas fumes!"

   e. The third party, who was the defendant's mistress, said, "He couldn't have killed Bob. He was with me last night."

8. During the course of a murder trial, a prosecuting attorney paraded through the courtroom carrying a hand that had been unearthed the day before and that had been widely publicized as belonging to the murder victim. The defense attorney strenuously objected on the ground that the hand was not relevant. Should the judge sustain the objection?

9. Determine whether each of the following statements is a statement of fact or a statement of opinion, and explain why:

   a. I am sure that the suspect took the money because when I saw him near the cash register, he looked around suspiciously and then tried to sneak away without being seen.

   b. The man who took the money from the cash register was wearing a green trench coat, brown pants, and black boots and was carrying a large tan briefcase.

10. Working in groups of three, role-play the initial client interview described in Chapter 6 between Katherine Baranski and the legal team—attorney Allen Gilmore and paralegal Elena Lopez. Attorney Gilmore will need to prepare a list of questions and will ask most of the questions during the interview. Paralegal Lopez will take notes during the interview, provide the retainer-agreement and release forms, and schedule the follow-up interview. Change roles if time allows.

▨ USING INTERNET RESOURCES

1. Access the following Web site to find the Federal Rules of Evidence:

   www.law.cornell.edu/rules/fre/overview.html#1007.

   Browse through these rules and then answer the following questions:

   a How do the Federal Rules of Evidence define "relevant evidence"?

   b. Summarize the "General Rule of Competency" set forth in the these rules.

   c. Look at Rule 803, which lists several exceptions to the "Hearsay Rule." List and describe five of these exceptions.

2. KnowX.com is a public records Web site. Much of the information that can be located at this site is information that a private investigator (or a paralegal) might want to find when investigating a case. Access the site at **www.KnowX.com**. From the information contained on the home page, what can you find using KnowX.com?

   a. Click on "Locate People." What databases does KnowX.com search to find people? Is there any cost involved? If so, how much does KnowX.com charge? Click on "Start the Demo" to run the "Quick Demo." What is the result of the search?

   b. Return to the home page and select "Research Businesses." Next, click on "The Ultimate Business Finder." What databases does KnowX.com search for business information?

   c. Return to the home page and choose "Run a Background Check." What types of background checks does KnowX.com perform? What databases does it search? Is there any cost involved? If so, how much does KnowX.com charge?

   d. Return to the home page. Click on "Other Searches." Make a list of five other searches that KnowX.com can perform.

CHAPTER 8
LEGAL RESEARCH, ANALYSIS, AND WRITING

Chapter Outline

▨ INTRODUCTION ▨ PRIMARY AND SECONDARY SOURCES
▨ THE RESEARCH PROCESS ▨ FINDING AND ANALYZING CASE LAW
▨ RESEARCHING STATUTORY LAW ▨ RESEARCHING ADMINISTRATIVE LAW
▨ FINDING CONSTITUTIONAL LAW
▨ UPDATING THE LAW ▨ LEGAL WRITING

After completing this chapter, you will know:

• The difference between primary and secondary sources of law and the importance of each type of source in legal research.

• The various steps involved in the research process.

• How to find and analyze case law, statutory law, and administrative law.

• How to find constitutional law.

• How to verify that your research results are up to date.

• Some important considerations in legal writing and the types of writing tasks often undertaken by paralegals.

• How to write an internal legal memorandum.

INTRODUCTION

For many paralegals, legal research is a fascinating part of their jobs. They find it intrinsically interesting to read the actual words of a court's opinion on a legal question or the text of a statute. Additionally, they acquire a firsthand knowledge of the law and how it applies to actual people and events. Research is also a crucial part of the paralegal's job, and the ability to conduct research thoroughly yet efficiently enhances a paralegal's value to the legal team.

As a paralegal, you may be asked to perform a variety of research tasks. Some research tasks will be simple. You may be asked to locate and copy a court case, for example. Other research tasks may take days or even weeks to complete. In almost all but the simplest of research tasks, legal research overlaps extensively with legal analysis, which is covered later in this chapter. To find relevant case law, for example, you need to be able to analyze the cases you find to ensure that they are indeed relevant. Keep in mind that the two processes, research and analysis, are closely related.

Many paralegals now conduct research without even entering a law library. Computerized legal services such as Westlaw® and Lexis® allow legal professionals to find the text of cases, statutes, and other legal documents without leaving their desks. As you will read in Chapter 9, these and an abundance of other sources are now available online. An increasing number of law firms today are also purchasing reference materials on CD-ROMs. To a great extent, how you do your research—that is, whether you conduct research online or in a law library—will depend on your employer and the computer facilities available to you. In some workplaces, paralegals are expected to conduct much of their research using computerized legal services or other online sources. In other workplaces, paralegals may be asked to do the bulk of their legal research using printed legal sources in law libraries.

Regardless of whether legal research is conducted online or in a law library, it is essential to know what sources to consult for different types of information. You will learn about these sources in this chapter. You will also learn how to make sure that the law you find is up to date and still "good law." Legal research also involves legal writing. When you complete a research assignment, for example, you will need to summarize your results in writing. As a paralegal, you will also be expected to draft legal correspondence and other documents. Because legal writing is also an important part of paralegal work, we conclude the chapter with a discussion of that subject.

PRIMARY AND SECONDARY SOURCES

Generally, research sources fall into two broad categories—primary sources and secondary sources. Printed decisions of the various courts in the United States, statutes enacted by legislative bodies, rules and regulations created by administrative agencies, presidential orders, and generally any documents that *establish* the law are **primary sources** of law. **Secondary sources** of law consist of books and articles that summarize, systematize, compile, or otherwise interpret the law. Legal encyclopedias, which summarize the law, are secondary sources of law.

Normally, researchers in any field or profession begin their research with secondary sources. Secondary sources are often referred to as *finding tools*, because they help the researcher to find primary sources on the topics they are researching and to learn how those sources have been interpreted by others. If you are asked to research case law on a certain issue, you should do likewise. You should first refer to secondary sources to learn about the issue and find relevant primary

Primary Source
In legal research, a document that establishes the law on a particular issue, such as a case decision, legislative act, administrative rule, or presidential order.

Secondary Source
In legal research, any publication that indexes, summarizes, or interprets the law, such as a legal encyclopedia, a treatise, or an article in a law review.

sources concerning it. Then you can go to the primary sources themselves (such as statutes or court cases) to research the established law on the issue.

In the following sections, you will read about the primary and secondary sources that are most frequently used in researching case law, statutory law and legislative history, administrative law, and constitutional law.

THE RESEARCH PROCESS

Any research project normally involves the following five steps:

- Defining the issue(s) to be researched.
- Determining the goal of the research project.
- Consulting relevant secondary sources.
- Researching relevant primary sources.
- Synthesizing and summarizing research results.

To illustrate how you would follow the first two steps when researching case law, we present a hypothetical case. The case involves one of your firm's clients, Trent Hoffman, who is suing Better Homes Store for negligence. During the initial client interview, Hoffman explained to you and your supervising attorney that he had gone to the store to purchase a large mirror. As he was leaving the store through the store's side entrance, carrying the bulky mirror, he ran into a large pole just outside the door. He did not see the pole because the mirror blocked his view. On hitting the pole, the mirror broke, and a piece of glass entered Hoffman's left eye, causing permanent loss of eyesight in that eye. Hoffman claims that the store was negligent in placing a pole so close to the exit and is suing the store for $3 million in damages.

After undertaking a preliminary investigation into the matter and obtaining evidence supporting Hoffman's account of the facts, your supervising attorney asks you to do some research. Your job is to research case law to find other cases with similar fact patterns and see how the courts decided the issue in those cases.

Defining the Issue

Before you consult any source, primary or secondary, you must know the legal issue that needs to be researched. Your first task will be to examine closely the facts of Hoffman's case to determine the nature of the legal issue involved. Based on Hoffman's description of the factual circumstances (verified through your preliminary investigation) and on his allegation that Better Homes Store should not have placed a pole just outside one of the store's entrances, you know that the legal issue relates to the tort of negligence—the failure to exercise reasonable care. As a starting point, you should therefore review what you know about negligence theory.

Determining Your Research Goals

Your next step is to determine your research goals. Remember that you are working on behalf of a client, who is paying for your services. Your overall goal is thus to find legal support for Hoffman's claim. To achieve this goal, you will want to do two things: find cases on point and cases that are mandatory authorities. Depending on what you find, you may also need to look for persuasive authorities.

DEVELOPING PARALEGAL SKILLS
Defining the Issues to Be Researched

Federal government agents observed Bernie Berriman in his parked car talking on his cellular phone. Later, other cars were seen driving up to Bernie's car and stopping. The drivers received brown paper bags in exchange for money. Bernie was questioned, and his car was searched. Cocaine was found in the car. He was arrested for transporting and distributing cocaine, and the police took his car and cellular phone. Bernie's lawyer is arguing that the government agents did not have the authority to require Bernie to forfeit his car and cellular phone. Natalie Martin, a legal assistant with the U.S. attorney's office, has been assigned the task of researching the federal statutes and cases on this issue.

Before Natalie can begin her research project, she must thoroughly review the case to determine what specific issues need to be researched. Using a checklist method that she learned in school, she breaks the facts of

the case down into five categories and inserts the relevant facts from her assignment:

- Parties: Who are the people involved in the action or lawsuit?
- Places and Things: Where did the events take place, and what items are involved in the action or lawsuit?
- Basis of Action or Issue: What is the legal claim or issue involved in the action or lawsuit?
- Defenses: What is the legal reason why the accused should not be held responsible?
- Relief Sought: What is the legal remedy or penalty sought in the case?

Now Natalie is ready to go to the library and begin her research.

CASES ON POINT. One of your research goals is to find a case (or cases) on point in which the court held for the plaintiff. A **case on point** is a previous case involving fact patterns and legal issues that are similar to those in a case that has not yet been decided by a court. The ideal case on point, of course, would be a case in which all four elements of a case (the parties, the circumstances, the legal issues involved, and the remedies sought by the plaintiff) are very similar. Such a case is called a **case on "all fours."**[1]

MANDATORY AUTHORITIES. In researching Hoffman's case, another goal is to find cases (on point or on "all fours") that are also mandatory authorities. A **mandatory authority** is any authority that the court must rely on in its determination of the issue. A mandatory authority may be a statute, regulation, or constitution that governs the issue, or it may be a previously decided court case that is controlling in your jurisdiction. For a case to serve as a mandatory authority, it must be on point and decided by a superior court. A lower court is bound to follow the decisions set forth by a higher court in the same jurisdiction. An appellate court's decision in a case involving facts and issues similar to a case brought in a trial court in the same jurisdiction would thus be a mandatory authority—the trial court would be bound to follow the appellate court's decision on the issue. A higher court is never required to follow an opinion written by a lower court in the same jurisdiction, however.

Case on Point
A case involving factual circumstances and issues that are similar to a case before the court.

Case on "All Fours"
A case in which all four elements of a case (the parties, the circumstances, the legal issues involved, and the remedies sought by the plaintiff) are very similar.

Mandatory Authority
Any source of law that a court must follow when deciding a case. Mandatory authorities include constitutions, statutes, and regulations that govern the issue before the court, and court decisions made by a superior court in the jurisdiction.

---

1. Some scholars maintain that this phrase originated from the Latin adage that "nothing similar is identical unless it runs on all four feet."

State courts have the final say on state law, and federal courts have the final say on federal law. Thus, except in deciding an issue that involves federal law, state courts do not have to follow the decisions of federal courts. In deciding issues that involve federal law, however, state courts must abide by the decisions of the United States Supreme Court.

 When you are performing research, look for cases on point decided by the highest court in your jurisdiction, because those cases carry the most weight.

Persuasive Authority
Any legal authority, or source of law, that a court may look to for guidance but on which it need not rely in making its decision. Persuasive authorities include cases from other jurisdictions and secondary sources of law, such as scholarly treatises.

PERSUASIVE AUTHORITIES.   A **persuasive authority** is not binding on a court. In other words, the court is not required to follow that authority in making its decision. Examples of persuasive authorities are (1) prior court opinions of other jurisdictions, which, although they are not binding, may be suggestive as to how a particular case should be decided; (2) legal periodicals, such as law reviews, in which the issue at hand is discussed by legal scholars; (3) encyclopedias summarizing legal principles or concepts relating to a particular issue; and (4) legal dictionaries that describe how the law has been applied in the past.

Often, a court refers to persuasive authorities when deciding a *case of first impression*, which is a case involving an issue that has never been addressed by that court before. For example, if in your research of Hoffman's claim you find that no similar cases have ever reached a higher court in your jurisdiction, you would look for similar cases decided by courts in other jurisdictions. If courts in other jurisdictions have faced a similar issue, the court may be guided by those other courts' decisions when deciding Hoffman's case. Your supervising attorney will want to know about these persuasive authorities so that he can present them to the court for consideration.

Consulting Secondary Sources

In researching the Hoffman issue, your next step will be to consult secondary sources of law to learn more about negligence theory and how negligence theory applies to the factual circumstances in Hoffman's case. You will also want to define more precisely the legal issue that needs to be researched and find references to relevant cases or other primary sources relating to that issue. The secondary sources described below will help you accomplish these aims.

LEGAL ENCYCLOPEDIAS.   Legal encyclopedias cover topics of law in a general manner. They explain subjects, define terms, and provide detailed summaries of legal concepts and rules. They are also helpful in finding primary sources of authority. The two major legal encyclopedias are *Corpus Juris Secundum (C.J.S.)*, published by West Group, and *American Jurisprudence 2d* (Am.Jur.2d)—"2d" means second edition—published by the Lawyers Cooperative Publishing Company, which is now a part of West Group. Each of these encyclopedias divides the law into more than four hundred topics. The legal discussions in these encyclopedias are valuable for the researcher because they provide both broad statements of accepted law and extensive footnotes to other legal sources, both primary and secondary.

Another helpful secondary source is *Words and Phrases,* a forty-six-volume encyclopedia of definitions and interpretations of legal terms and phrases published by West Group. The words and phrases covered are arranged in alphabetical order, and each word or phrase is followed by brief summary statements from federal or state court decisions in which that word or phrase has been interpreted or defined.

In researching Hoffman's claim, you could review the topic of *negligence* in a legal encyclopedia to learn more about the issue you are researching. The encyclopedia would also discuss the leading cases relating to that issue. A good starting point might be to look in *Words and Phrases* to find out how various courts have defined *negligence*. Part of the entry for this term is shown in Exhibit 8.1 on the next page.

Some states also have encyclopedias, such as *Texas Jurisprudence 3d*. A less technical reference is *The Guide to American Law: Everyone's Legal Encyclopedia*, which is published by West Group.

DIGESTS.   In addition to legal encyclopedias, digests are helpful finding tools for the legal researcher. **Digests** are indexes to American case law. There are digests for both the federal and state court systems. Digests consist primarily of case summaries, which are arranged topically, from each jurisdiction. The advantage of a digest is that researchers can review cases from, for example, all appellate courts for a ten-year period. The *American Digest System,* published by West Group, provides a master index of all cases published in West's National Reporter System (to be discussed later). The *American Digest System* includes the *Decennial Digest Series,* which is published every ten years,[2] and the *General Digest Series,* which is an annual publication.

There are other digests for specific jurisdictions and specialized interest areas. The *Lawyers' Edition of the Digest of the Supreme Court Reports* is published by West Group and is similar in organizational style to the West digests. The digest provides cross-references to the *American Law Reports* and other legal publications. Other publishers also publish state-specific digests, such as Callahan's *Michigan Digest.*

ANNOTATIONS: *AMERICAN LAW REPORTS.*   The *American Law Reports (A.L.R.)* and *American Law Reports Federal (A.L.R. Federal)*, published by West Group, are also useful resources for the legal researcher. An *A.L.R.* volume is shown in Exhibit 8.2 on page 259. These reports are multivolume sets that present the full text of selected cases in numerous areas of the law. They are helpful in finding cases from jurisdictions throughout the country with similar factual and legal issues. There are five different series of *American Law Reports,* covering case law since 1919. The fifth series *(A.L.R.5th)* is the current edition. *A.L.R. Federal*, the current edition for coverage of federal decisions, began in 1969.

The cases presented in these reporters are followed by **annotations**. In the *A.L.R.*, annotations consist of articles that focus on specific issues; these reports can therefore be an excellent source to turn to in researching case law. The annotations also present an overview of the specific area of law addressed by the case, indicate current trends in that area, and refer to other case law relating to the specific issue or issues.

TREATISES.   Law **treatises** are written by individuals such as law professors, legal scholars, and practicing attorneys. Law treatises are commentaries that summarize, interpret, or evaluate different areas of substantive and procedural law. Some treatises are published in multivolume sets, and others are contained in a single book. Paralegals who seek to familiarize themselves with a particular area of the law, such as torts or contracts, should review one of the many available hornbooks (single-volume treatises on a specific legal subject). For example, in researching the issue in Trent Hoffman's negligence case, you might want to locate

Digest
A compilation in which brief statements regarding court cases are arranged by subject and subdivided by jurisdiction and court.

Annotation
A brief comment, an explanation of a legal point, or a case summary found in a case digest or other legal source.

Treatise
In legal research, a text that provides a systematic, detailed, and scholarly review of a particular legal subject.

---

2. Because of the increased number of reported cases, West Group now publishes the "Decennial" digest every five years.

EXHIBIT 8.1
Excerpt from
Words and Phrases

Reproduced with permission of West Group.

NEGLIGENCE

Estoppel by Negligence
Fault
General Negligence
Gross Negligence
Hazardous Negligence
Heedlessness
High Degree of Negligence
Homicide by Negligence
Imputed Contributory Negligence
Imputed Negligence
Incurred Without Fault or Negligence
Independent Act of Negligence
Independent Negligence
Injury Resulting from Negligence
Insulated Negligence
Intentional Negligence
Joint Negligence
Legal Negligence
Liability Created by Law
Marine Cause
Mistake, Error or Negligence
Mutual Contributory Negligence
Negligent
Notice of Negligence
Nuisance
Nuisance Dependent Upon Negligence
Ordinary Care
Ordinary Negligence
Otherwise
Persistent Negligence
Preponderance
Presumption of Negligence
Prima Facie Case of Negligence
Prima Facie Negligence
Prior Negligence
Proof of Negligence
Proximate Contributory Negligence
Reckless; Recklessly; Recklessness
Separate Negligence
Simple Negligence
Situation Created by Actor's Negligence
Slight Negligence
Specific Negligence
Subsequent Negligence
Supervening Negligence
Trespass
Wanton Negligence
Wantonness
Willful and Intentional Negligence
Willful Negligence
Willfulness
Without Negligence

In general

"Negligence", in absence of statute, is defined as the doing of that thing which a reasonably prudent person would not have

In general—Cont'd

done, or the failure to do that thing which a reasonably prudent person would have done, in like or similar circumstances. Biddle v. Mazzocco, Or., 284 P.2d 364, 368.

"Negligence" is a departure from the normal or what should be the normal, and is a failure to conform to standard of what a reasonably prudent man would ordinarily have done under the circumstances, or is doing what such man would not have done under the circumstances. Moran v. Pittsburgh-Des Moines Steel Co., D.C.Pa., 86 F. Supp. 255, 266.

"Negligence" being failure to do that which ordinarily prudent man would do or doing of that which such a man would not do under same circumstances, an ordinary custom, while relevant and admissible in evidence of negligence, is not conclusive thereof, especially where it is clearly a careless or dangerous custom. Tite v. Omaha Coliseum Corp., 12 N.W.2d 90, 94, 144 Neb. 22, 149 A.L.R. 1164.

Whether or not an act or omission is "negligence" seems to be determined by what under like circumstances would men of ordinary prudence have done. Cleveland, C., C. & St. L. R. Co. v. Ivins, Ohio, 12 O.C.D. 570.

"Negligence" means simply the want of ordinary care under the circumstances surrounding that particular case and the transaction in question, and "negligently" simply means doing an act in such a manner that it lacks the care which men of ordinary prudence and foresight use in their everyday affairs of life under the same or similar circumstances. Smillie v. Cleveland Ry., Ohio, 31 O.C.D. 323, 325, 20 Cir.Ct.R.,N.S., 302.

"Negligence" is the failure to do what a reasonable and prudent man would ordinarily have done under circumstances of situation or doing what such a person, under existing circumstances, would not have done. Judt v. Reinhardt Transfer Co., 17 Ohio Supp. 105, 107, 32 O.O. 161.

By "negligence" is meant negligence of such character that in the discretion of the court, the defendant should have inflicted upon him the punative penalties of having his license suspended and that the public required such protection. Com. v. Galley, 17 Som. 54.

"Negligence" is a failure to use ordinary care, that is, such care as persons of ordinary prudence are accustomed to exercise

524

the learned treatise *Prosser and Keeton on the Law of Torts*, Fifth Edition, which is included in West's Hornbook Series. This text was written by distinguished lawyers from leading law schools and is frequently referred to by professionals, including court judges, as a (persuasive) authority on tort principles and doctrines.

RESTATEMENTS OF THE LAW. Other sources of general background information are the *Restatements of the Law*, produced by the American Law Institute (ALI), an organization established in 1923 by a group of prominent judges, law professors, and practicing attorneys. The *Restatements* present an overview of the basic principles of the common law in ten specific fields: agency law, conflict of laws, contracts, foreign relations law, judgments, property, restitution, security, torts, and trusts. Most of the *Restatements* have been updated by the issuance of second or third editions. The *Restatements* are often abbreviated when referred to by legal professionals. The *Restatement of the Law of Torts*, Second Edition, is often referred to as the *Restatement (Second) of the Law of Torts*, or, more simply, as the *Restatement (Second) of Torts*. The ALI is currently in the process of creating a new edition of the *Restatement of the Law of Torts*. To date, one volume has been completed, covering product liability. Exhibit 8.3 on next page shows a photograph of this volume.

Restatements are helpful resources when researching issues involving common law doctrines, such as negligence. Each section in the *Restatements* contains a statement of the principles of law that are generally accepted by the courts and/or embodied in statutes on the topic, followed by a discussion of these principles. The *Restatements* are useful research tools because they present particular cases as examples and also discuss variations on the general propositions of the law. Although the *Restatements* are *not* primary sources of law and therefore are not binding on the courts, they are highly respected secondary sources of law and are often referred to by the courts as the basis for their decisions.

LEGAL PERIODICALS. Legal periodicals, such as law reviews, are also important secondary sources of law. The contents of most law reviews include (1) commentaries about the law, usually written by law professors, judges, or practicing attorneys; (2) reviews of books recently written about the law; (3) comments by student writers explaining the meaning of selected recent cases; and (4) student notes on specific topics of law. Almost every accredited law school publishes a law review. The *Harvard Law Review* is one of the most prestigious law reviews. There are many more of equal quality. In addition to the general law reviews, many law schools also publish law journals on specific topics, such as environmental law or product liability.

To locate law-review articles relevant to your research topic, you can begin by looking in the subject index of a guide to legal periodicals. Every law library provides periodical guides, and if you are unfamiliar with them, ask the reference librarian for assistance.

FINDING AND ANALYZING CASE LAW

The primary sources of case law are, of course, the cases themselves. Once you have learned what cases are relevant to the issue that you are researching, you need to find the cases and examine the exact words of the court opinions.

Assume, for example, that in researching the issue in Hoffman's case, you learn that your state's supreme court, a few years ago, issued a decision on a case with a very similar fact pattern. In that case, the state supreme court upheld a lower court's judgment that a retail business owner had to pay extensive damages to a customer who was injured on the store's premises. You know that the state supreme court's decision is a mandatory authority, and to your knowledge, the decision has not been overruled or modified. Therefore, the case will likely provide weighty support to your attorney's arguments in support of Hoffman's claim. At this point, however, you have only read *about* the case in secondary sources.

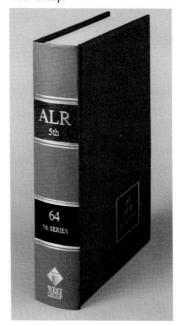

EXHIBIT 8.2
American Law Reports

Reproduced with permission of West Group.

On the Web
You can learn more about the American Law Institute (ALI) and its publications, including information on which *Restatements of the Law* are in the process of being revised, by accessing the ALI's Web site at **www.ali.org.**

EXHIBIT 8.3
***Restatement (Third)
of Torts: Products Liability***

Reproduced with permission of
West Group.

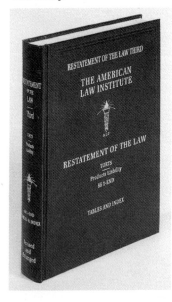

Reporter
A publication in which court cases
are published, or reported.

To locate the case itself and make sure that it is applicable, you need to understand the case reporting system and the legal "shorthand" employed in referencing court cases.

Finding Case Law

New York and a few other states publish selected opinions of their trial courts, but most state trial court decisions are not published. Decisions from the state trial courts are usually just filed in the office of the clerk of the court, where they are available for public inspection. Written decisions of the appellate courts, however, are usually published and distributed. The reported appellate decisions are published—in chronological order by date of decision—in **reporters,** the term generally given to any publication that "reports" (publishes) cases decided by the courts.

STATE COURT DECISIONS.   State appellate court decisions are found in the reports of that particular state. State court decisions are usually published in both official and unofficial reporters. The official reports are designated as such by the state legislature, are issued by the individual courts, and serve as the authoritative texts of case decisions. A few of the states, including New York and California, have more than one official state reporter.

WEST'S NATIONAL REPORTER SYSTEM.   Additionally, state court opinions appear in regional units of the National Reporter System, published by West Group. Most libraries have the West reporters because they report cases more quickly and are distributed more widely than the state-published reports. In fact, many states have eliminated their own reporters in favor of West's National Reporter System.

The National Reporter System divides the states into the following geographical areas: *Atlantic* (A. or A.2d), *South Eastern* (S.E. or S.E.2d), *South Western* (S.W. or S.W.2d), *North Western* (N.W. or N.W.2d), *North Eastern* (N.E. or N.E.2d), *Southern* (So. or So.2d), and *Pacific* (P. or P.2d). Note that the *2d* in the preceding abbrevia-

---

ETHICAL CONCERN
Avoiding Plagiarism

P lagiarism—copying the exact, or nearly exact, words of another without acknowledging the author of those words—may constitute a violation of federal copyright law. You should realize, though, that it is possible to plagiarize another's words *unintentionally*. Suppose, for example, that you are taking notes from a legal treatise, such as a treatise on the law of torts, and you copy several paragraphs word for word for your future reference. You don't enclose the paragraphs in quotation marks because you know you will remember that those are not your words but the words of the treatise's authors. A week or so later, you are preparing a brief and, referring to your notes, you include those paragraphs, assuming that they are your own version of what the authors said in the treatise. In short, you have plagiarized a substantial portion of another's copyrighted work without even being aware of it. To ensure that your employer will not face a lawsuit for copyright infringement, always remember to include quotation marks (and the exact source of the quoted material) when copying another's words.

Litigation Paralegal

PAMELA JO RAYBOURN *serves as a legal assistant in the areas of product liability, business and employment litigation, and antitrust. Her work includes undertaking factual investigations, drafting and responding to discovery requests (including motion practice), and organizing large documents. She has extensive experience in preparing for and assisting at trial, arbitration, and mediation. She is also involved in supervising and training support staff.*

Raybourn has served as chair of NFPA's Ethics Committee since 1998, has written numerous articles for newsletters published by the Oregon State Bar Association and the Oregon Legal Assistants Association, and was a PACE exam preparer for NFPA from 1996 to 1997.

What do you like best about your work?

"I like the responsibility of searching for the factual information that makes or breaks the case. I like digging and asking questions to gather all the information necessary to prepare the case. I also enjoy working with the employees of our corporate clients. It is easy to zealously represent a client when you know the client has integrity and strong business ethics."

What is the greatest challenge that you face in your area of work?

"It doesn't help the client if you complete the assignment and it sits on the attorney's desk for weeks. I find myself in the role of a prodder, checking to see that the work gets off the attorney's desk and out the door."

What advice do you have for would-be paralegals in your area of work?

"Get a well-rounded education in all areas of law. Because litigation can involve any legal theory, I have found it necessary to understand the legal principles involved in probate and estates, real estate, contracts, patents, bankruptcy, business organizations, and product liability in addition to understanding tort and negligence theory. The better you understand a legal theory, the more able you are to review documents and locate facts to support that theory."

"There is no such thing as a dumb question."

What are some tips for success as a paralegal in your area of work?

"Ask questions. There is no such thing as a dumb question. You will exert less wasted energy and effort if you ask a question to be sure you understand the assignment. Sometimes I go back to the attorney more than once to ensure that I am on the right track. Sometimes a review of documents will lead to other questions. If you ask questions, you can direct your efforts to efficiently completing the assignment. This will benefit you as well as the client."

tions refers to *Second Series*. In the near future, the designation *3d,* for *Third Series,* will be used for some of the reporters. The states included in each of these regional divisions are indicated in Exhibit 8.4 on the next page. Note that the names of the areas may not match the commonly used geographical terms. For example, the *North Western* reporter includes North Dakota, Minnesota, and other states located in the "old" Northwest—the Northwest in the United States in an earlier era.

EXHIBIT 8.4
National Reporter System—Regional and Federal

Regional Reporters	Coverage Beginning	Coverage
Atlantic Reporter (A. or A.2d)	1885	Connecticut, Delaware, Maine, Maryland, New Hampshire, New Jersey, Pennsylvania, Rhode Island, Vermont, and District of Columbia.
North Eastern Reporter (N.E. or N.E.2d)	1885	Illinois, Indiana, Massachusetts, New York, and Ohio.
North Western Reporter (N.W. or N.W.2d)	1879	Iowa, Michigan, Minnesota, Nebraska, North Dakota, South Dakota, and Wisconsin.
Pacific Reporter (P. or P.2d)	1883	Alaska, Arizona, California, Colorado, Hawaii, Idaho, Kansas, Montana, Nevada, New Mexico, Oklahoma, Oregon, Utah, Washington, and Wyoming.
South Eastern Reporter (S.E. or S.E.2d)	1887	Georgia, North Carolina, South Carolina, Virginia, and West Virginia.
South Western Reporter (S.W. or S.W.2d)	1886	Arkansas, Kentucky, Missouri, Tennessee, and Texas.
Southern Reporter (So. or So.2d)	1887	Alabama, Florida, Louisiana, and Mississippi.
Federal Reporters		
Federal Reporter (F., F.2d, or F. 3d)	1880	U.S. Circuit Court from 1880 to 1912; U.S. Commerce Court from 1911 to 1913; U.S. District Courts from 1880 to 1932; U.S. Court of Claims (now called U.S. Court of Federal Claims) from 1929 to 1932 and since 1960; U.S. Court of Appeals since 1891; U.S. Court of Customs and Patent Appeals since 1929; and U.S. Emergency Court of Appeals since 1943.
Federal Supplement (F.Supp.)	1932	U.S. Court of Claims from 1932 to 1960; U.S. District Courts since 1932; and U.S. Customs Court since 1956.
Federal Rules Decisions (F.R.D.)	1939	U.S. District Courts involving the Federal Rules of Civil Procedure since 1939 and Federal Rules of Criminal Procedure since 1946.
Supreme Court Reporter (S.Ct.)	1882	U.S. Supreme Court since the October term of 1882.
Bankruptcy Reporter (Bankr.)	1980	Bankruptcy decisions of U.S. Bankruptcy Courts, U.S. District Courts, U.S. Courts of Appeals, and U.S. Supreme Court.
Military Justice Reporter (M.J.)	1978	U.S. Court of Military Appeals and Courts of Military Review for the Army, Navy, Air Force, and Coast Guard.

NATIONAL-REPORTER-SYSTEM-MAP

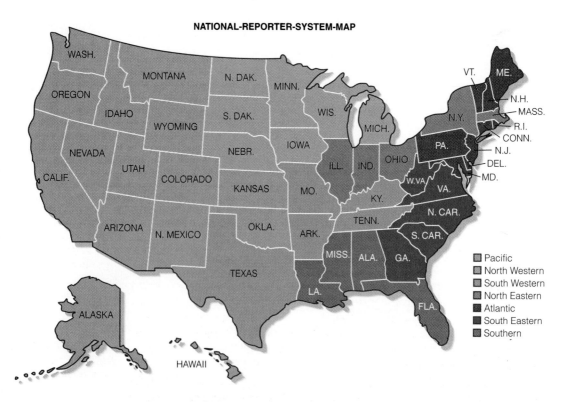

Legend:
- Pacific
- North Western
- South Western
- North Eastern
- Atlantic
- South Eastern
- Southern

DEVELOPING PARALEGAL SKILLS

Understanding Case Citations

Wendy Morgan is a legal secretary who is studying to become a paralegal. She has just read a chapter in her textbook on legal research and is studying the section on case citations. She shows a citation to Janet Honner, a legal assistant at the office, and asks Janet to go over the citation with her.

The name of the case is *O'Driscoll v. Hercules, Inc.,* and its citation is 55 F.3d 176 (10th Cir. 1999). Janet tells Wendy that the names in the case are the names of the parties to the lawsuit. Next is the volume number, which is 55. It is imprinted on the outside binding of the book or reporter in which the case is printed. The name, or abbreviation, of the reporter is F.3d, which stands for *West's Federal Reporter, Third Series.* The next number, 176, is the page number of volume 55 on which the case begins. The information in parentheses shows that the U.S. Court of Appeals for the Tenth Circuit decided the case in 1999. Wendy checks her understanding by reviewing the parts of another case citation.

Janet then explains to Wendy that citations for some cases (although not the *O'Driscoll* case) include a second

citation as well. The second citation, which is referred to as a parallel citation, indicates where the case can be found in a different reporter.

TIPS FOR UNDERSTANDING A CASE CITATION

- The case name usually appears first and includes the names of the parties to the lawsuit.
- The case name is either italicized or underlined.
- The first number is the volume number of the reporter in which the case appears.
- The reporter abbreviation is usually some combination of letters and/or numbers.
- The reporter abbreviation is followed by the page number on which the case begins.
- The material in parentheses contains at least the year that the court decided the case and, in some instances, the abbreviation of the name of the court that made the decision.

CITATION FORMAT. After an appellate decision has been published, it is normally referred to *(cited)* by the name of the case (often called the *style* of the case) and the volume number, abbreviated name, and page number of each reporter in which the case has been published. This information is included in what is called the **citation.** When more than one reporter contains the text of the same case, a reference to the other reporter or reporters in which the case can be found—called a **parallel citation**—is also included. The first citation will be to the state's official reporter (if different from West's National Reporter System). Note that in every citation to a reporter, the number preceding the abbreviated name of the reporter will be the volume number, and the first number following it will be the page number of the first page of the case.

To illustrate how to find case law from citations, suppose you want to find the following case: *Cirrincione v. Johnson,*184 Ill. 2d 109, 703 N.E. 2d 67 (1998). You can see that the opinion in this case may be found in volume 184 of the official *Illinois Reports, Second Series,* on page 109. The parallel citation is to volume 703 of West's *North Eastern Reporter, Second Series*, page 67. Exhibit 8.5, beginning on the next page, further illustrates how to read citations to state and federal court decisions, as well as to statutory law.

When conducting legal research, you need to include in your research notes the citations to the cases or other legal sources that you have consulted, quoted, or want to refer to in a written summary of your research results. Several guides have been published on how to cite legal sources. The most widely used guide is a book

Citation
In case law, a reference to the volume number, name, and page number of the reporter in which a case can be found. In statutory and administrative law, a reference to the title number, name, and section of the code in which a statute or regulation can be found.

Parallel Citation
A second (or third) citation to another case reporter in which a case has been published. When a case is published in more than one reporter, each citation is a parallel citation to the other(s).

EXHIBIT 8.5
How to Read Case Citations

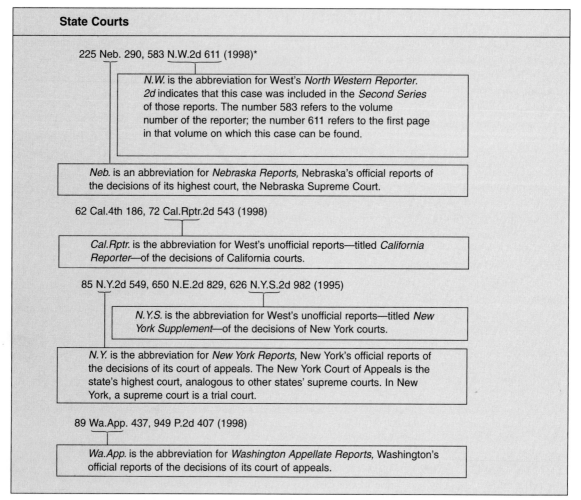

State Courts

225 Neb. 290, 583 N.W.2d 611 (1998)*

> *N.W.* is the abbreviation for West's *North Western Reporter.* *2d* indicates that this case was included in the *Second Series* of those reports. The number 583 refers to the volume number of the reporter; the number 611 refers to the first page in that volume on which this case can be found.

> *Neb.* is an abbreviation for *Nebraska Reports,* Nebraska's official reports of the decisions of its highest court, the Nebraska Supreme Court.

62 Cal.4th 186, 72 Cal.Rptr.2d 543 (1998)

> *Cal.Rptr.* is the abbreviation for West's unofficial reports—titled *California Reporter*—of the decisions of California courts.

85 N.Y.2d 549, 650 N.E.2d 829, 626 N.Y.S.2d 982 (1995)

> *N.Y.S.* is the abbreviation for West's unofficial reports—titled *New York Supplement*—of the decisions of New York courts.

> *N.Y.* is the abbreviation for *New York Reports,* New York's official reports of the decisions of its court of appeals. The New York Court of Appeals is the state's highest court, analogous to other states' supreme courts. In New York, a supreme court is a trial court.

89 Wa.App. 437, 949 P.2d 407 (1998)

> *Wa.App.* is the abbreviation for *Washington Appellate Reports,* Washington's official reports of the decisions of its court of appeals.

*The case names have been deleted from these citations to emphasize the publications. It should be kept in mind, however, that the name of a case is as important as the specific page numbers in the volumes in which it is found. If a citation is incorrect, the correct citation may be found in a publication's index of case names. The date of a case is also important because, in addition to providing a check on error in citations, the value of a recent case as an authority is likely to be greater than that of earlier cases.

On the Web
To find Supreme Court opinions and opinions issued by the federal appellate courts, a good starting point is FindLaw's site at **www.findlaw.com.**

entitled *The Bluebook: A Uniform System of Citation,* which is published by the Harvard Law Review Association. This book explains the proper format for citing cases, statutes, constitutions, regulations, and other legal sources. It is a good idea to memorize the basic format for citations to cases and statutory law because these legal sources are frequently cited in legal writing. Another popular guide is a small booklet entitled *The University of Chicago Manual of Legal Citation.*

FEDERAL COURT DECISIONS.   Court decisions from the U.S. district courts (federal trial courts) are published in West's *Federal Supplement* (F.Supp.), and opinions from the circuit courts of appeals are reported in West's *Federal Reporter* (F., F.2d, or F.3d). These are both unofficial reporters (there are no official reporters for these courts). Both the *Federal Reporter* and the *Federal Supplement* incorporate decisions from specialized federal courts. West also publishes separate reporters, such as its

EXHIBIT 8.5
How to Read Case Citations—Continued

Federal Courts

___ U.S. ___, 118 S.Ct. 2196, 141 L.Ed.2d 540 (1998)

> *L.Ed.* is an abbreviation for *Lawyers' Edition of the Supreme Court Reports,* an unofficial edition of decisions of the United States Supreme Court.

> *S.Ct.* is the abbreviation for West's unofficial reports—titled *Supreme Court Reporter*—of United States Supreme Court decisions.

> *U.S.* is the abbreviation for *United States Reports,* the official edition of the decisions of the United States Supreme Court. Volume and page numbers are not included in this citation because they have not yet been assigned.

Statutory and Other Citations

15 U.S.C. Section 1262(e)

> *U.S.C.* denotes *United States Code,* the codification of *United States Statutes at Large.* The number 15 refers to the statute's U.S.C. title number and 1262 to its section number within that title. The letter e refers to a subsection within the section.

UCC 2–206(1)(a)

> *UCC* is an abbreviation for *Uniform Commercial Code.* The first number 2 is a reference to an article of the UCC and 206 to a section within that article. The number 1 refers to a subsection within the section and the letter a to a subdivision within the subsection.

Restatement (Second) of Torts, Section 568

> *Restatement (Second) of Torts* refers to the second edition of the American Law Institute's *Restatement of the Law of Torts.* The number 568 refers to a specific section.

16 C.F.R. Section 453.2

> *C.F.R.* is an abbreviation for *Code of Federal Regulations,* a compilation of federal administrative regulations. The number 16 is a reference to the regulation's title number and 453.2 to a specific section within that title.

Bankruptcy Reporter, that contain decisions in certain specialized fields under federal law.

UNITED STATES SUPREME COURT DECISIONS.   Opinions from the United States Supreme Court are published in several reporters. The *United States Reports* (U.S.), published by the federal government, is the official edition of all decisions of the United States Supreme Court for which there are written opinions.

Syllabus
A brief summary of the holding and legal principles involved in a reported case, which is followed by the court's official opinion.

Headnote
A note near the beginning of a reported case summarizing the court's ruling on an issue.

Supreme Court cases are also published in West Group's *Supreme Court Reporter* (S.Ct.). West's *Supreme Court Reporter,* which is an unofficial edition of Supreme Court opinions, includes a brief **syllabus** (which summarizes the case) and **headnotes** (which summarize points of law or legal principles addressed by the case and the court's ruling on those issues) prepared by West Group editors.

Another unofficial edition of Supreme Court decisions is the *Lawyers' Edition of the Supreme Court Reports* (L.Ed.), published by West Group. Each case published in the *Lawyers' Edition, Second Series,* is preceded by a full summary of the case and a detailed discussion of selected cases of special interest to the legal profession. Also, the *Lawyers' Edition* is the only reporter of Supreme Court opinions that provides summaries of the briefs presented by counsel.

Virtually all Supreme Court decisions, as well as the text of many treaties and statutes, are now available in electronic format on the Internet. Supreme Court opinions are available on the Internet within minutes after their release. Thus, if you have access to the Internet and want to read the text of a Supreme Court decision made yesterday or even just hours ago, you may be able to view it on your computer screen.

Analyzing Case Law

One of the difficulties that all legal professionals face in analyzing case law is the sheer length and complexity of some court opinions. While certain court opinions may be only two or three pages in length, others can occupy hundreds of pages. Understanding the components of a case—that is, the basic format in which cases are presented—can simplify your task of reading and analyzing case law. You will find that over time, as you acquire experience, reading and analyzing cases becomes easier.

THE COMPONENTS OF A CASE.   Reported cases contain much more than just the court's decision. Cases have many different parts, and you should understand why each part is there and what information it communicates. The annotations on the sample court case shown in Exhibit 8.6 indicate the various components of a case.

The case presented in Exhibit 8.6 is an actual case that was decided by the United States Supreme Court in 1998. The lawsuit was initiated by Sidney Abbott, who was infected with the human immunodeficiency virus (HIV), against a dentist who refused to treat Abbott—fill a cavity—in the dental office. (The dentist offered to fill the cavity at the hospital, but Abbott refused.) In her suit, Abbott claimed that the dentist had violated the Americans with Disabilities Act (ADA) of 1990, which mandates the accommodation of persons with disabilities.

Important sections, terms, and phrases in the case are defined or discussed in the margins. You will note also that triple asterisks (* * *) and quadruple asterisks (* * * *) frequently appear in the exhibit. The triple asterisks indicate that we have deleted a few words or sentences from the opinion for the sake of readability or brevity. Quadruple asterisks mean that an entire paragraph (or more) has been omitted. Also, when the opinion cites another case or legal source, the citation to the referenced case or source has been omitted to save space and to improve readability.

CASE FORMAT.   The case presented in Exhibit 8.6 follows the typical format used in most case reporters. First, the case title, citation, and docket number are given. These are followed by the dates that the case was argued and decided, and the syllabus (in this case, prepared by the West Group editors). In the Westlaw®

On the Web
If you are interested in reading the entire opinion rendered by the United States Supreme Court in the sample case presented in Exhibit 8.6, you can access the case online at **www.findlaw.com.** Find the link to Supreme Court decisions, and then, when the link opens, click on "1998 cases." When that link opens, scroll down to *Bragdon v. Abbott* to access the case.

EXHIBIT 8.6
A Sample Court Case

Copr. © West 1999 No Claim to Orig. U.S. Govt. Works

___ U.S. ___ 118 S.Ct. 2196, 141 L.Ed.2d 540.

> The *citation.* The decision has not yet been published in the official *United States Reports,* so that parallel citation is not included here.

Randon BRAGDON, Petitioner,

v.

Sidney ABBOTT et al.

> The names set in capital letters indicate the names of the parties as they appear in the *case title,* which is *Bragdon v. Abbott.*

> The *docket number* assigned by the United States Supreme Court.

No. 97-156.

Argued March 30, 1998.

Decided June 25, 1998.

> The *dates on which the case was argued and decided.* In citing this case, you would include the year that the case was decided in parentheses after the citation(s).

> The *syllabus*—a brief summary of the issues and decisions in the case. Prepared by West Group editors.

Patient infected with the human immunodeficiency virus (HIV) brought action under the Americans with Disabilities Act (ADA) against dentist who refused to treat her in his office. The United States District Court for the District of Maine, 912 F.Supp. 580, granted summary judgment in favor of patient, and dentist appealed. The First Circuit Court of Appeals, 107 F.3d 934, affirmed. Dentist petitioned for **certiorari.** The Supreme Court, Justice Kennedy, held that * * * HIV infection is a "disability" under the ADA, even when the infection has not yet progressed to the so-called symptomatic phase, as a physical impairment which substantially limits the major life activity of reproduction * * * . **Vacated** and **remanded.**

> A Latin term (pronounced sur-shee-uh-*rah*-ree) meaning that the United States Supreme Court ordered the appellate court to send it the record of the case for review.

> Made void, nullified.

> Sent back to the trial court for further proceedings.

* * * *

Justice KENNEDY delivered the opinion of the Court.

> The *name of the justice* who authored the Supreme Court's opinion.

We address in this case the application of the Americans with Disabilities Act of 1990 (ADA) to persons infected with the human immunodeficiency virus (HIV). We granted *certiorari* to review * * * whether HIV infection is a disability under the ADA when the infection has not yet progressed to the so-called symptomatic phase * * * .

> The first paragraph of the *opinion* opens with a statement of the issue to be decided by the Court.

I

Respondent Sidney Abbott has been infected with HIV since 1986. When the incidents we recite occurred, her infection had not manifested its most serious symptoms. On September 16, 1994, she went to the office of petitioner Randon Bragdon in Bangor, Maine, for a dental appointment. She disclosed her HIV infection on the patient registration form. **Petitioner** completed a dental examination, discovered a cavity, and informed respondent of his policy against filling cavities of HIV-infected patients. He offered to perform the work at a hospital with no added fee for his services, though respondent would be responsible for the cost of using the hospital's facilities. Respondent declined.

> The *party against whom the appeal is brought.*

> The *party appealing the decision.*

EXHIBIT 8.6
A Sample Court Case—Continued

Respondent sued petitioner under * * * the ADA. * * *

* * * *

| The Court summarizes the rulings of the lower federal courts on the issue before the court. | * * * The District Court ruled in favor of [Abbott], holding that respondent's HIV infection satisfied the ADA's definition of disability. * * *

The Court of Appeals (affirmed.) It held respondent's HIV infection was a disability under the ADA, even though her infection had not yet progressed to the symptomatic stage. * * * |

| Confirmed, or ratified. |

II

| The Court cites the provision of the ADA that directly applies to the issue before the Court. | We * * * review the ruling that respondent's HIV infection constituted a disability under the ADA. The statute defines disability as:

(A) a physical or mental impairment that substantially limits one or more of the major life activities of such individual;

(B) a record of such an impairment; or

(C) being regarded as having such impairment. |

We hold respondent's HIV infection was a disability under subsection (A) of the definitional section of the statute. In light of this conclusion, we need not consider the applicability of subsections (B) or (C).

| The Court summarizes how it will proceed to analyze the issue. | Our consideration of subsection (A) of the definition proceeds in three steps. First, we consider whether respondent's HIV infection was a physical impairment. Second, we identify the life activity upon which respondent relies (reproduction and child bearing) and determine whether it constitutes a major life activity under the ADA. Third, tying the two statutory phrases together, we ask whether the impairment substantially limited the major life activity. * * * |

* * * *

1

| The Court begins the first step in its inquiry. | The first step in the inquiry under subsection (A) requires us to determine whether respondent's condition constituted a physical impairment. * * * |

* * * *

| The Court's conclusion on the first step. | In light of the immediacy with which the virus begins to damage the infected person's white blood cells and the severity of the disease, we hold it is an impairment from the moment of infection. * * * [I]nfection with HIV causes immediate abnormalities in a person's blood, and the infected person's white cell count continues to drop throughout the course of the disease, even when the attack is concentrated in the lymph nodes. In light of these facts, HIV infection must be regarded as a physiological disorder with a constant and detrimental effect on the infected person's hemic and lymphatic systems from the moment of infection. HIV infection satisfies the statutory and regulatory definition of a physical impairment during every stage of the disease. |

EXHIBIT 8.6
A Sample Court Case—Continued

2

The statute is not operative, and the definition not satisfied, unless the impairment affects a major life activity. Respondent's claim throughout this case has been that the HIV infection placed a substantial limitation on her ability to reproduce and to bear children. Given the pervasive, and invariably fatal, course of the disease, its effect on major life activities of many sorts might have been relevant to our inquiry. * * *

| The Court begins the second step in its inquiry.

From the outset, however, the case has been treated as one in which reproduction was the major life activity limited by the impairment. * * * We ask, then, whether reproduction is a major life activity.

| This is the essential question before the court in the second step of its inquiry.

We have little difficulty concluding that it is. As the Court of Appeals held, "[t]he plain meaning of the word 'major' denotes comparative importance" and "suggest[s] that the touchstone for determining an activity's inclusion under the statutory rubric is its significance." Reproduction falls well within the phrase "major life activity." Reproduction and the sexual dynamics surrounding it are central to the life process itself.

While petitioner concedes the importance of reproduction, he claims that Congress intended the ADA only to cover those aspects of a person's life which have a public, economic, or daily character. The argument founders on the statutory language. Nothing in the definition suggests that activities without a public, economic, or daily dimension may somehow be regarded as so unimportant or insignificant as to fall outside the meaning of the word "major." The breadth of the term confounds the attempt to limit its construction in this manner.

| The Court takes issue with the petitioner's argument.

* * * *

* * * Petitioner advances no credible basis for confining major life activities to those with a public, economic, or daily aspect. In the absence of any reason to reach a contrary conclusion, we agree with the Court of Appeals' determination that reproduction is a major life activity for the purposes of the ADA.

| The Court's conclusion on the second step.

3

The final element of the disability definition in subsection (A) is whether respondent's physical impairment was a substantial limit on the major life activity she asserts. * * *

| The Court begins the third and final step in its inquiry.

Our evaluation of the medical evidence leads us to conclude that respondent's infection substantially limited her ability to reproduce in two independent ways. First, a woman infected with HIV who tries to conceive a child imposes on the man a significant risk of becoming infected. * * * Second, an infected woman risks infecting her child during gestation and childbirth. * * *

| The Court's conclusion on the third step.

* * * *

The determination of the Court of Appeals that respondent's HIV infection was a disability under the ADA is affirmed. The judgment is vacated, and the case is remanded for further proceedings consistent with this opinion.

It is so ordered.

| The Court *summarizes its conclusion and gives its order* in the final portion of the opinion.

printout of this case, following the syllabus were a series of headnotes and the names of the lawyers representing the parties. We have not included these components in Exhibit 8.6 for reasons of space. The name of the judge or justice who authored the opinion in the case appears just above the opinion.

THE OPINION.   The term *opinion* is often used loosely to refer to a court case or decision. In fact, the term has a precise meaning. The formal **opinion** of the court contains the analysis and decision of the judge or judges that heard and decided the case. When researching case law, the opinion itself should receive your greatest attention. The other components of a case, including the syllabus and headnotes, are helpful guides to understanding the case, but they are not authoritative sources of law and should not be quoted or cited in your research summary.

When all of the judges unanimously agree in their legal reasoning and their decision, the opinion is deemed a *unanimous* opinion. When the opinion is not unanimous, a *majority* opinion is written, outlining the views of the majority of the judges deciding the case. There may also be a *concurring* opinion or a *dissenting* opinion. A concurring opinion is written by a judge who agrees with the majority's conclusion but who wants to either offer a different legal basis for the conclusion or shed additional light on the issue. A dissenting opinion is written by a judge who disagrees with the majority's decision. Although only the majority opinion is controlling (that is, mandatory authority for lower courts in that jurisdiction), concurrent and dissenting opinions may have future value as persuasive authorities.

THE COURT'S CONCLUSION.   In the opinion, the judges will indicate their conclusion, or decision, on the issue or issues before the court. If several issues are involved, as often happens, there may be a conclusion at the end of the discussion of each issue. Often, at the end of the opinion, the conclusions presented within the opinion will be briefly reiterated and summarized, or, if no conclusions were yet presented, they will be presented in the concluding section of the opinion.

An appellate court also specifies what the *disposition* of a case should be. If the appellate court agrees with a lower court's decision, it will *affirm* that decision, which means that the decision of the lower court remains unchanged. If the appellate court concludes that the lower court erred in its interpretation of the law, the court may *reverse* the lower court's ruling. Sometimes, if an appellate court concludes that further factual findings are necessary or that a case should be retried and a decision made that is consistent with the appellate court's conclusions of law, the appellate court will *remand* the case to the lower court for further proceedings consistent with its opinion. In the sample case presented in Exhibit 8.6, the United States Supreme Court vacated (nullified) the lower court's decision and remanded the case.

GUIDELINES FOR READING CASES.   When reading case law, you will inevitably find that some opinions are easier to understand than others. Some judges write more clearly and logically than others. You may need to reread a case (or a portion of a case) several times to understand what is being said, why it is being said at that point in the case, and what the judge's underlying legal reasoning is. Some cases contain several pages describing facts and issues of previous cases and how those cases relate to the one being decided by the court. You will need to distinguish between comments made in the previous case and comments that are being made about the case at bar (before the court).

Often, the judge writing the opinion provides some guideposts, perhaps by indicating sections and subsections within the opinion by numbers, letters, or sub-

Opinion
A statement by the court expressing the reasons for its decision in a case.

titles. Note that in Exhibit 8.6, Arabic numerals are used to divide the opinion into basic sections. Scanning through the opinion for these types of indicators can help orient you to the opinion's format.

In cases that involve dissenting or concurring opinions, you need to make sure that you identify these opinions so that you do not mistake one of them for the majority opinion. Generally, you should scan through the case a time or two to identify its various components and sections and then read the case (or sections of the case) until you understand the facts and procedural history of the case, the issues involved, the applicable law, the legal reasoning of the court, and how the reasoning leads to the court's conclusion on the issue or issues.

SUMMARIZING AND BRIEFING CASES.   After you have read and analyzed a case, you may decide that it is on point and that you want to include a reference to it in your legal writing. If so, you will want to summarize in your notes the important facts and issues in the case, as well as the court's decision, or holding, and the reasoning used by the court. This is called **briefing a case**.[3]

There is a fairly standard format you can use when you brief any court case. Although the format may vary, typically it presents the essentials of the case under headings such as those illustrated and described in Exhibit 8.7. As you can see in the exhibit, in a case brief, the name and citation for the case are given first. Then, the background and facts leading up to the lawsuit are included. Also, when more than one issue is involved in a case, the issues are combined in the *Issue* section, the decisions regarding each issue may be combined under the *Decision* section, and so on. Following the *Decision* section, the court's legal reasoning is set forth under the heading *Rationale*. Finally, the *Holding* section sets forth the rule of law for which the case stands. Depending on the issue you were researching, you would add a conclusion to the brief indicating how the Supreme Court's ruling affected that issue.

Briefing a Case
Summarizing a case. A typical case brief will indicate the case title and citation and then briefly state the factual background and procedural history of the case, the issue or issues raised in the case, the court's decision, the applicable rule of law and the legal reasoning on which the decision is based, and conclusions or notes concerning the case made by the one briefing it.

---

3. Note that a *case brief* is not the same is a *legal brief* that an attorney submits to a court.

---

1. **NAME (TITLE, OR STYLE) OF CASE.**   Give the full name of the case.

2. **CASE CITATION.**   Give the full citation for the case, including all parallel citations, the date the case was decided, and the name of the court deciding the case.

3. **FACTS.**   Briefly indicate a) the reasons for the lawsuit; b) the identity and arguments of the plaintiff(s) and defendant(s); and c) if the case was decided by an appellate court, the lower court's opinion on the issues.

4. **PROCEDURE.**   Summarize the judicial history of the case—that is, each court that has heard the case and each court's decision on the matter.

5. **ISSUE.**   Concisely phrase the essential legal issue(s) before the court.

6. **DECISION.**   Indicate here the court's decision on the issue(s).

7. **RATIONALE.**   Summarize as briefly as possible the legal reasoning on which the court based its decision.

8. **HOLDING.**   State the rule (or rules) of law for which the case stands.

EXHIBIT 8.7
Format for Briefing a Case

RESEARCHING STATUTORY LAW

Because of the tremendous growth in statutory and regulatory law in the last century, the legal issues dealt with by attorneys are frequently governed by statutes and administrative regulations. Indeed, in researching any legal issue, you will often find that you need to look not only at case law but also at statutory law, or vice versa. Although the issue in Hoffman's case will probably be decided on the basis of common law principles governing torts, as enunciated by the courts, other issues that you may be asked to research may be governed by statutory law.

To find the relevant statutory law governing a particular legal issue or area, you will need to know, first of all, the names of the various publications in which statutory law can be found. In this section, we look first at how federal statutes are published and how you can find, within these publications, statutes governing the issue you are researching. We then look at a more difficult task: how to read and analyze a statutory law.

Finding Statutory Law

When the U.S. Congress passes laws, they are collected in a publication entitled *United States Statutes at Large.* When state legislatures pass laws, they are collected in similar state publications. These publications arrange laws by date of enactment. Most frequently, however, laws are referred to in their codified form—that is, the form in which they appear in the federal and state codes. (A **code** is a systematic and logical presentation of laws, rules, or regulations.) Codes arrange statutory provisions by topic. When you are researching statutory law, a good beginning point is to review the topical index to a state, federal, or local code of laws to see if you can find statutes relevant to your issue.

Code
A systematic and logical presentation of laws, rules, or regulations.

THE *UNITED STATES CODE.*   Federal statutes enacted by Congress are published in their final form in the *United States Code (U.S.C.),* which is published by the U.S. government. The *U.S.C.* is divided into fifty topic classifications. As shown in Exhibit 8.8, each of these topics, called *titles* of the code, carries a descriptive title and a number. For example, laws relating to commerce and trade are collected in Title 15, and laws concerning the courts or judicial procedures are collected in Title 28. Titles are subdivided into *chapters* (sections) and *subchapters* (subsections). A citation to the *U.S.C.* includes title and section numbers. Thus, a reference to "28 U.S.C. Section 1346" means that the statute can be found in Section 1346 of Title 28. "Section" may also be designated by the symbol §, and "Sections" by §§.

One approach to finding statutory law in the *U.S.C.* is simply to refer to the title descriptions listed in the front of each volume. This approach is most beneficial for researchers who can quickly find the applicable title for the statute they are researching. Alternatively, the researcher can consult the index to the *U.S.C.* The index provides an alphabetical listing of all federal statutes by subject matter and by the name of the act. The index provides the exact location of the statute, by title and section number.

Sometimes a researcher may know the popular name of a legislative act but not its official name. In this situation, the researcher can consult the *U.S.C.* volume entitled *Popular Name Table,* which lists statutes by their popular names. Many legislative bills enacted into law are commonly known by a popular name. Some have descriptive titles reflecting their purpose; others are named after their sponsors. The Labor-Management Reporting and Disclosure Act of 1959, for example, is also known as the Landrum-Griffin Act. Searching by popular name will allow the researcher to find the title and section of the statute and therefore locate the statute in the *U.S.C.*

UNOFFICIAL VERSIONS OF THE FEDERAL CODE.   There are two unofficial versions of the federal code. These versions are similar to the *U.S.C.*, but they contain some important differences. They provide annotations describing cases and other sources that have applied or interpreted a given statute. Additionally, they contain more cross-references to related sections of the code than does the *U.S.C.*

One of these unofficial versions is the *United States Code Annotated (U.S.C.A.)*, published by West Group. The *U.S.C.A.* contains the full text of the *U.S.C.*, the U.S. Constitution, the Federal Rules of Evidence, and various other rules, including the Rules of Civil Procedure and the Rules of Criminal Procedure. This set of approximately two hundred volumes offers historical notes relating to the text of each statute and any amendments to the act. Locating statutory law in the *U.S.C.A.* is similar to locating statutes in the *U.S.C.* Researchers can use the

---

TITLES OF UNITED STATES CODE

*1. General Provisions.	27. Intoxicating Liquors.
2. The Congress.	*28. Judiciary and Judicial Procedure; and Appendix.
*3. The President.	
*4. Flag and Seal, Seat of Government, and the States.	29. Labor.
	30. Mineral Lands and Mining.
*5. Government Organization and Employees; and Appendix.	*31. Money and Finance.
†6. [Surety Bonds.]	*32. National Guard.
7. Agriculture.	33. Navigation and Navigable Waters.
8. Aliens and Nationality.	‡34. [Navy.]
*9. Arbitration.	*35. Patents.
*10. Armed Forces; and Appendix.	36. Patriotic Societies and Observances.
*11. Bankruptcy; and Appendix.	*37. Pay and Allowances of the Uniformed Services.
12. Banks and Banking.	
*13. Census.	*38. Veterans' Benefits.
*14. Coast Guard.	*39. Postal Service.
15. Commerce and Trade.	40. Public Buildings, Property, and Works.
16. Conservation.	41. Public Contracts.
*17. Copyrights.	42. The Public Health and Welfare.
*18. Crimes and Criminal Procedure; and Appendix.	43. Public Lands.
	*44. Public Printing and Documents.
19. Customs Duties.	45. Railroads.
20. Education.	*46. Shipping; and Appendix.
21. Food and Drugs.	47. Telegraphs, Telephones, and Radiotelegraphs.
22. Foreign Relations and Intercourse.	
*23. Highways.	48. Territories and Insular Possessions.
24. Hospitals and Asylums.	*49. Transportation; and Appendix.
25. Indians.	50. War and National Defense; and Appendix.
26. Internal Revenue Code.	

*This title has been enacted as law. However, any Appendix to this title has not been enacted as law.
†This title was enacted as law and has been repealed by the enactment of Title 31.
‡This title has been eliminated by the enactment of Title 10.

Page III

EXHIBIT 8.8

Titles in the *United States Code*

topical or index approach and, if necessary, look through the *Popular Name Table*.

The second unofficial statutory code is the *United States Code Service (U.S.C.S.)*, also published by West Group. The *U.S.C.S.* offers some of the same features offered by the *U.S.C.A.*, such as annotations. The *U.S.C.S.* and the *U.S.C.A.* are distinguishable by the research tools they provide. The research section of the *U.S.C.S.* provides references and citations to some sources that are not contained in the *U.S.C.A.*, such as *American Law Reports*, legal periodicals, and *American Jurisprudence*. Paralegals can begin statutory research in the *U.S.C.S.* by reviewing the subject index or tables listing the popular names of statutes. Both annotated codes also have conversion charts listing all public acts by public law number (P.L. number), *Statutes at Large* references, and *U.S.C.* title and section numbers.

STATE CODES.   State codes follow the *U.S.C.* pattern of arranging statutes by subject. They may be called codes, revisions, compilations, consolidations, general statutes, or statutes, depending on the preference of the states. In some codes, subjects are designated by number. In others, they are designated by name. For example, "13 Pennsylvania Consolidated Statutes Section 1101" means that the statute can be found in Section 1101 of Title 13 of the Pennsylvania code. "California Commercial Code Section 1101" means that the statute can be found in Section 1101 under the heading "Commercial" in the California code. Abbreviations may be used. For example, a reference to "13 Pennsylvania Consolidated Statutes Section 1101" may be abbreviated to "13 Pa.C.S. § 1101," and a reference to "California Commercial Code Section 1101" may be abbreviated to "Cal. Com. Code § 1101."

DEVELOPING PARALEGAL SKILLS
Researching the *U.S.C.A.*

Natalie Martin has completed her factual analysis of the case involving Bernie Berriman (see the earlier *Developing Paralegal Skills* feature entitled "Defining the Issues to Be Researched") and begins her research. The issue she is researching is whether the government, which arrested Bernie for the transportation and distribution of cocaine, had the authority to confiscate Bernie's car and car phone. Natalie's supervising attorney has told her to start her research by going to the *United States Code Annotated (U.S.C.A.)* to find the relevant federal statutes.

CHECKLIST FOR RESEARCHING THE *U.S.C.A.*

- Start with general index volumes unless the *U.S.C.A.* title (topic) number or a popular name is known.

- If the specific title number is known, begin in the title index. If the popular name of a statute is known, begin in the *Popular Name Table*.

- Look up topics, either by factual categories or legal categories, in the index. Here, the topic could be "drugs."

- Look up subtopics within topics. Here, "forfeiture" or "property" could be subtopics under "drugs."

- Write down the citations to the *U.S.C.A.* volumes containing the topics.

- Look up the citations in the volumes containing the various titles or topics.

- Read the relevant sections of the statute to determine if they apply to the research.

- Update the relevant sections of the statute to determine if they apply to the research.

- Check the annotations following the statute sections for case law in which the statute has been applied and interpreted.

- Review any cases that appear relevant.

- "Shepardize" both statutes and cases to make sure they are still "good law."

In many states, official codes are supplemented by annotated codes published by private publishers. Annotated codes follow the numbering scheme set forth in the official state code but provide outlines and indexes to assist in locating information. These codes also provide references to case law, legislative history sources, and other documents in which the statute has been considered or discussed.

Analyzing Statutory Law

As with court cases, some statutes are more difficult to read than others. Some are extremely wordy or lengthy or difficult to understand for some other reason. The kinds of information you want to look for when reading a statute will vary, depending on the nature of the issue you are researching. Generally, though, you should find answers to the following types of questions:

- Why was the statute enacted?
- When does the statute take effect? (The effective date of a statute may be a year or more after the statute was enacted by Congress.)
- To what class or group of people does the statute apply?
- What kind of conduct is being regulated by the statute, and in what circumstances is that conduct prohibited, required, or permitted?
- Are there any exceptions to the statute's applicability?

By carefully reading and rereading a statute, you can usually find answers to these questions.

Generally, when trying to understand the meaning of statutes, you should do as the courts do. When a court is unsure of how a particular statute applies to a given set of circumstances, the court will often research case law to see how other courts have applied the statute. You can find citations to court cases relating to specific statutes by referring to the annotated versions of state or federal statutory codes discussed above.

Another technique used by courts in interpreting a statute's meaning and applicability is to research the legislative history of the statute to discern what the legislators intended when they enacted the law. In researching the legislative history of a statute, you will want to locate and read through the reports of congressional committees, transcripts of congressional debates and proceedings, and other relevant documents. The easiest way to locate these sources is to refer to unofficial annotated versions of statutory codes. Unofficial versions of the federal code, such as the *U.S.C.A.,* often include references to sources that will provide you with more detailed information on a statute's legislative history.

RESEARCHING ADMINISTRATIVE LAW

Administrative rules and regulations also constitute a source of American law. As discussed in Chapter 5, Congress frequently delegates authority to administrative agencies through enabling legislation. All regulations issued by federal administrative agencies are published in their final form in the federal *Code of Federal Regulations (C.F.R.),* a U.S. government publication. The regulations are compiled from the *Federal Register,* a daily government publication in which regulations and presidential orders are initially published. The *C.F.R.* uses the same titles as the *U.S.C.* (shown previously in Exhibit 8.8). Each title of the *C.F.R.* is similarly divided into sections and subsections.

If you are searching for administrative regulations in the *C.F.R.*, you should begin with the index section of the *Index and Finding Aids* volume. This index will allow you to locate the relevant title and the section of the *C.F.R.* that pertains to your issue. The *Congressional Information Service (C.I.S.)* also provides an index to the *C.F.R.* The *C.I.S.* index is helpful in locating *C.F.R.* regulations by subject matter and also in determining the geographical areas affected by the regulation. The *American Digest System* can be of additional help because it provides coverage of court cases dealing with administrative questions. The digests, however, do not contain any agency rulings. Whenever you need to research administrative law, you may discover that the most efficient way to find what you are looking for is simply to call the agency and ask agency personnel how to access information relevant to your research topic.

Regulations issued by administrative agencies are as challenging to read as the laws, or statutes, enacted by legislatures. Generally, in reading and interpreting administrative law, you should apply the same techniques as you would when analyzing statutory law.

FINDING CONSTITUTIONAL LAW

The federal government and each of the fifty states have their own constitutions describing the powers, responsibilities, and limitations of the various branches of government. Constitutions can be replaced or amended, and it is important that researchers have access to both current and older versions.

The text of the U.S. Constitution can be found in a number of publications. A useful source of federal constitutional law is *The Constitution of the United States of America*, published under the authority of the U.S. Senate and available through the Library of Congress. It includes the full text of the U.S. Constitution, corresponding United States Supreme Court annotations, and a discussion of each provision, including background information on its history and interpretation. Additional constitutional sources are found in the *U.S.C.A.* and the *U.S.C.S.*, both of which contain the text of the U.S. Constitution and its amendments, as well as citations to cases discussing particular constitutional provisions. Annotated state codes provide a similar service for their state constitutions. State constitutions are usually included in the publications containing state statutes.

UPDATING THE LAW

Almost every day, new court decisions are made, new regulations are issued, and new statutes are enacted or existing statutes amended. Because the law is ever changing, a critical factor to consider when researching a topic or point of law is whether a given court opinion, statute, or regulation is still valid. A case decided six months ago may prove to be "bad law" today (if it has been reversed or significantly modified on appeal, for example). Similarly, statutes are frequently amended and new statutes enacted. This means that statutory law, too, is constantly changing. When conducting research, you must never assume that the law on a specific issue is the same today as it was last year or even last month.

Updating the law—making sure that your research results are still valid—is a crucial step in the research process.

One way to update your research results is to make sure that you check any supplemental publications to legal sources. For example, legal encyclopedias, case digests, and other sources are updated periodically by the publication of pam-

ETHICAL CONCERN
The Importance of Finding Current Law

It is easy to forget that the law is continually changing and, in certain areas, changing very quickly. Even though you might have researched a certain legal issue as recently as three months ago—and for a case very similar to the one your supervising attorney is now litigating—it is a mistake to assume that the earlier research results are still valid. Between then and now, a leading case on the issue might have been overruled or a statute amended or a regulatory guideline changed. Even though you may have checked the relevant printed volume of *Shepard's Citations*, you need to realize that the most recent changes in the law will not be included in printed legal reference materials. To make absolutely certain that your research results are still valid, you should use an online citator to see if recent cases or modifications to statutes or regulations affect your research. Failure to update your research results may seriously harm your attorney's chances at success in arguing a client's case. In sum, if your attorney trusts you to do legal research, never rely on yesterday's law.

phlets or **pocket parts** (small pamphlets that slip into the back cover of a bound volume).

You should also consult a citator to make sure that a law, such as a statute or case, has not been modified or overruled since the statute was enacted or the case decided. A **citator** provides a list of legal references that have cited or interpreted the case or law. A *case citator* provides, in addition, a history of the particular case.

Shepard's Citations

Shepard's Citations, which is published by Shepard's/McGraw-Hill, Inc., is a research tool with which all paralegals should become familiar. *Shepard's Citations* contains the most comprehensive system of case citators in the United States. *Shepard's* lists every case published in an official or unofficial reporter by its citation. *Shepard's* citators are available for many different jurisdictions. *Shepard's United States Citations* covers the decisions of the United States Supreme Court. *Shepard's* citators also exist for the reports of every state, the District of Columbia, and Puerto Rico. Every region of the National Reporter System is covered by *Shepard's*. Additionally, *Shepard's* citators cover statutory law, administrative regulations, constitutional law, and legal periodicals. Exhibit 8.9 shows a *Shepard's* citator.

You can use *Shepard's* citators to accomplish several research objectives. For example, *Shepard's* provides parallel citations for the cited case, thus allowing you to locate the case in other official or unofficial reporters. *Shepard's* also lists other cases ("citing cases") that have cited the main case (the "cited case"), which may provide you with useful information. For example, suppose that in researching Hoffman's claim you have found a case on point. You can check *Shepard's Citations* to see what other courts have cited the case (indicating that those courts must have discussed one or more of the issues involved in the cited case). Some of these citing cases may be on point and valuable to your research.

One of the most valuable functions of *Shepard's* is that it provides you with a means to verify the history of a case. For example, if you want to know whether

Pocket Part
A separate pamphlet containing recent cases or changes in the law that is used to update treatises, legal encyclopedias, and other legal authorities. It is called a "pocket part" because it slips into a sleeve, or pocket, in the back binder of the volume.

Citator
A book or online service that provides the subsequent history and intepretation of a court decision, statute, or regulation and a list of the cases, statutes, and regulations that have interpreted, applied, or modified a statute or regulation.

EXHIBIT 8.9
Shepard's Citations

Reproduced by permission of Shepard's. Further reproduction of any kind is strictly prohibited.

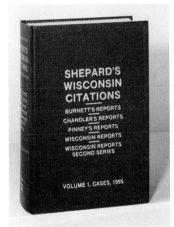

a certain court decision has been reversed by a higher court, *Shepard's* provides that information. Note, though, that it takes some time before the printed versions of *Shepard's* citators are updated. To make absolutely sure that your research is truly up to date, you will want to use an online citator.

Online Citators

Several computerized legal-research services provide online citators. Online citators are extremely useful to legal researchers because they are more up to date than the printed citators just discussed. You can access Westlaw® or Lexis® online to update the law within seconds. You can also learn the previous and subsequent history of a particular case, find out what other cases have cited it, and so on. You will read about online citators in further detail in Chapter 9.

LEGAL WRITING

As mentioned in this chapter's introduction, legal research and writing often go hand in hand. When you brief cases during the research process, for example, you are engaging in a form of legal writing. When you complete your research, you will need to create a memorandum in which you summarize the results of your research for your supervising attorney to review. As a paralegal, you will find that in addition to drafting research summaries, you will be expected to draft numerous other types of materials. In fact, much of your work as a paralegal will involve writing assignments. In the remainder of this chapter, we look at some of the basic requirements of legal writing and at the kinds of legal materials that paralegals create.

Important Considerations in Legal Writing

The legal profession is primarily a communications profession. Effective written communications are particularly crucial in the legal arena. For paralegals, good writing skills are linked with successful job performance. The more competent a writer you are, the more likely it is that your finished products will be satisfactory to the attorney with whom you are working. You should also keep in mind that some of your written work, such as correspondence, represents the firm for which you work. A well-written document is a positive reflection on the firm and upholds the firm's reputation for good work. Other important considerations in legal writing include those discussed below.

ACCURACY.   A crucial factor in legal writing is accuracy. All experienced writers in any business or other environment normally strive to produce accurate documents. In legal writing, however, accuracy is vital. A word or phrase that is ambiguous, erroneous, or unintentionally omitted from a document could jeopardize a client's legal rights. Generally, you should take special care to proofread carefully any document you write. You want to make sure not only that the document is free of grammatical or spelling errors but also that the information in the document is accurate in every respect and that no crucial clause or information has been omitted.

LEGAL TERMINOLOGY.   Always keep in mind that the purpose of any legal document is to *communicate* information. If you are writing a document to be read by an attorney, the use of legal terms presents no problem. When writing to non-

---

TECHNOLOGY AND TODAY'S PARALEGAL

Online "Plain English" Guidelines

The ability to write clearly and effectively is a valuable asset to any paralegal, because virtually every paralegal is required to do a certain amount of writing as a part of his or her job. As mentioned elsewhere, clear and effective writing means keeping "legalese"—legal terminology typically understood only by legal professionals—to a minimum, or even eliminating it entirely. The problem is, how can you do this without "dummying down" a legal concept or risking inaccuracy when describing that concept?

Today's paralegal need not go far to find helpful instructions in the art of writing in "plain English." Indeed, there are a number of sites on the Web you can turn to for guidance. You can find many helpful sites simply by doing a key-word search for "plain language" or "plain English" using a search engine such as Yahoo. Some sites, such as **www.deet.gov.au/pubs/plain_en/ writing.htm**, offer helpful writing tips in addition to specific examples of how you can replace cumbersome phrases (such as "at such time as" or "prior to and following") with a simpler term or phrase (such as "when" or "before and after"). Other sites, such as **www.web. net/~plain/PlainTrain** offer online training in the use of plain language in writing.

An excellent source for writing tips and using plain language is the "Plain English Handbook" that the Securities and Exchange Commission (SEC) recently published online at **www.sec.gov/consumer/plaine.htm#A3**. The purpose of the booklet is indicated by its subtitle: "How to Create Clear SEC Disclosure Documents." Paralegals working in the area of securities law will certainly find this handbook helpful. Yet the guidelines given in the booklet can apply to any written communication.

Paralegals can also turn to other online sources for ideas on how to use language that communicates well. For example, if you want to better understand a legal term (so that you can paraphrase it in language more understandable to your audience), you can check various online dictionaries, such as Black's Corporation Law Dictionary (at **www.alaska.net/~winter/black_law_dictionary.html**) or the 'Lectric Law Library's dictionary of legal terms (at **www.lectlaw.com/d-a.htm**). A particularly helpful online source is the "plain language" legal dictionary found at **www.wwlia.org/dicion.htm**. This dictionary defines and describes legal concepts in language most people can understand.

---

lawyers, however, you need to be especially careful when using legal terminology. Although a certain amount of legal terminology in legal writing is unavoidable, you should minimize the use of language that may confuse the reader. If you are writing a letter to a client, for example, either avoid using legal terms that the client may not understand or define such terms as you use them. For example, if you are advising a client of the date on which *voir dire* will take place, consider saying "jury selection"—or perhaps "*voir dire* (jury selection)"—instead. (See this chapter's *Technology and Today's Paralegal: Online "Plain English" Guidelines* for a discussion of online guidelines on how to use plain English in writing.)

WRITING APPROACH.   Another consideration in legal writing has to do with writing approach. You should determine at the outset of any writing assignment what type of writing is required. Many of your writing assignments will require *objective analysis,* which either focuses on facts or discusses fairly both sides of a legal matter. When you write a memorandum to your supervising attorney summarizing your research results, for example, you will want to be as objective as possible in summarizing how the law applies to a client's case. The attorney will need to know not only of those cases or other laws that support the client's position but also of any cases or laws that favor the opponent's position. To advise the client properly and develop a strategy for litigating or settling the dispute, the attorney must be aware of both the strengths and weaknesses of the client's case.

Other types of writing assignments will require *advocacy*, which involves presenting the facts and issues in a light most favorable to your client. If the writing assignment is intended to advocate a position, the style of writing will be somewhat different from the style in an objective discussion of the law. In advocating a position, you are primarily concerned with convincing the reader that the argument proposed is stronger than the opposing party's position. You will need to develop supportive legal arguments and present the matter in the light most favorable to the client. For example, suppose that you are asked to draft a *settlement letter* (a letter to an opposing party requesting that a case be settled out of court) to the defendant, Better Homes Store, in the Hoffman case. Your goal in writing is to convince the defendant of the strength of Hoffman's case against the store.

Pleadings and Discovery Documents

Many writing tasks undertaken by paralegals involve forms that must be submitted to the court or to opposing counsel before a trial begins or after the trial has commenced. These documents were discussed in Chapter 6. You can review that chapter for explanations and illustrations of the forms required for pretrial procedures (pleadings, discovery procedures, and pretrial motions) and for motions made during or just following the trial.

It is especially important that such documents contain the required information and be presented in the appropriate format. Form books and computerized forms offer guidelines, but you should always become familiar with the rules of the court with which the documents are being filed to ensure that you use the proper format.

General Legal Correspondence

Paralegals are often asked to draft letters to clients, witnesses, opposing counsel, and others. In this section, you will read about some typical requirements relating to legal correspondence. Keep in mind, though, that the particular law firm, corporate legal department, or government agency for which you work will probably have its own specific procedures and requirements that you will need to follow.

Informative Letter
A letter that conveys certain information to a client, a witness, an adversary's counsel, or other person regarding some legal matter (such as the date, time, place, and purpose of a meeting).

Confirmation Letter
A letter that states the substance of a previously conducted verbal discussion to provide a permanent record of the oral conversation.

Opinion (Advisory) Letter
A letter from an attorney to a client that contains a legal opinion on an issue raised by the client's question or legal claim. The opinion is based on a detailed analysis of the law.

TYPES OF LEGAL LETTERS.   There are several types of legal correspondence, and each type serves a different purpose. An **informative letter** conveys information to another party. As a paralegal, you will write many such letters—to clients, for example, to inform them of current developments in their cases or of upcoming procedures. Informative letters are also sent to opposing counsel, witnesses, or other persons that may be involved in a trial. Additionally, they may be used as transmittal (cover) letters when documents or other materials are sent to a client, a court, opposing counsel, or some other person. Paralegals also frequently write **confirmation letters**—letters that put into written form the contents of an oral discussion. In addition to providing attorneys with a permanent record of earlier conversations, confirmation letters also safeguard against any misinterpretation or misunderstanding of what was communicated orally.

The function of an **opinion letter**, or *advisory letter,* is to provide information and advice. In contrast to informative letters, opinion letters actually give a legal opinion about the matter discussed. Opinion letters provide a detailed analysis of the law as it applies to a particular claim or issue and gives the firm's conclusion, or opinion, on the matter.

Because opinion letters issued by a firm reflect legal expertise and advice on which a client may rely, they must always be signed by attorneys.

The signature of an attorney represents the attorney's acceptance of responsibility for what is stated in the document and can serve as the basis for liability.

Another basic type of letter is the demand letter. **Demand letters** are adversarial in nature and seek to advance the interests of a client. Whatever the content of a demand letter, its purpose is to demand something of the recipient on behalf of the client. A common form of demand letter in litigation firms is a settlement letter. Another example of a demand letter is a letter to a client's debtor, demanding payment for an amount owed.

GENERAL FORMAT FOR LEGAL CORRESPONDENCE.   Although there are many types of legal letters, the format used for each of these letters is very similar. A legal letter normally includes the components discussed below and illustrated and annotated in Exhibit 8.10 on the next page.

DATE, METHOD OF DELIVERY, AND ADDRESS BLOCK.   All legal correspondence must be *dated*. Dates serve an important function in legal matters. The date of a letter may be important in matters involving legal notice of a particular event. Additionally, legal correspondence normally is filed chronologically. Without any indication of when the letter was written, accurate filing of the letter would be difficult, if not impossible. As a general rule, you should always place a date on every written item that you create, including telephone messages, memos to file, and personal reminders to yourself.

Below the date is a line indicating how the letter was sent (if other than by U.S. mail) and the **address block**, which shows to whom the letter is addressed. This information is located on the upper part of the page at the left-hand margin. If the letter was sent by Federal Express, the line before the recipient's name and address will read VIA FEDERAL EXPRESS. If the letter is hand delivered, the line will read BY HAND DELIVERY. Communication by facsimile can be described by the words BY FAX or BY FACSIMILE. The address block should contain the name of the person to whom the letter is written, the person's title, and the name and address of the person's firm or place of business.

REFERENCE LINE AND SALUTATION.   Following the method of delivery and the address block, the writer may include a **reference line** identifying the matter discussed in the letter. In a letter regarding a pending lawsuit, the reference line may contain the name of the case, its case file (or docket) number, and a brief notation of the nature of the legal dispute. Many attorneys also include the firm's file number for the case. In an informative letter, the reference line may take the form of a title. For example, a reference line in a letter concerning the closing procedures for a financing transaction may read "RE: Closing Procedures for ABC Company's $4,000,000 Financing Package."

The **salutation**, which appears just below the reference line, is a greeting to the addressee. Because legal correspondence is a professional means of communication, the salutation, as well as the body of the letter, should be formal in tone. There are, of course, circumstances in which a formal greeting may not be necessary. For example, if the addressee is someone you know quite well, it may be appropriate to address the person by his or her first name, rather than by "Mr." or "Ms." In these situations, you must use your discretion to determine the appropriate level of formality. Generally, when in doubt, use a formal salutation.

Demand Letter
An adversarial letter that attempts to persuade the reader that he or she should accept a position that is favorable to the writer's client—that is, demanding that the reader do or not do a certain thing.

Address Block
That part of a letter that indicates to whom the letter is addressed. The address block is placed in the upper left-hand portion of the letter, above the salutation (or reference line, if one is included).

Reference Line
The portion of the letter that indicates the matter to be discussed in the letter, such as "RE: Summary of Cases Applying the Family and Medical Leave Act of 1993." The reference line is placed just below the address block and above the salutation.

Salutation
The formal greeting to the addressee of the letter. The salutation is placed just below the reference line.

EXHIBIT 8.10
Components of a Legal Letter

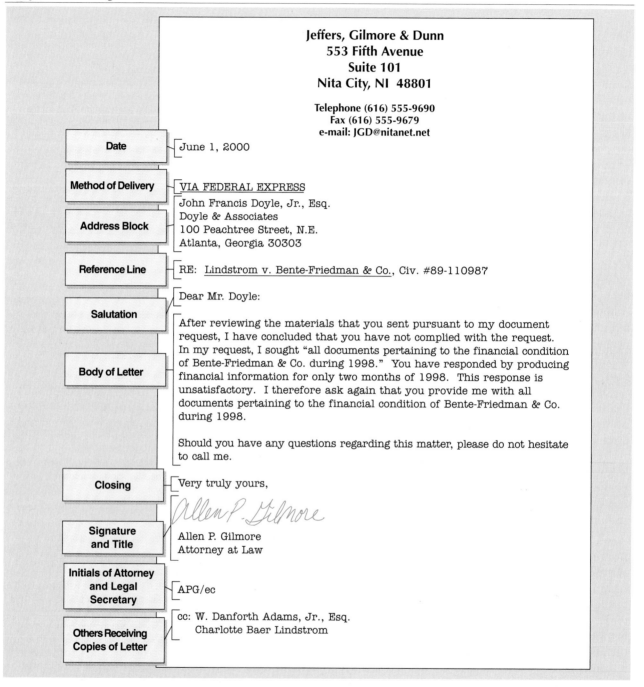

	Jeffers, Gilmore & Dunn **553 Fifth Avenue** **Suite 101** **Nita City, NI 48801** Telephone (616) 555-9690 Fax (616) 555-9679 e-mail: JGD@nitanet.net
Date	June 1, 2000
Method of Delivery	VIA FEDERAL EXPRESS
Address Block	John Francis Doyle, Jr., Esq. Doyle & Associates 100 Peachtree Street, N.E. Atlanta, Georgia 30303
Reference Line	RE: Lindstrom v. Bente-Friedman & Co., Civ. #89-110987
Salutation	Dear Mr. Doyle:
Body of Letter	After reviewing the materials that you sent pursuant to my document request, I have concluded that you have not complied with the request. In my request, I sought "all documents pertaining to the financial condition of Bente-Friedman & Co. during 1998." You have responded by producing financial information for only two months of 1998. This response is unsatisfactory. I therefore ask again that you provide me with all documents pertaining to the financial condition of Bente-Friedman & Co. during 1998. Should you have any questions regarding this matter, please do not hesitate to call me.
Closing	Very truly yours,
Signature and Title	Allen P. Gilmore Attorney at Law
Initials of Attorney and Legal Secretary	APG/ec
Others Receiving Copies of Letter	cc: W. Danforth Adams, Jr., Esq. Charlotte Baer Lindstrom

BODY AND CLOSING.   The main part of the letter is the body of the letter. The body of the letter should be formal and should effectively communicate information to the reader. As a representative of the firm, the paralegal must be careful to proofread all outgoing correspondence to ensure that the letter contains accurate information, is clearly written, and is free of any grammatical or spelling errors.

Following the body of the letter are standard concluding sentences. These final sentences are usually courteous statements such as "Thank you for your time

ETHICAL CONCERN
Letters and the Unauthorized Practice of Law

As has been stressed in other areas of this text, engaging in the unauthorized practice of law is one of the most serious potential ethical and legal problems facing paralegals. To avoid liability for the unauthorized practice of law, you should never sign opinion (advisory) letters with your own name, and when you sign other types of letters, you should always indicate your status as a paralegal. Even if the person to whom you are sending the letter knows you quite well and knows you are a paralegal, you should indicate your status on the letter itself. By doing so, you will prevent potential confusion as well as potential legal liability. Even if your name and status is included in the letterhead (as is permitted under some state laws), as a precaution, you should type your title below your name at the end of the letter as well.

and attention to this matter," or "Should you have any questions or comments, please call me at the above-listed number." These brief concluding statements are followed by the **closing**. The closing in legal correspondence is formal—for example, "Sincerely yours" or "Very truly yours."

Finally, you should always include your title in any correspondence written by you on behalf of the firm. Your title ("Paralegal" or "Legal Assistant" or other title) should immediately follow your name. This, of course, is not a concern when you prepare correspondence for an attorney who will provide a signature.

Closing
A final comment to a letter that is placed above the signature, such as "Very truly yours."

The Internal Memorandum

The internal legal memorandum, as the term implies, is prepared for internal use within a law firm, legal department, or other organization or agency. As a paralegal, you may be asked to draft a legal memorandum for your supervising attorney. Generally, the legal memo presents a thorough summary and analysis of a particular legal problem.

The attorney for whom the document is prepared may be relying on the memo for a number of reasons. For example, the attorney may be preparing a brief on behalf of a client or an opinion letter regarding a client's claim. Thus, if you are asked to draft the memo, you will want it to be extremely thorough and clearly written. Because the legal memo is directed to attorneys who are knowledgeable in the law, there is no need to avoid sophisticated legal terminology or to define basic legal theories or procedures.

The purpose of the memo is to provide an attorney with all relevant information regarding the case, so the document is written objectively. It is an explanatory memo informing the attorney of all sides of the issues presented, including both the strengths and weaknesses of the client's claim or defense. You should keep the following in mind:

> **Your goal in drafting a legal memorandum is to inform, explain, and evaluate the client's claim or defense.**

A legal memorandum is organized in a logical manner. Although there is no one way to structure the legal memo, most are divided into sections that perform distinct functions. Of course, if the law firm or the attorney for whom you are

FEATURED GUEST: RICHARD M. TERRY

Ten Tips for Effective Legal Writing

BIOGRAPHICAL NOTE

Richard M. Terry received his bachelor's degree and master's degree from the University of Baltimore. He worked as a legal assistant for ten years. During that time, he was a supervisor in the Office of the Public Defender for Baltimore City. Currently, he is an assistant professor and the coordinator of the legal-assistant program at Baltimore City Community College.

Writing is a major form of communication. As a paralegal, you will be asked to write constantly throughout your career. Writing in this profession can take many forms, depending on your specialty and employer. You may be asked to prepare letters to clients and reports on client interviews and investigations, as well as responses to legal questions you have researched. Make no mistake—every document you prepare will be important. The tips for effective legal writing given below are not cast in stone. They are general guidelines that will make you a better legal writer, not only while you are in school but also when you enter the profession.

1. Plan before You Write. In this age of computerized word processing, there is a tremendous temptation just to sit down at the keyboard and begin to type, creating as you go along. Avoid this temptation at all costs. Instead, prepare a plan of action before you put the first word on paper. Your plan of action will consist of a few simple steps. First, if your supervising attorney has asked you to write the document, make sure that he or she has spelled out clearly what is needed. Second, if you are drafting a particular type of document (such as a pleading or memorandum) for the first time, ask for or find a sample to use, perhaps in your firm's files. Third, outline the document before you begin writing. Making an outline is the key to producing a well-organized document. Fourth, just before printing out the final copy of the document, check with the attorney again, to make sure you have not missed any key points.

2. Write with a Purpose. Writing with a purpose means writing with an identifiable goal in mind. The document you produce must reflect that purpose. Generally, the purpose for any legal document is either objective or adversarial. A document with an objective purpose simply passes on information, without any appearance of bias. A document with an adversarial purpose emphasizes the strong points of one position versus the weak points of another. Adversarial writing will reflect a definite bias.

3. Write Clearly. Remember that simple is usually better. Try to say exactly what you mean, and use standard vocabulary and clear and concrete terms. It is not necessary to show that you have a mastery of legal language. Identify your audience, and write to the people who will ultimately read your document. The style and tone of your writing should change with the document's intended audience, as well as with the purpose of the document. When you write to a client, for example, try to avoid the use of technical or legal terms. Your tone should be explanatory, and you should define legal terms and describe the consequences of legal actions. In contrast, when you are writing to the court or to attorneys, you will not need to explain legal concepts or terms. Remember, too, that readers normally do not have time to figure out what you are trying to say. Structure what you write, get to the point, and stick to it.

4. Use Proper Grammar and Sentence Structure. Legal documents once were routinely written in highly formal, complex language, but over the past few years, writing in plain English has become the rule. As a result, legal documents are no longer as long and complicated as they once

FEATURED GUEST, *Continued*

were. No matter which style you use, however, you must observe the rules of basic grammar and punctuation you learned in junior and senior high school. Make sure, for example, that you write in complete sentences and punctuate long sentences correctly.

5. Use an Appropriate Writing Style. Style is a broad term. In a general sense, it refers to how you express what you have to say, as opposed to the content of your writing. For example, a piece of writing can have a formal or an informal style. More narrowly, style can refer to specific forms, such as the form of a legal citation or of the names of particular courts. A good style manual can assist in determining what is an appropriate style. Style manuals give many basic rules and explain how the rules apply in different contexts. Well-known style manuals include *The Elements of Style* by William Strunk, Jr., and E. B. White, and the *Chicago Manual of Style,* currently in its fourteenth edition. For the proper format for legal citations, the source to consult is *The Bluebook: A Uniform System of Citation.*

6. Edit Your Work. The first draft of a document is not necessarily cor-

rect in every detail. Always go back and review objectively what you have written. If possible, have someone else read it for you. If that is not possible, try reading the document backwards—that is, from the last line to the first line. More often than not, you will catch at least some spelling and punctuation errors this way.

7. Use Computers Effectively. The computer has come of age in the law office of the 1990s. Using computers saves time and reduces the potential for errors in legal writing. There is no excuse for sending out any document containing spelling and grammatical mistakes if the document was produced on a computer. Use the spell-checker and grammar-checker functions to ensure that the document has no spelling or grammatical errors before you print it. Because today's law office relies heavily on computers for both research and writing, legal assistants who wish to succeed on the job should become knowledgeable in the use of computers and legal software.

8. Keep Copies. Whenever you create a document, keep a copy for your files. For one thing, this will help you to create a "forms file." Legal writing is somewhat repetitive.

> **"Identify your audience, and write to the people who will ultimately read your document."**

The form stays the same, and only the names and facts are changed. Creating a forms file will, in the long run, save you time and effort.

9. Consider New Writing Methods and Styles. Keeping abreast of what others in the field are doing and how they write may affect the format and style of your writing. Read as many trade publications as possible. Papers such as the *National Law Journal* are great sources of information, and magazines such as *Legal Assistant Today* often give interesting writing tips. Another way of keeping up with current information is to network with others in the profession. Maybe another legal assistant has a method or style of writing that is suited to your situation. Don't close your mind to it.

10. Practice, Practice, Practice. Good, effective writing is an art that requires a great deal of practice. The more you write, the better you become.

working prefers a particular format, that format should be followed. Generally, legal memos contain the following sections:

- Heading.
- Statement of the facts.
- Questions presented.
- Brief conclusion in response to the questions presented.
- Discussion and analysis of the facts and the applicable law.
- Conclusion.

HEADING.   The *heading* of a legal memorandum contains four pieces of information:

- The date on which the memo is submitted.
- The name of the person submitting the memo.
- The name of the person for whom the memo was prepared.
- A brief description of the matter, usually in the form of a reference line.

Exhibit 8.11 illustrates a sample heading for a legal memorandum.

STATEMENT OF THE FACTS.   The *statement of the facts* introduces the legal issues by describing the factual elements of the dispute. Only the relevant facts are included in this section. Thus, a key requirement of paralegals is that they learn which facts are legally significant. In other words, as a paralegal, you will need to determine which facts have a bearing on the legal issues in the case and which facts are irrelevant.

Facts presented in a legal memo must not be slanted in favor of the client. The legal memo is not an adversarial argument on the client's behalf. Rather, it is an objective presentation of both the facts and the legal issues. Therefore, you should never omit facts that are unfavorable to the client's claim or defense. The attorney for whom you work needs to know all of the facts that will influence the outcome of the case.

The statement of the facts should contain a logical and concise description of the events surrounding the conflict. Presenting events chronologically often helps to clarify the factual pattern in a case. Alternatively, facts relating to the same issue can be grouped together. The latter organizational technique is especially useful when the facts are complicated and numerous legal issues are presented.

Exhibit 8.12 indicates what kinds of information are typically included in a statement of the facts. It also shows what writing style is generally used.

QUESTIONS PRESENTED.   The *questions presented* address the legal issues presented by the factual circumstances described in the statement of the facts. The questions should be specific and straightforward. They should refer to the parties by name, succinctly set out the legal problem, and specifically indicate the important and relevant events. The questions-presented section may involve just one simple issue or a number of complex issues. Regardless of the complexity of the matter, this section helps bring the main points of the conflict into focus. See Exhibit 8.13 on page 288 for an example of how the questions presented might be phrased.

EXHIBIT 8.11
Legal Memorandum—Heading

MEMORANDUM

DATE: August 6, 2000

TO: Allen P. Gilmore, Partner

FROM: Elena Lopez, Paralegal

RE: Neely, Rachel: Emotional Distress—File No. 00-2146
        Neely, Rachel, and Melanie: Emotional Distress—File
            No. 00-2147

EXHIBIT 8.12
**Legal Memorandum—
Statement of the Facts**

STATEMENT OF THE FACTS

Ms. Rachel Neely ("Neely") and Ms. Melanie Neely ("Melanie"), our clients, seek advice in connection with possible emotional distress claims against Mr. Miles Thompson ("Thompson"). The claims arose as a result of (1) Neely's distress at hearing a car crash, caused by Thompson and involving her eleven-year-old daughter, Melanie, and subsequently viewing Melanie's injuries; and (2) Melanie's distress related to statements made by Thompson.

In February 1998, Neely and Melanie moved to Union City from San Francisco. Neely immediately began working for an investment firm in downtown Union City. At that firm, she became acquainted with the defendant, Thompson. Thompson was Neely's boss. At first, the two had a friendly, professional relationship. During this time, Thompson and Neely spent much time together socially and learned much about each other. Thompson, for example, knew that Neely had left San Francisco after her marriage ended. Neely had confided in Thompson that the divorce and the events preceding it were extremely traumatic for herself and for Melanie. Melanie knew Thompson and was comfortable with him. Thompson had spent time with Melanie and knew that Melanie had suffered emotionally because of her parents' bitter divorce.

The relationship between Thompson and Neely became strained approximately six months after Neely began working with Thompson. Tension between the parties arose as a result of Thompson's expression of romantic interest in Neely. Neely, who was dating someone else, had no romantic interest in Thompson and communicated to him her lack of interest in pursuing that type of relationship with him.

On April 2, 2000, Thompson visited the Neely home. Melanie was not fully aware of the problem her mother was having with Thompson. Thompson came to the door, and Melanie, who was alone in the house, let him in. Thompson invited Melanie for a ride in his Corvette. Melanie willingly went with him. Meanwhile, Neely, who had gone to the grocery store to buy some milk, returned to the house to find Melanie missing. She panicked, called the neighbors, and then called the police.

Thompson, who claims that he took Melanie for a ride so that she could be informed about her mother's "bad behavior," drove around Union City with Melanie for approximately thirty minutes. During this ride, Thompson told Melanie that her mother was a "wicked, selfish, woman, who could care less about Melanie." Thompson also told Melanie that her mother was a "no good, sex-crazed woman who would leave Melanie once the right man came along." Upon returning to the Neely home, Thompson made a left turn from Oak Street onto Maple Road, and his car was hit by an oncoming vehicle. According to the police report of the accident, Thompson's blood-alcohol level indicated that he was intoxicated.

The Neely home is located on the corner of the intersection of Maple Road and Oak Street. Neely heard the crash and ran outside. Seeing the accident and recognizing Thompson's car, she approached the site of the accident. There she saw Melanie bleeding profusely from head injuries. As a result of the accident, Melanie spent two days at Union City Memorial Hospital, where she was kept under observation for possible internal injuries. Melanie continues to be severely depressed and emotionally unstable as a result of Thompson's comments. Additionally, she has frequent nightmares and finds it difficult to speak without stuttering. Since the time of the accident, she has been under psychiatric therapy for these problems. Neely, who fainted after viewing her daughter's injuries, spent one day in Union City Memorial Hospital for extreme anxiety and trauma.

BRIEF CONCLUSION.   The *brief conclusion* (or *short answer* or *brief answer*) sets forth succinct responses to the questions presented in the previous section. The responses may vary in length. For example, as indicated in Exhibit 8.14 on the next page, certain questions can be answered simply by "yes," "no," "probably so," or "probably not," followed by a brief sentence summarizing the reason for that answer. For complicated legal questions, a more detailed statement might be appropriate. Even so, each conclusion should be limited to a maximum of one paragraph. The discussion of the legal analysis, which is the main part of the memo, provides ample opportunity for supporting details.

DISCUSSION AND ANALYSIS.   The *discussion and analysis* section, as the phrase implies, discusses and analyzes each issue to be resolved. If the facts of the dispute concern only one legal issue, the entire discussion will revolve around that. When

EXHIBIT 8.13

**Legal Memorandum—
Questions Presented**

QUESTIONS PRESENTED

1. Does Neely have a claim for the negligent infliction of emotional distress as a result of viewing the injuries sustained by her daughter in a car accident caused by Thompson's negligence?

2. Does Melanie have a claim for the intentional infliction of emotional distress arising out of Thompson's statements to her on April 2, 2000?

multiple issues are involved, as is often the situation, you should organize the discussion into separate parts so that each legal issue can be analyzed separately. For example, if the dispute involves two potential legal claims, the discussion could be divided into two sections with a descriptive heading for each section.

The discussion is the core of the legal memo. This section provides an opportunity for paralegals to demonstrate good research and writing skills. After the research is completed, you must relate the legal findings to the facts of the matter. The reader expects to find a thorough analysis of the law. One method of legal reasoning and analysis commonly used by paralegals and other legal professionals is called the *IRAC method*. IRAC is an acronym consisting of the first letters of the following words: Issue, Rule, Application, and Conclusion. To use the IRAC method, you first state the issue you are researching. Then you state the rule of law that applies to the issue. The rule of law may be a rule stated by the courts in previous decisions, a state or federal statute, or a state or federal administrative agency regulation. Next, you apply the rule of law to the set of facts involved in the client's case. Finally, you set forth your conclusion on the matter. If there are two or more issues involved in the client's case, you can analyze each issue using the IRAC method.

The discussion section should contain a thorough analysis of the law as it applies to each issue, and you should support any conclusions you have drawn on the points of law discussed by including proper citations to legal authorities. Sometimes, it is effective to quote directly from the text of a statute, court opinion, or other legal source. You should not rely too heavily on quoted material, however. Although quotations from a case or other legal authority can lend extremely helpful support, you should always keep the following fact in mind:

 The attorney for whom the memo is prepared wants to see your analysis, not a reiteration of a court's opinion.

EXHIBIT 8.14

**Legal Memorandum—
Brief Conclusion**

BRIEF CONCLUSION

1. Probably not. Neely cannot recover under the rule that is currently applied in this jurisdiction. This rule requires that the plaintiff be present at the scene when the accident occurs.

2. Most likely, yes. Thompson's conduct toward Melanie appears to have been (1) reckless, (2) outrageous and extreme, and (3) the direct cause of Melanie's severe emotional distress.

EXHIBIT 8.15
Legal Memorandum—Discussion (Excerpt)

DISCUSSION (excerpt)

I. Negligent Infliction of Emotional Distress

<u>Recovery Restriction</u>

Issue   *Are there any restrictions on recovering for the negligent infliction of emotional distress?*

An individual's right to emotional tranquility is recognized by the law protecting persons against the negligent infliction of emotional distress. The method for determining whether protection should be afforded for emotional distress caused by the knowledge of a third person's injury as a result of a defendant's negligent

Rule   actions is clear in this jurisdiction. *The rule adopted in this jurisdiction is the "impact rule," which requires that a plaintiff alleging emotional distress must also suffer a direct, physical impact from the same force that injured the victim.* Saechao v. Matsskoun, *717 P.2d 165, 168 (Or.App. 1986).* This "bright line" rule provides the courts with a test from which they can easily determine the relationship between compensability and the defendant's breach of duty owed to the victim. *Id.* at 169.

Application   *Neely was in her house when the accident occurred. She heard the crash and ran outside. Recognizing Thompson's car, Neely approached it and found Melanie bleeding profusely from head injuries. Neely did not suffer any direct physical impact from the car accident which injured Melanie.* Thus, Neely could not recover under the impact rule because she did not suffer any direct physical impact and Thompson owed her no duty.

The impact rule, which evolved as a result of the law's early reluctance to acknowledge the authenticity of emotional distress claims, avoids the problems of floodgate litigation. *Id.* at 169. It strictly limits a victim's recovery. Some strong arguments can be made against the application of the impact rule. Although the rule limits a defendant's liability and offers an easy decision-making criterion for the courts, it also lends itself to arbitrary and often unjust results. The impact rule makes an after-the-fact determination of duty, protecting those suffering from emotional distress only if they also suffered harm directly and physically as a result of the defendant's negligence. *Id.* at 171.

Exhibit 8.15 presents a portion of a discussion section in a legal memorandum.

CONCLUSION.   The *conclusion* presents your opinion of how the issues discussed may be resolved. Exhibit 8.16 shows an example of a conclusion to a legal memorandum. The concluding section may acknowledge the fact that research into a particular area bore little fruit. The conclusion also may inform the

EXHIBIT 8.16
Legal Memorandum—Conclusion

CONCLUSION

It is unlikely that Neely has a cause of action against Thompson for the emotional distress that she allegedly suffered due to Thompson's negligence.

It is likely that Melanie has a cause of action for the intentional infliction of emotional distress based on Thompson's outrageous comments to her about her mother.

Note that Neely might pursue, on her own behalf, a claim for the intentional infliction of emotional distress against Thompson for Thompson's reckless behavior in taking Melanie from her home and telling Melanie outrageous things. I recommend that we speak with Neely about the effect on her of Thompson's statements to Melanie. This, in my opinion, is a strong claim. I believe that we could argue successfully that Thompson intended to injure Neely through this egregious act.

Preparing the Internal Memorandum

Ken Lawson, a legal assistant, works for Rhonda Mulhaven. Rhonda is representing the defendant, the Gourmet House Restaurant, in a slip-and-fall case. Ken is surprised that the plaintiff filed suit, because the plaintiff admitted that she saw water on the floor but walked through it anyway, apparently so that she could

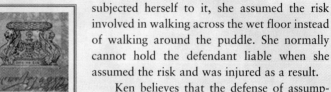

get to the telephone. Ken knows that there are several defenses available, including contributory or comparative negligence and assumption of risk.

RESEARCHING AND ANALYZING CASE LAW

Ken looks in a legal encyclopedia, which defines assumption of risk as follows:

> The plaintiff knew that the situation was dangerous and, despite her knowledge of the danger involved, voluntarily subjected herself to the danger or risk. When a plaintiff has assumed the risk of danger, then the plaintiff cannot recover from the defendant for her injuries.

Ken often uses the IRAC method to analyze legal problems. First, he states the issue. Second, he states the rule of law. Third, he applies the rule to the client's facts. And fourth, he reaches a conclusion. Ken has found this method useful because it helps him to think through all aspects of the problem and to apply the law to the facts to reach a conclusion. He decides to apply the IRAC method to the case on which he is working to determine whether the defense of assumption of risk could be successfully applied.

APPLYING THE IRAC METHOD

First, Ken identifies the issue in the case: Did the plaintiff assume the risk of falling when she walked across the wet floor? Next, Ken notes the applicable rule of law, as stated in the encyclopedia: a plaintiff who knows of a dangerous condition and voluntarily subjects himself or herself to it has assumed the risk and cannot hold a defendant liable. Ken then applies the rule of law to the facts of the case: the plaintiff knew of the dangerous condition, because she knew that the floor was wet. She voluntarily subjected herself to the danger by walking across the wet floor to get to the telephone. Ken then forms a conclusion: because the plaintiff knew of the dangerous condition and voluntarily

subjected herself to it, she assumed the risk involved in walking across the wet floor instead of walking around the puddle. She normally cannot hold the defendant liable when she assumed the risk and was injured as a result.

Ken believes that the defense of assumption of risk might be appropriate in the client's case. He decides to continue researching case law and looks through a state digest. There he finds several cases that contain a definition of assumption of risk similar to the one he read in the encyclopedia. He reviews the cases and then uses KeyCite to check each case on Westlaw® to make sure that it is still current law.

CREATING THE LEGAL MEMORANDUM

Ken sits down at his computer and prepares the following outline for a memorandum to Rhonda:

I. Statement of the Facts—A chronological statement of the events that led to the injury.

II. Question Presented—Did the plaintiff assume the risk of falling when she walked across the wet floor?

III. Brief Conclusion—Yes.

IV. Discussion
   A. Did the plaintiff assume the risk of falling when she walked across the wet floor?
   B. Check the encyclopedia's definition of assumption-of-risk defense and state case law supporting this definition.
   C. Apply the rules in B above to the facts in this case.

V. Conclusion—Based on the results of C above.

Having outlined the memo, Ken writes a first draft, edits and revises it, proofreads it carefully, and delivers it to Rhonda. The next day, she comes into his office and tells him that she is impressed with the quality and organization of his memo and with his analytical skills. She says that based on his research and the memorandum, she has been able to settle the case by convincing the plaintiff's attorney that his client has a weak case.

attorney that more information is needed or that a certain issue needs to be evaluated further. Finally, this section presents you with an opportunity to make strategical suggestions. Paralegals should feel comfortable—especially after a careful legal analysis—in recommending a course of action. Not only do your recommendations reflect thorough analysis, but they also indicate that you are willing to exercise initiative and make a mature judgment, which will be helpful to your supervising attorney.

KEY TERMS AND CONCEPTS

address block 281	confirmation letter 280	persuasive authority 256
annotation 257	demand letter 281	pocket part 277
briefing a case 271	digest 257	primary source 253
case on "all fours" 255	headnote 266	reference line 281
case on point 255	informative letter 280	reporter 260
citation 263	mandatory authority 255	salutation 281
citator 277	opinion 270	secondary source 253
closing 283	opinion (advisory) letter 280	syllabus 266
code 272	parallel citation 263	treatise 257

CHAPTER SUMMARY

1. Primary sources of law consist of all documents that establish the law, including court decisions, statutes, regulations, constitutions, and presidential orders. Secondary sources of law are sources written about the law, such as legal encyclopedias, case digests, annotations, *Restatements of the Law,* treatises, and periodicals.

2. The research process involves five steps: defining the issue, determining the goals of the research project, consulting secondary sources, researching primary sources, and summarizing research results. In researching case law, the researcher's goal is to find cases that are both on point (ideally, cases on "all fours") and mandatory authorities. Mandatory authorities are all legal authorities (statutes, regulations, constitutions, or cases) that courts must follow in making their decisions. In contrast, courts are not bound to follow persuasive authorities (such as cases decided in other jurisdictions).

3. Most state and federal trial court decisions are not published in printed volumes. State appellate court opinions, including those of state supreme courts, are normally published in state reporters, although many states have eliminated their own reporters in favor of West's National Reporter System. Federal trial court opinions are published unofficially in West's *Federal Supplement,* and opinions from the federal circuit courts of appeals are published unofficially in West's *Federal Reporter.* United States Supreme Court opinions are published officially in the *United States Reports,* published by the federal government, and unofficially in West's *Supreme Court Reporter* and the *Lawyers' Edition of the Supreme Court Reports,* which is also published by West Group.

4. In reading and analyzing case law, it is essential to understand the significance of the various components of a case. Legal professionals often use an analytical technique called case briefing to reduce the content of the case to its essentials.

5. Federal statutes are published officially in the *United States Code (U.S.C.).* The *U.S.C.* organizes statutes into fifty subjects, or titles, and further subdivides each title into chapters (sections) and subchapters. The researcher can find a statute in the *U.S.C.* by searching through the topical outlines, by

looking in the index, or by looking under the act's popular name in the volume entitled *Popular Name Table.* The *United States Code Annotated* and the *United States Code Service* are unofficial publications of federal statutes. Both of these sources are useful to researchers because they provide annotations and citations to other resources.

6. Reading and analyzing statutory language is often difficult. In reading statutory law, you should note the statute's provisions concerning its coverage and effective date, the class or groups of people to whom it applies, the type of conduct being regulated by the statute, and any exception to the statute's coverage. In interpreting statutory law, the paralegal can turn to previous judicial interpretations of the statute, if any exist, and the legislative history of the statute.

7. Regulations issued by federal administrative agencies are primary sources of law. Agency regulations are published in the *Code of Federal Regulations (C.F.R.),* which follows a format similar to that of the *U.S.C.* The U.S. Constitution can be found in a number of publications, including the extensively annotated official publication, which is available through the Library of Congress. Annotated versions of state constitutions are also available.

8. A critical requirement in legal research is making sure that the research results obtained are still valid. Printed legal sources are commonly updated through the periodic publication of supplemental pamphlets or pocket parts. The various volumes of *Shepard's Citations* allow the researcher to verify whether a case, statute, or regulation represents current law by indicating whether the case has been overruled or reversed, the statute repealed or amended, the regulation voided or superseded, and the like. Online citators enable the researcher to access recent cases, statutes, or regulations (or amendments or modifications to existing statutes or regulations) and thus ensure that research results are as up to date as possible.

9. Legal writing requires excellent writing skills, and special care must be taken to ensure that legal documents are free of grammatical and spelling errors. Other important considerations in legal writing include making sure that legal documents are accurate in every respect, using legal terminology appropriately, and knowing whether a writing project calls for an objective or adversarial writing approach.

10. Much legal writing consists of documents relating to litigation procedures, such as pleadings and discovery documents. These important forms of legal writing were discussed in Chapter 6.

11. Paralegals commonly draft the following types of letters: informative letters (to notify clients or others of some action or procedure or to transmit documents), confirmation letters (to create a written record of an oral transaction or agreement), opinion letters (to convey to a client or other party a formal legal opinion or advice on an issue), and demand letters (to advance the client's cause by demanding something from an adversarial party on the client's behalf).

12. The internal legal memorandum is a thoroughly researched and objectively written summation of the facts, issues, and applicable law relating to a particular legal claim. The purpose of the memo is to inform the attorney for whom the document is written of the strengths and weaknesses of the client's position. Generally, the legal memo is presented in a format that includes the following sections: heading, statement of the facts, questions presented, brief conclusion, discussion and analysis of the facts and the applicable law, and conclusion.

▓ QUESTIONS FOR REVIEW

1. What is the difference between primary and secondary sources of law? How are these sources used in legal research?

2. What is a case on point? What is a case on "all fours"? Why is finding such a case important when researching case law? What is the difference between a mandatory authority and a persuasive authority?

3. How are court decisions published? What information is contained in a case citation? What is a parallel citation? In what reporter would you find a case decided by a U.S. court of appeals?

4. What are the various components of a case? What is meant by "briefing a case"?

5. In what official publications would you find federal statutes and administrative regulations? How could you locate constitutional law?

6. What are some techniques for interpreting and analyzing statutory law?

7. Why is it important to find the most current law? How can you verify that your research results are up to date?

8. What are some important considerations in legal writing? What is the difference between objective and adversarial writing? When would each approach be appropriate?

9. What are the components of a legal letter? Name and describe four types of legal correspondence.

10. What are the components of an internal legal memorandum? What is the purpose of the memo, and for whom is it written?

ETHICAL QUESTIONS

1. Barbara Coltiers is a legal assistant in a very busy litigation practice. She gets a call from a nervous attorney in her firm thirty minutes before the attorney is to appear in court. He wants her to do some research before he goes to court. He has just heard about a case that might help him win and gives her the citation. Because he is in a hurry, he gives her the wrong volume number. She has a hard time finding the case, but after about fifteen minutes of searching turns to the table of cases and locates the citation. She quickly copies the case and runs to his office with it so that he can hurry across the street to the court for his appearance. She is in such a hurry that she forgets to check the subsequent history of the case.

   It turns out that the case had been overruled by the state supreme court and was therefore no longer controlling in the jurisdiction. The attorney is chastised by the judge for citing it. In fact, the judge is so annoyed with the attorney for making an argument that was not based on existing law that he denies the attorney's motion and makes the attorney pay the other side's court costs. When the client finds out why the motion was denied, she is irate. Does the client have any remedy against the attorney? Against Barbara?

2. John Hernandez is studying at a local college to be a legal assistant. The college has Westlaw® for its students to use. The software license specifically prohibits the faculty or students of the college from using the program for personal work. John knows that Kathy has a part-time job with a law firm, and he becomes aware that Kathy is using Westlaw® regularly to do research for her supervising attorney in that firm. What should John do?

3. David Thomas, a paralegal, is sending out a letter to a client. It is an informative letter advising the client of the status of her case and explaining what the next step in the litigation process will be. David signs the letter without including his title. He mails the letter to the client. The client has questions, and she calls David, thinking that he is an attorney. How should David handle this situation? What should he have done to prevent it?

PRACTICE QUESTIONS AND ASSIGNMENTS

1. Using the material presented in the chapter, identify the case name, volume number, reporter abbreviation, page number, and year of decision for each of the following case citations and their parallel cites:

   a. *Smith v. James,* 400 Mich.19, 630 N.W. 2d 98 (1999).

   b. *Johnson v. Fassler Wrecking, Inc.,* 10 Cal.4th 539, 27 Cal.Rptr.2d 201 (1999).

   c. *Barnes v. Barnes,* 95 N.Y.2d 101, 637 N.E. 2d 23, 654 N.Y.S. 13 (1999).

   d. *Miranda v. Arizona,* 384 U.S. 436, 86 S.Ct. 1602, 16 L.Ed.2d 694 (1966).

2. Using the material presented in the chapter, indicate whether the following sources are primary or secondary sources:

   a. Digests.

   b. Case reporters.

   c. Legal encyclopedias.

   d. Statutes.

   e. The *Code of Federal Regulations.*

3. Clip an article out of the newspaper or a news journal. Then follow the instructions and answer the questions given below:

a. Underline all of the active verbs and circle all of the passive verbs. Did the writer use more active verbs than passive verbs in writing the article?

b. Count the number of words in each sentence. What is the average sentence length? Do short sentences predominate?

c. Locate the topic sentence in each paragraph. Is the writer's paragraph construction effective?

d. Notice how the author uses transitional sentences when moving from one paragraph to the next. Underline the key transitional words or phrases.

4. Proofread the following paragraph, circling all of the mistakes. Then rewrite the paragraph.

> The defendent was aressted and chrge with drunk driving. Blood alcohol level of .15. He refused to take a breahalyzer test at first. After the police explained to him that he would loose his lisense if he did not take it, he concented. He also has ablood test to verify the results of the breathalyzer.

5. Using the material presented in this chapter, prepare an informative letter to a client using the following facts:

> The client, Dr. Brown, is being sued for medical malpractice and is going to be deposed on January 15, 1999, at 1:00 P.M. The deposition will take place at the law offices of Callaghan & Young. The offices are located at 151 East Jefferson Avenue, Cincinnati, Ohio. The client needs to call your supervising attorney's office to set up an appointment, so that the attorney can prepare Dr. Brown for the deposition.

▒ USING INTERNET RESOURCES

1. Go to the home page of the American Law Institute (ALI) at www.ali.org. Browse through this site and its offerings, and then answer the following questions:

a. Select "ALI Press Releases" and look over the list of new press releases. Have any new *Restatements* been published by the ALI? If so, on what topics?

b. Now access the ALI's "Catalogue of Publications." How many *Restatements of the Law* have been published by the ALI? Make a list of the topics covered in the *Restatements*.

2. The *United States Code,* which contains the statutes passed by Congress, can be accessed through Cornell Law School's Legal Information Institute at www.law.cornell.edu/uscode. Access this Web site and answer the following questions:

a. How many ways are there to access the *United States Code* within the Web site? What are they?

b. Scroll down to the title listing. How many titles are there? For what is "title" a synonym? Click on Title 42. What does it cover? How many chapters are in Title 42? In the "Search Title 42" box, enter "Superfund Act." What results do you obtain?

c. Go back to the *United States Code* home page. Using the section entitled "Find U.S. Code Materials by Title and Section," enter "42" in the title box and "9601" in the section box; then click on "Go to title and section." Describe what you find. In what chapter is this act located? In addition to the statutory section, what else is available?

3. The American Bar Association's (ABA's) Web site contains a helpful section on legal writing. Access the Web site at **www.abanet.org/lpm/writing**.

a. Click on the "Writing" button. What topics are listed? Which might be helpful?

b. Click on the "Style" button. What resources are available? Where are these resources available? Click on "Style Manuals." Give the names of the first two style manuals listed. Click on "Dictionaries." How does the Web site of Webster's Dictionary work? Access both the "Grammar" and "Miscellany" buttons and review the contents as well.

c. Click on the "Labs" button. What is accessible from this Web page? What information is accessible from the "Handouts" Web site? How might a student use this information? What is accessible from Purdue Lab? How might a student use this information?

COMPUTER-ASSISTED LEGAL RESEARCH

Chapter Outline

After completing this chapter, you will know:

- How CD-ROMs and legal-research services provided by Westlaw® and Lexis® help legal professionals in computer-assisted legal research (CALR).

- What the Internet is, and how it can be accessed and navigated.

- Some strategies for planning and conducting research on the Internet.

- How you can find people and investigate companies using Internet search tools and databases.

- How to find some of the best legal resources available on the Internet.

INTRODUCTION

Computers and online databases have greatly simplified the tasks of paralegals in all areas of legal work. This is particularly true in the area of legal research. One of the great benefits of computer technology for legal practitioners is **computer-assisted legal research (CALR)**. As you learned in Chapter 8, thorough and up-to-date legal research requires access to voluminous source materials, including state and federal court decisions and statutory law. Today, attorneys and paralegals can access many of these materials online—either through the use of proprietary software and a modem connection or via the Internet. Additionally, a number of primary and secondary legal sources are available on CD-ROMs.

An obvious advantage of CALR is that you can locate and print out court cases, statutory provisions, and other legal documents within a matter of minutes without leaving your work station. Another key advantage of CALR is that new case decisions and changes in statutory law are entered almost immediately into certain online legal databases, including those of Westlaw® and Lexis®. This means that you can find out easily and quickly whether a case decided three months ago is still "good law" today. The case may have been overturned by a higher court since then, and the only way you would know this would be through CALR (because the case would not yet be included in printed sources).

In this chapter, after a discussion of CD-ROMs and legal research, we look at the legal-research services available through Westlaw® and Lexis®. We then look at the Internet—what it is and how it can be used to conduct online research efficiently. You will learn about service providers, browsers, and search engines. You will discover how to evaluate whether the Internet is the best tool for particular research projects. You will also read about some of the best resources currently available on the Internet.

By the time you read this chapter, some of what we say will have changed, particularly with respect to Internet resources. Some of these resources may have improved, others may have been removed, and still others may have been added. The general approach to conducting research online will not have altered, however. If you master the basic principles of online research discussed in this chapter, you will be able to conduct research on the Internet no matter how much it changes.

CD-ROMS AND LEGAL RESEARCH

Increasingly, today's law firms are using research materials available in CD-ROM ("compact disk, read-only memory") format. CD-ROM technology allows the legal researcher to access data on a small, compact laser disk, much like the compact disks that are sold in music stores.

CD-ROMs are accessed through a CD-ROM reader, which reads and displays the contents of a CD-ROM when it is inserted into the reader. Depending on the computer system, the reader may be contained within the computer or attached to the computer with a cable. The software program accompanying a CD-ROM allows the computer operating system to communicate with the CD-ROM. A paralegal using CD-ROMs for legal research would find the CD-ROM containing the relevant reference materials—a legal encyclopedia, for example—and use the CD-ROM's index or search tool to quickly locate a given topic or subtopic.

Advantages of Using CD-ROMs

Most law firms have law libraries containing legal encyclopedias, case digests, statutory compilations, and other research materials frequently used by the firms'

Computer-Assisted Legal Research (CALR)
Any legal research conducted with the assistance of computers. CALR includes the use of CD-ROMs, fee-based legal services providers such as Westlaw® and Lexis®, and the Internet.

attorneys and paralegals. Law libraries and the physical space required to house them are expensive, particularly for small law firms. An obvious advantage of using legal reference materials on CD-ROMs is that they are far less costly to purchase and require much less space than their printed counterparts.

A CD-ROM holds the equivalent of over 600 megabytes of data. This means that one CD-ROM can store approximately 300,000 pages, or over one hundred volumes of legal reference materials. For example, the entire 215-volume *United States Code Annotated* (discussed in Chapter 8) is contained on only two CD-ROMs. Many federal government publications, legal encyclopedias, West reporters, and other research sources are also available in CD-ROM format. Exhibit 9.1 shows a photograph of CD-ROM legal libraries.

CD-ROMs can also be easily transported. They can be used (on laptop or notebook computers) while traveling or even in the courtroom. A further advantage of using CD-ROMs is that searches of materials contained on them can be conducted more easily and quickly than when using printed reference sources. For example, if you are researching a state statute, you can search through the statute for certain words or section numbers using the search command, which saves valuable research time. West's CD-ROM libraries offer the advantage of the key-number system. This system simplifies legal research by allowing you to search key numbers to find relevant case law or other legal sources. You can also copy segments of the statute directly to your computer, which reduces the amount of time you spend in document preparation as well as lessening the risk of error.

Disadvantages of Using CD-ROMs

The major disadvantage of using CD-ROMs in legal research is that, like their printed equivalents, they can become outdated. Suppose that you want to locate recent court cases interpreting a particular provision of the *United States Code*. If your CD-ROM containing the *United States Code Annotated* was purchased five years ago, clearly you will be unable to find the latest annotations on that CD-ROM. In other words, just as when conducting research using printed legal reference materials, you need to keep in mind the date of the materials included on the CD-ROM.

Note that even the most recently issued CD-ROM version of a legal encyclopedia or other reference work may be somewhat outdated, just as a printed text is, because of the time it takes to create and distribute the CD-ROM. The best way to ensure that your research is really up to date is to check an online legal database.

WESTLAW® AND LEXIS®

CALR has made it possible to access legal databases containing many of the most important legal resources. By accessing databases provided through commercial legal-research services, legal professionals can obtain case law or statutory law relating to a particular issue within seconds. Although not all printed legal sources are contained on these databases, many of them are. Two premier legal-research services often used by attorneys and paralegals are Westlaw® and Lexis®. To use these legal-research services, a law firm or other user signs a contract with the provider of the services. Charges for the service are typically based on either online time (Westlaw®) or the number of database searches performed (Lexis®).

The Westlaw® and Lexis® databases contain extensive legal and business information. Westlaw®, for example, is organized into more than ten thousand

EXHIBIT 9.1
West CD-ROM Libraries

Reproduced with permission of West Group.

databases covering all areas of the law. It is possible to access such primary sources as federal and state statutes, court cases, and administrative regulations. Some of the materials are also accessible through specialized databases, such as bankruptcy, insurance, and taxation. Secondary sources include legal texts and periodicals, public records, and other sources of business and financial information.

Accessing Westlaw® or Lexis®

To access Westlaw® or Lexis®, a subscriber can use the service's proprietary software, which allows the subscriber's computer to access the database through a modem connection over a telephone line. Traditionally, this was the only way that legal professionals could access these services. Today, both Westlaw® and Lexis® can be accessed online via the Internet as well—at **www.westlaw.com** and **www.lexis.com,** respectively. Special software is not needed to access either of these services via the Internet.

An advantage of accessing these databases on the Web is that research can be done easily with a standard browser (browsers are discussed later in this chapter) and without the extensive training needed to use the proprietary software. A disadvantage is that users who do not have the software also do not have the accompanying manuals that instruct them on how to use the services. "Help" links at both Web sites, however, give users instructions on how to perform various tasks. Another disadvantage for Lexis® users is that only a portion of the Lexis® databases are included on the Web site. In contrast, Westlaw® offers the full panoply of its services on the Web.

When you access Westlaw® or Lexis® (using proprietary software or via the Internet), you will be asked to sign onto the service with your password. After you sign on, a welcome page is displayed. (The welcome page of Westlaw® is shown in Exhibit 9.2.) From this page, you can begin your research. You can retrieve documents by citation, check citations, or search databases for cases, statutes, or other documents on a given topic or issue.

EXHIBIT 9.2
The Opening ("Welcome")
Page of Westlaw®

Reproduced with permission of West Group.

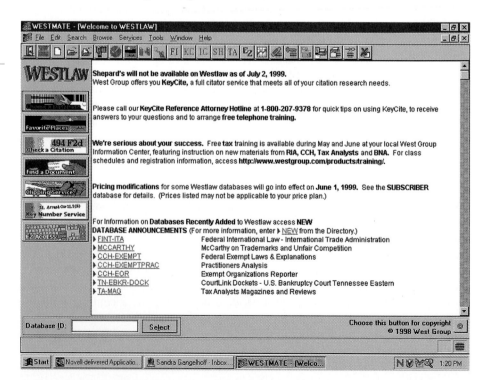

Retrieving a Document by Citation

If you have the citation for a document, such as a court case or statute, you can enter the citation and call up the document. For example, on Westlaw® you would click on the "Find a Document" box on the left side of the screen. This will open a query box into which you key the citation for a case, statute, regulation, or other document. Within seconds, the cited document will appear on the screen.

Checking a Citation

Westlaw® and Lexis® both provide online citators. Recall from Chapter 8 that a citator, such as one of *Shepard's* citators, shows the history of a case and provides a list of legal references that have cited or interpreted a particular case. Online citators are extremely useful to legal researchers because they are more up to date than printed citators. For example, suppose that you want to find out whether the holding in a particular case decided by a California appellate court is still "good law." If you are using Lexis®, you can use the **Auto-Cite** citator to find out if the decision was appealed to the California Supreme Court (or to the United States Supreme Court) and, if so, whether the holding was affirmed, overturned, or modified on appeal. You can also "Shepardize" the case to find out how courts in other jurisdictions have dealt with the same issue.

If you are using Westlaw®, you can use the **KeyCite** citator service. An important editorial enhancement to documents accessible through Westlaw® are the KeyCite case status flags, which indicate when there is case history that should be investigated. Depending on the color of the flag, you are warned that a case is not good law for at least one of its points, that the case has some negative history but its holding has not been reversed, or that the case has been overruled. KeyCite provides other features to make your research more efficient. When checking the citation of your case in the KeyCite database, stars added to the citation of a citing case show the extent to which your case is discussed in the citing case. For example, four stars indicate that the citing case contains an extended discussion of your case, usually more than a printed page of text. One star indicates the reference is brief, usually no more than as part of a list of case citations.

If your search results include a statute or an agency rule, when using Westlaw® you can check for any recent changes with the "Update" service. The service displays any documents on Westlaw® that amend or repeal the statute or rule you are viewing. The "General Materials" service retrieves references, notes, or annotations that apply to the title, chapter, or subchapter of a statute or rule you are viewing. This service also displays tables that track statute numbers through amendments and other changes.

These and other tools allow you to access updated law within seconds. As stressed in Chapter 8, a crucial part of legal research is making sure your findings are accurate and up to date. If your supervising attorney is preparing for trial, for example, the attorney will want to base his or her legal argument on current authorities. A precedential case that may have been good law yesterday may not remain so today.

 Making sure that your research results reflect current law is a crucial step in legal research.

Selecting a Database

Much of the legal research that paralegals perform involves searching legal databases for cases or statutes relating to certain topics or legal issues. To do this, you

Auto-Cite

An aid to legal research developed by the editors of Lexis®. On Lexis®, Auto-Cite can be used to find the history of a case, to verify whether the case is still good law, and to perform other functions.

KeyCite

An aid to legal research developed by the editors of Westlaw®. On Westlaw®, KeyCite can trace case history, retrieve secondary sources, categorize legal citations by legal issue, and perform other functions.

DEVELOPING PARALEGAL SKILLS

Cite Checking on Westlaw®

Katie, a paralegal, needs to quickly check a citation for a case from the court of appeals to see if it is still good law. Her supervising attorney wants to use the case in a brief that must be filed within a few hours. Katie accesses Westlaw®. She enters her password and client-identifying information. Once she has gained access, she clicks on the "Check This Citation" box and enters the case cite. Then she clicks on KeyCite. The search turns up a red flag, which means that the case has been reversed or overruled and is no longer good law. Katie clicks on the red flag, which takes her to the decision in which the case was reversed or overruled. It turns out that the case was reversed on different grounds. So the rule of law for which her supervising attorney wants to cite the case is still good

law. Katie and her supervisor can use the case in their brief after all.

TIPS FOR USING KeyCite

- A red flag means that a case has been reversed or overruled and must be reviewed.
- A yellow flag means that the case has been questioned and should be checked.
- Never cite a case without verifying that it is still good law.
- Always read a citing case to find why your case has a red or yellow flag and to determine what issue in your case has been questioned, reversed, or overruled.

first select a database that you want to search. If you are using Westlaw®, for example, you would click on the box labeled "Choose a Database," which would open a page containing the main directory. From that page, you could select "Federal Materials," "State Materials," or another topic and then click on "Expand" in the lower right-hand corner of the screen. Eventually, you will find the particular database you want.

For example, suppose that your supervising attorney has asked you to research case law on the liability of tobacco products manufacturers for cancer caused by the use of those products. To do a thorough investigation, you will need to search the databases containing decisions from all state courts as well as from all federal courts. To find these databases on Westlaw®, you would access the main directory, select "State Materials," and click on "expand." Then you would select "Case Law" to expand this database. Eventually, you will find the database containing decisions from all state courts ("allstates"). For federal court decisions, you would select "Federal Materials" from the main directory and continue the "expand" function until you reach the database containing decisions from all federal courts ("allfeds").

After you become familiar with the database identifiers on whatever service you are using, you can access that database more directly. For example, on the opening page of Westlaw® you can enter "allfeds" or "allstates" into the database box at the bottom of the screen.

Searching a Database

Once you have chosen a specific database, such as "allfeds," a search box will open on the screen into which you can enter your *search query*. Traditionally, searches of Westlaw® and Lexis® databases had to use the "terms and connectors" (Boolean) method of searching. Today, both services also allow users to draft search queries using natural language (or "plain English"). Before beginning your search, you should indicate in the search box which method you will use.

ETHICAL CONCERN
Cutting the Cost of Legal Research

As a paralegal, you have an ethical duty to the client to minimize costs, including the cost of computerized research—which, after all, is paid for by the client. One way you can reduce research costs is to plan your search queries carefully before accessing a service such as Lexis® or Westlaw®. This way, you do not have to spend online time making such decisions.

THE TERMS AND CONNECTORS METHOD.   In a search employing terms and connectors, you use numerical and grammatical connectors to specify the relationship between the terms. For example, to find cases on the liability of tobacco products manufacturers for cancer caused by the use of those products, you could type the following terms and connectors in the query box:

liability /p cancer /s tobacco

This would retrieve all cases in which the term *liability* is in the same paragraph ("/p") as the term *cancer,* with the term *cancer* in the same sentence ("/s") as the term *tobacco.* To restrict the scope of your search, you can add a field restriction. For example, you might want to retrieve only court opinions rendered after 1995. If you are using Westlaw®, you could add the following to your query to restrict the search results to cases decided after 1995:

& added date (after 1/1/1996)

Numerous other grammatical and numerical connectors can be used to efficiently search a database. These are listed in the instruction manuals provided to Lexis® and Westlaw® subscribers. Some of the most commonly used terms and connectors are indicated online when you are connected to one of these services. For example, on Westlaw® you will find a description of some options in the search box into which you enter your query.

Generally, when drafting queries, you want to make sure your query is not too broad (as it would be if you entered just the term *liability*). Your search will be futile because so many thousands of documents contain that term. At the same time, you do not want your search to be so narrow that no cases will be retrieved.

THE NATURAL LANGUAGE METHOD.   The natural language method (called "Freestyle" on Lexis® and WIN on Westlaw®—WIN is an acronym for "Westlaw® is Natural") allows you to type a description of an issue in plain English to retrieve the most relevant documents. In searching for cases relating to the topic in the previous example, your query might read as follows:

Is a tobacco manufacturer liable for cancer caused by the use of its products?

This query would retrieve the documents most closely matching your description. Exhibit 9.3 on the next page illustrates the results of running a search with these words on Westlaw®.

To include synonyms that might be necessary to produce more comprehensive results, there is a "Thesaurus" feature on Westlaw® that can suggest terms for your search. After entering your "natural language" query, click "Thesaurus." Select a term from the list for which you want suggestions. Then click "View

EXHIBIT 9.3
Search Results on Westlaw®

Reproduced with permission of West Group.

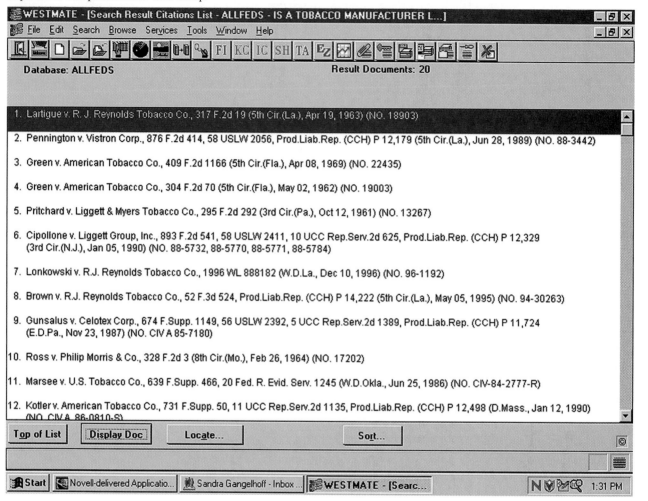

Related Terms." If you want to add one of the terms to your description, select the term and click "Add Term to Description."

Browser Enhancements

Suppose that your search resulted in a list of twenty cases relevant to your topic. At this point, there are internal browsing tools that can help you pinpoint your search more precisely. For example, Westlaw® browsing tools include "Term" browsing, "Best Section" browsing, and "Locate." Browsing by "Term" or "Best Section" allows you to find exact references to your search term.

The "Locate" tool allows you to scan the documents in your search result for terms that were not included in your query. For example, assume that your original request was, in natural language, "Is a tobacco manufacturer liable for cancer caused by the use of its products?" If you want to know whether "death" is discussed in any of your search-result documents, you can use the "Locate" tool (select "Locate" from the pull-down menu) and type "death" in the "Locate

Query" box; then click "Locate." Click the "Term" box at the bottom of the screen to continue the "Locate" function. To cancel "Locate," select "Cancel Locate" from the pull-down menu.

When browsing through your search results, remember that the time you spend using the service is costly. If you have found a case or cases that appear to be on point, you can print them out (or download them to your computer) for further study and analysis.

GOING ONLINE—INTERNET BASICS

Until the advent of the Internet, CALR generally meant research using CD-ROMs and databases provided by commercial computerized legal-research services, such as Westlaw® and Lexis®. Today, paralegals and other legal professionals can take advantage of the vast resources on the Internet to better serve their firms' clients.

As already mentioned, Westlaw® and Lexis® are both now "online"[1] (accessible through the Internet), as are numerous other legal-research services. Additionally, today's paralegals have access to a vast array of nonlegal online databases to quickly find other types of information they may be asked to locate.

In the remaining pages of this chapter, you will learn how the Internet can be used to conduct legal or fact-based research. You will also read about some of the best Web sites to access for particular types of information. We begin by looking at some Internet "basics"—what the Internet is and how it can be accessed and navigated to locate information.

What Is the Internet?

The Internet is a global communication network of interconnected computers. Business computers, university and college computers, government computers, your personal computer—all of these and more can be part of the "network of networks" that constitutes cyberspace, or the "information superhighway."

The Internet is growing so fast that estimates of its size are outdated before they make it into print. The technology that makes the Internet possible also changes quickly. The important point for a paralegal is how to use this technology to find information.

Internet Tools

User-friendly software, color monitors and printers, and faster processors have combined with other technological advances to open the Internet to anyone with a little computer knowledge. With a few points and clicks, a paralegal can get onto, and maneuver around, the Internet. Once online, the tools that a paralegal will find most useful include uniform resource locators, e-mail, file transfer protocol, and the World Wide Web.

UNIFORM RESOURCE LOCATORS.   A uniform resource locator (URL) is an Internet "address." A paralegal might think of a URL as an electronic citation. Nearly every resource on the Internet is identified by a URL.

---

1. Note that Westlaw® and Lexis® have been "online" for years, in the sense that their databases can be accessed electronically. In the remaining pages of this chapter, we use the term *online* to refer specifically to the Internet.

The basic format of a URL is "service://directorypath/filename." For example, http://www.westlegalstudies.com is the URL for the West Legal Studies Web site, a resource center for paralegal instructors, students, and professionals. This URL indicates that you use the "http" service to reach the directory path (or here, host computer) www.westlegalstudies.com. This site provides access to instructor resources, new textbook and learning material releases, and an online catalogue and bookstore.

Hypertext Transfer Protocol (http)
An interface program that enables computers to communicate. Hypertext is a database system by which distinct objects, such as text and graphics, can be linked. Protocol is a system of formats and rules, such as the speed of a transmission.

The letters **"http"** stand for **hypertext transfer protocol**. When something on the Internet is a site on the World Wide Web (to be discussed shortly), the first part of its address is "http." *Hypertext* is a database system by which disparate objects (text, graphics, and so on) can be linked to each other. With hypertext, you can move from one object to another even though their forms are different (for example, text and graphics have different forms). *Protocol* is the system of formats and rules that enables two computers to communicate. (Because "http://" is part of the URL of every site on the Web, we have omitted it from the rest of the URLs included in this chapter.)

World Wide Web
A hypertext-based system through which specially formatted documents are accessible on the Internet.

The letters "www" stand for World Wide Web. The **World Wide Web**, or simply the Web, is a hypertext-based service through which data is made available on the Internet.

To enter a URL into a browser, usually it is not necessary to type in "http" and "www." The browser will enter these terms automatically. This saves time.

E-MAIL.   One of the most common uses of the Internet today is for e-mail, and legal professionals and others often include e-mail addresses on their letterhead stationery and business cards. E-mail can at times be a research tool, as well. E-mail is the basis for services associated with listservs and newsgroups (discussed later in this chapter), for example.

An Internet service provider (to be discussed shortly) can supply an e-mail address and the software that allows a user to compose, send, and receive e-mail. The software is also available from other sources.

File Transfer Protocol (FTP)
An interface program that connects one computer to another over the Internet to copy files.

FILE TRANSFER PROTOCOL.   **File transfer protocol (ftp)** is a very basic interface that connects one computer to another to copy files. The files may contain text, graphics, or software. Ftp is the tool with which a computer (called a client) copies the files onto itself or from itself onto the host computer. A host computer set up to receive ftp requests is called a server.

To find files that are available from ftp servers, researchers use an online index called Archie. This index can be found at several Web sites, including ArchiePlex (www.lerc.nasa.gov/archieplex).

WORLD WIDE WEB.   The World Wide Web (the Web) is a data service on the Internet. The Web is accessed through a browser (browsers will be discussed shortly). The browser's basic user interface is hypertext, which means that communications between computers on the Web are primarily through links and menus (lists of commands).

Home Page
The main page of a Web site. Often, the home page serves as a table of contents to other pages at the site.

When most people think of the Internet, they think of the Web. The Web consists primarily of documents, which are referred to as Web pages (sometimes **home pages**) or Web sites. These pages or sites usually contain links in boldfaced, underlined, or colored text. By selecting or clicking on a link, a user can be transported to other pages or sites, or run other software.

For example, if you access the home page of the Legal Information Institute at Cornell Law School at www.law.cornell.edu (see Exhibit 9.4) which has one of the best law-related sites on the Internet, you will find numerous links. Among

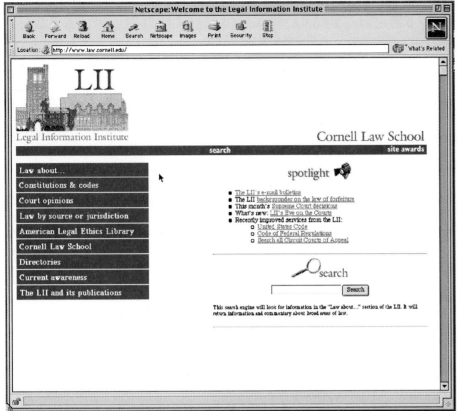

EXHIBIT 9.4
**The Home Page of the
Legal Information Institute**

Reproduced with permission.

other things, you will find links to the U.S. Constitution, the *United States Code,* and selected court cases—including the most recent United States Supreme Court decisions as well as some of the Court's historic decisions. You can download text, graphics, and software from Web sites (or "cut and paste" selected portions into a word-processing document).

Accessing the Internet

The Internet can be compared to an enormous library. Knowing how to get into the library—how to gain access to the information you need—is one of the most important parts of any research, and this is true of using the Internet. To get into a library, you need to know where it is and you need to go through the door. To get onto the Internet, you also need to find it and to go there—with a computer and an online service or an Internet service provider.

There are three basic types of *gateways* (methods of access) to the Internet. These methods differ in their cost and their ease of use. The most expensive method is to set up your own gateway, which a large law firm or business organization might do. This requires registering a domain name with the Internet Network Information Center (InterNIC) (see **www.internic.com**), paying a registration fee, and operating a computer work station with software connected to a special high-speed phone line. Other techniques to gain access are through commercial online services and Internet service providers.

COMMERCIAL ONLINE SERVICES.   Some small businesses and many individuals access the Internet through **commercial online services,** such as America Online

Commercial Online Services
Internet service providers that, for a fee, allow their subscribers access to resources that are otherwise restricted.

(**www.aol.com**). There are also online services, such as Counsel Connect (**www.americanlawyer.com**), designed for legal professionals. Each of these services has advantages and disadvantages.

The chief advantages of commercial online services are that they are generally designed to be easy to use and direct you to resources that are likely to meet your needs. The chief disadvantage is that the volume of users often surpasses the ability of a service's equipment to deliver data quickly (or sometimes to deliver it at all) and to provide other support that the service may advertise. Some services may also inhibit or prevent your viewing particular sites otherwise available on the Web.

Internet Service Provider (ISP)
A company that provides dedicated access to the Internet, generally through a local phone number.

INTERNET SERVICE PROVIDERS (ISPs).   An **Internet service provider (ISP)** is a service that provides dedicated access to the Internet. There are thousands of ISPs, which are usually the least expensive options for gaining access to the Internet. Most ISPs serve local regions, but there are national ISPs, including AT&T WorldNet (**www.att.com/worldnet**), Netcom (**www.netcom.com**), and Sprint Communications Company, L.P. (EarthLink Sprint TotalAccess can be accessed through **www.sprint.com**).

An ISP is often less consumer oriented than a commercial online service, while offering the same features, including basic Internet access, e-mail addresses, software, and other services. An advantage of an ISP is that it normally does not have the same volume of users as a commercial service and thus can deliver data faster. For the same reason, an ISP may respond more quickly with technical support, although it may not offer the same range of support as a commercial service advertises. A list of thousands of ISPs, organized by area code and country, is available at **thelist.internet.com**.

Navigating the Internet

Once you have access to the Internet, the next important step is to navigate through the vast number of Internet resources until you find the information you are seeking. As stated earlier, the Internet is similar to an enormous library, but there is a key difference—the Internet has no centralized, comprehensive card catalogue. In place of a card catalogue, a researcher uses browsers, guides, directories, and search engines.

BROWSERS.   A browser is software that allows a computer to roam the Web. Some commercial online services build browsers into their service. The most popular browsers, however, are Microsoft Explorer (**www.microsoft.com/ie**) and Netscape Navigator (**www.netscape.com/computering/download/index.html**). These browsers can be used with any Internet service.

Improvements and other changes in browser interfaces and capabilities are so rapid and ongoing that almost any discussion of specific features would be outdated before it was published. Although each browser (and each version of each browser) has its own features, all browsers perform the same basic functions. These functions include the ability to set up automatic links (referred to as "Favorites" in Explorer and "Bookmarks" in Netscape) to Internet sites, in order to access those links easily, and to travel back and forth from resource to resource on the Web. Browsers also make it possible to copy text from Web sites and paste it into a word-processing document. With a browser, you can download images, software, and documents to your computer. Finally, with a browser you can search a single document that appears in your window. This last feature is most helpful when the document is long and your time is short.

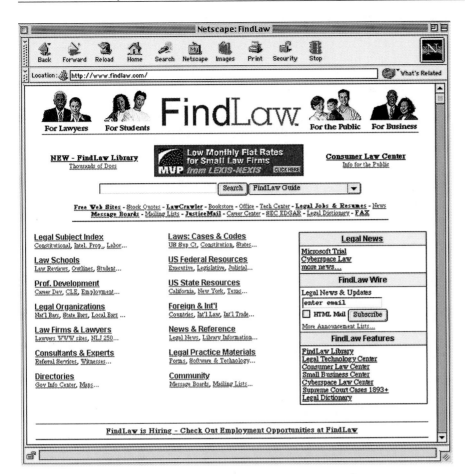

GUIDES AND DIRECTORIES.   The lack of a single, comprehensive catalogue of what's available on the Internet has led to hundreds of attempts to survey and map the Web. Lists of Web sites categorized by subject are organized into guides and directories, which can be accessed at Web sites online. These sites provide menus of topics that are usually subdivided into narrower subtopics, which themselves may be subdivided, until a list of URLs is reached. If you're uncertain of which menu to use, directories allow you to run a search of the directory site. Popular examples of online directories include Yahoo (**www.yahoo.com**) and, for legal professionals, FindLaw (**www.findlaw.com**). Exhibit 9.5 presents FindLaw's home page.

SEARCH ENGINES.   Next to browsers, the most important tools for conducting research on the Web are search engines. Search engines include the following:

- AltaVista (**altavista.digital.com**).
- Excite (**www.excite.com**).
- HotBot (**www.hotbot.com**).
- Infoseek (**www.infoseek.com**).
- Lycos (**www.lycos.com**).

A search engine scans the Web and indexes the contents of pages into a database. There are search engines that will search only specific categories of resources. For example, FindLaw, Inc., provides a tool at **www.findlaw.com** that searches only legal resources on the Web (see Exhibit 9.5). The FindLaw tool can be further limited to search specified databases, such as federal government sites.

Search engines vary in the size and scope of searches, in the flexibility of possible queries, and in the presentation of results. When contemplating whether the Internet is the best tool for a research project, however, you should always keep the following in mind:

 For legal research, even the best search engine cannot match the results of a search conducted with the internal search engine of a commercial fee-based database such as Lexis® or Westlaw®.

For example, all search engines have the capability to use connectors, such as "and," "or," and "not." For most search engines, this is the limit of their sophistication. More precise queries can be formulated with Westlaw® or Lexis®, especially for a researcher proficient in using the service. As discussed earlier in this chapter, search tools on Lexis® or Westlaw® allow a researcher to pinpoint anything in the service's database. As of this writing, universal Web search engines cannot match this capability.

Another difficulty with Web search engines is the quality of the results. In response to a search query, a search engine often lists irrelevant sources. Some of the best search engines will categorize results by, for example, the type of Web site (commercial, educational, personal, and so on—see, for instance, Northern Light at **www.nlsearch.com**). This can be helpful, but it does not eliminate irrelevant sites. Sometimes, irrelevant sites can be eliminated only when a researcher goes to the sites and scrolls through them. Ordinarily, however, the first few hits are likely to be the most useful, and a researcher with experience can often avoid others that are inappropriate.

 To obtain the best results, a researcher must know the features of each search engine and how to focus queries to take advantage of those features most effectively.

A capable researcher will also keep abreast of changes to the search engines. Each engine includes tips at its site for searching with it. Also, of course, with practice comes proficiency.

There are two basic kinds of searches: by key word and by concept. A keyword search generates Web sources that use the exact terms that the researcher types in. A concept search adds sources that use related words. In general, the best results are obtained in a search for Web pages that contain very specific terms. Exhibit 9.6 provides a look at the results of running a search in a search engine.

META SEARCH ENGINES.   Meta search engines run searches on more than one search engine simultaneously. They are the best tools for searching the most Web space possible. It should be noted that nothing searches the entire Web, however. The most capable search engine searches less than 10 percent of all of the Web pages on the Internet. These selected pages include those that receive the most hits. (This is in sharp contrast to searches in commercial databases such as Lexis® or Westlaw®.) Meta search engines include Metacrawler (**www.metacrawler.com**) and All In One Search (**www.AllOneSearch.com**).

Using search engines, including meta search engines, is often the starting point when conducting online research—a topic to which we now turn.

CONDUCTING ONLINE RESEARCH

Your goal when conducting online research is to find accurate, up-to-date information on the topic you are researching in a minimum amount of time. As anyone who has used the Internet knows, it is possible to spend hours navigating through

EXHIBIT 9.6
Results of a Search Using a Search Engine

Excite is a trademark of Excite, Inc., and may be registered in various jurisdictions. Excite screen display © 1995–1999 Excite, Inc.

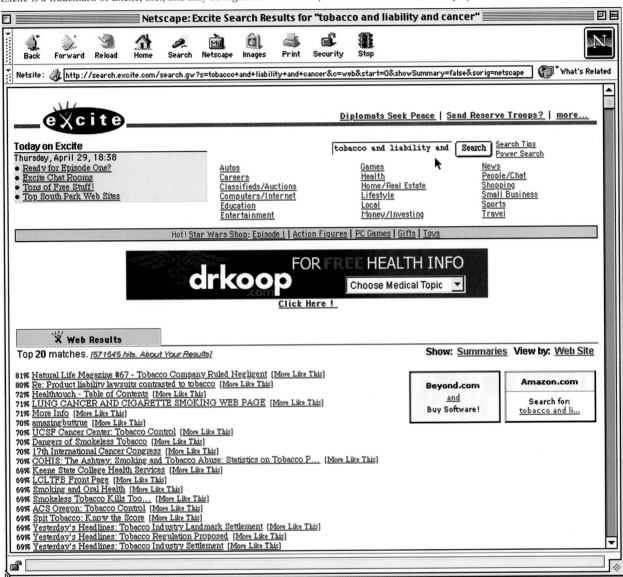

cyberspace to find specific data or information. Planning your research in advance and using various research strategies, such as those discussed in this section, can help you achieve your goal of conducting online research efficiently. First, though, as a preliminary matter, you need to decide whether the Internet is the right research tool for your project.

A Threshold Question: Is the Internet the Right Research Tool for Your Project?

The Internet is only one tool for doing research. Knowing which tool to use and when to use it is the key to obtaining quick, accurate results. Ask yourself the

Conducting Legal Research on the Internet

Robin Marks works as a paralegal for an attorney who practices constitutional law. Today is the first Monday in October 1999, and Robin has been assigned the task of obtaining a list of cases for which the United States Supreme Court granted *certiorari* for the Court's 1999–2000 term. Robin contemplates the fastest and most efficient method for obtaining this list of cases. She has used a United States Supreme Court Web site, www.usscplus.com, in the past for accurate information on pending Supreme Court decisions. Robin also knows from experience that the Internet is helpful for obtaining current legal information, such as recently issued court opinions. Robin turns to her computer and enters the URL into her browser to obtain the list of cases to be heard during the upcoming term.

TIPS FOR DOING LEGAL RESEARCH ON THE INTERNET

- Determine your research goals.
- Determine whether the legal material to be located is current or was published prior to 1990.
- Determine whether your legal issue is broad or narrow—narrow issues are easier to locate.
- Compile a list of legally related Web sites.
- Bookmark the Web sites that are most useful.

following questions: What sources are needed? Are they on the Internet? Are they available elsewhere? Either way, what is the cost? How much time do you have to produce results? The availability (accessibility) of a source, what it costs, and the time it would take to use it are the basic considerations. The Internet is most useful when the most recent information is needed.

Knowing what source to use is a skill that improves with time and experience. Being aware of a particular source is only the first step, however. A good researcher must be able to determine whether the source is available online and, if so, how to find the desired information within that source. Important points to keep in mind include the following:

- Discussion groups on the Internet cover nearly every conceivable topic.
- Most business firms, colleges, universities, and trade organizations have Web sites.
- Anything that can be subscribed to for a fee is available online, or will be available soon.
- Complete books are not online to the extent that fee-based periodicals are.

In terms of availability and cost, it should be remembered that many sources on the Internet are free, but some are not. It may be more cost effective to pull a book off a shelf than to pay for the same material online. It may also be faster to flip through the pages of a book, such as a dictionary, than to take the time to go online and click through a few links to find the same information. Additionally, if you are conducting serious legal research, the Internet may not be the research tool of choice. For other types of research, it may be the most efficient tool.

CONDUCTING LEGAL RESEARCH ON THE INTERNET.   Many primary sources of law—including federal and state statutes, federal and state regulations, and the decisions of numerous courts—are now accessible via the Internet. Later in this chapter, you will learn some of the best sites to access when you are looking for online legal resources. Among the primary sources of law that you can access online are the following documents:

- The United States Constitution, U.S. treaties, the Declaration of Independence, and other selected important historical documents.
- United States Supreme Court decisions.
- Decisions issued by the U.S. Courts of Appeals over at least the last two or three years.
- The entire *United States Code* (all federal statutes) and the entire *Code of Federal Regulations* (all federal administrative agency rules). See, for example, the U.S. House of Representatives Internet Law Library at **law.house.gov** (the home page of this site is illustrated in Exhibit 9.7 on the next page).
- Materials focused on specific areas of the law, such as intellectual property.
- Sources related to each state's laws—these vary in the depth of their coverage. There is a list of URLs for state resources included in "The Legal List" and indexed at **www.lcp.com/The-Legal-List/index5.html.**
- Foreign law, which can be hard to find in many law libraries, can be found at such sites as the European Union Internet Resources site at **www.lib.berkeley. edu/GSSI/eu.html.**

What is available online in terms of secondary sources of law (comments or explanations by experts on particular topics) varies. Traditional secondary sources, such as the legal encyclopedias and legal treatises familiar to paralegals and lawyers in their printed versions, are generally not available. Other types of secondary sources are online, however, and these can help a researcher focus his or her efforts (see, for example, the resources provided by Nolo Press at **www.nolo.com**). Many law firms provide background material at their sites (see, for example, the list of publications offered by Hale and Dorr, L.L.P., a Boston law firm, at **www.haledorr.com/ publications.html**).

THE LIMITED SCOPE OF ONLINE LEGAL SOURCES.   Although numerous legal materials are available online, their scope is limited.

> **For serious, in-depth legal research, as of the time this edition is being written, the free Web sites on the Internet are not excellent resources.**

For example, research into court cases to determine whether a law is constitutional must still be conducted in a law library or through a commercial, fee-based service. Although more legal resources are constantly being added to the Web, material that predates the 1990s is generally not available.

One reason for the limits to what is available online has to do with the expense of data compilation and storage. Most information providers selectively convert their data into an electronic resource. It also takes time to compile a large historical database. The limited facility of browsers and search engines also detracts from the usefulness of the free resources on the Internet for researching the law.

CONDUCTING FACT-BASED RESEARCH ON THE INTERNET.   While the Internet has drawbacks as far as serious legal research is concerned, it can be very useful when you need to find peripheral materials and information. Lawyers often need to know more than the law. For example, for a case involving a personal injury, medical research may be necessary. For other cases, scientific, technical, technological, or other types of research may be needed.

EXHIBIT 9.7

The Home Page of the U.S. House of Representatives Internet Law Library

Reproduced with permission.

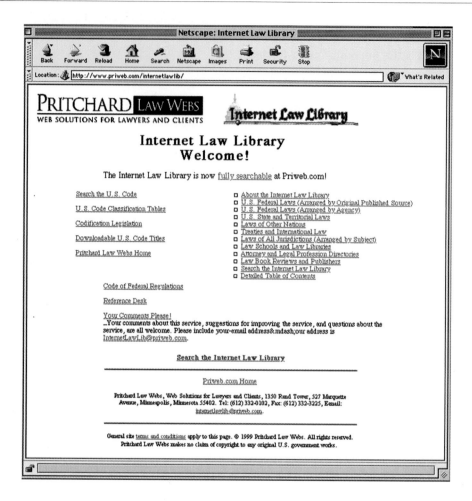

Online databases that focus on the law do not entirely fill this requirement. Other resources available on the Internet can be very useful to legal professionals, however.

 In fact, currently the great value of the Internet for legal professionals is the speed with which it allows them to locate people, investigate companies, and conduct other practical, fact-based research.

The numerous databases available on the Web make it possible to perform such research with great ease and speed. Of course, as with all research, the key to efficiency and obtaining successful results is careful planning.

Plan Ahead—Analyze the Facts and Identify the Issues

If you have decided that the Internet is the right tool for a particular research project, you should plan your research steps before going online. The first step is to know what it is you are seeking. To avoid wasting time and money, state your objectives clearly and be sure that you understand your goals. To narrow the scope

DEVELOPING PARALEGAL SKILLS
Medical Research on the Internet

Tom Shannon needs to locate information on bipolar disorder. Tom's supervising attorney is trying to prove that the defendant in a case has this mental disorder. Tom, who has worked as a paralegal for ten years, knows the Internet is an excellent source for medical information. Tom accesses the American Medical Association's Web site at www.ama-assn.org. He searches for articles describing this disorder. Tom finds several citations to articles, along with summaries of the articles, but the full text of the articles is not online. He prints out the information he found and goes to the library at the local medical school to obtain the full text of the articles.

TIPS FOR PERFORMING
MEDICAL RESEARCH ONLINE

- Become familiar with medical terminology.
- Search the appropriate medical categories on the Web site.
- Locate appropriate articles and summaries.
- If the full text of the articles is not available online, go to the nearest medical school's library to obtain them.

of your research, you may need to know the reason for the research or how the results will be used.

The second step is to determine which sources are most likely to lead you to the desired results. One way to gain a sense of where you want to look is to use a guidebook (see, for example, the most recent edition of *The Internet for Dummies,* written by John R. Levine, Carol Baroudi, and Margaret Levine Young, and published by IDG Books Worldwide, Inc.). A good guide can point you in the direction of the right Web sites to visit to begin your research, to narrow its focus, or to find exactly what you need. Once these steps are taken, your research can begin.

Starting Points

Sometimes, a research session begins with one of the online directories or guides discussed earlier in this chapter. For example, if the object of your search is to find information on a particular case, you could start with Yahoo's "Government" menu (www.yahoo.com/Government). This is broken into submenus, including one titled "Law," which is further broken down into submenus that include "Cases." See Exhibit 9.8 beginning on page 314.

A search engine or a meta search engine may be used to compile your own list of Web sites containing certain key words. A search engine tailored to zero in on specific topical sites may be more useful than either a general search engine or a meta search engine, depending on your research goals. Keep in mind the limitations of search engines, however. Your search may locate many irrelevant sources and may not spot every site that you would find helpful. Also, different search engines will yield different results. For this reason, it is best to use more than one search engine when conducting research.

From the preliminary results of a general search, you can click on the links to visit the sites and determine which are useful. Many sites include their own links to other sources you may find helpful. Some Web sites attempt to collect links to all online resources about particular topics. These include directories, which were discussed earlier, as well as other sites such as the Federal Web Locator (www.law.vill.edu/fed-agency/fedwebloc.html), which provides links to federal

EXHIBIT 9.8a
**www.yahoo.com/
Government/**

Reproduced with permission.

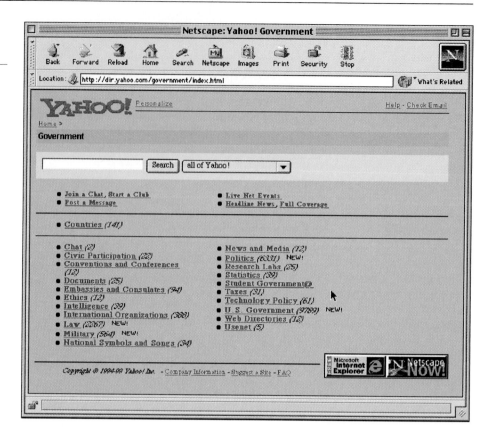

EXHIBIT 9.8b
**www.yahoo.com/
Government/Law/**

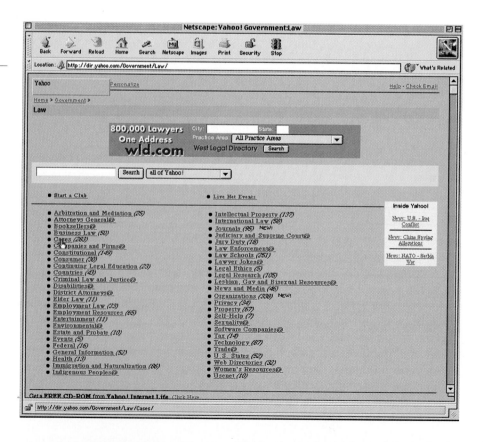

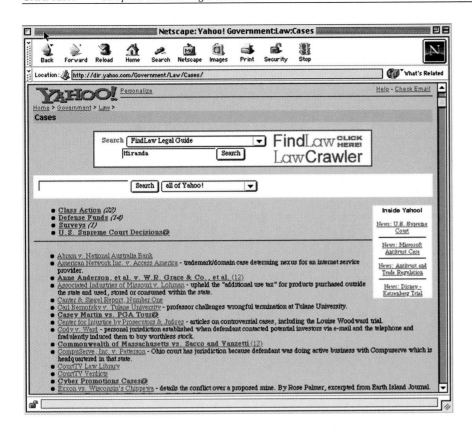

EXHIBIT 9.8c
**www.yahoo.com/
Government/Law/Case**

offices and agencies. For more experienced researchers, there is Hieros Gamos (**www.hg.org/hg**), which is an extensive guide to legal information available online. Some sites are more eclectic in what they offer (see, for example, the 'Lectric Law Library at **www.lectlaw.com**).

Discovering What Resources Are Available

Despite your best intentions and attempts to pinpoint your research, you may have to approach a project without a clear objective regarding what you need to find. Your initial research goal may be to discover the extent of resources available online, with your ultimate goal to obtain more precise results.

In addition to the popular guides and directories, such as Excite (**www.excite.com**), there are less familiar Web pages that contain links to important resources in particular topic areas. These pages often include directory-style menus and search utilities. For example, legal-resource search engines, such as CataLaw (see **www.catalaw.com**), are directed to find sites related to legal topics. Remember that these sources often change, and may even disappear, and new ones can develop overnight.

Many libraries provide access to their catalogues online (see, for example, the cataloguing available on the New York Public Library's Web site at **catnyp. nypl.org**). You can search these catalogues over the Internet in the same way that you would search them in the library. This can save the time that otherwise might be spent in a futile trip to the library. You can search the catalogues of your local libraries as well as those of more distant libraries. Often, you can arrange to have source material in a distant library delivered to a closer library, where you can more conveniently review it.

TECHNOLOGY AND TODAY'S PARALEGAL

Creative Online Searching

Information can be collected easily via the Internet. The only limit to what is collected and how it is analyzed is the ability of the researcher. What distinguishes a good researcher from an average researcher is the ability to obtain hard-to-find or obscure data from hard-to-reach sources that are especially reliable. Backing up a secondary source with hard-to-find primary data is qualitative, comprehensive research.

For example, the Web can be a good source for obtaining background information on people. Imagine that a lawyer for whom you work is scheduled to question a certain witness. Background information could be useful during the questioning. The witness's past can be investigated on the Web in several ways. A general search can be made to uncover any data concerning the witness. Newsgroups (discussed elsewhere in this chapter) can be searched to discover whether the person has said anything in these groups that relates to his or her testimony. Other ways to find people and information about them are discussed later in this chapter.

Interpreting the data in clever ways is another attribute that distinguishes good researchers. For example, one of your client's competitors advertises employment opportunities for engineers with certain skills. To an intelligent researcher, this may indicate a new direction for the competitor's research and development, or a new product line. A competitor's Web links could give your client insight into the competitor's operations or indicate a new market for your client's products. To discover sites that link to your competitor's home page, you could use a feature such as the Advanced Search tool at the Altavista search engine site (**www.altavista.com**). In that tool, as a search term, use **link: your competitor's home page address**.

Listserv List
A list of e-mail addresses of persons who have agreed to receive e-mail about a particular topic.

Newsgroup (Usenet Group)
An online bulletin board service (BBS). A newsgroup, or BBS, is a forum, or discussion group, that usually focuses on a particular topic.

Another way to find out what resources are available is to begin with a listserv list or a newsgroup. These can also be used to update your research.

A **listserv list** (or mailing list) is basically a list of e-mail addresses of persons interested in a particular topic. By placing their names on the list, they agree to receive e-mail from others about the topic. A message sent to the list's address is automatically sent to everyone on the list. Anyone on the list can respond to whoever sent the message. As a researcher, you might post a message that asks for suggestions about online resources for your research. You can also add your name to the list to receive the mass e-mailings. In some cases, you may be able to browse an archive of messages to see if another researcher has previously called attention to a resource that matches your search.

Listserv lists (see **tile.net/listserv**) provide more anonymity than newsgroups. There is a listserv list for paralegals and legal assistants. To subscribe to this list, send the message "subscribe paralegals <your e-mail address>" to **majordomo@ljx.com**. The address to post messages to the subscribers on this list is **PARALEGALS@ljx.com**. To add your e-mail address to other listserv lists, see **www.lawguru.com/subscribe/listtool.html**.

A **newsgroup** (also known as a **usenet group**) is a forum that resembles a community bulletin board. A newsgroup can be selected by topic. A researcher can post a question or problem (for example, "Does anyone know a good source for what I want to know?") and check back hours or days later for others' responses. A researcher might also browse the newsgroup's archive, although messages are typically stored only for limited periods of time. There are thousands of newsgroups (a few hundred of which focus on law-related topics). Newsgroup directories can be skimmed at such sites as Liszt (**www.liszt.com/news**). Newsgroups can be searched with specialized search engines, such as Dejanews (**www.dejanews.com**).

> ## ETHICAL CONCERN
> ## Surfing the Web
>
> A problem faced by paralegals who are novices in conducting online research is how to avoid spending hours surfing the Web for a site that contains the information being sought. You know the information is "out there" somewhere on the Web, but how can you locate it? What key terms can you use in your search that will find the information but that will also narrow the search sufficiently—so that you do not end up retrieving hundreds of thousands of documents? Over time, of course, you will become familiar with the best sites for information in your area of practice. In the meantime, how can you avoid giving the impression to your employer that you are "wasting" time surfing the Web? One thing you can do is explain to your employer at the outset that surfing the Web is part of the learning process and that this "learning time" is essential if you are to become efficient in online research.

Browsing the Links

Traveling around on the Internet to see what data are available is known as "surfing the Web" or "browsing the links." As you browse through the links that could be potentially useful for your research, two problems will become apparent. First, you need to keep track of the Web sites you visit. Second, the speed at which your computer browses can sometimes be slow.

A browser "Favorite" (Explorer) or "Bookmark" (Netscape) is an electronic substitute for keeping a book on your desk. With one of these tools, you can create an automatic link to any point on the Web and return to it at any time. For example, you might want to create a Favorite or Bookmark to the site at which you begin your research: a directory, a search engine, or one of the sites that have many links that relate to what you need.

Slow speed can be more of a problem. It may be the result of something, such as an outmoded browser, that you can correct. It is not always so easily overcome, however. It can result from bad phone lines, your service provider's problems, the limits of equipment (yours or someone else's), quirks in the weather, and so on.

Before going online, you may want to take steps to avoid some of the causes of slow speed. For example, to avoid the difficulty of accessing a popular site during its busiest times, you might go online early in the morning or late in the day. You should be aware that if traffic is heavy at a particular site, there could be a mirror site with the same data. A site will note on its home page if a **mirror site** is available. You might also avoid downloading or uploading large files at a site's busy times. It may be possible to increase your speed by selecting the text-only option when you browse. This may be particularly helpful when you use a low-performance computer or modem to access a site that has rich graphics. With some sites, this may not be an option, however, because the graphics may be necessary to navigate the sites.

Mirror Site
A Web site that duplicates an already existing site. A mirror site is used to improve the availability of access to a site that receives a lot of traffic or is distant from some users.

Narrowing Your Focus

Once you find a Web site that could be useful, you may need to zero in more precisely within that site on specific data. Many sites contain links to text and graphics within their pages. These links can be browsed to peruse documents within the site. Some sites include internal search utilities with which you can look for specific information within those sites. These utilities compare to an index in a book, except, of course, you choose the words in the index. Each site's internal utility can be different, but in general, it will work like a search engine. (See, for example, Harvard University's internal search tool at **search.harvard.edu:8765**.)

As pointed out earlier in this chapter, your browser also has the ability to search an individual Web page that you are viewing. This can be particularly helpful when scrolling through a document for a bit of information would be tedious and time consuming. Using your browser's "find" tool, you can search, for example, the text of a specific bill before Congress at the Library of Congress's THOMAS site (**thomas.loc.gov**), which contains legislative information. You might also use your find tool to search a company's document in the Electronic Data Gathering, Analysis, and Retrieval (EDGAR) database of the Securities and Exchange Commission (SEC) (**www.sec.gov/edgarhp.htm**). EDGAR is an indexed collection of documents and forms that public companies and others are required to file with the SEC. Exhibit 9.9 presents the first page of the EDGAR online collection.

Evaluating What You Find

After you have found what appears to be exactly what you are looking for, you need to consider its reliability. In evaluating data revealed through a search on the Internet, a researcher applies the same evaluative skills he or she would use to evaluate data found in other, more traditional ways. Because anyone with access to a computer can put anything on the Internet, however, you should abide by the following rule of thumb:

> **Every source of data obtained via the Internet needs to be evaluated carefully for its credibility.**

In evaluating a source's credibility, you need to ask yourself whether the source of the information is a primary, a secondary, or a tertiary source. Primary sources include experts and persons with firsthand knowledge. For example, the inventor of a product would be a primary source for information about his or her invention. Publicly filed documents are also good primary sources. For example, the legal forms that some companies are required to file with the Securities and Exchange Commission are good primary sources for the information that they contain (see the discussion of company investigations later in this chapter).

Secondary sources include books and periodicals (such as newspapers and magazines) and their online equivalents that contain "secondhand" information. Tertiary sources are any other sources that might be used in research.

A researcher needs to be aware, first of all, of whether online information is outdated. Often, it is difficult to ascertain when certain online articles, data, and other information were created. Also, a researcher needs to determine whether the source is reputable. A reputable source might be an organization that has established itself as an excellent resource in a particular field. A less reputable source might be an individual's own self-serving home page. Finally, the researcher should determine whether information was placed on the Web by a source that may be biased in a certain way.

In short, a researcher needs to keep in mind that anyone can provide information on the Web regardless of whether the person knows what he or she is talking about. People may not even be who they represent themselves to be. Because of this, whenever possible, you should do the following:

EXHIBIT 9.9

The Securities and Exchange Commission's EDGAR Database

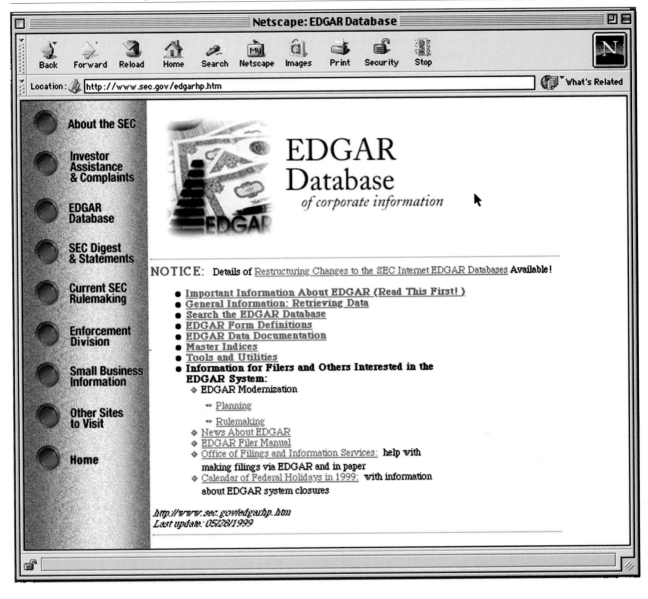

> Find and interpret primary sources yourself before you form any conclusions about information retrieved from the Web.

Updating Your Results

Staying current with events in the law, and in other areas that relate to your research, is important. The speed with which information is distributed via the Internet is a boon for paralegals and other researchers, because data are often online before they are available in other media. You can confirm whether your research results represent the most recent data available by going to relevant Web sites.

For certain types of research, you may want to check one of the news sites that abound on the Internet, such as CNN (see www.cnn.com). There are sites directed at those who may be interested only in updates in specific subjects. For updates on the legal news, you might check the site of FindLaw Legal News at www.findlaw.com. Corporate press releases—current and archival—can be reviewed at PRNewswire's site (www.prnewswire.com).

You can also arrange to have selected types of news articles sent immediately to your computer (see, for example, the Yahoo news ticker at www.my.yahoo.com/ticker.html or the Pointcast site at www.pointcast.com). Other sources for updating research results include newsgroups (or usenet groups) and listserv lists, both of which have already been discussed.

LOCATING PEOPLE AND INVESTIGATING COMPANIES

Paralegals often need to locate people or find out information about specific companies. As mentioned earlier, the Internet can be an especially useful research tool when searching for this type of information.

Finding People

A paralegal may need to find particular persons to assist a lawyer in collecting debts, administering an estate, preparing a case for court, and so on. Public records are helpful in looking for people, but some records (including most historic records) are not on the Internet. Despite this limitation, Web searches can be cheaper and faster than going to a government office or a library. Sometimes, using a commercial locator service or database can also be less costly than a trip out of the office.

BROAD SEARCHES.   On the Web, a researcher can run a broad search with a general search engine such as Infoseek (www.infoseek.go.com). A researcher might also narrow the focus of a search to, for example, all of the U.S. telephone books. There are several Web sites that provide telephone directories. Each of the sites has unique features. Some provide e-mail addresses (for example, Four11 Corporation at www.four11.com). Some include business listings (for example, www.companylink.com). Some can conduct a search with a telephone number or an e-mail address to reveal a name and a street address (for example, Database America at www.databaseamerica.com/html/index.htm or the Internet Address Finder at www.iaf.net). On some sites, such as WhoWhere (www.whowhere.com), a search can be based on personal characteristics, such as occupation, school, or affiliation with a certain organization. Some international telephone books can also be searched (see, for example, World Pages at www.worldpages.com).

NARROW SEARCHES.   If something is known about a person, the Web can be a good source for locating him or her. For example, if you are looking for an attorney, you can link to *West's Legal Directory,* which is a comprehensive compilation of lawyers in the United States, by going to www.westbuslaw.com. From the West Legal Studies Resource Center, click on the "Student Center" link in the "Support and Services" box in the left column. When the "Student Center" page appears, scroll down to "West's Legal Directory."

LOCATING EXPERT WITNESSES.   To find a person to serve as an expert witness, you can search the National Directory of Expert Witnesses at www.claims.com or choose a different Web source from the Expert Witness Info on the Internet list of the

PARALEGAL PROFILE

V. SHERI TOWNE   has a bachelor's degree in education from the University of Arkansas. She began her career in law while serving as an officer in the United States Navy. After graduating with honors from the U.S. Naval Justice School, she served as the non-lawyer legal officer for a naval air station and later as a member of a procurement fraud task force set up by the Navy and the Federal Bureau of Investigation. She has been with the firm of Pratt-Thomas, Pearce, Epting & Walker, P.A., since 1986, became a Certified Legal Assistant (CLA) in 1988, added the civil litigation specialist credential in 1994, and has served as her firm's lead paralegal since 1990. In addition to performing general paralegal responsibilities for Andrew K. Epting, Jr., Towne provides Internet research and litigation technology support for the fourteen-member firm and is responsible for designing and maintaining its Internet Web site at www.wiselaw.com. Ms. Towne has been actively involved with the National Association of Legal Assistants (NALA) and the South Carolina Alliance for Legal Assistant Associations (SCALAA). She is a founding member and past president of the Tri-County Paralegal Association.

Litigation Paralegal and Web Site Designer

What do you like best about your work?

"I like the intellectual challenge and the opportunity for creative problem solving, the satisfaction of knowing that your efforts contribute to making a difference in people's lives and (at times) when they feel helpless, vulnerable, or overcome by events."

What is the greatest challenge that you face in your area of work?

"My greatest challenge is keeping up with the ever-growing information and technology resources available to accomplish a given task and keeping those items in perspective such that in any given situation I can provide what is needed, when it is needed, in a cost-effective and efficient manner for both the firm and the client."

What advice do you have for would-be paralegals in your area of work?

"One of the most important skills to develop is that of a good listener. Pay close attention to what you are being told, not only by the attorneys who supervise your work but also by clients and others around you. Make sure you understand the ideas and concepts being imparted to you by the *other* person. Learn the resources that are available for finding information, including print material, online information, public and private libraries, and people. For any given situation, find the method to obtain the information needed that is both effective *and* efficient. Develop the habit of being methodical and paying attention to detail."

What are some tips for success as a paralegal in your area of work?

"Be flexible. Develop more than one method or option for accomplishing a task so that when conditions change, such as a deadline being shortened, you are still able to effectively and efficiently get the job done. Learn your supervising attorney's habits and patterns, and learn to think and plan ahead several steps. When you can anticipate what will be needed and have it ready almost as quickly as it is asked for, you will have made yourself a highly valued asset. Always keep your supervisors informed of problems, not just when they occur but also when they are anticipated—and have at least two suggestions for solving them available for discussion. Never be afraid to ask questions. No matter how busy you are, always take a moment to respond to requests for information or assistance from others. Never stop learning—the moment you think you know all there is to know is the exact moment you confirm that you don't."

> **"One of the most important skills to develop is that of a good listener."**

Northern California Association of Law Libraries (**www.nocall.org/experts.htm**). To look for a professor at a particular university or an employee at a certain company, the staff directory of the school or business firm may be available, and searchable, online. (See, for example, the directory for the faculty of Yale Law School at **elsinore.cis.yale.edu/lawweb/lawschool/facfp.htm**.)

SEARCHES BASED ON SPECIFIC CHARACTERISTICS.   A search for a person can be based on such characteristics as his or her professional status or where he or she went to school. With the right database (some sites charge a fee), a person's business license can be verified, a veteran may be located, information about a federal prison inmate can be accessed, and a federal employee can be found. (See, for example, the Federal Government Directory at **www.fed.gov**.)

Information can be obtained on persons who contribute to federal election campaigns (see the Federal Candidate Campaign Money Page at **www.tray.com/fecinfo**).

Adoptees and their birth parents may be located through certain databases on the Web such as the Webgator site at **www.inil.com/users/dguss/gator9.htm**. For genealogy searches, there are databases that include all persons who have died since 1962, American marriages before 1800, graves, and so on (see, for example, the Social Security Death Index at **www.ancestry.com**).

States' driving and vehicle registration records and motor vehicle accident data may be available on the Web (see, for example, the state of Texas list of licensed drivers at **www.publicdata.com**). Forwarding addresses and name changes for individuals and companies can be found at such databases as Semaphore Corporation's "Where Did They Go?" at **www.semaphorecorp.com/default.html**.

FEE-BASED SEARCHES.   Some commercial services provide access to their compilations of information only for a price. Some of the information mentioned above can be found in fee-based databases. There are pay services through which military personnel can be found (for example, MilitaryCity Online at **www.militarycity.com**). Through a service with access to states' incorporation data and other sources' information, people can be pinpointed based on their ownership interest in business organizations. Real-property records, bankruptcy filings, and documents relating to court dockets, lawsuits, and judgments can be searched through such sites as KnowX at **www.knowx.com**. Social Security numbers can also be verified (see **www.informus.com/ssnlkup.html**).

Investigating Companies

Lawyers often need to know about their clients' companies and the companies of their clients' competitors. For example, if a client suffered an injury caused by a defectively designed product, a lawyer will need to identify the defendant manufacturer, find out whether the manufacturer is the subsidiary of a larger company, and learn the defendant's address. If a client wants to acquire or invest in a particular business firm, research into the firm's background may be vital. There are many ways to find this type of information on the Web.

It is important to remember that sites on the Web can be searched online anonymously (without the awareness of the firm about which information is sought). Because of this anonymity, your clients may learn of competitive threats and opportunities without alerting their competitors.

FINDING COMPANY NAMES AND ADDRESSES.   A researcher can run a search with a telephone number to find a company's name and address (for example, see the GTE Superpages at **yp.gte.net**). Without a telephone number, a company's name and address can be found with the help of a directory that searches by industry and state (see the CompanyLink page at **www.companylink.com**, for example). A search with such a directory can also help determine whether a specific firm name is in use anywhere in the United States. The Internet Network Information Center maintains a database of registered domain names (see, for example, the Netpartners Company Site Locator at **www.netpartners.com/locator.htm**).

Uncovering Detailed Information about Public Companies.   To discover more information than a company name and address, an in-depth search is necessary. A guide to uncovering company information on the Web is located at **www.virtualchase.com/coinfo/index.htm**. Fuld & Company provides links to a variety of business research resources from its Competitive Intelligence Guide at **www.fuld.com**. Most companies maintain their own Web sites, which may contain the firm's annual reports, press releases, and price lists. Some companies put their staff directories online.

Information may be available through the sites of government agencies. For example, the Occupational Safety and Health Administration (OSHA) site (**www.osha.gov**) identifies manufacturers whose products have caused injuries or deaths at any time in the last twelve years, and the Consumer Product Safety Commission (CPSC) site (**www.cpsc.gov**) lists products that have been recalled. The Securities and Exchange Commission (SEC) regulates public companies and requires them to file documents and forms revealing certain information. The documents include annual reports and proxies, which contain information on directors and stock issues. This material can be accessed through the SEC's EDGAR database (at **www.sec.gov/edgarhp.htm**), as already mentioned.

Some states make their corporate records available online. For links to many states' records offices, see **w3.uwyo.edu/~prospect/secstate.html**.

Other information about public companies can be found at other free sites and pay sites. In general, the best free sites provide data on the companies and links to the companies' home pages, EDGAR, and other resources, such as news articles. See, for example, the Wall Street Research Network at **www.wsrn.com** or Yahoo Company Information at **biz.yahoo.com/news**. Pay sites sometimes include larger databases with archives of information that may span decades and may cover companies in other countries.

Learning about Private Companies.   Data on private companies is more difficult to find because these firms are not subject to the SEC's disclosure requirements. Much of the information that is available is only what the companies want to reveal. With this limitation in mind, there are a few sites that compile some of the data on private companies, associations, and nonprofit organizations. For example, Hoover's Online at **www.hoovers.com** provides brief profiles of many companies, with links to other sites, including search engines. For a fee, Hoover's will provide expanded profiles. Dun & Bradstreet provides, at its site (**www. companiesonline.com**), links to approximately one hundred thousand public and private companies.

Some of the Best Legal-Resource Sites on the Internet

As we have said elsewhere in this chapter, what is available on the Web changes rapidly. New sites come online. Old favorites disappear. Familiar sites move. URLs

FEATURED GUEST: JAN RICHMOND

Keeping Current on Computer Technology

BIOGRAPHICAL NOTE

Jan Richmond completed her master of arts degree in legal studies at Webster University in St. Louis, Missouri. As an undergraduate, she specialized in systems and data processing. She received her undergraduate degree from Washington University. Richmond has been an adjunct faculty member in the legal-assisting program at St. Louis Community College since 1989. Her teaching schedule includes courses in computers and the law, advanced computer utilization, and legal administration, in additon to classes in WordPerfect 5.1 and 6.0, and Windows, Excel, Lotus, and numerous other software applications. Richmond has been a consultant in law-office training for nine years. For the past four summers, she has offered computer classes for the Missouri Bar Association.

Computer technology is developing at such a rapid pace that you can almost rest assured that what's here today will be changed or gone tomorrow. That means that paralegals must learn to tackle the tremendous problem of keeping their computer systems up to date.

Here's an example: today, it is common to see a paralegal seated next to an attorney to assist with the marking of testimony that is being electronically captured by a court reporter and transmitted to the attorney's table. As testimony is being given, with the aid of online Westlaw® or Lexis®, research can begin in the electronic courtrooms of today. Courtroom presentations are no longer limited to paper-based media. PowerPoint or other software has made the changing visual image, manipulated by paralegals, instantly available as evidence in almost any jurisdiction.

There are several ways that you can learn about current developments in the area of computer technology and software. One way is to read computer magazines, such as those listed and described below. Other ways include attending computer workshops and seminars, participating in user groups, accessing online information, and attending software demonstrations or obtaining demonstration software diskettes, or "demos."

COMPUTER MAGAZINES

There are a number of monthly or bimonthly publications to which you or your firm can subscribe. By routinely scanning through some or all of these publications, you can keep abreast of what's happening in the computer world in regard to technology or software relating to law offices and legal research.

The Lawyer's PC (published by Shepard's/McGraw-Hill, P.O. Box 35300, Colorado Springs, CO 80935-3530) is a monthly publication for lawyers who use personal computers. Each month, a different topic is addressed. One issue, for example, featured an article entitled "Changing the Way We Work: Where Are Computers Taking Us?" The topic was right on target for attorneys and paralegals who wish to assess the impact of computer technology on their work habits. Each November, the entire issue is devoted to a list of application software for the law office. *The Perfect Lawyer,* a similar type of monthly publication also published by Shepard's/McGraw-Hill, deals with WordPerfect word-processing software and legal applications specific to that software.

Law Office Technology is a bimonthly publication that covers a wide variety of topics and deals with all aspects of law and computing. Topics covered range from the most commonly used WordPerfect macros to automating the job of estate management. To obtain information on this magazine, write to *Law Office Technology,* 3520 Cadillac Avenue, Suite E, Costa Mesa, CA 92626.

Legal Assistant Today (3520 Cadillac Avenue, Suite E, Costa Mesa, CA 92626) and *Legal Professional* (6060 North Central Expressway, Suite 670, Dallas, TX 75206-9947) are less oriented toward computer technology but do contain computing articles of interest and offer differing points of view on particular topics.

Last, but not least, is *AMLaw Tech* (345 Park Avenue South, New York, NY 10010), one of the newer publications that is heavily directed toward the use of technology in legal practice.

WORKSHOPS AND SEMINARS

Every professional organization offers workshops and seminars dealing with computers. If you are a member of an association for paralegals, you will

FEATURED GUEST, *Continued*

have an opportunity to meet and exchange ideas with others doing similar work. Check with your state, city, or county organization—or with the American Bar Association—to find out when seminars or workshops will be offered and on what specific topics. Computer workshops and seminars are not just for the technologically astute; even the novice can benefit from this type of meeting.

USER GROUPS

User groups come in two varieties: specific and generic. Specific groups deal with one particular product, such as WordPerfect. I have attended meetings of WordPerfect users in several cities and have found that those attending these meetings have the same common goal: to get the most out of the product. You can gain invaluable information from both knowledgeable members attending these meetings and WordPerfect personnel. You will pick up tips from both groups that can help make your tasks easier.

Generic groups include groups formed by IBM computer users, Macintosh users, and others. Such groups often meet on a monthly basis and discuss different software application packages that operate on personal computers. Usually, vendors attend these meetings and give away software to the groups for their use. Although the group's interests may not be the same as yours, you will not know until you attend a meeting or two.

Bar associations are beginning to sponsor special interest groups that exchange information. In addition, a number of state bar association meetings now address special topics at the end of each meeting. These topics may include vendor displays of new computer products and programs relating to law-office management, litigation, and so on.

USING THE INTERNET

With the explosion of the Internet, we could hardly overlook this wonderful and powerful communication tool. The amount of information that is now available to us worldwide is unbelievable and overwhelming. This tool can be used to research products and software, and even to gain access to online legal-research services such as Westlaw® and Lexis® via the Web. Often, attorneys access listservs for the purpose of exchanging information on a legal issue or a new technology tool available in the marketplace.

Be aware of the hazards as well as the benefits of using the Internet, however. One such potentially hazardous area might be using the Internet for transferring documents. Paralegals must keep their skills current on encryption software so they will be able to take advantage of sending information and documents to clients, other attorneys, medical facilities, and so on without the danger of a "surfer" picking up the firm's confidential material. There are paralegal listservs that allow paralegals and legal assistants across the world to share information.

SOFTWARE DEMONSTRATIONS

When a new software product piques your interest, you will not want to purchase it without having first had an opportunity to explore its capabilities and how it can be applied to your firm's needs. One way of evaluating new software is by contacting the vendor and requesting a demonstration by a local dealer. You might also request from the vendor the names of some other firms in your area using the product. Then make some telephone calls to those firms to see if

> "Paralegals must learn to tackle the tremendous problem of keeping their computer systems up to date."

they might be willing to discuss with you the advantages and disadvantages of the product. Usually, people are anxious to tell you about the problems they have experienced—which would be most helpful for you.

You can also ask the vendor for a demonstration diskette with supporting literature. Demonstration diskettes are usually very simple to use and very informative. Others in your firm can also view them and help in the evaluating process. Literature is always helpful because it will give you the hardware requirements of the program, such as how much space will be needed on the hard drive and how much internal memory is required for the program to run smoothly. The down side of demonstration diskettes is that you may receive an abbreviated version of the software and thus may not be able to see its full capabilities.

CONCLUSION

Computer technology is an ever-changing field. New kinds of hardware and software seem to appear every day. Keeping current in regard to computer technology can be frustrating, but it is also exciting. Generally, the best way to keep current is by reading computer literature and by communicating with others who share your needs and concerns.

change. This section lists selected sites that a legal professional might find helpful. Many of these sites are not otherwise noted in this chapter. Included are references to valuable sites that have been on the Web for some time and have been kept up to date.

Basic Resources

Important Web resources for a legal professional include more than law-related sites. As indicated earlier in this chapter, other important sites can include those of your clients' competitors. Sometimes, however, all that is needed is some basic information: the meaning of a word, the area code for a telephone number, or a local map, for example. Sites with such basic information include those mentioned here.

ALMANACS AND NONLEGAL ENCYCLOPEDIAS.   These may be found at a site maintained by Information Please at **www.infoplease.com**.

AREA CODES.   See Search.com at **www.555-1212.com/aclookup.html**.

CASE CITATION GUIDE.   *The Bluebook: A Uniform System of Citation* (discussed) in Chapter 8) is accessible online at **www.law.cornell.edu/citation/citation/table.html**.

DICTIONARIES.   "WWWebster Dictionary" (Merriam-Webster, Inc.) provides an online dictionary at **www.m-w.com/netdict.htm**. (Sites for legal dictionaries, multiple dictionaries, and specialized dictionaries will be mentioned shortly.)

E-MAIL ADDRESSES.   E-mail addresses may be located through the Internet @ddress.finder at **www.iaf.net**.

INTERNET DIRECTORIES.   A number of Internet directories, including Yahoo (**www.yahoo.com**) and Infoseek (**www.infoseek.com**), which were mentioned earlier in this chapter, are well known. Other Internet directories include "E-Map: The Electronic Map to the Internet" at **www.e-map.com**. A site titled "Librarians' Index to the Internet" is at **sunsite.berkeley.edu/internetindex**. The Magellan Internet Guide is online at **www.mckinley.com**. Another useful directory is Webcrawler at **Webcrawler.com**.

INTERNET SEARCH TOOLS.   Inference Find will organize your results by type of Web site—for example, commercial site, nonprofit site, and so on—at **www.inference.com/infind**. Northern Light at **www.nlsearch.com** will also categorize your search results by type of Web site. SavvySearch is a meta search engine at **www.savysearch.com**.

INTERNET SERVICE PROVIDERS.   To locate an Internet service provider, see the site ISP Finder at **www.ispfinder.com**. Another source for the names of providers is the "Internet Access Providers Meta-List" at **www.herbison.com/herbison/iap_meta_list.html**. The commercial service America Online can be accessed at **www.aol.com**.

LEGAL DICTIONARIES.   Black's Corporation Law Dictionary is online at **www.alaska.net/~winter/black_law_dictionary.html**. There is a European law dictionary at **www2.echo.lu/edic/**. The 'Lectric Law Library provides a dictionary of legal terms at **www.lectlaw.com/da.htm**. There is a "plain language" legal dictionary titled "WWLIA Legal Dictionary" at **www.wwlia.org/diction.htm**.

ETHICAL CONCERN
Finding Ethical Opinions on the Web

Paralegals can provide a valuable service to their employers by knowing how to access online the ethical opinions issued by the American Bar Association (ABA) or state bar associations. For example, suppose that your supervising attorney is defending a client in court, and the attorney learns that the client has given testimony that the attorney knows is false. What is the attorney's ethical responsibility in this situation? Should the attorney disclose the client's perjury to the court? Would this be a violation of the attorney-client privilege? Or suppose that the attorney learns that the client intends to testify falsely in court. Must the attorney inform the court of the client's intention? In these situations, the attorney may ask you to find out if the state bar association or the ABA has issued an ethical opinion on this issue. You can find this information quickly by going online and accessing **www.abanet.org/cpr/ethicopinions.html**, which is the page at the ABA's Web site where it posts summaries of its ethical opinions. To find ethical opinions issued by state bar associations, go to **www.legalethics/map.htm** and select "states" under the "EthicSites" heading in the index. When the link opens, click on your state.

LEGAL ETHICS.   One of the best sites on the Internet to find information on legal ethics, including articles dealing with ethical issues and ethical opinions issued by the American Bar Association (ABA) and state bar associations, is **www. legalethics.com**, a site maintained by Internet Legal Services. (You can also access the ABA or a state bar association through the Web sites given in the margins of Chapters 1 and 3. For Web sites concerning paralegal ethics, see Chapter 3.)

LIBRARY CATALOGUES.   For lists of links to the catalogues of libraries that may be accessed online, consult Yahoo's Library Collection at **www.yahoo.com/ Reference/Libraries.** The Library of Congress offers a collection of links to other libraries' catalogues at **lcWeb.loc.gov/z3950/gateway.html**. For a list of the catalogues of law libraries that may be available, see "Law Library Links" at **law.house.gov/114.htm.**

MAPS.   U.S. Street Maps is a site that provides what its name implies at **www.mapblast.com**. Another useful site is MapQuest at **www.mapquest.com**. See also World Maps at **www.lib.utexas.edu/Libs/PCL/Map_collection/Map_ collection.html.**

MULTIPLE DICTIONARIES.   On-Line Dictionaries includes links to more than 500 dictionaries in more than 140 languages at **www.facstaff.bucknell.edu/ rbeard/diction.html.**

SPECIALIZED DICTIONARIES.   One Look at **www.onelook.com** offers an engine that searches hundreds of dictionaries focused on such special topics as business, medicine, science, technology, and the Internet.

TELEPHONE DIRECTORIES.   All U.S. telephone books are online at Switchboard at **www.switchboard.com.** These books are also available at www.555-1212.com. A directory of toll-free numbers can be found at "AT&T Toll-Free Internet Directory"at **www.tollfree.att.net/dir800.**

THESAURI.   The WWWebster Dictionary site, produced by Merriam-Webster, Inc., includes a thesaurus at www.m-w.com/dictionary.htm. Roget's Thesaurus is accessible at online sites, including Web.cs.city.ac.uk/text/roget/thesaurus.html.

ZIP CODES.   For zip codes, see the U.S. Postal Service site at www.usps.gov/ncsc/lookups/lookup_zip+4.html.

University Sites

Many universities, colleges, law schools, and other academic institutions are dedicated to making the Internet and its related technology an essential part of professional research. Their Web sites are often good points from which to start because in general they provide updated material and links to other resources. These sites include those discussed in the following subsections.

LAW-RELATED STARTING POINTS.   The Legal Information Institute at Cornell Law School is a good starting place for online legal research. The URL is www.law.cornell.edu. This site includes many United States Supreme Court decisions (often within hours of their release) and links to many other law-related sites and services.

Another good site is the World Wide Web Virtual Law Library maintained by the Indiana University School of Law at www.law.indiana.edu/law/v-lib/lawindex.html. This is a comprehensive, up-to-date, subject index of law-related topics.

LawLists, a site produced at the University of Chicago, is online at www.lib.uchicago.edu/~llou/lawlists/info.html. This site contains an extensive listing of law-related discussion groups, including legal listservs.

Meta-Index for Legal Research at Georgia State University College of Law (gsulaw.gsu.edu/metaindex) enables a researcher to run a search in several Web sites' internal search tools simultaneously.

WashLaw WEB at www.washlaw.edu is produced by Washburn University. This site includes a comprehensive collection of links to legal resources on the Web.

Northwestern University, at Oyez Oyez Oyez: A Supreme Court Database (court.it-services.nwu.edu/oyez), provides digital audio (RealAudio) of the oral arguments in many important United States Supreme Court cases, as well as recordings of some of the announcements of the Court's opinions.

GOVERNMENT RESOURCES LISTINGS.   The site of the Documents Center of the University of Michigan Library is a reference point for local, state, federal, foreign, and international law resources on the Web. The URL is www.lib.umich.edu/libhome/Documents.center/index.html. This site is one of the most comprehensive lists of links to government documents on the Web, with descriptions of what is included at each link.

LAW-RELATED DISCUSSION GROUPS.   To receive information about new and updated resources related to the law, subscribe to LAWSRC-L by sending an e-mail note to mailto:listserve@listserve.law.cornell.edu. In the note, state, "subscribe LAWSRC-L <your name>."

NET-LAWYERS is a discussion group that involves primarily practicing attorneys in how to use the Internet. To subscribe, send an e-mail message to mailto:net-lawyers-request@Webcom.com. In the message, state, "subscribe NET-LAWYERS <your name>."

WEB SITE EVALUATIONS.   Questions to use when considering the reliability and accuracy of a particular Web site are listed at a site titled "Ten Cs for Evaluating Internet Resources." The URL is **www.uwec.edu/Admin/Library/10cs.html**.

Questions are also listed at "Thinking Critically about World Wide Web Resources." The URL for this site is **www.library.ucla.edu/libraries/college/instruct/web/critical.htm**.

Government Sites

The government—the federal government, in particular—provides many excellent resources online. Nearly every federal agency has its own Web site. The following are some of the most useful sites for a paralegal.

LAW-RELATED STARTING POINTS.   The House of Representatives Library at **www.house.gov** is one of the best government-supported sources of material on the Web. This site contains the full text of pending legislation and congressional testimony. The "Law Library" section contains a wealth of legal resources. The Library of Congress's THOMAS site (**thomas.loc.gov**) duplicates some of the House site's materials, but it does not include the "Law Library."

BUSINESS AND ECONOMIC INFORMATION.   The federal Department of Commerce, at **www.doc.gov**, provides a wealth of business and economic statistical data and other information. Some of it is available only for a fee. There are links to other government agencies' sites, including the home page of the U.S. Patent and Trademark Office.

INFORMATION ABOUT PUBLIC COMPANIES.   As mentioned earlier, the EDGAR database of the Securities and Exchange Commission (at **www.sec.gov/edgarhp.htm**) contains public companies' electronic filings of documents and forms that the commission requires. This is one of the best resources on the Web for information about public companies.

GOVERNMENT PUBLICATIONS.   GPO Access is the title of the Government Printing Office's database. This database contains the full text of the *Code of Federal Regulations,* the *Congressional Record,* the *Federal Register,* all versions of all bills introduced in Congress, the current edition of the *United States Government Manual,* the *United States Code,* and other government publications. The URL for this site is **www.access.gpo.gov/su_docs/index.html**.

DISCUSSION GROUP.   To learn about new government sources that appear on the Web, subscribe to GOVDOC-L. Send a message to **mailto:listserv@psuvm.psu.edu** or **mailto:listserv@psuvm.bitnet**. The message should read "subscribe GOVDOC-L <your name>."

Sites for Associations and Organizations

The following are some online databases that catalogue associations, professional organizations, and nonprofit organizations.

ASSOCIATIONS.   Associations Online includes Web links to more than five hundred associations divided into categories. The address is **www.ipl.org/ref/AON**.

Yahoo's directory includes a list of professional associations at **www.yahoo.com/Business_and_Economy/Organizations/Professional**.

PROFESSIONAL ORGANIZATIONS.   Professional organizations indexed according to business category (accounting, banking, law, and so on) can be found at **www.nvst.com/rsrc/proforg.htm**. (For Web sites for bar associations and paralegal organizations, see Chapters 1 and 3.)

NONPROFIT ORGANIZATIONS.   More than one million nonprofit organizations are included in a database maintained by the Internet Nonprofit Center at **www.nonprofits.org**. This site includes links to the Web pages of many nonprofit organizations.

Free Commercial Sites

Commercial sites are Web pages that are maintained or supported by for-profit organizations (as opposed to academic institutions, the government, and nonprofit organizations). Some commercial sites, such as Westlaw® and Lexis®, are fee-based, or pay, commercial sites. Other sites pay for themselves with on-site advertising. These are free commercial sites. Free commercial sites that may be of value to a legal professional include those discussed next.

ALL-PURPOSE STARTING POINTS.   Yahoo organizes, categorizes, and subdivides the most comprehensive list of URLs on the Web. New Web addresses are added at the rate of hundreds per day. Yahoo's address is **www.yahoo.com**.

Internet orientation, Internet tools, and Internet guides are the subjects of the Internet Web Text Index at **www.december.com/Web/text/index.html**.

A collection of references to various subject guides can be found at the Argus Clearinghouse site at **www.clearinghouse.net/searching/index.html**.

LAW-RELATED STARTING POINTS.   The West Legal Studies site (**www.westlegalstudies.com**) is a paralegal resource center. The site provides access to resources for professionals, students, and instructors, including links to nearly one thousand legal and paralegal information Web sites.

Another West site with a similar name—West Legal Studies Resource Center—is at **www.westbuslaw.com**. This site includes daily law highlights, an overview of the U.S. court system, study aids for students, links to a law dictionary and a lawyers' directory, and more.

The "Internet Legal Resource Guide," at **www.ilrg.com**, is an index of approximately four thousand law-related Web sites, categorized by topic. The site also includes the "LawRunner: A Legal Research Tool," which is preprogrammed to run your search terms in templates across as many as thirty million Web pages.

"The Legal List" at **www.lcp.com/The-Legal-List/TLL-home** is both a guide to research on the Web and a good starting point with links to other online resources.

The producers of the periodical *legal.online* offer links at their site at **www.legalonline.com** to legal resources on the Web that the producers find to be particularly useful. These resources include government sites, as well as sites maintained by libraries, law schools, law firms, private companies, and others.

Law-related search engines are linked at "Virtual Legal Search Engines," a site produced by Virtual Search Engines, at **www.dreamscape.com/frankvad/search.legal.html**. This site also includes a number of basic references (dictionaries, for example) and links to search engines for other topics.

Thousands of law-related materials and products are available through the 'Lectric Law Library at **www.lectlaw.com**. Most of the information files are not links to other sites but are actually at this site, with plain text and simple graphics

EXHIBIT 9.10
The Home Page of the 'Lectric Law Library

Reprinted with permission. Contact http://www.LectLaw.com or staff@LectLaw.com.

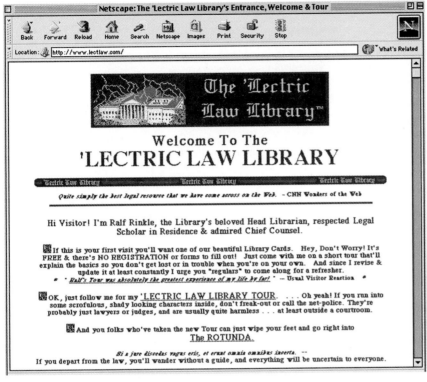

a) Home page

b) "Paralegal's Reading Room"
in "The Rotunda"

and without frames. Most of the larger items are compressed for downloading. Also included are legal forms and a law dictionary. An illustration of the home page of the 'Lectric Law Library is in Exhibit 9.10.

"Law Library Resource Xchange" (LLRX), at www.llrx.com, provides links to a number of resource sites on the net, ranging from legal research to library products and services. This site, which is maintained by Law Library Resource Xchange, L.L.C., includes timely and updated articles relating to research and library topics.

MEDIA DIRECTORY.   The American Journalism Review site contains more than eight thousand links to the online pages of newspapers, magazines, and other media, at www.newslink.org/menu.html.

TODAY'S PROFESSIONAL PARALEGAL

Locating Guardians and Wards

Patrick Mitchell works as a legal assistant for a sole practitioner, Anne Urso. Anne takes probate court assignments in which the court appoints her *guardian ad litem*. (A *guardian ad litem* is a special guardian appointed by a court to protect the interests of minors or incapacitated persons in legal proceedings.) This requires Anne to determine whether someone who had previously been appointed as a legal guardian for an incapacitated person needs to continue on as guardian. In order to make this determination, Anne must visit the ward and meet with the guardian.

Today, Anne has received an envelope in the mail appointing her *guardian ad litem* in five cases. The paperwork that comes from the court contains the names and addresses of both the guardian and the ward. Anne knows from experience that the court's records are often out of date and that this information needs to be updated.

Anne assigns the task of locating the guardians and wards to Patrick. He will call them first to see if the information from the court is accurate and to set up a meeting between them and either Anne or himself. The forms have to be submitted to the court within two weeks of their receipt by Anne, which is a quick turnaround time, especially in light of Anne's case load. Patrick calls the ward and the guardian on the first sheet and finds that their telephone numbers have been disconnected. He sets this sheet aside and calls the people listed on the next sheet. He succeeds in contacting the guardian and learns that the ward, an eighty-five-year-old man, Mr. Ahern, died almost a year ago. Patrick continues calling the guardians and wards listed on the sheets. He is able to contact the next three and sets up appointments with them.

Now Patrick must locate the guardian and the ward from the first sheet. He decides that the fastest way to do this is to use a people locator on the Internet. From past experience, Patrick is familiar with a number of reliable Web sites. These sites include KnowX, Bigfoot, and MapQuest. He accesses **www.bigfoot.com**. He enters the name of the ward, Thomas Ford, and the address, 1111 Three Mile Drive, Detroit, Michigan, and clicks on "Search." Within a few seconds, the computer retrieves a telephone number and an address for Mr. Ford. The telephone number is different from the one that was on the court's forms. Patrick runs another search for the guardian and turns up a new telephone number and address for him as well. Patrick then calls the guardian and the ward and schedules an appointment to meet with them.

Patrick then goes online to the Web site **www. knowx.com** to verify the death records of the second ward, Mr. Ahern. Using Mr. Ahern's Social Security number, he is able to access these records and print out a copy to include with his report. Patrick places a copy in the file.

Next, Patrick needs to use a mapping Web site to create maps for, and driving directions to, the five different locations to which he and Anne will need to go. Patrick accesses **www.mapquest.com**. He enters the address of the office and then the address of the first ward. He clicks on "Search," and a map with driving directions soon appears on the screen. Patrick prints out the maps with driving directions and places them in the file. Having finished this project, he then turns to his next task.

▨ KEY TERMS AND CONCEPTS

Auto-Cite   299

commercial online services   305

computer-assisted legal research (CALR)   296

file transfer protocol (ftp)   304

home page   304

hypertext transfer protocol (http)   304

Internet service provider (ISP)   306

KeyCite   299

listserv list   316

mirror site   317

newsgroup (usenet group)   316

World Wide Web   304

▨ CHAPTER SUMMARY

1. Computer-assisted legal research often involves using CD-ROMs. An advantage of using legal resources in CD-ROM format is that they are less costly to purchase and require less physical space than printed resources do. CD-ROMs can also be easily transported, which means they can be used while traveling, in the courtroom, or anywhere outside the office. The major disadvantage of using CD-ROMs in legal research is that they, like their printed equivalents, eventually become outdated.

2. For serious legal research, legal professionals often use online commercial legal-research services, particularly Lexis® and Westlaw®. Subscribers to these fee-based services can access the services' databases through the use of proprietary software and a modem connection via a telephone line, or via the Internet. Both Lexis® and Westlaw® provide their users with access to an extensive collection of legal, business, and other resources. Using these fee-paid legal services, paralegals can access specific documents, check citations, update the law, and search hundreds of databases. Both Lexis® and Westlaw® allow users to search databases with queries using "natural language" or "terms and connectors."

3. Today's legal professionals, including paralegals, can access a vast amount of information using the Internet, which is a global communication network of interconnected computers. Many online resources are available free, while others charge a fee for accessing their databases. The Internet tools most commonly used by paralegals include uniform resource locators (URLs), which are Internet "addresses"; e-mail, which transmits messages via the Internet to special e-mail addresses; file transfer protocol (ftp), which is a basic interface that connects computers and allows files to be transferred from one computer to another; and the World Wide Web, which is a data service on the Internet that is accessed through a browser.

4. The Internet is accessed through gateways, such as America Online or one of numerous Internet service providers. To navigate the Internet, which has no "card catalogue" as a library does, one must use browsers (software such as Microsoft Explorer or Netscape Navigator that allows a computer to roam the Web); guides and directories (menus of topics at various Web sites); and search engines (such as Alta Vista or Excite) that scan the Web for certain key words or concepts. Meta search engines run searches on more than one search engine simultaneously and thus are the best tools for searching the most Web space possible.

5. Before beginning an online research session, you should first decide whether the Internet is the right tool for your research project. At this time, there are insufficient primary and secondary legal sources on the Web to conduct in-depth legal research. For peripheral research, however, such as locating people or public records, the Internet offers an abundance of information. To avoid wasting time, you should also define what you are seeking and determine which sources are most likely to lead you to the desired results.

6. Once online, you can use various search tools and other resources (such as listservs and newsgroups) to locate data and information relevant to your topic. Often, researchers need to browse the Web (browse through the links provided at a site, which often provide links to other sites, and so on) for a time before finding a site that is particularly relevant and useful. In evaluating your research results, it is especially important to consider the reliability of any information obtained online. To update results, you can

access news sites online to see if there have been articles or press releases concerning a recent development in the area you are researching.

7. Paralegals often engage in online research to locate information about persons and to investigate companies. Sometimes, a person can be located through a broad search of the Web using a search engine such as Infoseek. Narrow searches can be conducted by accessing—for free or for a fee—specialized databases, such as compilations of physicians, lawyers, or expert witnesses. Searches for persons may also be conducted based on specific characteristics, such as professional status or campaign contributions. There are numerous online sites that contain information about both private and public companies.

8. Basic resources that you can find on the Web include almanacs, nonlegal encyclopedias, area codes, a case citation guide, dictionaries, e-mail addresses, information about the Internet, Internet directories, Internet search tools, Internet service providers, legal dictionaries, library catalogues, maps, multiple dictionaries, specialized dictionaries, telephone directories, thesauri, and zip codes. Various university and government sites offer links to a number of primary and secondary legal sources. There are also online databases that catalogue associations, professional organizations, and nonprofit organizations, as well as several free commercial sites that serve as all-purpose starting points for online research.

▨ QUESTIONS FOR REVIEW

1. What are some of the advantages and disadvantages of using legal resources in CD-ROM format when conducting legal research?

2. What is Westlaw®? What is Lexis®? How do legal professionals access these services? What kind of legal sources do these services make available to users?

3. How can these services be used to update the law? Describe two ways in which you can search databases on Lexis® and Westlaw®.

4. What is the difference between the Internet and the World Wide Web? Name and define four useful Internet tools.

5. Define and give two examples of an Internet gateway. What is a browser? What are Internet guides and directories?

6. What should you do before going online to conduct a research session? Is the Internet a good research tool for serious legal research? Why or why not?

7. What are some starting points when doing online research? How can one discover what resources are available on the Web? Why is it important to evaluate the reliability of information found online and to update the results of an Internet research session?

8. What online search techniques could you use when trying to find information on a specific person? How would you go about finding company names and addresses in an Internet search?

9. List five basic, nonlegal resources that can be accessed via the Internet. Name five universities whose law schools or legal institutes provide extensive Internet legal libraries or links to Internet legal resources.

10. What kinds of legal resources can be obtained at various government sites? What resources or search tools can be found at sites for associations and organizations and at free commercial sites?

▨ ETHICAL QUESTIONS

1. Janice, a paralegal in a labor-law firm, joins a listserv. It is called AWD@counterpoint.com. It is a discussion group about the Americans with Disabilities Act (ADA) of 1990 and related laws. Another member of the group posts a question about what companies the ADA applies to and whether his company is subject to the law. Janice knows the answer and could answer it. Should Janice answer the question? Why or why not?

2. The partners in the law firm of Dewey & Howe learn about a plane crash in the morning newspaper. They instruct their legal assistant to contact all of the families of the victims via e-mail to see if they are interested in filing a class-action lawsuit against the airline. Is this type of activity allowed under the ethical rules?

3. The law firm of Smith & Varney decides that it needs a Web page to advertise the law firm's services over

the Internet. It assigns the task to paralegal Mark Hampton. Mark develops a Web site for the firm. The site contains a biography of each attorney, e-mail addresses for all attorneys, and Web links to helpful and related practice areas. Is this type of Web site allowable advertising under the ethical rules?

4. Samantha, a paralegal, runs a credit check on a client over the Internet without using an encryption program. The client's Visa number is intercepted, and unauthorized charges of $4,320.00 are charged on the client's account. What kind of ethical problems result?

▨ Practice Questions and Assignments

1. Using the material presented in the chapter on Westlaw®, answer the following questions:

   a. How would you gain access to Westlaw®?

   b. How would you find the case *Del Monte Dunes at Monterey, Ltd. v. City of Monterey*, 95 F.3d 1422 (9th Cir. 1996)? How would you find out whether the holding in that case is still good law?

   c. What specific steps would you take to find the database of decisions made by courts in your state?

2. Suppose that one of your clients is suing a restaurant that served her tainted oysters. The oysters contained a bacteria that caused the client to suffer serious health injuries, including permanent nerve damage. What databases would you search on Westlaw® to find out whether there are any other cases involving this issue or a similar issue? How would you draft a query in natural language to retrieve these cases from the selected database(s)? To draft a query using terms and connectors, what key terms would you use?

3. Explain the parts of the following URL:

   http://www.urisko.edu

4. Create your own URL, using your name to create a Web site for commercial purposes.

5. Using the material presented in the chapter, make a list of the Web sites that you would search to find the name, address, and telephone number of a particular company. Would you search the same sites for more detailed information? If not, where would you search? Does it make a difference whether the company is public or private? If so, where would you search for information on public companies? Where would you search for information on private companies?

6. Assume that the legal researchers in the situations described below all have access to an excellent law library, to Westlaw® or Lexis®, and to the Internet. Which of these three research sources or tools would you advise the legal professional to use for his or her particular research need? Why?

   a. Matthew, a paralegal, needs to find out if a case cited in a legal motion he is drafting is still good law.

   b. Cindy, an attorney, needs to locate a psychiatric expert witness.

   c. Robert, a paralegal, has been asked to locate a statutory provision; he needs to make sure that the result is up to date.

   d. Tom, a paralegal, needs to locate a witness to a car accident.

   e. Megan, a paralegal, needs to find an heir who is to inherit $500,000 under her uncle's will.

▨ Using Internet Resources

1. In this chapter, you have learned many tips about how to use the Internet to do legal research and to find useful information relating to legal work. For an online article also dealing with legal research using the Internet, go to

   www.ali-aba.org/aliaba/intro.htm.

   Read through this guide to Internet research, and then answer the following questions:

   a. What does the article say about the reliability of information available on the Web?

   b. In the author's opinion, which search engine was the "hands-down winner" in his sample search? Why?

   c. Briefly summarize the author's recommendations on how to proceed with a search on a particular topic (see "A Search Example" at the end of the article).

2. The American Bar Association's Web site contains helpful information on legal-research sources on the Internet. Access the Web site at

www.abanet.org/lpm/writing/research.html

Answer the following questions about the research sources available online:

a. What categories of research materials are available?

b. Go to the "Legal Resources" category. Click on the "Johns Hopkins University Law Collection." How is the collection organized?

c. Click on the "Back" button. Select the "Legal Information Institute at Cornell Law School." How does it compare to the Johns Hopkins University collection? How is it organized? Which legal-research Web site would you prefer to use? Why?

APPENDIX A

NALA's
CODE OF ETHICS AND
PROFESSIONAL
RESPONSIBILITY

A legal assistant must adhere strictly to the accepted standards of legal ethics and to the general principles of proper conduct. The performance of the duties of the legal assistant shall be governed by specific canons as defined herein so that justice will be served and goals of the profession attained. (See Model Standards and Guidelines for Utilization of Legal Assistants, Section II.)

The canons of ethics set forth hereafter are adopted by the National Association of Legal Assistants, Inc., as a general guide intended to aid legal assistants and attorneys. The enumeration of these rules does not mean there are not others of equal importance although not specifically mentioned. Court rules, agency rules, and statutes must be taken into consideration when interpreting the canons.

Definition: Legal assistants, also known as paralegals, are a distinguishable group of persons who assist attorneys in the delivery of legal services. Through formal education, training, and experience, legal assistants have knowledge and expertise regarding the legal system and substantive and procedural law which qualify them to do work of a legal nature under the supervision of an attorney.

Canon 1

A legal assistant must not perform any of the duties that attorneys only may perform nor take any actions that attorneys may not take.

Canon 2

A legal assistant may perform any task which is properly delegated and supervised by an attorney, as long as the attorney is ultimately responsible to the client, maintains a direct relationship with the client, and assumes professional responsibility for the work product.

Canon 3

A legal assistant must not: (a) engage in, encourage, or contribute to any act which could constitute the unauthorized practice of law; and (b) establish attorney-client relationships, set fees, give legal opinions or advice, or represent a client before a court or agency unless so authorized by that court or agency; and (c) engage in conduct or take any action which would assist or involve the attorney in a violation of professional ethics or give the appearance of professional impropriety.

Canon 4

A legal assistant must use discretion and professional judgment commensurate with knowledge and experience but must not render independent legal judgment in place of an attorney. The services of an attorney are essential in the public interest whenever such legal judgment is required.

Canon 5

A legal assistant must disclose his or her status as a legal assistant at the outset of any professional relationship with a client, attorney, a court or administrative agency, or personnel thereof, or a member of the general public. A legal assistant must act prudently in determining the extent to which a client may be assisted without the presence of an attorney.

Canon 6

A legal assistant must strive to maintain integrity and a high degree of competency through education and training with respect to professional responsibility, local rules and practice, and through continuing education in substantive areas of law to better assist the legal profession in fulfilling its duty to provide legal service.

Canon 7

A legal assistant must protect the confidences of a client and must not violate any rule or statute now in effect or hereafter enacted controlling privileged communications.

Canon 8

A legal assistant must do all other things incidental, necessary, or expedient for the attainment of the ethics and responsibilities as defined by statute or rule of court.

Canon 9

A legal assistant's conduct is guided by bar associations' codes of professional responsibility and rules of professional conduct.

© Copyright 1998 NALA.

NALA's
Model Standards
and Guidelines
for the Utilization
of Legal Assistants

NALA's study of the professional responsibility and ethical considerations of legal assistants is ongoing. This research led to the development of the NALA Model Standards and Guidelines for Utilization of Legal Assistants. This guide summarizes case law, guidelines, and ethical opinions of the various states affecting legal assistants. It provides an outline of minimum qualifications and standards necessary for legal assistant professionals to assure the public and the legal profession that they are, indeed, qualified. The following is a listing of the standards and guidelines.

The annotated version of the Model was revised extensively in 1997. It is online (NALA Model Standards and Guidelines) and may be ordered through NALA headquarters.

Introduction

Proper utilization of the services of legal assistants affects the efficient delivery of legal services. Legal assistants and the legal profession should be assured that some measures exist for identifying legal assistants and their role in assisting attorneys in the delivery of legal services. Therefore, the National Association of Legal Assistants, Inc., hereby adopts these Model Standards and Guidelines as an educational document for the benefit of legal assistants and the legal profession.

Standards

A legal assistant should meet certain minimum qualifications. The following standards may be used to determine an individual's qualifications as a legal assistant:

1. Successful completion of the Certified Legal Assistant (CLA) certifying examination of the National Association of Legal Assistants, Inc.;

2. Graduation from an ABA-approved program of study for legal assistants;

3. Graduation from a course of study for legal assistants which is institutionally accredited but not ABA approved, and which requires not less than the equivalent of sixty semester hours of classroom study;

4. Graduation from a course of study for legal assistants, other than those set forth in (2) and (3)

above, plus not less than six months of in-house training as a legal assistant;

5. A baccalaureate degree in any field, plus not less than six months in-house training as a legal assistant;

6. A minimum of three years of law-related experience under the supervision of an attorney, including at least six months of in-house training as a legal assistant; or

7. Two years of in-house training as a legal assistant.

For purposes of these Standards, "in-house training as a legal assistant" means attorney education of the employee concerning legal assistant duties and these Guidelines. In addition to review and analysis of assignments, the legal assistant should receive a reasonable amount of instruction directly related to the duties and obligations of the legal assistant.

GUIDELINES

These Guidelines relating to standards of performance and professional responsibility are intended to aid legal assistants and attorneys. The responsibility rests with an attorney who employs legal assistants to educate them with respect to the duties they are assigned and to supervise the manner in which such duties are accomplished.

Guideline 1

Legal assistants should:

1. Disclose their status as legal assistants at the outset of any professional relationship with a client, other attorneys, a court or administrative agency or personnel thereof, or members of the general public;

2. Preserve the confidences and secrets of all clients; and

3. Understand the attorney's Code of Professional Responsibility and these guidelines in order to avoid any action which would involve the attorney in a violation of that Code, or give the appearance of professional impropriety.

Guideline 2

Legal assistants should not:

1. Establish attorney-client relationships; set legal fees, give legal opinions or advice; or represent a client before a court; nor

2. Engage in, encourage, or contribute to any act which could constitute the unauthorized practice of law.

Guideline 3

Legal assistants may perform services for an attorney in the representation of a client, provided:

1. The services performed by the legal assistant do not require the exercise of independent professional legal judgment;

2. The attorney maintains a direct relationship with the client and maintains control of all client matters;

3. The attorney supervises the legal assistant;

4. The attorney remains professionally responsible for all work on behalf of the client, including any actions taken or not taken by the legal assistant in connection therewith; and

5. The services performed supplement, merge with, and become the attorney's work product.

Guideline 4

In the supervision of a legal assistant, consideration should be given to:

1. Designating work assignments that correspond to the legal assistant's abilities, knowledge, training, and experience.

2. Educating and training the legal assistant with respect to professional responsibility, local rules and practices, and firm policies;

3. Monitoring the work and professional conduct of the legal assistant to ensure that the work is substantially correct and timely performed;

4. Providing continuing education for the legal assistant in substantive matters through courses, institutes, workshops, seminars, and in-house training; and

5. Encouraging and supporting membership and active participation in professional organizations.

Guideline 5

Except as otherwise provided by statute, court rule or decision, administrative rule or regulation, or the attorney's Code of Professional Responsibility and within the preceding parameters and proscriptions, a legal assistant may perform any function delegated by an attorney, including but not limited to the following:

1. Conduct client interviews and maintain general contact with the client after the establishment of the attorney-client relationship, so long as the client is aware of the status and function of the legal assis-

tant, and the client contact is under the supervision of the attorney.

2. Locate and interview witnesses, so long as the witnesses are aware of the status and function of the legal assistant.

3. Conduct investigations and statistical and documentary research for review by the attorney.

4. Conduct legal research for review by the attorney.

5. Draft legal documents for review by the attorney.

6. Draft correspondence and pleadings for review by and signature of the attorney.

7. Summarize depositions, interrogatories, and testimony for review by the attorney.

8. Attend executions of wills, real estate closings, depositions, court or administrative hearings and trials with the attorney.

9. Author and sign letters provided the legal assistant's status is clearly indicated and the correspondence does not contain independent legal opinions or legal advice.

The notes to accompany the NALA Model Standards and Guidelines for Utilization of Legal Assistants are updated regularly by the NALA Professional Development Committee. The standards and guidelines are adopted by the NALA membership, and changes to these provisions must be brought before NALA members during their annual meeting in July.

NFPA's
MODEL CODE OF ETHICS AND PROFESSIONAL RESPONSIBILITY AND GUIDELINES FOR ENFORCEMENT

Preamble

The National Federation of Paralegal Associations, Inc. ("NFPA") is a professional organization comprised of paralegal associations and individual paralegals throughout the United States and Canada. Members of NFPA have varying backgrounds, experiences, education, and job responsibilities that reflect the diversity of the paralegal profession. NFPA promotes the growth, development, and recognition of the paralegal profession as an integral partner in the delivery of legal services.

In May 1993 NFPA adopted its Model Code of Ethics and Professional Responsibility ("Model Code") to delineate the principles for ethics and conduct to which every paralegal should aspire.

Many paralegal associations throughout the United States have endorsed the concept and content of NFPA's Model Code through the adoption of their own ethical codes. In doing so, paralegals have confirmed the profession's commitment to increase the quality and efficiency of legal services, as well as recognized its responsibilities to the public, the legal community, and colleagues.

Paralegals have recognized, and will continue to recognize, that the profession must continue to evolve to enhance their roles in the delivery of legal services. With increased levels of responsibility comes the need to define and enforce mandatory rules of professional conduct. Enforcement of codes of paralegal conduct is a logical and necessary step to enhance and ensure the confidence of the legal community and the public in the integrity and professional responsibility of paralegals.

In April 1997, NFPA adopted the Model Disciplinary Rules ("Model Rules") to make possible the enforcement of the Canons and Ethical Considerations contained in the NFPA Model Code. A concurrent determination was made that the Model Code of Ethics and Professional Responsibility, formerly aspirational in nature, should be recognized as setting forth the enforceable obligations of all paralegals.

The Model Code and Model Rules offer a framework for professional discipline, either voluntarily or through formal regulatory programs.

§1. NFPA MODEL DISCIPLINARY RULES AND ETHICAL CONSIDERATIONS

1.1 A Paralegal Shall Achieve and Maintain a High Level of Competence.

ETHICAL CONSIDERATIONS

EC–1.1(a) A paralegal shall achieve competency through education, training, and work experience.

EC–1.1(b) A paralegal shall participate in continuing education to keep informed of current legal, technical, and general developments.

EC–1.1(c) A paralegal shall perform all assignments promptly and efficiently.

1.2 A Paralegal Shall Maintain a High Level of Personal and Professional Integrity.

ETHICAL CONSIDERATIONS

EC–1.2(a) A paralegal shall not engage in any *ex parte* communications involving the courts or any other adjudicatory body in an attempt to exert undue influence or to obtain advantage or the benefit of only one party.

EC–1.2(b) A paralegal shall not communicate, or cause another to communicate, with a party the paralegal knows to be represented by a lawyer in a pending matter without the prior consent of the lawyer representing such other party.

EC–1.2(c) A paralegal shall ensure that all timekeeping and billing records prepared by the paralegal are thorough, accurate, honest, and complete.

EC–1.2(d) A paralegal shall not knowingly engage in fraudulent billing practices. Such practices may include, but are not limited to: inflation of hours billed to a client or employer; misrepresentation of the nature of tasks performed; and/or submission of fraudulent expense and disbursement documentation.

EC–1.2(e) A paralegal shall be scrupulous, thorough, and honest in the identification and maintenance of all funds, securities, and other assets of a client and shall provide accurate accounting as appropriate.

EC–1.2(f) A paralegal shall advise the proper authority of nonconfidential knowledge of any dishonest or fraudulent acts by any person pertaining to the handling of the funds, securities, or other assets of a client. The authority to whom the report is made shall depend on the nature and circumstances of the possible misconduct (e.g., ethics committees of law firms, corporations and/or paralegal associations, local or state bar associations, local prosecutors, administrative agencies, etc.). Failure to report such knowledge is in itself misconduct and shall be treated as such under these rules.

1.3 A Paralegal Shall Maintain a High Standard of Professional Conduct.

ETHICAL CONSIDERATIONS

EC–1.3(a) A paralegal shall refrain from engaging in any conduct that offends the dignity and decorum of proceedings before a court or other adjudicatory body and shall be respectful of all rules and procedures.

EC–1.3(b) A paralegal shall avoid impropriety and the appearance of impropriety and shall not engage in any conduct that would adversely affect his/her fitness to practice. Such conduct may include, but is not limited to: violence, dishonesty, interference with the administration of justice, and/or abuse of a professional position or public office.

EC–1.3(c) Should a paralegal's fitness to practice be compromised by physical or mental illness, causing that paralegal to commit an act that is in direct violation of the Model Code/Model Rules and/or the rules and/or laws governing the jurisdiction in which the paralegal practices, that paralegal may be protected from sanction upon review of the nature and circumstances of that illness.

EC–1.3(d) A paralegal shall advise the proper authority of nonconfidential knowledge of any action of another legal professional that clearly demonstrates fraud, deceit, dishonesty, or misrepresentation. The authority to whom the report is made shall depend on the nature and circumstances of the possible misconduct, (e.g., ethics committees of law firms, corporations and/or paralegal associations, local or state bar associations, local prosecutors, administrative agencies, etc.). Failure to report such knowledge is in itself misconduct and shall be treated as such under these rules.

EC–1.3(e) A paralegal shall not knowingly assist any individual with the commission of an act that is in direct violation of the Model Code/Model Rules and/or the rules and/or laws governing the jurisdiction in which the paralegal practices.

EC–1.3(f) If a paralegal possesses knowledge of future criminal activity, that knowledge must be reported to the appropriate authority immediately.

1.4 A Paralegal Shall Serve the Public Interest by Contributing to the Delivery of Quality Legal Services and the Improvement of the Legal System.

ETHICAL CONSIDERATIONS

EC–1.4(a) A paralegal shall be sensitive to the legal needs of the public and shall promote the development and implementation of programs that address those needs.

EC–1.4(b) A paralegal shall support bona fide efforts to meet the need for legal services by those unable to pay reasonable or customary fees; for example, participation in *pro bono* projects and volunteer work.

EC–1.4(c) A paralegal shall support efforts to improve the legal system and access thereto and shall assist in making changes.

1.5 A Paralegal Shall Preserve All Confidential Information Provided by the Client or Acquired from Other Sources before, during, and after the Course of the Professional Relationship.

ETHICAL CONSIDERATIONS

EC–1.5(a) A paralegal shall be aware of and abide by all legal authority governing confidential information in the jurisdiction in which the paralegal practices.

EC–1.5(b) A paralegal shall not use confidential information to the disadvantage of the client.

EC–1.5(c) A paralegal shall not use confidential information to the advantage of the paralegal or of a third person.

EC–1.5(d) A paralegal may reveal confidential information only after full disclosure and with the client's written consent; or, when required by law or court order; or, when necessary to prevent the client from committing an act which could result in death or serious bodily harm.

EC–1.5(e) A paralegal shall keep those individuals responsible for the legal representation of a client fully informed of any confidential information the paralegal may have pertaining to that client.

EC–1.5(f) A paralegal shall not engage in any indiscreet communications concerning clients.

1.6 A Paralegal Shall Avoid Conflicts of Interest and Shall Disclose Any Possible Conflict to the Employer or Client, as Well as to the Prospective Employers or Clients.

ETHICAL CONSIDERATIONS

EC–1.6(a) A paralegal shall act within the bounds of the law, solely for the benefit of the client, and shall be free of compromising influences and loyalties. Neither the paralegal's personal or business interest, nor those of other clients or third persons, should compromise the paralegal's professional judgment and loyalty to the client.

EC–1.6(b) A paralegal shall avoid conflicts of interest which may arise from previous assignments whether for a present or past employer or client.

EC–1.6(c) A paralegal shall avoid conflicts of interest which may arise from family relationships and from personal and business interests.

EC–1.6(d) In order to be able to determine whether an actual or potential conflict of interest exists a paralegal shall create and maintain an effective record-keeping system that identifies clients, matters, and parties with which the paralegal has worked.

EC–1.6(e) A paralegal shall reveal sufficient nonconfidential information about a client or former client to reasonably ascertain if an actual or potential conflict of interest exists.

EC–1.6(f) A paralegal shall not participate in or conduct work on any matter where a conflict of interest has been identified.

EC–1.6(g) In matters where a conflict of interest has been identified and the client consents to continued representation, a paralegal shall comply fully with the implementation and maintenance of an Ethical Wall.

1.7 A Paralegal's Title Shall Be Fully Disclosed.

ETHICAL CONSIDERATIONS

EC–1.7(a) A paralegal's title shall clearly indicate the individual's status and shall be disclosed in all business and professional communications to avoid misunderstandings and misconceptions about the paralegal's role and responsibilities.

EC–1.7(b) A paralegal's title shall be included if the paralegal's name appears on business cards, letterhead, brochures, directories, and advertisements.

EC–1.7(c) A paralegal shall not use letterhead, business cards, or other promotional materials to create a fraudulent impression of his/her status or ability to practice in the jurisdiction in which the paralegal practices.

EC–1.7(d) A paralegal shall not practice under color of any record, diploma, or certificate that has been illegally or fraudulently obtained or issued or which is misrepresentative in any way.

EC–1.7(e) A paralegal shall not participate in the creation, issuance, or dissemination of fraudulent records, diplomas, or certificates.

1.8 A Paralegal Shall Not Engage in the Unauthorized Practice of Law.

ETHICAL CONSIDERATIONS

EC–1.8(a) A paralegal shall comply with the applicable legal authority governing the unauthorized practice of law in the jurisdiction in which the paralegal practices.

§2. NFPA GUIDELINES FOR THE ENFORCEMENT OF THE MODEL CODE OF ETHICS AND PROFESSIONAL RESPONSIBILITY

2.1 Basis for Discipline

2.1(a) Disciplinary investigations and proceedings brought under authority of the Rules shall be conducted in accord with obligations imposed on the paralegal professional by the Model Code of Ethics and Professional Responsibility.

2.2 Structure of Disciplinary Committee

2.2(a) The Disciplinary Committee ("Committee") shall be made up of nine (9) members including the Chair.

2.2(b) Each member of the Committee, including any temporary replacement members, shall have demonstrated working knowledge of ethics/professional responsibility–related issues and activities.

2.2(c) The Committee shall represent a cross section of practice areas and work experience. The following recommendations are made regarding the members of the Committee.

1. At least one paralegal with one to three years of law-related work experience.
2. At least one paralegal with five to seven years of law-related work experience.
3. At least one paralegal with over ten years of law-related work experience.

4. One paralegal educator with five to seven years of work experience; preferably in the area of ethics/professional responsibility.
5. One paralegal manager.
6. One lawyer with five to seven years of law-related work experience.
7. One lay member.

2.2(d) The Chair of the Committee shall be appointed within thirty (30) days of its members' induction. The Chair shall have no fewer than ten (10) years of law-related work experience.

2.2(e) The terms of all members of the Committee shall be staggered. Of those members initially appointed, a simple majority plus one shall be appointed to a term of one year, and the remaining members shall be appointed to a term of two years. Thereafter, all members of the Committee shall be appointed to terms of two years.

2.2(f) If for any reason the terms of a majority of the Committee will expire at the same time, members may be appointed to terms of one year to maintain continuity of the Committee.

2.2(g) The Committee shall organize from its members a three-tiered structure to investigate, prosecute, and/or adjudicate charges of misconduct. The members shall be rotated among the tiers.

2.3 Operation of Committee

2.3(a) The Committee shall meet on an as-needed basis to discuss, investigate, and/or adjudicate alleged violations of the Model Code/Model Rules.

2.3(b) A majority of the members of the Committee present at a meeting shall constitute a quorum.

2.3(c) A Recording Secretary shall be designated to maintain complete and accurate minutes of all Committee meetings. All such minutes shall be kept confidential until a decision has been made that the matter will be set for hearing as set forth in Section 6.1 below.

2.3(d) If any member of the Committee has a conflict of interest with the Charging Party, the Responding Party, or the allegations of misconduct, that member shall not take part in any hearing or deliberations concerning those allegations. If the absence of that member creates a lack of a quorum for the Committee, then a temporary replacement for the member shall be appointed.

2.3(e) Either the Charging Party or the Responding Party may request that, for good cause shown, any member of the Committee not participate in a hearing or deliberation. All such requests shall be honored. If the absence of a Committee member under those circumstances creates a lack of a quorum for the Committee, then a temporary replacement for that member shall be appointed.

2.3(f) All discussions and correspondence of the Committee shall be kept confidential until a decision has been made that the matter will be set for hearing as set forth in Section 6.1 below.

2.3(g) All correspondence from the Committee to the Responding Party regarding any charge of misconduct and any decisions made regarding the charge shall be mailed certified mail, return receipt requested, to the Responding Party's last known address and shall be clearly marked with a "Confidential" designation.

2.4 Procedure for the Reporting of Alleged Violations of the Model Code/Disciplinary Rules

2.4(a) An individual or entity in possession of nonconfidential knowledge or information concerning possible instances of misconduct shall make a confidential written report to the Committee within thirty (30) days of obtaining same. This report shall include all details of the alleged misconduct.

2.4(b) The Committee so notified shall inform the Responding Party of the allegation(s) of misconduct no later than ten (10) business days after receiving the confidential written report from the Charging Party.

2.4(c) Notification to the Responding Party shall include the identity of the Charging Party, unless, for good cause shown, the Charging Party requests anonymity.

2.4(d) The Responding Party shall reply to the allegations within ten (10) business days of notification.

2.5 Procedure for the Investigation of a Charge of Misconduct

2.5(a) Upon receipt of a Charge of Misconduct ("Charge"), or on its own initiative, the Committee shall initiate an investigation.

2.5(b) If, upon initial or preliminary review, the Committee makes a determination that the charges are either without basis in fact or, if proven, would not constitute professional misconduct, the Committee shall dismiss the allegations of misconduct. If such determination of dismissal cannot be made, a formal investigation shall be initiated.

2.5(c) Upon the decision to conduct a formal investigation, the Committee shall:

1. mail to the Charging and Responding Parties within three (3) business days of that decision

notice of the commencement of a formal investigation. That notification shall be in writing and shall contain a complete explanation of all Charge(s), as well as the reasons for a formal investigation and shall cite the applicable codes and rules;

2. allow the Responding Party thirty (30) days to prepare and submit a confidential response to the Committee, which response shall address each charge specifically and shall be in writing; and

3. upon receipt of the response to the notification, have thirty (30) days to investigate the Charge(s). If an extension of time is deemed necessary, that extension shall not exceed ninety (90) days.

2.5(d) Upon conclusion of the investigation, the Committee may:

1. dismiss the Charge upon the finding that it has no basis in fact;

2. dismiss the Charge upon the finding that, if proven, the Charge would not constitute Misconduct;

3. refer the matter for hearing by the Tribunal; or

4. in the case of criminal activity, refer the Charge(s) and all investigation results to the appropriate authority.

2.6 Procedure for a Misconduct Hearing before a Tribunal

2.6(a) Upon the decision by the Committee that a matter should be heard, all parties shall be notified and a hearing date shall be set. The hearing shall take place no more than thirty (30) days from the conclusion of the formal investigation.

2.6(b) The Responding Party shall have the right to counsel. The parties and the Tribunal shall have the right to call any witnesses and introduce any documentation that they believe will lead to the fair and reasonable resolution of the matter.

2.6(c) Upon completion of the hearing, the Tribunal shall deliberate and present a written decision to the parties in accordance with procedures as set forth by the Tribunal.

2.6(d) Notice of the decision of the Tribunal shall be appropriately published.

2.7 Sanctions

2.7(a) Upon a finding of the Tribunal that misconduct has occurred, any of the following sanctions, or others as may be deemed appropriate, may be imposed upon the Responding Party, either singularly or in combination:

1. letter of reprimand to the Responding Party; counseling;

2. attendance at an ethics course approved by the Tribunal; probation;

3. suspension of license/authority to practice; revocation of license/authority to practice;

4. imposition of a fine; assessment of costs; or

5. in the instance of criminal activity, referral to the appropriate authority.

2.7(b) Upon the expiration of any period of probation, suspension, or revocation, the Responding Party may make application for reinstatement. With the application for reinstatement, the Responding Party must show proof of having complied with all aspects of the sanctions imposed by the Tribunal.

2.8 Appellate Procedures

2.8(a) The parties shall have the right to appeal the decision of the Tribunal in accordance with the procedure as set forth by the Tribunal.

DEFINITIONS

APPELLATE BODY   means a body established to adjudicate an appeal to any decision made by a Tribunal or other decision-making body with respect to formally heard Charges of Misconduct.

CHARGE OF MISCONDUCT   means a written submission by any individual or entity to an ethics committee, paralegal association, bar association, law enforcement agency, judicial body, government agency, or other appropriate body or entity, that sets forth nonconfidential information regarding any instance of alleged misconduct by an individual paralegal or paralegal entity.

CHARGING PARTY   means any individual or entity who submits a Charge of Misconduct against an individual paralegal or paralegal entity.

COMPETENCY   means the demonstration of: diligence, education, skill, and mental, emotional, and physical fitness reasonably necessary for the performance of paralegal services.

CONFIDENTIAL INFORMATION   means information relating to a client, whatever its source, that is not public knowledge nor available to the public. ("Nonconfidential Information" would generally include the name of the client and the identity of the matter for which the paralegal provided services.)

DISCIPLINARY HEARING   means the confidential proceeding conducted by a committee or other designated body or entity concerning any instance of alleged misconduct by an individual paralegal or paralegal entity.

DISCIPLINARY COMMITTEE   means any committee that has been established by an entity such as a paralegal association, bar association, judicial body, or government agency to: (a) identify, define, and investigate general ethical considerations and concerns with respect to paralegal practice; (b) administer and enforce the Model Code and Model Rules and; (c) discipline any individual paralegal or paralegal entity found to be in violation of same.

DISCLOSE   means communication of information reasonably sufficient to permit identification of the significance of the matter in question.

ETHICAL WALL   means the screening method implemented in order to protect a client from a conflict of interest. An Ethical Wall generally includes, but is not limited to, the following elements: (1) prohibit the paralegal from having any connection with the matter; (2) ban discussions with or the transfer of documents to or from the paralegal; (3) restrict access to files; and (4) educate all members of the firm, corporation, or entity as to the separation of the paralegal (both organizationally and physically) from the pending matter. For more information regarding the Ethical Wall, see the NFPA publication entitled "The Ethical Wall—Its Application to Paralegals."

EX PARTE   means actions or communications conducted at the instance and for the benefit of one party only, and without notice to, or contestation by, any person adversely interested.

INVESTIGATION   means the investigation of any charge(s) of misconduct filed against an individual paralegal or paralegal entity by a Committee.

LETTER OF REPRIMAND   means a written notice of formal censure or severe reproof administered to an individual paralegal or paralegal entity for unethical or improper conduct.

MISCONDUCT   means the knowing or unknowing commission of an act that is in direct violation of those Canons and Ethical Considerations of any and all applicable codes and/or rules of conduct.

PARALEGAL   is synonymous with "Legal Assistant" and is defined as a person qualified through education, training, or work experience to perform substantive legal work that requires knowledge of legal concepts and is customarily, but not exclusively performed by a lawyer. This person may be retained or employed by a lawyer, law office, governmental agency, or other entity or may be authorized by administrative, statutory, or court authority to perform this work.

PROPER AUTHORITY   means the local paralegal association, the local or state bar association, Committee(s) of the local paralegal or bar association(s), local prosecutor, administrative agency, or other tribunal empowered to investigate or act upon an instance of alleged misconduct.

RESPONDING PARTY   means an individual paralegal or paralegal entity against whom a Charge of Misconduct has been submitted.

REVOCATION   means the rescission of the license, certificate, or other authority to practice of an individual paralegal or paralegal entity found in violation of those Canons and Ethical Considerations of any and all applicable codes and/or rules of conduct.

SUSPENSION   means the suspension of the license, certificate, or other authority to practice of an individual paralegal or paralegal entity found in violation of those Canons and Ethical Considerations of any and all applicable codes and/or rules of conduct.

TRIBUNAL   means the body designated to adjudicate allegations of misconduct.

APPENDIX D

THE ABA'S MODEL GUIDELINES FOR THE UTILIZATION OF LEGAL ASSISTANT SERVICES

PREAMBLE

State courts, bar associations, or bar committees in at least seventeen states have prepared recommendations[1] for the utilization of legal assistant services.[2] While their content varies, their purpose appears uniform: to provide lawyers with a reliable basis for delegating responsibility for performing a portion of the lawyer's tasks to legal assistants. The purpose of preparing model guidelines is not to contradict the guidelines already adopted or to suggest that other guidelines may be more appro-

priate in a particular jurisdiction. It is the view of the Standing Committee on Legal Assistants of the American Bar Association [ABA], however, that a model set of guidelines for the utilization of legal assistant services may assist many states in adopting or revising such guidelines. The Standing Committee is of the view that guidelines will encourage lawyers to utilize legal assistant services effectively and promote the growth of the legal assistant profession.[3] In undertaking this project, the Standing Committee has attempted to state guidelines that conform with the American Bar Association's

---

1. An appendix identifies the guidelines, court rules, and recommendations that were reviewed in drafting these Model Guidelines. [This appendix is not included in *West's Paralegal Today.*]

2. On February 6, 1986, the ABA Board of Governors approved the following definition of the term "legal assistant":

    A legal assistant is a person, qualified through education, training, or work experience, who is employed or retained by a lawyer, law office, governmental agency, or other entity in a capacity or function which involves the performance, under the ultimate direction and supervision of an attorney, of specifically delegated substantive legal work, which work, for the most part, requires a sufficient knowledge of legal concepts that, absent such assistant, the attorney would perform the task. In some contexts, the term

    "paralegal" is used interchangeably with the term legal assistant. {Note: The ABA has since modified this decision. See Chapter 1.]

3. While necessarily mentioning legal assistant conduct, lawyers are the intended audience of these Guidelines. The Guidelines, therefore, are addressed to lawyer conduct and not directly to the conduct of the legal assistant. Both the National Association of Legal Assistants (NALA) and the National Federation of Paralegal Associations (NFPA) have adopted guidelines of conduct that are directed to legal assistants. See NALA, "Code of Ethics and Professional Responsibility of the National Association of Legal Assistants, Inc." (adopted May 1975, revised November 1979 and September 1988); NFPA, "Affirmation of Responsibility" (adopted 1977, revised 1981).

A-13

Model Rules of Professional Conduct, decided authority, and contemporary practice. Lawyers, of course, are to be first directed by Rule 5.3 of the Model Rules in the utilization of legal assistant services, and nothing contained in these guidelines is intended to be inconsistent with that rule. Specific ethical considerations in particular states, however, may require modification of these guidelines before their adoption. In the commentary after each guideline, we have attempted to identify the basis for the guideline and any issues of which we are aware that the guideline may present; those drafting such guidelines may wish to take them into account.

Guideline 1

A lawyer is responsible for all of the professional actions of a legal assistant performing legal assistant services at the lawyer's direction and should take reasonable measures to ensure that the legal assistant's conduct is consistent with the lawyer's obligations under the ABA Model Rules of Professional Conduct.

COMMENT TO GUIDELINE 1. An attorney who utilizes a legal assistant's services is responsible for determining that the legal assistant is competent to perform the tasks assigned, based on the legal assistant's education, training, and experience, and for ensuring that the legal assistant is familiar with the responsibilities of attorneys and legal assistants under the applicable rules governing professional conduct.[4]

Under principles of agency law and rules governing the conduct of attorneys, lawyers are responsible for the actions and the work product of the non-lawyers they employ. Rule 5.3 of the Model Rules[5] requires that partners and supervising attorneys ensure that the conduct of non-lawyer assistants is compatible with the

lawyer's professional obligations. Several state guidelines have adopted this language. E.g., Commentary to Illinois Recommendation (A), Kansas Guideline III(a), New Hampshire Rule 35, Sub-Rule 9, and North Carolina Guideline 4. Ethical Consideration 3–6 of the Model Code encouraged lawyers to delegate tasks to legal assistants provided the lawyer maintained a direct relationship with the client, supervised appropriately, and had complete responsibility for the work product. The adoption of Rule 5.3, which incorporates these principles, implicitly reaffirms this encouragement.

Several states have addressed the issue of the lawyer's ultimate responsibility for work performed by subordinates. For example, Colorado Guideline 1.c, Kentucky Supreme Court Rule 3.700, Sub-Rule 2.C, and Michigan Guideline I provide: "The lawyer remains responsible for the actions of the legal assistant to the same extent as if such representation had been furnished entirely by the lawyer and such actions were those of the lawyer." New Mexico Guideline X states "[the] lawyer maintains ultimate responsibility for and has an ongoing duty to actively supervise the legal assistant's work performance, conduct and product." Connecticut Recommendation 2 and Rhode Island Guideline III state specifically that lawyers are liable for malpractice for the mistakes and omissions of their legal assistants.

Finally, the lawyer should ensure that legal assistants supervised by the lawyer are familiar with the rules governing attorney conduct and that they follow those rules. See Comment to Model Rule 5.3; Illinois Recommendation (A)(5), New Hampshire Supreme Court Rule 35, Sub-Rule 9, and New Mexico, Statement of Purpose; see also NALA's Model Standards and Guidelines for the Utilization of Legal Assistants, guidelines IV, V, and VIII (1985, revised 1990) (hereafter "NALA Guidelines").

The Standing Committee and several of those who have commented upon these Guidelines regard Guideline 1 as a comprehensive statement of general principle governing lawyers who utilize legal assistant services in the practice of law. As such it, in effect, is a part of each of the remaining Guidelines.

Guideline 2

Provided the lawyer maintains responsibility for the work product, a lawyer may delegate to a legal assistant any task normally performed by the lawyer except those tasks proscribed to one not licensed as a lawyer by statute, court rule, administrative rule or regulation, controlling authority, the ABA Model Rules of Professional Conduct, or these Guidelines.

---

4. Attorneys, of course, are not liable for violation of the ABA Model Rules of Professional Conduct ("Model Rules") unless the Model Rules have been adopted as the code of professional conduct in a jurisdiction in which the lawyer practices. They are referenced in this model guideline for illustrative purposes; if the guideline is to be adopted, the reference should be modified to the jurisdiction's rules of professional conduct.

5. The Model Rules were first adopted by the ABA House of Delegates in August of 1983. Since that time many states have adopted the Model Rules to govern the professional conduct of lawyers licensed in those states. Since a number of states still utilize a version of the Model Code of Professional Responsibility ("Model Code"), which was adopted by the House of Delegates in August of 1969, however, these comments will refer to both the Model Rules and the predecessor Model Code (and to the Ethical Considerations and Disciplinary Rules found under the canons in the Model Code).

COMMENT TO GUIDELINE 2.   The essence of the definition of the term legal assistant adopted by the ABA Board of Governors in 1986 is that, so long as appropriate supervision is maintained, many tasks normally performed by lawyers may be delegated to legal assistants. Of course, Rule 5.5 of the Model Rules, DR 3–101 of the Model Code, and most states specifically prohibit lawyers from assisting or aiding a non-lawyer in the unauthorized practice of law. Thus, while appropriate delegation of tasks to legal assistants is encouraged, the lawyer may not permit the legal assistant to engage in the "practice of law." Neither the Model Rules nor the Model Code define the "practice of law." EC 3–5 under the Model Code gave some guidance by equating the practice of law to the application of the professional judgment of the lawyer in solving clients' legal problems. Further, ABA Opinion 316 (1967) states: "A lawyer can employ lay secretaries, lay investigators, lay detectives, lay researchers, accountants, lay scriveners, nonlawyer draftsmen or nonlawyer researchers. In fact, he may employ nonlawyers to do any task for him except counsel clients about law matters, engage directly in the practice of law, appear in court or appear in formal proceedings as part of the judicial process, so long as it is he who takes the work and vouches for it to the client and becomes responsible for it to the client."

Most state guidelines specify that legal assistants may not appear before courts, administrative tribunals, or other adjudicatory bodies unless their rules authorize such appearances; may not conduct depositions; and may not give legal advice to clients. E.g., Connecticut Recommendation 4; Florida EC 3–6 (327 So.2d at 16); and Michigan Guideline II. Also see NALA Guidelines IV and VI. But it is also important to note that, as some guidelines have recognized, pursuant to federal or state statute legal assistants are permitted to provide direct client representation in certain administrative proceedings. E.g., South Carolina Guideline II. While this does not obviate the attorney's responsibility for the legal assistant's work, it does change the nature of the attorney supervision of the legal assistant. The opportunity to use such legal assistant services has particular benefits to legal services programs and does not violate Guideline 2. See generally ABA Standards for Providers of Civil Legal Services to the Poor, Std. 6.3, at 6.17–6.18 (1986).

The Model Rules emphasize the importance of appropriate delegation. The key to appropriate delegation is proper supervision, which includes adequate instruction when assigning projects, monitoring of the project, and review of the completed project. The Supreme Court of Virginia upheld a malpractice verdict against a lawyer based in part on negligent actions of a legal assistant in performing tasks that evidently were properly delegable. *Musselman v. Willoughby Corp.*, 230 Va. 337, 337 S.E.2d 724 (1985). See also C. Wolfram, *Modern Legal Ethics* (1986), at 236, 896. All state guidelines refer to the requirement that the lawyer "supervise" legal assistants in the performance of their duties. Lawyers should also take care in hiring and choosing a legal assistant to work on a specific project to ensure that the legal assistant has the education, knowledge, and ability necessary to perform the delegated tasks competently. See Connecticut Recommendation 14, Kansas Standards I, II, and III, and New Mexico Guideline VIII. Finally, some states describe appropriate delegation and review in terms of the delegated work losing its identity and becoming "merged" into the work product of the attorney. See Florida EC 3–6 (327 So.2d at 16).

Legal assistants often play an important role in improving communication between the attorney and the client. EC 3–6 under the Model Code mentioned three specific kinds of tasks that legal assistants may perform under appropriate lawyer supervision: factual investigation and research, legal research, and the preparation of legal documents. Some states delineate more specific tasks in their guidelines, such as attending client conferences, corresponding with and obtaining information from clients, handling witness execution of documents, preparing transmittal letters, maintaining estate/guardianship trust accounts, etc. See, e.g., Colorado (lists of specialized functions in several areas follow guidelines); Michigan, Comment to Definition of Legal Assistant; New York, Specialized Skills of Legal Assistants; Rhode Island Guideline II; and NALA Guideline IX. The two-volume *Working with Legal Assistants*, published by the Standing Committee in 1982, attempted to provide a general description of the types of tasks that may be delegated to legal assistants in various practice areas.

There are tasks that have been specifically prohibited in some states, but that may be delegated in others. For example, legal assistants may not supervise will executions or represent clients at real estate closings in some jurisdictions, but may in others. Compare Connecticut Recommendation 7 and Illinois State Bar Association Position Paper on Use of Attorney Assistants in Real Estate Transactions (May 16, 1984), which proscribe legal assistants conducting real estate closings, with Georgia "real estate job description," Florida Professional Ethics Committee Advisory Opinion 89–5 (1989), and Missouri, Comment to Guideline I, which permit legal assistants to conduct real estate closings. Also compare Connecticut Recommendation 8 (prohibiting attorneys from authorizing legal assistants to supervise will executions) with Colorado "estate planning job description," Georgia "estate, trusts, and wills job description," Missouri, Comment to Guideline I, and Rhode Island Guideline II (suggesting that legal assistants may supervise the execution of wills, trusts, and other documents).

Guideline 3

A lawyer may not delegate to a legal assistant:

(a) **Responsibility for establishing an attorney-client relationship.**
(b) **Responsibility for establishing the amount of a fee to be charged for a legal service.**
(c) **Responsibility for a legal opinion rendered to a client.**

COMMENTS TO GUIDELINE 3. The Model Rules and most state codes require that lawyers communicate with their clients in order for clients to make well-informed decisions about their representation and resolution of legal issues. Model Rule 1.4. Ethical Consideration 3–6 under the Model Code emphasized that "delegation [of legal tasks to nonlawyers] is proper if the lawyer *maintains a direct relationship with his client*, supervises the delegated work and has complete professional responsibility for the work product." (Emphasis added.) Accordingly, most state guidelines also stress the importance of a direct attorney-client relationship. See Colorado Guideline 1, Florida EC 3–6, Illinois Recommendation (A)(1), Iowa EC 3–6(2), and New Mexico Guideline IV. The direct personal relationship between client and lawyer is necessary to the exercise of the lawyer's trained professional judgment.

An essential aspect of the lawyer-client relationship is the agreement to undertake representation and the related fee arrangement. The Model Rules and most states require that fee arrangements be agreed upon early on and be communicated to the client by the lawyer, in some circumstances in writing. Model Rule 1.5 and Comments. Many state guidelines prohibit legal assistants from "setting fees" or "accepting cases." See, e.g., Colorado Guideline 1 and NALA Guideline VI. Connecticut recommends that legal assistants be prohibited from accepting or rejecting cases or setting fees "if these tasks entail any discretion on the part of the paralegals." Connecticut Recommendation 9.

EC 3–5 states: "[T]he essence of the professional judgment of the lawyer is his educated ability to relate the general body and philosophy of law to a specific legal problem of a client; and thus, the public interest will be better served if only lawyers are permitted to act in matters involving professional judgment." Clients are entitled to their lawyers' professional judgment and opinion. Legal assistants may, however, be authorized to communicate legal advice so long as they do not interpret or expand on that advice. Typically, state guidelines phrase this prohibition in terms of legal assistants being forbidden from "giving legal advice" or "counseling clients about legal matters." See, e.g., Colorado Guideline 2, Connecticut Recommendation 6, Florida DR 3–104, Iowa EC 3–6(3), Kansas Guideline I, Kentucky Sub-Rule 2, New Hampshire Rule 35, Sub-Rule 1, Texas Guideline I, and NALA Guideline VI. Some states have more expansive wording that prohibits legal assistants from engaging in any activity that would require the exercise of independent legal judgment. Nevertheless, it is clear that all states, as well as the Model Rules, encourage direct communication between clients and a legal assistant insofar as the legal assistant is performing a task properly delegated by a lawyer. It should be noted that a lawyer who permits a legal assistant to assist in establishing the attorney-client relationship, communicating a fee, or preparing a legal opinion is not delegating responsibility for those matters and, therefore, may be complying with this guideline.

Guideline 4

It is the lawyer's responsibility to take reasonable measures to ensure that clients, courts, and other lawyers are aware that a legal assistant, whose services are utilized by the lawyer in performing legal services, is not licensed to practice law.

COMMENT TO GUIDELINE 4. Since, in most instances, a legal assistant is not licensed as a lawyer, it is important that those with whom the legal assistant deals are aware of that fact. Several state guidelines impose on the lawyer responsibility for instructing a legal assistant whose services are utilized by the lawyer to disclose the legal assistant's status in any dealings with a third party. See, e.g., Michigan Guideline III, part 5, New Hampshire Rule 35, Sub-Rule 8, and NALA Guideline V. While requiring the legal assistant to make such disclosure is one way in which the attorney's responsibility to third parties may be discharged, the Standing Committee is of the view that it is desirable to emphasize the lawyer's responsibility for the disclosure and leave to the lawyer the discretion to decide whether the lawyer will discharge that responsibility by direct communication with the client, by requiring the legal assistant to make the disclosure, by a written memorandum, or by some other means. Although in most initial engagements by a client it may be prudent for the attorney to discharge the responsibility with a writing, the guideline requires only that the lawyer recognize the responsibility and ensure that it is discharged. Clearly, when a client has been adequately informed of the lawyer's utilization of legal assistant services, it is unnecessary to make additional formalistic disclosures as the client retains the lawyer for other services.

Most state guidelines specifically endorse legal assistants signing correspondence so long as their status as a legal assistant is indicated by an appropriate title. E.g., Colorado Guideline 2; Kansas, Comment to Guideline IX; and North Carolina Guideline 9; also see ABA Informal Opinion 1367 (1976). The comment to New Mexico Guideline XI warns against the use of the title "associate" since it may be construed to mean associate-attorney.

Guideline 5

A lawyer may identify legal assistants by name and title on the lawyer's letterhead and on business cards identifying the lawyer's firm.

COMMENT TO GUIDELINE 5. Under Guideline 4, above, an attorney who employs a legal assistant has an obligation to ensure that the status of the legal assistant as a non-lawyer is fully disclosed. The primary purpose of this disclosure is to avoid confusion that might lead someone to believe that the legal assistant is a lawyer. The identification suggested by this guideline is consistent with that objective, while also affording the legal assistant recognition as an important part of the legal services team.

Recent ABA Informal Opinion 1527 (1989) provides that non-lawyer support personnel, including legal assistants, may be listed on a law firm's letterhead and reiterates previous opinions that approve of legal assistants having business cards. See also ABA Informal Opinion 1185 (1971). The listing must not be false or misleading and "must make it clear that the support personnel who are listed are not lawyers."

Nearly all state guidelines approve of business cards for legal assistants, but some prescribe the contents and format of the card. E.g., Iowa Guideline 4 and Texas Guideline VIII. All agree the legal assistant's status must be clearly indicated and the card may not be used in a deceptive way. New Hampshire Supreme Court Rule 7 approves the use of business cards so long as the card is not used for unethical solicitation.

Some states do not permit attorneys to list legal assistants on their letterhead. E.g., Kansas Guideline VIII, Michigan Guideline III, New Hampshire Rule 35, Sub-Rule 7, New Mexico Guideline XI, and North Carolina Guideline 9. Several of these states rely on earlier ABA Informal Opinion 619 (1962), 845 (1965), and 1000 (1977), all of which were expressly withdrawn by ABA Informal Opinion 1527. These earlier opinions interpreted the predecessor Model Code and DR 2–102(A), which, prior to *Bates v. State Bar of Arizona*, 433 U.S. 350 (1977), had strict limitations on the information that could be listed on letterheads. States which do permit attorneys to list names of legal assistants on their stationery, if the listing is not deceptive and the legal assistant's status is clearly identified, include: Arizona Committee on Rules of Professional Conduct Formal Opinion 3/90 (1990); Connecticut Recommendation 12; Florida Professional Ethics Committee Advisory Opinion 86–4 (1986); Hawaii, Formal Opinion 78–8–19 (1978, as revised 1984); Illinois State Bar Association Advisory Opinion 87–1 (1987); Kentucky Sub-Rule 6; Mississippi State Bar Ethics Committee Opinion 93 (1984); Missouri Guideline IV; New York State Bar Association Committee on Professional Ethics Opinion 500 (1978); Oregon, Ethical Opinion No. 349 (1977); and Texas, Ethics Committee Opinion 436 (1983). In light of the United States Supreme Court opinion in *Peel v. Attorney Registration and Disciplinary Commission of Illinois*, 496 U.S. 91, 110 S.Ct. 2281 (1990), it may be that a restriction on letterhead identification of legal assistants that is not deceptive and clearly identifies the legal assistant's status violates the First Amendment rights of the lawyer.

Guideline 6

It is the responsibility of a lawyer to take reasonable measures to ensure that all client confidences are preserved by a legal assistant.

COMMENT TO GUIDELINE 6.   A fundamental principle underlying the free exchange of information in a lawyer-client relationship is that the lawyer maintain the confidentiality of information relating to the representation. "It is a matter of common knowledge that the normal operation of a law office exposes confidential professional information to non-lawyer employees of the office. This obligates a lawyer to exercise care in selecting and training his employees so that the sanctity of all confidences and secrets of his clients may be preserved." EC 4–2, Model Code.

Rule 5.3 of the Model Rules requires "a lawyer who has direct supervisory authority over the non-lawyer [to] make reasonable efforts to ensure that the person's conduct is compatible with the professional obligations of the lawyer." The Comment to Rule 5.3

makes it clear that lawyers should give legal assistants "appropriate instruction and supervision concerning the ethical aspects of their employment, particularly regarding the obligation not to disclose information relating to the representation of the client." DR 4–101(D) under the Model Code provides that: "A lawyer shall exercise reasonable care to prevent his employees, associates and others whose services are utilized by him from discharging or using confidences or secrets of a client. . . ."

It is particularly important that the lawyer ensure that the legal assistant understands that *all* information concerning the client, even the mere fact that a person is a client of the firm, may be strictly confidential. Rule 1.6 of the Model Rules expanded the definition of confidential information ". . . not merely to matters communicated in confidence by the client but also to all information relating to the representation, whatever its source."[6] It is therefore the lawyer's obligation to instruct clearly and to take reasonable steps to ensure the legal assistant's preservation of client confidences. Nearly all states that have guidelines for the utilization of legal assistants require the lawyer "to instruct legal assistants concerning client confidences" and "to exercise care to ensure that legal assistants comply" with the Code in this regard. Even if the client consents to divulging information, this information must not be used to the disadvantage of the client. See, e.g., Connecticut Recommendation 3; New Hampshire Rule 35, Sub-Rule 4; NALA Guideline V.

Guideline 7

A lawyer should take reasonable measures to prevent conflicts of interest resulting from a legal assistant's other employment or interests insofar as such other employment or interests would present a conflict of interest if it were that of the lawyer.

---

6. Rule 1.05 of the Texas Disciplinary Rules of Professional Conduct (1990) provides a different formulation, which is equally expansive:

   "Confidential information" includes both "privileged information" and "unprivileged client information." "Privileged information" refers to the information of a client protected by the lawyer-client privilege of Rule 503 of the Texas Rules of Evidence or the Rule 503 of the Texas Rules of Criminal Evidence or by the principles of attorney-client privilege governed by Rule 501 of the Federal Rules of Evidence for United States Courts and Magistrates. "Unprivileged client information" means all information relating to a client or furnished by the client, other than privileged information, acquired by the lawyer during the course of or by reason of the representation of the client.

COMMENT TO GUIDELINE 7. A lawyer must make "reasonable efforts to ensure that [a] legal assistant's conduct is compatible with the professional obligations of the lawyer." Model Rule 5.3. These professional obligations include the duty to exercise independent professional judgment on behalf of a client, "free of compromising influences and loyalties." ABA Model Rules 1.7 through 1.13. Therefore, legal assistants should be instructed to inform the supervising attorney of any interest that could result in a conflict of interest or even give the appearance of a conflict. The guideline intentionally speaks to other employment rather than only past employment, since there are instances where legal assistants are employed by more than one law firm at the same time. The guideline's reference to "other interests" is intended to include personal relationships as well as instances where a legal assistant may have a financial interest (i.e., as stockholder, trust beneficiary or trustee, etc.) that would conflict with the client's in the matter in which the lawyer has been employed.

"Imputed Disqualification Arising from Change in Employment by Non-lawyer Employee," ABA Informal Opinion 1526 (1988), defines the duties of both the present and former employing lawyers and reasons that the restrictions on legal assistants' employment should be kept to "the minimum necessary to protect confidentiality" in order to prevent legal assistants from being forced to leave their careers, which "would disserve clients as well as the legal profession." The Opinion describes the attorney's obligations (1) to caution the legal assistant not to disclose any information and (2) to prevent the legal assistant from working on any matter on which the legal assistant worked for a prior employer or respecting which the employee has confidential information.

If a conflict is discovered, it may be possible to "wall" the legal assistant from the conflict area so that the entire firm need not be disqualified and the legal assistant is effectively screened from information concerning the matter. The American Bar Association has taken the position that what historically has been described as a "Chinese wall" will allow non-lawyer personnel (including legal assistants) who are in possession of confidential client information to accept employment with a law firm opposing the former client so long as the wall is observed and effectively screens the non-lawyer from confidential information. ABA Informal Opinion 1526 (1988). See also Tennessee Formal Ethics Opinion 89–F–118 (March 10, 1989). The implication of this Informal Opinion is that if a wall is not in place, the employer may be disqualified from representing either party to the controversy. One court has so held. *In re: Complex Asbestos Litigation*, No. 828684 (San Francisco Superior Court, September 19, 1989).

It is not clear that a wall will prevent disqualification in the case of a lawyer employed to work for a law firm representing a client with an adverse interest to a client of the lawyer's former employer. Under Model Rule 1.10, when a lawyer moves to a firm that represents an adverse party in a matter in which the lawyer's former firm was involved, absent a waiver by the client, the new firm's representation may continue only if the newly employed lawyer acquired no protected information and did not work directly on the matter in the former employment. The new Rules of Professional Conduct in Kentucky and Texas (both effective January 1, 1990) specifically provide for disqualification. Rule 1.10(b) in the District of Columbia, which became effective January 1, 1991, does so as well. The Sixth Circuit, however, has held that the wall will effectively insulate the new firm from disqualification if it prevents the new lawyer-employee from access to information concerning the client with the adverse interest. *Manning v. Waring, Cox, James, Sklar & Allen*, 849 F.2d 222 (6th Cir. 1988). [As a result of the Sixth Circuit opinion, Tennessee revised its formal ethics opinion, which is cited above, and now applies the same rule to lawyers, legal assistants, law clerks, and legal secretaries.] See generally NFPA, "The Chinese Wall—Its Application to Paralegals" (1990).

The states that have guidelines that address the legal assistant conflict of interest refer to the lawyer's responsibility to ensure against personal, business or social interests of the legal assistant that would conflict with the representation of the client or impinge on the services rendered to the client. E.g., Kansas Guideline X, New Mexico Guideline VI, and North Carolina Guideline 7. Florida Professional Ethics Opinion 86–5 (1986) discusses a legal assistant's move from one firm to another and the obligations of each not to disclose confidences. See also Vermont Ethics Opinion 85–8 (1985) (a legal assistant is not bound by the Code of Professional Responsibility and, absent an absolute waiver by the client, the new firm should not represent client if legal assistant possessed confidential information from old firm).

Guideline 8

A lawyer may include a charge for the work performed by a legal assistant in setting a charge for legal services.

COMMENT TO GUIDELINE 8.   The U.S. Supreme Court in *Missouri v. Jenkins,* 491 U.S. 274 (1989), held that in setting a reasonable attorney's fee under 28 U.S.C. §1988, a legal fee may include a charge for legal assistant services at "market rates" rather than "actual cost" to the attorneys. This decision should resolve any question concerning the propriety of setting a charge for legal services based on work performed by a legal assistant. Its rationale favors setting a charge based on the "market" rate for such services, rather than their direct cost to the lawyer. This result was recognized by Connecticut Recommendation 11, Illinois Recommendation D, and Texas Guideline V prior to the Supreme Court decision. See also Fla.Stat.Ann. §57.104 (1991 Supp.) (adopted in 1987 and permitting consideration of legal assistant services in computing attorney's fees) and Fla.Stat.Ann. §744.108 (1991 Supp.) (adopted in 1989 and permitting recovery of "customary and reasonable charges for work performed by legal assistants" as fees for legal services in guardianship matters).

It is important to note, however, that *Missouri v. Jenkins* does not abrogate the attorney's responsibilities under Model Rule 1.5 to set a reasonable fee for legal services and it follows that those considerations apply to a fee that includes a fee for legal assistant services. Accordingly, the effect of combining a market rate charge for the services of lawyers and legal assistants should, in most instances, result in a lower total cost for the legal service than if the lawyer had performed the service alone.

Guideline 9

A lawyer may not split legal fees with a legal assistant nor pay a legal assistant for the referral of legal business. A lawyer may compensate a legal assistant based on the quantity and quality of the legal assistant's work and the value of that work to a law practice, but the legal assistant's compensation may not be contingent, by advance agreement, upon the probability of the lawyer's practice.

COMMENT TO GUIDELINE 9.   Model Rule 5.4 and DR 3–102(A) and 3–103(A) under the Model Code clearly prohibit fee "splitting" with legal assistants, whether characterized by splitting of contingent fees, "forwarding" fees, or other sharing of legal fees. Virtually all guidelines adopted by state bar associations have continued this prohibition in one form or another.[7] It appears clear that a legal assistant may not be compensated on a contingent basis for a particular case or paid for "signing up" clients for a legal practice.

---

7. Connecticut Recommendation 10; Illinois Recommendation D; Kansas Guideline VI; Kentucky Supreme Court Rule 3.700, Subrule 5; Michigan Guideline III, part 2; Missouri Guideline II; New Hampshire Rule 35, Sub-Rules 5 and 6; New Mexico Guideline IX; Rhode Island Guideline VIII and IX; South Carolina Guideline V; Texas Guideline V.

Having stated this prohibition, however, the guideline attempts to deal with the practical consideration of how a legal assistant properly may be compensated by an attorney or law firm. The linchpin of the prohibition seems to be the advance agreement of the lawyer to "split" a fee based on a pre-existing contingent agreement.[8] There is no general prohibition against a lawyer who enjoys a particularly profitable period recognizing the contribution of the legal assistant to that profitability with a discretionary bonus. Likewise, a lawyer engaged in a particularly profitable specialty of legal practice is not prohibited from compensating the legal assistant who aids materially in that practice more handsomely than the compensation generally awarded to legal assistants in that geographic area who work in law practices that are less lucrative. Indeed, any effort to fix a compensation level for legal assistants and prohibit greater compensation would appear to violate the federal antitrust laws. See, e.g., *Goldfarb v. Virginia State Bar*, 421 U.S. 773 (1975).

Guideline 10

A lawyer who employs a legal assistant should facilitate the legal assistant's participation in appropriate continuing education and *pro bono publico* activities.

COMMENT TO GUIDELINE 10. While Guideline 10 does not appear to have been adopted in the guidelines of any state bar association, the Standing Committee on Legal Assistants believes that its adoption would be appropriate.[9] For many years the Standing Committee on Legal Assistants has advocated that the improvement of formal legal assistant education will generally improve the legal services rendered by lawyers employing legal assistants and provide a more satisfying professional atmosphere in which legal assistants may work. See, e.g., ABA Board of Governors, Policy on Legal Assistant Licensure and/or Certification, Statement 4 (February 6, 1986); ABA, Standing Committee on Legal Assistants, "Position Paper on the Question of Legal Assistant Licensure or Certification" (December 10, 1985), at 6 and Conclusion 3. Recognition of the employing lawyer's obligation to facilitate the legal assistant's continuing professional education is, therefore, appropriate because of the benefits to both the law practice and the legal assistant and is consistent with the lawyer's own responsibility to maintain professional competence under Model Rule 1.1. See also EC 6–2 of the Model Code.

The Standing Committee is of the view that similar benefits will accrue to the lawyer and legal assistant if the legal assistant is included in the *pro bono publico* legal services that a lawyer has a clear obligation to provide under Model Rule 6.1 and, where appropriate, the legal assistant is encouraged to provide such services independently. The ability of a law firm to provide more *pro bono publico* services will be enhanced if legal assistants are included. Recognition of the legal assistant's role in such services is consistent with the role of the legal assistant in the contemporary delivery of legal services generally and is consistent with the lawyer's duty to the legal profession under Canon 2 of the Model Code.

THE STANDING COMMITTEE ON LEGAL
ASSISTANTS OF THE AMERICAN BAR
ASSOCIATION
May 1991

ADOPTED BY ABA HOUSE OF DELEGATES
August 1991

---

8. In its Rule 5.4, which [became] effective on January 1, 1991, the District of Columbia will permit lawyers to form legal service partnerships that include non-lawyer participants. Comments 5 and 6 to that rule, however, state that the term "non-lawyer participants" should not be confused with the term "non-lawyer assistants" and that "[n]on-lawyer assistants under Rule 5.3 do not have managerial authority or financial interests in the organization."

9. While no state has apparently adopted a guideline similar to Model Guideline 10, parts 4 and 5 of NALA Guideline VIII suggest similar requirements. Sections III and V of NFPA's "Affirmation of Professional Responsibility" recognize a legal assistant's obligations to "maintain a high level of competence" (which "is achieved through continuing education") and to "serve the public interest." NFPA has also published a guide to assist legal assistant groups in developing public service projects. See NFPA, "*Pro Bono Publico* (For the Good of the People)" (1987).

PARALEGAL ETHICS AND REGULATION:

HOW TO FIND STATE-SPECIFIC INFORMATION

NALANet

One resource for finding state-specific information is NALANet. This is an online information service for the legal-assistant profession. NALANet reports on relevant topics such as ethics, guidelines, membership, case law updates, legislative activities, bar activities, significant research projects, and articles about the utilization of legal assistants on a state-by-state basis. The Florida example, shown below, illustrates the type of information provided for each state. NALANet is available to members of NALA. For further information, contact NALA at (918) 587-6828, or visit its Web site at **www.nala.org**.

FLORIDA

Ethics

FL Opinion 86-4 8/1/86
(business cards, letterhead)

FL Opinion 88-15
(solicitation of clients, confidentiality, attorneys' fees)

FL Opinion 89-4 8/29/90
(nonlawyers, attorneys' fees, solicitation of clients, business cards)

FL Advisory Opinion 74479
(unauthorized practice of law)

FL Bar Re Advisory Opinion Hrs
Non-Lawyer Counselor FLA Sup Ct
No 70615 5/25/89
(nonlawyers)

FL Ethics Guide for Legal Assistants 86
(definitions, attorneys' fees, business cards, supervision, unauthorized practice of law, letterhead, ethics, qualifications)

FL Opinion 88-6 4/15/88
(initial interview, supervision, nonlawyers)

FL Opinion 87-11
Signing Lawyer Name/Pleadings &
Notices
(nonlawyers, unauthorized practice of
law, supervision)

FL Bar Advisory Opinion Non-Lawyer
Pre of Living Trusts FL Supreme Court
Case No. 78358
(nonlawyers, unauthorized practice
of law)

FL Supreme Court Review of Opinion
Unauthorized Practice of Law Comm
Re Non-Lawyer Prep of Pension Plans
11/29/90
(nonlawyers, unauthorized practice
of law)

FL Advisory Opinion 74479 Undated
(unauthorized practice of law)

FL Opinion 86-5 8/1/86
(conflict of interest, confidentiality)

FL Opinion 88-6 4/15/88
(supervision, unauthorized practice of
law, work product)

FL Opinion 89-5
(real property, nonlawyers)

Rule 10-1.1(B), Rules Regulating
Florida Bar (6/20/91) Forms Approved
for Use by Lawyers/Non-Lawyers

FL Opinion 92-3 (10/1/92)
(nonlawyers, attorneys' fees, solicitation of clients)

Guidelines

FL Ethics Guide for Legal Assistants 86
(definitions, attorneys' fees, business
cards, supervision, unauthorized

practice of law, letterhead, ethics,
qualifications)

Membership

FL Family Law Section Florida Bar
(certification, American Bar
Association Approved School, experience)

FL Orange County Bar
(affiliate membership)

FL General Practice Section Florida Bar
(certification, American Bar
Association Approved School, experience)

FL Local Government Section Florida
Bar
(certification, Florida member)

FL Health Law Section Florida Bar
(open)

FL Practice Management &
Technology Florida Bar

(certification, American Bar
Association Approved School,
experience)

FL Real Property Probate & Trust
Section
(certification, American Bar
Association Approved School,
experience)

FL Trial Lawyers Section Florida Bar
(certification, American Bar
Association Approved School,
experience)

FL Environmental & Land Use Section
(open)

FL Broward County Bar

Cases

The Celotex Corp-Mid Dist.
FL 90-10016-8B1 and
90-10017-8B1
(bankruptcy, attorneys' fees)

FL Bar v. Mitchell, 569 So. 2d 424
(FLA Sup. Ct. 1990)
(nonlawyers, supervision by lawyer)

Florida Bar v. Carter, 502 So. 2d 904
(FLA Sup. Ct. 1987)
(supervision)

FL Bar Re Advisory Opinion Hrs
Nonlawyer Counselor FLA Sup. Ct.
No. 70615 5/25/89
(nonlawyers)

FL Bar Advisory Opinion Nonlawyer
Prep of Living Trusts FL Supreme
Court Case No. 78358
(nonlawyers, unauthorized practice
of law)

FL Supreme Court Review of Opinion
UPL Comm Re Nonlawyer Prep of
Pension Plans 11/29/90
(nonlawyers, unauthorized practice
of law)

FL Advisory Opinion 73306 6/1/89
(forms, representation, unauthorized
practice of law)

In Re Christopher Backmann, BR
1990 (Bkrtcy S.D. FL, No. 88-94588-
BKC-AJC, 3/30/90)
(unauthorized practice of law,
supervision, bankruptcy, forms)

Security First Fed. v. Broom et al.,
DCA No 89-01814, 4/18/90
(qualifications, regulation, real
property)

Florida Bar v. Brumbaugh, No. 48803
S.Ct. Florida
(unauthorized practice of law, forms,
constitutional law)

Florida Bar v. Furman, No. 51226
S.Ct. Florida
(unauthorized practice of law, constitutional law, nonlawyers, forms)

*Std Guaranty Ins. v. Brenda L.
Quanstrom,* No 72100 Sup. Ct. of
Florida 1/11/90
(fees, Missouri)

*Town of Windermere v. Isleworth
Golf & CC,* Circuit Ct. 9th Judicial
District, Orange County Florida, CI
87-2677
(attorneys' fees)

Ray v. Cutter Labs, 746 F. Supp. (MD
FLA 1990)
(privilege waived, unintentional act,
privilege)

Corn v. City of Lauderdale Lakes, 794
F. Supp. 364 (S.D. Fla. 1992)
(attorneys' fees, market rate fees if pre-
vailing practice)

The Florida Bar v. Daniel E. Shramek,
Case No 77,871
(nonlawyers, unauthorized practice
of law)

Ippolito v. Florida, Case No. 92-880-
Civ.T-99
(nonlawyers, unauthorized practice of
law, legal technicians)

*Ibanez v. Florida Dept of Bus. & Prof.
Regulation,* 114 S.Ct. 2084 (1994)
7/18/94
(professional designation)

Legislation

FL Statute 57.104 Computation of
Attorney Fee
(definitions, attorneys' fees)

FL Senate Bill 2770 10/1/90 Passed
Public Law Paralegal Fees in
Guardianship Law
(attorneys' fees, supervision)

Articles

Amendment to Rule 4-6.1 of Rules Regulating the Florida Bar, Fla Sup. Ct., No 74,538 2/20/92 Pro Bono (*pro bono*)

Florida Legal Technician Committee 6/1/92 Preliminary Report Summary (legal technicians, unauthorized practice of law, regulation)

Rule 10-1.1(B), Rules Regulating Florida Bar (6/20/91) Forms Approved for Use by Lawyers/Nonlawyers (nonlawyers, forms)

What's in a Name? 8/1/94 Outlines Difference between Legal Assistant & Technician—Bar News Article Tech (definitions, certification)

Other

Florida Legal Technician Committee 6/1/92 Preliminary Report Summary (legal technicians, unauthorized practice of law, regulations)

A P P E N D I X   F

PARALEGAL ASSOCIATIONS

PARALEGAL ASSOCIATIONS

NFPA Associations

REGION I

Alaska Association of Legal Assistants
P.O. Box 101956
Anchorage, AK 99510-1956

Arizona Association of Professional
    Paralegals, Inc.
P.O. Box 430
Phoenix, AZ 85001

California Association of Independent
    Paralegals
39120 Argonaut Way, #114
Fremont, CA 94538

Hawaii Association of Legal Assistants
P.O. Box 674
Honolulu, HI 96809

Los Angeles Paralegal Association
P.O. Box 7803
Van Nuys, CA 91409
818/347-1001

Oregon Legal Assistants Association
P.O. Box 8523

Portland, OR 97207
503/796-1671

Sacramento Association of Legal
    Assistants
P.O. Box 453
Sacramento, CA 95812-0453
916/763-7851

San Diego Association of Legal
    Assistants
P.O. Box 87449
San Diego, CA 92138-7449
619/491-1994

San Francisco Paralegal Association
P.O. Box 2110
San Francisco, CA 94126-2110

Washington State Paralegal
    Association
P.O. Box 48153
Burieu, WA 98148
800/288-WSPA

REGION II

Dallas Area Paralegal Association
P.O. Box 12533
Dallas, TX 75225
972/991-0853

Illinois Paralegal Association
P.O. Box 8089
Bartlett, IL 60103-8089
630/837-8088

Kansas City Paralegal Association
8826 Santa Fe Drive, Suite 208
Overland Park, KS 66212
913/381-4458

Kansas Paralegal Association
P.O. Box 1675
Topeka, KS 66601

Legal Assistants of New Mexico
P.O. Box 1113
Albuquerque, NM
87103-1113
515/260-7104

Manitoba Association of Legal
    Assistants, Inc.
22-81 Tyndall Avenue
Winnipeg, Manitoba R2X 2W2

Minnesota Paralegal Association
1711 W. County Rd. B, #300N
Roseville, MN 55113
612/633-2778

New Orleans Paralegal Association
P.O. Box 30604

New Orleans, LA 70190
504/467-3136

Northwest Missouri Paralegal
  Association
Box 7013
St. Joseph, MO 64507

Paralegal Association of
  Wisconsin, Inc.
P.O. Box 510892
Milwaukee, WI 53203-0151
414/272-7168

Rocky Mountain Paralegal Association
P.O. Box 481864
Denver, CO 80248
303/370-9444

REGION III

Baltimore Association of Legal
  Assistants
P.O. Box 13244
Baltimore, MD 21203
301/567-BALA

Cincinnati Paralegal Association
P.O. Box 1515
Cincinnati, OH 45201
513/244-1266

Cleveland Association of Paralegals
P.O. Box 14517
Cleveland, OH 44114
216/556-5437

Georgia Association of Paralegals, Inc.
1199 Euclid Avenue, NE
Atlanta, GA 30307
404/522-1457

Greater Dayton Paralegal Association
P.O. Box 515
Mid-City Station
Dayton, OH 45402

Greater Lexington Paralegal
  Association, Inc.
P.O. Box 574
Lexington, KY 40586

Indiana Paralegal Association
P.O. Box 44518
Indianapolis, IN 46204

Legal Assistants of Central Ohio
P.O. Box 15182
Columbus, OH 43215-0182
614/224-9700

Louisville Association of Paralegals
P.O. Box 962
Louisville, KY 40201

Maryland Association of Paralegals
P.O. Box 13244
Baltimore, MD 21203
410/576-2252

Memphis Paralegal Association
P.O. Box 3646
Memphis, TN 38173-0646

Michiana Paralegal Association
P.O. Box 11458
South Bend, IN 46634

Mobile Association of Legal Assistants
P.O. Box 1852
Mobile, AL 36633

National Capital Area Paralegal
  Association
P.O. Box 27607
Washington, DC 20038-7607
202/659-0243

Northeast Indiana Paralegal
  Association, Inc.
P.O. Box 13646
Fort Wayne, IN 46865

Northeastern Ohio Paralegal
  Association
P.O. Box 80068
Akron, OH 44308-0068

Palmetto Paralegal Association
P.O. Box 11634
Columbia, SC 29211-1634

Roanoke Valley Paralegal Association
P.O. Box 1505
Roanoke, VA 24007

REGION IV

Central Connecticut Paralegal
  Assoc., Inc.
P.O. Box 230594
Hartford, CT 06123-0594

Central Massachusetts Paralegal
  Association
P.O. Box 444
Worcester, MA 01614

Central Pennsylvania Paralegal
  Association
P.O. Box 11814
Harrisburg, PA 17108

Chester County Paralegal Association
P.O. Box 295
West Chester, PA 19381-0295

Connecticut Association of
  Paralegals, Inc.
(Fairfield County)

P.O. Box 134
Bridgeport, CT 06601-0134

Delaware Paralegal Association
P.O. Box 1362
Wilmington, DE 19899

Long Island Paralegal Association
1877 Bly Road
East Meadow, NY 11554-1158

Manhattan Paralegal Association, Inc.
521 Fifth Avenue, 17th Floor
New York, NY 10175
212/330-8213

Massachusetts Paralegal Association
c/o Offtech Management Services
99 Summer Street, Suite L-150
Boston, MA 02110
800/637-4311

Paralegal Association of Rochester, Inc.
P.O. Box 40567
Rochester, NY 14604
716/234-5923

Philadelphia Association of Paralegals
P.O. Box 59179
Philadelphia, PA 19102-9179
610/825-6504

Pittsburgh Paralegal Association
P.O. Box 2845
Pittsburgh, PA 15230
412/344-3904

Prudential Insurance Company of
  America—Paralegal Council
751 Broad Street
Newark, NJ 07102

Rhode Island Paralegal Association
P.O. Box 1003
Providence, RI 02901

South Jersey Paralegal Association
P.O. Box 355
Haddonfield, NJ 08033

Southern Tier Association
  of Paralegals
P.O. Box 2555
Binghamton, NY 13902

Vermont Paralegal Organization
P.O. Box 6238
Rutland, VT 05702

West/Rock Paralegal Association
P.O. Box 668
New City, NY 10956

Western Massachusetts Paralegal
  Association

P.O. Box 30005
Springfield, MA 01103

Western New York Paralegal
   Association, Inc.
P.O. Box 207
Niagara Square Station
Buffalo, NY 14201
716/635-8250

NALA State and Local Affiliates

Alabama

Alabama Association of Legal
   Assistants
P.O. Box 55921
Birmingham, AL 35255

Legal Assistant Society of Southern
   Institute/PJC
Birmingham, AL

Legal Society of Virginia College
Dept. of Paralegal Studies
800 28th Avenue, South
Birmingham, AL 35209
205/802-1596

Sanford Paralegal Association
Birmingham, AL

Alaska

Fairbanks Association of Legal
   Assistants
P.O. Box 73503
Fairbanks, AK 99707

Arizona

Arizona Paralegal Association
2700 N. Central Avenue, #1400
Phoenix, AZ 85004-1122
602/285-4400

Legal Assistants of Metropolitan
   Phoenix
Maricopa County Attorney's Office
301-W Jefferson, 9th Floor
Phoenix, AZ 85003

Tucson Association of Legal Assistants
W. J. Harrison & Associates
3561 E. Sunrise, Suite 201
Tucson, AZ 85718

Arkansas

Arkansas Association of Legal
   Assistants

P.O. Box 2162
Little Rock, AR 72203

California

Legal Assistants Association of Santa
   Barbara
P.O. Box 2695
Santa Barbara, CA 93120
805/965-7319

Orange County Paralegal Association
6 Hutton Centre Drive
Santa Ana, CA 92707

Palomar College Paralegal Studies Club
1140 W. Mission Road
San Marcos, CA 92069-1487

Paralegal Association of Santa Clara
   County
P.O. Box 26736
San Jose, CA 95159

San Joaquin Association of Legal
   Assistants
3729 N. Claremont
Fresno, CA 93727

Ventura County Association of Legal
   Assistants
P.O. Box 24229
Ventura, CA 93002

Colorado

Association of Legal Assistants of
   Colorado
105 E. Vermijo Avenue, Suite #415
Colorado Springs, CO 80903

Legal Assistants of the Western Slope
P.O. Box 1487
Montrose, CO 81402
970/249-2546

Florida

Central Florida Paralegal Association
1664 Wild Fox Drive
Casselberry, FL 32707

Dade Association of Legal Assistants
9100 S. Dadeland Blvd., Suite 404
Miami, FL 33156
305/670-2690

Florida Legal Assistants, Inc.
756 Beachland Blvd.
Vero Beach, FL 32963
407/774-7880

Gainesville Association of Legal
   Assistants
1110-C NW 8th Avenue
Gainesville, FL 32601
352/955-2260

Jacksonville Legal Assistants
1660 Prudential Drive, Suite 200
Jacksonville, FL 32207
904/346-3800

Legal Assistants of SW Florida, Inc.
1549 Ringling Blvd., Suite 600
Sarasota, FL 34236
941/365-0140

Pensacola Legal Assistants
220 W. Garden Street, Suite 801
Pensacola, FL 32501
850/434-6223

Phi Lambda Alpha Legal Assisting
   Society
2602 SE 23rd Avenue
Cape Coral, FL 33904
941/275-6659

Volusia Association of Legal Assistants
213 Silver Beach Avenue
Daytona Beach, FL 32118
904/254-2941

Georgia

Georgia Legal Assistants
1808 Seminole Trail
Waycross, GA 31501-4132
912/632-8693

Georgia Paralegal Association
P.O. Box 1802
Atlanta, GA 30301
707/433-5252

South Georgia Assn. of Legal
   Assistants
P.O. Box 25
Valdosta, GA 31603-0025
912/242-2211

Southeastern Assn. of Legal Assistants
   of Georgia
P.O. Box 9086
120 West Liberty
Savannah, GA 31401
912/232-6423

Idaho

Gem State Association of Legal
   Assistants
P.O. Box 1118
Burley, ID 83318-1118
208/678-9181

Illinois

Central Illinois Paralegal Association
One State Farm Plaza, E8
Bloomington, IL 61710

Heart of Illinois Paralegal Association
331 Fulton, Suite 704
Peoria, IL 61602
309/674-4222

Indiana

Indiana Legal Assistants
14669 Old State Road
Evansville, IN 47711-9408

Iowa

Iowa Association of Legal Assistants
410 Washington Street
Iowa City, IA 52240
319/356-5032

Nebraska Assn. of Legal Assistants
P.O. Box 1588
Council Bluffs, IA 51502

Kansas

Kansas Association of Legal Assistants
P.O. Box 2975
Wichita, KS 67201
316/828-8712

Kentucky

Western Kentucky Paralegals
P.O. Box 447
Benton, KY 42025
502/527-5500

Louisiana

Louisiana State Paralegal Association
306-B Windermere Place
Alexandria, LA 71303

Northwest Louisiana Paralegal
    Association
330 Marshall Street, Suite 1410
Shreveport, LA 71101
318/222-9100

Maine

Maine State Association of Legal
    Assistants
2211 Congress Street, Mail Stop M194
Portland, ME 04122
207/770-3229

Michigan

Legal Assistants Association of
    Michigan
P.O. Box 80857
Lansing, MI 48908-0857
517/886-7176

Mississippi

Mississippi Association of Legal
    Assistants
P.O. Box 22567
Jackson, MS 39225-2564
601/973-1499

USM Society for Paralegal Studies
P.O. Box 5108
Hattiesburg, MS 39406-5108

Missouri

Kansas Association of Legal Assistants
4420 Madison Avenue, Suite 150
Kansas City, MO 64111
816/753-3000

St. Louis Association of Legal
    Assistants
10 South Broadway, Suite 1500
St. Louis, MO 63102
314/241-6566

Montana

Montana Association of Legal
    Assistants
P.O. Box 9197
Missouri, MT 59807-9197
406/721-6655

Nebraska

Nebraska Assn. of Legal Assistants
1650 Farnam
Omaha, NE 68102
402/346-6000

Nevada

Clark Co. Org. of Legal
    Assistants, Inc.
302 East Carson, #1100
Las Vegas, NV 89101
702/385-3373

Sierra Nevada Association of
    Paralegals
290 S. Arlington Avenue, #200
Reno, NV 89501
702/322-3811

New Hampshire

Paralegal Association of New
    Hampshire
1819 Elm Street
Manchester, NH 03104
603/627-1819

New Jersey

Legal Assistants of New Jersey
P.O. Box 142
Caldwell, NJ 07006

New Mexico

Southwestern Assn. of Legal Assistants
49 FW/JA
490 First Street, Suite 1940
Hollomon AFB, NM 88330-8277
505/475-7217

North Carolina

Coastal Carolina Paralegal Club
444 Western Blvd.
Jacksonville, NC 28546-6877
910/958-6351

Metrolina Paralegal Association
2400 Yorkmont Road
Charlotte, NC 28217
704/329-4016

North Carolina Paralegal
    Association, Inc.
P.O. Box 130
Linvlle Falls, NC 28647-0130
828/765-8897

North Dakota

Red River Valley Legal Assistants
101 10th Street N., #110
Fargo, ND 58102
701/293-8425

Western Dakota Assn. of Legal
    Assistants
P.O. Box 1000
Minot, ND 58702-1000
701/852-0381

Ohio

Toledo Association of Legal Assistants
416 N. Erie Street, #500
Toledo, OH 43624

Oklahoma

City College Legal Association
1370 North Interstate Drive
Norman, OK 73072
405/329-5627

Oklahoma Paralegal Association
P.O. Box 1108
Enid, OK 73701
405/233-2020

TJC Student Association of Legal
    Assistants
909 South Boston, Room 416
Tulsa, OK 741919-2095
918/595-7317

Tulsa Association of Legal Assistants
525 S. Main Street, Suite 1000
Tulsa, OK 74103-4514
918/583-7129

Oregon

Pacific Northwest Legal Assistants
112 W. 4th
The Dalles, OR 97058
541/296-5424

Pennsylvania

Keystone Legal Assistant Association
60 W. Pomfret Street
Carlisle, PA 17013
717/249-2353

South Carolina

Central Carolina Tech. College
   Paralegal Assn.
506 N. Guignard Drive
Sumter, SC 29150-2499
803/778-7859

Charleston Association of Legal
   Assistants
P.O. Box 340
Charleston, SC 29402
803/720-4449

Grand Strand Paralegal Association
743 Hemlock Avenue
Myrtle Beach, SC 29577

Greenville Association of Legal
   Assistants
108 Whitsett Street
Greenville, SC 29601
802/298-0089

Tri-County Paralegal Association
P.O. Box 993
Charleston, SC 29402
803/724-6665

South Dakota

National American University Student
   Assn. of Legal Assistants
317 N. Dakota Street, Suite 834
Vermillion, SD 57069-2332

South Dakota Legal Assistants
   Association
P.O. Box 8108
Rapid City, SD 57709-8108
605/348-7516

Tennessee

Greater Memphis Legal
   Assistants, Inc.
80 North Front Street, Suite 850
Memphis, TN 38103

Tennessee Paralegal Association
124 East Court Square

Trenton, TN 38382
901/855-9584

Texas

Capital Area Paralegal Association
600 Congress Avenue, Suite 2700
Austin, TX 78701
512/495-8516

El Paso Association of Legal Assistants
11104 Paducah
El Paso, TX 79936
915/598-0067

Legal Assistants Association
400 West Illinois, Suite 1640
Midland, TX 79701
915/683-8844

Northeast Texas Assn. of Legal
   Assistants
2020 Bill Owens Parkway, Suite 200
Longview, TX 75604-6213
903/759-2020

Nueces County Assn. of Legal
   Assistants
711 N. Carancahua, #1508
Corpus Christi, TX 78475
512/883-5786

Southeast Texas Assn. of Legal
   Assistants
2380 Eastern Freeway Beaumont, TX
   77703
409/898-2123

Texarkana Association of Legal
   Assistants
P.O. Box 6671
Texarkana, TX 75505

Texas Panhandle Assn. of Legal
   Assistants
P.O. Box 9142
Amarillo, TX 79105
806/345-3107

Tyler Area Assn. of Legal Professionals
P.O. Box 2013
Tyler, TX 75710
903/595-3573

West Texas Association of Legal
   Assistants
P.O. Box 10104
Lubbock, TX 79408
806/763-3661

Utah

Legal Assistants Association of Utah
230 S. 500 E, Suite 460

Salt Lake City, UT 84102
801/521-6666

Virgin Islands

Virgin Islands Association of Legal
   Assistants
P.O. Box 70
St. Thomas, VI 00804
809/774-6680

Virginia

Peninsula Legal Assistants, Inc.
601 Thimble Shoals Blvd., Suite 202
Newport News, VA 23606
757/873-9425

Richmond Association of Legal
   Assistants
901 E. Cary Street
One James Center
Richmond, VA 23219-4030
804/775-7540

Tidewater Association of Legal
   Assistants
910 W. Mercury Blvd., Suite 2A
Hampton, VA 23666
757/825-0400

Washington

Association of Paralegals and Legal
   Assistants of Washington State
929 Sprague Avenue West
Spokane, WA 92204

West Virginia

Legal Assistants of
   West Virginia, Inc.
121 North Queen Street
Martinsburg, WV 25401
304/262-9300

Wisconsin

Madison Area Paralegal Association
P.O. Box 927
Madison, WI 53701-0927
608/257-9521

Wyoming

Legal Assistants of Wyoming
P.O. Box 8498
235 East Broadway
Jackson, WY 83002
307/733-8668

Other Law-Related Associations

American Association of Law Libraries (AALL)
53 West Jackson Boulevard, Suite 940
Chicago, IL 60604
312/939-4764

American Association for Paralegal Education (AafPE)
2965 Flowers Road S, Suite 105
Atlanta, GA 30342
404/367-4770

American Bar Association (ABA)
Standing Committee on Legal Assistants
750 North Lake Shore Drive
Chicago, IL 60611
312/988-5000

Association of Legal Administrators (ALA)
104 Wilmot Road, Suite 205
Deerfield, IL 60015-5195
312/940-9240

Legal Assistant Management Association (LAMA)
2965 Flowers Road S, Suite 105
Atlanta, GA 30341
404/367-4770

National Association for Independent Paralegals
585 5th St. W
Sonoma, CA 95476

National Paralegal Association
P.O. Box 406
Solebury, PA 18963
215/297-8333

State and Major Local Bar Associations

Alabama

Alabama State Bar
Founded 1879
P.O. Box 671
Montgomery, AL 36101
205/269-1515
fax: 205/261-6310

Birmingham Bar Assn.
Founded 1885
2021 2d Avenue N
Birmingham, AL 35203
205/251-8006
fax: 205/251-7193

Alaska

Alaska Bar Assn.
Founded 1955
P.O. Box 100279
Anchorage, AK 99510
907/272-7469
fax: 907/272-2932

Arizona

Maricopa County Bar Assn.
Founded 1914
303 E. Palm Lane
Phoenix, AZ 85004-1532
602/257-4200
fax: 602/257-0522

State Bar of Arizona
Founded 1933
111 W. Monroe Street
Phoenix, AZ 85003-1742
602/252-4804
fax: 602/271-4930

Arkansas

Arkansas Bar Assn.
Founded 1899
400 W. Markham
Little Rock, AZ 72201
501/375-4605
fax: 501/375-4901

California

Bar Assn. of San Francisco
Founded 1872
685 Market Street, Suite 700
San Francisco, CA 94105
415/267-0709
fax: 415/546-9223

Beverly Hills Bar Assn.
Founded 1931
300 S. Beverly Drive, #201
Beverly Hills, CA 90212
310/553-6644
fax: 310/284-8290

Eastern Alameda County Bar Assn.
Founded 1877
360 22nd Street, #800
Oakland, CA 94612
510/893-7160
fax: 510/893-3119

Lawyers' Club of Los Angeles
Founded 1930
601 W. 5th Street, #203
Los Angeles, CA 90017-2000
213/624-4223

Lawyers' Club of San Francisco
Founded 1946
685 Market Street, Suite 750
San Francisco, CA 94105
415/882-9150
fax: 415/882-7170

Los Angeles County Bar Assn.
Founded 1878
P.O. Box 55020
Los Angeles, CA 90055
213/896-6424
fax: 213/896-6500

Orange County Bar Assn.
601 Civic Center Drive W
Santa Ana, CA 92710-4002
714/541-6222
fax: 714/541-1482

Sacramento County Bar Assn.
Founded 1925
901 H. Street, Suite 101
Sacramento, CA 95814
916/448-1087
fax: 916/448-6930

San Diego County Bar Assn.
Founded 1920
1333 Seventh Avenue
San Diego, CA 92101
619/231-0781
fax: 619/338-0042

Santa Clara County Bar Assn.
Founded 1917
4 N. Second Street, Suite 400
San Jose, CA 95113
408/287-2557
fax: 408/287-6083

State Bar of California
Founded 1927
555 Franklin Street
San Francisco, CA 94012
415/561-8200
fax: 415/561-8305

Colorado

The Colorado Bar Assn.
Founded 1897
1900 Grant Street, #950
Denver, CO 80203
303/860-1115
fax: 303/894-0821

Denver Bar Assn.
Founded 1891
1900 Grant Street, #950
Denver, CO 80203-4309
303/860-1115
fax: 303/894-0821

Connecticut

Connecticut Bar Assn.
Founded 1875
101 Corporate Place
Rocky Hill, CT 06067
203/721-0025
fax: 203/257-4125

Hartford County Bar Assn.
Founded 1783
61 Hungerford Street
Hartford, CT 06106
203/525-8106
fax: 203/293-1345

Delaware

Delaware State Bar Assn.
Founded 1923

1225 King Street
Wilmington, DE 19801
302/658-5279
fax: 302/658-5212

District of Columbia

Bar Assn. of the Dist. of Columbia
Founded 1871
1819 H Street, NW, 12th Floor
Washington, DC 20006-3690
202/223-6600
fax: 202/293-3388

The District of Columbia Bar
Founded 1972
1250 H Street NW, 6th Floor
Washington, DC 20005-3908
202/737-4700
fax: 202/626-3473

Florida

Dade County Bar Assn.
Founded 1920
123 NW First Avenue, #214
Miami, FL 33128
305/371-2220
fax: 305/539-9749

The Florida Bar
Founded 1950
650 Apalachee Parkway
Tallahassee, FL 32399-2300
904/561-5600
fax: 904/561-5827

Hillsborough County Bar Assn.
Founded 1937
315 E. Madison, Suite 1010
Tampa, FL 33602
813/226-6431
fax: 813/223-3946

Orange County Bar Assn.
880 N. Orange Avenue, #100
Orlando, FL 32801
407/422-4551
fax: 407/843-3470

Georgia

Atlanta Bar Assn.
Founded 1888
2500 The Equitable Bldg.
100 Peachtree Street NW
Atlanta, GA 30303
404/521-0781
fax: 404/522-0269

State Bar of Georgia
Founded 1964
800 The Hurt Bldg.
50 Hurt Plaza

Atlanta, GA 30303
404/527-8755
fax: 404/527-8717

Hawaii

Hawaii State Bar Assn.
Founded 1899
Penthouse 1, 9th Floor
1136 Union Mall
Honolulu, HI 96813
808/537-1868
fax: 808/521-7936

Idaho

Idaho State Bar
Founded 1923
P.O. Box 895
Boise, ID 83701
208/334-4500
fax: 208/334-4515

Illinois

The Chicago Bar Assn.
Founded 1874
321 Plymouth Court
Chicago, IL 60604
313/554-2000
fax: 312-554-2054

Chicago Council of Lawyers
Founded 1969
220 S. State Street, Room 800
One Quincy Court
Chicago, IL 60604
312/427-0710
fax: 312/427-0181

Illinois State Bar Assn.
Founded 1877
424 S. Second Street
Springfield, IL 62701
217/525-1760
fax: 217/525-0712

Indiana

Indiana State Bar Assn.
Founded 1896
230 E. Ohio, 4th Floor
Indianapolis, IN 46204
317/639-5465
fax: 317/266-2588

Indianapolis Bar Assn.
Founded 1878
Market Tower,
10 W. Market, Suite 440
Indianapolis, IN 46204
317/269-2000
fax: 317/464-8118

Iowa

The Iowa State Bar Assn.
Founded 1874
521 E. Locust
Des Moines, IA 50309
515/243-3179
fax: 515/243-2511

Kansas

Kansas Bar Assn.
Founded 1882
P.O. Box 1037
Topeka, KS 66601-1037
913/234-5696
fax: 913/234-3813

Kentucky

Kentucky Bar Assn.
Founded 1871
514 West Main Street
Frankfort, KY 40601-1883
501/564-3795
fax: 502/564-3225

Louisville Bar Assn.
Founded 1900
717 W. Main Street
Louisville, KY 40202
502/583-5314
fax: 502/583-4113

Louisiana

Louisiana State Bar Assn.
Founded 1941
601 St. Charles Avenue
New Orleans, LA 70130
504/566-1600
fax: 504/566-0930

New Orleans Bar Assn.
Founded 1924
228 Saint Charles Avenue, Suite 1223
New Orleans, LA 70130
504/525-7453
fax: 504/525-6549

Maine

Maine State Bar Assn.
Founded 1891
P.O. Box 788
Augusta, ME 04332-0788
207/622-7523
fax: 207/623-0083

Maryland

Bar Assn. of Baltimore City
Founded 1880
111 N. Calvert Street, Suite 627

Baltimore, MD 21202
410/539-5936
fax: 401/685-3420

Bar Association of Montgomery
   County
Founded 1894
27 W. Jefferson Street
Rockville, MD 20850
301/424-3454
fax: 301/217-9327

Maryland State Bar Assn., Inc.
Founded 1896
520 W. Fayette Street
Baltimore, MD 20201
410/685-7878
fax: 410/837-0518

Massachusetts

Boston Bar Assn.
Founded 1761
16 Beacon Street
Boston, MA 02018
617/742-0615
fax: 617/523-0127

Massachusetts Bar Assn.
Founded 1911
20 West Street
Boston, MA 02111-1218
617/542-3602

Michigan

Detroit Bar Assn.
Founded 1836
2380 Penobscot Bldg.
Detroit, MI 48226
313/961-6120
fax: 313/965-0842

Oakland County Bar Assn.
Founded 1934
760 S. Telegraph, Suite 100
Bloomfield, MI 48302-0181
810/334-3400
fax: 810/334-7757

State Bar of Michigan
Founded 1936
306 Townsend Street
Lansing, MI 48933-2083
517/372-9030

Minnesota

Hennepin County Bar Assn.
Founded 1919
514 Nicollet Mall, #350
Minneapolis, MN 55402
612/340-0022
fax: 612/340-9518

Minnesota State Bar Assn.
Founded 1883
513 Nicollet Mall, #300
Minneapolis, MN 55402
612/333-1183
fax: 612/333-4927

Ramsey County Bar Assn.
Founded 1883
332 Minnesota Street, E-1312
St. Paul, MN 55101
612/222-0846
fax: 612/223-8344

Mississippi

Mississippi Bar
Founded 1905
P.O. Box 2168
Jackson, MS 39225-2168
601/948-4471
fax: 601/355-8635

Missouri

Bar Assn. of Metropolitan St. Louis
Founded 1874
One Metropolitan Square, Suite 1400
St. Louis, MO 63102
314/421-4134
fax: 314/421-0013

Kansas City Metropolitan Bar
   Association
Founded 1884
1125 Grand, Suite 400
Kansas City, MO 64106
816/474-4322
fax: 816/474-0103

The Missouri Bar
Founded 1944
P.O. Box 119
Jefferson City, MO 65102
314/635-4128
fax: 314/635-2811

Montana

State Bar of Montana
Founded 1975
P.O. Box 577
Helena, MT 59624
406/442-7660
fax: 406/442-7763

Nebraska

Nebraska State Bar Assn.
Founded 1877
P.O. Box 81809
Lincoln, NE 68501
402/475-7091
fax: 402/475-7098

Nevada

State Bar of Nevada
Founded 1928
201 Las Vegas Blvd., Suite 200
Las Vegas, NV 89101
702/383-2200
fax: 702/385-2878

New Hampshire

New Hampshire Bar Assn.
Founded 1873
112 Pleasant Street
Concord, NH 03301
603/224-6942
fax: 603/224-2910

New Jersey

Bergen County Bar
Founded 1898
61 Hudson Street
Hackensack, NJ 07601
201/488-0044
fax: 201/488-0073

Essex County Bar Assn.
Founded 1898
One Newark Center,
16th Floor
Newark, NJ 07102
201/622-6207
fax: 201/622-4341

New Jersey State Bar Assn.
Founded 1899
New Jersey Law Center
One Constitution Square
New Brunswick, NJ 08901-1500
908/249-5000
fax: 908/249-2815

New Mexico

State Bar of New Mexico
Founded 1886
P.O. Box 25883
Albuquerque, NM 87125
505/842-6132
fax: 505/843-8765

New York

The Assn. of the Bar of the City of
   New York
Founded 1871
42 W. 44th Street
New York, NY 10036
212/382-6620
fax: 212/302-8219

Bar Assn. of Erie County
Founded 1887
1450 Statler Towers
Buffalo, NY 14202
716/852-8687
fax: 716/856-7641

Bar Assn. of Nassau County, Inc.
Founded 1899
15th & West Streets
Mineola, NY 11501
516/747-4070
fax: 516/747-4147

Brooklyn Bar Assn.
Founded 1872
23 Remsen Street
Brooklyn, NY 11201-4212
718/624-0675
fax: 718/797-1713

Monroe County Bar Assn.
Founded 1892
One Exchange Street, 5th Floor
Rochester, NY 14614
716/546-1817
fax: 716/546-1807

New York County Lawyers Assn.
Founded 1908
14 Vesey Street
New York, NY 10007
212/267-6646
fax: 212/406-9252

New York State Bar Assn.
Founded 1876
One Elk Street
Albany, NY 12207
518/463-3200
fax: 518/463-4276

Queens County Bar Assn.
Founded 1876
90-35 148th Street
Jamaica, NY 11435
718/291-4500
fax: 718/657-1789

Suffolk County Bar Assn.
Founded 1908
560 Wheeler Road
Hauppauge, NY 11788-4357
516/234-5511
fax: 516/234-5899

Westchester County Bar Assn.
Founded 1896
300 Hamilton Avenue, Suite 400
White Plains, NY 10601
914/761-3707
fax: 914/761-9402

North Carolina

North Carolina Bar Assn.
Founded 1899
P.O. Box 12806
Raleigh, NC 27605
919/677-0561
fax: 919/677-0761

North Carolina State Bar
Founded 1933
208 Fayetteville Street Mall
P.O. Box 25908
Raleigh, NC 27605
919/828-4620
fax: 919/821-9168

10th Judicial District Bar Assn.
P.O. Box 10625
Raleigh, NC 27605
919/677-9903
fax: 919/677-0761

North Dakota

State Bar Assn. of North Dakota
Founded 1921
P.O. Box 2136
Bismark, ND 58502-2136
701/255-1404
fax: 701/224-1621

Ohio

Cincinnati Bar Assn.
Founded 1873
35 E. Seventh Street, 8th Floor
Cincinnati, OH 45202-2492
513/381-8213
fax: 513/381-0528

Cleveland Bar Assn.
Founded 1873
113 St. Clair Avenue NE
Cleveland, OH 44114-1253
216/696-3525
fax: 216/696-2413

Columbus Bar Assn.
Founded 1869
175 South 3rd Street
Columbus, OH 43215-5134
614/221-4112
fax: 614/221-4850

Cuyahoga County Bar Assn.
Founded 1928
500 The Terminal Tower
50 Public Square
Cleveland, OH 44113-2203
216/621-5112
fax: 216/523-2259

Ohio State Bar Assn.
Founded 1880
1700 Lake Shore Drive
Columbus, OH 43216-6562
614/487-2050
fax: 614/487-1008

Oklahoma

Oklahoma Bar Assn.
Founded 1939
1901 N. Lincoln
P.O. Box 53036
Oklahoma City, OK 73152
405/524-2365
fax: 405/524-1115

Oklahoma County Bar Assn.
Founded 1902
119 N. Robinson, Suite 240
Oklahoma, OK 73102
405/236-8421
fax: 405/232-2210

Tulsa County Bar Assn.
Founded 1903
1446 South Boston
Tulsa, OK 74119
916/584-5243
fax: 918/592-0208

Oregon

Multnomah Bar Assn.
Founded 1906
630 SW Fifth Avenue, Suite 200
Portland, OR 97204
503/222-3275
fax: 503/243-1881

Oregon State Bar
Founded 1890
P.O. Box 1689
Lake Oswego, OR 97035
503/620-0222
fax: 503/684-1366

Pennsylvania

Allegheny County Bar Assn.
Founded 1870
Kopper's Building, 4th Floor
Pittsburgh, PA 15219
412/261-6161
fax: 412/261-3622

Pennsylvania Bar Assn.
Founded 1895
P.O. Box 186
Harrisburg, PA 17108
717/238-6715
fax: 717/238-1204

Philadelphia Bar Assn.
Founded 1802
1101 Market Street, 11th Floor
Philadelphia, PA 19107-2911
215/238-6338
fax: 215/238-1267

Puerto Rico

Puerto Rico Bar Assn.
Founded 1840
P.O. Box 1900
San Juan, PR 00903
809/721-3358
fax: 809/725-0330

Rhode Island

Rhode Island Bar Assn.
Founded 1898
115 Cedar Street
Providence, RI 02903
401/421-5740
fax: 401/421-2703

South Carolina

South Carolina Bar
Founded 1975
950 Taylor Street
Columbia, SC 29202
803/799-6653
fax: 803/799-4118

South Dakota

State Bar of South Dakota
Founded 1931
222 E. Capitol
Pierre, SD 57501
605/224-7554
fax: 605/224-0282

Tennessee

Nashville Bar Assn.
Founded 1831
221 Fourth Avenue N, Suite 400
Nashville, TN 37129-2100
615/242-9272
fax: 615/255-3026

Tennessee Bar Assn.
Founded 1881
3622 West End Avenue
Nashville, TN 37205-2403
615/383-7421
fax: 615/297-8058

Texas

Dallas Bar Assn.
Founded 1873

2101 Ross Avenue
Dallas, TX 75201
214/969-7066
fax: 214/880-0807

Houston Bar Assn.
Founded 1870
1001 Fannin, Suite 1300
Houston, TX 77002-6708
713/759-1133
fax: 713/759-1710

San Antonio Bar Assn.
Founded 1916
Bexar County Courthouse, 5th Floor
San Antonio, TX 78205
210/227-8822
fax: 210-271-9614

State Bar of Texas
Founded 1939
P.O. Box 12487
Austin, TX 78711
512/463-1463 or
800/204-2222
fax: 512/463-7388

Utah

Utah State Bar
Founded 1931
645 S. 200 East, #310
Salt Lake City, UT 84111
801/531-9077
fax: 801/531-0660

Vermont

Vermont Bar Assn.
Founded 1878
P.O. Box 100
Montpelier, VT 05601
802/223-2020
fax: 802/223-1573

Virginia

Fairfax Bar Assn.
Founded 1935
4110 Chain Bridge Road, #303
Fairfax, VA 22030
703/246-2740
fax: 703/273-1274

Virginia Bar Assn.
Founded 1888
7th & Franklin Bldg.
701 E. Franklin Street, #1515
Richmond, VA 23219
804/644-0052

Virginia State Bar
Founded 1938

707 E. Main Street, Suite 1500
Richmond, VA 23219-2803
804/775-0500
fax: 804/775-0501

Washington

King County Bar Assn.
Founded 1906
The Bank of CA Bldg., Suite 600
900 4th Avenue
Seattle, WA 98164
206/624-9365
fax: 206/382-1270

Washington State Bar Assn.
Founded 1890
500 Westin Bldg.
2001 6th Avenue
Seattle, WA 98121-2599
206/727-8200
fax: 206/727-8320

West Virginia

West Virginia Bar Assn.
Founded 1886

904 Security Bldg.
101 Capitol Street
P.O. Box 346
Charleston, WV 23507
304/342-1474
fax: 304/345-5864

West Virginia State Bar
Founded 1947
2006 Kanawha Blvd. E
Charleston, WV 25311
304/558-2456
fax: 304/558-2567

Wisconsin

Milwaukee Bar Assn.
Founded 1858
533 East Wells Street
Milwaukee, WI 53202
414/274-6760
fax: 414/274-6765

Wyoming

Wyoming State Bar
Founded 1915

P.O. Box 109
Cheyenne, WY 82003-0109
307/632-9061
fax: 307/632-3737

Guam

Guam Bar Assn.
259 Martyr Street, Suite 101
Agana, Guam 96910
011/671/472-6848
fax: 011/671/472-1246

Northern Mariana Islands Bar Assn.
Founded 1985

Virgin Islands

Virgin Islands Bar Assn.
Founded 1921
P.O. Box 4108
Christiansted, VI 00822
809/778-7497
fax: 809/773-5060

APPENDIX H

INFORMATION ON NALA's CLA AND CLAS EXAMINATIONS

BACKGROUND AND NUMBERS

Established in 1976, the Certified Legal Assistant program has enabled the profession to develop a strong and responsive self-regulatory program offering a nation-wide credential for legal assistants. The Certified Legal Assistant program establishes and serves as a:

- National professional standard for legal assistants
- Means of identifying those who have reached this standard
- Credentialing program responsive to the needs of legal assistants and responsive to the fact that this

form of self-regulation is necessary to strengthen and expand development of this career field

- Positive, ongoing, voluntary program to encourage the growth of the legal-assistant profession, attesting to and encouraging a high level of achievement.

As of January 1999, there are 9,594 Certified Legal Assistants and over 700 Certified Legal Assistant Specialists in the United States. Approximately 19,000 legal assistants have participated in this program. The distribution of CLAs is as follows:

CLA Examination Data States Represented at Time of Certification as of January 22, 1999

Alabama	117	Nebraska	89
Alaska	78	Nevada	175
Arizona	715	New Hampshire	45
Arkansas	58	New Jersey	45
California	442	New Mexico	154
Colorado	181	New York	43
Connecticut	4	North Carolina	221
Delaware	1	North Dakota	87
District of Columbia	2	Ohio	76
Florida	2,577	Oklahoma	398
Georgia	127	Oregon	97
Hawaii	2	Pennsylvania	61
Idaho	37	Puerto Rico	1
Illinois	40	Rhode Island	4
Indiana	39	South Carolina	78
Iowa	99	South Dakota	86
Kansas	175	Tennessee	159
Kentucky	16	Texas	1,993
Louisiana	133	Utah	99
Maine	47	Vermont	2
Maryland	8	Virginia	184
Massachusetts	14	Virgin Islands	24
Michigan	114	Washington	45
Minnesota	16	West Virginia	49
Mississippi	104	Wisconsin	27
Missouri	77	Wyoming	78
Montana	49		

On December 31, 1990, 3,974 legal assistants had achieved the CLA designation. As of the December 1998 testing session, there were 9,594 Certified Legal Assistants. This represents an increase of over 100 percent in the number of Certified Legal Assistants in the last eight years. Since the examination was first administered in 1976, over 19,000 legal assistants have participated in this program.

In order to pass, a legal assistant must successfully complete the seven sections of the CLA examination. Approximately 48 percent of the examinees pass all seven sections on the first sitting; over 90 percent of the examinees pass four or more sections of the examination on the first sitting.

Use of the CLA credential signifies that a legal assistant is capable of providing superior services to firms and corporations. National surveys consistently show Certified Legal Assistants are better paid and better utilized in a field where attorneys are looking for a credible, dependable way to measure ability. The credential has been recognized by the American Bar Association as a designation which marks a high level of professional achievement. The CLA credential has also been recognized by over forty-seven legal-assistant organizations and numerous bar associations.

For information concerning standards of professional credentialing programs, see the article "The Certified Legal Assistant Program and the United States Supreme Court Decision in *Peel v. Attorney Registration and Disciplinary Committee of Illinois.*" In this case, the United States Supreme Court addressed the issue concerning the utilization of professional credentials awarded by private organizations. In *Peel v. Attorney Registration and Disciplinary Committee of Illinois*, 110 S.Ct. 2281 (1990), the Court suggested that a claim of certification is truthful and not misleading if it meets certain standards. This article details those standards in terms of the standards of the NALA Certified Legal Assistant Program.

CLA and CLA Specialist are certification marks duly registered with the U.S. Patent and Trademark Office (No. 113199 and No. 1751731 respectively). Any unauthorized use of these credentials is strictly forbidden.

Administration

The Certifying Board for Legal Assistants is responsible for content, standards, and administration of the Certified Legal Assistant Program. It is composed of legal assistants who have received a CLA Specialist designation, attorneys, and legal-assistant educators. In the technical areas of statistical analyses, examination construction, reliability, and validity tests, the Board contracts with a professional consulting firm offering expertise in these areas as well as in occupational research. Technical analyses of the CLA examination are conducted on an ongoing basis to ensure the integrity of the examination. Content analyses of the test design, accuracy of questions, and topic/subject mix for each exam section are ongoing processes of the Certifying Board. The Board also utilizes the occupational data available through surveys of legal assistants and other means, including review of textbooks and research within the field of legal-assistant education. Through these analyses and procedures, the Board is assured that the examination reflects and responds to workplace realities and demands.

The Examination— Eligibility Requirements

To be eligible for the CLA examination, a legal assistant must meet one of the following alternate requirements:

1. Graduation from a legal-assistant program that is:
- Approved by the American Bar Association; or
- An associate degree program; or
- A postbaccalaureate certificate program in legal-assistant studies; or
- A bachelor's degree program in legal-assistant studies; or
- A legal-assistant program which consists of a minimum of 60 semester hours (900 clock hours or 225 quarter hours) of which at least 15 semester hours (90 clock hours or 22.5 quarter hours) are substantive legal courses.

2. A bachelor's degree in any field plus one year's experience as a legal assistant. Successful completion of at least 15 semester hours (or 22.5 quarter hours or 225 clock hours) of substantive legal courses will be considered equivalent to one year's experience as a legal assistant.

3. A high school diploma or equivalent plus seven (7) years' experience as a legal assistant under the supervision of a member of the Bar, plus evidence of a minimum of twenty (20) hours of continuing legal education credit to have been completed within a two (2) year period prior to the examination date.

EXAMINATION SUBJECTS

The Certified Legal Assistant examination is a two-day comprehensive examination based on federal law and procedure. The major subject areas of the examination are:

- Communications
- Ethics
- Legal Research
- Human Relations and Interviewing Techniques
- Judgment and Analytical Ability
- Legal Terminology

Substantive Law—This section consists of five mini-examinations covering (1) the American Legal System and four (4) of the areas listed below as selected by examinees:

- Administrative Law
- Bankruptcy
- Business Organizations/Corporations
- Contracts
- Family Law
- Criminal Law and Procedure
- Litigation

- Probate and Estate Planning
- Real Estate

CLA SPECIALTY EXAMINATIONS

Those who have achieved the CLA credential may seek advanced certification in specialty practice areas. Specialty certification examinations are available in the areas of Bankruptcy, Civil Litigation, Corporations/Business Law, Criminal Law and Procedure, Intellectual Property, Estate Planning and Probate, and Real Estate. Each of these is a four-hour examination written to test specialized knowledge of the practice area.

The CLA Specialty program began in 1982 with the examinations for those working in the areas of Civil Litigation and Probate and Estate Planning. In 1984, the Corporations/Business and Criminal Law and Procedure examinations were offered. A Real Estate specialty examination was offered for the first time in 1987; Bankruptcy in 1992; and Intellectual Property in 1995. As of the December 1998 CLA Specialty examinations, 771 CLAs have received a CLA Specialist designation, as follows:

Bankruptcy	36
Civil Litigation	402
Corporate/Business	39
Criminal Law and Procedure	35
Intellectual Property	13
Probate and Estates	87
Real Estate	159

NALA is also working with individual states to established advanced specialty certification programs designed to test knowledge of state law and procedures. State certification programs are available to legal assistants in California, Florida, and Louisiana.

MAINTAINING PROFESSIONAL CERTIFICATION

The Certified Legal Assistant credential is awarded for a period of five years. To maintain Certified Legal Assistant status, legal assistants must submit proof of participation in a minimum of fifty hours of continuing legal education programs or individual study programs. Credit is also awarded for significant achievement in the area of continuing legal-assistant education such as successful completion of a state certification test, completion of a CLA Specialty examination, or teaching in a legal-assistant program.

REVOCATION OF THE CLA CREDENTIAL

The Certified Legal Assistant designation may be revoked for any one of the following reasons:

1. Falsification of information on the application form.
2. Subsequent conviction of the unauthorized practice of law.
3. Failure to meet educational and other recertification requirements.
4. Divulging the contents of any examination question or questions.
5. Subsequent conviction of a felony.
6. Violation of the NALA Code of Ethics and Professional Responsibility.

DATES AND DEADLINES AND TESTING CENTERS AND FEES

The CLA examination is offered three times a year: March/April (depending on the holiday schedule); July, and December. Application forms and the requisite fees must be received by the published filing dates. Filing deadline dates are January 15 for the March/April examination, May 15 for the July examination, and October 1 for the December examination session.

Many schools, universities, and junior colleges serve as testing centers through an arrangement with NALA. In cities in which a school testing center is not already established, NALA will establish a testing center where ten or more legal assistants apply. All testing center locations are subject to minimum registration.

The fee for the CLA examination is $225 for NALA members and $250 for nonmembers of NALA. Retake fees are $50 per section. CLA Specialty examination fees are $100 for NALA members and $125 for nonmembers.

STUDY MATERIALS

The CLA Review Manual is available from West Publishing Company, an imprint of Delmar Publishers, and International Thomson Publishing Company. Delmar Publishers also publishes the NALA CLA Study Guide and Mock Examination, a 250-page guide consisting of outlines for a nine-week study program with practice tests and a mock examination. The CLA Study Guide and Mock Examination is available from NALA Headquarters at a cost of $18 to NALA members, $21

to nonmembers. Study material is also available online at **NALA Campus.com.**

A series of study guides for those preparing for a CLA Specialty Examination were published through 1997 and 1998. The first, Real Estate Law Review Manual, is now available from West Legal Studies.

CALIFORNIA ADVANCED SPECIALIZATION CERTIFICATION FOR PARALEGALS

Established in 1995, the California Advanced Specialist (CAS) Certification was created for California paralegals who have achieved the national CLA (Certified Legal Assistant) credential and want to demonstrate advanced knowledge of California law and procedure. To qualify for the California Advanced Examination, these legal assistants have successfully completed a two-day examination covering general skills and knowledge required of legal assistants, and have demonstrated proficiency in the specialty practice area. Specialty certification in California is available in the areas of Civil Litigation, Business Organizations/Business Law, Real Estate, Estates and Trusts, and Family Law. As of July 1997, there are thirteen legal assistants in California who have achieved the CAS credential. For further details about the program, contact NALA Headquarters or the Commission for Advanced California Paralegal Specialization, Inc., P.O. Box 22433, Santa Barbara, California 93121.

Application Deadline Date	January 15, 1999
Examination Date	March 27, 1999
July 24, 1999	May 15, 1999
December 4, 1999	October 1, 1999

FLORIDA CERTIFICATION PROGRAMS

In 1980, Florida Legal Assistants, Inc. (FLA, Inc.), established its Certification Program to complement NALA's CLA program. Its purpose is to provide a standard for measurement of advanced skills and knowledge in Florida law of those persons who have already achieved the national CLA certification. FLA, Inc., began administering the CFLA exam in 1983. Florida, through FLA, Inc., was the first state to administer such an exam. As of December 1996, there were eighty-four CFLAs in the state of Florida.

The CFLA examination is administered through the Certifying Board of FLA, Inc., in conjunction with the FLA, Inc., midyear meeting in the spring and the annual meeting in September. A two-day CFLA review course has been established and is offered prior to the midyear and annual meetings.

FLA, Inc., has developed a CFLA study guide which is available from FLA, Inc., headquarters at a cost of $37.50 plus shipping.

The exam takes three hours and is limited to Florida law. The first part of the exam covers ethics and general Florida law which includes the Florida court system and terminology. All questions must be answered. Part Two covers seven substantive areas:

(1) real estate law
(2) civil litigation
(3) criminal law
(4) family law
(5) probate and estate planning
(6) corporate and business law, and
(7) contract law

There are three questions from each of the substantive areas. An examinee must answer a total of six questions and may select any combination of questions from the substantive areas. The examinee may not answer more than six questions. Only the first six questions answered are graded.

The test comprises true/false questions, short-answer essay questions, and multiple-choice questions.

Upon successful completion of the CFLA examination, a legal assistant becomes authorized to use the designation "CLA, CFLA."

CFLAs are required to have thirty hours of continuing legal education credit over a five-year period to maintain their CFLA certification which must be directly applicable to Florida law. Proof of continuing legal education must be submitted to and is maintained by the Certifying Board.

Information regarding the dates of the next study course and examination may be obtained from the headquarters office of FLA, Inc., as follows:

Florida Legal Assistants, Inc.
11812-A North 56th Street
Tampa, Florida 33617
Tel: 813-985-2044
800-433-4FLA (4352)
Fax: 813-988-5837

LOUISIANA CERTIFIED PARALEGAL PROGRAM

At its 1992 annual meeting, the members of the Louisiana State Paralegal Association (LSPA) passed a resolution which endorsed voluntary certification as a means of establishing professional standards and promoting recognition of the paralegal profession. Subsequently, the LSPA determined a state voluntary certification credential should be developed and made available to all Louisiana paralegals who desire to demonstrate comprehensive knowledge, a high degree of proficiency in Louisiana law, and adherence to a Code of Ethics to enhance the quality of paralegal services available to the Louisiana legal community and to the public it serves.

The resulting certification program requires the candidate to sit for both the LCP (Louisiana Certified Paralegal) and CLA (Certified Legal Assistant) examinations. The LCP examination is designed to test the examinee's knowledge and understanding of the Louisiana legal and judicial system, Louisiana general law, ethics, civil procedure, and four areas of Louisiana substantive law. The CLA examination offered by the National Association of Legal Assistants tests the core paralegal skills, knowledge of the American legal and judicial system, and four areas of substantive law based on federal law and common law principles.

To qualify for the examination, one must either have a valid CLA credential or meet one of the alternate eligibility requirements of the CLA examination.

Testing Sessions

The examination will be offered twice a year, in October and in the spring (March or April).

Subjects

As a state-specific examination, the LCP examination is designed to test a paralegal's knowledge and comprehension of the law in the state of Louisiana. Each examinee will be required to take the general law, ethics, and civil procedures sections and must select four law topics, from a list of eight, that will comprise the substantive law section of that examinee's test. The substantive law areas are:

• Business Organizations
• Contracts/Obligations
• Criminal Law and Procedure
• Wills/Probate/Successions/Trusts
• Family Law
• Property
• Torts
• Evidence

Preparation

Those individuals who have not had formal substantive law paralegal courses in Louisiana would benefit from study of a current textbook covering the topics selected for the substantive law section. Much of the material covered in this section of the examination is acquired through experience in the legal field.

The LSPA will offer a review course once a year to assist interested parties in preparing for the examination. Written materials and a videotape of the seminar sessions are available from the Louisiana State Paralegal Association in care of NALA Headquarters, 1516 S. Boston, #200, Tulsa, OK 74119, (918) 587-6828.

APPENDIX I

INFORMATION ON NFPA's PACE EXAMINATION

INTRODUCTION

The legal service industry is facing great change. While containing costs, it is trying to respond to an increased number of pending cases, rapid changes in technology, and increased demands from consumers for a higher level of client service.

The paralegal profession is facing possible regulation through certification, licensing, or other means.

The National Federation of Paralegal Associations, Inc., a grass-roots organization, is addressing this issue. During the NFPA's 1994 midyear meeting, the membership voted to develop an exam to test the competency level of experienced paralegals.

PACE = Paralegal Advanced Competency Exam

Offering experienced paralegals an option to

- validate their experience and job skills;
- establish credentials; and
- increase their value to their organizations and clients.

The only exam of its kind, PACE

- was developed by a professional testing firm;
- is administered by an independent test administration company;
- provides results across practice areas, and when available, for state-specific laws;
- offers the profession a national standard of evaluation; and
- is offered at multiple locations on numerous dates and at various times.

PACE = Personal Advancement for the Experienced Paralegal

The development of this exam is a conscientious effort by paralegals to direct the future of the paralegal profession and acknowledges the vital role of paralegals within the legal service industry. It is a direct response to states that are considering regulation of the paralegal profession and are seeking a method to measure job competency. While the NFPA believes in the criteria established by its members to take this exam, it recognizes that any state may adopt the exam and modify the criteria.

The Paralegal Advanced Competency Exam (PACE) will be developed in two stages, identified as tiers. Tier I, comprising general and ethics questions, is available; state-specific modules will be developed within particular jurisdictions as the need arises. Tier II will comprise specialty sections.

Paralegals receive two major benefits by taking PACE. The exam

- provides a fair evaluation of the competencies of paralegals across practice areas; and
- creates a professional level of expertise by which all paralegals can be evaluated.

EXPERIENCE AND EDUCATION

Requirements for a paralegal to take either tier of PACE include work experience and education. The paralegal cannot have been convicted of a felony nor be under suspension, termination, or revocation of a certificate, registration, or license by any entity. PACE has generated a great deal of interest since the resolution to develop it was passed. Based on this interest, and the number of paralegals who may apply to take the exam (a number

reported by the U.S. Department of Labor to exceed 113,000), a need exists for global grandparenting.

The global grandparenting period for paralegals to apply to take the exam expires December 31, 2000. Paralegals who intend to substitute work experience for the educational requirements must apply to take the test by December 31, 2000.

During the grandparenting period, paralegals have time to learn about PACE and understand the option of substituting extensive work experience for the educational requirements. After December 31, 2000, the educational standards originally established for PACE will be mandatory.

Requirements for Tier I

- a minimum of four years' work experience as a paralegal if application is made within the global grandparenting period, or
- a bachelor's degree, and completion of a paralegal program within an institutionally accredited school (which may be embodied in the bachelor's degree), and a minimum of two years' work experience as a paralegal.

Requirements for Tier II

- successful completion of Tier I, and one of the following
- a minimum of six years' work experience as a paralegal, if application is made within the global grandparenting period, or

- a bachelor's degree, and completion of a paralegal program within an institutionally accredited school (which may be embodied in the bachelor's degree), and a minimum of four years' work experience as a paralegal.

INDEPENDENCE AND FAIRNESS

The NFPA strongly believes PACE must produce legitimate and verifiable results and consistently pass only paralegals who demonstrate an established level of knowledge, skills, and competency. PACE was developed in cooperation with the independent test development firm, Professional Examination Service (PES).

PES was selected through an extensive proposal process and a personal interview with the NFPA Board of Directors. PES has developed professional exams for more than fifty years for groups such as the Federal Reserve System, the National Association of Securities Dealers, Inc., the Environmental Protection Agency, and the Emergency Medical Technicians and Paramedics Association. PES currently works with more than seventy-five professional associations and more than three hundred licensing boards in sixty-two jurisdictions in the United States and Canada.

PES does not work alone. An independent task force of paralegals, paralegal educators, attorneys, and other content specialists are assisting in every step, from the preparation of the job analysis for paralegals through creation of the initial exam and ongoing revisions.

To ensure test results are valid, the test is administered by PES, an independent firm.

All profits received from the exam will be passed to the "Foundation for the Advancement of the Paralegal Profession," an independent foundation, and will be used to further the entire paralegal profession.

CREDENTIAL

Those who pass PACE and maintain the continuing education requirement may use the designation "PACE–Registered Paralegal" or "RP."

HOW TO PREPARE AND REGISTER

To prepare for the exam, paralegals may use any of the following options:

- a study manual
- a practice diskette

- seminars sponsored by local paralegal associations and the NFPA;
- a video of an "Overview for PACE" seminar; or
- study information provided through the Internet.

To register to take the exam (details on application process), send $15 to NFPA, P.O. Box 33108, Kansas City, MO 64114-0108, for a Candidate Handbook, which includes an application, information on exam content, sample exam questions, and logistical information on taking the exam. The $15 fee will be applied to the overall examination fee of $225. Once the application has been approved, the exam must be taken within ninety days.

PACE is a four-hour, computer-generated test and is offered at more than two hundred Sylvan Technology Centers throughout the country. Once approved, each applicant can schedule the date and time to take the test at his or her convenience on any day except Sundays and holidays.

To maintain the RP credential, twelve hours of continuing legal or specialty education is required every two years, with at least one hour in legal ethics.

PREPARING FOR THE FUTURE

The PACE exam provides hard facts about the competency of experienced paralegals. While PACE does not address all the issues of regulation, including certification and licensing, it does provide the legal service industry with an option to evaluate the competency level of experienced paralegals.

As members of a self-directed profession, all paralegals should consider the vital role the profession performs within the legal service industry. PACE is independently monitored and well structured. PACE provides test results across practice areas.

The NFPA is committed to ensuring that the paralegal profession responds to the changing needs of the public and legal service industry.

THE NFPA'S ROLE

First organized in 1974, the NFPA was created to provide a communications network and develop channels to expand the role of the paralegal profession. In addition, the NFPA has assisted the profession in evaluating educational standards and responding to organizations and entities interested in regulating the profession.

NFPA membership has significantly increased since its inception. In 1998, it included fifty-four associations located throughout the United States, with more than 17,000 members.

THE CONSTITUTION OF THE UNITED STATES

Preamble

We the People of the United States, in Order to form a more perfect Union, establish Justice, insure domestic Tranquility, provide for the common defence, promote the general Welfare, and secure the Blessings of Liberty to ourselves and our Posterity, do ordain and establish this Constitution for the United States of America.

Article I

SECTION 1. All legislative Powers herein granted shall be vested in a Congress of the United States, which shall consist of a Senate and House of Representatives.

SECTION 2. The House of Representatives shall be composed of Members chosen every second Year by the People of the several States, and the Electors in each State shall have the Qualifications requisite for Electors of the most numerous Branch of the State Legislature.

No Person shall be a Representative who shall not have attained to the Age of twenty five Years, and been seven Years a Citizen of the United States, and who shall not, when elected, be an Inhabitant of that State in which he shall be chosen.

Representatives and direct Taxes shall be apportioned among the several States which may be included within this Union, according to their respective Numbers, which shall be determined by adding to the whole Number of free Persons, including those bound to Service for a Term of Years, and excluding Indians not taxed, three fifths of all other Persons. The actual Enumeration shall be made within three Years after the first Meeting of the Congress of the United States, and within every subsequent Term of ten Years, in such Manner as they shall by Law direct. The Number of Representatives shall not exceed one for every thirty Thousand, but each State shall have at Least one Representative; and until such enumeration shall be made, the State of New Hampshire shall be entitled to chuse three, Massachusetts eight, Rhode Island and Providence Plantations one, Connecticut five, New York six, New Jersey four, Pennsylvania eight, Delaware one, Maryland six, Virginia ten, North Carolina five, South Carolina five, and Georgia three.

When vacancies happen in the Representation from any State, the Executive Authority thereof shall issue Writs of Election to fill such Vacancies.

The House of Representatives shall chuse their Speaker and other Officers; and shall have the sole Power of Impeachment.

SECTION 3. The Senate of the United States shall be composed of two Senators from each State, chosen by the Legislature thereof, for six Years; and each Senator shall have one Vote.

Immediately after they shall be assembled in Consequence of the first Election, they shall be divided as equally as may be into three Classes. The Seats of the Senators of the first Class shall be vacated at the Expiration of the second Year, of the second Class at the Expiration of the fourth Year, and of the third Class at the Expiration of the sixth Year, so that one third may be chosen every second Year; and if Vacancies happen by Resignation, or otherwise, during the Recess of the Legislature of any State, the Executive thereof may make temporary Appointments until the next Meeting of the Legislature, which shall then fill such Vacancies.

No Person shall be a Senator who shall not have attained to the Age of thirty Years, and been nine Years a Citizen of the United States, and who shall not, when elected, be an Inhabitant of that State for which he shall be chosen.

The Vice President of the United States shall be President of the Senate, but shall have no Vote, unless they be equally divided.

The Senate shall chuse their other Officers, and also a President pro tempore, in the Absence of the Vice President, or when he shall exercise the Office of President of the United States.

The Senate shall have the sole Power to try all Impeachments. When sitting for that Purpose, they shall be on Oath or Affirmation. When the President of the United States is tried, the Chief Justice shall preside: And no Person shall be convicted without the Concurrence of two thirds of the Members present.

Judgment in Cases of Impeachment shall not extend further than to removal from Office, and disqualification to hold and enjoy any Office of honor, Trust, or Profit under the United States: but the Party convicted shall nevertheless be liable and subject to Indictment, Trial, Judgment, and Punishment, according to Law.

SECTION 4. The Times, Places and Manner of holding Elections for Senators and Representatives, shall be prescribed in each State by the Legislature thereof; but the Congress may at any time by Law make or alter such Regulations, except as to the Places of chusing Senators.

The Congress shall assemble at least once in every Year, and such Meeting shall be on the first Monday in December, unless they shall by Law appoint a different Day.

SECTION 5. Each House shall be the Judge of the Elections, Returns, and Qualifications of its own Members, and a Majority of each shall constitute a Quorum to do Business; but a smaller Number may adjourn from day to day, and may be authorized to compel the Attendance of absent Members, in such Manner, and under such Penalties as each House may provide.

Each House may determine the Rules of its Proceedings, punish its Members for disorderly Behavior, and, with the Concurrence of two thirds, expel a Member.

Each House shall keep a Journal of its Proceedings, and from time to time publish the same, excepting such Parts as may in their Judgment require Secrecy; and the Yeas and Nays of the Members of either House on any question shall, at the Desire of one fifth of those Present, be entered on the Journal.

Neither House, during the Session of Congress, shall, without the Consent of the other, adjourn for more than three days, nor to any other Place than that in which the two Houses shall be sitting.

SECTION 6. The Senators and Representatives shall receive a Compensation for their Services, to be ascertained by Law, and paid out of the Treasury of the United States. They shall in all Cases, except Treason, Felony and Breach of the Peace, be privileged from Arrest during their Attendance at the Session of their respective Houses, and in going to and returning from the same; and for any Speech or Debate in either House, they shall not be questioned in any other Place.

No Senator or Representative shall, during the Time for which he was elected, be appointed to any civil Office under the Authority of the United States, which shall have been created, or the Emoluments whereof shall have been increased during such time; and no Person holding any Office under the United States, shall be a Member of either House during his Continuance in Office.

SECTION 7. All Bills for raising Revenue shall originate in the House of Representatives; but the Senate may propose or concur with Amendments as on other Bills.

Every Bill which shall have passed the House of Representatives and the Senate, shall, before it become a Law, be presented to the President of the United States; If he approve he shall sign it, but if not he shall return it, with his Objections to the House in which it shall have originated, who shall enter the Objections at large on their Journal, and proceed to reconsider it. If after such Reconsideration two thirds of that House shall agree to pass the Bill, it shall be sent together with the Objections, to the other House, by which it shall likewise be reconsidered, and if approved by two thirds of that House, it shall become a Law. But in all such Cases the Votes of both Houses shall be determined by

Yeas and Nays, and the Names of the Persons voting for and against the Bill shall be entered on the Journal of each House respectively. If any Bill shall not be returned by the President within ten Days (Sundays excepted) after it shall have been presented to him, the Same shall be a Law, in like Manner as if he had signed it, unless the Congress by their Adjournment prevent its Return in which Case it shall not be a Law.

Every Order, Resolution, or Vote, to which the Concurrence of the Senate and House of Representatives may be necessary (except on a question of Adjournment) shall be presented to the President of the United States; and before the Same shall take Effect, shall be approved by him, or being disapproved by him, shall be repassed by two thirds of the Senate and House of Representatives, according to the Rules and Limitations prescribed in the Case of a Bill.

SECTION 8.   The Congress shall have Power To lay and collect Taxes, Duties, Imposts and Excises, to pay the Debts and provide for the common Defence and general Welfare of the United States; but all Duties, Imposts and Excises shall be uniform throughout the United States;

To borrow Money on the credit of the United States;

To regulate Commerce with foreign Nations, and among the several States, and with the Indian Tribes;

To establish an uniform Rule of Naturalization, and uniform Laws on the subject of Bankruptcies throughout the United States;

To coin Money, regulate the Value thereof, and of foreign Coin, and fix the Standard of Weights and Measures;

To provide for the Punishment of counterfeiting the Securities and current Coin of the United States;

To establish Post Offices and post Roads;

To promote the Progress of Science and useful Arts, by securing for limited Times to Authors and Inventors the exclusive Right to their respective Writings and Discoveries;

To constitute Tribunals inferior to the supreme Court;

To define and punish Piracies and Felonies committed on the high Seas, and Offenses against the Law of Nations;

To declare War, grant Letters of Marque and Reprisal, and make Rules concerning Captures on Land and Water;

To raise and support Armies, but no Appropriation of Money to that Use shall be for a longer Term than two Years;

To provide and maintain a Navy;

To make Rules for the Government and Regulation of the land and naval Forces;

To provide for calling forth the Militia to execute the Laws of the Union, suppress Insurrections and repel Invasions;

To provide for organizing, arming, and disciplining, the Militia, and for governing such Part of them as may be employed in the Service of the United States, reserving to the States respectively, the Appointment of the Officers, and the Authority of training the Militia according to the discipline prescribed by Congress;

To exercise exclusive Legislation in all Cases whatsoever, over such District (not exceeding ten Miles square) as may, by Cession of particular States, and the Acceptance of Congress, become the Seat of the Government of the United States, and to exercise like Authority over all Places purchased by the Consent of the Legislature of the State in which the Same shall be, for the Erection of Forts, Magazines, Arsenals, dock-Yards, and other needful Buildings;—And

To make all Laws which shall be necessary and proper for carrying into Execution the foregoing Powers, and all other Powers vested by this Constitution in the Government of the United States, or in any Department or Officer thereof.

SECTION 9.   The Migration or Importation of such Persons as any of the States now existing shall think proper to admit, shall not be prohibited by the Congress prior to the Year one thousand eight hundred and eight, but a Tax or duty may be imposed on such Importation, not exceeding ten dollars for each Person.

The privilege of the Writ of Habeas Corpus shall not be suspended, unless when in Cases of Rebellion or Invasion the public Safety may require it.

No Bill of Attainder or ex post facto Law shall be passed.

No Capitation, or other direct, Tax shall be laid, unless in Proportion to the Census or Enumeration herein before directed to be taken.

No Tax or Duty shall be laid on Articles exported from any State.

No Preference shall be given by any Regulation of Commerce or Revenue to the Ports of one State over those of another: nor shall Vessels bound to, or from, one State be obliged to enter, clear, or pay Duties in another.

No Money shall be drawn from the Treasury, but in Consequence of Appropriations made by Law; and a regular Statement and Account of the Receipts and Expenditures of all public Money shall be published from time to time.

No Title of Nobility shall be granted by the United States: And no Person holding any Office of Profit or

Trust under them, shall, without the Consent of the Congress, accept of any present, Emolument, Office, or Title, of any kind whatever, from any King, Prince, or foreign State.

SECTION 10.   No State shall enter into any Treaty, Alliance, or Confederation; grant Letters of Marque and Reprisal; coin Money; emit Bills of Credit; make any Thing but gold and silver Coin a Tender in Payment of Debts; pass any Bill of Attainder, ex post facto Law, or Law impairing the Obligation of Contracts, or grant any Title of Nobility.

No State shall, without the Consent of the Congress, lay any Imposts or Duties on Imports or Exports, except what may be absolutely necessary for executing its inspection Laws: and the net Produce of all Duties and Imposts, laid by any State on Imports or Exports, shall be for the Use of the Treasury of the United States; and all such Laws shall be subject to the Revision and Controul of the Congress.

No State shall, without the Consent of Congress, lay any Duty of Tonnage, keep Troops, or Ships of War in time of Peace, enter into any Agreement or Compact with another State, or with a foreign Power, or engage in War, unless actually invaded, or in such imminent Danger as will not admit of delay.

Article II

SECTION 1.   The executive Power shall be vested in a President of the United States of America. He shall hold his Office during the Term of four Years, and, together with the Vice President, chosen for the same Term, be elected, as follows:

Each State shall appoint, in such Manner as the Legislature thereof may direct, a Number of Electors, equal to the whole Number of Senators and Representatives to which the State may be entitled in the Congress; but no Senator or Representative, or Person holding an Office of Trust or Profit under the United States, shall be appointed an Elector.

The Electors shall meet in their respective States, and vote by Ballot for two Persons, of whom one at least shall not be an Inhabitant of the same State with themselves. And they shall make a List of all the Persons voted for, and of the Number of Votes for each; which List they shall sign and certify, and transmit sealed to the Seat of the Government of the United States, directed to the President of the Senate. The President of the Senate shall, in the Presence of the Senate and House of Representatives, open all the Certificates, and the Votes shall then be counted. The Person having the greatest Number of Votes shall be the President, if such Number

be a Majority of the whole Number of Electors appointed; and if there be more than one who have such Majority, and have an equal Number of Votes, then the House of Representatives shall immediately chuse by Ballot one of them for President; and if no Person have a Majority, then from the five highest on the List the said House shall in like Manner chuse the President. But in chusing the President, the Votes shall be taken by States, the Representation from each State having one Vote; A quorum for this Purpose shall consist of a Member or Members from two thirds of the States, and a Majority of all the States shall be necessary to a Choice. In every Case, after the Choice of the President, the Person having the greater Number of Votes of the Electors shall be the Vice President. But if there should remain two or more who have equal Votes, the Senate shall chuse from them by Ballot the Vice President.

The Congress may determine the Time of chusing the Electors, and the Day on which they shall give their Votes; which Day shall be the same throughout the United States.

No person except a natural born Citizen, or a Citizen of the United States, at the time of the Adoption of this Constitution, shall be eligible to the Office of President; neither shall any Person be eligible to that Office who shall not have attained to the Age of thirty five Years, and been fourteen Years a Resident within the United States.

In Case of the Removal of the President from Office, or of his Death, Resignation or Inability to discharge the Powers and Duties of the said Office, the same shall devolve on the Vice President, and the Congress may by Law provide for the Case of Removal, Death, Resignation or Inability, both of the President and Vice President, declaring what Officer shall then act as President, and such Officer shall act accordingly, until the Disability be removed, or a President shall be elected.

The President shall, at stated Times, receive for his Services, a Compensation, which shall neither be increased nor diminished during the Period for which he shall have been elected, and he shall not receive within that Period any other Emolument from the United States, or any of them.

Before he enter on the Execution of his Office, he shall take the following Oath or Affirmation: "I do solemnly swear (or affirm) that I will faithfully execute the Office of President of the United States, and will to the best of my Ability, preserve, protect and defend the Constitution of the United States."

SECTION 2.   The President shall be Commander in Chief of the Army and Navy of the United States, and of the Militia of the several States, when called into the actual Service of the United States; he may require the Opinion, in writing, of the principal Officer in each of the executive Departments, upon any Subject relating to the Duties of their respective Offices, and he shall have Power to grant Reprieves and Pardons for Offenses against the United States, except in Cases of Impeachment.

He shall have Power, by and with the Advice and Consent of the Senate to make Treaties, provided two thirds of the Senators present concur; and he shall nominate, and by and with the Advice and Consent of the Senate, shall appoint Ambassadors, other public Ministers and Consuls, Judges of the supreme Court, and all other Officers of the United States, whose Appointments are not herein otherwise provided for, and which shall be established by Law; but the Congress may by Law vest the Appointment of such inferior Officers, as they think proper, in the President alone, in the Courts of Law, or in the Heads of Departments.

The President shall have Power to fill up all Vacancies that may happen during the Recess of the Senate, by granting Commissions which shall expire at the End of their next Session.

SECTION 3. He shall from time to time give to the Congress Information of the State of the Union, and recommend to their Consideration such Measures as he shall judge necessary and expedient; he may, on extraordinary Occasions, convene both Houses, or either of them, and in Case of Disagreement between them, with Respect to the Time of Adjournment, he may adjourn them to such Time as he shall think proper; he shall receive Ambassadors and other public Ministers; he shall take Care that the Laws be faithfully executed, and shall Commission all the Officers of the United States.

SECTION 4. The President, Vice President and all civil Officers of the United States, shall be removed from Office on Impeachment for, and Conviction of, Treason, Bribery, or other high Crimes and Misdemeanors.

Article III

SECTION 1. The judicial Power of the United States, shall be vested in one supreme Court, and in such inferior Courts as the Congress may from time to time ordain and establish. The Judges, both of the supreme and inferior Courts, shall hold their Offices during good Behaviour, and shall, at stated Times, receive for their Services a Compensation, which shall not be diminished during their Continuance in Office.

SECTION 2. The judicial Power shall extend to all Cases, in Law and Equity, arising under this Constitution, the Laws of the United States, and Treaties made, or which shall be made, under their Authority;—to all Cases affecting Ambassadors, other public Ministers and Consuls;—to all Cases of admiralty and maritime Jurisdiction;—to Controversies to which the United States shall be a Party;—to Controversies between two or more States;—between a State and Citizens of another State;—between Citizens of different States;—between Citizens of the same State claiming Lands under Grants of different States, and between a State, or the Citizens thereof, and foreign States, Citizens or Subjects.

In all Cases affecting Ambassadors, other public Ministers and Consuls, and those in which a State shall be a Party, the supreme Court shall have original Jurisdiction. In all the other Cases before mentioned, the supreme Court shall have appellate Jurisdiction, both as to Law and Fact, with such Exceptions, and under such Regulations as the Congress shall make.

The Trial of all Crimes, except in Cases of Impeachment, shall be by Jury; and such Trial shall be held in the State where the said Crimes shall have been committed; but when not committed within any State, the Trial shall be at such Place or Places as the Congress may by Law have directed.

SECTION 3. Treason against the United States, shall consist only in levying War against them, or, in adhering to their Enemies, giving them Aid and Comfort. No Person shall be convicted of Treason unless on the Testimony of two Witnesses to the same overt Act, or on Confession in open Court.

The Congress shall have Power to declare the Punishment of Treason, but no Attainder of Treason shall work Corruption of Blood, or Forfeiture except during the Life of the Person attainted.

Article IV

SECTION 1. Full Faith and Credit shall be given in each State to the public Acts, Records, and judicial Proceedings of every other State. And the Congress may by general Laws prescribe the Manner in which such Acts, Records and Proceedings shall be proved, and the Effect thereof.

SECTION 2. The Citizens of each State shall be entitled to all Privileges and Immunities of Citizens in the several States.

A Person charged in any State with Treason, Felony, or other Crime, who shall flee from Justice, and be found in another State, shall on Demand of the executive Authority of the State from which he fled, be delivered up, to be removed to the State having Jurisdiction of the Crime.

No Person held to Service or Labour in one State, under the Laws thereof, escaping into another, shall, in Consequence of any Law or Regulation therein, be discharged from such Service or Labour, but shall be delivered up on Claim of the Party to whom such Service or Labour may be due.

SECTION 3. New States may be admitted by the Congress into this Union; but no new State shall be formed or erected within the Jurisdiction of any other State; nor any State be formed by the Junction of two or more States, or Parts of States, without the Consent of the Legislatures of the States concerned as well as of the Congress.

The Congress shall have Power to dispose of and make all needful Rules and Regulations respecting the Territory or other Property belonging to the United States; and nothing in this Constitution shall be so construed as to Prejudice any Claims of the United States, or of any particular State.

SECTION 4. United States shall guarantee to every State in this Union a Republican Form of Government, and shall protect each of them against Invasion; and on Application of the Legislature, or of the Executive (when the Legislature cannot be convened) against domestic Violence.

Article V

The Congress, whenever two thirds of both Houses shall deem it necessary, shall propose Amendments to this Constitution, or, on the Application of the Legislatures of two thirds of the several States, shall call a Convention for proposing Amendments, which, in either Case, shall be valid to all Intents and Purposes, as part of this Constitution, when ratified by the Legislatures of three fourths of the several States, or by Conventions in three fourths thereof, as the one or the other Mode of Ratification may be proposed by the Congress; Provided that no Amendment which may be made prior to the Year One thousand eight hundred and eight shall in any Manner affect the first and fourth Clauses in the Ninth Section of the first Article; and that no State, without its Consent, shall be deprived of its equal Suffrage in the Senate.

Article VI

All Debts contracted and Engagements entered into, before the Adoption of this Constitution shall be as valid against the United States under this Constitution, as under the Confederation.

This Constitution, and the Laws of the United States which shall be made in Pursuance thereof; and all Treaties made, or which shall be made, under the Authority of the United States, shall be the supreme Law of the Land; and the Judges in every State shall be bound thereby, any Thing in the Constitution or Laws of any State to the Contrary notwithstanding.

The Senators and Representatives before mentioned, and the Members of the several State Legislatures, and all executive and judicial Officers, both of the United States and of the several States, shall be bound by Oath or Affirmation, to support this Constitution; but no religious Test shall ever be required as a Qualification to any Office or public Trust under the United States.

Article VII

The Ratification of the Conventions of nine States shall be sufficient for the Establishment of this Constitution between the States so ratifying the Same.

Amendment I [1791]

Congress shall make no law respecting an establishment of religion, or prohibiting the free exercise thereof; or abridging the freedom of speech, or of the press; or the right of the people peaceably to assembly, and to petition the Government for a redress of grievances.

Amendment II [1791]

A well regulated Militia, being necessary to the security of a free State, the right of the people to keep and bear Arms, shall not be infringed.

Amendment III [1791]

No Soldier shall, in time of peace be quartered in any house, without the consent of the Owner, nor in time of war, but in a manner to be prescribed by law.

Amendment IV [1791]

The right of the people to be secure in their persons, houses, papers, and effects, against unreasonable searches and seizures, shall not be violated, and no Warrants shall issue, but upon probable cause, supported by Oath or affirmation, and particularly describing the place to be searched, and the persons or things to be seized.

Amendment V [1791]

No person shall be held to answer for a capital, or otherwise infamous crime, unless on a presentment or indictment of a Grand Jury, except in cases arising in the land or naval forces, or in the Militia, when in actual service in time of War or public danger; nor shall any person be subject for the same offence to be twice put in jeopardy of life or limb; nor shall be compelled in any criminal case to be a witness against himself, nor be deprived of life, liberty, or property, without due process of law; nor shall private property be taken for public use, without just compensation.

Amendment VI [1791]

In all criminal prosecutions, the accused shall enjoy the right to a speedy and public trial, by an impartial jury of the State and district wherein the crime shall have been committed, which district shall have been previously ascertained by law, and to be informed of the nature and cause of the accusation; to be confronted with the witnesses against him; to have compulsory process for obtaining witnesses in his favor, and to have the Assistance of Counsel for his defence.

Amendment VII [1791]

In Suits at common law, where the value in controversy shall exceed twenty dollars, the right of trial by jury shall be preserved, and no fact tried by jury, shall be otherwise re-examined in any Court of the United States, than according to the rules of the common law.

Amendment VIII [1791]

Excessive bail shall not be required, nor excessive fines imposed, nor cruel and unusual punishments inflicted.

Amendment IX [1791]

The enumeration in the Constitution, of certain rights, shall not be construed to deny or disparage others retained by the people.

Amendment X [1791]

The powers not delegated to the United States by the Constitution, nor prohibited by it to the States, are reserved to the States respectively, or to the people.

Amendment XI [1798]

The Judicial power of the United States shall not be construed to extend to any suit in law or equity, commenced or prosecuted against one of the United States by Citizens of another State, or by Citizens or Subjects of any Foreign State.

Amendment XII [1804]

The Electors shall meet in their respective states, and vote by ballot for President and Vice-President, one of whom, at least, shall not be an inhabitant of the same state with themselves; they shall name in their ballots the person voted for as President, and in distinct ballots the person voted for as Vice-President, and they shall make distinct lists of all persons voted for as President, and of all persons voted for as Vice-President, and of the number of votes for each, which lists they shall sign and certify, and transmit sealed to the seat of the government of the United States, directed to the President of the Senate;—The President of the Senate shall, in the presence of the Senate and House of Representatives, open all the certificates and the votes shall then be counted;—The person having the greatest number of votes for President, shall be the President, if such number be a majority of the whole number of Electors appointed; and if no person have such majority, then from the persons having the highest numbers not exceeding three on the list of those voted for as President, the House of Representatives shall choose immediately, by ballot, the President. But in choosing the President, the votes shall be taken by states, the representation from each state having one vote; a quorum for this purpose shall consist of a member or members from two-thirds of the states, and a majority of all states shall be necessary to a choice. And if the House of Representatives shall not choose a President whenever the right of choice shall devolve upon them, before the fourth day of March next following, then the Vice-President shall act as President, as in the case of the death or other constitutional disability of the President.—The person having the greatest number of votes as Vice-President, shall be the Vice-President, if such number be a majority of the whole number of Electors appointed, and if no person have a majority, then from the two highest numbers on the list, the Senate shall choose the Vice-President; a quorum for the purpose shall consist of two-thirds of the whole number of Senators, and a majority of the whole number shall be necessary to a choice. But no person constitutionally ineligible to the office of President shall be eligible to that of Vice-President of the United States.

Amendment XIII [1865]

SECTION 1. Neither slavery nor involuntary servitude, except as a punishment for crime whereof the party shall have been duly convicted, shall exist within the United States, or any place subject to their jurisdiction.

SECTION 2.   Congress shall have power to enforce this article by appropriate legislation.

Amendment XIV [1868]

SECTION 1.   All persons born or naturalized in the United States, and subject to the jurisdiction thereof, are citizens of the United States and of the State wherein they reside. No State shall make or enforce any law which shall abridge the privileges or immunities of citizens of the United States; nor shall any State deprive any person of life, liberty, or property, without due process of law; nor deny to any person within its jurisdiction the equal protection of the laws.

SECTION 2.   Representatives shall be apportioned among the several States according to their respective numbers, counting the whole number of persons in each State, excluding Indians not taxed. But when the right to vote at any election for the choice of electors for President and Vice President of the United States, Representatives in Congress, the Executive and Judicial officers of a State, or the members of the Legislature thereof, is denied to any of the male inhabitants of such State, being twenty-one years of age, and citizens of the United States, or in any way abridged, except for participation in rebellion, or other crime, the basis of representation therein shall be reduced in the proportion which the number of such male citizens shall bear to the whole number of male citizens twenty-one years of age in such State.

SECTION 3.   No person shall be a Senator or Representative in Congress, or elector of President and Vice President, or hold any office, civil or military, under the United States, or under any State, who having previously taken an oath, as a member of Congress, or as an officer of the United States, or as a member of any State legislature, or as an executive or judicial officer of any State, to support the Constitution of the United States, shall have engaged in insurrection or rebellion against the same, or given aid or comfort to the enemies thereof. But Congress may by a vote of two-thirds of each House, remove such disability.

SECTION 4.   The validity of the public debt of the United States, authorized by law, including debts incurred for payment of pensions and bounties for services in suppressing insurrection or rebellion, shall not be questioned. But neither the United States nor any State shall assume or pay any debt or obligation in-curred in aid of insurrection or rebellion against the United States, or any claim for the loss or emancipation of any slave; but all such debts, obligations and claims shall be held illegal and void.

SECTION 5.   The Congress shall have power to enforce, by appropriate legislation, the provisions of this article.

Amendment XV [1870]

SECTION 1.   The right of citizens of the United States to vote shall not be denied or abridged by the United States or by any State on account of race, color, or previous condition of servitude.

SECTION 2.   The Congress shall have power to enforce this article by appropriate legislation.

Amendment XVI [1913]

The Congress shall have power to lay and collect taxes on incomes, from whatever source derived, without apportionment among the several States, and without regard to any census or enumeration.

Amendment XVII [1913]

SECTION 1.   The Senate of the United States shall be composed of two Senators from each State, elected by the people thereof, for six years; and each Senator shall have one vote. The electors in each State shall have the qualifications requisite for electors of the most numerous branch of the State legislatures.

SECTION 2.   When vacancies happen in the representation of any State in the Senate, the executive authority of such State shall issue writs of election to fill such vacancies: *Provided*, That the legislature of any State may empower the executive thereof to make temporary appointments until the people fill the vacancies by election as the legislature may direct.

SECTION 3.   This amendment shall not be so construed as to affect the election or term of any Senator chosen before it becomes valid as part of the Constitution.

Amendment XVIII [1919]

SECTION 1.   After one year from the ratification of this article the manufacture, sale, or transportation of intoxicating liquors within, the importation thereof into, or the exportation thereof from the United States and all territory subject to the jurisdiction thereof for beverage purposes is hereby prohibited.

SECTION 2. The Congress and the several States shall have concurrent power to enforce this article by appropriate legislation.

SECTION 3. This article shall be inoperative unless it shall have been ratified as an amendment to the Constitution by the legislatures of the several States, as provided in the Constitution, within seven years from the date of the submission hereof to the States by the Congress.

Amendment XIX [1920]

SECTION 1. The right of citizens of the United States to vote shall not be denied or abridged by the United States or by any State on account of sex.

SECTION 2. Congress shall have power to enforce this article by appropriate legislation.

Amendment XX [1933]

SECTION 1. The terms of the President and Vice President shall end at noon on the 20th day of January, and the terms of Senators and Representatives at noon on the 3d day of January, of the years in which such terms would have ended if this article had not been ratified; and the terms of their successors shall then begin.

SECTION 2. The Congress shall assemble at least once in every year, and such meeting shall begin at noon on the 3d day of January, unless they shall by law appoint a different day.

SECTION 3. If, at the time fixed for the beginning of the term of the President, the President elect shall have died, the Vice President elect shall become President. If the President shall not have been chosen before the time fixed for the beginning of his term, or if the President elect shall have failed to qualify, then the Vice President elect shall act as President until a President shall have qualified; and the Congress may by law provide for the case wherein neither a President elect nor a Vice President elect shall have qualified, declaring who shall then act as President, or the manner in which one who is to act shall be selected, and such person shall act accordingly until a President or Vice President shall have qualified.

SECTION 4. The Congress may by law provide for the case of the death of any of the persons from whom the House of Representatives may choose a President whenever the right of choice shall have devolved upon them, and for the case of the death of any of the persons from whom the Senate may choose a Vice President whenever the right of choice shall have devolved upon them.

SECTION 5. Sections 1 and 2 shall take effect on the 15th day of October following the ratification of this article.

SECTION 6. This article shall be inoperative unless it shall have been ratified as an amendment to the Constitution by the legislatures of three-fourths of the several States within seven years from the date of its submission.

Amendment XXI [1933]

SECTION 1. The eighteenth article of amendment to the Constitution of the United States is hereby repealed.

SECTION 2. The transportation or importation into any State, Territory, or possession of the United States for delivery or use therein of intoxicating liquors, in violation of the laws thereof, is hereby prohibited.

SECTION 3. This article shall be inoperative unless it shall have been ratified as an amendment to the Constitution by conventions in the several States, as provided in the Constitution, within seven years from the date of the submission hereof to the States by the Congress.

Amendment XXII [1951]

SECTION 1. No person shall be elected to the office of the President more than twice, and no person who has held the office of President, or acted as President, for more than two years of a term to which some other person was elected President shall be elected to the office of President more than once. But this Article shall not apply to any person holding the office of President when this Article was proposed by the Congress, and shall not prevent any person who may be holding the office of President, or acting as President, during the term within which this Article becomes operative from holding the office of President or acting as President during the remainder of such term.

SECTION 2. This article shall be inoperative unless it shall have been ratified as an amendment to the

Constitution by the legislatures of three-fourths of the several States within seven years from the date of its submission to the States by the Congress.

Amendment XXIII [1961]

SECTION 1.   The District constituting the seat of Government of the United States shall appoint in such manner as the Congress may direct:

A number of electors of President and Vice President equal to the whole number of Senators and Representatives in Congress to which the District would be entitled if it were a State, but in no event more than the least populous state; they shall be in addition to those appointed by the states, but they shall be considered, for the purposes of the election of President and Vice President, to be electors appointed by a state; and they shall meet in the District and perform such duties as provided by the twelfth article of amendment.

SECTION 2.   The Congress shall have power to enforce this article by appropriate legislation.

Amendment XXIV [1964]

SECTION 1.   The right of citizens of the United States to vote in any primary or other election for President or Vice President, for electors for President or Vice President, or for Senator or Representative in Congress, shall not be denied or abridged by the United States, or any State by reason of failure to pay any poll tax or other tax.

SECTION 2.   The Congress shall have power to enforce this article by appropriate legislation.

Amendment XXV [1967]

SECTION 1.   In case of the removal of the President from office or of his death or resignation, the Vice President shall become President.

SECTION 2.   Whenever there is a vacancy in the office of the Vice President, the President shall nominate a Vice President who shall take office upon confirmation by a majority vote of both Houses of Congress.

SECTION 3.   Whenever the President transmits to the President pro tempore of the Senate and the Speaker of the House of Representatives his written declaration that he is unable to discharge the powers and duties

of his office, and until he transmits to them a written declaration to the contrary, such powers and duties shall be discharged by the Vice President as Acting President.

SECTION 4.   Whenever the Vice President and a majority of either the principal officers of the executive departments or of such other body as Congress may by law provide, transmit to the President pro tempore of the Senate and the Speaker of the House of Representatives their written declaration that the President is unable to discharge the powers and duties of his office, the Vice President shall immediately assume the powers and duties of the office as Acting President.

Thereafter, when the President transmits to the President pro tempore of the Senate and the Speaker of the House of Representatives his written declaration that no inability exists, he shall resume the powers and duties of his office unless the Vice President and a majority of either the principal officers of the executive department or of such other body as Congress may by law provide, transmit within four days to the President pro tempore of the Senate and the Speaker of the House of Representatives their written declaration that the President is unable to discharge the powers and duties of his office. Thereupon Congress shall decide the issue, assembling within forty-eight hours for that purpose if not in session. If the Congress, within twenty-one days after receipt of the latter written declaration, or, if Congress is not in session, within twenty-one days after Congress is required to assemble, determines by two-thirds vote of both Houses that the President is unable to discharge the powers and duties of his office, the Vice President shall continue to discharge the same as Acting President; otherwise, the President shall resume the powers and duties of his office.

Amendment XXVI [1971]

SECTION 1.   The right of citizens of the United States, who are eighteen years of age or older, to vote shall not be denied or abridged by the United States or by any State on account of age.

SECTION 2.   The Congress shall have power to enforce this article by appropriate legislation.

Amendment XXVII [1992]

No law, varying the compensation for the services of the Senators and Representatives, shall take effect, until an election of Representatives shall have intervened.

Spanish Equivalents for Important Legal Terms in English

Abandoned property: bienes abandonados
Acceptance: aceptación; consentimiento; acuerdo
Acceptor: aceptante
Accession: toma de posesión; aumento; accesión
Accommodation indorser: avalista de favor
Accommodation party: firmante de favor
Accord: acuerdo; convenio; arreglo
Accord and satisfaction: transacción ejecutada
Act of state doctrine: doctrina de acto de gobierno
Administrative law: derecho administrativo
Administrative process: procedimiento o metódo administrativo
Administrator: administrador (-a)
Adverse possession: posesión de hecho susceptible de proscripción adquisitiva
Affirmative action: acción afirmativa
Affirmative defense: defensa afirmativa
After-acquired property: bienes adquiridos con posterioridad a un hecho dado
Agency: mandato; agencia
Agent: mandatorio; agente; representante
Agreement: convenio; acuerdo; contrato
Alien corporation: empresa extranjera
Allonge: hojas adicionales de endosos
Answer: contestación de la demande; alegato

Anticipatory repudiation: anuncio previo de las partes de su imposibilidad de cumplir con el contrato
Appeal: apelación; recurso de apelación
Appellate jurisdiction: jurisdicción de apelaciones
Appraisal right: derecho de valuación
Arbitration: arbitraje
Arson: incendio intencional
Articles of partnership: contrato social
Artisan's lien: derecho de retención que ejerce al artesano
Assault: asalto; ataque; agresión
Assignment of rights: transmisión; transferencia; cesión
Assumption of risk: no resarcimiento por exposición voluntaria al peligro
Attachment: auto judicial que autoriza el embargo; embargo

Bailee: depositario
Bailment: depósito; constitución en depósito
Bailor: depositante
Bankruptcy trustee: síndico de la quiebra
Battery: agresión; física
Bearer: portador; tenedor
Bearer instrument: documento al portador
Bequest or legacy: legado (de bienes muebles)

Bilateral contract: contrato bilateral
Bill of lading: conocimiento de embarque; carta de porte
Bill of Rights: declaración de derechos
Binder: póliza de seguro provisoria; recibo de pago a cuenta del precio
Blank indorsement: endoso en blanco
Blue sky laws: leyes reguladoras del comercio bursátil
Bond: título de crédito; garantía; caución
Bond indenture: contrato de emisión de bonos; contrato del ampréstito
Breach of contract: incumplimiento de contrato
Brief: escrito; resumen; informe
Burglary: violación de domicilio
Business judgment rule: regla de juicio comercial
Business tort: agravio comercial

Case law: ley de casos; derecho casuístico
Cashier's check: cheque de caja
Causation in fact: causalidad en realidad
Cease-and-desist order: orden para cesar y desistir
Certificate of deposit: certificado de depósito

Certified check: cheque certificado

Charitable trust: fideicomiso para fines benéficos

Chattel: bien mueble

Check: cheque

Chose in action: derecho inmaterial; derecho de acción

Civil law: derecho civil

Close corporation: sociedad de un solo accionista o de un grupo restringido de accionistas

Closed shop: taller agremiado (emplea solamente a miembros de un gremio)

Closing argument: argumento al final

Codicil: codicilo

Collateral: garantía; bien objeto de la garantía real

Comity: cortesía; cortesía entre naciones

Commercial paper: instrumentos negociables; documentos a valores commerciales

Common law: derecho consuetudinario; derecho común; ley común

Common stock: acción ordinaria

Comparative negligence: negligencia comparada

Compensatory damages: daños y perjuicios reales o compensatorios

Concurrent conditions: condiciones concurrentes

Concurrent jurisdiction: competencia concurrente de varios tribunales para entender en una misma causa

Concurring opinion: opinión concurrente

Condition: condición

Condition precedent: condición suspensiva

Condition subsequent: condición resolutoria

Confiscation: confiscación

Confusion: confusión; fusión

Conglomerate merger: fusión de firmas que operan en distintos mercados

Consent decree: acuerdo entre las partes aprobado por un tribunal

Consequential damages: daños y perjuicios indirectos

Consideration: consideración; motivo; contraprestación

Consolidation: consolidación

Constructive delivery: entrega simbólica

Constructive trust: fideicomiso creado por aplicación de la ley

Consumer-protection law: ley para proteger el consumidor

Contract: contrato

Contract under seal: contrato formal o sellado

Contributory negligence: negligencia de la parte actora

Conversion: usurpación; conversión de valores

Copyright: derecho de autor

Corporation: sociedad anónima; corporación; persona jurídica

Co-sureties: cogarantes

Counterclaim: reconvención; contrademanda

Counteroffer: contraoferta

Course of dealing: curso de transacciones

Course of performance: curso de cumplimiento

Covenant: pacto; garantía; contrato

Covenant not to sue: pacto or contrato a no demandar

Covenant of quiet enjoyment: garantía del uso y goce pacífico del inmueble

Creditors' composition agreement: concordato preventivo

Crime: crimen; delito; contravención

Criminal law: derecho penal

Cross-examination: contrainterrogatorio

Cure: cura; cuidado; derecho de remediar un vicio contractual

Customs receipts: recibos de derechos aduaneros

Damages: daños; indemnización por daños y perjuicios

Debit card: tarjeta de dé bito

Debtor: deudor

Debt securities: seguridades de deuda

Deceptive advertising: publicidad engañosa

Deed: escritura; título; acta translativa de domino

Defamation: difamación

Delegation of duties: delegación de obligaciones

Demand deposit: depósito a la vista

Depositions: declaración de un testigo fuera del tribunal

Devise: legado; deposición testamentaria (bienes inmuebles)

Directed verdict: veredicto según orden del juez y sin participación activa del jurado

Direct examination: interrogatorio directo; primer interrogatorio

Disaffirmance: repudiación; renuncia; anulación

Discharge: descargo; liberación; cumplimiento

Disclosed principal: mandante revelado

Discovery: descubrimiento; producción de la prueba

Dissenting opinion: opinión disidente

Dissolution: disolución; terminación

Diversity of citizenship: competencia de los tribunales federales para entender en causas cuyas partes intervinientes son cuidadanos de distintos estados

Divestiture: extinción prematura de derechos reales

Dividend: dividendo

Docket: orden del día; lista de causas pendientes

Domestic corporation: sociedad local

Draft: orden de pago; letrade cambio

Drawee: girado; beneficiario

Drawer: librador

Duress: coacción; violencia

Easement: servidumbre

Embezzlement: desfalco; malversación

Eminent domain: poder de expropiación

Employment discrimination: discriminación en el empleo

Entrepreneur: empresario

Environmental law: ley ambiental

Equal dignity rule: regla de dignidad egual

Equity security: tipo de participación en una sociedad

Estate: propiedad; patrimonio; derecho

Estop: impedir; prevenir

Ethical issue: cuestión ética

Exclusive jurisdiction: competencia exclusiva

Exculpatory clause: cláusula eximente

Executed contract: contrato ejecutado

Execution: ejecución; cumplimiento

Executor: albacea

Executory contract: contrato aún no completamente consumado

Executory interest: derecho futuro

Express contract: contrato expreso

Expropriation: expropriación

Federal question: caso federal

Fee simple: pleno dominio; dominio absoluto

Fee simple absolute: dominio absoluto

Fee simple defeasible: dominio sujeta a una condición resolutoria

Felony: crimen; delito grave

Fictitious payee: beneficiario ficticio

Fiduciary: fiduciaro

Firm offer: oferta en firme

Fixture: inmueble por destino, incorporación a anexación

Floating lien: gravamen continuado

Foreign corporation: sociedad extranjera; U.S. sociedad constituída en otro estado

Forgery: falso; falsificación

Formal contract: contrato formal

Franchise: privilegio; franquicia; concesión

Franchisee: persona que recibe una concesión

Franchisor: persona que vende una concesión

Fraud: fraude; dolo; engaño

Future interest: bien futuro

Garnishment: embargo de derechos

General partner: socio comanditario

General warranty deed: escritura translativa de domino con garantía de título
Gift: donación
Gift *causa mortis*: donación por causa de muerte
Gift *inter vivos*: donación entre vivos
Good faith: buena fe
Good-faith purchaser: comprador de buena fe

Holder: tenedor por contraprestación
Holder in due course: tenedor legítimo
Holographic will: testamento ológrafico
Homestead exemption laws: leyes que exceptúan las casas de familia de ejecución por duedas generales
Horizontal merger: fusión horizontal

Identification: identificación
Implied-in-fact contract: contrato implícito en realidad
Implied warranty: guarantía implícita
Implied warranty of merchantability: garantía implícita de vendibilidad
Impossibility of performance: imposibilidad de cumplir un contrato
Imposter: imposter
Incidental beneficiary: beneficiario incidental; beneficiario secundario
Incidental damages: daños incidentales
Indictment: auto de acusación; acusación
Indorsee: endorsatario
Indorsement: endoso
Indorser: endosante
Informal contract: contrato no formal; contrato verbal
Information: acusación hecha por el ministerio público
Injunction: mandamiento; orden de no innovar
Innkeeper's lien: derecho de retención que ejerce el posadero
Installment contract: contrato de pago en cuotas
Insurable interest: interés asegurable
Intended beneficiary: beneficiario destinado
Intentional tort: agravio; cuasi-delito intencional
International law: derecho internacional
Interrogatories: preguntas escritas sometidas por una parte a la otra o a un testigo
***Inter vivos* trust:** fideicomiso entre vivos
Intestacy laws: leyes de la condición de morir intestado
Intestate: intestado
Investment company: compañia de inversiones
Issue: emisión

Joint tenancy: derechos conjuntos en un bien inmueble en favor del beneficiario sobreviviente
Judgment *n.o.v.*: juicio no obstante veredicto
Judgment rate of interest: interés de juicio
Judicial process: acto de procedimiento; proceso jurídico
Judicial review: revisión judicial
Jurisdiction: jurisdicción

Larceny: robo; hurto
Law: derecho; ley; jurisprudencia
Lease: contrato de locación; contrato de alquiler
Leasehold estate: bienes forales
Legal rate of interest: interés legal
Legatee: legatario
Letter of credit: carta de crédito
Levy: embargo; comiso
Libel: libelo; difamación escrita
Life estate: usufructo
Limited partner: comanditario
Limited partnership: sociedad en comandita
Liquidation: liquidación; realización
Lost property: objetos perdidos

Majority opinion: opinión de la mayoría
Maker: persona que realiza u ordena; librador
Mechanic's lien: gravamen de constructor
Mediation: mediación; intervención
Merger: fusión
Mirror image rule: fallo de reflejo
Misdemeanor: infracción; contravención
Mislaid property: bienes extraviados
Mitigation of damages: reducción de daños
Mortgage: hypoteca
Motion to dismiss: excepción parentoria
Mutual fund: fondo mutual

Negotiable instrument: instrumento negociable
Negotiation: negociación
Nominal damages: daños y perjuicios nominales
Novation: novación
Nuncupative will: testamento nuncupativo

Objective theory of contracts: teoria objetiva de contratos
Offer: oferta
Offeree: persona que recibe una oferta
Offeror: oferente
Order instrument: instrumento o documento a la orden

Original jurisdiction: jurisdicción de primera instancia
Output contract: contrato de producción

Parol evidence rule: regla relativa a la prueba oral
Partially disclosed principal: mandante revelado en parte
Partnership: sociedad colectiva; asociación; asociación de participación
Past consideration: causa o contraprestación anterior
Patent: patente; privilegio
Pattern or practice: muestra o práctica
Payee: beneficiario de un pago
Penalty: pena; penalidad
Per capita: por cabeza
Perfection: perfeción
Performance: cumplimiento; ejecución
Personal defenses: excepciones personales
Personal property: bienes muebles
Per stirpes: por estirpe
Plea bargaining: regateo por un alegato
Pleadings: alegatos
Pledge: prenda
Police powers: poders de policia y de prevención del crimen
Policy: póliza
Positive law: derecho positivo; ley positiva
Possibility of reverter: posibilidad de reversión
Precedent: precedente
Preemptive right: derecho de prelación
Preferred stock: acciones preferidas
Premium: recompensa; prima
Presentment warranty: garantía de presentación
Price discrimination: discriminación en los precios
Principal: mandante; principal
Privity: nexo jurídico
Privity of contract: relación contractual
Probable cause: causa probable
Probate: verificación; verificación del testamento
Probate court: tribunal de sucesiones y tutelas
Proceeds: resultados; ingresos
Profit: beneficio; utilidad; lucro
Promise: promesa
Promisee: beneficiario de una promesa
Promisor: promtente
Promissory estoppel: impedimento promisorio
Promissory note: pagaré; nota de pago
Promoter: promotor; fundador
Proximate cause: causa inmediata o próxima
Proxy: apoderado; poder
Punitive, or exemplary, damages: daños y perjuicios punitivos o ejemplares

Qualified indorsement: endoso con reservas
Quasi contract: contrato tácito o implícito
Quitclaim deed: acto de transferencia de una propiedad por finiquito, pero sin ninguna garantía sobre la validez del título transferido

Ratification: ratificación
Real property: bienes inmuebles
Reasonable doubt: duda razonable
Rebuttal: refutación
Recognizance: promesa; compromiso; reconocimiento
Recording statutes: leyes estatales sobre registros oficiales
Redress: reporacíon
Reformation: rectificación; reforma; corrección
Rejoinder: dúplica; contrarréplica
Release: liberación; renuncia a un derecho
Remainder: substitución; reversión
Remedy: recurso; remedio; reparación
Replevin: acción reivindicatoria; reivindicación
Reply: réplica
Requirements contract: contrato de suministro
Rescission: rescisión
Res judicata: cosa juzgada; res judicata
Respondeat superior: responsabilidad del mandante o del maestro
Restitution: restitución
Restrictive indorsement: endoso restrictivo
Resulting trust: fideicomiso implícito
Reversion: reversión; sustitución
Revocation: revocación; derogación
Right of contribution: derecho de contribución
Right of reimbursement: derecho de reembolso
Right of subrogation: derecho de subrogación
Right-to-work law: ley de libertad de trabajo
Robbery: robo
Rule 10b-5: Regla 10b-5

Sale: venta; contrato de compreventa
Sale on approval: venta a ensayo; venta sujeta a la aprobación del comprador
Sale or return: venta con derecho de devolución
Sales contract: contrato de compraventa; boleto de compraventa
Satisfaction: satisfacción; pago
Scienter: a sabiendas
S corporation: S corporación
Secured party: acreedor garantizado
Secured transaction: transacción garantizada

Securities: volares; titulos; seguridades
Security agreement: convenio de seguridad
Security interest: interés en un bien dado en garantía que permite a quien lo detenta venderlo en caso de incumplimiento
Service mark: marca de identificación de servicios
Shareholder's derivative suit: acción judicial entablada por un accionista en nombre de la sociedad
Signature: firma; rúbrica
Slander: difamación oral; calumnia
Sovereign immunity: immunidad soberana
Special indorsement: endoso especial; endoso a la orden de una person en particular
Specific performance: ejecución precisa, según los términos del contrato
Spendthrift trust: fideicomiso para pródigos
Stale check: cheque vencido
Stare decisis: acatar las decisiones, observar los precedentes
Statutory law: derecho estatutario; derecho legislado; derecho escrito
Stock: acciones
Stock warrant: certificado para la compra de acciones
Stop-payment order: orden de suspensión del pago de un cheque dada por el librador del mismo
Strict liability: responsabilidad unconditional
Summary judgment: fallo sumario

Tangible property: bienes corpóreos
Tenancy at will: inguilino por tiempo indeterminado (según la voluntad del propietario)
Tenancy by sufferance: posesión por tolerancia
Tenancy by the entirety: locación conyugal conjunta
Tenancy for years: inguilino por un término fijo
Tenancy in common: specie de copropiedad indivisa
Tender: oferta de pago; oferta de ejecución
Testamentary trust: fideicomiso testamentario
Testator: testador (-a)
Third party beneficiary contract: contrato para el beneficio del tercero-beneficiario
Tort: agravio; cuasi-delito
Totten trust: fideicomiso creado por un depósito bancario
Trade acceptance: letra de cambio aceptada
Trademark: marca registrada
Trade name: nombre comercial; razón social
Traveler's check: cheque del viajero

Trespass to land: ingreso no autorizado a las tierras de otro
Trespass to personal property: violación de los derechos posesorios de un tercero con respecto a bienes muebles
Trust: fideicomiso; trust

Ultra vires: ultra vires; fuera de la facultad (de una sociedad anónima)
Unanimous opinion: opinión unámine
Unconscionable contract or clause: contrato leonino; cláusula leonino
Underwriter: subscriptor; asegurador
Unenforceable contract: contrato que no se puede hacer cumplir
Unilateral contract: contrato unilateral
Union shop: taller agremiado; empresa en la que todos los empleados son miembros del gremio o sindicato
Universal defenses: defensas legitimas o legales
Usage of trade: uso comercial
Usury: usura

Valid contract: contrato válido
Venue: lugar; sede del proceso
Vertical merger: fusión vertical de empresas
Voidable contract: contrato anulable
Void contract: contrato nulo; contrato inválido, sin fuerza legal
Voir dire: examen preliminar de un testigo a jurado por el tribunal para determinar su competencia
Voting trust: fideicomiso para ejercer el derecho de voto

Waiver: renuncia; abandono
Warranty of habitability: garantía de habitabilidad
Watered stock: acciones diluídos; capital inflado
White-collar crime: crimen administrativo
Writ of attachment: mandamiento de ejecución; mandamiento de embargo
Writ of *certiorari*: auto de avocación; auto de certiorari
Writ of execution: auto ejecutivo; mandamiento de ejecutión
Writ of mandamus: auto de mandamus; mandamiento; orden judicial

GLOSSARY

ABA-Approved Program A legal or paralegal educational program that satisfies the standards for paralegal training set forth by the American Bar Association.

Active Listening The act of listening attentively to the speaker's verbal or nonverbal messages and responding to those messages by giving appropriate feedback.

Address Block That part of a letter that indicates to whom the letter is addressed. The address block is placed in the upper left-hand portion of the letter, above the salutation (or reference line, if one is included).

Administrative Agency A federal or state government agency established to perform a specific function. Administrative agencies are authorized by legislative acts to make and enforce rules relating to the purpose for which they were established.

Administrative Law A body of law created by administrative agencies in the form of rules, regulations, orders, and decisions in order to carry out their duties and responsibilities.

Affidavit A written statement of facts, confirmed by the oath or affirmation of the party making it and made before a person having the authority to administer the oath or affirmation.

Affiliate An entity that is connected (or affiliated) with another entity. State and local branches of national or regional paralegal associations are often referred to as affiliates.

Affirmative Defense A response to a plaintiff's claim that does not deny the plaintiff's facts but attacks the plaintiff's legal right to bring an action.

Allegation A party's statement, claim, or assertion made in a pleading to the court. The allegation sets forth the issue that the party expects to prove.

Alternative Dispute Resolution (ADR) The resolution of disputes in ways other than those involved in the traditional judicial process. Mediation and arbitration are forms of ADR.

American Arbitration Association (AAA) The major organization offering arbitration services in the United States.

American Association for Paralegal Education (AAfPE) A national organization of paralegal educators; the AAfPE was established in 1981 to promote high standards for paralegal education.

American Bar Association (ABA) A voluntary national association of attorneys. The ABA plays an active role in developing educational and ethical standards for attorneys and in pursuing improvements in the administration of justice.

Annotation A brief comment, an explanation of a legal point, or a case summary found in a case digest or other legal source.

Answer A defendant's response to a plaintiff's complaint.

Appeal The process of seeking a higher court's review of a lower court's decision for the purpose of correcting or changing the lower court's judgment or decision.

Appellate Court A court that reviews decisions made by lower courts, such as trial courts; a court of appeals.

Appellate Jurisdiction The power of a court to hear and decide an appeal; that is, the power and authority of a court to review cases that already have been tried in a lower court and the power to make decisions about them without actually holding a trial. This process is called appellate review.

Arbitration The settling of a dispute by submitting it to a disinterested third party (other than a court), who renders a decision that may or may not be legally binding.

Arbitration Clause A clause in a contract that provides that, in case of a dispute, the parties will determine their rights by arbitration rather than through the judicial system.

Associate's Degree An academic degree signifying the completion of a two-year course of study, normally at a community college.

Attorney-Client Privilege A rule of evidence requiring that confidential communications between a client and his or her attorney (relating to their professional relationship) be kept confidential, unless the client consents to disclosure.

Authentication Establishing the genuineness of an item that is to be introduced as evidence in a trial.

Auto-Cite An aid to legal research developed by the editors of Lexis®. On Lexis®, Auto-Cite can be used to find the history of a case, to verify whether the case is still good law, and to perform other functions.

Bachelor's Degree An academic degree signifying the completion of a four-year course of study at a college or university.

Bankruptcy Court A federal court of limited jurisdiction that hears only bankruptcy proceedings.

Bankruptcy Law The body of federal law that governs bankruptcy proceedings. The twin goals of bankruptcy law are (1) to protect a debtor by giving him or her a fresh start, free from creditors' claims; and (2) to ensure that creditors who are competing for a debtor's assets are treated fairly.

Bill of Rights The first ten amendments to the Constitution.

Billable Hours Hours or fractions of hours that attorneys and paralegals spend in work that requires legal expertise and that can be billed directly to clients.

Bonus An end-of-the-year payment to a salaried employee in appreciation for that employee's overtime work, work quality, diligence, or dedication to the firm.

Breach To violate a legal duty by an act or a failure to act.

Briefing a Case Summarizing a case. A typical case brief will indicate the case title and citation and then briefly state the factual background and procedural history of the case, the issue or issues raised in the case, the court's decision, the applicable rule of law and the legal reasoning on which the decision is based, and conclusions or notes concerning the case made by the one briefing it.

Case Law Rules of law announced in court decisions.

Case on "All Fours" A case in which all four elements of a case (the parties, the circumstances, the legal issues involved, and the remedies sought by the plaintiff) are very similar.

Case on Point A case involving factual circumstances and issues that are similar to a case before the court.

Certification Formal recognition by a private group or a state agency that an individual has satisfied the group's standards of proficiency, knowledge, and competence; ordinarily accomplished through the taking of an examination.

Certified Legal Assistant (CLA) A legal assistant whose legal competency has been certified by the National Association of Legal Assistants (NALA) following an examination that tests the legal assistant's knowledge and skills.

Certified Legal Assistant Specialist (CLAS) A legal assistant whose competency in a legal specialty has been certified by the National Association of Legal Assistants (NALA) following an examination of the legal assistant's knowledge and skills in the specialty area.

Challenge An attorney's objection, during *voir dire,* to the inclusion of a particular person on the jury.

Challenge for Cause A *voir dire* challenge for which an attorney states the reason why a prospective juror should not be included in the jury.

Charge The judge's instruction to the jury, following the attorneys' closing arguments, setting forth the rules of law that the jury must apply in reaching its decision, or verdict.

Circumstantial Evidence Indirect evidence that is offered to establish, by inference, the likelihood of a fact that is in question.

Citation In case law, a reference to the volume number, name, and page number of the reporter in which a case can be found. In statutory and administrative law, a reference to the title number, name, and section of the code in which a statute or regulation can be found.

Citator A book or online service that provides the subsequent history and interpretation of a court decision, statute, or regulation, and a list of the cases, statutes, and regulations that have interpreted, applied, or modified a statute or regulation.

Civil Law The branch of law dealing with the definition and enforcement of all private or public rights, as opposed to criminal matters.

Closed-Ended Question A question that is phrased in such a way that it elicits a simple "yes" or "no" answer.

Closing A final comment to a letter that is placed above the signature, such as "Very truly yours."

Closing Argument An argument made by each side's attorney after the cases for the plaintiff and defendant have been presented. Closing arguments are made prior to the jury charge.

Code A systematic and logical presentation of laws, rules, or regulations.

Commercial Online Services Internet service providers that, for a fee, allow their subscribers access to resources that are otherwise restricted.

Common Law A body of law developed from custom or judicial decisions in English and U.S. courts and not attributable to a legislature.

Complaint The pleading made by a plaintiff or a charge made by the state alleging wrongdoing on the part of the defendant.

Computer-Assisted Legal Research (CALR) Any legal research conducted with the assistance of computers. CALR includes the use of CD-ROMs, fee-based legal-services providers such as Westlaw® and Lexis®, and the Internet.

Concurrent Jurisdiction Jurisdiction that exists when two different courts have the power to hear a case. For example, some cases can be heard in either a federal or a state court.

Confirmation Letter A letter that states the substance of a previously conducted verbal discussion to provide a permanent record of the oral conversation.

Conflict of Interest A situation in which two or more duties or interests come into conflict, as when an attorney attempts to represent opposing parties in a legal dispute.

Conflicts Check A procedure for determining whether an agreement to represent a potential client will result in a conflict of interest.

Contempt of Court The intentional obstruction or frustration of the court's attempt to administer justice. A party to a lawsuit may be held in contempt of court (punishable by a fine or jail sentence) for refusing to comply with a court's order.

Contingency Fee A legal fee that consists of a specified percentage (such as 30 percent) of the amount the plaintiff recovers in a civil lawsuit. The fee must be paid only if the plaintiff prevails in the lawsuit (recovers damages).

Corporate Law Law that governs the formation, financing, merger and acquisition, and termination of corporations, as well as the rights and duties of those who own and run the corporation.

Criminal Law The branch of law that governs and defines those actions that are crimes and that subjects persons convicted of crimes to punishment imposed by the government.

Cross-Examination The questioning of an opposing witness during the trial.

Damages Money sought as a remedy for a civil wrong, such as a breach of contract or a tortious act.

Default Judgment A judgment entered by a clerk or court against a party who has failed to appear in court to answer or defend against a claim that has been brought against him or her by another party.

Defendant A party against whom a lawsuit is brought.

Demand Letter An adversarial letter that attempts to persuade the reader that he or she should accept a position that is favorable to the writer's client—that is, demanding that the reader do or not do a certain thing.

Deponent A party or witness who testifies under oath during a deposition.

Deposition A pretrial question-and-answer proceeding, usually conducted orally, in which an a party or witness answers an attorney's questions. The answers are given under oath, and the session is recorded.

Deposition Transcript The official transcription of the recording taken during a deposition.

Digest A compilation in which brief summaries of court cases are arranged by subject and subdivided by jurisdiction and court.

Direct Evidence Evidence establishing the existence of a fact that is in question without relying on inferences.

Direct Examination The examination of a witness by the attorney who calls the witness to the stand to testify on behalf of the attorney's client.

Disbarment A severe disciplinary sanction in which an attorney's license to practice law in the state is revoked because of unethical or illegal conduct.

Discovery Formal investigation prior to trial. During discovery, opposing parties use various methods, such as interrogatories and depositions, to obtain information from each other and from witnesses to prepare for trial.

Diversity of Citzenship Under Article III, Section 2, of the Constitution, a basis for federal court jurisdiction over certain disputes, including disputes between citizens of different states.

Docket The list of cases entered on a court's calendar and thus scheduled to be heard by the court.

Double Billing Billing more than one client for the same billable time period.

Elder Law A term used to describe a relatively new legal specialty that involves servicing the needs of older clients, such as estate planning and making arrangements for long-term care.

Employment Manual A firm's handbook or written statement that specifies the policies and procedures that govern the firm's employees and employer-employee relationships.

Enabling Legislation A statute enacted by a legislature that authorizes the creation of an administrative agency and specifies the name, purpose, composition, and powers of the agency being created.

Environmental Law All state and federal laws or regulations enacted or issued to protect the environment and preserve environmental resources.

Estate Planning Making arrangements, during a person's lifetime, for the transfer of that person's property or obligations to others on the person's death. Estate planning often involves executing a will, establishing a trust fund, or taking out a life insurance policy to provide for others, such as a spouse or children, on one's death.

Ethical Wall A term that refers to the procedures used to create a screen around a legal employee to shield him or her from information about a case in which there is a conflict of interest.

Evidence Anything that is used to prove the existence or nonexistence of a fact.

Exclusive Jurisdiction Jurisdiction that exists when a case can be heard only in a particular court, such as a federal court.

Expense Slip A slip of paper on which any expense, or cost, that is incurred on behalf of a client (such as the payment of court fees or long-distance telephone charges) is recorded.

Expert Witness A witness with professional training or substantial experience qualifying him or her to testify on a particular subject.

Eyewitness A witness who testifies about an event that he or she observed or has experienced firsthand.

Family Law Law relating to family matters, such as marriage, divorce, child support, and child custody.

Federal Question A question that pertains to the U.S. Constitution, acts of Congress, or treaties. A federal question provides a basis for jurisdiction by the federal courts. This jurisdiction is authorized by Article III, Section 2, of the Constitution.

Federal Rules of Civil Procedure (FRCP) The rules controlling all procedural matters in civil trials brought before the federal district courts.

File Transfer Protocol (FTP) An interface program that connects one computer to another over the Internet to copy files.

Fixed Fee A fee paid to the attorney by his or her client for having rendered a specified legal service, such as the creation of a simple will.

Forms File A reference file containing copies of the firm's commonly used legal documents and informational forms. The documents in the forms file serve as a model for drafting new documents.

Freelance Paralegal A paralegal who operates his or her own business and provides services to attorneys on a contractual basis. A freelance paralegal works under the supervision of an attorney, who assumes responsibility for the paralegal's work product.

Friendly Witness A witness who gives voluntary testimony at an attorney's request on behalf of the attorney's client; a witness who is prejudiced against the client's adversary.

General Licensing A type of licensing in which all individuals within a specific profession or group (such as paralegals) must meet licensing requirements imposed by the state before they may legally practice their profession.

Headnote A note near the beginning of a reported case summarizing the court's ruling on an issue.

Hearsay An oral or written statement made by an out-of-court declarant that is later offered in court by a witness (not the declarant) concerning a matter before the court. Hearsay is generally not admissible as evidence.

Home Page The main page of a Web site. Often, the home page serves as a table of contents to other pages at the site.

Hostile Witness A witness for the opposing side in a lawsuit or other legal proceeding; an adverse witness.

Hypertext Transfer Protocol (http) An interface program that enables computers to communicate. Hypertext is a database system by which distinct objects, such as text and graphics, can be linked. Protocol is a system of formats and rules, such as the speed of a transmission.

Hypothetical Question A question based on hypothesis, conjecture, or fiction.

Immigration Law All laws that set forth the requirements that persons must meet if they wish to visit or immigrate to the United States.

Impeach To call into question the credibility of a witness by challenging the truth or accuracy of his or her trial statement.

Independent Paralegal A paralegal who offers services directly to the public, normally for a fee, without attorney supervision. Independent paralegals assist consumers by supplying them with forms and procedural knowledge relating to simple or routine legal procedures.

Informative Letter A letter that conveys certain information to a client, a witness, an adversary's counsel, or other person regarding some legal matter (such as the date, time, place, and purpose of a meeting).

Intellectual Property Property that results from intellectual, creative processes. Copyrights, patents, and trademarks are examples of intellectual property.

Internet Service Provider (ISP) A company that provides dedicated access to the Internet, generally through a local phone number.

Interrogatories A series of written questions for which written answers are prepared and then signed under oath by a party to a lawsuit (the plaintiff or the defendant).

Interviewee The person who is being interviewed.

Investigation Plan A plan that lists each step involved in obtaining and verifying the facts and information that are relevant to the legal problem being investigated.

Judgment The court's final decision regarding the rights and claims of the parties to a lawsuit.

Jurisdiction The authority of a court to hear and decide a specific action.

KeyCite An aid to legal research developed by the editors of Westlaw®. On Westlaw®, KeyCite can trace case history, retrieve secondary sources, categorize legal citations by legal issue, and perform other functions.

Law A body of rules of conduct with legal force and effect, prescribed by the controlling authority (the government) of a society.

Law Clerk In the context of law-office work, a law student who works as an apprentice, during the summer or part-time during the school year, with an attorney or a law firm to gain practical legal experience.

Lay Witness A witness who can truthfully and accurately testify on a fact in question without having specialized training or knowledge; an ordinary witness.

Leading Question A question that suggests, or "leads to," a desired answer. Interviewers may use leading questions to elicit responses from witnesses who otherwise would not be forthcoming.

Legal Administrator An administrative employee of a law firm who manages the day-to-day operations of the firm. In smaller law firms, legal administrators are usually called office managers.

Legal-Assistant Manager An employee in a law firm who is responsible for overseeing the paralegal staff and paralegal professional development.

Legal Nurse Consultant (LNC) A nurse who consults with legal professionals and others about medical aspects of legal claims or issues. Legal nurse consultants normally must have at least a bachelor's degree in nursing and a significant amount of nursing experience.

Licensing A government's official act of granting permission to an individual, such as an attorney, to do something that would be illegal in the absence of such permission.

Limited Licensing A type of licensing in which a limited number of individuals within a specific profession or group (such as independent paralegals within the paralegal profession) must meet licensing requirements imposed by the state before those individuals may legally practice their profession.

Listserv List A list of e-mail addresses of persons who have agreed to receive e-mail about a particular topic.

Litigation Paralegals Paralegals who specialize in assisting attorneys in the litigation process.

Litigation The process of working a lawsuit through the court system.

Long Arm Statute A state statute that permits a state to obtain jurisdiction over nonresident individuals and corporations. Individuals or corporations, however, must have certain "minimum contacts" with that state for the statute to apply.

Malpractice Professional misconduct or negligence—the failure to exercise due care—on the part of a professional, such as an attorney or a physician.

Managing Partner The partner in a law firm who makes decisions relating to the firm's policies and procedures and who generally oversees the business operations of the firm.

Mandatory Authority Any source of law that a court must follow when deciding a case. Mandatory authorities include constitutions, statutes, and regulations that govern the issue before the court, and court decisions made by a superior court in the jurisdiction.

Mediation A method of settling disputes outside of court by using the services of a neutral third party, who acts as a communicating agent between the parties; a method of dispute settlement that is less formal than arbitration.

Memorandum of Law A document (known as a brief in some states) that delineates the legal theories, statutes, and cases on which a motion is based.

Mirror Site A Web site that duplicates an already existing site. A mirror site is used to improve the availability of access to a site that receives a lot of traffic or is distant from some users.

Motion A procedural request or application presented by an attorney to the court on behalf of a client.

Motion for a Directed Verdict (Motion for Judgment as a Matter of Law) A motion requesting that the court grant a judgment in favor of the party making the motion on the ground that the other party has not produced sufficient evidence to support his or her claim.

Motion for a New Trial A motion asserting that the trial was so fundamentally flawed (because of error, newly discovered evidence, prejudice, or other reason) that a new trial is needed to prevent a miscarriage of justice.

Motion for Judgment Notwithstanding the Verdict A motion (also referred to as a motion for judgment as a matter of law in federal courts) requesting that the court grant judgment in favor of the party making the motion on the ground that the jury verdict against him or her was unreasonable or erroneous.

Motion for Judgment on the Pleadings A motion, which can be brought by either party to a lawsuit after the pleadings are closed, for the court to decide the issue without proceeding to trial. The motion will be granted only if no facts are in dispute and the only issue concerns how the law applies to a set of undisputed facts.

Motion for Summary Judgment A motion requesting the court to enter a judgment without proceeding to trial. The motion can be based on evidence outside the pleadings and will be granted only if no facts are in dispute and the only issue concerns how the law applies to a set of undisputed facts.

Motion to Dismiss A pleading in which a defendant admits the facts as alleged by the plaintiff but asserts that the plaintiff's claim fails to state a cause of action (that is, has no basis in law) or that there are other grounds on which a suit should be dismissed.

National Association of Legal Assistants (NALA) One of the two largest national paralegal associations in the United States; formed in 1975. NALA is actively involved in paralegal professional development.

National Federation of Paralegal Associations (NFPA) One of the two largest national paralegal associations in the United States; formed in 1974. NFPA is actively involved in paralegal professional development.

Negotiation A method of alternative dispute resolution in which disputing parties, with or without the assistance of their attorneys, meet informally to resolve the dispute out of court.

Networking Making personal connections and cultivating relationships with people in a certain field, profession, or area of interest.

Newsgroup (Usernet Group) An online bulletin board service (BBS). A newsgroup, or BBS, is a forum, or discussion group, that usually focuses on a particular topic.

Office Manager An administrative employee who manages the day-to-day operations of a business firm. In larger law firms, office managers are usually called legal administrators.

Open-Ended Question A question that is phrased in such a way that it elicits a relatively detailed discussion of an experience or event.

Opening Statement An attorney's statement to the jury at the beginning of the trial. The attorney briefly outlines the evidence that will be offered during the trial and the legal theory that will be pursued.

Opinion A statement by the court setting forth the applicable law and the reasons for its decision in a case.

Opinion (Advisory) Letter A letter from an attorney to a client that contains a legal opinion on an issue raised by the client's question or legal claim. The opinion is based on a detailed analysis of the law.

Ordinance An order, rule, or law enacted by a municipal or county government to govern a local matter unaddressed by state or federal legislation.

Original Jurisdiction The power of a court to take a case, try it, and decide it.

Overtime Wages Wages paid to workers who are paid an hourly wage rate to compensate them for overtime work (hours worked beyond forty hours per week). Under federal law, overtime wages are at least one and a half times the regular hourly wage rate.

Paralegal (or Legal Assistant) A person sufficiently trained or experienced in the law and legal procedures to assist attorneys in the delivery of legal services to the public or to perform legal work as otherwise authorized by law.

Paralegal Certificate A certificate awarded to an individual with a high school diploma or its equivalent who has successfully completed a paralegal program of study at a private, for-profit business school, trade school, or college.

Parallel Citation A second (or third) citation to another case reporter in which a case has been published. When a case is published in more than one reporter, each citation is a parallel citation to the other(s).

Partner A person who has undertaken to operate a business jointly with one or more other persons. Each partner is a co-owner of the business firm.

Partnership An association of two or more persons to carry on, as co-owners, a business for profit.

Peremptory Challenge A *voir dire* challenge to exclude a potential juror from serving on the jury without any supporting reason or cause. Peremptory challenges based on racial or gender criteria are illegal.

Personal Liability An individual's personal responsibility for debts or obligations. The owners of sole proprietorships and partnerships are personally liable for the debts and obligations incurred by their business firms. If their firms go bankrupt or cannot meet debts as they become due, the owners will be personally responsible for paying the debts.

Persuasive Authority Any legal authority, or source of law, that a court may look to for guidance but on which it need not rely in making its decision. Persuasive authorities include cases from other jurisdictions and secondary sources of law, such as scholarly treatises.

Plaintiff A party who initiates a lawsuit.

Pleadings Statements by the plaintiff and the defendant that detail the facts, charges, and defenses involved in the litigation.

Pocket Part A separate pamphlet containing recent cases or changes in the law that is used to update treatises, legal encyclopedias, and other legal authorities. It is called a "pocket part" because it slips into a sleeve, or pocket, in the back binder of the volume.

Postdegree Certificate A certificate awarded by a college or university to an individual who, having already completed an associate's degree or bachelor's degree program, successfully completes a paralegal program of study.

Precedent A court decision that furnishes an example or authority for deciding subsequent cases in which identical or similar facts are presented.

Pressure Question A question intended to make the interviewee feel uncomfortable and respond emotionally. Pressure questions are sometimes used by interviewers to elicit answers from interviewees who may otherwise be unresponsive.

Pretrial Conference A conference prior to trial in which the judge and the attorneys litigating the suit discuss settlement possibilities, clarify the issues in dispute, and schedule forthcoming trial-related events.

Primary Source In legal research, a document that establishes the law on a particular issue, such as a case decision, legislative act, administrative rule, or presidential order.

Privileged Information Confidential communications between certain individuals, such as an attorney and his or her client, that are protected from disclosure except under court order.

Probate The process of "proving" the validity of a will and ensuring that the instructions in a valid will are carried out.

Probate Court A court having jurisdiction over proceedings concerning the settlement of a person's estate.

Procedural Law Rules that define the manner in which the rights and duties of individuals may be enforced.

Professional Corporation (P.C.) A firm that is owned by shareholders, who purchase the corporations stock, or shares. The liability of shareholders is often limited to the amount of their investments.

Professional Portfolio A job applicant's collection of selected personal documents (such as school transcripts, writing samples, and certificates) for presentation to a potential employer.

Real Estate Land and things permanently attached to the land, such as houses, buildings, and trees and foliage.

Recross-Examination The questioning of an opposing witness following the adverse party's redirect examination.

Redirect Examination The questioning of a witness following the adverse party's cross-examination.

Reference Line The portion of the letter that indicates the matter to be discussed in the letter, such as "RE: Summary of Cases Applying the Family and Medical Leave Act of 1993." The reference line is placed just below the address block and above the salutation.

Relevant Evidence Evidence tending to make a fact in question more or less probable than it would be without the evidence. Only relevant evidence is admissible in court.

Reporter A publication in which court cases are published, or reported.

Reprimand A disciplinary sanction in which an attorney is rebuked for his or her misbehavior. Although a reprimand is the mildest sanction for attorney misconduct, it is nonetheless a serious one and may significantly damage the attorney's reputation in the legal community.

Retainer An advance payment made by a client to a law firm to cover part of the legal fees and/or costs that will need to be incurred on that client's behalf.

Retainer Agreement A signed document stating that the attorney or the law firm has been hired by the client to provide certain legal services and that the client agrees to pay for those services in accordance with the terms set forth in the retainer agreement.

Return-of-Service Form A document signed by a process server and submitted to the court to prove that a defendant received a summons.

Rule of Four A rule of the United States Supreme Court under which the Court will not issue a writ of *certiorari* unless at least four justices approve of the decision to issue the writ.

Rules of Evidence Rules governing the admissibility of evidence in trial courts.

Salutation The formal greeting to the addressee of the letter. The salutation is placed just below the reference line.

Secondary Source In legal research, any publication that indexes, summarizes, or interprets the law, such as a legal encyclopedia, a treatise, or an article in a law review.

Self-Regulation The regulation of the conduct of a professional group by members of the group themselves. Self-regulation usually involves the establishment of ethical or professional standards of behavior with which members of the group must comply.

Service of Process The delivery of the summons and the complaint to a defendant.

Settlement Agreement An out-of-court resolution to a legal dispute, which is agreed to by the parties in writing. A settlement agreement may be reached at any time prior to or during a trial.

Shareholder One who purchases corporate stock, or shares, and who thus becomes an owner of the corporation.

Sole Proprietorship The simplest form of business, in which the owner is the business. Anyone who does business without creating a formal business entity has a sole proprietorship.

Staff Attorney An attorney who is hired by a law firm as an employee and who has no ownership rights in the firm.

Stare Decisis A flexible doctrine of the courts, recognizing the value of following prior decisions (precedents) in cases similar to the one before the court; the courts' practice of being consistent with prior decisions based on similar facts.

State Bar Association An association of attorneys within a state. Membership in the state bar association is mandatory in over two-thirds of the states—that is, before an attorney can practice law in a state, he or she must be admitted to that state's bar association.

Statute A written law enacted by a legislature under its constitutional lawmaking authority.

Statute of Limitations A statute setting the maximum time period within which certain actions can be brought or rights enforced. After the period of time has run, no legal action can be brought.

Statutory Law Laws enacted by a legislative body.

Subpoena A document commanding a person to appear at a certain time and place to give testimony concerning a certain matter.

Substantive Law Law that defines the rights and duties of individuals with respect to each other, as opposed to procedural law, which defines the manner in which these rights and duties may be enforced.

Summons A document served on a defendant in a lawsuit informing the defendant that a legal action has been commenced against him or her and that the defendant must appear in court on a certain date to answer the plaintiff's complaint.

Support Personnel Those employees who provide clerical, secretarial, or other support to the legal, paralegal, and administrative staff of a law firm.

Supremacy Clause The provision in Article VI of the U.S. Constitution that provides that the Constitution, laws, and treaties of the United States are "the supreme Law of the Land." Under this clause, state and local laws that directly conflict with federal law will be rendered invalid.

Suspension A serious disciplinary sanction in which an attorney who has violated an ethical rule or a law is prohibited from practicing law in the state for a specified or an indefinite period of time.

Syllabus A brief summary of the holding and legal principles involved in a reported case, which is followed by the court's official opinion.

Third Parties Persons or entities that are not directly involved in an agreement (such as a contract), legal proceeding (such as a lawsuit), or relationship (such as an attorney-client relationship).

Time Slip A record documenting, for billing purposes, the hours (or fractions of hours) that an attorney or a paralegal worked for each client, the date on which the work was done, and the type of work that was undertaken.

Trade Journal A newsletter, magazine, or other periodical that provides a certain trade or profession with information (products, trends, or developments) relating to that trade or profession.

Treatise In legal research, a text that provides a systematic, detailed, and scholarly review of a particular legal subject.

Trial Court A court in which most cases usually begin and in which questions of fact are examined.

Trial Notebook A binder that contains copies of all of the documents and information that an attorney will need to have at hand during the trial.

Trust An arrangement in which title to property is held by one person (a trustee) for the benefit of another party (a beneficiary).

Trust Account A bank or escrow account in which one party (the trustee, such as an attorney) holds funds belonging to another person (such as a client); a bank account into which funds advanced to a law firm by a client are deposited.

Unauthorized Practice of Law (UPL) The act of engaging in actions defined by a legal authority, such as a state legislature, as constituting the "practice of law" without legal authorization to do so.

Venue The geographical district in which an action is tried and from which the jury is selected.

Verdict A formal decision made by a jury.

Voir Dire A proceeding in which attorneys for the plaintiff and the defendant ask prospective jurors questions to determine whether potential jury members are biased or have any connection with a party to the action or with a prospective witness.

Will A document directing how and to whom the maker's property and obligations are to be transferred on his or her death.

Witness A person who is asked to testify under oath at a trial.

Witness Statement The written transcription of a statement made by the witness during an interview and signed by the witness.

Work Product An attorney's mental impressions, conclusions, and legal theories regarding a case being prepared on behalf of a client. Work product normally is regarded as privileged information.

Workers' Compensation Statutes State laws establishing an administrative procedure for compensating workers for injuries that arise in the course of their employment.

World Wide Web A hypertext-based system through which specially formatted documents are accessible on the Internet.

Writ of *Certiorari* A writ from a higher court asking the lower court for the record of a case for review.

INDEX